Readings in Labor Economics and Labor Relations

Readings in Labor Economics and Labor Relations

Edited by
RICHARD L. ROWAN
The Wharton School
University of Pennsylvania

1985 Fifth Edition

RICHARD D. IRWIN, INC.   Homewood, Illinois   60430

© RICHARD D. IRWIN, INC., 1968, 1972, 1976, 1980, and 1985

ISBN 0-256-03000-6
Library of Congress Catalog Card No. 84-80447
Printed in the United States of America
1 2 3 4 5 6 7 8 9 0 K 2 1 0 9 8 7 6 5

Preface

The general lack of readily available supplementary reading resources to meet the needs of students creates the need for this book of readings. I have been met with the classic economic problem of choosing among alternatives for this book. It is hoped that professors and students will continue to find the book helpful in the areas of labor history, labor economics, collective bargaining, industrial relations, and human resource management. Supplementation of basic texts has been the major criterion in the selection of articles. Particular emphasis has been placed on making available articles that libraries cannot stock in quantities, and an attempt has been made to select judiciously from both the classics and the current literature.

The book is organized in such a way that it can be used as an integrated whole, or any one section may be used to enhance the student's understanding in a particular area. Brief introductory remarks are provided for each section of the volume to give some assistance to the reader. An explanatory note highlighting the major points dealt with by the author in each essay enables the reader to determine the relative use of the material quickly and rather easily.

Permission from authors and publishers to reprint materials in this volume is acknowledged with sincere appreciation. Their kind cooperation has meant that a much finer book could be prepared than would have been possible otherwise.

I would like to thank Benn Steil, my student assistant, and Cynthia Smith and Rita Gorman, my secretaries, all of whom performed many details in a good-natured and efficient manner. The many students whom I have taught in the Wharton School have also served as excellent critics of the materials included in this volume.

In the final analysis, the success of the book depends on the excellence of the articles selected; this, of course, means that the editor has a special sense of indebtedness to the authors whose research, analysis, and opinions are herein made available.

Richard L. Rowan

CONTENTS

PART ONE
Labor Force Characteristics

Students in industrial relations, personnel, human resource management, as well as other fields, should have a firm understanding of the concept of the labor force. Federal, state, and local government officials use labor force statistics in designing legislation and allocating resources. Private manpower planners also are interested in labor force statistics and, in particular, the trends in the composition of the labor force that may impact on planners' ability to operate in an effective manner. It is important that labor force measurements reflect an accurate picture of those who work as well as those actively searching for work.

The first article in this section elaborates on the concepts and methods used in the preparation of labor force statistics by the U. S. government. The definition of the labor force is one that includes all those in the noninstitutional population, 16 years of age and over, who during a survey week are either employed or unemployed, according to certain classifications. The first article discusses the types of data collected and published by the government, the definition of the employed and unemployed in the labor force, the survey design, and the manner in which the data are collected.

Women workers constitute a growing portion of the labor force. Indeed, this may be the most important single characteristic of the labor force in the 20th century. This phenomenon will impact heavily on both labor unions and management. Ray Marshall presents a "perspective on basic trends affecting women's jobs and opportunities" in the second article.

The third article in this section discusses the position of blacks in the labor force. Blacks have consistently made up approximately 10 percent of the population in the United States and about 10 percent of the labor force. Distribution of blacks in the labor force, however, has shown them to be historically at the lower end of the blue-collar ladder. Diane Nilsen stresses the status of blacks in the labor force in the recent decade and finds that "more blacks obtained white-collar jobs but fewer penetrated higher-salary positions; mobility in higher-paid blue-collar jobs was somewhat more impressive."

The last article in this section deals with the complex question pertaining to job-creating possibilities arising out of a move toward high-tech industries. It appears from the research presented in this article that these industries are expected to provide a small proportion of the jobs created between 1982 and 1995.

READING 1

Concepts and Methods Used in Labor Force Statistics*

U.S. Departments of Commerce and Labor

This report describes the concepts and methods used in the Census Bureau's Current Population Survey which is conducted each month with a scientifically selected sample representing the noninstitutional civilian population of the United States. This survey provides monthly statistics on employment, unemployment, and related subjects which are analyzed and published by the Bureau of Labor Statistics of the U.S. Department of Labor.[1]

These monthly statistics are first issued in a summary press release within two weeks after completion of the survey. More detailed information is published in the Labor Department's *Employment and Earnings*. Both publications also incorporate data from surveys of business establishments.

Data Collected and Published

The Current Population Survey (CPS) provides a large amount of detail not otherwise

*From U.S. Department of Commerce, Bureau of the Census, and U.S. Department of Labor, Bureau of Labor Statistics, *Concepts and Methods Used in Labor Force Statistics Derived from the Current Population Survey*, BLS Report No. 463, Series P-23, No. 62, issued October 1976, pp. 1–8. *Note:* This report supersedes *BLS Report No. 313* and *Current Population Reports*, Series P-23, No. 22, issued jointly by the Bureau of Labor Statistics and the Bureau of the Census in June 1967. It incorporates changes instituted in the program since that date.

[1]In addition to the collection of labor force data, the Current Population Survey is used by the Bureau of the Census to collect statistics on education, migration, family size and composition, income, fertility, and housing vacancies. On an increasing scale, it has also been used to collect information for many other government agencies on a wide range of subjects which are best approached through household interviews

available on the economic status and activities of the population of the United States. In general, it is not possible to develop one or two overall figures, such as the number of unemployed, that will be adequate to describe the whole complex of labor market phenomena. Consequently, the Current Population Survey is designed to provide a large amount of detailed and supplementary data which are available for use in interpreting and adjusting the broad totals to meet a wide variety of needs on the part of users of labor market information. It is the only source of monthly estimates of total employment, both farm and nonfarm; of nonfarm self-employed persons, domestics, and unpaid helpers in nonfarm family enterprises as well as wage and salaried employees; and of total unemployment, whether or not covered by unemployment insurance. It is the only comprehensive source of information on the personal characteristics of the total population (both in and out of the labor force), such as age and sex, race, marital and family status, veteran status, educational background, and ethnic origin.

It provides the only available distributions of workers by the numbers of hours worked (as distinguished from aggregate or average hours for an industry), permitting separate analyses of part-time workers, workers on overtime, etc. The survey is also the only comprehensive current source of information on the occupation of workers. It also provides statistics on the industries in which they work.

Information is available from the survey not only for persons currently in the labor force but also for those who are outside the labor force. The characteristics of such persons—whether married women with or without young children, disabled persons, students, older retired workers, etc.—can be determined. Information on their current desire for work, their past work experience, and their intentions as to jobseeking are available from a subsample consisting of the outgoing rotation groups.

Monthly Publication. Each month, a significant amount of information about the labor force is published by the Labor Department in *Employment and Earnings*. The following major categories of data are provided:

1. Unemployment

   a. Number of unemployed persons and rates of unemployment by sex, age, race, marital status, and relationship to the household head.

   b. Rates of unemployment by industry and occupation.

   c. Unemployed persons by duration of unemployment, including a distribution of the long-term unemployed by sex, age, race, marital status, and major industry and occupational group.

   d. Unemployed persons by whether seeking full-time or part-time work, by sex, age, and major occupational group.

   e. Unemployed persons by their status at the time they became unemployed (their reason for unemployment), sex, age, race, and duration of unemployment.

   f. Unemployed persons according to the job search methods used, by age, sex, race, and reason for unemployment.

   g. A measure of labor force time lost through unemployment and involuntary part-time employment.

2. Employment

   a. Persons employed in agriculture and in nonagricultural industries by sex, age, class of worker, occupational group, race, and number of hours worked during the survey week.

   b. Total and nonagricultural employed persons by full- or part-time status and reasons for working part time.

   c. For persons at work in nonagricultural industries, distribution by full- or part-time status and number of hours worked, by major industry group (wage and salary workers only), major occupational group, sex and age, marital status, and race. In these distributions, part-time workers (reporting less that 35 hours) are further divided into those working limited hours because of economic factors and those on part time by choice or for other noneconomic reasons.

   d. Persons with a job but not at work during the survey week by reason for not working and whether paid for time off.

3. Labor force. Total and civilian labor force by sex, age, and race; and labor force participation rates.
4. Not in labor force. Persons not in the labor force by sex, age, and race, by main activity during survey week (keeping house, going to school, unable to work, and other).
5. Seasonally adjusted data. Adjusted data are provided for many series, including unemployment rates for all civilian workers, adult men, adult women, teenagers, household heads, and experienced wage and salary workers. A short description of the method of seasonal adjustment for labor force data is published each year in the February issue of *Employment and Earnings*.

THE SURVEY DESIGN

Concepts

Concepts of the labor force, employment, and unemployment similar to those now in use were introduced in the latter stages of the depression of the 1930s, chiefly in the interest of deriving more objective measurements of unemployment and employment than were previously available. These concepts have been modified but not substantially altered since the inception of the survey in 1940.

Prior to the 1930s, and aside from attempts in some of the decennial censuses, there were no direct measurements of the number of jobless persons. Because of the development of mass unemployment in the early 30s, the need for statistics became urgent, and widely conflicting estimates based on a variety of indirect techniques began to make their appearance.

Dissatisfied with these methods, many research groups, as well as state and municipal governments, began experimenting with direct surveys of the population or samples of the population. In these surveys, an attempt was made to classify the population as in or out of the labor force, or as employed or unemployed, by means of a varied series of questions addressed to each individual. In most of the surveys, the unemployed were defined as those who were not working but were "willing and able to work." This concept, however, did not meet the standards of objectivity that many technicians felt were necessary in order to measure not only the level of unemployment at a point in time but changes over periods of time. The criterion "willing and able to work," when applied in specific situations, appeared to be too intangible and too dependent upon the interpretation and attitude of the person being interviewed.

Out of this experimentation, a new set of concepts was developed in the late 1930s which sought to meet these criticisms. According to these concepts, the classification of an individual was to be dependent principally upon his actual activity within a designated time period, i.e., whether working or looking for work, or doing something else. These concepts were adopted for the national sample survey initiated by the Works Progress Administration in 1940. Although there have been improvements in measurement techniques, these concepts have been used in substantially unchanged form since that date, both in the Current Population Survey and in the decennial censuses.

In measuring activity and status, the time period selected for the monthly survey was a calendar week. Several considerations led to adopting a calendar week as the survey reference period. First, the period used must be short enough so that the data obtained would be "current," and the time reference would not tax the memory of the person giving the information. Second, it must not be so short that the occurrence of holidays or other accidental events would cause extremely erratic fluctuations in the information obtained. A calendar week seemed to fulfill these conditions as well as being a convenient and easily defined period of time. Also, most employers pay on a weekly basis so that this is a natural unit of time for collecting data from establishments, which are frequently studied in conjunction with these data. Since July 1955 the calendar week, Sunday through Saturday, which includes the 12th day of the month has been the reference week. The actual survey is conducted during the following week which is the week containing the 19th day of the month.

The official measures relate to persons 16 years old and over, although separate data are collected for 14 and 15 year-olds. In the United States most children under 16 are prevented from working because of child labor laws, compulsory school attendance, and general social custom.

The criteria used in classifying persons on the basis of their activity are described below:

Employed Persons. Employed persons comprise (1) all civilians who, during the specified week, did any work at all as paid employees or in their own business or profession, or on their own farm, or who worked 15 hours or more as unpaid workers on a farm or in a business operated by a member of the family, and (2) all those who were not working but who had jobs or businesses from which they were temporarily absent because of illness, bad weather, vacation, or labor-management dispute, or various personal reasons whether or not they were paid for the time off and whether or not they were seeking other jobs. Excluded from the employed group are persons whose only activity consisted of work around the house (such as own home housework, painting or repairing own home, etc.,) or volunteer work for religious, charitable, and similar organizations.

Unemployed. Unemployed persons are those civilians who had no employment during the survey week, were available for work, and

1. Had engaged in any specific jobseeking activity within the past four weeks. Principal activities include: registering at a public or private employment office; meeting with prospective employers; checking with friends or relatives; placing or answering advertisements; writing letters of application; or being on a union or professional register.
2. Were waiting to be called back to a job from which they had been laid off, or

3. Were waiting to report to a new wage or salary job scheduled to start within the following 30 days.

Labor Force. The civilian labor force consists of the total of all civilians classified as employed or unemployed in accordance with the criteria described above. These data are obtained from the monthly survey, which is confined to the civilian noninstitutional population. The published report also contains estimates of the total labor force, which includes members of the Armed Forces stationed either in the United States or abroad. Information on the size of the Armed Forces is obtained from the official records of the Department of Defense.

Not in Labor Force. All persons who are not classified as employed, unemployed, or in the Armed Forces are defined as "not in labor force." These persons are further classified as "engaged in own home housework," "in school," "unable to work" (because of long-term physical or mental illness), "retired," and "other." The "other" group includes individuals reported as too old or temporarily unable to work, the voluntarily idle, seasonal workers for whom the survey week fell in an "off" season and who were not reported as looking for work, and persons who did not look for work because they believed that no jobs were available in the area, or that no jobs were available for which they could qualify. Persons doing only incidental unpaid family work (less than 15 hours in the specified week) are also classified as not in labor force. Inmates of institutions (such as penal institutions, homes for the aged, tuberculosis sanitoriums, etc.) were also sampled annually until 1970 for purposes of special tabulations and comparisons with previous decennial census data. The inmate population, when covered, was classified as not in the labor force. This annual sample of inmates was dropped from the survey after 1970 because of its small size and resultant high sampling variability.

For persons not in the labor force, detailed questions are asked about previous work experience, intentions to seek work, desire for a job at the time of interview, and reasons for not looking for work. The questions for persons not in the labor force are asked only in those households that are leaving the sample after their first or second four-month interviewing period. Prior to 1970, these questions were asked in those households entering the sample for the first time and those returning for the second four months of interviewing.

The Classification Scheme. As discussed earlier, the basis of the labor force classification used in the CPS is the activity and status of an individual during a particular calendar week each month. Obviously, a person could have engaged in more than one activity during the period. Thus, in classifying persons, it is necessary to assign a priority to the various activities for which information was obtained. In this way, an individual is classified in only one group, and unduplicated totals of the employed, the unemployed, and persons outside the labor force can be obtained.

In this classification system, the highest priority is assigned to the activity "working." Thus, if a person did any work—as defined in the concepts—during the survey week (that is, 1 hour or more for pay or profit, or 15 hours or more without pay in a family-operated enterprise), he is classified as "at work" and is included with the employed, even though he may also have looked for work, gone to school, or done something else.

Second priority is assigned to the remaining employed—those who during the survey week had a job or business from which they were temporarily absent. Although this requires some modification of the "activity" concept, it is recognized that, if activity alone during a calendar week is considered, large numbers of persons who have definite job attachments but are temporarily absent from work in the survey week for reasons such as illness, vacation, or bad weather would be excluded from the labor force count. Because, in most cases, their absence would not exceed a week or two, it is believed that their exclusion from the labor force would result in an unrealistic count of the economically active population. Moreover, they most logically belong with the employed because they have jobs reserved for them in the economy. Therefore, a second category is set up consisting of persons who are not working but who have jobs or businesses from which they were temporarily absent because of illness, vacation, bad weather, or some other such reason during the survey week. This group, "persons with jobs but not at work," is measured separately but is added to the "at work" group to derive estimates of the total number of employed persons.

The activity "looking for work" is given third priority in the classification scheme. If a person did not work at all or did not have a job during the survey week but had engaged in some specific jobseeking activity within the past four weeks and was currently available for work, he is regarded as being in the market for a job and is classified as "unemployed." In defining this group, a slight departure is again made from the strict "activity" concept for some cases. Under certain circumstances, some persons, although unemployed in a realistic sense, might not be looking for work continuously. Thus the definition of unemployed persons was expanded to include those waiting to be recalled from layoff, as well as those waiting to start a new wage or salary job within 30 days.

The classification of persons at work in the survey week as employed regardless of the number of hours they worked has been the subject of much discussion. It has been suggested that when hours of work fall below a certain level (less than 35 hours, for example) these persons are more properly classified as partially unemployed. Although the official definition continues to count all part-time workers as employed, very detailed information is provided in the published reports each month on hours worked by employed persons, so that the changes in the extent of full-time or part-time work and the characteristics of full-time and part-time workers can be readily observed. Furthermore, the questions asked each month of part-time workers show how many are working short hours because of economic factors and how many are doing so because they want, or are available for, only part-time employment.

The Reference Period. The use of a fairly short period of reference (one week each month) imposes certain limitations on the interpretation of the data, particularly in trend analysis. Although the effects of factors such as adverse weather conditions, strikes, holidays, etc., are less marked in a one-week period than they would be if the time reference were shorter, say one day, they may nevertheless significantly influence the figures when they occur during the survey week. For example, unfavorable weather in some parts of the country may result in an apparent decline in farm employment in a given week as compared with the same period in the preceding year although no significant change in the underlying economic situation has actually taken place. A legal holiday during the survey week is not likely to affect employment levels appreciably, but reported hours of work will decline. Consequently, such factors must be taken into account in any interpretation and evaluation of the published figures.

Sample Selection

The CPS sample is located in 461 sample areas comprising 923 counties and independent cities with coverage in every state and the District of Columbia. In all, some 55,000 housing units or other living quarters are assigned for interview each month; about 47,000 of them, containing about 100,000 persons 16 years and over, are occupied by households eligible for interview. The remainder are units found to be vacant, converted to nonresidential use, containing persons with residence elsewhere, and others for which no interview is required. Of the occupied units eligible for enumeration, about three to five percent are not interviewed in a given month because the residents are not found at home after repeated calls, are temporarily absent, or are unavailable for other reasons.[2]

[2]The detailed description of the sample design and other technical phases of the program in U.S. Bureau of the Census, *Technical Paper No. 7,* "The Current Population Survey—A Report on Methodology," Washington, D.C., 1963, is still largely applicable to the present survey.

Selection of Sample Areas. In the process of selecting the sample following the 1970 Census of Population and Housing, the entire area of the United States, consisting of 3,146 counties and independent cities, was divided into 1,931 primary sampling units. With some minor exceptions, a primary sampling unit (PSU) consists of a county or a number of contiguous counties. Each of the 238 standard metropolitan statistical areas (SMSAs) as defined by the Office of Management and Budget through OMB Transmittal memorandum No. 13, dated February 21, 1971, constituted a separate PSU. Outside SMSAs, counties normally were combined, except where the geographic area of the single county was excessive. In combining counties to form PSUs, each PSU was defined so as to be as heterogeneous as possible. Greater heterogeneity could be accomplished by including more counties. Moreover, another important consideration was to have the PSU sufficiently compact in area so that a small sample spread throughout it could be efficiently canvassed by one interviewer without undue travel cost. A typical PSU, for example, included both urban and rural residents of both high and low economic levels and encompassed, to the extent feasible, diverse occupations and industries.

The PSUs were then grouped into 376 strata. Among these PSUs, 146 of the largest SMSAs (including all those with more than 250,000 inhabitants) and 10 other areas (not SMSAs) were strata by themselves. In general, however, a stratum consisted of a set of PSUs as much alike as possible in various characteristics such as geographic region, rate of growth in the 1960–1970 decade, proportion of blacks and other minorities, principal industry, percent of population living in urban areas, and so on. Except for the 156 areas mentioned above, each of which is a complete stratum, the strata were established so that their sizes in terms of 1970 population were approximately equal. Where a PSU was a stratum by itself, it automatically fell in the sample. The other 220 strata were divided into two random halves. From each strata falling in one half, one PSU was selected in a random manner for inclusion in the sample, the selection having been made in such a way that the probability of selection of any one unit was proportionate to its 1970 population. For example, within a stratum the chance that a PSU with a population of 50,000 would be selected was twice that of a unit with a population of 25,000.

In each of the other 110 strata, two PSUs were selected independently for inclusion in the sample, again in such a way that the probability of selection of each PSU was proportionate to its 1970 population. Since within each such stratum the two PSUs were selected with replacement, it sometimes happened that the same PSU was selected both times. This occurred in 25 cases; in the other 85 strata two separate PSUs were selected, giving a total of 170.

The resulting 461 areas are those in which the survey is being conducted. For the most part, these areas would remain in the sample until the results of the next decennial census (1980) become available.

Selection of Sample Households. The overall sampling ratio used at the present time (1975) in the 461-area design is about 1 in 1,490. The sampling ratio is reduced slightly each month in order to keep the sample relatively constant despite the overall growth of the population. The within-PSU sampling ratio is determined in such a way that the overall sampling rate for each household included in the survey is equal.

Within each of the 461 PSUs, the number of households to be enumerated each month is determined by the application of the within-PSU sampling ratio rather than through the assignment of a fixed quota. This procedure makes it possible for the sample to reflect any shifts in population. For example, if on the basis of the 1970 census a sample ratio of 1 in every 150 is used in a sample area, the number of households found in the sample will be larger than that obtained by a fixed quota in areas where the number of households has increased since the census. In areas where the number of households has declined, the number of sample households selected will be smaller. In this way, the sample properly reflects the changing distribution of the population and avoids the distortion which would result from the application of fixed quotas of households, or persons, based on the population at an earlier date.

Within each designated PSU, several stages of sampling may be used in selecting the units to be enumerated. The first step is the selection of a sample of census enumeration districts (EDs), which are administrative units used in the 1970 census and contain, on the average, about 350 households. These are selected systematically from a geographically arranged listing, so that the sample EDs are spread over the entire PSU. The probability of selection of any one ED is proportionate to its 1970 population.

The next step is to select a cluster of approximately four households to be enumerated within each designated ED. This is done, wherever possible, from the list of addresses for the ED compiled during the 1970 census or, if the addresses are incomplete or inadequate, by area sampling methods. The address lists are used in about two thirds of the cases, primarily in urban areas, whereas area sampling is applied in the remainder. In using the census lists, small multiunit addresses (two-four units) are almost always kept intact within a single cluster. This improves the ability of the interviewer to cover all households designated for the sample. Subject to this restriction, clusters consist of addresses as geographically contiguous as possible.

The list sample is supplemented by a selection of the appropriate proportion of units newly constructed in the PSU since the census date, which is obtained mainly from records of building permits maintained by the offices responsible for issuing permits in that area. A special procedure is also followed to include units in the CPS sample that had been missed in the census.

In those EDs where area sampling methods are used—mainly rural areas—they are subdivided into small land areas with well-defined boundaries having in general an expected "size" of about 7 to 20 housing units or other living quarters. For each subdivided ED, one land area is designated for the sample, with the probability of selection proportionate to the estimated "size" of the land

area. Where available, advance information indicates that a selected segment contains about four households, all units within the land area are included in the sample. In cases where the advance information indicates the "size" of a land area is several times four units, a field listing is made of all living quarters in the area, and a systematic sample drawn so as to achieve the equivalent of a four-household cluster which is canvassed completely.

Rotation of Sample. Part of the sample is changed each month. A primary reason for rotating the sample is to avoid the problems of lack of cooperation which arise when a constant panel is interviewed indefinitely. Another reason for replacing households is to reduce the cumulative effect of biases in response, which are sometimes observed when the same persons are interviewed indefinitely. For each sample, eight systematic subsamples (rotation groups) of segments are identified. A given rotation group is interviewed for a total of eight months, divided into two equal periods. It is in the sample for four consecutive months one year, leaves the sample during the following eight months, and then returns for the same four calendar months of the next year. In any one month, one eighth of the sample segments are in their first month of enumeration, another eighth are in their second month, and so on, with the last eighth in the eighth time (the fourth month of the second period of enumeration). Under this system, 75 percent of the sample is common from month to month and 50 percent from year to year. This procedure provides a substantial amount of month-to-month and year-to-year overlap in the panel (reducing discontinuities in the series of data) without burdening any specific group of households with an unduly long period of inquiry.

Measuring the Accuracy of Results. Modern sampling theory provides methods for measuring the range of errors due to sampling, where, as in the case of the CPS sample, the probability of selection of each member of the population is known. Methods are also available for measuring the effect of response variability in the CPS. A measure of sampling variability indicates the range of difference that may be expected because only a sample of the population is surveyed. A measure of response variability indicates the range of difference that may be expected as a result of compensating types of errors arising from practices of different interviewers and the replies of respondents. In practice, these two sources of error—sampling and response variability, as defined above—are estimated jointly from the results of the survey. The computations do not, however, incorporate the effect of response bias as would occur, for example, if respondents, by and large, tended to overstate hours worked. Response biases occur in the same way in a complete census as in a sample, and, in fact, they may be smaller in a well-conducted sample survey because there it is feasible to pay the price necessary to collect the information more skillfully.

Estimates of sampling and response variability combined are provided in *Employment and Earnings* and in other reports based on the CPS, thus permitting the user to take this factor into account in interpreting the data. In general, smaller figures and small differences between figures are subject to relatively large variation and should be interpreted with caution.

DATA COLLECTION

Field Procedures

The field organization of the Census Bureau consists of 12 Regional Offices, each staffed by a regional director and a staff of program assistants. During CPS enumeration week each month and all or part of the preceding and following week, the majority of the supervisory staff members devote their time to preparations for control and supervision of this survey. During other periods, the staff collects statistics concerning business and various other subjects. They supervise, in total, a staff of about 1,500 part-time interviewers, of whom about 1,000 are CPS interviewers.

The Interview. During the calendar week containing the 19th day of each month, these interviewers contact some responsible person in each of the sample households in the CPS. At the time of the first enumeration of a household, the interviewer visits the household and prepares a roster of the household members, including their personal characteristics (date of birth, sex, race, marital status, educational attainment, veteran status, origin or descent, etc.) and their relationship to the household head. This roster is brought up to date at each subsequent interview to take account of new or departed residents, changes in marital status, and similar items. The information on personal characteristics is thus available each month for identification purposes and for cross-classification with economic characteristics of the sample population.

Personal visits are required in the first, second, and fifth month that the household is in the sample. In other months, the interview may be conducted by telephone if the respondent agrees to this procedure. Also, if no one is at home when the interviewer visits, the household may be contacted by telephone after the first month. Approximately 50 percent of the households in any given month are interviewed by telephone.

At each monthly visit, the interviewer asks a series of standard questions on economic activity during the preceding week (the calendar week containing the 12th day of the month, called the "survey week") for each household member of working age. The primary purpose of these questions is to classify the sample population into three basic economic groups—the employed, the unemployed, and those not in the labor force.

Questions are asked in depth each month to help clarify the information on labor force status. For the employed, information is obtained on hours worked during the survey week, together with a description of the current job. If these persons worked less than 35 hours during the survey week, information is obtained on the reasons they were working part time, primarily to distinguish between those whose hours are restricted because of slack work conditions or other economic factors and those working part time by choice or for personal or noneconomic reasons. For those temporarily away from their jobs, the reason for not working during the survey week is obtained as well as information on whether they were paid for the time off and whether they usually work 35 hours or more at their job.

For the unemployed, information is obtained on what method they used during the last four weeks to find work, why they started looking for work, the length of time they have been looking for work, whether they are seeking full- or part-time work, when they last worked at a full-time job or business lasting two consecutive weeks or more, and a description of their last full-time civilian job.

For those outside the labor force, their principal activity during the survey week—whether keeping house, going to school, or doing something else—is recorded and information obtained on when they last worked, reasons for leaving their last job, a description of that job, whether they want to work at the present time and, if so, the reason they are not seeking work currently; and, finally, intentions to seek work in the next 12 months.

Quality Control Program

Classification errors in labor force surveys may be particularly large in the case of persons with marginal attachments to the labor force. These errors may be caused by interviewers, respondents, or both, or may arise from faulty questionnaire design. The CPS interviewers are chiefly part-time workers, although most of the staff at any time consists of persons who have had repeated experience on the survey for some years. They are given intensive training when first recruited and also have either direct or home study training each month prior to the survey. Moreover, through editing of their completed questionnaires, repeated observation during enumeration, and a systematic reinterview of part of their assignments by the field supervisory staff, the work of the interviewers is kept under control and errors or deficiencies are brought directly to their attention.

In spite of these controls, interviewers may not always ask the questions in the prescribed fashion. To the extent that varying the wording of the questions results in differences in response, this factor may result in some errors or lack of uniformity in the statistics.

Similarly, the data are limited by the adequacy of the information possessed by the respondent and the willingness to report accurately. Usually a single respondent, generally the wife, reports for the entire family. The respondent may not know all the facts about family members or may be unable to report adequately on their attitudes or intentions. For example, the wife will probably know that her husband is working, but she may not always know exactly how many hours he worked or the precise nature of his job.

Because of the crucial role of the interviewers in securing accurate and complete returns, a great deal of time and resources are devoted to maintaining the quality of their work. The major aspects of this program are described briefly below:

1. **Initial Training.** New interviewers recruited for the survey are given special intensive training the first three months they are on the job. The program includes approximately 12½ hours of advance home study; 1½ days of classroom lectures, discussions, and practice; at least three days of on-the-job training and observation; and, in subsequent months, special followup home-study and review materials.

2. **Refresher Training.** Prior to each monthly enumeration, experienced interviewers are given two to three hours of home study, including review exercises and similar materials. Several times a year the interviewers are convened for day-long group training and review sessions.

3. **Observation.** At least once a year, each experienced interviewer is accompanied by a supervisor for about one day in the course of the actual survey, in order to determine how well he or she understands and applies the concepts and procedures. In addition to such corrective action and retraining as may be needed, a rating sheet is prepared in the course of observation which becomes part of the interviewer's record. Interviewers requir-

ing additional attention are observed more frequently, at the option of the Regional Office.

4. Reinterview. On the average of twice a year, a subsample of the work of each interviewer is reinterviewed (through a second interview with the household) by a supervisor in order to determine whether the correct information was obtained. The interviewers do not know when their work will be checked or which units will be in the subsample, although they are aware of the general nature of the reinterview program. Where the information differs between the reinterview and and the initial interview, the supervisor seeks to determine which answers were correct and (where the original information was incorrect) the reasons for the discrepancies. Errors attributable to the interviewers are brought to their attention and—where the discrepancies exceed certain prescribed limits—special training, observation, and further checking

are provided. In addition to its value as a check on particular interviewers, this system provides some data on the quality of the survey in general.[3]

5. Inspection of Returns. In addition to these other measures, the completed questionnaires are carefully inspected each month both in Regional Offices and in the processing center at Jeffersonville, Indiana. The results of this inspection, together with information from the observation and reinterview programs, serve as a basis for orienting training materials to the indicated needs of the interviewers. The results of these various checks may also lead to the replacement of interviewers who—in spite of special attention and training—are unable to meet the prescribed standards of quality.

---

[3]See Bureau of the Census, *Technical Paper No. 19*, "The Current Population Survey Reinterview Program— January 1961 through December 1966," December 1968.

READING 2

Work and Women in the 1980s: A Perspective on Basic Trends Affecting Women's Jobs and Job Opportunities*

Ray Marshall†

FOREWORD‡

If we as a society are to adapt productively to change, if we are to solve the brand-new problems it creates and the long-standing problems it reveals, and, above all, if we are to take advantage of the opportunities it presents, we must understand and accept the nature and dimensions of the change. This is why Ray Marshall's wise and thoughtful analysis, *Work and Women in the 1980s: A Perspective on Basic Trends Affecting Women's Jobs and Job Opportunities,* is so important.

Although, as he points out, it has not happened overnight, what Mr. Marshall documents is a revolutionary change. Today's women are joining the work force in unprecedented numbers, they are staying in the work force for unprecedented lengths of time, and they are expecting to stay in the work force for most of their lives. Millions of American families depend for their very sustenance on working women. Many more millions of families depend on women's earnings to help provide a decent standard of living, a home of their own, or a college education for their children. Our economy has come to depend heavily on the contributions that women make as workers and as consumers. These things are facts of life; we could not—even if we wanted to—undo this revolution.

But, like all revolutions, this one has had its human costs and dislocations, and it has made long-time inequities more glaring. Members of Congress and others who seek to solve these problems—and to turn this revolution to the best possible account for our society, and the individuals and families that compose it—will find a valuable resource in Mr. Marshall's overview. He looks not only at history, and at the widely publicized factors relating to working women, but also at more subtle and complex economic and societal factors. These, too, must be understood as we consider the kind of work that both women and men will be doing, what value will be placed on their work, and how they can best be helped to handle their responsibilities to both families and jobs.

Mr. Marshall's paper is the first in a series of policy-relevant analyses that WREI will publish in the next year as part of its effort to illuminate some of the longer-term issues of importance to women. We look forward to the rest of the series.

INTRODUCTION

The increasing labor force participation of women is perhaps the most important labor market development of this century. Women have always worked, of course, but in the preindustrial society the family was the basic producing unit and the work of women was an integral part of that unit. Industrialization caused the labor market to expand and the basic producing unit to be external to the family. In the new division of labor, women were considered to be peripheral and temporary participants in the male-dominated market economy. Market values gave inadequate attention to the importance of home work, and women were viewed as temporary participants in the market economy. Wages and other conditions

---

*Reproduced from a publication of WREI, Women's Research and Education Institute of the Congressional Caucus for Women's Issues, 1983.

†*Ray Marshall is Professor of Economics and Public Policy at the University of Texas at Austin; Professor Marshall was U.S. Secretary of Labor under President Carter.*

‡Foreword written by The Honorable Patricia Schroeder, M.C., and The Honorable Olympia Snowe, M.C., *Co-Chairs, Congressional Caucus for Women's Issues.*

Figure 1

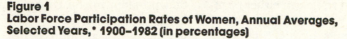

Figure 1
**Labor Force Participation Rates of Women, Annual Averages,
Selected Years,* 1900–1982 (in percentages)**

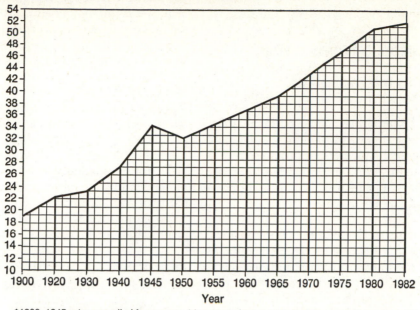

*1900–1945 rates compiled for persons 14 years and over; rates for later years for persons 16 and over.

Sources; 1900–1970: U.S. Department of Commerce, Bureau of the Census, *Historical Statistics of the United States, Colonial Times to 1970,* Series D 29–41 (Washington, D.C.: U.S. Government Printing Office, September 1975); 1975–1980: U.S. Department of Labor, Bureau of Labor Statistics, *Employment and Training Report of the President* (Washington, D.C.: U.S. Government Printing Office, 1982), Table A–3; 1982: U.S. Department of Labor, Bureau of Labor Statistics, *Employment and Earnings* (Washington, D.C.: U.S. Government Printing Office, January 1983), Table 4, annual averages.

of employment were made on the assumption that men would be the main wage earners; this "traditional model" was the dominant pattern in the United States until the 1960s.

The increased labor force participation of women (Figure 1) changed the character of the work force but has not changed many of the assumptions about typical family patterns. In other words, conditions of employment have not changed to reflect the new realities, where women are not peripheral but integral parts of the work force, where most women spend more time working than they do bearing children, and where male and female expectations about self-realization from jobs and careers are converging.

The tensions and relationships produced by increased labor force participation of women have very important social and economic implications. The way traditional labor, management, and governmental institutions re-

spond to these new realities will affect their institutional strength as well as the conditions of women and men and, indeed, the health and stability of the entire society.

The purpose of this paper is to trace some of the trends that form the complex constellation of forces affecting women's issues during the 1980s and beyond. My focus will be primarily on the workplace, because that is the area I know best. Moreover, the workplace will be even more important in the lives of people in the future than in the past because work is becoming more universal with the increasing labor force participation of women and young people. Despite talk about the decline of the work ethic, most people want to work. Work is both the way most adults identify themselves and the central organizing principle of our lives.

The work institutions and relationships of the future are not predetermined. There are some strong trends, but these can either be reinforced or changed by positive intervention. However, the effectiveness of intervention requires an understanding of the trends.

TRENDS AFFECTING WOMEN'S ISSUES

Increasing International Interdependence

In the United States, international trade accounted for 9 percent of GNP in 1950 and about 25 percent in 1980; in other countries international trade is even more important. Some implications of this increasing interdependence include:

Developments in the World Economy. Jobs in each country depend on developments in the world economy, over which national leaders have limited control. However, both the quality of jobs and the number will require greater attention to such matters as international trade, immigration, monetary reform, and cooperation in solving international problems. A major regulatory problem results from the fact that problems have become international, while policy instruments are mainly national.

The Role of Multinationals. Multinational enterprises are generating competition and jobs and transmitting labor standards and work practices throughout the world. The multinationals have done a much better job than unions and other organizations in integrating international activities. The policies of these institutions with respect to the employment of women are therefore very important. Moreover, without greater countervailing power, the multinationals will continue to gain economic power over unions and governments. The mobility of capital strengthens the multinationals' bargaining power.

International Migration. The importance of the international migration of workers is growing, especially migration from the Third World, where 600–700 million jobs must be created in the next two decades just to keep unemployment from rising. This is an impor-

tant problem in the United States, where illegal immigration perpetuates bad jobs and will limit the job options of low-wage workers. Worldwide unemployment, especially in the low-wage and basic manufacturing jobs where many women workers are concentrated, will be a serious problem for the rest of the decade. Industrial market economies (IMECs) and Third World leaders have strong mutual interests in job development and labor standards, including the employment conditions of women in the Third World, as well as in developed countries. IMEC countries, especially, must broaden the scope of their self-interest to include job creation and labor standards in the Third World countries because these standards have a direct impact on labor standards in the industrial countries.

International Competition. Internationalization limits the effectiveness of traditional domestic economic policies, thus requiring international solutions. For example, monetarist attempts to control inflation are limited by the internationalization of money in an age of instantaneous electronic communications. In addition, there are limits to how much a domestic economy can expand in a relatively free and open international trading system that attracts imports and immigrants.

A natural tendency exists in such circumstances to restrict immigration and protect domestic economies, but most IMECs have become so internationalized that this will be a very expensive alternative. Small open economies have therefore found it necessary to adopt wage and price formulas that keep their export sectors competitive, causing "sheltered" and internationally competitive sectors to become more differentiated.

International competition is particularly important to women, who are much more heavily concentrated in jobs unfavorably affected by international trade than they are in those that benefit from trade. For example, a 1980 study of the impact of international trade by the Department of Labor concluded that "females comprised an average of 41.1 percent of the work force in the unfavorably affected industries compared with 29.4 percent of those favorably affected" (U.S. Department of Labor, Bureau of International Labor Affairs, 1980: 5).

Above all, jobs have been subjected to the efficiency requirements of intensified international competition. In order to protect job options, the IMECs must give careful attention to the rules within which international trade takes place. This will require attention to minimum international labor standards in some areas to prevent international competition from eroding labor standards in the IMEC and Third World countries. In short, because of the spread of international corporations and the greater mobility of capital and technology, an interdependent and competitive international market tends to erode labor standards in the high-wage countries.

Declining Rates of Growth in Productivity

The declining rates of growth in both productivity and GNP in most industrial market economies limit job options, exacerbate internal conflicts, weaken international competitiveness, and intensify inflationary pressures. The reasons for the decline in the growth of productivity are not fully understood, but improvements can and will be sought in management systems and job practices.

Declining productivity and GNP growth have important implications for women. In the past, wages, fringe benefits, and social services were often based on the assumption of continued growth. Consequently, private pension systems could be on a pay-as-you-go basis on the assumption that growth would continue, but now they must be put on a more actuarially sound basis. Similarly, growth permitted collective bargaining mainly to involve ways to share gains rather than how to share losses or gain greater efficiency. With high productivity growth, greater attention could be given to stability, equity, and certainty than to efficiency and flexibility.

The greater competitiveness of other models has caused questioning of the traditional authoritarian management system. In particular, there is growing interest in the Japanese system of quality control circles, long-term employment expectations, cooperative

labor-management relations at the firm level, emphasis on nonequity financing, greater cooperation between the public and private sectors, greater attention to long-run technical and economic viability, and incentive systems that provide greater worker identification with company objectives. All of these features contrast vividly with the U.S. pattern of adversarial relations between labor and management and between the public and private sectors, oligopolistic pricing, employment insecurity, short-run political and business decisions, and pattern bargaining. However, concentration on these positive elements tends to obscure the fact that the Japanese system applies mainly to the export sector (about one third of the work force) and is possible only because some groups (especially women) and sectors (along with subcontracting, production sharing, and the bonus system) act as shock absorbers for the more stable, competitive core.

It is, however, easy to exaggerate the uniqueness of the "Japanese model" and to stereotype both that model and the so-called "American management style." There is great diversity in the United States and in Japan, although what has come to be known as the Japanese Management System is fairly uniform in the Japanese large-firm and export sector. However, average productivity in the United States is about 25–30 percent higher than it is in Japan. Moreover, while the Japanese have successfully competed with some U.S. firms, those firms are in the minority. On the whole, there are more U.S. companies with which the Japanese are not competitive. The key seems to be whether American companies adjusted mainly to oligopolistic conditions in domestic markets rather than being required to compete in domestic and international markets. Under the latter conditions, American firms have been more productive and competitive. If American firms are to survive pressures for markets from international exporters, their management systems must be adaptive and competitive.

Moreover, there seems to be little that is truly unique about the Japanese system. There is, after all, considerable international borrowing of business practices. Indeed, much of what is regarded as the "Japanese" system was taught to them by American management experts.

Finally, Japanese and American management systems are subsystems of larger political and economic systems. The Japanese have been able to become highly competitive in certain industries by careful attention to co-ordinated export-driven industrial policies, as well as to highly productive and coordinated enterprise management systems. This contrasts vividly with laissez-faire, uncoordinated, discontinuous, and adversarial economic policies in the United States. When all of the evidence is in, it probably will reveal that national economic policy has at least as much to do with the relatively successful performance of the Japanese economy and the competitiveness of favored industries as the Japanese management system (Marshall, 1983).

While there are common features of good management systems everywhere, each system has to be adapted to national political, social, and economic realities. The Japanese work force is much more homogeneous than the American, and the Japanese have therefore devoted much less attention to equal opportunity and affirmative action. Moreover, the discriminatory treatment of women in the Japanese system would be unacceptable and even illegal in the United States. Indeed, some observers believe that the so-called Japanese Management System tends to be male-dominated and discriminatory with respect to outsiders wherever it is used (Ouchi, 1981). Those who are concerned about the employment of women and minorities in nontraditional jobs must therefore give careful, critical scrutiny to the so-called Japanese model. In the American system, efficiency and stability require equal employment opportunity for legal and equity reasons, but also because that is the only way to avoid conflict and realize the advantages of a multiracial, multicultural society.

Stagflation

Keynesian demand-management techniques were relatively successful in the 1950s and 1960s but became less effective in the 1970s, mainly because structural changes in domestic economies and international economic shocks aggravated domestic inflationary pressures. Demand management alone could not eliminate structural problems or external supply and price shocks, especially with the inflationary biases created by traditional income support, industrial relations, and internal pricing arrangements. Indeed, demand-management policies and private sector adjustment to those policies created inflationary biases within the system.

Unemployment

High unemployment will limit job options and exacerbate social problems. The concern about inflation will cause unemployment to be neglected by policymakers in the short run. But the futility of attempting to solve the inflation problem with high unemployment will become very clear by the middle of this decade, causing strong public pressures to seek sensible ways to achieve price stability and full employment. The desire for jobs is very strong in all sections of the population and will grow during this decade.

The solution to our problems will be found in increasing output and employment, not limiting it. However, the job problem will be complicated by the fact that the demand for jobs is such that we have had to create two or three jobs to reduce unemployment by one. Full employment is particularly important for women. Tight labor markets facilitate the advancement of women, their employment in nontraditional jobs, and greater management attention to their specific labor market needs.

Demographic and Labor Market Trends

A number of very strong demographic and labor market trends will influence the employment options of men and women. These include:

Increased Labor Force Participation by Women. Women will constitute two thirds of the growth in the labor force during this decade. In 1950, 70 percent of American house-

Table 1
Labor Force Participation Rates of Women 20 Years and over by Year of Birth and Age, Annual Averages, Selected Years, 1955–1979 (in percentages)

Year of Birth	1955 Age	1955 Rate	1960 Age	1960 Rate	1965 Age	1965 Rate
1956–60						
1951–55						
1946–50						
1941–45					20–24	50.0%
1936–40			20–24	46.2%	25–29	38.9
1931–35	20–24	46.0%	25–29	35.7	30–34	38.2
1926–30	25–29	35.3	30–34	36.3	35–39	43.6
1921–25	30–34	34.7	35–39	40.8	40–44	48.5
1916–20	35–39	39.2	40–44	46.8	45–49	51.7
1911–15	40–44	44.1	45–49	50.7	50–54	50.1
1906–10	45–49	45.9	50–54	48.8	55–59	47.1
1901–05	50–54	41.5	55–59	42.2	60–64	34.0
1896–1901	55–59	35.6	60–64	31.4	65–69	17.4
1895 or before	60–64	29.0	65–69	17.6	70 and over	6.1
	65–69	17.8	70 and over	6.8		
	70 and over	6.4				

Year of Birth	1970 Age	1970 Rate	1975 Age	1975 Rate	1979 Age	1979 Rate
1956–60					20–24	69.1%
1951–55			20–24	64.1%	25–29	65.7
1946–50	20–24	57.8%	25–29	57.0	30–34	61.8
1941–45	25–29	45.2	30–34	51.7	35–39	63.4
1936–40	30–34	44.7	35–39	54.9	40–44	63.9
1931–35	35–39	49.2	40–44	56.8	45–49	60.4
1926–30	40–44	52.9	45–49	55.9	50–54	56.5
1921–25	45–49	55.0	50–54	53.3	55–59	48.7
1916–20	50–54	53.8	55–59	47.9	60–64	33.9
1911–15	55–59	49.0	60–64	33.3	65–69	15.3
1906–10	60–64	36.1	65–69	14.5	70 and over	4.7
1901–05	65–69	17.3	70 and over	4.8		
1896–1901	70 and over	5.7				
1895 or before						

Source: U.S. Department of Labor, Bureau of Labor Statistics, *Perspectives on Working Women: A Databook* (Washington, D.C.: U.S. Government Printing Office, October 1980), Bulletin 2080.

holds were headed by men whose income was the sole source of family income; today, less than 15 percent of households fit this "traditional" model, even though many of the nation's employment policies assume it still to be pervasive. The evidence also suggests that the labor force participation of women is increasing for minorities as well as whites and that younger women have higher labor force participation rates than their mothers and grandmothers (Table 1). Labor force participation rates tend to decline for women in the 25–29 age category and then to increase for older age groups.

Job practices and family practices become more closely related. The absence of such family-enhancing advantages as flexible working time, child care facilities, and maternity leave will have a strong impact on American families, and this in turn may have a major impact on delinquency, child development, and other social problems.

The greater availability of such social services probably is an important reason for the relatively superior position of working women in other industrialized countries. Such services as child allowances, health care, child care facilities, pregnancy leave, and flexible working time all facilitate the continuity of employment by women and therefore their more equal wage-earning profiles. Of course, the opportunities for women were facilitated by tighter labor markets in Europe during most of the post-war period. In addition, the European school child typically spends more hours and days in school than American children—240 days versus 160 in the United States; hence the need for child care facilities for school-age children is less.

There is no evidence that the great increase in the number of mothers who work outside the home has had a negative impact on childraising. In fact, the mothers' self-images and the families' economic and emotional well-being are heavily conditioned by the ability of the mother and the father to work. A paid job has become an important symbol of self-worth and personal independence for women, even though most women work for economic reasons. The mechanization of household work and increasing life expectancy have created much more time for women to pursue careers. Around 1900, the average life expectancy for a woman was 48 years, 18 of which were spent childbearing; today, life expectancy is about 78 years, only 10 of which are devoted to childbearing (although more is devoted to childrearing).

Demographic trends show some of the general changes in the dimension of women's employment patterns. Because minorities have different life expectancies, the impact of trends can be seen more clearly by looking at the experiences of white women. In 1900, the life expectancy of a white woman at age 20 was about 64 years. She could expect, on the average, to be widowed at 52 and to die before her last child left home. In 1980, a white woman who married at 22 could expect to live about 79 years, and to stop having children at age 30. Her last child would leave home when she was 48. However, there was a 47 percent chance that her first marriage would end in divorce. Davis and van den Oever (1982) observe:

Underlying demographic changes thus force women to reduce the importance of marriage in their lives. The prospect is that two thirds of their adult years will be spent without children in the household and half to two thirds without a husband.

Education. The educational level of the work force has increased significantly since World War II. Between 1966 and 1974, the number of people receiving bachelor degrees doubled and the number receiving masters and Ph.D. degrees increased about as fast. Between 1970 and 1980, the proportion of all workers 16 to 64 who had completed at least one year of college increased from one fourth to over one third. Moreover, women are increasing their share of the professional degrees awarded, and undergraduate degrees are converging for men and women.

These educational developments have a number of implications:

Increasing education and training have been responsible for sustaining economic growth, though at a diminishing rate in the 1970s.

The higher levels of educational attainment intensify competition for good jobs, placing those with limited education or training at a serious labor market disadvantage.

Higher levels of education have reinforced other factors tending to change traditional attitudes about work. There is a strong demand for "good" jobs and a growing tendency to avoid marginal, disagreeable, low-wage jobs, a tendency that many use to justify continuing immigration to fill these positions instead of improving those jobs or raising wages to attract workers. More highly educated workers wish to become more involved in on-the-job decisions traditionally handled by management. Demand for such worker participation in managerial decisions has not reached the intensity it has in Europe, where workers participate more at every level of management, or in Japan, where workers participate in many production decisions through quality control circles. Nonetheless, the desire for participation, plus the greater perceived efficiency achieved through worker participation in Japan, Germany, and Scandinavia, will undoubtedly intensify pressures for some form of participation in the United States. However, the main form of participation in the United States undoubtedly will be an extension of collective bargaining to younger, better-educated workers and participation in government-mandated protective programs like occupational safety and health, rather than participation on boards of directors or in works councils.

Still, the pressures to improve productivity and efficiency are such that efforts will be made to increase worker participation in quality control and productivity improvement programs. Many of these efforts will end in collective bargaining, especially in the public sector. These participatory processes also could give women workers a means to express their job needs.

The significance of this trend for women is that any system to provide greater participation will cause employment systems to be more responsive to the unique needs of women workers.

Fertility. Declining fertility rates also have been an important trend reflecting and affecting changes in women's employment. The average birthrate has declined from 22.3 per thousand in the 1935–55 period to 19.5 per thousand between 1955 and 1978 and is expected to be 15.8 for 1975 through 1995–2000 (United Nations, 1979). These declines in birthrates reflect changing employment and lifestyles for women. They mean, for instance, that more time can be devoted to work outside the home. They also mean that in the future domestic population increases will be less of a factor in the competition for jobs than they have been. Moreover, declining birthrates, if sustained, would imply an aging population. Associated with the decline in fertility rates is the fact that young women are delaying marriage. In 1960 only 28 percent of 20–24 year-old women had never been married; by 1980 this proportion had increased to 52 percent and it is expected to reach 55 percent by 1995.

Age Composition of the Labor Force. Some significant changes in the age composition of the work force have occurred, and these will continue during the 1980s. Youth job pressure will be alleviated somewhat because four million fewer 16–24 year-olds will enter the work force. The most dramatic change involves the 25–44 year age group, reflecting the aging of the post-war baby boom. In 1975, there were only 39 million people in this category; by 1990 there will be over 60 million. This will greatly intensify job competition among workers between the ages of 25 and 44, who will constitute over half of the work force in 1990. Intensified competition for jobs probably will make this group less supportive of affirmative action programs for women and minorities unless special efforts are made to gain support.

There are those who believe that the decline in the number of 16–24 year-olds will create labor shortages in this category. I do not share this belief because I do not think we will reduce immigration very much, and the desire for jobs is such that competition with young people for jobs in the secondary labor market will continue. If, however, temporary labor shortages should occur among young people, it would improve their relative earnings and lead to improvements in the nature of jobs they hold. Moreover, the projections of labor shortages assume a continuation of the patterns of "male" and "female" jobs. These shortages could be overcome and labor markets made more efficient by the reduction of labor market segregation. Unfortunately, however, analysts probably are correct in assuming that these patterns will change relatively slowly.

Men 55–64 have been withdrawing from the work force and a larger proportion of the population is over 65. This will continue to strain pension funds and the social security system because the ratio of workers to nonworkers might continue to decline. In 1935, when the social security system was established, there were 11 workers for each person 65 and older; today, the ratio is three to one. The much-documented strains on the social security system are particularly important to women, who constitute a majority of social security recipients. However, this burden would be even greater were it not for the growth in labor force participation by women, which has increased the number of contributors to social security.

The growing proportion of older women in the population will require greater attention to the special needs of this group. These needs include work opportunities as well as special income support for those who cannot work or who have inadequate retirement systems because those systems have discriminated against women. Older workers also have special housing and health needs.

Occupational Distribution. There have been some important occupational trends away from goods producing to services, especially information occupations, which were 17 percent of jobs in 1950 but 60 percent today. This change has contributed to the decentralization of industry to rural areas and the sunbelt and reduced the size of producing units. It has also increased the number of service jobs regarded by employers as "women's jobs," increasing the demand for women workers.

Rapidly changing information technology and intensified international competition have created serious job problems in the industrial heartland, especially for relatively high-wage union workers in basic industries. Minorities have also been heavily concentrated in jobs in basic industries. The future of the industrial heartland and of America's competitiveness will depend on the development of effective industrial policies. General policies that favor newer places and enterprises will accelerate the decline of our basic industries.

All of these changes have caused work forces to be more diverse than they were 30 years ago. This diversity will lead to pressures to increase job options in order to meet workers' diverse needs, because work forces have changed more than jobs. As Clark Kerr has observed:

The nontraditional worker, the educated worker, the mobile worker . . . lead to pressures for more variations [on the job]; to electives at the place of work as in the school; to special arrangements in the office—to options in work time, in retirement plans, in job tasks; to choices about when to work, when to learn, when to take leisure time, when to retire, rather than follow a set schedule; the multiple option society rather than the society of the common rule (Kerr and Rosow, 1979, xxvi–xxvii).

WOMEN'S EMPLOYMENT PATTERNS

The nature and dimensions of women's extraordinary increase in labor force participation is suggested by some highlights:

During the 1970s, 60 percent of the growth in the work force came from women whose numbers in the labor force increased by 12 million. About half of these were relatively young women 25–34 years of age, a remarkable 64 percent of whom were looking for work in 1979 and the first half of 1980; 54 percent of the mothers in this group were in the labor force. Put another way, in March 1981, of the almost 32 million children under 18, 54 percent had working mothers, compared with only 39 percent in 1970. Both the unemployment (11.9 percent) and labor force participation rates (67.9 percent) were higher for women with children under 18 in March 1981 than for women who maintained families containing no children under 18 (5.3 percent unemployment, 49.2 percent labor force participation).

Although a large percentage of women remained in traditional occupations, significant increases were evident in nontraditional areas like medicine, law, and accounting. In 1970, 60 percent of all female professional and/or technical workers were in the traditional occupations of nursing and pre-college teaching; by 1979 this percentage had dropped to about 52 percent.

Figure 2 gives a breakdown of the occupational distribution of employed women between 1950 and 1979. The percentage of women in professional, managerial, and clerical jobs increased, the percentage in sales decreased slightly, and the percentage in private household, operative, and farm occupations declined significantly.

Other data show considerable variation in occupational patterns by race and sex. Males are much more heavily concentrated in craft jobs and females in clerical jobs. Nonwhites and females are more heavily concentrated in service and operative categories.

Figure 2
Occupational Distribution of Employed Women, Annual Averages, Selected Years, 1950–1979 (in percentages)

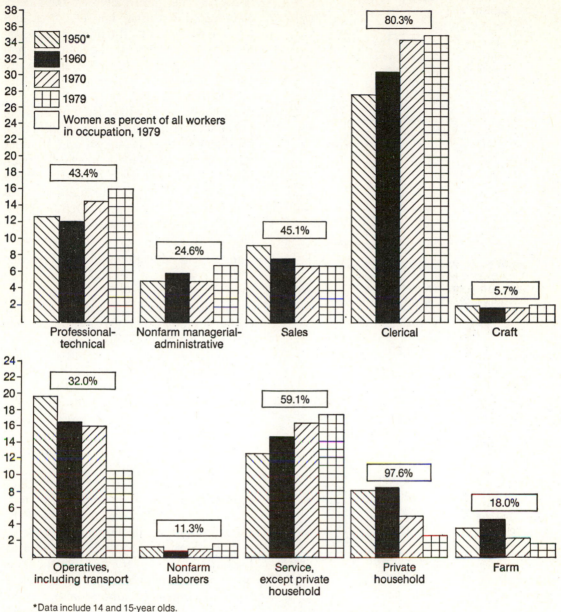

*Data include 14 and 15-year olds.
Source: See Table 1.

The proportions of the total professional labor force represented by different groups can be seen in Table 2's figures from the Equal Employment Opportunity Commission (EEOC). As these data show, white women have made particularly impressive gains in broad professional occupations. However, as will be seen later, there is still considerable job segregation within these broad classifications.

The labor force participation rate for women has risen from 33.9 percent in 1950 to over 52 percent in 1981, while the rate for men declined from 86.4 percent in 1950 to

Table 2
Total Professional Labor Force by Sex and Race, 1966 and 1979 (in percentages)

Race and Sex	Year 1966	Year 1979
White women	13.0	31.6
Black women	0.6	2.2
Black men	0.7	1.9
White men	83.5	58.9
Other	2.2	5.4

Sources: U.S. Equal Employment Opportunity Commission, Report No. 1, *Job Patterns for Minorities and Women in Private Industry, 1966* (Washington, D.C.: U.S. Government Printing Office, n.d.), Part II, p. 51; 1979 Report: *Minorities and Women in Private Industry* (Washington, D.C.: U.S. Government Printing Office, 1981), vol. 1, Table 1.

Table 3
Labor Force Participation Rates of Women and Men, Annual Averages, Selected Years, 1950–1979 and January–June 1980 (in percentages)

Year	Participation Rate Women	Participation Rate Men
1950	33.9	86.4
1952	34.7	86.3
1954	34.6	85.5
1956	36.9	85.5
1958	37.1	84.2
1960	37.7	83.3
1962	37.9	82.0
1964	38.7	81.0
1966	40.3	80.4
1968	41.6	80.1
1970	43.3	79.7
1972	43.9	79.0
1974	45.6	78.7
1976	47.3	77.5
1978	50.0	77.9
Jan.–June 1980	51.2	77.2

Source: See Table 1.

(e.g., 1961–62 and 1970–71) temporarily halted the growing labor force participation of women and increased the unemployment differentials between men and women, while during the present recession the labor force participation rates for women have continued to increase, and the unemployment rate for men has risen faster than that for women.

However, women have been much more vulnerable than men to increasing unemployment in the managerial and administrative occupations; in October 1982, when overall unemployment in this category was 3.6 percent, the unemployment rate for women was 4.7 percent. By October 1982, overall unemployment rates were 9.8 percent for men and 8.6 percent for women.

The median educational levels of women and men are about equal and have been since 1970: 12.4 years for both men and women in 1970 and 12.6 years in 1979. The proportion of women (31 percent in 1970 and 23 percent in 1979) and men (37 percent in 1970 and 26 percent in 1979) in the labor force who have completed less than four years of high school has declined markedly, while the proportion who have completed four years of college has increased: for women, under 11 percent in 1970 and 15 percent in 1979; for men, 14 percent in 1970 and almost 20 percent in 1979.

Men, however, are still more likely to be college graduates and women are more likely to finish high school only, though the education gaps are declining.

The educational upgrading of the work force is suggested by the fact that the number of workers who have had some college is approaching the number who did not continue beyond high school. In March 1981, 40 percent of all workers between the ages of 25 and 64 had completed a year or more of college; in 1970, this proportion was only 25 percent. This increase reflects primarily the entry of the baby boom generation into the work force and the tendency of older workers with less education to retire early.

Data on the proportion of women who have had four or more years of college indi-

77.2 percent in January–June 1980 (Table 3). Women increased their proportion of the total labor force from 29.6 percent in 1950 to 42.5 percent in January–June 1980 (Figure 3).

The unemployment rates for women generally have been higher than those for men overall, 5.9 percent and 4.4 percent in 1970, but the differential was eliminated during the early 1980s. The present recession is unique in that previous recessions

Figure 3
Women in the Labor Force, Annual Averages, Selected Years, 1950–1979 and January–June 1980

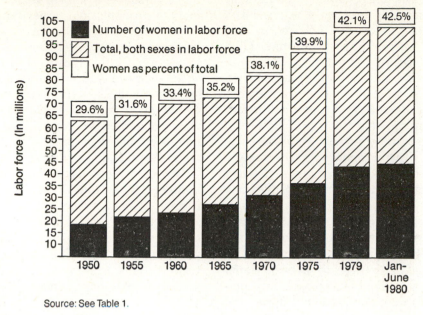

Source: See Table 1.

cate significant differences among age groups. Young women 18–24 years of age are more likely than men in their age group to have had four or more years, but the reverse is true for the older age categories. In every age category, a larger proportion of men than of women did not complete four years of high school, as shown by the data in Table 4.

Labor force participation rates are higher and unemployment rates are lower for whites than for minorities at every educational level; at higher levels of education, that labor force participation rises and unemployment declines for all groups.

Women's Earnings

At the beginning of the 1980s, despite some occupational upgrading, women had about the same earnings relative to men that they had at the beginning of the 1970s. Women who worked full time earned about 60 percent as much as men. Although women almost achieved earnings parity in some newer occupations like computer science, they ordinarily were concentrated in lower-paying jobs in each occupation.

In the 51 percent of families where husbands and wives worked, median income was $23,000 in 1978, compared with $17,000 for families where only the husband worked. Working wives who worked all year contributed 38 percent to family income, but they contributed only 11 percent to the family income

Table 4
Educational Levels of Persons in the Labor Force, March 1981, by Age and Sex

Age and Sex	Percent of Labor Force with	
	Less than Four Years of High School	Four Years of College
18–24 years		
Women	14.7	9.3
Men	23.9	6.4
25–34 years		
Women	11.2	24.7
Men	13.2	27.8
35–64 years		
Women	22.6	15.2
Men	27.5	22.2

Source: U.S. Department of Labor, Bureau of Labor Statistics, *Employment in Perspective: Working Women*, (Washington, D.C.: U.S. Department of Labor, 1981), Report 650.

if they worked part time or less than 26 weeks full time.

In 1978, male-female earnings differentials varied considerably by race; it was smallest among blacks (72 percent), followed by Hispanics (69.8 percent), and then whites (59.5 percent). In the second quarter of 1981, the median weekly earnings of white married families ($474) were about 18 percent higher than for black families ($401), despite the fact that a slightly higher percentage of black families had two or more workers. Median weekly earnings of Hispanic families ($396) were similar to those of blacks, even though relatively fewer Hispanic families had more than one wage earner.

A major way families are able to maintain relatively high incomes in the face of inflation is for both husband and wife to work. The dual-earning family therefore became dominant during the 1970s. In 1920, only nine percent of wives were employed, but during the late 1960s, there was a dramatic increase in working wives; by 1968, as many families (45 percent) had dual earners as had only husbands working. By 1978, 51 percent of all families had dual earners; in just 31 percent was only the husband working (Hayghe, 1981). There was a tendency for wives to work in the same general occupational category as their husbands. A study that compared dual-earner families with "traditional" single-earner families showed that the former were generally younger, were almost as likely to have children under 18 (58 percent versus 60 percent), were better educated, were more prevalent among blacks than among either whites or Hispanics, and had 20 percent higher incomes, primarily because of the wives' earnings.

It is, however, difficult to measure real income differentials between dual- and traditional single-earner families. The former tend to spend about the same proportions of their income as traditional families on durable goods, but spend much more on convenience items and services and transportation. Dual-earner families tend to save less than their traditional counterparts. Moreover, tax and pension laws often discriminate against dual-earner families.

Dual-earner families are much less likely to fall below the official poverty line than traditional families (1.8 percent versus 5.5 percent in 1978). Among dual-earner families, those below the poverty line tend to be younger and have less education, but a major reason for their poverty is that they work less than those above the poverty line. In 1978, 62 percent of husbands and 22 percent of wives in dual-earner poor families worked full time 40 weeks or more; the comparable figures for nonpoor dual-earner families were 88 percent for husbands and 51 percent for wives.

Unemployment has a particularly severe impact on the earnings of dual-earner families if the husband becomes unemployed. In the second quarter of 1980, dual-earner family median weekly earnings were $532 (compared with only $375 for the traditional family). However, if the husband were unemployed, median weekly family income fell to about $190; if the wife were unemployed, it fell to $310, but where both spouses were working and some other family member was unemployed, it averaged between $570 and $580.

To some extent, these occupational and earnings patterns reflect differences in education, continuity of employment, and work experience. However, there is no doubt that a large residual, estimated by one study to be between one half and one third of the earnings differentials between men and women, cannot be accounted for after controlling for these factors (*Economic Report of the President*, 1974; 155: U.S. DOL, Women's Bureau, 1979).

Studies controlling for educational attainment show wide differentials in earnings and career patterns between men and women. A recent study by Bailey and Burrell (1980) found that seven years after graduating from Harvard Law School, 25 percent of men and only 1 percent of women were partners in law firms. The average salaries of graduates of Harvard School of Public Health were $37,800 a year for men and $21,300 for women. This survey also examined the careers of 1972 graduates of Harvard's schools of dentistry, design, divinity, education, public health, and arts and sciences seven years after students were awarded advanced degrees. As

Figure 4
Mean Money Earnings of Year-Round, Full-Time Workers by Sex, 1979

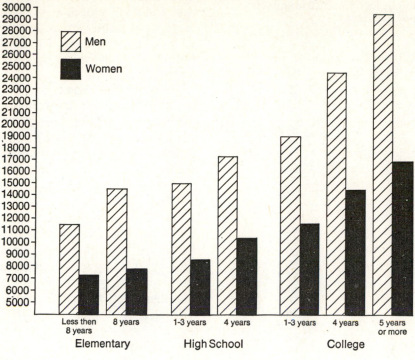

Source: U.S. Bureau of the Census, *Current Population Reports,* Series P-60, No. 129, *Money Income of Families and Persons in the United States: 1979* (Washington, D.C.: U.S. Government Printing Office, 1981), Table 53.

with law graduates, women graduates in other fields had consistently lower salaries regardless of marital or family status. The study concluded that there was "convincing evidence that subtle biases continue to constrain the career development of many women."

Both black and white men with eight years of education earn more than black or white women with one to three years of college. Overall, men with eight years of schooling earn more than women with four years of college (Figure 4).

In all industrialized countries there has been a long-run trend toward increased labor force participation on the part of women, accelerated in recent years by inflation and the growth of the service sector, where women are concentrated (Hewlett, 1981). In 1981, the participation rate of women in the United States was 52 percent, compared with 48 percent in the United Kingdom, 62 percent in Sweden, and 45 percent in France.

Although the United States has the increased labor force participation of women in common with other countries, the earnings of women relative to men are higher in most other countries and have increased, while, as seen in Table 5 since the mid-1950s the relative position of American women has declined. In France, for example, women earned 86 percent as much as men in 1981, in Greece 70 percent, and in Sweden 88 percent. Moreover, the earnings differentials are narrowing in other countries. Between 1968 and 1977, the ratio in West Germany changed from 69 percent to 72 percent. Between 1970 and 1976, the ratio changed from 63 percent to 74 percent in Britain and from 73 percent to 80 percent in Italy.

One of the reasons for women's lower earning rates is their concentration in low-paying jobs. Moreover, the age-earnings profiles for women are flat relative to men's; the earnings peak tends to occur much earlier for women.

Table 5
Year–Round, Full–Time Workers 14 Years and over: Women's Earnings as a Percent of Men's

Year*	Women's Earnings as Percent of Men's
1955	63.9
1956	63.3
1957	63.8
1958	63.0
1959	61.3
1960	60.8
1961	59.4
1962	59.5
1963	59.6
1964	59.6
1965	60.0
1966	58.0
1967	57.8
1968	58.2
1969	60.5
1970	59.4
1971	59.5
1972	57.9
1973	56.6
1974	58.6
1975	58.8
1976	60.2
1977	58.9
1978	59.4

*Data for 1955 to 1966 are for wage and salary workers only and exclude self-employed persons.
Source: See Table 1.

One explanation for this pattern advanced by human capital theorists, as Hartmann and Reskin (1982) point out, is the fact that women anticipate periods of withdrawal from the labor market for childbearing and therefore choose occupations where the withdrawal penalties are low and the lifetime earnings growth is relatively low (Mincer and Polachek, 1974, 1978; Polachek, 1976, 1979, and 1981).

However, this theory has been challenged by studies which attribute the sex earnings ratios more to employment policies and labor market discrimination and less to choices made by women. These studies show that women lose relatively little from withdrawal and recoup their losses relatively fast when they reenter the work force. (For reviews of these theories, see Hartmann and Reskin, 1982.)

A more plausible explanation for the lower job growth of women is the fact that women have less seniority in the labor force and interrupt their job tenure for childbearing. Employers apparently structure jobs for women with this pattern in mind and provide less opportunity for on-the-job training that leads to higher-paying jobs.

However, the experience factor is becoming more favorable to women because the main reason for their increased labor force participation rates (LFPR) is not new entry rates but the fact that experienced women are reentering or remaining in the work force (Barrett, 1980).

While labor market factors account for some of the male-female earnings differentials, careful studies have found that less than half of the gross earnings differentials can be accounted for by such human capital factors as education, training, experience, and skill requirements (Hartmann and Reskin, 1982). The large, unexplained residual is attributable to overt and institutional discrimination, especially job segregation.

As noted, there have been large earnings differentials between predominantly male and female occupations. A 1981 study of 1970 data found that workers in predominantly female occupations averaged $4,000 less than those in predominantly male occupations (Treiman and Hartmann, 1981). Of course, some of these earnings differentials can be explained by the characteristics of occupations in which men and women are concentrated, but the impact of occupational segregation appears to be larger the more detailed the occupational classification; the most detailed census data make it possible to attribute over one third of the sex differential to job segregation. This is probably an understatement because the earnings in different occupations are themselves affected by job segregation. It has been found, for example, that sex earnings differentials are largest in those occupations dominated by males (Treiman and Hartmann, 1981), even though the highest-paying occupations for women are those dominated by men.

These trends suggest that women have made some progress integrating occupations, but are a long way from equality. While conclusive proof is not available, there is little doubt that a major factor responsible for the integration of nontraditional occupations has been pressure from the federal government to enforce antidiscrimination legislation and the affirmative action requirements of government contractors. Surveys suggest that women in managerial positions, particularly, feel that discrimination is the main barrier to their advancement and that during the early 1980s, ". . . businesses sense less federal pressure to hire and promote women as part of affirmative action requirements" (Lublin, 1982).

The future enforcement of antidiscrimination measures will depend heavily on public support for affirmative action programs. There is a danger that with prolonged unemployment, competition for jobs will lead to white male resistance to upgrading of women and minorities. There also is some concern that the upgrading of white women will be at the expense of blacks. For example, a 1982 *New York Times* survey concluded that "many black men and women are becoming increasingly convinced that they are not making the kinds of gains in white collar jobs that white women are making. And that impression appears to be fueling tensions among groups as they compete for work in a recession" (Rule, 1982).

These kinds of tensions are likely to become more pronounced as unemployment persists, giving women and minorities a special stake in full employment.

A favorable factor in the future employment of women in professional, technical, and managerial jobs is their rapidly growing share of college and professional degrees. The percentage of women among law degree recipients increased from 5 percent in 1970 to 32 percent in 1981, among medical degree recipients from 8 percent to 25 percent, and among MBA recipients from 4 percent to 25 percent. Furthermore, the ratio of women to men awarded undergraduate degrees in many fields of study is becoming more equal.

However, the main determinants of future employment growth for women will be the growth of nonprofessional occupations because this is where most of the jobs are. These will, in turn, depend on general economic conditions and the extent to which women are able to break into nontraditional occupations.

Unions

Another determinant of future economic prospects for women will be their relationship with unions. Although unions have been male-dominated institutions in the United States and abroad, women are increasing their absolute union membership (from 2.95 million in 1954 to 6.86 million in 1978) and are a larger percentage of total union membership (17 percent in 1954 versus 24 percent in 1978). If employee associations are included, 6.9 million women were union members, constituting 28 percent of total union membership; 15 percent of women workers and 28 percent of men were in labor organizations in 1978 (U.S. Department of Labor, Bureau of Labor Statistics, 1980).

Reflecting their occupational segregation, women are heavily concentrated in a few unions. In 1978, women constituted at least 50 percent of the membership in 26 unions— 39, counting associations (out of 208 unions and associations). In 1978, 18 unions and associations reported no women members. The unions with the most female members in 1978 were: Teamsters (480,000); American Federation of State, County and Municipal Employees (AFSCME, 409,000); Retail Clerks (375,105); Clothing and Textile Workers (330,660); Service Employees (312,500); International Brotherhood of Electrical Workers (303,510); Teachers (300,000); and the International Ladies' Garment Workers (274,000). These eight unions accounted for about half of all female union members in 1978.

Women are also increasingly found in labor movement leadership positions, but their share of these positions remains small relative to their share of the rank and file membership. The first woman was elected to the AFL–CIO Executive Council in 1980. Women constituted about 7 percent of union board members in 1978 and 24 percent of total union membership; the comparable figures for associations were 35 percent of board members and 60 percent of the membership.

A 1980 study of the determinants of female union membership, which controlled for education, age, location, and incidence of part-time work, found that differences in occupational and industrial status account for over half of the male-female union membership differential. The point estimate in this study suggests that if female and male workers were identical in other ways, changing their occupational-industrial patterns would increase female union membership by roughly 50 percent, leaving a large portion of the gender differential in union membership unexplained by changes in occupational-industrial patterns. Increasing the female proportion of union membership to the male proportion would also reduce the male-female wage differential by nine percent (Antos, Chandler and Mellow, 1980).

Because of the growth in female labor force participation rates, the relationship between women and unions is mutually important. Unions are major economic and political forces whose policies will affect female as well as male workers. Indeed, unions form the main interest group for programs of concern to *all* workers. The objectives of some unions will sometimes conflict with those of women's groups—like the establishment of goals and timetables for women in the construction industry, or challenges to established union seniority systems in order to improve the job opportunities for women—but there will be broad overlapping interests between unions and women's groups, making their cooperation mutually advantageous.

However, neither unions nor women's organizations are monolithic. Some women's groups and unions will have stronger interests in the problems of working women than others. Unions with large female memberships or potential memberships naturally will have a stronger interest in women's issues than others. The AFL-CIO and state and local federations will have an interest in coalitions with women's organizations because the federations are mainly political organizations. Moreover, unions are means to achieve the ends of their members, so women can work within unions to achieve their economic and political objectives.

Comparable Worth

An illustration of the kinds of things unions can do and have done to promote female (and therefore their own) economic interests is illustrated by the pay equity, comparable worth, or "equal pay for equal value" issue which has become a major women's economic issue of the 1980s. This movement originated from the growing realization that equal pay for equal work would do little to improve the economic conditions of women because men and women typically do not have the same jobs. It has been demonstrated that "women's" jobs often have lower pay than "men's" jobs with equal or greater value to the employer—measured by such standard job analyses as skill, effort, responsibility, and working conditions. Moreover, this kind of discrimination is generally not reached by the Equal Pay Act, which applies only to those job classifications in which men and women are employed and to employees in "female" jobs who are performing essentially the same work as men in historically male-dominated jobs.

Industrial relations systems have considerable experience with these job rate inequity problems, which frequently are resolved through collective bargaining and arbitration. Moreover, the Gunther and Westinghouse cases establish that sex-based discrimination violates Title VII of the Civil Rights Act (6.31 F.2d [3rd Cir. 1980], cert denied, 49 U.S.L.W. 3954, June 22, 1981).

AFSCME, a union with a large female membership, has made litigation a major component of its collective bargaining program on pay equity and has made pay equity an organizing tool. In San Jose, California, for example, a job evaluation undertaken jointly by AFSCME and the city revealed that predominantly women's jobs averaged 15 percent less pay than predominantly men's jobs with the same point values. After a year of efforts to bargain over pay equity, AFSCME filed charges with the EEOC and conducted the first major successful strike over pay equity. Other job evaluation studies in Connecticut and Washington show similar pay equity differentials.

Although pay equity is difficult to measure or to apply precisely in concrete situations, this is a characteristic of most pay problems. Some will argue that pay differentials relate to demand and supply conditions in female-dominated labor markets and not to discrimination. However, while the labor market does function in a very rough way, it is very imprecise and erodes discrimination very slowly. Moreover, the crowding of women into segregated jobs because of discrimination increases the supply of women in occupations like nursing, which has relatively low earnings despite what is perceived by employers to be a shortage at existing wages.

One careful observer of this issue concludes:

In the foreseeable future it does not seem likely that federal agencies will take action to correct sex-based discrimination. The Reagan Administration has made it clear that it is not interested in the problem of wage discrimination or other forms of class action or systemic discrimination.

Management and union representatives agree that immediate comparable worth initiatives "will not come from the government," but rather from "private plaintiffs and predominantly labor unions in the public sector." Unions have a distinct advantage over private plaintiffs. Through their knowledge of employer practices, and their access to . . . information from employees, unions are in an excellent position to identify discriminatory practices which may otherwise have gone unrecognized.

Unions are also able to inform . . . workers about their rights and to assist them in bringing their complaints before the proper authorities (Newman, 1981).

The AFL–CIO's interest in this issue is suggested by the fact that its 1981 convention adopted a resolution calling on its affiliates to:

1. Treat sex-based pay inequities in contract negotiations like all other inequities which must be corrected,
2. Initiate joint union-employer pay equity studies, as AFSCME has already done with a number of public employers, and
3. Take all other appropriate action to bring about true equality in pay for work of comparable value and to remove all barriers to equal opportunity for women.

Newman believes that "while the litigative route is an essential backstop, the more traditional collective bargaining approach offers a far more effective method of handling the massive amount of pay discrimination that exists" (Newman, 1981).

Unions could also join women's groups in promoting greater equity in retirement and pregnancy benefits.* In addition, they could help prevent (and bring charges against those guilty of) sexual harassment, a very important problem for women that appears not to be very well understood by many men.

CONCLUSIONS

The leadership challenge of the future will be how to shape these dynamic, diverse trends and values into viable, efficient systems that will at the same time satisfy changing human needs for self-fulfillment.

These trends have important implications for all of the principal actors in the labor market—women's groups, labor organizations, management, and government. Experience suggests that the major impetus for change must come from women themselves and that effective change requires careful analyses of institutions and power relationships and the development of effective tactics to achieve change. Other institutions can facilitate change or even come to advocate it, but they are not likely to do so without pressure from those who are adversely affected by present arrangements.

Labor organizations have a major stake in women's issues. As these issues become more important politically and economically, the support by women of the unions' goals and objectives will be important determinants of

---

*After the Supreme Court nullified the EEOC's guidelines making pregnancy benefits a part of such leave and disability benefits available to other workers, President Carter signed the 1978 Pregnancy Disability Act amendment to Title VII of the Civil Rights Act, requiring employers to make pregnancy benefits a part of insurance and other benefits, making it illegal to discriminate against pregnant workers in hiring or promotion, and protecting the reinstatement rights of women on leave for pregnancy-related reasons.

union power and viability. Similarly, the extent to which women are active in and influence unions will determine the extent to which labor organizations can be induced to support women's issues.

Similarly, management and management organizations must be concerned not only about the political and economic power of women and their organizations, but also about the extent to which the equitable integration of women into the work force produces greater productivity, efficiency, and profits.

National policy must give greater weight to women's issues because the effective and equitable development of female human resources will have important implications for the nation's political, social, and economic health.

The federal government's antidiscrimination and economic and social policies have helped improve the economic position of women as well as minorities. However, although cooperative relationships between enforcement agencies and between those agencies and the private sector are desirable objectives, there will always be some who will not cooperate, so voluntary efforts must be backed by sufficient penalties to encourage cooperation and deter violations. The arguments about quotas and reverse discrimination are false issues which divert attention from the real problem—the need to take positive measures to break down institutionalized patterns of discrimination against people for reasons unrelated to their merit and ability. Goals and timetables are not quotas, and special programs to help people overcome the consequences of past discrimination are not necessarily reverse discrimination.

The United States derives rich benefits from being a multiracial, multicultural society. But it is hard to see how we can derive the benefits of such a system and avoid dangerous and debilitating social strife without equal opportunity, and it is hard to see how equal opportunity can be a reality in the face of institutionalized discrimination without affirmative action.

Antidiscrimination programs alone, however, are not sufficient to make significant improvements in the economic condition of women. General economic policies to reduce unemployment and foster full utilization of our resources, and special targeted programs to deal with the needs of particular groups, also are required. In this connection, continuing high levels of unemployment, especially among workers in lower-paying jobs, will cause great difficulty for women. Both the 1981 tax and subsequent spending cuts adversely affect women. Heavily concentrated in low-income jobs, women will realize little or no benefit from the tax cuts, which are targeted toward high-income earners. Moreover, women are bearing the main brunt of cuts in human resource development programs. Over 70 percent of the cuts now in place affect programs serving low-income groups, in which women predominate. These include education, jobs and training, Medicaid, housing aid, food stamps, school nutrition, aid to poor families with children, energy assistance, and unemployment compensation.

Finally, there is a need for the United States to develop more systematic policies which deal with the reality that women are permanent and integral parts of the labor force and that the "traditional" pattern of men being the only family income earners is obsolete. This requires particular attention to the labor market needs of women at different stages in their lives: career selection and development, childbearing and reentry into the work force, the ability to enter nontraditional jobs, a policy with respect to caring for children of working mothers (especially for low-income working mothers), health care for women and children, and the special housing, income support, and health care needs of older women who will be an increasing proportion of the population.

REFERENCES

Antos, Joseph; Mark Chandler; and Wesley Mellow. "Sex Differences in Union Membership." *Industrial and Labor Relations Review* 33, January 1980, pp. 162–69.

Bailey, Susan, and Barbara Burrell. *Second Century Radcliffe News*, Winter 1980.

Barrett, Nancy. *Productivity Impact of the*

Housework Shift. Washington, D.C.: U.S. Department of Labor, May 1980.

Corcoran, Mary. "Women's Experience, Labor Force Withdrawals, and Women's Wages: Empirical Results Using the 1976 Panel of Income Dynamics." In *Women in the Labor Market,* ed. Cynthia B. Lloyd; Emily S. Andrews; and Curtis L. Gilroy. New York: Columbia University Press, 1979.

Davis, Kingsley, and Pietronella van den Oever. "The Demographics of Feminism." *Washington Times,* July 1, 1982.

Economic Report of the President, 1974. Washington, D.C.: U.S. Government Printing Office, 1974.

Hartmann, Heidi, and Barbara Reskin. "Job Segregation: Trends and Prospects." Appendix B in *Occupational Segregation and Its Impact on Working Women,* ed. Cynthia H. Chertos; Lois Haignere; and Ronnie J. Steinberg. Report of a conference held at the Ford Foundation, June 9, 1982. Albany: State University of New York, Center for Women in Government, 1982.

Hayghe, Howard. "Husbands and Wives as Earners." *Monthly Labor Review* 104, February 1981, pp. 46–53.

Hewlett, Sylvia Ann. *"Women and Work: Lessons from Other Civilized Nations."* Mimeographed. 1982.

Kerr, Clark, and Jerome Rosow, eds. *Work in America: The Decade Ahead.* New York: Van Nostrand Reinhold, 1979.

Lloyd, Cynthia B., and Beth T. Niemi. *The Economics of Sex Differentials.* New York: Columbia University Press, 1979.

Lublin, Joann S. "White-Collar Cutbacks Are Falling More Heavily on Women than Men." *The Wall Street Journal,* November 9, 1982.

Marshall, Ray; Charles Knapp; Malcolm Liggett; and Robert Glover. *Employment Discrimination: The Impact of Legal and Administrative Remedies.* New York: Praeger Publishers, 1978.

Marshall, Ray. *Management and Productivity.* Discussion paper for United Nations Association Economic Policy Council, 1983.

Mincer, Jacob, and Solomon W. Polachek. "Family Investments in Human Capital: Earnings of Women." *Journal of Political Economy* 82, 1974, pp. S76–S108.

———. "Women's Earnings Reexamined." *Journal of Human Resources* 13, 1978, pp. 118–34.

Newman, Winn. "Combatting Occupational Segregation: Presentation III." In *Women and the Workplace: The Implications of Occupational Segregation,* ed. Martha Blaxall and Barbara Reagan. Chicago: University of Chicago, 1976.

———. "Pay Equity: An Emerging Labor Issue." Paper presented to the Industrial Relations Research Association annual meeting, December 29, 1981.

Ouchi, William. *Theory Z.* New York: Avon Books, 1981.

Polachek, Solomon W. "Occupational Segregation: An Alternative Hypothesis." *Journal of Contemporary Business* 5, 1976, pp. 1–2.

———. "Occupational Segregation Among Women: Theory, Evidence, and a Prognosis." In *Women in the Labor Market,* ed. Cynthia B. Lloyd; Emily Andrews; and Curtis Gilroy. New York: Columbia University Press, 1979.

———. "Occupational Self-Selection: A Human Capital Approach to Sex Differences in Occupational Structure." *The Review of Economics and Statistics* 63, 1981, pp. 60–69.

Remick, Helen. "Beyond Equal Pay for Equal Work: Comparable Worth in the State of Washington." In *Equal Employment Policy for Women: Strategies for Implementation in the United States, Canada, and Western Europe,* ed. Ronnie Steinberg Ratner. Philadelphia: Temple University Press, 1980.

Rule, Sheila. "Blacks Believe White Women Lead in Job Gains." *New York Times,* March 25, 1982.

Treiman, Donald J., and Heidi Hartmann, eds. *Women, Work, and Wages: Equal Pay for Jobs of Equal Value.* Committee on Occupational Classification and Analysis, Assembly of Behavioral and Social Sciences, National Research Council. Washington, D.C.: National Academy Press, 1981.

United Nations. *World Population Trends and Prospects by Country, 1950–2000: Summary Report of the 1978 Assessment.* New York: United Nations, 1979.

U.S. Department of Labor, Bureau of Labor Statistics. *Directory of National Unions and Employee Associations,* 1979.

———. Bulletin 2079, September 1, 1980.

U.S. Department of Labor, Bureau of International Labor Affairs. *Demographic and Occupational Characteristics of Workers in Trade-Sensitive Industries.* Economic Discussion Paper no. 2, 1980.

U.S. Department of Labor, Women's Bureau. *The Employment of Women: General Diagnosis of Development and Issues,* April 1979.

READING 3

Blacks in the 1970s: Did They Scale the Job Ladder?*

Diane M. Nilsen†

More blacks obtained white-collar jobs but fewer penetrated higher-salaried positions; mobility in higher-paid blue-collar jobs was somewhat more impressive.

The proportion of workers holding white-collar jobs has increased steadily over the past few decades as employment grew quite rapidly in the professional and clerical fields. Accompanying this movement were substantial declines among private household workers and farmworkers. Each of these trends has had an impact on the employment patterns of black workers.[1] Blacks made some advances in the more highly skilled occupational groups. For example, in 1960, 11 percent of black workers were in professional and technical and craft worker positions; by 1980, their proportion had almost doubled to 21 percent.

Throughout the 1960s, blacks advanced both socially and economically, making notable strides in a number of areas including educational attainment, voting rights, equal housing opportunities, and earnings, as well as in employment.[2] These advancements came about during a period of favorable economic conditions; however, it was also a time of social change which saw the passage of the Civil Rights Act of 1964 and the establishment of the Equal Employment Opportunity Commission. During the 1970–80 period, however, job opportunities and occupational mobility slowed considerably as the nation underwent three recessions. With each contraction came periods of sustained and progressively higher levels of unemployment, accompanied by severe inflationary pressures which failed to subside over the course of the decade. Movement up the occupational scale for blacks progressed more slowly during the 1970s, as the number of black professional and craft workers increased only about half as fast as during the 1960s. Clearly, economic disruptions affected the occupational advancement not only of blacks, but of all workers as well.

Between 1972[3] and 1980, the number of employed blacks increased by 1.3 million, or 17 percent. Their proportion of the nation's employed work force—9.4 percent—did not change, as the white employment level rose by 18 percent. The largest employment gains for blacks occurred in the white-collar occupations, where the four major subcategories—professional and technical, managerial and administrative, sales, and clerical—increased very sharply. (See Table 1.) While their advancement in these occupational categories was proportionately greater than for whites, it was not sufficient to alter materially the overall black-white proportions of the previous decade, and blacks continued to represent a disproportionately small number of white-collar workers.

This article examines the occupational shifts of black workers between 1972 and 1980, using Current Population Survey data on employment by detailed occupation, race, and sex. To further assess the extent of occupational mobility among blacks during this period, occupational data by area of residence and usual weekly earnings are also analyzed.

---

*From U.S. Department of Labor, *Monthly Labor Review* 105, no. 6 (June 1982), pp. 29–37.

†*Diane M. Nilsen is an economist in the Division of Employment and Unemployment Analysis, Bureau of Labor Statistics.*

[1] Unless otherwise stated, the term *black* in this article refers exclusively to the "black only" population and not to the "black and other" category which is made up of blacks, American Indians, Alaskan Natives, and Asian and Pacific Islanders.

[2] See Sylvia Small, *Black Americans, A Decade of Occupational Change*, Bulletin 1760 (Bureau of Labor Statistics, revised 1972). For a short history of occupational change among blacks, see "The Social and Economic Status of the Black Population in the U.S.: An Historical View, 1790–1978," *Current Population Reports*, Series P-23, No. 80 (Bureau of the Census), pp. 61–63.

[3] The year 1972 was chosen for comparison with 1980, rather than 1970, because occupational data before that time are not strictly comparable with data for later years due to classification changes.

Table 1
Employment Change by Occupation and Race, 1972 and 1980, Annual Averages (000)

Occupation	Black Employment Change, 1972–80		White Employment Change, 1972–80	
	Number	Percent	Number	Percent
Total employment	1,344	17.3	13,306	18.2
White-collar workers	1,185	55.3	10,022	27.4
Professional and technical	354	55.4	3,592	33.8
Managers and administrators	168	69.1	2,639	34.2
Sales	88	51.9	698	13.5
Clerical	580	52.7	3,094	23.8
Blue-collar workers	215	6.8	1,760	7.0
Craft and kindred workers	217	32.3	1,427	14.2
Operatives, except transport	73	5.8	− 209	− 2.3
Transport equipment operatives	41	9.0	204	7.5
Nonfarm laborers	− 116	− 14.7	337	10.0
Service workers	21	1.0	1,826	21.2
Private household workers	− 238	− 41.8	− 159	− 18.6
Other service workers	259	15.9	1,985	25.6
Farmworkers	− 74	− 31.9	− 302	− 10.8
Farm managers	− 23	− 51.1	− 187	− 11.4
Farm laborers	− 51	− 27.3	− 116	− 9.9

Table 2
Percent Distribution of Employed Persons by Occupation, Race, and Sex, 1972 and 1980

Occupation	Black Men		White Men		Black Women		White Women	
	1972	1980	1972	1980	1972	1980	1972	1980
Total employed	4,347	4,704	45,769	5,033	3,406	4,394	27,305	36,043
Percent	100.0	100.0	100.0	100.0	100.0	100.0	100.0	100.0
Professional and technical	6.4	8.2	14.3	16.1	10.6	13.8	14.9	17.0
Managers and administrators	4.0	5.6	14.0	15.3	2.1	3.4	4.8	7.4
Sales	1.7	2.5	6.6	6.4	2.5	2.8	7.8	7.3
Clerical	7.6	8.4	6.8	6.2	22.7	29.3	36.2	36.0
Craft and kindred workers	14.8	17.6	21.2	21.5	.9	1.4	1.3	1.9
Operatives, except transport	17.4	15.5	12.1	10.7	14.8	13.8	12.5	9.4
Transport equipment operatives	10.3	9.9	5.7	5.4	.4	.7	.4	.7
Nonfarm laborers	17.4	13.0	6.8	6.5	.9	1.4	.9	1.2
Farm and farm managers	1.0	.4	3.4	2.6	—	—	.4	.4
Farm laborers and foremen	3.5	2.4	1.7	1.5	1.1	.5	1.5	1.3
Private household workers	.3	.1	—	—	16.4	7.4	3.0	1.9
Other service workers	15.8	16.4	7.3	7.9	27.6	25.4	16.2	16.0

Black-White Employment Changes

Between 1972 and 1980, employment in the professional and technical occupations expanded rapidly, and both blacks and whites increased their participation in these fields accordingly. The number of black men in professional positions grew at a slightly faster pace than that of white males during the decade. Still, in 1980, 16 percent of all white men were employed as professional workers, twice the black male proportion. This 2-to-1 ratio is only slightly lower than that which prevailed in 1972. (See Table 2.)

Relative to their white counterparts, black women strengthened their foothold as professional workers.[4] Black women professionals, who had accounted for nearly 11 percent of all employed black women in 1972, made up

---

[4]For a recent analysis of the employment situation of black women, see Phyllis A. Wallace, *Black Women in the Labor Force* (Cambridge, Mass.: MIT Press, 1980).

14 percent of the total in 1980, a proportion approaching that for white women.

Jobs for managers and administrators also increased during the decade. Black men and women shared more than proportionately in the gains but were still much less likely to be employed in these fields than their white counterparts. For example, in 1980, 15 percent of all white men were engaged as managers or administrators, compared with fewer than 6 percent of black men.

Employment in clerical occupations rose rapidly between 1972 and 1980. Among women—who make up four-fifths of all clerical workers—the increase was proportionately much greater for blacks than for whites. Black men also increased their participation in this field, while white men experienced a decline. There was a similar occurrence in sales, where both black men and women increased their representation, while white participation declined.

Blue-collar jobs grew at a relatively slow pace during the 1970s. Overall, the proportion of black men who were blue-collar workers was down somewhat from 1972. This stemmed from reduced participation in the relatively undesirable operative and nonfarm laborer jobs, as their representation in the skilled craft and kindred trades actually rose. By 1980, the largest proportion of black men in any single occupational group was in skilled craftwork; this has long been true for white men. Despite this improvement, there were still relatively high concentrations of black men in the less skilled job categories. For example, they were still twice as likely to be in laborer jobs as their white counterparts.

After the craft trades, service work employed more black men than any other occupation. One-sixth of all employed black men were engaged in service work (excluding private household) in 1980—not much different than in 1972. Blacks continued to be more than twice as likely to have service jobs as white men.

The most substantial movement among black women during the 1970s occurred in private household work, as their proportion fell from 16 to 7 percent. One-fourth of employed black women had jobs in other service occupations in 1980—a small decline from 1972. Only clerical work was more prevalent among black women, accounting for 29 percent of those employed. Like private household workers, farmworkers registered an employment drop between 1972 and 1980; black men left this occupation more quickly than white men.

Clearly, the movement out of the lower-paying nonfarm-labor, service, and farm jobs and into mid- and upper-level jobs in the white-collar occupations and craft trades was sustained during the 1970s, although the changes were not as dramatic as those which occurred in the previous decade. But while blacks moved into higher-skilled (and more highly paying) occupations in greater numbers and, correspondingly, diminished their proportions in the less desirable job groups, they still accounted for a disproportionately large share of private household workers, nonfarm laborers, and transport equipment operatives, while constituting a disproportionately small share among most white-collar jobs—clerical workers being the exception.

Specific Job Changes

It is important to know the specific job markets in which blacks have actually made headway relative to their white counterparts. Are blacks increasingly more likely to become physicians or accountants or are they still, as in the past, finding teaching and technicians jobs their primary source of entry into the professional occupations? If the jobs blacks hold are found in the lesser-skilled and lower-paying professional positions, then the conclusion that there has been significant occupational upgrading may not be justified. Detailed occupational data permit a finer analysis of the areas of the job market in which blacks are overrepresented and those in which their entry seems to have been restricted. An examination of occupational participation rates[5] during the 1970s is a useful yardstick of progress in this area.

---

[5]For the purposes of this analysis, an occupational participation rate is defined as the ratio of black men employed in a given occupational group to all men in that oc-

Overall, black occupational advancement in the 1970s is not particularly impressive when the detailed occupational data are examined. In most cases, black workers were concentrated in the same jobs in which they were employed in 1972. In other words, although a higher proportion of blacks could be found among the professional and technical occupations in 1980 than in 1972, they were concentrated in jobs at the lower end of the professional pay scale, such as nursing, technical trades, and vocational and educational counseling. And even though their numbers have expanded in some of the more desirable and better-paid jobs, there are few examples where black men and women have been able to significantly increase their representation in a particular job.

Black Men. Despite a substantial increase in the proportion of black men in the professional and technical occupations, their proportion of all employed men in this category rose only slightly over the 1972–80 period, from 4.0 to 4.4 percent. By way of comparison, black men accounted for 8.4 percent of employed men in 1980, a small drop from the 8.6 percent in 1972. The 1980 recession undoubtedly had an impact on the employment of black men. In the previous year, 1979, black men had accounted for 8.6 percent of employment, the same as in 1972. (See Table 3.)

In 1980, black males in the professional and technical occupations accounted for eight percent or more of all men employed as health technicians, nurses, social and recreational workers, vocational and educational counselors, and personnel and labor relations workers. In every case, these were the same professions in which they were concentrated in 1972.

The proportions of black men in certain higher-status professional occupations—such as accountants, computer specialists, engineers, and lawyers—showed some increases over the period, but were still disproportionately low. The proportion employed as physicians, at 2.1 percent, did not increase at all between 1972 and 1980.

The overall black occupational participation rates for managers and administrators rose slightly—but to only 3.2 percent—with bank officials and financial managers showing a healthy increase. Nevertheless, blacks in 1980, as well as 1972, were most likely to be employed as managers of restaurants, cafeterias, and bars, and as school administrators. Black employment in school administration actually declined during the 1972–80 period, while those working as food establishment managers showed a rise.

Overall, employment growth in sales was rather sluggish during the 1970s, yet black men were able to increase their proportion of those employed from 2.4 to 3.5 percent. However, gains occurred in occupations in which blacks have traditionally been concentrated— retail salesclerks and insurance agents.

Some of the largest occupational gains among black men during the decade occurred in the clerical occupations, in particular as banktellers, bookkeepers, estimators and investigators, office machine operators, statistical clerks, and secretaries—jobs that had shown substantial growth during the 1970s. For example, the participation rate of black men who were estimators and investigators rose from 3 to 6 percent and the rate for office machine operators increased from 10 to 14 percent. Areas in which black men had been highly concentrated in 1972 (15 percent or more)—file clerks, mailhandlers, messengers and office boys, and postal clerks—showed little growth or declined by 1980, although they still accounted for a significant proportion of black male employment.

To capsulize, black men were able to realize greater participation in a substantial number of white-collar occupations over the decade. One significant exception was the better-paying professional and technical jobs, in which they advanced, but not significantly. Despite some progress in the professional ranks, they were concentrated in the same occupations as they were almost a decade earlier.

cupation and black women to all women. It is appropriate to examine data for men and women separately, as occupational differences between the sexes are so pronounced. Though this statistic is not unique, the term *occupational participation rate* was made popular by Stuart Garfinckle back in 1974 in his article, "Occupations of Women and Black Workers, 1962–1974," *Monthly Labor Review*, November 1975, pp. 25–35.

Table 3
Employed Blacks as a Percent of All Employed Men and Women in Selected Detailed Occupations, 1972 and 1980, Annual Averages

Occupation	Black Men 1972	Black Men 1980	Black Women 1972	Black Women 1980
Total	8.6	8.4	11.0	10.6
Professional and technical	4.0	4.4	8.0	8.8
Accountants	2.1	3.6	5.2	7.4
Computer specialists	3.5	4.1	6.5	9.3
Engineers	1.4	2.2	(¹)	(¹)
Personnel and labor relations	6.1	7.9	12.5	10.8
Physicians, dentists, and related practitioners	2.1	2.1	(¹)	5.0
Nurses,dietitians, therapists	8.6	13.2	6.1	8.2
Health technologists and technicians	12.4	8.4	7.8	9.2
Lawyers and judges	1.3	3.1	(¹)	7.1
Religious workers	10.0	5.7	(¹)	(¹)
Social and recreation workers	13.8	16.4	17.4	17.4
Teachers, college and university	3.6	3.3	5.4	5.3
Teachers, except college and university	7.0	5.5	9.0	10.2
Engineering and science technicians	3.5	5.6	(¹)	6.7
Vocational and educational counselors	9.0	15.2	13.4	17.8
Writers, artists, and entertainers	4.2	4.1	2.8	3.6
Managers and administrators	2.6	3.2	5.0	5.2
Bank officials and financial managers	(¹)	2.6	(¹)	4.6
Restaurant, cafeteria, and bar managers	4.8	5.7	10.6	7.9
School administrators, elementary and secondary	6.7	6.0	6.9	12.2
Sales	2.4	3.5	3.8	4.4
Insurance agents, brokers, and underwriters	2.3	4.3	7.8	8.2
Sales clerks, retail trade	4.2	7.0	4.1	5.0
Clerical	9.5	10.9	7.2	8.9
Bank tellers	(¹)	10.3	4.0	5.9
Bookkeepers	3.7	6.7	2.4	3.4
Cashiers	7.5	8.7	6.5	8.6
Counter clerks, except food	4.7	5.4	6.2	8.6
Estimators and investigators	2.5	6.0	7.3	11.7
File clerks	22.0	25.6	16.0	18.2
Library attendants and assistants	(¹)	(¹)	8.7	8.5
Mail carriers, post office	13.1	11.6	(¹)	(¹)
Mail handlers, except post office	25.0	22.1	12.5	17.9
Messengers and office helpers	16.4	16.9	(¹)	(¹)
Office machine operators	9.8	14.0	11.9	15.1
Postal clerks	16.0	14.8	26.7	32.7
Receptionists	(¹)	(¹)	6.4	6.4
Secretaries	(¹)	12.1	4.4	5.5
Shipping and receiving clerks	13.0	13.1	13.4	8.3
Statistical clerks	8.0	11.8	7.1	11.3
Stock clerks and storekeepers	12.2	10.5	10.3	11.0
Teachers aides	(¹)	(¹)	21.2	17.3
Telephone operators	(¹)	(¹)	(¹)	14.8
Typists	(¹)	(¹)	10.9	13.2
Craft and kindred workers	6.2	7.0	8.0	8.1
Carpenters	5.1	4.4	(¹)	(¹)
Brickmasons and stonemasons	13.6	14.6	(¹)	(¹)
Bulldozer operators	13.6	11.7	(¹)	(¹)
Cement and concrete finishers	33.3	31.0	(¹)	(¹)
Electricians	2.8	4.1	(¹)	(¹)
Excavating, grading, and road machinery operators	6.6	8.2	(¹)	(¹)
Painters, construction and maintenance	9.3	10.5	(¹)	(¹)
Plumbers and pipe fitters	5.1	8.5	(¹)	(¹)
Machinists and jobsetters	5.6	6.3	(¹)	(¹)
Metal craftsmen, except mechanical, machinery, and jobsetters	4.9	6.2	(¹)	(¹)
Mechanics, automotive	7.4	7.7	(¹)	(¹)
Mechanics, except automotive	4.5	6.1	(¹)	8.9
Printing craftsmen	4.5	7.3	8.5	8.6
Cranesmen, derrickmen, hoistmen	15.5	16.3	(¹)	(¹)

Table 3 *(concluded)*

Occupation	Black Men 1972	Black Men 1980	Black Women 1972	Black Women 1980
Operatives, except transport	11.9	11.7	12.7	14.6
Assemblers	13.3	11.2	11.8	11.9
Checkers, examiners, and inspectors (manufacturing)	7.6	9.6	9.3	10.8
Clothing ironers and pressers	28.9	(¹)	38.4	40.4
Furnacemen, smeltermen, and pourers	23.9	25.4	(¹)	(¹)
Garage workers and gas station attendants	7.3	7.9	(¹)	(¹)
Laundry and drycleaning operators	24.0	21.9	28.7	23.3
Meatcutters and butchers	9.4	8.5	19.4	18.6
Packers and wrappers	12.6	20.4	13.4	15.4
Painters, manufacturing articles	14.5	10.7	(¹)	(¹)
Precision machine operators	6.9	6.7	10.3	18.2
Punch and stamping press	10.5	11.0	11.6	9.1
Sawyers	19.1	17.4	(¹)	(¹)
Sewers and stichers	(¹)	14.3	11.3	13.8
Textile operatives	18.9	22.1	12.4	20.7
Welders and flamecutters	9.4	9.8	(¹)	(¹)
Transport equipment operatives	14.5	14.7	9.0	11.2
Busdrivers	21.7	24.0	7.0	13.1
Deliverypersons and routepersons	10.0	9.2	(¹)	5.1
Forklift and tow motor operators	21.7	18.8	(¹)	(¹)
Taxicab drivers and chauffeurs	22.5	24.0	(¹)	(¹)
Truck drivers	13.9	13.5	(¹)	7.3
Laborers, except farm	19.2	15.5	12.0	12.2
Construction laborers	24.7	15.4	(¹)	(¹)
Freight and material handlers	21.7	17.5	17.8	19.7
Garbage collectors	33.3	32.8	(¹)	(¹)
Gardeners and groundskeepers	16.5	14.1	(¹)	(¹)
Stockhandlers	8.8	10.4	10.7	10.0
Vehicle washers and equipment cleaners	21.9	18.4	(¹)	(¹)
Farm and farm managers	2.6	1.6	3.0	(¹)
Farmers (owners and tenants)	2.6	1.6	3.0	(¹)
Farm laborers and foremen	16.1	12.7	8.1	7.0
Farm laborers, wage workers	19.3	14.3	23.5	15.7
Service workers, except private household	16.8	15.7	17.3	15.9
Cleaning service workers	25.4	22.8	35.3	30.2
Food service workers	12.8	11.5	11.2	10.1
Health service workers	24.5	32.1	23.7	21.0
Personal service workers	13.9	15.0	11.2	12.6
Protective service workers	9.2	9.8	16.9	17.4
Private household workers	(¹)	(¹)	39.8	31.9
Child care	(¹)	(¹)	8.0	7.0
Maids and servants	(¹)	(¹)	71.1	52.5

¹Data not shown where numerator is less than 4,000 or denominator is less than 35,000.

Blue-collar occupations expanded much less rapidly than white-collar jobs over the decade. The occupational participation rate of black men held steady for both transport equipment and other operatives, declined among laborers, but rose in the craft trades. However, even with the rise from 6 to 7 percent, the craft trades remained the only major blue-collar category in which black men accounted for less than their proportion of overall employment.

Black men increased their share in a number of the more highly skilled job categories including electricians, painters, plumbers, metal and printing craftsmen, and excavating and grading road machine operators. However, the two largest job concentrations of black men continued to be as cement and concrete finishers and crane operators.

The overall participation of black men in operative and transport equipment operative positions held steady between 1972 and 1980, with blacks continuing to represent a dispro-portionately large number of employed persons in these occupations. They made up about 20 percent or more of all men employed as clothing ironers and pressers, furnacemen, laundry and drycleaning operatives, sawyers, textile operatives, busdrivers, forklift operatives, and taxicab drivers. For the most part, participation of black men in these occupations increased or was about the same between 1972 and 1980, because white men were moving out of these jobs.

In the nonfarm laborer and service worker occupations—which also have relatively large numbers of black men—there were declines in the proportion engaged in these jobs. The number of laborers dropped substantially during the 1970s, but the employment of black men in these occupations fell even more rapidly.

Black Women. Despite the fact that they made up a smaller percentage of employed women in 1980 than in 1972—because of the huge influx of white women into the labor force—black women were able to increase their proportions in most of the professional and technical job categories. (See Table 3.) And a definite occupational shift occurred over the period. In 1972, black women had participation rates of 12 percent or more in three occupations—social and recreation work, vocational and educational counseling, and personnel and labor relations work. By 1980, although they were still highly visible in these three areas, their concentration in other professional occupations had broadened considerably. The most notable change occurred in the fast growing computer field, where black women increased their participation by 2.8 percentage points to 9.3 percent. Other noteworthy gains were among accountants, nurses, dieticians and therapists, engineering and science technicians, and vocational and educational counselors. Still, in contrast to developments in the 1960s, growth in the professional and technical occupations among black women continued to be relatively slow.

Limited gains among black women were realized in most managerial and administrative positions and sales occupations. The rate of employment participation among school administrators, insurance agents, and bank officials increased, while there was a declining rate among restaurant managers.

Black women made some progress moving out of salesclerk positions, although their participation rate actually increased during the 1970s as white women left this occupation in even greater numbers. In 1972, 75 percent of all black women in sales were retail clerks, but by 1980, this proportion had fallen to 68 percent. Black women accounted for about five percent of employed women in this field.

Employment gains of black women in the fast-growing clerical field were widespread as their overall participation rate moved from seven to nine percent over the eight-year period—still somewhat below the percentage of all employed women who were black. Gains were strong for black women as estimators and investigators, mailhandlers, postal clerks, statistical clerks, and telephone operators. The largest numbers of black women were employed as cashiers, typists, and secretaries.

Although blue-collar occupations are generally male dominated, black women made a number of inroads into some job fields. It should be noted that the occupational participation rates of black women in the better-paying craft trades are difficult to measure, as the actual numbers engaged in these jobs were very low. While some increases in specific crafts were registered, the overall proportion of black women in the craft trades remained about the same over the period, at 8.1 percent.

The largest concentration of black women in blue-collar jobs was in the operative category, a group in which black women have been traditionally overrepresented relative to their employment total. In 1980, black women had participation rates of 18 percent or more in six occupational categories; this compares with three such categories in 1972. Among transport equipment operatives, black women advanced rather strongly as busdrivers, reaching 13 percent in 1980. They also registered strong growth in two occupations in which they had shown little representation in the past—delivery persons and truckdrivers.

The participation rate of black women in

occupations at the lower end of the earnings ladder was unchanged for laborers and declined among household workers during the 1970s. Furthermore, the drop in the rate among black women engaged in private household services, from 40 to 32 percent, is particularly important, given the large concentration of women in this occupation and the fact that black women are moving out at a faster rate than white women.

Residential Location

To better understand the growth of blacks in certain occupations and their decline in others, it is helpful to examine their residential location. In 1980, approximately 55 percent of all blacks lived in central cities, with the other 45 percent divided almost equally between suburban and nonmetropolitan areas. In contrast, only 24 percent of all whites lived in central cities, with the bulk residing in suburban rings (42 percent). This concentration of blacks in the central city becomes particularly important when one realizes that it is the suburban rather than city blacks who were the recipients of most of the occupational upgrading during the 1970s.

Overall, the occupational distribution of black men and women residing in the suburbs was similar to that of their counterparts living in central cities in 1973.[6] However, by 1980, this was no longer the case. While virtually all occupational changes among residents of both cities and suburbs were in the same direction, blacks in the suburbs fared better than those in the central cities or nonmetropolitan areas during the 1970s. This is evident from the rather impressive increases in the proportion holding white-collar jobs, particularly professional and technical and managerial positions. For example, black suburban men had a 91-percent rise in employment in the professional fields, compared with a 16-percent increase among city residents. Likewise, black suburban women had a 158-

percent increase in the managerial ranks, compared with 63 percent among their city counterparts. (These increases may be partially explained by the migration of successful white-collar blacks from the cities to the suburbs.)

In 1973, black workers in blue-collar occupations were predominant in central cities and suburban areas. However, by 1980, while both areas had made the shift to a predominance of white-collar jobs, the changes were more pervasive in the suburbs. Cities and suburbs alike experienced drop in the percentage of men holding semi-skilled and unskilled blue-collar jobs. Metropolitan women also contributed to this growth in white-collar jobs, as they left the service occupations in great numbers.

Nonmetropolitan area blacks also moved into white-collar jobs during this period, though not to as great an extent as blacks living in the cities and suburbs. The proportion of blacks in blue-collar jobs remained unchanged between 1973 and 1980, while blacks moved out of service and farm jobs. In general, the occupational distribution of nonmetropolitan workers is very much different from that of their metropolitan counterparts in that a much larger proportion are engaged in blue-collar work and comparatively few are in white-collar occupations.

That blacks are moving into the professional, clerical, and craft occupations is readily apparent, but nowhere more so than for those who live in the suburbs.[7] And that blacks are still disproportionately concentrated in the less skilled and service jobs is also evident, particularly for those residing in the city and nonmetropolitan areas. In part, central city, suburban, and nonmetropolitan employment differences reflect the strong growth of white-collar occupations in the metropolitan areas and the predominance of blue-collar jobs available in the nonmetropolitan areas. Black occupational advancement is some-

---

[6]Data by area of residence are not available for 1972. Also, the term *blacks* in this section refers to persons classified as blacks and other minorities, as area of residence data by occupation are not presently available for the "black only" category.

[7]For a detailed account on the growth of white-collar jobs by area and how it relates to black employment, see Brian J. O'Connell, *Blacks in White-Collar Jobs* (New Jersey: Allanheld, Osmum, 1979). Also see Thomas M. Stanback, Jr. and Richard Knight, *Suburbanization and the City* (Cambridge, Mass.: Ballinger, 1974).

what related to residential location, in that most workers have jobs in the geographic area in which they live.[8] However, individual levels of educational attainment, skill, and ability are the predominant factors in determining one's occupational classification.

Earnings

Because the white-collar professions are considered among the most powerful and prestigious occupations in American society, it is easy to assume that the growing proportions of workers in these jobs are a sign of achievement. While white-collar jobs are often associated with higher pay status and most blue-collar and service jobs are equated with lower-paying positions, movement of workers from blue-collar to white-collar jobs should not be construed as an improvement in one's relative economic position. Earnings differentials by occupation are more complex than the relationship noted above. There is a broad range of earnings within each major occupational category. (See Exhibit 1.) In a number of instances, blue-collar trades have higher earnings than white-collar jobs, particularly those in the skilled craft occupations.

Median weekly earnings for all workers were $265 in 1980. Managers and administrators had the highest weekly earnings, $380, followed by professional and technical workers, $341; craft and kindred workers, $328; transport equipment operatives, $286; and sales workers, $279. Those occupations with earnings below the overall median were farmers and farm managers, $243; operatives, $225; nonfarm laborers, $220; clerical and kindred workers, $215; service workers, except private household, $184; farm laborers and foremen, $167; and private household workers, $94. Exhibit 1 shows specific occupations which are above or below the median level for four key occupational groups. The highest-paid professional and technical jobs—engineers, lawyers, physicians, and scientists—are all categories in which blacks were underrep-

resented in both 1972 and 1980. By contrast, health technologists, social and recreational workers, nurses, and teachers were among the lowest-paid professional positions and the ones in which blacks continued to be concentrated.

Black workers in management and sales professions were concentrated in jobs that paid below the median for the overall occupation. Only in the clerical field were black workers well dispersed and advancing in some of the better-paying positions, such as postal clerks, stock clerks, and shipping and receiving clerks.

Blacks in the craft trades were able to advance in a number of the higher-paid positions, including plumbers and electricians, though they were still underrepresented in the latter. In contrast to the professional and managerial fields, blacks in craft jobs were more widely dispersed and not relegated to the lower-paid positions.

Between 1973[9] and 1980, black full-time workers increased their earnings by 68 percent, compared with 65 percent for whites. Blacks posted larger gains than whites in the blue-collar occupations, while white workers outpaced blacks in white-collar jobs. Even though blacks were entering the white-collar professions in increasing numbers, they were generally concentrated in the lower-paying jobs of those particular occupations. In addition, their pay increases were smaller relative to those of whites in the white-collar occupations. Consequently, the earnings of black workers relative to whites in white-collar jobs, which had averaged 91 percent in 1973, dropped to 86 percent in 1980. However, blacks were able to advance in occupational standing in the blue-collar professions, as they increased their earnings relative to whites in a number of the higher-paying jobs. (See Table 4.) For example, in 1973, black transport

---

[8]See Diane N. Westcott, "Employment and Commuting Patterns: A Residential Analysis," *Monthly Labor Review*, July 1979, pp. 3–9.

[9]Earnings data used in this article are collected through the *Current Population Survey*. For purposes of comparability, it was necessary to compare May 1973 data with that for the second quarter 1980, as earnings data were not available on an annual average basis prior to 1979. Also, data for black and other races were the only race data available in 1973; by 1980, however, earnings data were tabulated for blacks only, excluding other minorities. Hence, the data are not strictly comparable but do provide very close estimations of earnings changes during this period for blacks.

Exhibit 1
Occupations above and below the Median Weekly Earnings of Full-Time Wage and Salary Workers in Selected Occupational Groups, 1980

Professional and Technical Workers
Above median
  Accountants
  Computer specialists
  Engineers
  Lawyers and judges
  Life and physical scientists
  Personnel and labor relations workers
  Physicians, dentists, and related practitioners
  Vocational and educational counselors
Below median
  Engineering and science technicians
  Health technologists and technicians
  Nurses, dietitians, and therapists
  Social and recreation workers
  Teachers, except college and university

Craft and Kindred Workers
Above median
  Brickmasons and stonemasons
  Cement and concrete finishers
  Cranemen, hoistmen, and derrickmen
  Electricians
  Machinists and jobsetters
  Plumbers and pipefitters
Below median
  Bulldozer operators
  Carpenters
  Excavating, grading, and road machine operators
  Mechanics and repairers
  Painters, construction and maintenance
  Printing craftsmen

Operatives
Above median
  Checkers, examiners, and inspectors
  Furnacemen, smeltermen, and pourers
  Meatcutters and butchers

Painters, manufactured articles
Precision machine operators
Punch and stamping press operators
Welders and flamecutters
Below median
  Assemblers
  Clothing ironers and pressers
  Garage workers and gas station attendants
  Laundry and dry cleaning operators
  Packers and wrappers
  Sawyers
  Sewers and stitchers
  Textile operatives

Clerical and Kindred Workers
Above median
  Mail carriers, post office
  Office machine operators
  Postal clerks
  Shipping and receiving clerks
  Statistical clerks
  Stock clerks and storekeepers
  Telephone operators
Below median
  Bank tellers
  Bookkeepers
  Cashiers
  Counter clerks
  Estimators and investigators
  File clerks
  Library attendants
  Mail handlers, except post office
  Receptionists
  Secretaries
  Teachers' aids
  Typists

equipment operatives made 73 percent of the earnings of their white counterparts; by 1980, this percentage had risen to 85 percent—evidence of their penetration into some of the better-paid positions.

Differences in earnings by race were more discernible among men than among women. In 1980, black males made about 80 percent of the earnings of white men in both the white-collar and blue-collar occupations. However, black women made almost the same as their counterparts in white-collar jobs and over 90 percent of white women's earnings in the blue-collar trades. The following tabulation shows the 1980 black-to-white earnings differential by sex and occupation:

	Male	Female
Total	75.1	92.2
White-collar	79.2	98.7
Professional and technical	85.5	97.6
Managerial	76.7	105.9
Sales	69.2	99.4
Clerical	80.7	98.5
Blue-collar	81.4	93.9
Craft	86.9	99.5
Operatives, except transport	86.8	94.3
Transport equipment operatives	82.6	97.2
Laborers	86.2	100.6
Service	86.6	102.7
Private household workers	73.5	140.7
Other	86.6	103.9
Farm	78.3	81.4

Table 4
Earnings Data by Race and Occupation for May 1973 and Second Quarter 1980

Occupation	Percent Increase in Earnings, 1973–1980		Black/White Earnings Ratio	
	Black	White	1973	1980
Total	68.2	65.4	79.6	81.0
White-collar workers	53.2	63.6	91.3	85.5
Professional and technical	58.3	57.5	89.7	90.2
Managers and administrators	42.4	58.2	87.9	79.1
Sales	76.9	64.0	71.3	77.0
Clerical	47.5	63.6	107.8	97.2
Blue-collar workers	77.2	69.9	77.9	81.2
Craft and kindred workers	61.7	66.5	84.8	82.3
Operatives, except transport	77.4	70.4	85.2	88.7
Transport equipment operatives	89.9	63.6	73.3	85.1
Nonfarm laborers	58.0	56.6	83.2	83.9
Service Workers	74.0	65.1	88.1	92.8
Private household workers	123.5	157.6	154.5	133.1
Other service workers	67.0	64.3	92.0	93.3
Farmworkers	73.7	67.3	75.2	78.1

Note: May 1973 data are for black and other races; second-quarter 1980 data are for blacks only.

Black women, while still at the bottom of the earnings hierarchy, have narrowed the earnings gap between themselves and white women in most occupational categories, much more so than black men have succeeded in doing with respect to white men. This is because women are more concentrated in lesser-skilled, lower-paying jobs which traditionally have been easier for blacks to enter.[10]

Overview

Black occupational status improved somewhat during the 1970s, as proportionately more blacks moved into white-collar jobs, although few penetrated the higher-salaried professional and managerial positions. In fact, the black-to-white earnings differential was unchanged for professional and technical workers between 1973 and 1980, and, even more importantly, black earnings relative to those of whites fell in the fast-growing clerical field. Black mobility in the blue-collar, service,

and farm occupations was more impressive, as blacks moved out of unskilled work—especially private household and laborer positions—and into the craft trades. The growth of black employment in the expanding skilled craft area was particularly important, in that blacks were able to move into some of the better-paid positions, and, for the most part, were able to increase their earnings relative to their white counterparts in the blue-collar occupations.

Overall, shifts by blacks into the higher-salaried occupations were rather limited; this was most apparent for those who resided in the central city areas. The majority of blacks lived in central cities, which have high concentrations of office and other business district-type activities. Yet, by 1980, central city blacks had made little progress in increasing their proportion in white-collar occupations. Most of the occupational upgrading occurred among the smaller number of blacks who resided in suburban areas. Furthermore, the progress that did occur among blacks living in the city was mostly accounted for by women, whereas, in the suburbs, black men and women shared equally in the gains. This indicates that black women in both areas competed successfully for jobs in those occupations in which women are heavily recruited. Clearly,

[10]The earnings gains of black women have been attributed to a reduction in racial discrimination among the female sex. For an explanation of these and other findings on black male/female earnings, see Ronald N. Oaxaca, "The Persistence of Male-Female Earnings Differentials," and others in *The Distribution of Economic Well-Being*, ed. F. Thomas Juster (Cambridge, Mass.: Ballinger, 1977).

black workers, especially black men and city dwellers, need to gain more access to the higher-skilled, better-paying jobs in the rapidly growing white-collar fields, if their earnings are to increase.

Note: The statistics are based on the 1970 Decennial Census population counts, adjusted for the aging of the population, deaths, and net migration. The Bureau of Labor Statistics has subsequently converted Current Population Survey estimates to reflect the 1980 census, which enumerated 4.7 million more people than had been estimated in updating the 1970 figure. Because this difference was so much larger than previous censuses, historical CPS data series are also being revised, including broad occupational employment categories. However, the full range of revised data for detailed occupational categories was not available at this writing; indeed, revisions of some of the detailed series may not be undertaken. Even if revised data were available, their validity might be questionable at the level of detail in this analysis.

Editor's Note: One table, Occupational Distribution of Employed Blacks, by Sex and Area of Residence, 1973 and 1980; and one chart, Percent Distribution of Full-Time Weekly Earnings by Occupation, 1980, Annual Average, have been eliminated from the original article.

READING 4

High Technology Today and Tomorrow: A Small Slice of the Employment Pie*

Richard W. Riche, Daniel E. Hecker, and John U. Burgan†

High-tech industries are expected to provide only a small proportion of the jobs created between 1982 and 1995, under three concepts which embrace from 6 to 48 industries

High technology enjoys high visibility. Industry developments are tracked closely in the United States and abroad, and the implications for productivity, international competition, national defense, and the general standard of living are of increasing interest. Many states and some major cities have established task forces to assess the potential of high technology to provide employment opportunities and to develop incentives to attract high-tech industries.

Although industries that manufacture computers and office equipment, electronic components and new drugs and medicines generally are among those classified as high-tech industries, experts differ as to the make-up of the high-tech group. There is no widely accepted definition of high-technology industries, and they have been defined in many ways. In this article, we set forth various concepts of high technology and consider its effect on employment during the 1970s and through the mid-1990s.

The criteria generally used to classify high-

tech industries are research and development (R&D) expenditures, the use of scientific and technical personnel relative to total employment, and product sophistication. Employing these criteria, we developed three definitions of high tech to analyze employment trends in these industries. Our analysis indicates that:

Employment in high-tech industries increased faster than average industry growth during the 1972–82 period.

High-tech industries accounted for a relatively small proportion of all new jobs nationwide, but provided a significant proportion of new jobs in some states and communities.

About 6 out of 10 high-tech jobs are located in the 10 most populous states.

States with relatively high proportions of employment in high-tech industries are generally small; most are in the Northeast.

Through 1995, employment in high-tech industries is projected to grow somewhat faster than in the economy as a whole.

High-tech industries, even broadly defined, will account for only a small proportion of new jobs through 1995.

Scientific and technical workers, while critical to the growth of industry and the economy, will account for only 6 percent of all new jobs through 1995.

A Look at the Concepts

Our examination of published reports on high technology prepared by private organizations and federal and state agencies indicates a variety of approaches to identifying high-technology industries. One approach used by a state agency, for example, involved a review of the U.S. Government's Standard Industrial Classification (SIC) manual in which 20 industry groups were designated as high tech based on the perceived degree of technical sophistication of the products.[1] One limitation of this method, and others which focus on the nature of the product, is that it is highly sub-

*From U.S. Department of Labor, *Monthly Labor Review* 106, no. 11 (November 1983), pp. 50–51.

†*Richard W. Riche is an economist in the Office of Productivity and Technology, Daniel E. Hecker is an economist in the Office of Economic Growth and Employment Projections, and John U. Burgan is an economist in the Office of Employment and Unemployment Statistics, Bureau of Labor Statistics.*

[1]Robert Vinson and Paul Harrington, *Defining High-Technology Industries in Massachusetts* (Boston, Mass.: Department of Manpower Development, September 1979).

jective. Moreover, as Robert Vinson and Paul Harrington point out in an article on high-technology industries in Massachusetts, the degree of technical sophistication of the product is of less significance than the complexity of the production process for those interested in the implications of high tech for capital and labor force requirements.[2]

A concept of high technology included in a document prepared by the Congressional Office of Technology Assessment illustrates a much broader and complex approach in which a series of factors are considered in developing a concept of high-tech firms and industries.[3] The office describes high-technology firms as "companies that are engaged in the design, development, and introduction of new products and/or innovative manufacturing processes through the systematic application of scientific and technical knowledge." It points out that these companies typically use state-of-the-art techniques, have a high proportion of R&D costs; employ a high proportion of scientific, technical, and engineering personnel; and serve small, specialized markets. The report goes on to say, "A high-technology industry is a group of firms, producing similar or related products, that includes a high proportion of high-technology firms."

As suggested earlier, definitions of high technology vary considerably. Federal agencies, including the Department of Defense, the Securities and Exchange Commission, and the Department of Commerce have formulated definitions of high technology to suit their own particular research needs.

An example: the set of definitions included in a report by the International Trade Administration, Department of Commerce, which examines U.S. competitiveness in high-technology industries.[4] Four techniques for

defining technology-intensive trade are presented; one identifies industries and three focus on products.

The industry-based definition of technology-intensive trade, developed by Michael Boretsky, uses the two measures frequently employed in examining high technology: R&D expenditures as a percentage of industry value added, and industry employment of scientists, engineers, and technicians as a proportion of the industry work force.[5] He identified two groups of industries based on the magnitude of R&D expenditures and employment of scientists, engineers, and technicians: technology-intensive industries and high-technology industries. Technology-intensive products and others are not separately identified. The three product-based definitions also help in evaluating competitiveness in high-technology industries. In the mid-1970s, Regina Kelly used R&D expenditures by product field and value of product shipments to develop intensity ratios.[6] She ranked products by R&D "intensity" and classified them by technology. Kelly designated the first quartile of R&D intensities as high-technology goods. Subsequently, she refined her analysis and considered product groups with above average R&D intensities as technology intensive. In 1980, C. Michael Aho and Howard Rosen basically used the Kelly methodology to identify technology-intensive product groups.[7]

[2]Ibid.

[3]Technology, Innovation, and Regional Economic Development (Washington, D.C.: U.S. Congress, Office of Technology Assessment, September 9, 1982). This 14-page report describes a project to assess the implications of high technology to include factors which promote the development of high-technology industries in states and localities.

[4]An Assessment of U.S. Competitiveness in High-Technology Industries (Washington, D.C.: U.S. Department of Commerce, International Trade Administration,

February 1983), 68 pp. See, particularly, Appendix A. "Defining Technology Intensive Trade," pp. 33–37.

[5]Ibid. See also Michael Boretsky, "Concerns about the Present American Position in International Trade," Technology and International Trade (Washington, D.C.: National Academy of Sciences, 1971), and "The Threat to U.S. High-Technology Industries: Economic and National Security Implications," draft (Washington, D.C.: U.S. Department of Commerce, International Trade Administration, March 1982).

[6]Ibid. See also Regina Kelly, "Research and Development in U.S. Trade in Manufactures," paper prepared for International Economics Course, George Washington University, 1974, and "The Impact of Technological Innovation on International Trade Patterns," Staff Economic Report (Washington, D.C.: U.S. Department of Commerce, Office of Economic Research, December 1977).

[7]Ibid. See also C. Michael Aho and Howard F. Rosen, "Trends in Technology-Intensive Trade," Economic Discussion Paper 9 (Washington, D.C.: U.S. Department of Labor, Bureau of International Labor Affairs, October 1980).

These researchers used more recent data and the Standard International Trade Classification. More recently, Lester Davis used input-output analysis and R&D expenditure and shipment data by product group to develop an index of technological intensity.[8] Using an input-output matrix, Davis determined the value of R&D embodied in the various inputs used to make the products and the percentage of R&D embodied in the final product. He then arrived at total R&D by combining the indirect R&D (R&D contributed by inputs) with the value of direct R&D (R&D expenditures on product development). Davis ranked product groups according to total R&D to shipments intensity, with only those goods showing a significant R&D intensity (rather than simply above average) designated as high-tech products.

A definition by Ann Lawson in an article in the Department of Commerce's *Industrial Economic Review* includes industries "possessing above average levels of scientific and engineering skills and capabilities, compared to other industries; and currently experiencing the accelerating technological growth associated with the germination and evolution stages along their respective S-curves."[9]

Selecting Three Groups of Industries

Because there is no widely accepted definition of high-technology industries, we believe it is useful to illustrate employment trends under a range of concepts. As indicated, the concepts underlying most definitions of high technology use one or a combination of three factors (1) the utilization of scientific and technical workers, (2) expenditures for research and development, and (3) the nature of the product of the industry. We have selected three groups of high-technology industries based on these concepts.

[8] Ibid. See also Lester A. Davis, "Technology Intensity of U.S. Output and Trade" (Washington, D.C.: U.S. Department of Commerce, International Trade Administration, July 1982.)

[9] Ann M. Lawson, "Technological Growth and High Technology in U.S. Industries," *Industrial Economics Review* (Washington, D.C.: U.S. Department of Commerce, Bureau of Industrial Economics, Spring 1982), p. 12.

We have defined industries according to the Standard Industrial Classification (SIC) at the 3-digit detail. We would have preferred to use 4-digit detail, but data were not available. We made an exception for R&D laboratories (SIC 7391), because, for this industry, data were available, and the other industries in SIC 739 have high levels of employment but little or no involvement with high technology. We defined scientific and technical workers as engineers, life and physical scientists, mathematical specialists, engineering and science technicians, and computer specialists. We refer to these workers as *technology-oriented workers*. We excluded government, colleges, and universities, although some of their activities are no doubt high-tech-oriented, such as some research conducted in higher educational institutions and in some government agencies. There was no realistic way to estimate the small proportion of employment associated with these activities.

Data on research and development expenditures are compiled annually through surveys conducted by the National Science Foundation. The most recent data available are for 1980. Statistics on employment of scientific and technical workers by industry are presented in the Bureau's national industry-occupation matrix. The most current matrix available presents data for 1982.

Group I. The criterion for inclusion in this group is solely the utilization of technology-oriented workers. We included an industry if technology-oriented workers accounted for a proportion of total employment that was *at least one and a half times the average for all industries* (See Table 1.)

To provide a reasonable definition but very broad coverage, we set the cutoff at 5.1 percent of total employment. However, we excluded industries with fewer than 25,000 workers. A total of 48 industries makes this the broadest of the three groups. As indicated in Table 1, manufacturing industries account for 3 of every 4 industries in this category, with the remainder in mining, construction, transportation and public utilities, and trade and services.

Table 1
Employment in High-Technology Industries, 1972, 1980, and 1982 (000)

SIC	Industry	High-Tech Group[1] I	II	III	Employment 1972	1980	1982	Percent Change 1972–80	1972–82
131	Crude petroleum and natural gas	X			139.3	219.6	281.7	57.7	102.2
162	Heavy construction, except highway and street	X			495.1	658.5	633.9	33.0	28.1
281	Industrial inorganic chemicals	X		X	141.2	161.1	153.5	14.1	8.7
282	Plastic materials and synthetics	X		X	228.7	204.8	182.7	− 10.0	− 20.1
283	Drugs	X	X	X	159.2	196.1	199.8	23.2	25.5
284	Soaps, cleaners, and toilet preparations	X		X	122.4	140.9	145.3	15.1	18.7
285	Paints and allied products	X		X	68.6	65.1	59.7	− 5.1	− 13.0
286	Industrial organic chemicals	X		X	142.8	174.1	174.3	21.9	22.1
287	Agricultural chemicals	X		X	56.4	72.0	67.1	27.7	19.0
289	Miscellaneous chemical products	X		X	90.0	93.3	91.5	3.7	1.7
291	Petroleum refining	X		X	151.4	154.8	169.0	2.3	11.6
301	Tires and inner tubes	X			122.1	114.8	101.9	6.0	− 16.5
324	Cement, hydraulic	X			31.9	30.9	28.5	− 3.1	− 10.6
348	Ordance and accessories	X		X	81.9	63.4	71.4	− 25.6	− 12.8
351	Engines and turbines	X		X	114.6	135.2	114.8	18.0	0.2
352	Farm and garden machinery	X			135.0	169.1	130.8	25.3	− 3.1
353	Construction, mining, and material handling machinery	X			293.7	389.3	340.9	32.6	16.1
354	Metalworking machinery	X			286.0	373.1	320.3	30.5	12.0
355	Special industry machinery, except metalworking	X		X	176.9	207.3	179.4	17.2	1.4
356	General industrial machinery	X			267.5	323.7	283.2	21.0	5.9
357	Office, computing, and accounting machines	X	X	X	259.6	432.2	489.7	66.5	88.6
358	Refrigeration and service industry machinery	X			164.4	174.2	161.3	6.0	− 1.9
361	Electric transmission and distribution equipment	X		X	128.4	122.5	110.1	− 4.6	− 14.2
362	Electrical industrial apparatus	X		X	209.3	239.9	211.8	14.6	1.2
363	Household appliances	X			186.9	163.2	142.0	− 12.7	− 25.0
364	Electric lighting and wiring equipment	X			204.4	209.2	186.9	2.4	− 8.6
365	Radio and TV receiving equipment	X		X	139.5	108.8	94.6	− 22.0	− 32.2
366	Communication equipment	X	X	X	458.4	541.4	555.7	18.1	21.2
367	Electronic components and accessories	X	X	X	354.8	553.6	568.7	56.0	60.3
369	Miscellaneous electrical machinery	X		X	131.7	152.1	141.3	15.5	7.3
371	Motor vehicles and equipment	X			874.8	788.8	690.0	− 9.8	− 21.1
372	Aircraft and parts	X	X	X	494.9	652.3	611.8	31.8	23.6
376	Guided missiles and space vehicles	X	X	X	92.5	111.3	127.3	20.3	37.5
381	Engineering, laboratory, scientific, and research instruments	X		X	64.5	76.8	75.7	19.1	17.4
382	Measuring and controlling instruments	X		X	159.6	245.3	244.3	53.7	53.1
383	Optical instruments and lenses	X		X	17.6	33.0	32.5	87.5	84.7
384	Surgical, medical, and dental instruments	X		X	90.5	155.5	160.4	71.8	77.2
386	Photographic equipment and supplies	X		X	117.1	134.6	138.3	15.0	18.1
483	Radio and TV broadcasting	X			142.7	199.6	216.4	39.9	51.6
489	Communication services, n.e.c.[2]	X			29.7	66.1	91.0	122.6	206.4
491	Electric services	X			312.0	391.0	415.1	25.3	33.0
493	Combination electric, gas and other utility services	X			183.4	196.7	198.4	7.3	8.2
506	Wholesale trade, electric goods	X			331.2	421.4	434.9	27.2	31.3

[1]*Group I:* Includes industries with a proportion of technology-oriented workers (engineers, life and physical scientists, mathematical specialists, engineering and science technicians, and computer specialists) at least 1.5 times the average for all industries.
Group II: Includes industries with a ratio of R&D expenditures to net sales at least twice the average for all industries.
Group III: Includes manufacturing industries with a proportion of technology-oriented workers equal to or greater than the average for all manufacturing industries, and a ratio of R&D expenditures to sales close to or above the average for all industries. Two nonmanufacturing industries which provide technical support to high-tech manufacturing industries also are included.
[2]Not elsewhere classified.

Table 1 *(concluded)*

SIC	Industry	High-Tech Group[1]			Employment			Percent Change	
		I	II	III	1972	1980	1982	1972–80	1972–82
508	Wholesale trade, machinery, equipment, and supplies	X			868.6	1,307.7	1,344.9	50.6	54.8
737	Computer and data processing services	X		X	106.7	304.3	357.5	185.2	235.1
7391	Research and development laboratories	X		X	110.7	163.1	162.7	47.3	47.0
891	Engineering, architectural, and surveying services	X			339.3	544.9	568.7	60.1	67.6
892	Noncommercial educational, scientific and research organizations	X			111.8	113.5	117.8	1.5	5.4

[1]*Group I:* Includes industries with a proportion of technology-oriented workers (engineers, life and physical scientists, mathematical specialists, engineering and science technicians, and computer specialists) at least 1.5 times the average for all industries.

Group II: Includes industries with a ratio of R&D expenditures to net sales at least twice the average for all industries.

Group III: Includes manufacturing industries with a proportion of technology-oriented workers equal to or greater than the average for all manufacturing industries, and a ratio of R&D expenditures to sales close to or above the average for all industries. Two nonmanufacturing industries which provide technical support to high-tech manufacturing industries also are included.

[2]Not elsewhere classified.

Group II. R&D expenditures were the factor used to select this group of industries. We included an industry if its *ratio of R&D expenditures to net sales was at least twice the average for all industries.* The cutoff point, 6.2 percent, was set high to capture only those industries, such as drugs and communication equipment, heavily involved in developing new products. Because the National Science Foundation data show little R&D outside of manufacturing, we excluded other industries. This group, with only six industries, is the narrowest of the three groups of high tech industries. The industries, as expected, fall into all three groups.

Group III. The criteria for this group are both the utilization of technology-oriented workers and R&D expenditures. In addition, we excluded some industries based on their major products.

We included manufacturing industries if the proportion of technology-oriented workers relative to total employment in the industry was *equal to or greater than the average for all manufacturing industries (6.3 percent) and the ratio of R&D expenditures to sales was close to or above the average for all industries (3.1 percent).* We added two industries which provide technical support to manufacturing industries, computer and data processing services (SIC 737) and R&D laboratories.

Group III, with 28 industries, provides a scope of coverage between groups I and II. It excludes most nonmanufacturing industries that are in group I but which have little R&D activity (and therefore little new product development), such as engineering and architectural services and radio and TV broadcasting. The exclusion of nonmanufacturing industries is common in definitions of high-tech industries. Group III also excludes some manufacturing industries found in group I, such as motor vehicles, which did not meet both criteria, and certain machinery industries, which met the criteria, but whose products we did not consider high technology. However, using both criteria, we included some manufacturing industries not in group II, such as those in the instruments, chemicals, and electrical equipment groups, industries with moderately high R&D to sales ratios that appear on many lists of high technology.

Employment Trends during 1972–1982

Employment in high-technology industries, no matter which of the three definitions is used, increased faster than all wage and salary employment between 1972 and 1982. (See Ta-

Editor's Note: Former Table 1: The proportion of high-technology workers by State in 48 industries compared with the average for all industries, 1982, *and* former Table 2: The proportion of high-technology workers by state in six industries compared with the average for all industries, 1982, have been eliminated from the original article.

Table 2
Employment in Three Groups¹ of High-Technology Industries, 1972, 1980, 1982, and Projected 1995 (000)

Employment Grouping	Employment			Projected 1995 Employment Alternatives			Percent Change							
									1980–95			1982–95		
	1972	1980	1982	Low	Moderate	High	1972–80	1972–82	Low	Moderate	High	Low	Moderate	High
All wage and salary workers	76,547.0	92,611.2	91,950.1	115,382.9	117,744.9	120,531.1	21.0	20.1	24.6	27.1	30.1	25.5	28.1	31.1
Group I	9,989.7	12,550.1	12,349.6	16,260.7	16,612.9	16,931.6	25.6	23.6	29.6	32.4	34.9	31.7	34.5	37.1
Percent of total employment	13.1	13.6	13.4	14.1	14.1	14.0	—	—	—	—	—	—	—	—
Group II	1,819.4	2,486.9	2,543.0	3,517.5	3,409.6	3,452.9	36.7	39.8	41.4	37.1	38.8	38.3	34.1	35.8
Percent of total employment	2.4	2.7	2.8	3.0	2.9	2.9	—	—	—	—	—	—	—	—
Group III	4,468.9	5,694.8	5,691.1	7,746.6	7,719.8	7,890.0	27.4	27.3	36.0	35.6	38.5	36.1	35.6	38.6
Percent of total employment	5.8	6.2	6.2	6.7	6.6	6.5	—	—	—	—	—	—	—	—

¹Each group equals the sum of employment in detailed industries listed in Table 1.

ble 2.) Group II employment, however, increased significantly faster, 39.8 percent, nearly twice as fast as the 20.1-percent increase in total employment. Group III employment increased 27.3 percent and group I, only 23.6 percent. Over the period, each group increased slightly as a percentage of total wage and salary employment, group I from 13.1 to 13.4 percent, group II from 2.4 to 2.8 percent, and group III from 5.8 to 6.2 percent.

The contribution of high-tech industries to total employment growth over this period, no matter how high tech is defined, was relatively small. Group I accounted for 15.3 percent of new wage and salary jobs, group II, 4.7 percent, and group III, 7.9 percent.

Growth was not steady. For example, when wage and salary employment declined below its 1980 level during the 1981–82 recession, employment in group I, which includes some *cyclical* industries, also declined. During this period, employment in group III held steady, and group II continued to grow, despite the recession.

Among the industries included in the high-technology groups, growth rates varied widely during 1972–82. Computer and data processing services had the fastest growth, 235.1 percent; followed by communication services, 206.4; crude petroleum and natural gas extraction, 102.2; office, computing, and accounting machines, 88.6; and optical instruments, 84.7. Radio and TV receiving equipment declined by 32.2 percent; household appliances

by 24.0; motor vehicles by 21.2; and plastic materials and synthetics, by 20.1 percent. Some of the declines in employment are directly attributed to the 1981–82 recession.

Employment through 1995

Every other year, the bureau prepares employment projections of roughly 12 years by industry under alternative scenarios. The latest projections of moderate, high, and low growth extend through 1995.[10] Because of employment declines in certain industries in 1981 and 1982, projected growth in wage and salary employment and employment in groups I and III is actually greater from 1982 to 1995 than from 1980. In group II, which had increasing employment from 1980 to 1982, this is not the case. For each of the three groups, using either 1980 or 1982 as a base, high-tech employment is projected to grow somewhat faster than total wage and salary employment under all three alternatives. (See Table 2.)

For group II, the low growth alternatives shows higher 1995 employment than the moderate alternative. This is because higher defense spending is assumed in the low alternative than in the moderate alternative, and

[10]See Arthur J. Andreassen, Norman C. Saunders, and Betty W. Su, "The Economic Outlook for the 1990s: Three Scenarios for Economic Growth"; Valerie A. Personick, "The Job Outlook through 1995: Industry Output and Employment Projections"; and Howard N. Fullerton and John Tschetter, "The 1995 Labor Force: A Second Look," *Monthly Labor Review*, November 1.

Table 3
Occupational Distribution in Selected *Rapidly Growing* High-Technology Industries and the Motor Vehicle Manufacturing and Blast Furnaces and Basic Steel Industries, 1980 (in percentages)

Occupation	Office, Computing, and Accounting Machines	Electronic Components	Computer and Data Processing Services	Blast Furnaces and Basic Steel Products	Motor Vehicles
Total	100.0%	100.0%	100.0%	100.0%	100.0%
White-collar	66.3	37.7	96.0	17.7	20.2
Tech-oriented	27.3	15.0	26.0	3.9	5.9
Engineers	11.9	7.2	1.7	1.8	3.4
Life and physical scientists	.1	.2	.1	.2	.1
Mathematical specialists	(¹)	(¹)	(.3)	(¹)	(.2)
Engineering and science technicians	8.8	6.4	2.7	1.5	1.7
Computer specialists	6.5	1.2	21.2	.4	.5
Blue collar	32.7	61.0	3.4	80.2	76.8
Service	1.0	1.3	.6	2.1	3.0

¹Less than 0.1 percent.

group II has a high proportion of its employment in three defense-related industries, communication equipment, aircraft and parts, and guided missiles and space vehicles. In addition, these projections indicate that certain industries which grew very rapidly over the 1972–82 period, including computer and data processing services and office, computing, and accounting machines, will grow at a slower rate over the 1982–95 period, although still well above average for all industries.

High-Tech and Displaced Workers. The bureau's projections indicate that between 23.4 and 28.6 million new wage and salary jobs will be created between 1982 and 1995. We estimate that between 1.0 and 4.6 million of these jobs will be in high-technology industries. Growth in group I will account for 16 or 17 percent of all new jobs, depending on the projection used, while growth in group II will account for 3 or 4 percent and group III, 8 or 9 percent. The great majority of new jobs will be in industries other than high technology. Therefore, displaced workers and others seeking jobs, and governmental and community organizations seeking to attract jobs to their regions, would be well advised not to limit their search to high-tech industries only.

One additional factor may have a negative effect on the ability of high-tech industries to save economically depressed industries and provide jobs for displaced workers. The occupational composition of many rapidly growing high-tech industries is significantly different from other manufacturing industries that have suffered in recent years. For example, about three-fourths of the workers in the blast furnaces and basic steel industry and the motor vehicles industry are blue-collar workers. These are the workers who have been displaced. However, many high-tech industries, especially those projected to grow the fastest, have a much smaller proportion of their workers in these occupations. (See Table 3.)

High-Technology Occupations

High-technology occupations have also been the subject of much concern recently, although here too data on current and projected employment and clear definitions of what occupations are included have been lacking.

Occupations which clearly meet the definition of high-technology workers are engineers, life and physical scientists, mathematical specialists, engineering and science technicians, and computer specialists. Most workers in these technology-oriented occupations are directly involved in developing or applying new technologies.[11] Their work requires in-depth knowledge of theories and principles of sci-

[11]Some managerial jobs also involve the development and application of technology, and many of these jobs are

Table 4
Projected 1982–1995 Growth in Technology-Oriented Occupations (000)

| Occupational Group | Employment | | | | Change 1982–95 | | | | | |
| | | Projected 1995 | | | Number | | | Percent | | |
	1982	Low	Moderate	High	Low	Moderate	High	Low	Moderate	High
All occupations	101,510	124,846	127,110	129,902	23,336	25,600	28,392	23.0	25.2	28.0
Professional	16,584	21,545	21,775	22,325	4,961	5,191	5,741	29.9	31.3	34.6
Technology-oriented	3,287	4,777	4,795	4,907	1,490	1,508	1,620	45.3	45.9	49.3

ence, engineering, and mathematics underlying technology—a knowledge which distinguishes them from computer operators, computer service technicians and other high-tech machinery repairers, or workers in a wide range of occupations who use word processing machines, computers, or other high-technology products, but rarely have—or need—such in-depth knowledge. Workers in these technology-oriented occupations generally need specialized post-high school education in some field of technology—ranging from an associate degree or its equivalent to a doctorate—education with a thorough high school preparation in science and mathematics as a prerequisite.

Technology-oriented workers, while essential to the development of technology, are relatively few in number and will account for a relatively small proportion of new jobs through 1995. In 1982, technology-oriented employment totaled 3.3 million, or about 3.2 percent of total employment. (See Table 4.) Through 1995, this employment is projected to show growth ranging from 45.3 to 49.3 percent, much faster than the 23- to 28-percent increase projected for all wage and salary workers. This growth is expected to generate between 1.5 and 1.6 million new jobs over the 13-year period. These occupations are projected to account for six percent of all new jobs in the economy, roughly the same proportion as during the 1970s.

Local Employment Levels

High-technology employment is not expected to take up the slack in job generation caused by the long-term decline in heavy du-

rable goods industries, including those we have defined as high tech. What is true for the nation as a whole of course, does not hold for certain states and areas. (See Table 5.) High-technology employment can have a large impact on a local economy. Local success stories include California's Silicon Valley and the Route 128 area in Massachusetts and New Hampshire.[12] In a relatively short period, these areas have developed substantial industrial bases built on high-technology industries.

We analyzed data on the distribution of high-technology employment in three states —California, Michigan, and Texas. The results are shown in Table 5.[13]

Regardless of the definition used, we found most employment to be located in the largest metropolitan areas. The top five areas in each state accounted for between 72.7 and 93.2 percent of the high-tech jobs, depending on the state and definition used. Nonagricultural employment in these areas ranged from 63.7 to 74.2 percent of all employment in each state.

[12]"America Rushes to High Technology for Growth," *Business Week*, March 28, 1983, p. 87.

[13]The industry employment statistics cited in this study are from two Bureau of Labor Statistics payroll employment programs. The industry classifications are taken from the 1972 *Standard Industrial Classification Manual*, Office of Management and Budget.

Employment estimates for the nation were compiled from the Current Employment Statistics program. These data are produced from employer payroll records reported to the bureau on a voluntary basis each month. Self-employed persons and others not on a regular civilian payroll are outside the scope of the survey.

State and county data were compiled from the ES-202 program, which collects information on the employment and wages of workers covered by unemployment insurance programs. Each quarter all covered employers submit mandatory reports of employment and wages to the appropriate State Employment Security Agency. These reports are edited and summarized by county, state, and detailed industry, and forwarded to the bureau. Self-employed persons are not covered in this statistical program.

filled by workers transferring from these "technology-oriented" occupations. Data are not available to identify this group.

Table 5
Metropolitan Areas Ranked by High-Technology Employment Levels and Percentages of Total Nonagricultural Employment in Three States, September 1982 (000)

State	Group I			Group II			Group III		
	SMSA[1]	Number of Employees	Percent	SMSA[1]	Number of Employees	Percent	SMSA[1]	Number of Employees	Percent
California, total		1,523.3			616.3			930.0	
Top 5 areas, total		1,321.1			574.5			848.4	
Top 5 areas as percent of state's high-tech employment		86.7			93.2			91.2	
	Los Angeles	606.3	17.2	Los Angeles	259.5	7.4	Los Angeles	365.0	10.4
	San Jose	261.3	37.5	San Jose	169.5	24.3	San Jose	227.7	32.7
	Anaheim	175.7	20.9	Anaheim	78.4	9.3	Anaheim	121.3	14.4
	San Francisco	173.0	11.1	San Diego	45.1	6.8	San Francisco	67.4	4.3
	San Diego	104.8	15.8	San Francisco	22.0	1.4	San Diego	67.0	10.1
Texas, total		1,016.8			154.4			362.3	
Top 5 areas, total		739.2			134.0			286.3	
Top 5 areas as percent of state's high-tech employment		72.7			86.8			79.0	
	Houston	349.1	22.0	Dallas	102.0	6.6	Dallas	140.9	9.1
	Dallas	284.5	18.4	Houston	10.4	.7	Houston	86.9	5.5
	San Antonio	36.4	8.7	Austin	10.4	3.8	Beaumont	24.0	16.2
	Beaumont	35.3	23.8	San Antonio	7.1	1.7	Austin	21.6	8.1
	Austin	33.9	12.6	Lubbock	4.3	4.8	San Antonio	12.9	3.1
Michigan, total		623.4			28.8			118.4	
Top 5 areas, total		490.3			24.5			88.3	
Top 5 areas as percent of state's high-tech employment		78.6			85.1			74.6	
	Detroit	325.5	21.0	Detroit	11.7	.8	Detroit	48.1	3.1
	Flint	59.2	33.9	Kalamazoo	7.9	7.5	Grand Rapids	15.8	6.0
	Ann Arbor	37.4	28.5	Muskegon	2.2	3.9	Kalamazoo	10.6	10.0
	Grand Rapids	34.9	13.3	Grand Rapids	1.4	.6	Ann Arbor	9.5	7.2
	Lansing	33.3	18.6	Benton Harbor	1.3	2.4	Muskegon	4.3	7.6

[1]Standard Metropolitan Statistical Area.

Table 6
Employment in Three Groups of High-Technology Industries in 10 States with Highest Levels of High-Technology Employment, Annual Averages[1] 1982 (000)

Group I		Group II		Group III	
Total, United States	13,038.3	Total, United States	2,633.7	Total, United States	5,943.4
Top 10 States	7,489.5	Top 10 States	1,737.4	Top 10 States	3,566.6
California	1,527.5	California	610.6	California	933.1
Texas	1,068.4	New York	205.3	New York	493.4
New York	924.0	Massachusetts	160.7	Texas	372.0
Ohio	683.0	Texas	157.6	New Jersey	316.8
Illinois	672.0	New Jersey	116.9	Massachusetts	305.5
Michigan	651.0	Florida	108.1	Pennsylvania	277.0
Pennsylvania	615.4	Connecticut	98.5	Illinois	261.5
New Jersey	521.7	Illinois	96.2	Ohio	247.8
Massachusetts	450.0	Pennsylvania	93.3	Connecticut	185.8
Florida	376.5	Washington	90.2	Florida	173.7

[1]Because fourth-quarter 1982 data were not available at the time of publication, a 9-month average was used.

Thus, the distribution of high-technology employment appears to be concentrated within the states.

In California, the Los Angeles area, with a large aerospace industry, shows the highest level of high-technology employment by a large margin over San Jose. However, the San Jose area, which contains "Silicon Valley," has the highest proportion of high-tech jobs in California, regardless of definition. In the San Jose area, from a quarter to more than one third of the jobs are in high-tech industries.

Texas ranked second, third, and fourth in the *number* of high-technology jobs. Because of its size and large employment base, however, it ranked no higher than eighth in the *proportion* of workers in high-tech jobs. When scrutinized at the metropolitan level, however, several Texas areas emerge as high-technology centers.

Dallas provided over 100,000 high-technology jobs, regardless of definition. The Houston area is also a major source of jobs, while Beaumont shows a large proportion of high-tech jobs in groups I and III, primarily because of its chemical and petroleum refining industries.

Michigan has a high proportion of high-technology jobs in group I, which includes auto manufacturing. (See Table 6.) With groups II and III, Michigan ranks 14th and 39th among all states. Detroit, under the group III definition, shows almost 50,000 high-technology jobs, and the Kalamazoo area displays a smaller proportion of high-tech workers (7.5 and 10.0 percent in groups II and III).

Outside of those two areas, high-technology industry does not appear to be a major factor in the Michigan economy unless auto manufacturing remains in the high-technology definition.

If we look at the nonmetropolitan proportion of high-tech employment in the three states, we find that California has 1.6 percent in group I, .4 percent in group II, and .5 percent in group III; Texas, 10.4, 4.0, and 5.8; and Michigan, 9.5, 7.8, and 15.6.

Few counties outside metropolitan areas have many high-tech jobs. (Hutchinson County in Texas is an exception, with more than 5,000 in group 1, and almost 2,500 in group III.)

Employment by State

In 1982, the share of the nation's high-technology employment in the 10 states with the highest levels of high-tech employment ranged from 57.4 to 66 percent among our three groups, while these states had only 54.1 percent of the total U.S. nonfarm employment. (See Table 6.) Eight states—California, New York, Texas, Massachusetts, New Jersey, Florida, Illinois, and Pennsylvania—appear on all three lists. All were also among the 10 states with the most nonagricultural employment in 1982. Only two states not among the top 10 in employment appear on the three

Table 7
High-Technology Employment as a Percent of Total Nonagricultural Employment in Top 10 States under Three Definitions, 1982 Annual Average[1]

Group I		Group II		Group III	
Total, United States	13.4%	Total, United States	2.8%	Total, United States	6.2%
Delaware	24.0	New Hampshire	7.2	Delaware	16.2
New Hampshire	21.0	Vermont	7.0	Connecticut	13.0
Michigan	20.4	Connecticut	6.9	New Hampshire	12.5
Connecticut	20.3	Arizona	6.8	Vermont	11.7
Vermont	18.9	California	6.2	Massachusetts	11.7
Indiana	17.6	Massachusetts	6.1	New Jersey	10.3
Massachusetts	17.2	Washington	5.7	California	9.5
Texas	17.0	Kansas	4.7	Arizona	9.0
New Jersey	16.9	Utah	4.2	Washington	8.2
Kansas	16.5	Colorado	3.9	Kansas	7.8
Ohio	16.5				

[1] 9-month average.

lists—Washington and Connecticut—largely because each had more than 10 percent of the national employment in aircraft and parts (SIC 372), which appears in all three high-technology definitions.

California not only heads each list but does so by a large margin. New York's total nonagricultural employment was 74 percent of California's in 1982, but it had only half of California's high-technology employment in group III, and about a third of its group II employment, illustrating the importance of definitions.

Has the concentration of high-tech employment within the larger states increased over the last several years? The following shows the percentage of total U.S. high-technology employment in the top 5 states under each definition for selected years from 1975 to 1982:

	1975	1977	1979	1982
Group I	38.4	37.8	38.3	37.4
Group II	46.7	47.1	47.6	47.5
Group III	41.6	40.9	40.4	40.7

The concentration of high-technology employment in the largest states does not appear to be increasing, regardless of the definition used.

As we have seen, comparing a state's high-technology employment to its total nonagricultural employment produces a much different picture than looking at absolute levels. Small states appear on these lists, as a broad spectrum of industries in large states tends to overshadow small groups of emerging industries. Only under the broadest definition—group I—do as many as 5 of the 10 states with the most nonfarm employment qualify. Under the most restrictive definition—group II—only two large states are included. It is noteworthy that Massachusetts, despite its size, is on all three lists. (See Table 7.)

Turning again to group I, we find 46 states had 10 percent or more of their nonagricultural employment in high-technology industries. However, in group II no state had more than 7.2 percent of high-tech employment.

The performance of Delaware under the three definitions is quite interesting. It tops groups I and III with 24.0 and 16.2 percent of its nonfarm employment in high technology. In group II, however, Delaware places 42nd in the nation, with only .8 percent. Groups I and III both include the entire chemical manufacturing industry (SIC 28). Group II only includes drug manufacturing (SIC 283). Because more than 10 percent of the total employment in Delaware is in chemical manufacturing (about 10 times the national proportion), any high-technology definition which includes the entire chemical industry places Delaware at or near the top in the proportion of high-tech employment.

Table 8
High-Technology Employment as a Percentage of Total Nonagricultural Employment Growth in Top 10 States, 1975–1982, under Three Definitions

Group I		Group II		Group III	
Total, United States	21.0%	Total, United States	5.8%	Total, United States	11.3%
South Dakota	49.1	Massachusetts	18.3	Massachusetts	30.0
New Hampshire	43.1	New Hampshire	15.8	Vermont	26.9
Vermont	38.7	Vermont	11.5	South Dakota	25.1
Massachusetts	35.2	Arizona	10.6	New Hampshire	25.0
Nebraska	33.1	Maine	10.1	Connecticut	21.4
Rhode Island	32.6	California	10.0	Idaho	19.9
Idaho	32.4	Oregon	10.0	Maryland	19.9
Montana	31.5	South Dakota	10.0	District of Columbia	19.8
Delaware	30.7	Washington	10.0	Rhode Island	19.2
Colorado	30.3	Rhode Island	9.1	Oregon	18.0

A Regional Pacesetter

The relative importance of high technology among states, however, no matter how defined, shows that the New England states lead other regions in the proportion of high-technology employment. The New England area has provided the ideal environment for these industries. Preeminent educational institutions provide the needed skilled workers. Also, for many decades the area has had a decaying industrial base. In 1947, Massachusetts' leading nondurable manufacturing industries were textiles, apparel, and leather, with a total employment of almost 250,000 workers. In 1982, employment in those industries totaled slightly more than 75,000 workers. The departure of the textile and apparel industry to the South and overseas left behind an industrial infrastructure, coupled with an awareness of the need to attract and foster industrial development. New England states (with the exception of Massachusetts) also tend to be small, making, as noted, the impact of high-technology employment more noticeable.[14]

Although for the nation as a whole, high-technology industries generated only between 4.7 and 15.3 percent of the new jobs in the United States during 1972–82, several states showed greater growth. Even in narrowly defined group II, nine states saw high-tech jobs

account for 10 percent or more of the rise in their total employment between 1975 and 1982. In Massachusetts, growth exceeded 18 percent. (See Table 8.) Maine, absent from the top 10 in percentage of high-tech employment, appears to have experienced significant job-generating effects from high-tech expansion under the group II definition.

However, care must be used in analyzing the impact of high-technology growth in a state. A state may register a large increase in high-tech jobs in a generally expanding economy, or a modest gain in a stagnant economy. Examples of both situations appear in all three groups of high-tech industries. Massachusetts, which tops groups II and III and ranks fourth in group I, is an example of the first situation. Massachusetts ranked 10th in total job creation between 1975 and 1982 and depending on definition, 3rd, 2nd, or 4th in high-tech job generation. South Dakota, which ranks 1st, 8th, and 3rd in percentage growth of high-tech jobs, added a total of only about 20,000 new jobs, one of the smallest increases in the country. However, a large proportion (10.0 to 49.1 percent—according to definition) were high-tech, such as those within electrical and nonelectrical machinery manufacturing (SIC 35 and 36).

It should be reiterated that even when high-tech is very broadly defined, as in group I, it has provided and is expected to provide a relatively small proportion of employment. Thus, for the foreseeable future the bulk of employment expansion will take place in non-high-tech fields.

---

[14]For more on the factors which enabled New England to become a leading area in high technology, see Lynn E. Browne and John S. Hekman, "New England's Economy in the 80s," *New England Economic Review*, January–February 1981, pp. 5–16.

PART TWO

The American Labor Movement: Theories and Explanation

During the past century, serious students of the American labor movement have attempted to explain the "how" and "why" of the development of labor organizations. The classical studies made by the Webbs, Hoxie, Commons, Marx, and others have contributed a great deal toward an explanation of the labor movement. These studies, however, have not been completely satisfactory. John T. Dunlop, in the first article, presents a brief summary of the leading explanations of the labor movement and attempts to test them against some important questions: How is one to account for the origin or emergence of labor organizations? What explains the pattern of growth and development of labor organizations? What are the ultimate goals of the labor movement? Why do individual workers join labor organizations? Subsequent to his investigation, Dunlop finds that none of the theories of the labor movement answers all of the questions; indeed, the questions themselves are nowhere explicitly stated. He suggests that the labor movement may be more rewardingly studied by examining four interrelated factors: (1) technology, (2) market structures and character of competition, (3) wider community institutions, and (4) ideas and beliefs. This method would not constitute a theory but it would greatly implement the development of a theoretical system.

In the second article, one of the most famous labor historians, John R. Commons, presents an explanation for the rise of the labor movement. What was an early labor organization like in terms of its goals and functions? What motivated employees to form America's first labor union? Commons discusses the cordwainers (shoemakers) as illustrative of the American craft workers. Investigation of the activities of the cordwainers reveals a great deal concerning industrial evolution, market expansion, and conditions in America during the 19th century that led to the development of permanent trade unions.

The second and third articles in this section were prepared by the AFL-CIO in celebration of the 1981 centennial of American labor. The brief history of the American labor movement over the 100-year period, 1881-1981, is presented and the activities of the early leaders in the labor movement are highlighted. Samuel Gompers, William Green, and John L. Lewis were pioneers in the development of the American Federation of Labor and the Congress for Industrial Organization. In the concluding article in this section, Edwin E. Witte discusses "the crisis in American unionism" from the perspective of the 1950s. Witte's admonition "that there is developing a crisis in labor unionism in this country is known to everyone" is perhaps just as relevant in the 1980s as it was in the 1950s. Students will find a striking similarity between the issues raised by Witte in this article and by writers in articles in the following section, where the current status of the unions is analyzed.

READING 5

The Development of Labor Organization: A Theoretical Framework*

John T. Dunlop†

"The facts do not tell their own story; they must be cross-examined. They must be carefully analyzed, systematized, compared, and interpreted."[1] This conclusion is an indictment of the all too frequent approach to the development of the labor movement,[2] in which "history" and "theory" are separate and nonpermeable compartments.

Under the caption of "history of labor" are chronicled what purport to be collections of fact and sequences of fact. Under the heading of "theory of labor organization" are found "explanations" conjured out of inner consciousness with only occasional and convenient reference to the past. The "history" and "theory" of the labor movement can have little meaning in isolation.[3] But it is particularly the failure of theoretical apparatus that accounts for the lack of greater understanding of the development of the labor movement and the paucity of significant research. Indeed, despite all the epoch-making developments in the field of labor organization in the past 15 years, there has been virtually no contribution to the "theory" and scarcely a reputable narrative of this period exists.[4]

This essay constitutes a reexamination of fashions of thinking in theories of the labor movement. It proceeds from the initial conviction that any theory of the labor movement must first establish its criteria. Just what questions is a theory of labor organization supposed to answer? Only after this task has been explicitly recognized can there be critical discussion of the development of the labor movement.

The body of economic theory attempts to explain the allocation of resources.[5] Business cycle theories present systems of propositions to make intelligible the fluctuations of the economic system. In similar terms, what is the *pièce de résistance* of a theory of the labor movement? By what standards or tests is it possible to prefer one theory to another? What behavior must such a theory explain to be judged a "closer fit" than another model?

EXPLANATIONS OF THE LABOR MOVEMENT

The literature on theories of the labor movement, carefully analyzed, reveals at least four questions which have been the concern of investigators. As far as can be determined, however, nowhere are these questions posed explicitly.

1. How is one to account for the origin or emergence of labor organizations? What conditions are necessary and what circumstances stimulate the precipitation of labor organization? Why have some workers organized and others not?

2. What explains the pattern of growth and development of labor organizations? What factors are responsible for the sequence and form in which organizations have emerged in various countries, industries,

*Reprinted with permission of the publisher from R. A. Lester and J. Shister (eds.), *Insights into Labor Issues*, pp. 163–93. Copyright 1948 by the Macmillan Company.

†*Lamont Professor, Harvard University*. This essay has benefited from helpful comments by J. A. Schumpeter, A. P. Usher, and Selig Perlman.

[1]Talcott Parsons, *The Structure of Social Action* (New York: McGraw-Hill, 1937), p. 698.

[2]See E. Wight Bakke, *Mutual Survival, The Goal of Unions and Management* (New Haven: Labor and Management Center, Yale University, 1946), p. 12, for a contrast between a "movement" and a "business."

[3]J. B. Bury, *The Ideas of Progress* (New York: Macmillan, 1932). See the Introduction by Charles A. Beard, pp. ix–xl.

[4]Selig Perlman's *Theory of the Labor Movement* (New York: Macmillan) was published in 1928. See Horace B. Davis, "The Theory of Union Growth," *Quarterly Journal of Economics* 55 (August 1941), pp. 611–37; and Russel Bauder, "Three Interpretations of the American Labor Movement," *Social Forces* 22 (December 1943), pp. 215–24.

[5]Frank H. Knight, *Risk, Uncertainty, and Profit* (London: London School of Economics and Political Science, 1933), Preface to reissue.

crafts, and companies? Since there is great diversity in the patterns of development, any theory of the labor movement must account for these differences.

3. What are the ultimate goals of the labor movement? What is its relationship to the future of capitalism? What is its role in the socialist or communist state?

4. Why do individual workers join labor organizations? What system of social psychology accounts for this behavior of the employee?

Most writings on theories of the labor movement have in effect been concerned with one or several of these questions. They show a tendency to seek a single and usually oversimplified statement of the development of labor organization. But the labor movement is highly complex and many-sided. The "history" does not readily lend itself to any single formula.

The pages immediately following constitute a brief summary of the principal contributions to theories of the labor movement. No attempt will be made to present a detailed appraisal of these views; the summary cannot be an exegesis. The discussion is necessarily sketchy. It may be helpful, however, to have in brief compass a summary of views since none exists. Brevity at times has the virtue of concentrating on and compelling attention to essentials.

Frank Tannenbaum[6]

To Tannenbaum "the labor movement is the result and the machine is the major cause."[7] The machine threatens the security of the individual worker and the wage earner reacts in self-defense through a union to attempt to control the machine. The individual worker seeks to harness the machine and to stem the tide of insecurity by which his life is menaced.

He intends little more than this security when joining a union, but "in the process of carrying out the implications of defense against the competitive character of the capitalist system he contributes to the well-being of present-day society—a contribution which represents a by-product of the more immediate and conscious attempt to find security in an insecure world."[8] Tannenbaum sees the labor movement ultimately displacing the capitalistic system by "industrial democracy," "an achievement which is implicit in the growth and development of the organized labor movement."[9]

Tannenbaum provides an answer of sorts to at least three of the four questions posed above; he does not examine the pattern of growth of the labor movement. While not concerned with historical data, Tannenbaum finds the origin of labor organizations in a reaction to the machine (Question 1). The labor movement creates a new society (Question 3). The individual worker joins the union in self-defense in quest of security (Question 4).

Sidney and Beatrice Webb[10]

A trade union is a "continuous association of wage-earners for the purpose of maintaining or improving the conditions of their working lives."[11] Its fundamental objective, according to the Webbs, is "the deliberate regulation of the conditions of employment in such a way as to ward off from the manual-working producers the evil effects of industrial competition."[12] The labor organization utilizes, in the well-known schema of the Webbs, the "methods" of mutual insurance, collective bargaining, and the legal enactment. The labor organization chooses among these "methods" depending on the stage of development

[6]Frank Tannenbaum, *The Labor Movement, Its Conservative Functions and Social Consequences* (New York: G. P. Putnam's Sons, 1921).

[7]Ibid., p. 29. As a statement of the origin of labor organizations, this view is to be contrasted with that of John R. Commons, "Whatever may have been its origin in other countries, the labor movement in America did not spring from factory conditions. It arose as a protest against the merchant-capitalist system." *A Documentary History of American Industrial Society* (Glendale, Calif.: Arthur H. Clark, 1910), vol. 5, p. 23, with Helen L. Sumner.

[8]Ibid., p. 32. These lines are in italics in the original.

[9]Ibid., p. 44.

[10]Sidney Webb and Beatrice Webb, *Industrial Democracy* (New York: Longmans, Green, 1897); and *History of Trade Unionism* (New York: Longmans, Green, 1894). Also see Margaret Cole, *Beatrice Webb* (New York: Harcourt Brace Jovanovich, 1946), pp. 73–83.

[11]Webb, *History of Trade Unionism* (1920 ed.), p. 1.

[12]*Industrial Democracy* (1914 printing), p. 807.

of the society. An era of the master system requires the enforcement of common rules against "industrial parasitism"; the existence of trusts makes legal enactment the only effective method in many cases. The assumption by government of the responsibility for social risks, such as old age and unemployment, greatly curtails the use of the method of mutual insurance on the part of labor organizations.

In the view of the Webbs, trade unionism is "not merely an incident of the present phase of capitalist industry but has a permanent function to fulfill in the democratic state."[13] The special function of the trade union is in the democratic administration of industry. While consumers acting through cooperatives or entrepreneurs may determine *what* is produced, the democratic society requires a labor organization to provide for the participation of workers in the conditions of sale of their services. In the type of democratic society the Webbs eventually expected (the little profit-taker and the trust superseded by the salaried officer of the cooperative and by government agencies), the unions would more and more assume the character of professional associations.

The Webbs used the term *theory of trade unionism*[14] not to refer to answers to any of the four questions posed in the preceding section but as a statement of the economic consequences of a labor organization, virtually a theory of wages or collective bargaining. The trade union is pictured as having only two "expedients" for the improvement of conditions of employment:[15] the restriction of numbers in the trade and the establishment of uniform minimum standards required of each firm. The Webbs condemned the former monopolist policy. They endorsed the latter application of the Common Rule, for it transfers competition from wages to quality. The device of the Common Rule envisages the gradual improvement in these minimum standards of wages and conditions. It is the duty of the labor organization to strive perpetually to raise the level of its common rules. This process may be carried on by collective bargaining or by the use of legislation.[16] Such is the Webbs' "theory of trade unionism," an economic rationalization for the establishment of minimum standards.

What the Webbs called their "theory of trade unionism" would not ordinarily be called a theory of the development of the labor movement. While the Webbs made fundamental and pioneer contributions to the study of trade union government and the narrative of labor organization history, they formulated no systematic, conceptual answers to the first two questions posed in the previous section (the emergence of labor organization and the patterns of development). As for ultimate goals (Question 3), the Webbs see the labor union as an instrument of the democratization of both the work community and the wider society as a whole.

Robert F. Hoxie[17]

Hoxie starts from the proposition that wage earners in similar social and economic environments tend to develop a "common interpretation of the social situation."[18] The union emerges when group sentiments have been crystallized. It appears as a "group interpretation of the social situation in which the workers find themselves, and a remedial program in the form of aims, policies, and methods."[19] To Hoxie, the union constitutes a common interpretation and set of beliefs concerned with the problems confronting the worker and a generalized program of amelioration. Such a persistent group "viewpoint or interpretation"[20] Hoxie calls a *functional* type of union-

---

[13]Ibid., p. 823.

[14]Ibid., pp. viii and 795. See note 16.

[15]Ibid., p. 560.

[16]"the whole community of wage-earners . . . may be a persistent and systematic use of the Device of the Common Rule secure an indefinite, though the course not an unlimited, rise in its Standard of Life. And in this universal and elaborate application of the Common Rule, the economist finds a *sound and consistent theory of Trade Unionism*, adapted to the conditions of modern industry." Ibid., p. 795. (Italics added.)

[17]Robert F. Hoxie, *Trade Unionism in the United States* (New York: Appleton-Century-Crofts, 1921). See the introduction by E. H. Downey.

[18]Ibid., p. 58.

[19]Ibid., p. 60.

[20]Ibid., p. 69.

ism. His name has come to be associated almost exclusively with classification of the functional type he suggests (business unionism, uplift unionism, revolutionary unionism, predatory unionism, and dependent unionism) to the detraction of an understanding of his significant contribution.

The account of the origin of labor organizations which Hoxie gives—a crystallization of group viewpoint and programme of action—leads him to question whether the labor movement has any unity: "Seen from the standpoint of aims, ideals, methods, and theories, there is no normal type to which all union variants approximate, no single labor movement which has progressively adapted itself to progressive change of circumstances, no one set of postulates which can be spoken of as *the* philosophy of unionism. Rather they are competing, relatively stable union types."[21]

Since the labor movement is nonunitary, Hoxie rejects interpretations that look upon trade unionism as fundamentally an economic manifestation of changing methods of production or market developments.[22] The fact of different functional types compels Hoxie to renounce any explanation in environmental terms alone. The subjective factor emphasized in the concept of functional types is equally important.

Hoxie provides an answer to the problem of the emergence of labor organization (Question 1) in terms of "group psychology." He accounts for the divergent forms of unionism but is comparatively unconcerned with an explanation of historical development. One of the factors affecting the classification of functional types is the program for social action developed by the group. In this sense, Hoxie indicates the different answers that have been posed to the problem of the relation of the labor movement to the future of capitalism (Question 3). But there is no sense of historical development here again, for Hoxie is reticent to generalize to a "labor movement as a whole" from his functional types."[23]

Selig Perlman[24]

Perlman finds that in any "modern labor situation" there may be said to be three factors operative: "First, the resistance of capitalism, determined by its own historical development; second, the degree of dominance over the labor movement by the intellectual's 'mentality,' which regularly underestimates capitalism's resistance power and overestimates labor's will to radical change; and third, the degree of maturity of a trade union 'mentality.'"[25] By this last factor Perlman means the extent to which the trade union is conscious of job scarcity. "It is the author's contention that manual groups . . . have had their economic attitudes basically determined by a consciousness of scarcity of opportunity. . . . Starting with this consciousness of scarcity, the 'manualist' groups have been led to practicing solidarity, to an insistence upon an 'ownership' by the group as a whole of the totality of economic opportunity extant, to a 'rationing' by the group of such opportunity among the individuals constituting it, to a control by the group over its members in relation to the conditions which they as individuals are permitted to occupy a portion of that opportunity."[26]

Perlman suggests that there are three basic economic philosophies, those of the manual laborer just indicated, the businessman, and the intellectual. In the United States a "stabilized" unionism was delayed until the labor movement developed job consciousness, until it came to assert a "collective mastery over job opportunities and employment bargains," until wage earners dissociated themselves from "producers" generally who were imbued with the doctrine of abundance and who organized under the slogan of antimonopoly. The American Federation of Labor constitutes a shift in the psychology of the labor move-

---

[21]E. H. Downey, Introduction to *Trade Unionism in The United States*, pp. xxiii–xxiv.

[22]See the discussion under the heading of John R. Commons which follows in the text.

[23]See, however, Hoxie, *Trade Unionism*, note 3, p. 59.

[24]Perlman, *Labor Movement.*

[25]Ibid., p. x.

[26]Ibid., p. 4; also see pp. 237–53. The importance attached to job consciousness is the outcome of one of the few explicit statements on the requirements of a theory of the labor movement. "A theory of the labor movement should include a theory of the psychology of the laboring man" (p. 237).

ment, a recognition of the scarcity of opportunity.[27]

Perlman apparently gives a certain primacy to the role of job consciousness in the labor movement. In fact a labor organization can be regarded as fundamentally a manifestation of "economic attitudes" (see quotation cited below in note 26). Nonetheless, labor history cannot deny a "truly pivotal part" to the intellectual. The character of the labor movement in any particular country must depend on the particular combination of the role of the intellectual, the resistance of capitalism, and the development of job consciousness.

Perlman is seen to treat one way or another all four criteria posed in the previous section. Labor organizations develop from a concern with the scarcity of job opportunities (Questions 1 and 4). The pattern of development of organization in a particular country depends upon the particular combination of the three factors operative in any "modern labor situation" (Question 2). The relation of the labor movement to the future of capitalism is peculiarly influenced by the role of the intellectual (Question 3).

John R. Commons[28]

Commons believed that labor history should be understood in terms of the interaction of "economic, industrial, and political conditions with many varieties of individualistic, socialistic, and protectionist philosophies."[29] He treats labor history as a part of its industrial and political history.

Commons' thinking on the origin and

emergence of labor organization involved an appraisal of the writings of Marx, Schmoller, and Bucher. He posed the problem of explaining the emergence of the labor movement in terms of the growth of new bargaining classes—the wage earner and the employer. He traced the gradual evolution of the employee-employer relationship from the merchant-capitalist dealings with a journeyman. The growth of the market separates from the merchant-capitalist the functions of the custom merchant, the retail merchant, and the wholesale merchant. The employer remains.[30]

While Commons recognized that the changing modes of production influenced to some extent the emergence of labor organization, he attached primary importance to the market expansion. "The extension of the market took precedence over the mode of production as an explanation of the origin of new class alignments."[31]

The pattern of uneven growth in the American labor movement Commons attributed to the fluctuations in economic conditions. Periods of prosperity produced organization while depressions saw the labor movement subside or change its form to political or social agitation.[32]

The theoretical system of Commons seems to have been concerned only with the emergence and the pattern of development of the labor movement (Questions 1 and 2 above).

The Marxist View

To Karl Marx, the trade union was first and foremost an "organizing center."[33] It provided the locus for collecting the forces of the working class. Without organization, workers competed with each other for available employment. "The trade union developed originally out of the spontaneous attempts of the workers to do away with this competition, or at least to restrict it for the purpose of obtaining

---

[27]Perlman disagrees with the Webbs' view that there is a tendency for unionism to give up the principle of restriction of numbers in favor of the device of the Common Rule, Ibid., pp. 295–98. Also see *Labor in the New Deal Decade*, Three Lectures by Selig Perlman . . . at the ILGWU Officers Institute, New York City, 1943–45 (Educational Department, International Ladies' Garment Workers' Union, 1945).

[28]John R. Commons, ed., A *Documentary History of American Industrial Society*, 11 vols. (Glendale, Calif.: Arthur H. Clark, 1910–11). In particular see the Introduction, vol. 5, pp. 19–37, written with Helen L. Sumner. Also John R. Commons and Associates, *History of Labor in the United States*, 2 vols. (New York: Macmillan, 1918), in particular vol. 1, pp. 3–21.

[29]Commons et al., *History of Labor*, Vol. 1, Introduction, p. 3.

[30]Ibid., p. 106.

[31]Ibid., p. 28.

[32]Commons, ed., *Documentary History*, vol. 5, p. 19.

[33]A. Lozovsky, *Marx and the Trade Unions* (New York: International Publishers, 1935), p. 15.

at least such contractual conditions as would raise them above the status of bare slaves."[34]

The labor organization provided for Marx the focal point for the functional organization of the working class toward a change in the structure of society. Just as the medieval municipalities and communities were the center of organization of the bourgeoisie, so the trade union for the proletariat. Thus, in addition to its original tasks, the trade union was to learn to take on additional duties, to become the center for organizing the working class for its political emancipation.[35]

It is imperative to distinguish the role of the trade union under capitalism from that after the successful revolution of the proletariat. Left to themselves, labor organizations would remain within the capitalistic framework. Lenin has put this point succinctly: "The spontaneous labour movement, able by itself to create (and inevitably will create) only trade unionism, and working-class trade-union politics are precisely working-class bourgeois politics."[36]

In terms of the fundamental questions posed above, it is apparent that Marx and Lenin, insofar as they formulated a theory of the labor movement, were concerned with the origin or emergence of labor organizations (Question 1) and their ultimate relationship to capitalistic society (Question 3).

A critical comparison of these views is beyond the scope of this essay. There are important similarities of analysis and emphasis that appear at once and more that would be evident save for differences in language. A rather sharp cleavage emerges, however, between writers such as the Webbs and Commons, who look upon the labor movement primarily as the manifestation of economic developments, and those, such as Perlman and Hoxie, who choose to emphasize the habits of mind of wage earners. Compare the *key concepts* of "Common Rule" (Webbs) and "expansion of the market" (Commons) on the one hand with "job consciousness" (Perlman) and "functional type" (Hoxie, a persistent exponent of the group viewpoint or interpretation). The Webbs and Commons built their models of the trade union out of changes in observable economic institutions. Hoxie and Perlman were imbued with the necessity of a "psychology" of the labor movement and hold the notion that the outlook of the worker upon his world and his destiny is the cornerstone of a model of trade union development.

This cleavage represents a fundamental failure in the formulation of "theories of the labor movement." For certainly there are significant interrelations between the outlook of members of a community and the economic institutions. Consider, for instance, the shedding of the "producer class" complex of the American labor movement. Commons explains the development in terms of the final development of the national market, while Perlman emphasizes that job consciousness and the belief in scarcity of work opportunities had asserted itself. These developments are clearly not independent.

The sections which follow are intended to present a more generalized and more integrated understanding of the development of the labor movement. The next section provides a scaffolding or generalized theoretical framework for an approach to the labor movement.

THE DETERMINANTS OF LABOR ORGANIZATION

The labor movement, or any similarly complex social organization, may be fruitfully explored by an examination of four interrelated factors: technology; market structures and the character of competition; community institutions of control; and ideas and beliefs.

1. Technology. This term includes not only changes in machinery and in methods of production but concomitant developments in the size and organization of production and distribution units.

2. Market Structures and Character of Competition. The term comprehends the

---

[34]Ibid., p. 16. (Italics deleted.)

[35]Paul M. Sweezy, *The Theory of Capitalist Development* (New York: Oxford University Press, 1942), pp. 312–13.

[36]V. L. Lenin, *What Is To Be Done?* Reprinted from *The Iskra Period* (New York: International Publishers, 1929), p. 90.

growth of markets, the changes in the focus of financial control as distinguished from the size of production units, the development of buying and selling institutions in both product and factor markets, and the emergence of specialized functions and personnel within these organizations.

3. Wider Community Institutions. This phrase is intended to include among others the role of the press, radio, and other means of communication in the society; the formal educational system for both general and vocational training; the courts, governmental administrative agencies; and political parties and organizations.

4. Ideas and Beliefs. This caption is a short cut for the value judgments and mores that permeate and identify a social system.

Such a comprehensive scaffolding or method of approach does not in itself constitute a theory of the labor movement. It claims only to facilitate the development of such a theoretical system. It compels reflection on the range of mutual influences operative in any society. Such a comprehensive framework of reference assists in asking significant questions; the complex interrelations between the labor movement and any society are sharpened. The labor movement is seen in the context of its "total" environment. The fourfold scheme is a set of preliminary tools through which the labor movement may be reconnoitered and analyzed. The facts of labor history may more readily be cross-examined.

It must be emphasized that these four factors are intended not merely to facilitate the cross-sectional study of the labor movement at any one given time but even more to assist in the analysis of the growth and change of the labor movement over time. The interaction among technological and market factors, community institutions, and ideas and beliefs must be used to account for the development of the labor movement.

Social systems or institutions go through periods of relative stability and through other periods of spectacular and tortuous change. Periods of stability may be regarded as involving a certain equilibrium among these four factors. That is, a given system of technology and markets requires or is compatible with only a limited number of community institutions and value judgments and ideas. The converse is equally true; a given system of ideas and community organization is compatible only with particular types of market and technological arrangements. In these terms, equilibrium in the social system may be said to exist when these four groups of factors are compatible one with another. Equilibrium may involve an unchanging condition or rates of change among the factors which are congruous. Change the technology of a system and there are required alterations in the other three factors, or change the value judgments and ideas of a community and there must be changes in market systems and technology.

The actual course of history does not disclose the isolated reaction to the change in a single factor any more than a series of prices reveals directly the unique effects of shifts in demand or movements along demand schedules. A comprehensive theory of a society should indicate the result of varying one of these factors—the others unchanged—when the system as a whole is in initial equilibrium. The actual course of events consists in continuous and inseparable interaction between the secondary effects of the initial change and new impacts on the social system.

The procedure suggested in this section would analyze the labor movement by indicating the change in each of these four factors over the past and the consequent impact on the emergence and the manner of growth of the labor movement. The labor movement is seen as the product of its total environment. As labor organizations grow they become an independent factor affecting the course of their own destiny.

LONG-RUN TRENDS IN UNION GROWTH

In thinking of the development of the labor movement, it will be helpful to distinguish between long-term trends and variations around these tendencies. The evolution of social institutions does not take place at uniform rates. The process is more like waves eating away at the base of a cliff, which eventually crashes into the sea.[37] The present section will be concerned with the trend aspects of the development of the labor movement, while that which follows will adapt this analysis to the pulsation of growth of labor organization.

No working community is ever completely unorganized. Any group of human beings associated together for any length of time develops a community in which there are recognized standards of conduct and admitted leaders. "In industry and in other human situations the administrator is dealing with well-knit human groups and not with a horde of individuals."[38] A group of workers which continues together will establish standards of a "fair" day's work and acceptable norms of behavior in the views of the working group as a whole. Not everyone, of course, will conform to these standards, but there will be recognized norms. In the same way one worker will soon be recognized as a person whose judgment is sought on personal problems; another will be regarded as having superior skill, whose advice on the technical aspects of the job is highly regarded; still another will be accepted as spokesman in expressing the feelings of the group to the management. At times these functions may be combined in the same person. Whenever human beings live or work together the informal group develops. This fact is true today; it no doubt preceded the first formal labor organization.

Formal trade union organization has on many occasions been precipitated out of this type of informal organization. Some danger to the stability and security of the informal group frequently serves as the immediate occasion for formalizing an organization. The threat may come from the management in the form of a wage reduction or a substitution of women on men's jobs, or the arbitrary discipline of a member of the work community.

The threat may have its origin outside the firm, as in the introduction of machinery made necessary by competitive conditions. Very frequently the formal organization may last for a short time, only during the period of greatest immediacy of the danger.

The formal group may be assisted and encouraged by outside organizers. The initiative may be taken by the professional organizer, or he may be called in after an initial step. The congealing of these informal organizations into formal structures follows no uniform pattern. The "intellectual" does not here receive the prominence in the development of the labor movement subscribed to by some writers. There can be little doubt that, in any going institution, "rationalizations" are developed—a task necessarily intellectual in content. Such formal statements often help in extending organization. The processes of rationalization are here treated as an essential step in the growth of the union movement, but the "intellectual" does not have a dominant role.

Wage earners join unions for a great many different reasons. They generally involve various aspects of the relation of the individual workman to his immediate work community and, at times, his relation to the larger locality and national life.[39] The fundamental point, however, is that any analysis of the development of labor organizations must proceed from the recognition that work communities, prior to formal organization, are not simply random aggregates of individual workmen. Typically, informal coagulations exist. While every labor organization probably has not grown out of nor adopted the leadership of the informal group, it is difficult to conceive of a labor organization which has not been substantially influenced by these basic facts of any work community.

There have been, no doubt, many cases in which the informal organization has been precipitated into dramatic formal action only to lapse quickly and pass away. There have been many such outbursts against arbitrary behavior and substantial grievances. But in some circumstances continuing organization has developed and in others it has lapsed. The dis-

---

[37]For a discussion of historical change refer to Melvin M. Knight, Introduction to Henri Sée, *The Economic Interpretation of History* (New York: Adelphi, 1929), pp. 9–37.

[38]Elton Mayo, *The Social Problems of an Industrial Civilization* (Cambridge, Mass.: Harvard University Press, 1945), p. 111. Also see F. J. Roethlisberger and William J. Dickson, *Management and the Worker* (Cambridge, Mass.: Harvard University Press, 1940); F. J. Roethlisberger, *Management and Morale* (Cambridge, Mass.: Harvard University Press, 1942).

[39]E. Wight Bakke, "Why Workers Join Unions," *Personnel* 22, no. 1 (1945).

cussion which follows suggests, with reference to the American scene, two factors that were necessary to the emergence of organization historically and two that have been decisive in determining the trend of development.

1. How is the student of labor organization to account for the location in the productive process of the emergence of continuing unions? Successful organization has required that workmen occupy a *strategic* position in the technological or market structures. In any *technological* process for producing and distributing goods and services, there are some workers who have greater strategic position than others; that is, these workers are able to shut down, to interrupt, or to divert operations more easily than others. They furnish labor services at decisive points in the productive stream where the withdrawal of services quickly breaks the whole stream. The productive process has its bottlenecks. Frequently these workers are skilled. The term *strategic*, however, is not identical with skill. It means sheer bargaining power by virtue of location and position in the productive process. Locomotive engineers, loom fixers in the textile industry, molders in the casting industry, and cutters in the garment industry well illustrate the concept. The withdrawal of the services of these relatively few almost immediately compels, for technological reasons, the complete shutting down or diversion of operations of the plant.

Analogously, in the *structure of markets* there are firms, and consequently there are employees, who are in strategic positions to affect the whole stream of production and distribution. Employees are technologically strategic by virtue of their position *within* an individual firm. Workers are in a strategic position, marketwise, by virtue of their position in the structure of markets. In the market framework they can most readily exact a price. Not only are the teamsters in a position to tie up operations (technological position), but also their employers are in a position to pass on cost increases to their customers (market position). Another illustration would be a craft, such as the bricklayers, where cost increases may be passed on to the small housebuilder whose bargaining position is such as to

force absorption. The musicians constitute probably an even better example. The technological and market strategic positions are never completely disassociated, although it is helpful to make the conceptual distinction.

Labor organization emerges among employees who have strategic market or technological positions. They have bargaining power. They can make it hurt. These strategic employees may be regarded as "points of infection" or "growth cones," to borrow the latter term from embryology, for the spread of labor organization.

How far will organization spread around the original "point of infection?" In some instances organization is confined to these most strategic workers and a pure craft union may result. In other instances these workers become the nucleus of the organization that encompasses other workers in the same plant. The cell wall of the organization may be pushed coextensively with the plant and an industrial union result. The boundary line may be drawn any place in between and may in fact fluctuate a good deal over time. The analogous point applies to the growth of unions in different types of firms. The boundary line of the union may be stopped from crossing into firms with different product market conditions. The phenomenon of a union organized in commercial building but unable or uninterested in pushing into housing is familiar in construction.

There are barriers to extending the cell wall of organization that arise within the strategic groups of workers themselves as well as from the opposition of those outside this nucleus. On occasions, the most strategic group will prefer to remain so purist that developments resulting in differentiation of work among these strategic workers will produce a split in the cell and two organizations result. Expanding the group would dilute the gains of organization for the existing nucleus. Labor organizations in the printing industry in this country have taken this pattern of development. From the original group of strategically positioned printers have split off the pressmen, the photo-engravers, the stereo-typers, the bookbinders, and others, as specialized operations have developed.

Resistance to the expansion of the strategic group may arise from the fact that those outside the nucleus may have such high rates of turnover as to make organization impossible. Thus the butchers in retail outlets did not originally include part-time employees around these stores. The boundary line of the union may be confined because those outside may feel that they can enjoy any benefits won by the strategic group without the costs of organization. It is a mistake to interpret historically the structure (in the sense of boundary lines) of American trade unionism, primarily in terms of a slavish following of the "principle of craft unionism." This analysis suggests a more general view.

Necessary to the emergence and growth of permanent labor organizations have been workers who are located in strategic positions in the market or technological framework. Organization may be treated as expanding from these centers in different patterns and to varying extents. It may be helpful to illustrate this formal analysis with examples from the early growth of labor organizations. In both the men's and women's clothing industry the first group organized was the cutters.[40] Their key position in the technological operation of the making of garments gave them a dominant position in early organizations in these industries. For a while, organization was concentrated in this group. Later the cutters became the nucleus in the women's garment industry for the International Ladies' Garment Workers' Union.

Consider the development of the coal mining industry. Organization was first significant among the contract miners. As a "petty contractor," the miner owned his own tools, purchased his own powder, and worked without supervision. Starting from these strategic employees in the early coal mining industry as a nucleus, organization among the miners gradually expanded to include in a single organization all employees, including those who worked above ground as well as underground.[41]

In the cotton textile industry, the loom fixer has had a position of technological prominence. The failure to keep the looms in running order would soon force the shutdown of the weaving shed. There are other strategic groups of employees, such as the spinners and the slasher tenders. In a sense, one finds multiple points of organization in this industry. In some cases the craft-like union resulted and in others the nucleus expanded to include sufficient other groups to be designated as a semi-industrial arrangement.

In the steel industry, the Amalgamated Iron, Tin, and Steel Workers Union was formed out of strategically located groups in various branches of the industry. The boilers and puddlers in the making of iron, and the heaters, rollers, and roughers from the finishing operations, formed the bulk of organization.[42] This nucleus failed to expand and in fact could not maintain its own position until the emergence of the CIO. These illustrations could be multiplied many times: the linemen in the growth of the Brotherhood of Electrical Workers,[43] the jiggermen and kilnmen in the pottery industry,[44] and the blowers, gatherers, flatteners, and cutters in the flat glass industry.[45] A union leader described an organizing drive as follows: "we had all of the polishing department, and those men were the core of our whole organization."[46] Such instances provide flesh and blood to the formal scheme outlined above. The simple notion again is a strategic nucleus, which may expand in different patterns, depending on conditions and ideas within the union and the environment without.

[40]See Joel Seidman, *The Needle Trades* (New York: Farrar and Rinehart, 1942), pp. 81–92; also Elden La Mar, *The Clothing Workers in Philadelphia* (Philadelphia Joint Board, Amalgamated Clothing Workers, 1940), pp. 46–47.

[41]Edward A. Wieck, *The American Miners' Association* (New York: Russel Sage Foundation, 1940), pp. 75–77, 85–86.

[42]J. S. Robinson, *The Amalgamated Association of Iron, Steel, and Tin Workers* (Baltimore: The Johns Hopkins Press, 1920), pp. 9–21.

[43]Michael A. Mulcaire, *The International Brotherhood of Electrical Workers* (Washington, D.C.: The Catholic University of America, Studies in the Social Sciences, 1923), vol. 5.

[44]David A. McCabe, *National Collective Bargaining in the Pottery Industry* (Baltimore: The Johns Hopkins Press, 1932), pp. 4–7.

[45]Window Glass Cutters League of America. "*A History of Trade Unions in the Window Glass Industry,*" reprinted from the *Glass Cutter*, March–September 1943.

[46]"From Conflict to Cooperation," *Applied Anthropology* 5 (Fall 1946), p. 9.

The analysis that has just been outlined must be thought of as applicable to the task of understanding the development of the American labor movement in the context of community institutions which prevailed prior to the Wagner Act. Organization by ballot rather than by the picket line places much less emphasis upon strategic employees in the technological and market scene. Organization may proceed instead from those most susceptible to union appeals for votes. Furthermore, the unit or boundary which a union would select for an election is apt to be quite different from that which it would select to defend on the picket line. It has not been generally recognized that the Wagner Act has had as much effect on the organizing strategy and structure of labor organizations as upon relations with the employer.[47]

The concept of strategic workers cannot be as useful to an understanding of the development of the labor movement today as it is for the explanation of the past. Still it may help to explain stresses and strains within unions and particular wage policies.

2. A second necessary condition in the emergence of organization is the view of the employees that they shall look forward to spending a substantial proportion of their lifetime as workmen. This factor has been gradually developing over the past 100 years and has been influenced by the rate of increase in gainful employment. It is also necessary that a substantial proportion in any given work community look forward to remaining in the same or similar work community. Negatively, organization is difficult, if not impossible, where individuals expect to work themselves out of the status of wage earners, or where they expect to remain wage earners but a short time because of anticipated withdrawals from the labor market, or where the rate of turnover and migration is so rapid and so erratic and random as to preclude stability in organization. In a period or in situations in which individual employees expect to become foremen and then owners of their own business, permanent and stable organization is virtually impossible. One of the problems of organizing women arises from the fact that they expect only a short working life and then plan to retire to the more arduous duties of the household. Migratory labor has been notoriously difficult to form into permanent organizations.[48]

3. Certain types of community institutions stimulate, and others retard, the emergence and growth of labor organizations. "There had developed, in effect a double standard of social morality for labor and capital. The story of the gradual modification of this double standard can be read in the history of labor organization and in the record of social legislation on state and federal governments over the past 50 years."[49] The legal system may actually preclude organization as would have been the case had the doctrine of the early conspiracy cases been generally applied. This is not to suggest that the passage of a law could have wiped out all organization. Such a legal doctrine, however, acted as an obstruction to the growth of organization. Analogously, a policy of government to encourage organization, such as adopted in the Wagner Act, tends to accelerate the growth of labor unions.

The role of the wider community influence on the emergence and pattern of growth of the labor movement must be more broadly conceived than the legal system.[50] Both the struggle for free public schools and the impact of widespread general and technical education have left their mark on the American labor movement. The labor press has drawn heavily on the conventions of the daily newspaper. The hostility of the ordinary press to labor organizations over much of the past in

[47]The interpretation of the rise of the CIO as a repudiation of the principle of craft unionism neglects the adaptation in structure to these new conditions. A fruitful research enterprise would study these effects of the Wagner Act on union structure.

[48]Carleton H. Parker, *The Casual Laborer and Other Essays* (New York: Harcourt Brace Jovanovich, 1920). Also see Stuart Jamieson, *Labor Unionism in American Agriculture*, Bulletin 836 (Washington: Bureau of Statistics, 1945).

[49]Samuel Eliot Morrison and Henry Steel Commager, *The Growth of the American Republic*, rev. and enlarged ed. (New York: Oxford University Press, 1937), vol. 2, p. 153.

[50]See W. Lloyd Warner and J. O. Low, "The Factory in the Community," in *Industry and Society*, ed. William F. Whyte (New York: McGraw-Hill, 1946), pp. 21–45.

this country in turn helped to set the tone of the labor press.

The *emergence* of labor organizations has been related in preceding pages to the strategic position of wage earners in a market and technological setting. But the subsequent form of the labor organization will be decisively molded by the environment of these wider community and national institutions. In some contexts the labor organization has developed into an almost exclusively political body; in others political activity is minor. Special local or industry conditions, such as prevail in the field of municipal employment, may lead to substantial political activity even though the dominant pattern in the country may involve little such action.

The relation of the labor movement to the future of capitalism (Question 3) must not be viewed narrowly as an issue of the extent or character of political activity. The growth in modern technology in the setting of the business corporation has gradually yielded a society predominantly made up of wage and salary earners. Wage earners have constituted a minor element in previous communities made up largely of self-employed farmers, serfs, slaves, or peasants. Unique in human history has been the creation of a society where the vast majority of persons earn a livelihood as wage and salary earners. (Two thirds of the national income is wage and salary payment.) Under these circumstances when wage earners organize into labor organizations, as traced in previous sections, these bodies may be expected to exercise considerable political power in the community. The center of political power ultimately shifts as the character of the groups within the community changes.

If the locus of political power shifts to the degree that the labor organization becomes the dominant political power, there is growing evidence that the function and role of the union changes. The attitude toward the right to strike, compulsory arbitration, and production drives shifts away from the customary patterns under capitalism. This transition cannot but involve serious controversy within the labor movement.

4. Over and above these technological, market, and community influences on the la-

bor movement has been the system of values, the ethos, and the beliefs of the community. Professor Schlesinger has summarized the traditional attributes to the American most noted by foreign observers: "a belief in the universal obligation to work; the urge to move about; a high standard of comfort for the average man; an absence of permanent class barriers; the neglect of abstract thinking and of the aesthetic side of life."[51] Many of these characteristics are to be traced to the "long apprenticeship to the soil."

It should not be hard to understand why labor organization would be difficult in a day in which men believed that individual advancement was to be achieved solely by work,[52] where leisure was a vice, where economic destiny depended solely upon one's ability to work and save, where poverty could only be the reward for sloth, where the poor deserved their fate, and where the public care of the impoverished was regarded as encouragement of idleness. As Poor Richard says:

Employ thy Time well, if thou meanst to gain Leisure;
And, since thou art not sure of a Minute, throw not away an Hour.
Trouble springs from Idleness, and grievous Toil from needless Ease.
For Age and Want, save while you may,
No Morning Sun lasts a whole day.
I think the best way of doing good to the poor, is, not making them easy *in* poverty but leading or driving them *out* of it.

These admonitions of Benjamin Franklin[53] are hardly the ideal text for the organization of a labor union. This set of ethical standards which has pervaded the ethos of the American community until recently places the economic destiny of a workman in his own hands rather than in a labor union.

The political and economic philosophy of the founding fathers, beyond standards of in-

---

[51]Arthur Meier Schlesinger, "What Then Is the American, This New Man?" reprinted from the *American Historical Review* 48 (January 1943), pp, 3–4.

[52]"What qualities of the national character are attributable to this long-persistent agrarian setting? First and foremost is the habit of work." (Ibid., p. 10.)

[53]"The Way to Wealth," Preface to *Poor Richard Improved* (1758).

dividual behavior, came to be adapted to the advancing order of corporate business. "This ideology was derived in part from deep-rooted folk ideas, in part from the sanctions of religion, in part from concepts of natural science. But whatever the source, its arguments rested upon the concepts of individualism, equality of opportunity, and the promise of well-being under a profit economy. The conservative defense, crystallized by business leaders and by allied members of the legal, educational, and literary professions, was popularized in sermons, speeches, novels, slogans, and essays. It became part and parcel of American popular thought."[54]

Moreover, the dominant economic thinking on the determination of wage rates (the wage-fund doctrine), by the community, could hardly have been favorable a hundred years ago to the growth of labor organizations. "There is no use in arguing against any one of the four fundamental rules of arithmetic. The question of wages is a question of division. It is complained that the quotient is too small. Well, then, how many ways are there to make a quotient larger? Two ways. Enlarge your dividend, the divisor remaining the same, and the quotient will be larger; lessen your divisor, the dividend remaining the same, and the quotient will be larger."[55] There was no place for a union; it could serve no legitimate function. The intellectual climate of political economy changed and became more conducive to labor organization over the years.

The *trend* of standards of personal morality and social and economic philosophy has moved in directions more congenial to the flowering of unionism. Contrast the entreaties of Poor Richard and Horatio Alger with the admonitions of Sir William Beveridge! Leisure is now a virtue rather than a vice; saving may be a

community vice rather than the epitome of individual morality; the economically less fortunate are to be sustained by comprehensive social security rather than to be left to sink or swim. The trade union has a more nourishing ethos.

The dominant ethical judgments pervading the community have been a vital factor influencing the growth of labor organization not only as they affect the individual workman but also as they shape and mold the character of the labor organization itself. The primacy of property rights in the American tradition is partly responsible for the dominance of the concept of exhaustive jurisdiction in the American Federation of Labor constitution. Each union "owns" its jurisdiction in the same way that a businessman owns a piece of property. These community values have also decisively determined the attitude of the community toward social insurance. It is no accident that the American Federation of Labor was opposed to a program of compulsory insurance until 1932.[56]

The environment of ideas and beliefs in which the labor organization developed has included the special role of the labor intelligentsia or the intellectual. "Capitalist evolution produces a labor movement which obviously is not the creation of the intellectual group. But it is not surprising that such an opportunity and the intellectual demiurge should find each other. Labor never craved intellectual leadership, but intellectuals invaded labor politics. They had an important contribution to make: They verbalized, supplied theories and slogans for it, made it conscious of itself and in so doing changed its meaning."[57] The formulation of a creed or folklore or rationalization is an important function in the development of the labor movement, just as in any organization. The function needs to be kept in proportion. In the American scene this process seems not to have been the province of a special class nor fashioned through different means in labor organizations than in

---

[54]Merle Curti, *The Growth of American Thought* (New York: Harper & Row, 1943), p. 656. See pp. 605–56. Also, Vernon Louis Parrington, *Main Currents in American Thought*, vol. 3, *The Beginning of Critical Realism in America* (New York: Harcourt Brace Jovanovich, 1927).

[55]A. L. Perry, *Political Economy*, p. 123, quoted in Francis A. Walker, *The Wage Question* (New York: Henry Holt, 1886), p. 143. Compare this with the statement by the Webbs, "Down to within the last 30 years it would have been taken for granted, by every educated man, that Trade Unionism . . . was against Political Economy." *Industrial Democracy*, p. 603.

[56]See George G. Higgins, *Voluntarism in Organized Labor in the United States, 1930–40* (Washington, D.C.: Catholic University of America Press, 1944).

[57]Joseph A. Schumpeter, *Capitalism, Socialism, and Democracy* (New York: Harper & Row, 1942), pp. 153–54.

other groups in the community. The English and continental experience is different in this respect.

This section has sketched some suggestions toward an analytical view of the emergence and development of the labor movement out of its total environment, regarding that environment as the technological processes, the market structure, the community institutions, and the value judgments of the society. The emphasis has been upon the long-term *trend* of development.

SHORT-RUN VARIATIONS IN TRADE UNION MEMBERSHIP

The growth of the labor movement has not been uniform and the four factors which have been used to approach the long-term trends in the labor movement were not all operative at the same rate. This section is concerned with the deviations from trend, in particular, the periods of advance in labor organization.

Even a cursory view of the American labor movement identifies seven major periods of rapid expansion in organization. The following tabulation identifies these periods; it also notes the estimated membership[58] of the organizations at the end of a given period.

Periods*	Dates	Membership (000)
Awakening	1827–1836	300
Nationalism	1863–1872	300
Great Upheaval	1881–1886	1,000
Mass Advancement	1896–1904	2,000
First World War	1917–1920	5,000
New Deal	1933–1937	8,000
Second World War	1941–1945	14,000

*The titles used in Commons and Associates, *History of Labor,* have been adopted for the first four periods. The membership figures for these periods are from the same source.

These seven periods can be divided into two distinct types. The dominant characteristics of a period do not preclude some elements of the opposite type. The first group of periods were years of wartime, with rapid in-creases in the cost of living and stringency in the labor market. This group includes the periods of Nationalism (1863–72), Mass Advancement (1896–1904), the First World War (1917–20), and the Second World War (1941–45). The rapid expansion in membership is to be explained almost entirely by developments in the labor market: the rapid rise in the cost of living and the shortage of labor supply relative to demand. Under these circumstances a trade union helped to enable wage earners to increase their wages to an extent more closely approximating the rise in prices. The individual worker joined unions to push up his wages; the tightness in the labor market and the general level of profits enabled the union to achieve results. Organization in these instances may be regarded as predominately a market reflex.

Contrasting with these years is the second type of period—to be regarded as one of fundamental unrest. Organization of unions represented a basic dissatisfaction with the performance of the economic system and the society in general. Such were the years of Awakening (1827–36), the Great Upheaval (1881–86), and the New Deal (1933–37). It is these three periods which call for special explanation.

It is well established in the analysis of economic fluctuations that modern capitalism has moved in certain long waves.[59] These long waves or Kondratieff cycles are generally regarded as approximately 50 years in length with 25 years of good times and 25 years of bad times, and are distinguished from the shorter business cycles. Professor Alvin H. Hansen's dating scheme is typical.[60] The long wave represents a fundamental structural period in modern capitalism. The first of these

Good Times	Bad Times
1787–1815	1815–43
1843–1873	1873–97
1897–1920	1920–40
1940–	

[58]In any organization it is not always clear who should be counted as a "member." In the case of a union, depending upon the purpose, the significant figure may be those who have signed membership cards, pay dues regularly, attend meetings, vote for the union in a NLRB election, or support the union by joining a strike.

[59]Joseph A. Schumpeter, *Business Cycles: A Theoretical, Historical, and Statistical Analysis of the Capitalist Process* (New York: McGraw-Hill, 1939).

[60]Alvin H. Hansen, *Fiscal Policy and Business Cycles* (New York: W. W. Norton, 1940), p. 30.

waves has been designated as that of the Industrial Revolution, the second the Age of Railroads, and the third the Electrical Period.[61] The fourth may be known as that of the airplane and atomic power.

For the present purposes it is significant to note that each one of the three periods of major upheaval and fundamental unrest came at the bottom of the period of bad times in the long wave. The period of good times in the long wave is associated with a cluster of major innovations. There follows a period of generally declining prices (1815–43, 1873–97, 1920–40), during which the shorter business cycles are severe and intense. The three major periods of upheaval follow severe depressions. It is suggested that after prolonged periods of high unemployment for a substantial number in the work force and after years of downward pressure on wages exerted by price declines, labor organizations emerge which are apt to be particularly critical of the fundamental tenets of the society and the economy.

These three fundamental periods of upsurge in the labor movement must also be related to important developments in community institutions and ideas or value judgments. Thus, the first period was the Age of Jacksonian Democracy, the second the Populist, and the third the New Deal. The labor movement of 1827–36 has been treated as an alignment of "producer classes."[62] The Knights of Labor in the period 1881–86 has been referred to as the last great middle-class uprising. The expansion of the labor movement in the New Deal period was primarily a working class movement. The first period rallied around the slogan of free education, the second used the watchword of shorter hours, the third was characterized by the accent on security.

CONCLUDING REMARKS

The scaffolding may now be removed. In the distinctive pattern of growth of the labor movement in this country, one sees in outline form the way in which technology, market structure, community institutions, and the ethos factors have interacted together to yield the labor movement considered as a whole. Special types of these factors in operation in specific industries and localities account for the divergent types and forms of unionism which have developed within the generalized framework. For example, the migratory character of agricultural work and the lumber industry, together with the absence of stability of community, help to account for the type of unionism that originally emerged in this sector, illustrated by the IWW. The unions in the field of local or national government employment have become lobbying agencies by virtue of the practical prohibitions to effective collective bargaining. These specialized forms or species are variations from the main pattern of growth and development arising from special types of environments. In the same way, peculiar national characteristics shape the operation of these factors in comparing labor movements in various countries.

The framework of approach to the labor movement presented here is intended to be suggestive for a renewed interest in the writing of the history of the labor movement in general and in particular sectors. The emphasis upon the interrelations and mutual dependence of four groups of factors has served as the basis for this analysis. Not only is the analysis schematic, but it must be recognized that any simplified schemata must abstract from many complexities of behavior. The formal analysis must not leave the impression of the labor organization as primarily rationalistic. Professor Knight has well said that there is need for "some grasp of the infinitely complex, intangible, and downright contradictory character of men's interests, conscious and unconscious, and their interaction with equally intricate mechanical, biological, neural, and mental processes in forming the pattern of behavior. The great vice is oversimplification."[63]

---

[61]Schumpeter, *Business Cycles*, vol. 1, pp. 220–448.

[62]At the third meeting of the Working Men's Party in New York it was not the employers who were given five minutes to withdraw but "persons not living by some useful occupation, such as bankers, brokers, rich men, etc." Commons, ed., *Documentary History*, vol. 5, p. 24.

[63]Knight in Introduction to Sée, *Economic Interpretation*, p. xxix.

R E A D I N G 6

American Shoemakers, 1648–1895*

John R. Commons

The boot and shoe makers, either as shoemakers or "cordwainers," have been the earliest and the most strenuous of American industrialists in their economic struggles. A highly skilled and intelligent class of tradesmen, widely scattered, easily menaced by commercial and industrial changes, they have resorted with determination at each new menace to the refuge of protective organizations. Of the 17 trials for conspiracy prior to 1842, the shoemakers occasioned 9. Taking the struggles of this harassed trade, it is possible to trace industrial stages by American documents from the guild to the factory. Organizations whose records give us this picture of industrial evolution under American conditions are the "Company of Shoomakers," Boston, 1648; the "Society of the Master Cordwainers," Philadelphia, 1789; the "Federal Society of Journeymen Cordwainers," Philadelphia, 1794; the "United Beneficial Society of Journeymen Cordwainers," Philadelphia, 1835; the Knights of St. Crispin, 1868; the Boot and Shoe Workers' Union, 1895. Each of these organizations stands for a definite stage in industrial evolution, from the primitive itinerant cobbler to the modern factory; each represents an internal contention over the distribution of wealth provoked by external conditions of marketing or production; each was productive of written documents preserving to us the types of social organization that struggled for adaption to the evolving economic series.

THE "COMPANY OF SHOOMAKERS," BOSTON, 1648

Probably the first American guild was that of the "shoomakers of Boston," and its charter of incorporation, granted by the Colony of the Massachusetts Bay, on October 18, 1648, is the only complete American charter of its kind, of which I have knowledge.[1] The coopers were granted a similar charter on the same date. The act recited that on petition of the "shoomakers" and on account of the complaints of the "damage" which the country sustained "by occasion of bad ware made by some of that trade," they should meet and elect a master, two wardens, four or six associates, a "clarke," a sealer, a searcher, and a beadle, who should govern the trade. The "commission" was to continue in force for three years.

A contemporary reference to this incorporation of shoemakers is that of Edward Johnson, in his "Wonder-Working Providence of Sion's Savior in New England," 1651. Speaking of the material progress of the colony and the rapid division of labor, he says,[2] "All other trades have here fallen into their ranks and places, to their great advantage; especially Coopers and Shoomakers, who had either of them a Corporation granted, inriching themselves by their trades very much."

In the charter of the Boston guild, the main object of the shoemakers was the suppression of inferior workmen, who damaged the country by "occasion of bad ware." The officers were given authority to examine the shoemakers, and to secure from the courts of the colony an order suppressing any one whom they did not approve "to be a sufficient workman." They were also given authority to regulate the work of those who were approved, and thus to "change and reforme" the trade and "all the affayres thereunto belonging." And they were erected into a branch of government with power to annex "reasonable

*From *Labor and Administration* (New York: Macmillan, 1913), pp. 210–64. Reprinted by permission of the publishers from *The Quarterly Journal of Economics*, vol. 24 (November 1909), Cambridge, Mass.: Harvard University Press. References are to reprints in *Documentary History of American Industrial Society*, edited by Commons, Phillips, Gilmore, Sumner, and Andrews, and published by A. H. Clark, Glendale, California.

[1]See Appendix to this reading.

[2]Collections of the Massachusetts Historical Society 3, 2d series (Boston, 1826), p. 13.

pennalties" and to "levie the same by distresse."

At the same time it was evident that the colonial authorities took pains to protect the inhabitants from abuse of these powers by placing their determination "in case of difficultie" in the hands of the judges of the county, and by allowing appeals to the county court. The two substantial reservations which the colony withholds from the company are the "inhancinge the prices of shooes, bootes, or wages," and the refusal to make shoes for inhabitants "of their owne leather for the use of themselves and families," if required by the latter.

From these reservations we are able to infer the industrial stage which the industry had reached at the time of incorporation.[3] It was the transition from the stage of the itinerant shoemaker, working up the raw material belonging to his customer in the home of the latter, to the stage of the settled shoemaker, working up his own raw material in his own shop to the order of his customer. The reservation for the protection of inhabitants is suggestive of statutes of the 15th and 16th centuries imposing penalties on guild members who refused to work in the house of their customer.[4] The fact that the colony, while granting power to reform the trade, nevertheless thought it necessary to require the shoemaker to continue that he need not go to the house of the customer, indicates the source of the abuses from which the shoemakers were endeavoring to rid themselves. The itinerant was likely to be poorly trained, and he could escape supervision by his fellow craftsmen. He was dependent on his customer who owned not only the raw material, but also the workplace, the lodging, and the food supplies of the shoemaker, leaving to the latter only the mere hand tools. He worked under the disadvantage of a new workplace for each new order, without the conveniences and equipment necessary for speedy and efficient work. He had to seek the customer, and consequent-ly was at a disadvantage in driving a bargain. This made him, however, a serious menace to the better-trained shoemaker, working in his own shop and on his own material, but waiting for the customer to come.

The Boston guild represented the union in one person of the later separated classes of merchant, master, and journeyman. Each of these classes has a different function. The merchant-function controls the kind and quality of the work, and its remuneration comes from ability to drive the bargain with the customer in the process of adjusting price to quality. The master-function, on the other hand, controls the workplace and the tools and equipment, and passes along to the journeyman the orders received from the merchant. Its remuneration comes from management of capital and labor. The journeyman-function, finally, is remunerated according to skill and quality of work, speed of output, and the amount and regularity of employment.[5]

Thus, from the standpoint of each of the functions that later were separated, did this primitive guild in self-interest set itself against the "bad ware" of the preceding itinerant stage. From the merchant standpoint the exclusion of bad ware removed a menace to remunerative prices for good ware. From the master standpoint the exclusion of the itinerant transferred the ownership of the workshop and the medium of wage payments from the consumer to the producer. From the journeyman standpoint, this exclusion of the itinerant eliminated the truck-payment of wages in the form of board and lodging by substituting piece wages for a finished product. And this control of the finished product through all the stages of production gave a double advantage to the craftsman. It transferred to him the unskilled parts of the work hitherto done by the customer's family, thus enabling him at one and the same stroke both to increase the amount of his work and to utilize the bargaining leverage of his skills to get skilled wages for unskilled work.

By this analysis we can see that when the three functions of merchant, master, and

---

[3]See Bücher, "Die Entstehung der Volkswirtschaft." Citations are from Wickett's translation, "Industrial Evolution" (New York, 1901). Also Sombart, "Der Moderne Kapitalismus," vol. 1, pp. 93–94.

[4]Bücher, "Die Entstehung," p. 169.

[5]Table 1, showing industrial stages, classes, and organizations, should be consulted in reading this and the following analysis.

Table 1
Industrial Stages, Classes, and Organizations of American Shoemakers

Extent of Market	Kind of Bargain	Capital Ownership (customer, merchant, employer, laborer)	Industrial Classes	Kind of Work	Competitive Menace	Protective Organizations	Case
Itinerant	Wages	Customer-Employer Material Board and lodging	Farm family Skilled helper Journeyman Hand tools	Skilled supervision	Family workers	None	Itinerant individuals 1648
Personal	Custom order	Merchant-Master-Journeyman Material Hand tools Home shop Journeyman / Hand tools	Merchant-Master-journeyman	"Bespoke"	"Bad Ware"	Craft guild	Boston "Company of Shoemakers," 1648
Local	Retail	Merchant-master Material Finished stock Short credits Sales shop Journeyman / Hand tools / Home shop	Merchant-master-journeyman	"Shop"	"Market" work "Advertisers" Auctions	Retail merchants' association	Philadelphia "Society of the Master Cordwainers," 1789
Water-ways	Wholesale order	Merchant-master Material Finished stock Long credits Store-room Journeyman / Hand tools / Home shop	Merchant-master-journeyman	"Order"	"Scabs" Interstate producers	Journeymen's society Masters' society	Philadelphia "Federal Society of Journeymen Cordwainers," 1794–1806
High-ways	Wholesale speculative	Merchant-Capitalist Material Finished stock Bank credits Warehouse "Manufactory" Contractor / Work shop Journeyman / Hand tools	Merchant-Capitalist Contractor Contractor Journeyman	Team work	Prison Sweatshop "Foreigner" "Speeding up"	Journeymen's society Manufacturers' association* Employers Association	Philadelphia "United Beneficial Society of Journeymen Cordwainers," 1835
Rail	Wholesale speculative	Merchant-Jobber Material Finished stock Bank credits Warehouse "Manufactory" Contract Manu-facturer / Work shop Journeyman / Footpower Machines	Merchant-Jobber "Manu-facturer" Journey-man	Team work	"Green hands" Chinese Women Children Prisoners Foreigners	Trade union Employers' association Manufacturers' association*	Knights of St. Crispin, 1868–72
World	Factory order	Manufacturer Material Stock Credits Power machinery Factory Laborer / None	Manufacturer Wage-earners	Piece work	Child labor Long hours Immigrants Foreign products	Industrial union Employers' association Manufacturers' association*	Boot and Shoe Workers' Union, 1895

*The "Manufacturer's Association" is based on the merchant or price-fixing function.

journeyman were united in the same person, the merchant-function epitomized the other two. It is the function by which the costs of production are shifted over to the consumer. The master looks to the merchant for his profits on raw material, workshop, tools, and wages, and the journeyman looks to him for the fund that will pay his wages.

Now, there is a prime consideration in the craft-guild stage that enhances the power of the merchant to shift his costs to the consumer. This is the fact that his market is a personal one, and the consumer gives his order before the goods are made. On the other hand, the bargaining power of the merchant is menaced by the incapacity of customers accurately to judge the quality of goods, as against their capacity clearly to distinguish prices. Therefore, it is enough for the purposes of a protective organization in the custom-order stage of the industry, to direct attention solely to the quality of the product rather than the price or the wage, and to seek only to exclude bad ware and the makers of bad ware. Thus the Boston shoemakers and coopers, though enlisting the colonial courts only in the laudable purpose of redressing "the damag which the country sustaynes by occasion of bad ware," succeeded thereby in "inriching themselves by their trades very much." In this they differed from later organizations, based on the separation of classes, to whom competition appeared as a menace primarily to prices and wages, and only secondarily to quality.

THE "SOCIETY OF MASTER CORDWAINERS," 1789, AND THE "FEDERAL SOCIETY OF JOURNEYMEN CORDWAINERS," 1794, PHILADELPHIA

The separation of classes first appears in the case of the cordwainers of Philadelphia, a century and a half later. Here appeared the first persistent discord that broke the primitive American harmony of capital and labor. So intense were the passions aroused, and so widespread was the popular irritation, that they have left their permanent record in 159 pages of "The Trial of the Boot and Shoemakers of Philadelphia, on an indictment for a combination and conspiracy to raise their

wages."[6] Here we have a fairly full record of the first American association of employers and the first trade union. They were the "Society of the Master Cordwainers of the City of Philadelphia," 1789, and the "Federal Society of Journeymen Cordwainers" of the same city, organized in 1794.

Other journeymen may have had organizations prior to that time. Mr. Ethelbert Stewart[7] has, indeed, unearthed records showing that the printers in New York as early as 1776, and in Philadelphia as early as 1786, were organized for the purpose of supporting their demands by means of strikes. But these were temporary organizations, falling apart after a brief strike; whereas the cordwainers of Philadelphia in 1799 conducted a strike and lockout of 9 or 10 weeks. To them goes the distinction of continuing their organization for at least 12 years, and aggressively driving their demands at the end of that period to the extent that the public took notice and the employers sought refuge behind the arm of the law. And it is to this junction of popular excitement and judicial interposition that we owe the record which exhibits the earliest struggle of capital and labor on American soil.

The indictment charged the journeymen with conspiring not to work except at prices and rates in excess of those "which were then used and accustomed to be paid and allowed to them"; with endeavoring "by threats, menaces, and other unlawful means" to prevent others from working at less than these excessive prices; and with adopting "unlawful and arbitrary by-laws, rules, and orders" and agreeing not to work for any master who should employ any workman violating such rules, and agreeing "by threats and menaces and other injuries" to prevent any workman from working for such a master.

The conspiracy and strike occurred in November 1805, and the matter came to trial in the Mayor's court in March 1806. The court permitted the witnesses to recite the entire history of this and the preceding strikes, as well as the history of the preceding combina-

---

[6]Commons et al., *Documentary History*, vol. 3, pp. 59–248.

[7]*Bulletin of U.S. Bureau of Labor*, no. 61, p. 860.

tions both of journeymen and employers. Consequently we are able to trace from the year 1789 to the year 1806 the development of the boot and shoe industry in Philadelphia, along with the accompanying separation of the interests of the journeymen from those of the masters.

I do not find any record of a guild organization like that in Boston, but there had been a "charitable society" to which both employers and journeymen belonged, and this was still in existence in 1805.[8] It was the masters who first formed themselves, in April 1789, into a separate organization. Their early constitution was laid before the court, showing the purpose of their organization to be that of "taking into consideration the many inconveniences which they labour under, for want of proper regulations among them, and to provide remedies for the same."[9] They were to "consult together for the general good of the trade, and determine upon the most eligible means to prevent irregularities in the same." They were to "consult together for the general good of the trade, and determine upon the most eligible means to prevent irregularities in the same." They were to hold four general meetings each year, and they had a committee of seven "to meet together as often as they think necessary." The society terminated in 1790, after the fifth quarterly meeting.

Apparently the masters had at that time just two kinds of "inconveniences": the competition of cheap grades of goods offered for sale at the "public market," and the competition of masters who offered bargain prices by public advertisement. This is shown by their qualifications for membership, "No person shall be elected a member of this society who offers for sale any boots, shoes, etc., in the public market of this city, or advertises the prices of his work, in any of the public papers or handbills, so long as he continues in these practices."

Evidently this society of masters was not organized as an employers' association, for nothing is said of wages or labor. It was organized by the masters merely in their function of retail merchant. The attorneys for the journeymen tried to make out that when the latter organized separately in 1794 they did so in self-defense, as against the masters' association, and they contended that in the masters' constitution were to be found "ample powers" not only to regulate prices, but also "to form a league to reduce the wages of their journeymen."[10] And although they admitted that the association had terminated in 1790, yet they held "it was a Phoenix that rose from its ashes."[11] But it was brought out clearly in evidence that the subsequent resurrections in 1799 and 1805 were provoked by the journeymen's aggressive society and were but temporary organizations. The Phoenix that kept on repeatedly rising was not the one that had disappeared. In 1789 it had been an organization of masters in their function of retail merchant. In its later stages it was an organization of masters in their function of employer. The distinction, fundamental in economics, caused a realignment in *personnel*, as will be shown presently. The early organization regulated prices and followed the vertical cleavage between producer and consumer. The later organization regulated wages and followed the horizontal cleavage between employer and laborer. In the early organization the journeyman's interest was the same as the master's. In the later ones the journeyman's interest was hostile to both consumer and master.

The foregoing considerations, as well as the transition to later stages, will become more apparent if we stop for a moment to examine the economic conditions that determine the forms of organization. These conditions are found, not so much in the technical "instruments of production," as in the development of raw markets. The economic development of the market proceeded as follows: The cordwainer of the Boston guild made all his boots and shoes to the order of his customer, at his home shop. His market was a custom-order market, composed of his neighbors. His product, in the terminology in 1806, was a "bespoke" product. He was in his own person master, custom-merchant, and journeyman.

---

[8]Commons et al., *Documentary History,* vol. 3, p. 99.
[9]Ibid, p. 128.

[10]Ibid., p. 166.
[11]Ibid., pp. 129, 174.

Next, some of the master cordwainers begin to stock up with standard sizes and shapes, for sale to sojourners and visitors at their shops. They cater to a wider market, requiring an investment in capital, not only in raw material, but also in finished products and personal credits. They give out the material to journeymen to be made up at their homes and brought back to the shop. In addition to "bespoke work," the journeyman now makes "shop work" and the master becomes retail merchant and employer. This was the stage of the industry in Philadelphia in 1789—the retail-shop stage.

Next, some of the masters seek an outside or foreign market. They carry their samples to distant merchants and take "orders" for goods to be afterwards made and delivered. They now become wholesale merchant-employers, carrying a larger amount of capital invested in material, products, and longer credits, and hiring a larger number of journeymen. In addition to "bespoke" and "shop" work the journeyman now makes "order work" for the same employer. This is the wholesale-order stage of the industry.

This was the stage in Philadelphia in 1806. At that time we find the journeyman engaged on one kind and quality of work, with the same tools and workshops, but with four different destinations for his product. Each destination was a different market, with a different level of competition, leading ultimately, after a struggle, to differences in quality. The terms employed at the time recapitulate the evolution of the industry. "Bespoke work" recalls the primitive custom market of the Boston guild, now differentiated as the market offered by the well-to-do for the highest quality of work at the highest level of competition. "Shop work" indicates the retail market of less particular customers at a wider but lower level of competition and quality. "Order work" indicates a wholesale market made possible by improved means of transportation, but on a lower level of strenuous competition and indifferent quality projected from other centres of manufacture. "Market work"—i.e., cheap work sold in the public market—indicates the poorest class of customers, and consequently the lowest level of competition, undermining especially the shop-work level, and to a lesser degree, the order-work level, but scarcely touching the "bespoke" level.

It was the widening of these markets with their lower levels of competition and quality, but without any changes in the instruments of production, that destroyed the primitive identity of master and journeyman cordwainers and split their community of interest into the modern alignment of employers' association and trade union. The struggle occurred, not as a result of changes in tools or methods of production, but directly as a result of changes in markets. It was a struggle on the part of the merchant-employer to require the same *minimum quality* of work for each of the markets, but lower rates of wages on work destined for the wider and lower markets. It was a struggle on the part of the journeymen to require the same *minimum wage* on work destined for each market, but with the option of a higher wage for a higher market. The conflict came over the wage and quality of work destined for the widest, lowest, and newest market. This will appear from the evidence brought out at the trial.

In the Boston guild it does not appear that there were any journeymen. Each "master" was at first a traveller, going to the homes of his customers and doing the skilled part of the journeyman's work. Next he was the all-around journeyman, not only "his own master" but, more important, his own merchant. The harmony of capital and labor was the identity of the human person. The market was direct, the orders were "bespoke."

Even in Philadelphia, in 1789, when the masters had added "shop work" and had separated themselves out as an association of retail merchants, the interests of the journeymen coincided with theirs. The journeymen were even more distressed by "market work" than were the masters. At the "market" there was no provision for holding back goods for a stated price. Everything had to be sold at once and for cash. Goods were not carried in stock. Consequently, the prices paid were exceedingly low. Job Harrison, the "scab," testified that, whereas he was regularly paid 9s. for making a pair of shoes, he could get only 3s. to 3s. 6d. on "market work." If he should quit his job by joining the "turnout" under orders from the society, he would be "driven to market work," at which he could not get half a living.[12] So also declared Andrew Dunlap and James Cummings, members of the society who had resorted to "market work" during the turnout.[13] The journeymen's society, in its contest with the masters, permitted its members to send their product to the public market, or to work for merchants who supplied that market. The society members pieced out their strike benefits and what they could get by "cobbling," with what they could get at "market work."[14] "You were at liberty to make market work, or any other work you could get, except of master workmen?" "Yes," was the answer of Job Harrison.[15] This was evidently a war measure, and not an indication that the journeymen were less hostile than the retail merchant toward the public market.

The two other kinds of work that prevailed in 1789 were "shop" work and "bespoke" work. The prices paid to the journeymen for these two kinds of work were originally the same. If they differed in quality, the difference was paid for at a specific price for extra work, as when Job Harrison got 6d. extra a pair if he would "side line" his shoes with silk.[16] But the payment for extras was the same for shop work as it was for "bespoke" work. The same workman made both, and made them in the same way, with the same tools. One of the grievances of the journeymen was the innovation attempted in 1798 by one of the employers to reduce the price for shop work. "I made some work for Mr. Ryan," said John Hayes, "and he made a similar reduction upon me, because they were to go into the shop, when he used before to give the same price for shop goods as he did for bespoke work."[17] The society demanded similar pay for similar work,

whether shop or bespoke. "None are to work under the price," said Keegan, a member of the committee that met the employers: "a good workman may get more."[18]

Thus the journeymen were at one with the masters in their opposition to "market work." For the journeyman it was a menace to his wages on shop work. For the master it was a menace to his business as a retail storekeeper.

It was the third, or "export" stage of the market, with its wholesale "order" work, that separated the interests of the journeyman from those of the master. Here the retail merchant adds wholesale orders to his business.

On the other hand, employers who were not branching out for export work were willing to pay the wages demanded and unwilling to join the employers' association. Wm. Young had belonged to the masters' association in 1789, when it was only a retail merchants' association, and in 1805 he was still doing only bespoke and shop work.

Likewise, the journeymen who did only bespoke and shop work were not inclined to stand by the union for the increase in prices. Job Harrison said,[19] "If shoes were raised to 9s. I should not be benefitted, for I had that price already, but you know it cannot be given only on customers' work." Afterwards he was asked:

Q. Did I understand you to be satisfied all this time with the wages you had been accustomed to receive from Mr. Bedford, and yet they compelled you to turn out?
A. I had as much as any man, and I could not expect more: but they did not compel me to turn out, any other way than by making a *scab* of me. At length I received a note from Mr. Bedford, informing me that if I did not turn in to work I should hereafter have no more than common wages.[20]

The same was true of inferior workmen who could not command the wages demanded. These were doubtless kept on "order" work, and when the union demanded that the price on that work should be brought up to the same level as shop and bespoke work, they secretly worked "under wages." The union

[12]Commons et al., *Documentary History*, vol. 3, pp. 74, 83.
[13]Ibid., pp. 91, 96.
[14]Ibid., pp. 83, 91, 93, 96.
[15]Ibid., p. 88.
[16]Ibid., p. 94.
[17]Ibid., p. 121.

[18]Ibid., p. 120.
[19]Ibid., p. 82.
[20]Ibid., p. 84.

had a committee, "to hunt up cases of the kind," and to demand of employers that such men be discharged.[21]

Thus, as intimated above, the organization of the masters according to their employer-function, as compared with their former organization according to their merchant-function, caused a realignment of *personnel*. Both the employer and the workman on high-class custom-work "scabbed" on their respective class organizations struggling to control wholesale-order work.

The several steps in this alignment of interests will appear in the history of the journeymen's society. The first society of the journeymen was organized in 1792, two years after the master's society had dissolved. This was apparently a secret society. At any rate it did not submit a scale of prices to the employers, and did not call a strike, but merely contented itself with a "solemn" oath taken by each member to the effect, "I will support such and such wages, to the utmost of my power, etc." But a number of the journeymen secretly violated their pledge. "I know a number," testified Samuel Logan, at that time a journeyman, but now a master, "to work under wages they had solemnly promised to support. I therefore requested a repeal of this affirmation, which broke up the society."[22] The society dissolved in 1792, the year of its organization.

This society, however, must have had some effect on the price of shoes, for the price which had originally been 4s. 6d.[23] had been raised to 6s. before 1794.

It was in 1794 that the permanent society was organized, which continued until the time of the prosecution in 1806.[24] It secured in that year, and again in 1796, an increase in the price of shoes, first, to something under $1, then to $1 a pair.[25] These increases, affected, however, only shop and bespoke work, so that after 1796 the "settled price" was 7s. 6d.; but Job Harrison, by making a lighter shoe with silk lining "so as to come nearer to London

dress-shoes," was paid 9s. a pair.[26] At the other and lowest extreme, only "five eleven penny bits" were paid for "order work." These prices prevailed until 1806. The bespoke and shop work was said to be sold to customers at $2.75 a pair, but the order work was sold to retailers at $1.80 a pair.[27] Thus it was that for nominally the same quality of shoe the journeymen's society was able almost to double their wages on the custom and retail work, but had brought about an increase of only a few cents on the wholesale-order work. In other words, the employer as retail merchant gave to his employees an advance out of the advanced retail price of his goods, but as a wholesale merchant he was not able to give a similar advance. Naturally the better class of workmen gravitated toward the custom and retail work, and the inferior workmen toward the wholesale work so that what was originally the same quality of work, and nominally remained the same, became eventually different in quality.

Notice now the characteristic features of the retail and wholesale-order stages of the industry. The master workman at the retail stage has added a stock of finished goods to his business of custom work. This requires a shop on a business street accessible to the general public, with corresponding high rents. It involves also a certain amount of capital tied up in short credits and accounts with customers. In his shop he has a stock of raw material, besides finished and partly finished goods. The merchant-function has thus become paramount, and has drawn with it the master-function. The two functions have equipped themselves with capital—merchant's capital in the form of finished stock, retail store, and short credits; employer's capital in the form of raw material undergoing manufacture by workmen under instructions. The journeymen are left with only their hand tools and their home workshop.

Thus the retail market has separated the laborer from the merchant. Labor's outlook now is solely for wages. The merchant's outlook is for quality and prices. But the separation is not antagonism. The employer-func-

---

[21]Ibid., p. 92.

[22]Ibid., p. 93.

[23]Ibid., p. 118.

[24]Ibid., pp. 174, 217–18.

[25]Ibid., pp. 72, 93.

[26]Ibid., pp. 74, 86.

[27]Ibid., p. 86.

tion is as yet at a minimum. Profit is not dependent on reducing wages so much as increasing prices. Indeed, the journeymen are able almost to double their wages without a strike, and the merchants pass the increase along to the customers.

But it is different when the merchant reaches out for wholesale orders. Now he adds heavy expenses for solicitation and transportation. He adds a storeroom and a larger stock of goods. He holds the stock a longer time and he gives long and perilous credits. At the same time he meets competitors from other centers of manufacture, and cannot pass along his increased expenses. Consequently the wage-bargain assumes importance, and the employer-function comes to the front. Wages are reduced by the merchant as employer on work destined for the wholesale market. The conflict of capital and labor begins.

Before we can fully appreciate the significance and the economic interpretation of these revolutionizing facts, we shall need to consider the next succeeding stage, that of the merchant-capitalist.

THE "UNITED BENEFICIAL SOCIETY OF JOURNEYMEN CORDWAINERS," PHILADELPHIA, 1835

The organizations of masters and journeymen of 1805 continued more or less until 1835. Then a new and more revolutionary stage of the industry is ushered in. This time it is the merchant-capitalist, who subdues both the master and the journeyman through his control of the new widespread market of the South and West. We read of his coming in the address "to the Journeymen Cordwainers of the City and County of Philadelphia," issued by the 200 members of the "United Beneficial Society of Journeymen Cordwainers."[28] This organization took the lead in bringing together the several trade societies of Philadelphia into the Trades' Union, and in conducting the first great general 10-hour strike in this country. The reasons for their aggressiveness may be inferred from their "Address." They recite that the wages of $2.75 formerly paid for

[28]*Pennsylvanian*, April 4, 1835; Commons et al., *Documentary History*, vol. 6, pp. 21–27.

boots have fallen to $1.12½; that their earnings of $9 to $10 a week have fallen to $4 to $6; that, in order to earn such wages they must work, in many instances, 14 hours a day; and that other skilled tradesmen are earning $8 to $12 dollars a week, often "only working 10 hours a day." This depression, they explain, has occurred since "a few years ago." It began with an "unfortunate" cooperative experiment of the journeymen in "opening shops for the manufacture of cheap goods" for the purpose of winning a strike. It was intensified by the appearance of the merchant-capitalist. We are told that

"The cunning men of the East" have come to our city, and having capital themselves, or joining with those who have had, have embarked in our business, and realized large fortunes, by reducing our wages, making large quantities of work and selling at reduced price, while those who had served their time at the trade, and had an anxious desire to foster and cherish its interests, have had to abandon the business or enter into the system of manufacturing largely (i.e., on a large scale) in order to save themselves from bankruptcy.

Then they explain how this has come about "without any positive reduction of our wages."

The answer is plain and simple—by making cheap work, triple the quantity has to be made to obtain a living; this produces, at dull seasons, a surplus of work in the market; and these *large* manufacturers, taking advantage of the times, have compelled their journeyman to make the work so far superior to the manner in which it was originally made for the wages given, that it is now brought into competition with first-rate work. This again lessens the quantity of first-rate work made, and the journeymen, formerly working for employers who gave them $2.75 for each pair of boots made, are forced to seek employment of the very men who had ruined their business.

The dubious position of the employers also, at this stage of the industry, is shown by the action of "a large adjourned meeting of the ladies'-shoe dealers and manufacturers." They unanimously adopted a preamble and resolution presented by a committee appointed at a previous meeting reciting that,

Whereas, the laboring portion of this community have made a general strike for what they consider their just rights, knowing that if they were longer to permit the growing encroachments of capital upon labor, they would soon be unable to make any resistance . . . we feel a desire to aid and encourage them in their effort to obtain an adequate compensation for their labor. Knowing that the pittance hitherto earned by them is entirely insufficient for their support, we do hereby agree to and comply with their demands generally, and pledge ourselves to do all in our power to support and sustain them. Believing also that a trifling advance in the price of shoes would scarcely be felt by general society . . . we will agree to be governed hereafter by a list of prices for our work, which will render our business uniform and permanent.[29]

Nine months later these employers were forced by the exactions of the union and their inability to control the merchant-capitalist to take the other side of the question, organizing as an employers' association and making a determined fight against the union.[30]

At this stage of the industry we have reached the market afforded by highway and canal, as well as ocean and river. The banking system has expanded, enabling the capitalist to convert customers' credit into bank credits and to stock up a surplus of goods in advance of actual orders. The market becomes speculative, and the warehouse of the wholesale-merchant-master takes the place of the storeroom of the retail capitalist. The former master becomes the small manufacturer or contractor, selling his product to the wholesale-manufacturer, the merchant-capitalist. The latter has a wide range of option in his purchase of goods, and consequently in his ability to compel masters and journeymen to compete severely against each other. He can have his shoes made in distant localities. The cordwainers relate[31] that

there are many employers of this city who have made off of the labor of journeymen a liberal fortune, and now refuse to accede to the justice of our demands, and in order to evade the same they are preparing materials (in this city) in order to send them into the towns of the Eastern states (where living and labor are cheaper and workmanship not so good) to get the same made into shoes, then to be brought here and sold for Philadelphia manufacture.

The merchant-capitalist can also discover new fields for the manufacturer of cheap work, and for the first time we read of the competition of convict labor. The cordwainers publish an advertisement[32] warning their members against a firm who "are now getting work manufactured by convicts in the Eastern Penitentiary at less than one-half what our bill of rates call for." And one of their resolutions asserts that "shoemaking is found to be the most convenient and most lucrative employment of convicts, consequently almost *one half* of the convicts in our different penitentiaries are taught shoemaking."[33]

The merchant-capitalist has also the option of all the different methods of manufacture and shop organization. He can employ journeymen at his warehouse as cutters, fitters, and pattern makers; he can employ journeymen at their homes to take out material and bring back finished work; but, more characteristic of his methods, he can employ small contractors, the specialized successors of the master cordwainer, who in turn employ one to a dozen journeymen, and by division of labor and "team work" introduce the sweating system.[34]

Through these different methods of manufacture we are able to see how it is that the merchant-capitalist intensifies and even creates the antagonism of "capital and labor." He does this by forcing the separation of functions and classes a step further than it had been forced in the wholesale-order stage. First, he takes away from the retail merchant his wholesale-order business. He buys and

[29]*Pennsylvanian*, June 15, 1835; Commons et al., *Documentary History*, vol. 6, pp 27–28.

[30]*Pennsylvanian*, March 28, 1836; Commons et al., *Documentary History*, vol. 6, pp. 32–35.

[31]*Pennsylvanian*, June 20, 1835; Commons et al., *Documentary History*, vol. 6, pp. 29–30.

[32]*Pennsylvanian*, September 5, 1835.

[33]*Pennsylvanian*, October 1, 1835.

[34]The term *manufactory*, as distinguished from *factory*, occurs in the merchant-capitalist stage to indicate the combined warehouse and place of employment where material is prepared to be taken out by journeymen or contractors. It is the "inside shop" of the ready-made clothing trade, the contractor's shops being known as "outside shops." See Commons, "Trade Unionism and Labor Problems," p. 316 (1905), article on "sweating system."

sells in large quantities; he assembles the cheap products of prison labor, distant localities, and sweatshops; he informs himself of markets, and beats down the charges for transportation. Thus he takes the wholesale business and leaves to the merchant the retail trade.

Second, he drives off from the retail merchant his employer-function. The retail merchant can no longer afford to employ journeymen on "shop" work, because he can purchase more cheaply of the merchant-capitalist. A few years ago, say the cordwainers in their "Address," "such an article as boots was then unknown in the Market street shops: The manufacturing of that article being confined exclusively to those, who having served an apprenticeship to the business, knew best its value."[35]

Thus the merchant-capitalist strips the former merchant-master both of his market and his journeymen. The wholesale market he takes to himself; the journeymen he hands over to a specialist in wage-bargaining. This specialist is no longer known as "master"—he takes the name of "boss,"[36] or employer. He is partly a workman, having come up through the trade, like the master, and continuing to work alongside his men. He is an employer without capital, for he rents his workshop, and the merchant-capitalist owns the raw material and the journeymen own the tools. His profits are not those of the capitalist, neither do they proceed from his ability as a merchant, since the contract-prices he gets are dictated by the merchant-capitalist. His profits come solely out of wages and work. He organizes his workmen in teams, with the work subdivided in order to lessen dependence on skill and to increase speed of output. He plays the less skilled against the more skilled, the speedy against the slow, and reduces wages while enhancing exertion. His profits are

"sweated" out of labor, his shop is the "sweatshop," he the "sweater."

Thus the merchant-capitalist, with his widespread, wholesale-speculative market, completes the separation and specializes the functions of the former homogeneous craftsman. The merchant-function, which was the first to split off from the others, is now itself separated into three parts—custom merchant, retail merchant, wholesale merchant—corresponding to the three levels of market competition. The journeyman-function is now segregated on two levels of competition, the highest level of custom work and the lowest level menaced by prison and sweatshop work. The employer-function, the last to split off, makes its first appearance as a separate factor on the lowest level of market competition. Evidently the wide extension of the market in the hands of the merchant-capitalist is the cataclysm in the position of the journeyman. By a desperate effort of organization he struggles to raise himself back to his original level. His merchant-employers at first sympathize with him and endeavor to pass over to their customers his just demand for a higher wage. But they soon are crushed between the level of prices and the level of wages. From the position of a merchants' association striving to hold up prices, they shift to that of an employers' association endeavoring to keep down wages. The result of these struggles of protective organizations will appear when we analyze more closely the economic forces under which they operate. These forces turn on the nature of the bargain, the period and risk of investment and the level of the competitive menace.

*　*　*　*　*

We have already seen the cumulative effect in 1806 and 1835, of these three sets of circumstances in dragging down the entire body of workmen. We now proceed to notice the resistance of protective organizations and their ultimate effect in bringing about a segregation of work and workers on noncompeting levels.

This may be seen by following again the movement of wages in Philadelphia from 1789 to 1835, on the different classes of work.

---

[35]*Pennsylvanian*, April 4, 1835; Commons et al., *Documentary History*, vol. 6, p. 22.

[36]The first use that I have found of the Dutch word "bos," meaning manager of a group of workmen, is in the organ of the New York Trades Union, *The Man*, May 30, 1834; Commons et al., *Documentary History*, vol. 6, p. 92. It was spelled with one "s," though the obstinacy of the printer of the *Documentary History* finally succeeded in using two in the reprint.

Prior to 1792, on common boots, the journeyman's wages were $1.40 a pair on both bespoke and shop work. In the course of 15 years the price advanced to $2.75, and this price was paid for both bespoke and shop work, but a concession of $0.25 was made on wholesale-order work, bringing that price to $2.50. In 1835 the price had fallen to $1.12½ for wholesale work, while retail work had dropped out or had come down to the same price as wholesale work, leaving custom work at a higher figure. In the course of this movement, the better class of workmen restricted themselves as much as possible to custom work, and the quality of this kind of work was improved. On the other hand, the wholesale-order and the wholesale-speculative work tended throughout to fall into the hands of inferior workmen, and this brought about an inferiority in quality. These inferior goods, made by inferior workmen, became more and more a menace to the superior goods and the superior journeymen, both on account of the lower levels of the marginal producers and on account of the smaller demand relatively for the production of superior goods.

Herein was the necessity of protective organizations. In order that these organizations might succeed, it was just as necessary to set up protection against inferior goods as against low wages. In the guild stage of the industry, when the three functions of journeyman, master, and workman were united in one person, the protection sought was against the "bad ware" made by some of the trade. By "supressing" those who made bad ware, the customers would be compelled to turn to those who were "sufficient" workmen and made good ware. Since the bargain was a separate one for each article, so that the price could be adjusted to the quality before the work was done, nothing more was needed on the part of the guild members for the purpose of "inriching themselves by their trades very much."

But in the later stages of the industry, the merchant-function, and afterwards the employer-function, were separated from the journeyman-function. It is the special function of the merchant to watch over and guard the quality of the work, because his bargain with the consumer is an adjustment of the price to the quality demanded. The journeyman's function is simply that of making the kind and quality of goods ordered by the merchant. The merchant, in his function as employer, gives these orders to the journeyman, and consequently, when the employer-function is separated from the journeyman-function, the employer, as the representative of the merchant, attends to the quality of the work. In this way the journeyman has lost control over quality and is forced to adapt his quality to his price, instead of demanding a price suited to his quality. So, when he forms his protective organization, his attention is directed mainly to the compensation side of the bargain. In proportion as the quality of his work depends on his rate of pay, he directly controls the quality, but the primary purpose of his organization is to control the rate of pay. This he does, first, by demanding the same minimum rate of pay for all market destinations of the same kind of work. It was this demand that forced the alignment of classes and drove the sympathetic merchant over into the hostile employers' association. The employer could yield if he confined himself to the narrow field of the "bespoke" market, but not if he was menaced by the wider field of the wholesale market. On this account it was possible in the retail-shop stage for the interests of employer and workmen to be harmonious. But the employer could not yield in the merchant-capitalist stage, on that part of the field menaced by prison and sweatshop labor. Consequently, the outcome of the strikes of 1835 was the differentiation of the market into two noncompeting levels, the higher level of custom and high-grade shop work, controlled more or less by the cordwainers' societies for the next 25 years[37] and the lower level of inferior work controlled by prison and sweatshop competition.[38]

---

[37]E. T. Freedley, "Philadelphia and Its Manufactories," p. 187, says in 1858: "Making men's wear and making women's wear are distinct branches. The Men's men and Women's men, as the workmen are distinguished, have separate organizations, and neither know nor mingle with each other."

[38]"In addition to these there are a large number whose operations, though in the aggregate important, cannot easily be ascertained. They are known by a term more expressive than euphonious, 'garret bosses' who employ

KNIGHTS OF ST. CRISPIN, 1868

We come now to an entirely different step in the progress of industrial stages. Hitherto, the only change requiring notice has been that produced by the extension of the market and the accompanying credit system. These changes were solely external. The next change is internal. Prior to 1837 there had been scarcely a hundred inventions affecting the tools used by the cordwainer. All of these may be described as "devices" rather than machines. Even as late as 1851 all of the labor in the manufacture of shoes was hand labor. In 1852, the sewing machine was adapted to the making of uppers, but this did not affect the journeyman cordwainer because the sewing of uppers had been the work of women. Even the flood of inventions that came into use during the decade of the 50s were aids to the journeyman rather than substitutes for his skill. Indeed, some of them probably operated to transfer the work of women to men, for they required greater physical strength and endurance in order to develop their full capacity. Whether operated by foot power or merely facilitating the work of his hands, they were essentially shop tools and not factory machines. Such were the tin patterns for cutting, the stripper and sole-cutter, adjustable lasts, levellers, skivers, and the machines for heel making, lasting, and sandpapering. Quite different were the pegging machine, introduced in 1857, and especially the McKay sole-sewing machine, introduced in 1862. These usurped not only the highest skill of the workman, but also his superior physique. The McKay machine did in 1 hour what the journeyman did in 80. These machines were quickly followed by others, either machines newly invented or old ones newly adapted, but all of them belted up to steam. The factory system, aided by enormous demand of government for its armies, came suddenly forth, though it required another 15 years to reach perfection. It was at the middle of this transition period, 1868 to 1872, that the Knights of St. Crispin appeared and flourished beyond anything theretofore known in the history of American organized labor. Its membership mounted to 40,000 or 50,000 whereas the next largest unions of the time claimed only 10,000 to 12,000. It disappeared as suddenly as it had risen, a tumultuous, helpless protest against the abuse of machinery. For it was not the machine itself that the Crispins were organized to resist, but the substitution of "green hands" for journeymen in the operation of the machines. There was but one law which they bound themselves by constitutions, rituals, oaths, and secret confederacy to enforce and to support each other in enforcing: refusal to teach "green hands" except by consent of the organization. This at least was the object of the national organization. When local unions once were established, they took into their own hands the cure of other ills, and their strikes and lockouts were as various as the variety of shops and factories in which they were employed. The Knights of St. Crispin were face to face with survivals from all of the preceding stages of industrial evolution, as well as the lusty beginnings of the succeeding stages. They were employed in custom shops, in retail and wholesale-order shops, in the shops of the merchant-capitalist and his contractors, in the factories of the manufacturer-capitalist. A comparison of the objects of their strikes reveals the overlapping of stages. All of their strikes turned directly or indirectly on two issues, resistance to wage reductions and refusal to teach "green hands." The wage strikes took place mainly in the shops of the merchant-capitalist, the "green hand" strikes in the factories.[39] The merchant-capitalist was forced by the competition of the manufacturer, either to become a manufacturer himself (or to purchase from the manufacturer), or to cut the wages of his journeymen and the prices paid to his contractors. Neither the journeyman's devices nor his foot power ma-

---

from 1 to 12 men each; and having but little capital, make boots and shoes in their own rooms, and sell them to jobbers and retailers in small quantities at low rates for cash. One retailer, who sells $20,000 worth per annum, buys three-fourths of his stock from these makers." Freedley, p. 188.

[39]For the detailed study upon which this brief summary of the Knights of St. Crispin is based, I am indebted to Mr. D. D. Lescohier, member of my research group. See *Bulletin* No. 355 of the University of Wisconsin, Economics and Political Science Series 7, no. 1.

chines yielded a sufficient increase of output to offset his wage reductions. His aggravation was the more intense in that the wage reductions occurred only on shop work and not on custom work. The anomaly of different prices for the same grade of work, which had showed itself with the extension of markets, was now still more exaggerated and more often experienced under the competition of factory products. Even prison labor and Chinese labor were not cheap enough to enable the merchant-capitalist to compete with the product of "green hands" and steam power.

The factory succeeded also in producing a quality of work equal or even superior to that produced by the journeyman. Consequently its levelling agencies reached upward to all but the topmost of the noncompeting levels on which the journeymen had succeeded in placing themselves, and brought them down eventually to its own factory level. The Grand Lodge of the Knights of St. Crispin was the protest of workmen whose skill of work, quality of product, and protective unions had for a generation preceding saved for themselves the higher levels of the merchant-capitalist system against the underwash of prison and sweatshop competition. It was their protest against the new menace of cheap labor and "green hands" utilized by the owners of steam power and machinery. Suffice it to note that in the shoe industry the factory system was established in substantially its present form in the early part of the 80s; that detailed piece-work has taken the place of team-work and hand-work; that the last vestige of property-right has left the worker; that the present form of labor organization, the Boot and Shoe Workers' Union, has endeavored, since 1895, to bring together all classes of employees, men and women, in a single industrial union rather than a partial trade union; and that the two classes of protective organizations have asserted their political power for protection against low levels of competition, the merchant-manufacturer against free trade in foreign products, the wage earner against foreign immigrants, prison labor, child labor, and long hours of labor.

APPENDIX

"COMPANY OF SHOOMAKERS," BOSTON, 1648[40]

Vppon the petition of the shoomakers of Boston, & in consideration of the complaynts which haue bin made of the damag which the country sustaynes by occasion of bad ware made by some of that trade, for redresse hereof, its ordred, & the Court doth hereby graunt libtie & powre vnto Richard Webb, James Euerill, Robt Turner, Edmund Jackson, & the rest of the shoomakers inhabiting & howskeepers in Boston, or the greatest number of them, vppō due notice giuen to the rest, to assemble & meete together in Boston, at such time & times as they shall appoynt, who beinge so assembled, they, or the greater number of them, shall haue powre to chuse a master, & two wardens, with fowre or six associats, a clarke, a sealer, a searcher, & a beadle, with such other officers as they shall find nessessarie; & these officers & ministers, as afforesd, every yeare or oftener, in case of death or departure out of this jurisdiction, or remoueall for default, &c., which officers & ministers shall each of them take an oath sutable to theire places before the Gounor or some of the magists, the same beinge pscribed or allowed by this Court; & the sd shoomakers beinge so assembled as before, or at any other meettinge or assembly to be appoynted from time to time by the master & wardens, or master or wardens with two of the associats, shall haue power to make orders for the well gouerninge of theire company, in the mannaginge of their trade & all the affayres therevnto belonging, & to change & reforme the same as occasion shall require & to anex reasonable pennalties for the breach of the same; provided, that none of theire sd orders, nor any alteration therein, shalbe of force before they shalbe pvsed & allowed of by the Court of that county, or by the Court of Assistants. And for the better executing such orders, the sd master & wardens, or any two of them with

---

[40]"The records of the Colony of Massachusetts Bay in New England," 3, p. 132.

4 or 6 associats, or any three of them, shall haue power to heare & determine all offences agaynst any of theire sd orders, & may inflict the pennalties pscribed as aforesd, & assesse fines to the vallew of forty shillings or vnder for one offence, & the clarke shall giue warrent in writinge to the beadle to leuie the same, who shall haue power therevppon to leuie the same by distresse, as is vsed in other cases; & all the sd fines & forfeitures shalbe imployd to the benefit of the sd company of shoomakers in generall, & to no other vse. And vppon the complaynt to the sd master & wardens, or theire atturny or advocate, in the County Court, of any pson or psons who shall vse the art or trade of a shoomaker, or any pt thereof, not beinge approused of by the officers of ye sd shoomakers to be a sufficient workman, the sd Court shall haue power to send for such psons, & suppresse them; provided also, that the prioritie of theire graunt shall not giue them precedency of other companies that may be graunted; but that poynt to be determined by this Court when there shalbe occasiō thereof; provided also, that no vnlawful combination be made at any time by the sd company of shoomakers for inhancinge the prices of shooes, bootes, or wages, whereby either or owne people may suffer; provided also, that in cases of dificultie, the sd officers & associats doe not pceede to determine the cause but by the advice of the judges of that county; provided, that no shoomaker shall refuse to make shooes for any inhabitant, at reasonable rates, of theire owne leather, for the vse of themselues & families. only if they be required therevnto; provided, lastly, that if any pson shall find himselfe greiued by such excessiue fines or other illegal pceedinges of the sd officers, he may complayne thereof at the next Court of that county, who may heare & determine the cause. This commission to continue & be of force for three yeares, & no longer, vnles the Court shall see cause to continue the same.

The same cōmission, verbatim, with the same libtie & power for the same ends, vpon the like grounds is giuen vnto Thomas Venner, John Millum, Samuel Bidfeild, James Mattocks, Wm. Cutter, Bartholomew Barlow, & the rest of the coops of Boston & Charlestowne, for the pventing abuses in theire trade. To continue only for three years, as the former, mutatis mutandis.

READING 7

A Short History of American Labor*

AFL–CIO

This brief history of the 100 years of the modern trade union movement in the United States can only touch the high spots of activity and identify the principal trends of a "century of achievement." In such a condensation of history, episodes of importance and of great human drama must necessarily be discussed far too briefly, or in some cases relegated to a mere mention.

What is clearly evident, however, is that the working people of America have had to unite in struggle to achieve the gains that they have accumulated during this century. Improvements did not come easily. Organizing unions, winning the right to representation, using the collective bargaining process as the core of their activities, struggling against bias and discrimination, the working men and women of America have built a trade union movement of formidable proportions.

Labor in America has correctly been described as a stabilizing force in the national economy and a bulwark of our democratic society. Furthermore, the gains that unions have been able to achieve have brought benefits, direct and indirect, to the public as a whole. It was labor, for example, that spearheaded the drive for public education for every child. The labor movement, indeed, has served as a force for American progress.

AMERICAN LABOR'S SECOND CENTURY

Now, in the 1980s, as the American trade union movement looks toward its second cen-

*Reprinted from AFL–CIO, *American Federationist* 88, no. 3, March 1981, pp. 1–16. *This article is excerpted from the AFL–CIO publication,* A Short History of American Labor, *prepared for the 1981 Centennial of American labor.*

tury, it takes pride in its first "century of achievement" as it recognizes a substantial list of goals yet to be achieved.

In this past century, American labor has played a central role in the elevation of the American standard of living. The benefits which unions have negotiated for their members are, in most cases, widespread in the economy and enjoyed by millions of our fellow citizens outside the labor movement. It is often hard to remember that what we take for granted—vacations with pay, pensions, health and welfare protection, grievance and arbitration procedures, holidays—never existed on any meaningful scale until unions fought and won them for working people.

Through these decades, the labor movement has constantly reached out to groups in the American society striving for their share of opportunity and rewards . . . to the blacks, the Hispanics, and other minorities . . . to women striving for jobs and equal or comparable pay . . . to those who work for better schools, for the freedom of speech, press, and assembly guaranteed by the Bill of Rights . . . to those seeking to make our cities more livable or our rural recreation areas more available . . . to those seeking better health for infants and more secure status for the elderly.

Through these decades, in addition, the unions of America have functioned in an economy and a technology marked by awesome change. When the Federation of Organized Trades and Labor Unions gathered in convention in 1881, Edison had two years earlier invented the electric light, and the first telephone conversation had taken place just five years before. There were no autos, no airplanes, no radio, no television, no air conditioning, no computers or calculators, no electronic games. For our modest energy needs—coal, kerosene, and candles—we were independently self-sufficient.

The labor movement has seen old industries die (horse-shoeing was once a major occupation) and new industries mature. The American work force, once predominantly "blue-collar," now finds "white-collar" employees and the "grey-collar" people of the service industries in a substantial majority.

The work force in big mass production industries has contracted, and the new industries have required employees with different skills in different locations. Work once performed in the United States has been moved to other countries, often at wage levels far below the American standards. Multinational, conglomerate corporations have moved operations around the globe as if it were a mammoth chessboard. The once thriving U.S. merchant marine has shriveled.

A new kind of "growth industry"—consultants to management skilled in the use of every legal loophole that can frustrate union organizing, the winning of representation elections, or the negotiation of a fair and equitable collective bargaining agreement—has mushroomed in recent years, and threatens the stability of labor-management relationships. A group of organizations generally described as the "new right" enlist their followers in retrogressive crusades to develop an anti-union atmosphere in the nation, and to repeal or mutilate various social and economic programs that have brought a greater degree of security and peace of mind to the millions of American wage earners in the middle and lower economic brackets.

Resistance to modest proposals like the labor law reform bill of 1977, and the use of lie detectors and electronic surveillance in probing the attitudes and actions of employees are a reminder that opposition to unions, while changing in style from the practices of a few decades ago, is still alive and flourishing—often financed by corporate groups, trade associations, and extremist ideologues.

Yet through this dizzying process of change, one need remains constant—the need for individual employees to enjoy their human rights and dignity, and to have the power to band together to achieve equal collective status in dealing with multimillion and multibillion dollar corporations. In other words, there is no substitute for the labor union.

American labor's responsibility in its second century is to adjust to the new conditions, so that it may achieve optimum ability to represent its members and contribute to the evolutionary progress of the American democratic society.

AFL–CIO President Lane Kirkland expressed that concept in his formal statement on labor's centennial in 1981:

Labor has a unique role in strengthening contemporary American society and dealing adequately and forcefully with the challenge of the future.

We shall rededicate ourselves to the sound principle of harnessing democratic tradition and trade union heritage with the necessity of reaching out for new and better ways to serve all working people and the entire nation.

TOWARD A FEDERATION OF LABOR

The roots of our country's trade unions extend deep into the early history of America. Several of the Pilgrims arriving at Plymouth Rock in 1620 were working craftsmen. Captain John Smith, who led the ill-fated settlement in 1607 on Virginia's James River, pleaded with his sponsors in London to send him more craftsmen and working people.

Primitive unions, or guilds, of carpenters and cordwainers, cabinet makers and cobblers made their appearance, often temporary, in various cities along the Atlantic seaboard of colonial America. Workers played a significant role in the struggle for independence; carpenters disguised as Mohawk Indians were the "host" group at the Boston Tea Party in 1773. The Continental Congress met in Carpenters Hall in Philadelphia, and there the Declaration of Independence was signed in 1776. In "pursuit of happiness" through shorter hours and higher pay, printers were the first to go on strike, in New York in 1794; cabinet makers struck in 1796; carpenters in Philadelphia in 1797; cordwainers in 1799. In the early years of the 19th century, recorded efforts by unions to improve the workers' conditions, through either negotiation or strike action, became more frequent.

By the 1820s, various unions involved in the effort to reduce the working day from 12 to 10 hours began to show interest in the idea of federation—of joining together in pursuit of common objectives for working people.

Puny as these first efforts to organize may have been, they reflected the need of working people for economic and legal protection from exploiting employers. The invention of the steam engine and the growing use of water power to operate machinery were developing a trend toward a factory system not much different from that in England which produced misery and slums for decades. Starting in the 1830s and accelerating rapidly during the Civil War, the factory system accounted for an ever-growing share of American production. It also produced great wealth for a few, grinding poverty for many.

With workers recognizing the power of their employers, the number of local union organizations increased steadily during the mid-19th century. In a number of cities, unions in various trades joined together in citywide federations. The National Trades' Union, formed in 1834 by workers in five cities, was an early attempt at countrywide federation—but the financial panic of 1837 put an end to its efforts. In 1866 several national associations of unions functioning in one trade—printers, machinists, stone cutters, to name a few—sent delegates to a Baltimore meeting that brought forth the National Labor Union. Never very strong, it was a casualty of the sweeping economic depression of 1873.

Five years later, the Knights of Labor captured the public imagination. The Knights were an all-embracing organization committed to a cooperative society. Membership was not limited to wage earners; it was open to farmers and small business people—everybody, that is, except lawyers, bankers, stockbrokers, professional gamblers, and anyone involved in the sale of alcoholic beverages. The Knights achieved a membership of nearly 750,000 during the next few years, but the skilled and unskilled workers who had joined the Knights in hope of improvement in their hours and wages found themselves frustrated by the Knights' vague organizational structure, by its officers' aversion to strikes against employers, and by its leaders' reliance on the promise of future social gains instead of the hard day-to-day work of building and operating a union organization. So the stage was set for the creation of a down-to-earth, practical labor federation which could combine long-range objectives of a better society with the practical activity of day-to-day union functions.

FEDERATION OF ORGANIZED TRADES AND LABOR UNIONS

The first practical step in response to the need for a united labor movement was a meeting of workers' representatives from a few trades and industries at Pittsburgh on November 15, 1881. The delegates came from the carpenters, the cigar makers, the printers, merchant seamen, and the steel workers, as well as from a few city labor bodies and a sprinkling of delegates from local units of the Knights of Labor.

The new Federation of Organized Trades and Labor Unions which they created had a constitution inspired by that of the British Trades Union Congress—which then was about a dozen years old. Its principal activity was legislative, its most important committee was concerned with legislation. The chairman of that committee was 31-year-old Samuel Gompers of the Cigar Makers Union, serving in the earliest phase of a career that was to make him the principal leader and spokesman for labor in America for the next four decades.

The Federation of Organized Trades and Labor Unions was a good deal less than a strongly effective organization. In its third year, it collected just $508 in dues, and its 1884 convention brought together merely 18 delegates. Yet its fingers were clearly on the pulse of America's working class; it passed a resolution decreeing that "eight hours shall constitute a legal day's labor from and after May 1, 1886." It recommended to its affiliated unions that they "so direct their laws as to conform to this resolution by the time named." In the words of a much later cliché, the federation's call for the eight-hour day was clearly "an idea whose time had come." It touched off, or accelerated, a strong and vociferous national clamor for the shorter work week.

Despite the popularity of that call for action, Gompers and a number of his associates—among them, particularly, Peter J. McGuire of the Brotherhood of Carpenters—felt the time had come for reorganizing the Federation to make it a more effective center for the trade unions of the country. So, on December 8, 1886, they and a few other delegates met in Columbus, Ohio, to create a renovated organization.

It was at this meeting that the American Federation of Labor evolved from the earlier Federation of Organized Trades and Labor Unions. The action was a giant step forward toward the development of a modern trade union movement in America. Gompers was elected president, McGuire secretary. Gompers, born in 1850, came as a boy with his parents to America from the Jewish slums of London; he entered the cigar-making trade and received much of his education as a "reader"—a worker who read books, newspaper stories, poetry and magazine articles to fellow employees to help break the monotony of their work in the shop—and became a leader of his local union and of the national Cigar Makers Union.

A statement by the founders of the AFL expressed their belief in the need for more effective union organization. "The various trades have been affected by the introduction of machinery, the subdivision of labor, the use of women's and children's labor, and the lack of an apprentice system—so that the skilled trades were rapidly sinking to the level of pauper labor," the AFL declared. "To protect the skilled labor of America from being reduced to beggary and to sustain the standard of American workmanship and skill, the trades unions of America have been established."

The leadership of the early labor movement showed a keen awareness that the unions could not succeed with a "men only" philosophy, even though men were then the clearly dominant element in the labor force. In 1882 the Federation extended to "all women's labor organizations representation . . . on an equal footing." Even more explicitly—and rather grandiloquently—the AFL convention in 1894 adopted a resolution that "women should be organized into trade unions to the end that they may scientifically and permanently abolish the terrible evils accompanying their weakened, unorganized state; and we demand that they receive equal compensation with men for equal services performed."

The new AFL, with its 300,000 members in 25 unions, came on the national scene in a time of discord and struggle. Earlier in 1886,

railroad workers in the Southwest had been involved in a losing strike against the properties of Jay Gould, one of the more flamboyant of the so-called "robber barons" of the post-Civil War period. On May 1, 1886, some 200,000 workers had struck in support of the effort to achieve the eight-hour day.

While the national eight-hour-day strike movement was generally peaceful, and frequently successful, it led to an episode of violence in Chicago that resulted in a setback for the new labor movement. The McCormick Harvester Company in Chicago, learning in advance of the planned strike, locked out all its employees who held union cards. Fights erupted and the police opened fire on the union members, killing four of them. A public rally at Haymarket Square to protest the killings drew a large and peaceful throng. As the meeting drew to a close, a bomb exploded near the lines of police guards, and seven of the uniformed force were killed, with some 50 persons wounded. The police began to fire into the crowd; several more people were killed and about 200 were wounded.

Eight anarchists were arrested and charged with a capital crime. Four were executed; four others were eventually freed by Governor John P. Altgeld of Illinois after he concluded that the trial had been unfairly conducted. No one knows for certain who planted the bomb. But as Gompers ruefully commented some time later: "The bomb not only killed the policemen, but it killed our eight-hour movement for a few years after."

The new AFL, breaking with the cloudy organizational structure that had hampered the Knights of Labor and other previous attempts at federation, placed emphasis on the autonomy of each affiliated union in its jurisdiction, and encouraged the development of practical collective bargaining to gain improvements for the membership. But it takes two to make collective bargaining work—employers and workers—and as American industry moved into a period of immense growth and power in the latter part of the 19th century, the lords of industry were little inclined to negotiate with the unions of their employees. The Sherman Antitrust Act, designed to break up the power of monopoly corporations, was used very strongly against small unions, contrary to its intent. And so, the companies grew in strength while their lawyers fought successful rearguard actions to make the law inoperative.

Thus the decade of the 1890s and the early years of the 20th century witnessed many intense struggles between essentially weak unions seeking to liberate their members from back-breaking toil under often unsafe and unhealthy working conditions for very low wages, and powerful corporations with heavy financial resources, the active or passive support of the government and its police forces, and the backing of much of the press and the general public. It was a perfect climate for union-busting and violence.

In 1891 steel boss Henry C. Frick broke a Pennsylvania strike of coke oven workers seeking the eight-hour day. But that was just a warmup event for Frick, who as head of the Carnegie Steel Company in 1892, ordered a pay cut ranging from 18 to 26 percent. The Amalgamated Association of Iron and Steel Workers—one of the stronger unions of the period—called a strike at the Carnegie plant at Homestead, Pennsylvania, to seek a rescinding of the cut in wages. Pitched battles followed between the strikers and a boatload of 300 armed Pinkerton detectives. The strikers won the battle and the Pinkertons retreated, with a death toll of seven workers, three strikebreakers, and scores of wounded. The state militia then took over the town. Indictments poured out, but no one was convicted; and Frick had succeeded in breaking the strike.

The next big confrontation, in 1894, was at the Pullman plant near Chicago. The American Railroad Union—not affiliated with the AFL and led by Eugene V. Debs, a leading American socialist—struck the company's manufacturing plant, and called for a boycott of the handling of Pullman's sleeping and parlor cars on the nation's railroads. Within a week, 125,000 railroad workers were engaged in a sympathy protest strike. The government swore in 3,400 special deputies; later, at the request of the railroad association, President Cleveland moved in federal troops to break the strike—despite a plea by Governor Alt-

geld of Illinois that their presence was unnecessary. Finally a sweeping federal court injunction forced an end to the sympathy strike, and many railroad workers were blacklisted. The Pullman strikers were essentially starved into submissive defeat.

The strike illustrated the increasing tendency of the government to offer moral support and military force to break strikes. The injunction, issued usually and almost automatically by compliant judges on the request of government officials or corporations, became a prime legal weapon against union organizing and action.

A TESTING PERIOD AND GROWTH

A better method of federal intervention occurred during a 1902 strike of anthracite coal miners, under the banner of the United Mine Workers. More than 100,000 miners in northeastern Pennsylvania called a strike on May 12, and kept the mines closed all that summer. When the mine owners refused a UMW proposal for arbitration, President Theodore Roosevelt intervened on October 3, and on October 16 appointed a commission of mediation and arbitration. Five days later the miners returned to their jobs, and five months later the Presidential Commission awarded them a 10 percent wage increase and shorter work days—but not the formal union recognition they had sought.

The difficulties that unions experienced in fashioning their strategies for bringing workers into membership and fighting low-wage nonunion competition could best be observed in a long court fight which became nationally known as the Danbury Hatters case. In 1902, the AFL hatters union instituted a national boycott of a nonunion company in Danbury, Connecticut. The company, charging a conspiracy in restraint of trade, under the provisions of the antitrust law, filed a damage suit in the state court but lost.

The case worked its way through the federal courts over the next few years, and in 1908 the U.S. Supreme Court ruled in a 5–4 decision against the union. It held that the Hatters Union had participated in an illegal secondary boycott, which was subject to federal injunctive restraint. The decision was a clear signal to the federal judiciary and to the corporations that injunctions could be used to stop various kinds of labor strikes and strike-support actions. In addition, the individual strikers were fined a total of nearly $250,000. In 1915, the AFL proclaimed a Hatters' Day, in which workers voluntarily contributed an hour's pay to help pay off the fines. The money thus collected kept 184 individual Danbury hat workers from having their homes seized in order to pay the court-ordered levy. [It is important to differentiate between direct consumer boycotts or "unfair to labor" or "don't buy" activities, which are recognized as perfectly legal when conducted in connection with or in support of labor union disputes with employers—and, on the other hand, secondary boycotts, which were the issue in the Danbury Hatters case and which were made illegal under the 1947 Taft-Hartley Act. A secondary boycott is one directed at companies or stores to try to force them not to use, or to offer for sale, products which have been made by a company involved in a strike or otherwise deemed "unfair" by the legitimate union. The secondary boycott has all but disappeared since Taft-Hartley was passed. It should be noted, however, that the courts have ruled that the Constitution's free speech provisions legally permit a union to place "informational pickets" outside a store selling "unfair" goods and calling attention to labor's "don't buy" campaign—so long as they do not call the store itself "unfair" or ask the public not to patronize the establishment.]

This was not to be the first or last example of the way in which employers have sought to redirect the thrust of laws designed to regulate corporations and instead aimed them toward labor unions and their members. Indeed, even at the current time, efforts are still being made to include labor under the antitrust and other laws originally aimed at corporations.

Not all the strikes and struggles of the period were conducted by the "sons of toil" in the nation's heavy industries. Long before the rise of the contemporary feminist movement, large numbers of women were at work—particularly in the big cities and in the men's and women's garment industry. Their grievances were real and tangible in both the textile and garment industries. Their pay was often at sweatshop levels, their hours too long, the speed-up rampant, the working conditions dreadful. Conditions such as these led in 1909 to a strike known widely as "The Uprising of the Twenty Thousand." The strikers, mostly women, almost all of them recent immigrants from eastern Europe, conducted the first big protest in the needle trades under the banner of the Ladies' Garment Workers against shirtwaist and dress manufacturers. Their plight brought widespread public support, and they gained the 52-hour work week and wage increases.

In 1910, some 50,000 cloakmakers called a strike in New York. Thanks to the efforts of Louis D. Brandeis, a lawyer later named to the U.S. Supreme Court, the dispute ended on a constructive note. A "protocol of peace" designed by Brandeis established procedures for conciliation and arbitration of future grievance disputes, as well as such important advances as the abolition of homework, the free use of electricity, 10 paid holidays a year, and piece work at rates fixed by joint union-management committees.

But a reminder that the garment industry was a good deal this side of paradise occurred in 1911, when a fire broke out at the Triangle Shirtwaist Company on New York's lower east side. About 150 employees—almost all of them young women—perished when the fire swept through the upper floors of the loft building in which they worked. Many burned to death; others jumped and died. Why so large a casualty list? The safety exits on the burning floors had been securely locked, allegedly to prevent "loss of goods." New York and the country were aroused by the tragedy. A state factory investigation committee headed by Frances Perkins (she was to become Franklin Roosevelt's secretary of labor in 1933, the first woman cabinet member in history) paved the way for many long-needed reforms in industrial safety and fire prevention measures.

Another of the historic industrial conflicts

Women In the Unions

A noteworthy event in the labor movement of the early 1900s was the creation of the Women's Trade Union League, to help educate women workers about the advantages of union membership, to support their demands for better working conditions, and to acquaint the public with the serious exploitation of the rising number of women workers, many of them in "home industries" or industrial sweatshops.

It was founded by Mary O'Sullivan, a bindery worker who became the first woman organizer employed by the AFL; Jane Addams, the noted social worker and founder of Chicago's Hull House; Mary Kehew, a Boston philanthropist, and women who were officials in the unions of the garment and textile industries.

For much of its first century, the labor movement was—in huge majority—composed of men. Except in a few occupations—clerical work and the garment, textile, retail, and hotel industries—the labor force was essentially male.

This began to change in World War II when women moved for the first time into many occupations formerly the domain solely of men. It has changed even more since the 1960s, with the increasing prevalence of two-wage-earner families at almost every income level.

More frequently now, women are being elected and appointed to prominent union positions, and the first woman member of the AFL–CIO Executive Council was elected in 1980. Some organizing efforts are now primarily directed at enlisting the support of nonunion women employees.

---

prior to World War I occurred in 1912 in the textile mills of Lawrence, Massachusetts. It was led not by an AFL union but by the radical Industrial Workers of the World—the IWW, or the Wobblies, as they were generally known—an organization in frequent verbal and physical conflict with the AFL and its affiliates. The strike in Lawrence started when the mill owners, responding to a state legislature action reducing the work week from 54 to 52, coldly and without prior notice cut the pay rates by a 3½ percent. The move produced predictable results: a strike of 50,000 textile workers; arrests; fiery statements by the IWW leaders; police and militia attacks on peaceful meetings; and broad public support for the strikers. Some 400 children of strikers were "adopted" by sympathizers. When women strikers and their children were attacked at the railroad station by the police after authorities had decided no more youngsters could leave town, an enraged public protest finally forced the mill owners not only to restore the pay cuts but to increase the workers' wages to more realistic levels.

Perhaps the temper of the times in which working men and women sought to build their unions was epitomized by the attitude of George Baehr, head of the Philadelphia and Reading Railway Company, at the time of the 1902 coal strike. In Mr. Baehr's publicly expressed view, "the rights and interests of the labor man will be protected and cared for not by the labor agitators but by the Christian men to whom God in His infinite wisdom has given the control of the property interests of the country and upon the successful management on which so much depends." Such an attitude did not leave much room for flexibility in developing more equitable labor-management relationships.

Yet not all of the news was of strike and struggle. By 1904, the AFL could claim a membership in its affiliated unions of nearly

1,700,000 members. Ten years later, at the eve of World War I, it had climbed to about 2 million.

There were, furthermore, important legislative accomplishments. Congress, at the urging of the AFL, created a separate U.S. Department of Labor with a legislative mandate to protect and extend the rights of wage earners. A Children's Bureau, with a major concern to protect the victims of job exploitation, was created. The LaFollette Seaman's Act required urgently needed improvements in the working conditions on ships of the U.S. merchant marine. Of crucial importance, the Clayton Act of 1914 made explicit the legal concept that "the labor of a human being is not a commodity or article of commerce" and hence not subject to the kind of Sherman Act provisions which had been the issue in the Danbury Hatters case. The act gave a legal basis in the federal jurisdiction to strikes and boycotts and peaceful picketing, and dramatically limited the use of injunctions in labor disputes. Little wonder that AFL President Gompers hailed the Clayton Act as a "magna carta," probably not foreseeing that future court decisions and interpretations would seriously undermine the power of the language of the law.

The Adamson Act passed by Congress in 1916 concerning work hours on the railroads was an important milestone in the decades-long effort to achieve the eight-hour day, an objective of the Federation of Organized Trades and Labor Unions in 1884 and of many subsequent strikes. The 10-hour day—an improvement in its era—was introduced for federal government employees in 1840, but it took until the early years of the 20th century before the eight-hour work day became broadly accepted in the private sector, particularly in the printing and building trades. The mass production industries and the railroads continued their refusal to grant it.

The Adamson Act brought the shorter work day to railroad employees. It came in other industries through the impact of strikes, collective bargaining, state laws, and two federal statutes: the Public Contracts Act in 1936, requiring contractors on government jobs to observe the eight-hour day, and the Fair Labor Standards Act of 1938 which provided a maximum work week for employers in interstate commerce—first a maximum of 44 hours and, after two years, 40 hours a week.

WARTIME GAINS AND POST-WAR CHALLENGES

When the United States entered World War I in April 1917, the AFL under President Gompers' leadership worked in close cooperation with President Wilson to ensure industrial peace and a steady flow of military equipment and armaments for the American Expeditionary Force in Europe. As head of the War Committee on Labor and member of the Council for National Defense, Gompers and the unions he represented played an increasingly important role in national affairs. A wartime disputes board helped avoid strikes and maintain production; it had the support and cooperation of the labor movement. With the vast expansion of production for military and civilian needs, unions grew rapidly during the wartime years.

A symbolic recognition of labor's new status was President Wilson's visit to Buffalo in 1917 to address the annual AFL convention—the first time a President had made such an appearance. In succeeding administrations most Presidents, Republican and Democratic alike, spoke to the labor conventions.

One effort in which Gompers worked hard and successfully was for the creation of the International Labor Organization, an intergovernmental body headquartered in Geneva, with government, labor, and employer delegates and advisers, to discuss international problems directly affecting workers and to seek the elevation of work standards and the rights of workers in every country. The ILO was established under the Treaty of Versailles that followed World War I. Although the U.S. Senate finally refused to ratify the treaty, the American labor movement played an important role in ILO affairs beginning in 1934, and more intensely after World War II when the ILO became a specialized international agency of the United Nations.

During the years following World War I, however, the labor movement suffered setbacks and difficulties.

While AFL membership had reached almost 4 million by 1919, the post-war reaction from employers and their allies was swift and predictable. Elbert Gary, head of U.S. Steel (the company bestowed his name on the Indiana city), refused to meet with striking workers. The AFL endorsed and supported a strike of steel workers committed to such objectives as the end of the 12-hour day, the dismantlement of company-dominated "unions," collective bargaining, and wage increases. Using massive propaganda which sought to depict the strike as "unpatriotic," plus such time-tested favorites as strikebreakers, spies, armed guards, and cooperative police departments, "Big Steel" finally wore down the strikers, and they were forced to return to work early in 1920 under the old conditions.

Both the steel strike and an early post-war meat packing strike found employers—not for the first time nor the last—importing blacks from southern rural areas and Mexican peasants in order to serve as strikebreakers, usually without advance knowledge of that fact until they had to face the ordeal of being escorted through hostile picket lines. These random events, however, did not prevent the labor movement from playing a role of support for future civil rights activities and legislation.

The "Roaring Twenties," nostalgically depicted in some movies and musical comedies as an era of unbounded prosperity and champagne-induced gaiety, fell a good deal short of those marks for most American working people. Throughout the decade, unemployment rose, quietly, almost anonymously. It was a time of considerable hardship for many of the unemployed long before the days of unemployment insurance or supplementary benefits.

The postwar depression brought wages down sharply and caused major erosion of union membership—a loss of about a million members in the years from 1920 to 1923. The difficulties were multiplied by the decision of the National Association of Manufacturers and other antiunion "open shop" groups to wipe out or seriously diminish the status of

American unions. The fear of "Bolsheviks," often hysterical, that was nurtured by the Russian communist revolution was used gleefully by the antiunion forces. As early as 1913, President John Kirby of the NAM had decided the trade union movement was "an un-American, illegal, and infamous conspiracy." As the Senate Civil Liberties Committee, headed by Senator Robert LaFollette, Jr., reported years later, such demands as "union recognition, shorter hours, higher wages, regulation of child labor and the hours and wages of women and children in industry" came to be seen—under the influence of the NAM-sponsored "American Plan"—as aspects of the alleged communist revolution from which the antilabor employers wanted to save the nation. Strikebreaking, blacklisting, and vigilanteeism became, for a time, acceptable aspects of this new and spurious brand of patriotism.

The "yellow dog contract," which workers had to sign in order to get a job, bound them never to join a union; at the same time, the corporations promoted employee representation plans or company unions—pale and generally useless imitations of the real thing.

In 1924, faced with continual attacks and decisions by the Republican and Democratic parties to present the voters with the very limited choice between President Coolidge, a laissez faire conservative, and John W. Davis, a corporation lawyer, the AFL voted to support "neither of the above" but to make an endorsement for the first time in a presidential election. Senator LaFollette of Wisconsin, an old line friend of labor and the farmers, ran on the Progress Party ticket with strong AFL backing. He drew an impressive 17 percent of the total vote.

That same year, Samuel Gompers died, leaving a heritage of admiration and respect and a philosophy of trade unionism that still today underlies much of labor's thinking. His successor was William Green, who guided the destinies of the Federation until his death in 1952. Green, born in Coshocton, Ohio, in 1873, left school to become a coal miner, joined the union, and served as Mine Workers secretary-treasurer for a dozen years before being elected AFL president. An earnest and dedicated trade unionist, Green presided over

From Murdered Miners to Shiny Dimes

One chapter of the history of early-century industrial conflicts involved John D. Rockefeller, the first tycoon of the age of energy and the creator of the Standard Oil complex of corporations.

Rockefeller controlled the Colorado Fuel and Iron Corporation, whose coal miners went on strike in 1914. With their families, they were promptly evicted from company-owned homes in Ludlow, Colorado.

They moved into a cluster of tents, around which National Guard soldiers took positions and at night occasionally fired their rifles into the colony. To protect the children, the miners dug a cave under the largest tent. But on Easter night 1914, company-hired gunmen and some of the National Guard poured oil over the strikers' tents and set them on fire.

As the frantic miners and their families ran for safety in the night, they were machine-gunned. Some escaped, some were wounded, and 13 children and a pregnant woman in the recently dug cave all died—some with gun wounds, some from suffocation.

The nationwide protest against the killings on Rockefeller property were immediate and long sustained. Eventually, it led Rockefeller, the nation's first billionaire, to hire Ivy Lee, an early public relations man, to repair John D.'s sullied reputation.

Even as an old man, Rockefeller continued to hand out shiny new dimes to little children in the effort to erase the Ludlow image—but among the miners and workers in many other unions, the memory of Ludlow persists like an endless bad dream.

---

the AFL with calm dignity during a difficult period—the depression years and the years of the division of the labor movement.

The decade of the 1920s drifted on a downhill course for the labor movement. Virulent antiunionism, the steady, creeping ascent of unemployment, and the complacent political climate engendered by the Hoover Administration, had a decidedly negative effect on the fortunes of the AFL, its unions, and America's working men and women in every part of the country, in every sector of the economy.

DEPRESSION, WAR, AND A LABOR SCHISM HEALED

December 1931—the 50th anniversary of the creation of the modern labor movement—found America and much of the world sliding down the much steeper slope of a cataclysmic economic depression. Business enterprises failed by the thousands, production plummeted, unemployment went through the roof. By 1932, when Franklin D. Roosevelt was elected president, the American economy was in chaos—and the American trade union movement was but a ghost of its former strength and numbers.

Roosevelt, taking the leadership of the all but paralyzed nation on March 4, 1933, undertook a number of programs designed to recharge the economy, feed the unemployed, and restore confidence. At his urging, Congress passed the National Recovery Administration; the NRA's Section 7a specifically placed on the statute books the right of unions to exist and to negotiate with employers. Although it had no real enforcement powers, Section 7a was seen by millions of workers as a green light—if not a government invitation—to join a union.

Many AFL unions took quick advantage of the new atmosphere and soon began to register spectacular gains in membership. Some issued leaflets suggesting that "President Roosevelt wants you to join the union."

The Supreme Court soon declared NRA unconstitutional, and Section 7a was no more. Under the leadership of Senator Robert F. Wagner of New York, Congress in 1936 enacted the National Labor Relations Act—known as the Wagner Act. It went beyond "7a" to establish a legal basis for unions; set collective bargaining as a matter of national policy required by the law; provided for secret ballot elections for the choosing of unions; and protected union members from employer intimidation and coercion. That law, as amended in 1947 by the Taft-Hartley Act and in 1959 by the Landrum Griffin Act, is still in force.

The surge in union membership in the early years of the New Deal, and the potential for organizing the important nonunion mass production industries like steel, automobile, rubber, textile, and others, led directly to the most serious schism in the history of the modern labor movement. Heads of a number of the industrial unions in the AFL, led by John L. Lewis of the Mine Workers, called upon the AFL to finance and support big organizing campaigns in the nonunion industries on a basis that all the workers in each industry would belong to one industrial, or "vertical," union. Most of the leaders of the AFL unions presided over craft, or "horizontal," unions, and they maintained that employees of the same skills or crafts in the unorganized industries should sooner or later belong to their organizations.

In November 1935, Lewis announced the creation of the CIO—the Committee for Industrial Organization—composed of about a dozen leaders of AFL unions, to carry on the effort for industrial unionism. Lewis, born in Iowa in 1880 of Welsh immigrant parents, went to work in the coal mines and became president of the Mine Workers in 1920. An orator of remarkable virtuosity, Lewis voiced increasingly bitter attacks on his colleagues on the AFL Executive Council; his words helped speed the break. In 1936, the various CIO unions were expelled from the Federation—because, said Lewis, they favored industrial unionism; because, said AFL President Green, they had flouted procedures and rules of the AFL. In 1938 the CIO held its first constitutional convention and became the Congress of Industrial Organizations.

In any event, the CIO began a remarkably successful series of organizing campaigns—and in rapid succession, over the next few years, brought industrial unionism to large sectors of basic American industry. After U.S. Steel signed with the CIO Steel Workers in the spring of 1937, major organizing efforts brought, during the next few years, first signed agreements—most frequently after strike action—with major corporations in the steel, auto, rubber, glass, maritime, meat packing, and other mass production industries. At the same time the unions remaining in the AFL registered even more substantial gains in membership.

The growth in union strength of both the AFL and CIO throughout the period, coupled with Roosevelt's domestic program, led to passage of a number of national social programs long advocated by the labor movement: among them, the national social security program, unemployment compensation, workers' compensation, and a federal minimum wage-hour law (the original minimum hourly pay set by the 1938 statute was 25 cents an hour).

During World War II, the AFL and CIO, while preserving areas of disagreement, began to find more substantial bases for working together on problems affecting all workers. Philip Murray, who succeeded Lewis as president of the CIO, and AFL President Green served jointly and cooperatively on a number of government commissions involved in the war effort. Murray, born in Scotland in 1886, came as a boy to the coal fields of western Pennsylvania, and through his negotiating talents and oratorical ability rose through the Mine Workers ranks to vice president. Murray headed the CIO's Steel Workers Organizing Committee in 1936, and in 1942 he was elected president of the new United Steelworkers, a position he retained while serving as head of the CIO.

In 1952, Murray died, and was succeeded by Walter P. Reuther of the United Automobile Workers. Reuther, born in 1907 as one of four sons of a socialist brewery worker in Wheeling, West Virginia, moved to Detroit during the depression and became a skilled worker in the auto industry. He was one of the prime organizers of the Auto Workers and after World War II won a closely contested battle for the UAW presidency, a post he held until his death in an airplane crash in 1970. Just a few weeks after Murray's death, William Green died, and was succeeded by George Meany, the AFL secretary-treasurer. Many of the old antagonisms had died out, many of the old issues had been resolved, and the stage was set for merger of the two labor groups. They were reunited into the AFL–CIO at a convention in New York opening on December 5, 1955.

George Meany was unanimously elected president of the merged labor federation, and a new chapter opened for the American labor movement. Meany, born in the Bronx, New York, in 1894, followed his father's footsteps as a plumber, became active in his local union, and was elected president of the New York State Federation of Labor in 1934. On the basis of a brilliant record of helping win enactment of state labor and social legislation, he was elected AFL secretary-treasurer, to fill a vacancy, in 1939.

THE AFL-CIO YEARS

George Meany's commitment to "the traditional objectives of the labor movement" was expanded in his role as AFL–CIO president, to include labor's "full contribution to the welfare of our neighbors, to the communities in which we live, and to the nation as a whole." In the 25 years after the merger, a number of important issues and trends emerged; they embrace both the tradition or improving working conditions and a new emphasis on issues involved in local, state, national, and international affairs.

While labor's interest in politics was by no means new, the development of COPE—the AFL–CIO's Committee on Political Education—brought to labor a more efficient and practical means of achieving these three goals: (1) To make workers aware of the records and promises of the candidates running for public office, (2) To encourage workers to register and to vote, and (3) To endorse candidates at local, state, and national levels.

The AFL–CIO merger and its accompanying agreements brought about the virtual elimination of jurisdictional disputes between unions that had plagued the labor movement and alienated public sympathy in earlier years. The unions placed a new priority on organizing workers in areas, industries, and plants where no effective system of labor representation yet existed. In many cases, it meant crossing the barriers of old thinking and tired methods to reach the employees of companies which for years had resisted unions.

A major phenomenon of this period was the rapid growth of unions of government employees—federal, state, and local. For many decades, postal employees, teachers, the fire fighters, and building and metal trades workers in some federal installations represented about the only substantially unionized part of public sector employment. With increasing economic pressures, more public employees turned to unions—a trend spurred on by such developments as an Executive Order by President Kennedy in 1962 underscoring the right of federal employees to join unions and negotiate on many issues, and by various statutes in the states and cities providing for various forms of collective bargaining with their personnel.

Throughout the years after World War II, women entered the work force in ever-increasing numbers, and especially significant was their entry into "nontraditional" occupations. A long-sought objective—equal pay for equal work—was passed by Congress in 1963, prohibiting economic discrimination on the basis of sex.

Five years later, the Age Discrimination Act was passed to assist persons in the older brackets of the work force.

The Civil Rights Act of 1964, strongly supported by the AFL–CIO, was a significant forward step toward equal rights for blacks and other minorities, at the workplace and in the community. President Johnson, in signing the act into law, acknowledged that it could not have happened without the affirmative support of the AFL–CIO.

The Civil Rights Act could trace its legislative history back to the days of World War II, when A. Philip Randolph, president of the AFL Sleeping Car Porters, persuaded President Roosevelt to issue an Executive Order establishing a Fair Employment Practices Commission. Randolph, a brilliant union officer and civil rights champion, managed to convince FDR that governmental action to stop discrimination in hiring and promotion was essential to the wartime production effort.

The words of Dr. Martin Luther King, Jr., illustrate the common bonds among labor, blacks, Hispanics, and other minority groups: "Our needs are identical with labor's needs— decent wages, fair working conditions, livable housing, old age security, health and welfare measures, conditions in which families can grow, have education for their children and respect in the community."

Throughout these years, the AFL–CIO was forced to resist various efforts to limit the rights of unions. The so-called "right-to-work" bills, which in fact were aimed at outlawing contract language providing union security, arose in many states. In Congress there were continued efforts to expand the Hobbs Act to make every picket-line scuffle or act of violence a federal case, even though they are currently covered by state and local laws.

The increasing interest in safety on the job, heightened by the introduction of new and potentially dangerous materials used in a wide variety of industries, gave rise to labor's intensive support for a federal Occupational Safety and Health Act, which became law in 1970. Specifically, the act authorized the secretary of labor to establish health and safety standards, to enforce them, and to listen to employees' legitimate complaints about conditions at the workplace.

Full employment was and continues to be a first-rank concern of the AFL–CIO, with its vivid recollection of past unemployment. The unions have kept insisting that whoever is able and willing to work should not be denied this opportunity. The full employment concept was endorsed by labor in its successful drive for passage of the Employment Act of 1946, which had the support of President Truman. The Humphrey-Hawkins Act of 1978 re-expressed the need to direct full attention to the problem of unemployment in the United States.

Recognition that workers have interests as consumers as well as producers has been apparent in the labor movement for many decades. Unions have played an active role in the formation of consumer cooperatives, and at both national and local levels have worked with other citizen groups for the enactment of various forms of consumer protection legislation. At the same time unions have voiced concern that apparent "bargains" of goods imported from low-wage countries may in fact be of inferior quality or workmanship and thus, in the long run, more expensive for the consumer. In recent years, there has been a vast increase in imported manufactured goods—often produced by corporations directly or indirectly related to American conglomerate companies—and the AFL–CIO has called for a revitalization of American manufacturing industries.

The strengthening of free unions throughout the world is another ongoing objective of the AFL–CIO. Special agencies functioning within the framework of the AFL–CIO carry out many of labor's efforts to move toward this goal, which was constantly expressed by George Meany: to build strong, free, noncommunist unions in the democratic societies of the free world and to resist all forms of tyranny and political repression. In fact, resistance to domination of workers and their organizations by governments or by political parties, or the control of unions by right-wing or left-wing extremist groups, has been a constant theme of American labor during the entire post-war period.

The broadening range of the union movement's interest and activities which began during the Roosevelt years with the expansion of federal government programs relating to the nation's economic and social problems, has been reflected in the size of the Federation's operating staff. In the early years of the AFL, that staff consisted of few persons beyond the officers' secretaries and a janitor.

During the past half-century, however, the Federation has endeavored to meet the challenges of the times and to function as the "people's lobby." In pursuit of these goals, the AFL–CIO has built a corps of specialized professional personnel: legislative representatives, lawyers, research experts, writers, and publicists, as well as departments of education, safety and health, social security, community services, civil rights, and international affairs.

In addition groups of unions have developed autonomous departments of the AFL–CIO to meet specialized needs. The first of these, the Building and Construction Trades, was set up back in 1916. The Industrial Union Department was created in the AFL–CIO merger agreement. Other departments include the Union Label and Service Trades, Maritime Trades, Metal Trades, Food and Beverage, Professional Employees, and Public Employees.

The George Meany Center for Labor Studies, established in 1969, plays an increasingly important role in training labor union staff and officials through a range of courses from techniques of collective bargaining to labor law institutes.

Meany retired at the AFL–CIO convention in 1979, at the age of 85; he nominated Lane Kirkland as his successor, and Thomas R. Donahue was elected secretary-treasurer. Kirkland, born in South Carolina in 1922, had been a merchant marine officer during World War II, and became a member of the Master, Mates, and Pilots Union. He joined the staff of the AFL in the post-war years; filled a number of increasingly responsible positions, including that of executive assistant to Meany; and was elected secretary-treasurer of the Federation in 1969. Donahue, born in New York in 1928, served in many capacities for the Service Employees Union, both with its Local 32B in New York and as vice president of the international union. He was named in 1973 as executive assistant to Meany.

READING 8

Early Leaders in the American Labor Movement: Samuel Gompers, William Green, and John L. Lewis

A. Samuel Gompers versus Horatio Alger: Defining the Work Ethic*

Stuart B. Kaufman†

Horatio Alger and Samuel Gompers were contemporaries. This is a strange confluence to puzzle out. How could the spirit of a single age have launched both of these careers? And what could this tell us about the spirit of the modern American labor movement?

Horatio Alger's novel *Ragged Dick*, about the rise of a young bootblack, is still selling well in a paperback edition more than 100 years after it was written. Alger described his protagonist this way: "Dick's appearance as he stood beside the box was rather peculiar. His pants were torn in several places, and had apparently belonged in the first instance to a boy two sizes larger than himself. He wore a vest, all the buttons of which were gone except two, out of which peeped a shirt which looked as if it had been worn a month. To complete his costume he wore a coat too long for him,

*Reprinted from AFL–CIO, *American Federationist* 88, no. 2 (February 1981), pp. 7–12.

†*Stuart B. Kaufman, an associate professor of history at the University of Maryland, is editor of The Samuel Gompers Papers. This article is taken from a paper he delivered at an AFL–CIO Centennial seminar in January 1981 at the George Meany Center for Labor Studies. Kaufman is the author of "Samuel Gompers and the Origins of the AFL" and is working on a history of the Tobacco Workers.*

dating back, if one might judge from its general appearance, to a remote antiquity."

This was the young man who, before Alger was finished with him, emerged as the distinguished Richard Hunter, the protector of an equally ragged youngster, Mark the Match Boy, who was similarly successful in his rise from rags to riches. Alger ground out the same story with little variation more than a hundred times—the poor young man making it by a combination of intelligence, aggressiveness, and inner moral spirit. He sold some 200 million copies of his books before World War I; his success bred imitation in a proliferation of success stories in dime novels—those cheap weekly publications that anyone could buy and, to judge by late-19th-century figures, almost everyone did. "Pluck and Luck" was one of these; "Fame and Fortune Weekly," subtitled "Stories of Boys Who Make Money," was another.

This is a starting place for understanding the modern American labor movement. Horatio Alger and Samuel Gompers were contemporaries: the American labor movement as we know it today got its start in the midst of a society that was frantically and passionately insisting that there was room at the top for everyone with the gumption, the pluck to pull themselves up by their own bootstraps.

It is precisely in the overblown and exaggerated form of the Horatio Alger success story that we come to grips with the workplace anxiety of the modern age. Americans had for a long time prided themselves that, unlike Europe, here in America the race of life was open to all, any right-living common man could win the race. Inherited riches were a marginal advantage at best. Historian Stephen Thernstrom relates a story from a mid-century New England newspaper about an Edward Marvel, an unskilled English laborer. Out of work for weeks, Marvel returns home one night to tell his wife Agnes, "The native independence of my character revolts at our present condition . . . every avenue is crowded." His wife answers, "There is another land where, if what we hear be true, ability finds employment, and talent a sure reward." Edward pauses: "America," he says, and the couple resolves to emigrate to the New World.

And this, after all, was fundamental to American culture—the work ethic, that cluster of values that suggested that doing one's work well and with satisfaction was a man's calling before God. At the end of the 17th century the Puritan clergyman Cotton Mather declared, "Every Christian ordinarily should have a Calling. That is to say, there should be some Special Business, and some Settled Business, wherein a Christian should for the most part spend the most of his Time; and this, that so he may Glorify God, by doing Good for others, and getting of Good for himself." It was at work that an individual practiced piety and came to terms with existence. Mather asked, "Why do you find so many Occupations mentioned in the Scriptures? 'Tis partly, that so you may think on the Scriptures in the midst of your Occupations. The Carpenter may pray: 'May I be built up in my most Holy Faith!' The Goldsmith: 'May I be Enriched with the true God tried in the Fire.' The Tailor: 'May my Soul be furnished with the Garments of Salvation!'"

The message from Mather, then, was that if in the course of working, one also rose in one's trade to the status of an independent craftsman, perhaps with some journeymen of one's own, an apprentice or two, owning one's shop, sitting in the better pews in church, this was the natural course of things: not so much the purpose of a life of honest toil as the God-given recognition of a life well lived.

Until the late 19th century, a labor movement like the Knights of Labor could still be built to a membership of hundreds of thousands upon the idea that the decent folk of this country, the individuals who labored with their hands, worked hard, gave good value, lived temperately and morally—in a word, the producers—could derive meaning and dignity from their work and should expect to achieve some economic independence and, symbolic of that, a measure of regular, meaningful political participation in their communities. Until that time farmers, workers, and small shopkeepers could still think of themselves as having something in common: their work was the central defining element in their lives.

Yet in the impersonal, commercialized, and industrializing economy of that period,

self-esteem in the workplace was eluding most workers, and the best the General Master Workman of the Knights of Labor, Terence Powderly, could propose was that workers try to form cooperative shops to recover collectively the independence that was out of their reach as individuals. Failing that, there was every prospect that most American workers would have to look outside their work life for something to give meaning to their existence.

Already the culture of the day was beckoning to them to begin defining themselves by a new measure—not by what they did at work but rather by what they consumed. Pioneering in this seductive message by the 1880s and 1890s was the cigarette industry, whose testimonials reached down into the darker recesses of the psyche with a brashness that still embarrasses in the 1980s and which presaged the 20th-century assault by Madison Avenue on our sensibilities and our senses: "In Spain," one read, "The dark-eyed, olive-skinned Spanish beauty puffs her cigarette with a grace and sangfroid that is enchanting to behold. Lying on her couch, or reclining in an easy chair, surrounded by the prolific and beautiful shrubbery and flowers of her native land, a handsome gallant at her side whispering sweet nothings in her ear, she daintily smoking her cigarette, makes a sensuous dreamy picture well nigh indescribable." And another related, "I have seen some women smoke a cigarette so daintily that it was a beautiful sight to watch the delicate smoke circling up from their rosy lips."

In the face of all this, what Samuel Gompers did was to embody in a new organization, the American Federation of Labor, a reformulation of the work ethic and a rededication to it. For most workers, he was to repeat over and over again, there was no escape from the working class. This was an idea difficult for many craftsmen to accept then, just as it is today for many teachers and other so-called professionals of the white-collar world. We cannot look to rise into independence individually, he argued; we can only achieve it in the workplace collectively. We are, he said, permanently members of the working class. We must devise ways to have a say in all decisions affecting our work lives because only then can we workers perform what is needed of us with dignity and self-esteem.

Gompers said, "To be free, the workers must have choice. To have choice they must retain in their own hands the right to determine under what conditions they will work." This assertion of the right to be free within the context of a shop or factory or workplace owned by another implied a modification of the traditional definition of property rights, and indeed Gompers was fully aware of that: "One of the greatest impediments to a better appreciation by the capitalists of the devoted efforts of the Trade Unions to establish harmony in the industrial relations has been the perverted view taken by the capitalists in regarding their capital as essentially if not absolutely their own, whereas the Trade Unions, taking a more comprehensive and purer view, regard all capitalists, large and small, as the fruits of labor's economies and discoveries, inventions, and institutions."

Such an assertion of rights by Gompers flowed naturally from the aggressive spirit of the craftsmen of the cigar shops in which Gompers had worked. One is carried back to an episode Gompers recalled in his autobiography as happening in the Eagle Cigar Company in New York City where he worked:

"One of the men was named Cohen. He was a small man, a weakling about 45 years or so, whose sight was considerably impaired. The loft was lighted by windows in front. Long rows of seats extended across the room with benches or worktables between. These were extended back into the room four or five rows. I had a seat in the first row as did Cohen, or 'Conchy' as we all called him. Of course, the light was much better nearer the windows than in the back row. One Monday morning, I came into the shop and found that some fellow, who had been a strikebreaker in one of the lockouts, was seated at the front bench against the window, in Conchy's seat. Conchy had been removed to one of the seats or benches in the rear. I went up to Conchy and said: 'What is the matter with you?' In a very plaintive tone he said, 'Well, they put me back here this morning and gave the other fellow my seat near the window.' 'What for?' I said.

Conchy replied, 'Well, they just put the new fellow there, that's all, just put him there.' I left him, went back to my seat, and called one of the call boys . . . and told him to go down to Mr. Smith, the new foreman, and tell him I wanted to see him. Finally, Mr. Smith came up and said, 'Well, what do you want?' I said, 'Why did you put Conchy away back there in that dark seat for and put the young fellow down there in the light?' The foreman replied, 'None of your damned business.' 'Do you mean to say that you are going to let this young fellow keep that front seat and make Conchy stay back there?' 'Yes, I am. What are you going to do about it?' Smith replied. I began gathering up my tools as I replied, 'Not much except that he can have this seat, too.' Then as if an explosion had occurred, every man in that shop—there were about 50 of us—rose and reiterated one after another. 'Yes, and he can have this seat too.' 'And this seat,' . . . 'and this seat.' Conchy got his old seat and then we went to work."

Consistently over the next century the labor movement recruited its leaders and organizers heavily from among the aristocrats of the labor force. The stratum of skilled workers, as Andrew Dawson has pointed out, remained remarkably constant even in the face of mechanization. Technology diluted some trades to the point they were no longer skilled—cigarmaking, for instance, and shoemaking and tailoring. In other areas, however, such as construction, skilled workers like the bricklayers and carpenters could not be replaced. Other skilled workers such as the machinists proved remarkably adaptable in redefining their skills in relationship to new machinery without missing a step in maintaining their status on the job. In some cases industrialization actually created whole new skilled occupations.

In order to preserve control of their work lives, the organized skilled workers began to adapt their unions; they organized select groups of lesser-skilled production workers who came into competition with them and amalgamated unions of related crafts in order to maintain the greatest possible leverage in the workplace. To protect the skilled carpenter, for instance, the Carpenters union aggressively expanded its jurisdiction during the 20th century to take in the woodworking industry, the lumber industry, and eventually much of the work that had only at one time involved working with wood; in the course of doing so, it became not so much a craft organization as a mixed craft-industrial organization. The same was true of other AFL unions, such as the Electrical Workers and the Teamsters.

The more we study the advent of the CIO in the 1930s to organize the mass-production workers in steel, automobiles, textiles, rubber, and so forth, the more clear it becomes that despite differences in strategy between the AFL and CIO, much of the motivation to organize and much of the field leadership of the CIO organizational campaign came from the craft elite among the mass-production workers. They were the ones most likely to feel they were making a substantial contribution to the production process and to be proportionately more aware that they were powerless individually to maintain a control and discretion over their work lives consistent with dignity and self-esteem.

There were, of course, other impulses to organization besides those emanating from these skilled workers. John Brophy, the miners and CIO leader, remembered the particular quality of coal miners. The coal miner, he said, was "his own boss. His judgment was at work as well as his muscles, and he made his own decisions—how deeply to undercut the face, how much powder to use, how to pace himself in loading the car." That independence at work, coupled with the almost total isolation of the mining communities under an oppressive hegemony of the coal companies and their political allies, seemed consistently to generate a militant leadership for the coal miners. Many people with a mine union background later led locals in the mass-production industries.

William Banks, a black organizer and later vice president of the Tobacco Workers, recalled how he was drawn to the union during the Great Depression: "I went into the factory because my father got me there. He was one

of those men to kinda fit in with the policies, you know how they call 'em. He fit in with the big man . . . you couldn't hardly find a job then. Well anyhow I got a job in the factory through my father. Another man was in there who'd been with the company 30-some years. I'll never forget it. The man took me on and went to that man and told him that that was his last day there. And I remember that man standing up there crying just like a baby. That changed my whole outlook. From that day on the union was in my mind."

Rose Schneiderman rose to leadership in the Ladies' Garment Workers out of a poor Orthodox Russian-Jewish immigrant family background through the camaraderie of her fellow cap makers and the socialism of a family close to her. Schneiderman came to the belief that trade unionism was "so much more than getting that loaf of bread, buttered or not. To me it is the spirit of trade unionism that is most important, the service of fellowship, the feeling that the hurt of one is the concern of all and that the work of the individual benefits all. I came to see that poverty is not ordained by Heaven, that we could help ourselves, that we could bring about a decent standard of living for all and work-hours that would leave us time for intellectual and spiritual growth."

For all these workers, organization promised greater control and dignity in the workplace and in their lives. Rose Schneiderman's contention that trade unionism had something to do with intellectual and spiritual growth was not such a strange notion. It was the essential, humanistic core of the labor movement from its beginnings, though I think it was obscured by the unusual faith Gompers had, for his day, that the workers could be trusted to find their way toward these lofty ends for themselves. Gompers lived in an age in which engineering students in the most prestigious engineering schools were, by the end of the century, beginning to sign up for a curriculum called the "humanistic-social stem" in hopes of learning more about how to manipulate workers the way they manipulated physical material in the workplace. When the field of occupational psychology took off in the 1920s, it was based heavily on Sigmund Freud's insights into the irrational side of man's behavior.

Yet Gompers was building a movement dedicated to the rationality of the workers. In his younger days he would have said: "The emancipation of the working class must be achieved by the working class itself." In his legendary battle with the socialists for the leadership of the labor movement he put it this way: "I have always been impressed with the belief that it was our duty to arouse a spirit of independence, to instill in the hearts and minds of the toilers that it was essential to promote and protect their class interests in order to reach and elevate the entire human family, and that any tangible action that will lead them to take the aggressive in the contest to solidify their ranks, to crystalize their thoughts and to concentrate their efforts was a 'progressive movement.' "

Of late, many outsiders have devised programs for increasing job satisfaction by the reorganization of one or another feature of work, only to find many workers suspicious of outsiders bearing gifts, and obsessed with such supposedly mundane features of their work lives as the grievance procedure, job benefits, the seniority system, job security provisions, pensions, holidays, changes in productivity, and even the pay check. And yet it is difficult to look at these provisions that workers have achieved for themselves without seeing in them a structure of protection against some of the most glaring indignities of workplaces past. What, for example, would an effective grievance procedure mean to someone like Joe Morrison, a southwestern Indiana coal miner who told Studs Terkel: "In '34 I got discharged over a hassle we had with the mine company. I was on the union's grievance committee. They had me blacklisted in the fields there. I never got a job until I went to work in the steel mills in '36. I bummed around a little in some temporary jobs, anything I could get. Had a big family, seven children, they were all small."

Similarly, the seniority system gave universal recognition and just recompense to a central ethical component of American work lives, durability—the dedication to giving full measure over time. All these provisions, collectively won, were the inheritance that gave workers a modicum of independence, control, and reward consistent with a dignified and satisfying work life.

In a piece called "What Does Labor Want?" Samuel Gompers called the trade unions the "only hope of civilization." I have looked in vain for the statement usually attributed to Gompers, that what the labor movement wants, pure and simply, is "more." Taken from context and worded that way, it seems to imply that the sole motivation of the labor movement was simply acquisitiveness. What Gompers said, however, was: "We want more school houses and less jails; more books and less arsenals; more learning and less vice; more constant work and less crime; more leisure and less greed; more justice and less revenge; in fact, more of the opportunities to cultivate our better natures, to make manhood more noble, womanhood more beautiful, and childhood more happy and bright."

In both Horatio Alger and Samuel Gompers we find a reborn faith in the ability of the individual spirit at work to survive and find dignity. Alger reiterated the scenario that was familiar to the 19th-century American, who rose, in his words, "By a series of upward steps, partly due to good fortune, but largely to his own determination to improve, and hopeful energy."

Samuel Gompers gave us a new scenario, a collective one for the people whom Ragged Dick and Mark the Match Boy left behind.

B. Birth of a Federation: Mr. Gompers Endeavors 'Not to Build a Bubble'*

Stuart Bruce Kaufman†

Contemporary account notes the role of the longtime AFL president in the founding 100 years ago of an earlier federation of unions, to which the AFL–CIO traces its origin

The centennial celebration this year by the AFL–CIO, marking the founding in 1881 of the AFL's immediate predecessor, the Federation of Organized Trades and Labor Unions of the United States and Canada, comes in the seventh year of a scholarly research project known as the Samuel Gompers Papers. The project's staff is gathering the papers of Samuel Gompers (1850–1924), the cigar-maker who became the AFL's first president in 1886 and continued in office, with the exception of one year, until his death 38 years later. This collection now includes almost a million pages of Gompers' correspondence, writings, and speeches, and other important documents drawn from unions, repositories, and private individuals, and is located at the University of Maryland and Pace University. The project's editors plan to produce a comprehensive microfilm for scholars, students, and researchers, and to publish 12 volumes of the most important papers for general readers. The first series of microfilm appeared in 1979.[1]

A hundred years ago a reporter from the Pittsburgh *Commercial Gazette* witnessed the four-day founding convention, in that city, of the Federation of Organized Trades and Labor Unions of the United States and Canada. Although the reporter's interpretation of events on the first day did not please Samuel Gompers, by the end of the convention the *Gazette* must have felt satisfaction as Gompers himself led the assembly in thanking the paper for its fair reporting of the proceedings. The excerpts from the *Gazette's* coverage that follow give a good sense of the range of federation concerns in 1881, and of the reaction of one representative of the daily press to the convention and what it portended. They are adapted from the first volume of the Gompers Papers, which the University of Illinois Press published in 1983. For the most part, the text is rendered as it appeared in the original.

PITTSBURGH COMMERCIAL GAZETTE

Wednesday, November 16, 1881

At two o'clock yesterday afternoon the delegates to the National Labor Congress assembled . . . from Massachusetts, New York, Pennsylvania, Ohio, Michigan, Illinois, Missouri, California, Maryland, West Virginia, Indiana, and Wisconsin. Short speeches advancing ideas to be discussed at some future time, were made by a number of gentlemen. All were conservative in tone, and, while the difference between labor and capital was referred to as a conflict that was irrepressible, none of the speeches were in the slightest degree communistic. On the contrary, the intelligence and moderation displayed was remarkable. All the speakers expressed themselves as being in favor of the greatest moderation. Mr. Gompers, the representative of the International Cigar Makers' Union, said he had come to Pittsburgh, not to air his opinions, but to work, not to build a bubble, but to lay the foundation for a superstructure that would be solid, and that would be a true federation of trade unions. He was in favor of progressing slowly, and wanted the organization to be emphatically a workingmen's organization; one that is not defiled by money, but which will in itself contain the elements of strength.

Among the delegates mentioned for permanent chairman . . . [is] Mr. Gompers, of the

---

*From U.S. Department of Labor, *Monthly Labor Review* 104, no. 11 (November 1981), pp. 23–26.

†*Stuart Bruce Kaufman is editor of the Samuel Gompers Papers and associate professor of history at the University of Maryland. This article was prepared with the assistance of an associate editor of the project, Peter J. Albert.*

[1]*American Federation of Labor Records: The Samuel Gompers Era* (Microfilming Corporation of America, 1979).

International Cigar Makers' Union. The latter is the leader of the Socialistic element, which is pretty well represented in the Congress, and one of the smartest men present. It is thought that an attempt will be made to capture the organization for Mr. Gompers, as the representative of the Socialists, and if such an attempt is made, whether it succeeds or not, there will likely be some lively work, as the delegates opposed to Socialism are determined not to be controlled by it. If the Socialists do not have their own way, they may bolt, as they have always done in the past. If they do bolt, the power of the proposed organization will be so seriously crippled as to almost destroy its usefulness.

The majority of the delegates realize the importance of effecting an organization that will harmonize all differences likely to arise, and last evening seemed hopeful that this could be accomplished. They think that the Committee on Organization will present the name of Mr. Rankin[2] of this city, or some western man, for permanent chairman, and that the Socialistic element will be prevented not only from capturing the organization, but from introducing any of their peculiar ideas into the declaration of principles to be prepared.

Thursday, November 17, 1881

Mr. Gompers took occasion to deny the statement that he was a leader of the Socialistic element, and that the committee had been captured for him, saying that he had attended the Congress only for the purpose of assisting in the federation of labor organizations. A number of delegates differed with him, however.

For a time it looked as if the chairmanship would be hotly contested, but Mr. Gompers poured oil on the troubled waters by stating that he was thoroughly devoted to trade unionism, and in order to facilitate the work of completing the organization, would withdraw his name. Mr. Powers[3] gracefully fol-

lowed suit, and Mr. Jarrett[4] was unanimously chosen permanent chairman. Messrs. Powers and Gompers were chosen vice presidents.

Friday, November 18, 1881

It was four o'clock, and the whole day had been consumed in the discussion of four or five subjects.[5] President Jarrett took the chair, however, and by a little ruse succeeded in expediting business wonderfully. At a previous meeting a rule had been adopted making it imperative for a vote to be taken on any questions whenever seven members called for the "question." This rule had not been enforced by Mr. Gompers, but when President Jarrett took the chair he enforced it in a manner that made it resemble a self-inflicted gag law. As soon as a motion had been stated, he would ask, "Are you ready for the question?" Immediately the "question" would be called for by a number of delegates, who thought that by so doing they would place the motion in proper shape for debate. But Mr. Jarrett was not of the same mind, and the last three sections of the "plan" were railroaded through with a speed that was highly creditable to Mr. Jarrett's conception of the rule, but not entirely satisfactory to those delegates who thought they should be permitted to air their opinions on every question that came before the house.

The chairman of the committee appointed to prepare a declaration of principles, then read their report, which, as adopted, is as follows:

Whereas, a Struggle is going on in the nations of the civilized world, between the oppressors and the oppressed of all countries, a struggle between capital and labor which must grow in intensity from year to year and work disastrous results to the toiling millions of all nations, if not combined for mutual protection and benefits. The history of the wage workers of all countries is but the history of constant struggle and misery, engendered by

---

[2]Alexander C. Rankin (b. 1849?) represented Iron Molders' local 14 of Pittsburgh at this convention.

[3]Richard Powers (1850–1929), president of the Chicago Lake Seamen's Union from 1878 to 1887.

[4]John Jarrett (1843–1918), president of the National Amalgamated Association of Iron and Steel Workers.

[5]These included discussions on the name of the organization and the basis of representation.

ignorance and disunion, whereas the history of the nonproducers of all countries proves that a minority thoroughly organized may work wonders for good or evil. It behooves the representatives of the workers of North America in congress assembled, to adopt such measures and disseminate such principles among the people of our country as will unite them for all time to come, to secure the recognition of the rights to which they are justly entitled. Conforming to the old adage, "In union there is strength," a formation embracing every trade and labor organization in North America, a union founded upon the basis as broad as the land we live in, is our only hope. The past history of trade unions proves that small organizations, well conducted, have accomplished great good, but their efforts have not been of that lasting character which a thorough unification of all the different branches of industrial workers is bound to secure.

Conforming to the spirit of the times, and the necessities of the industrial classes, we declare the following:

Resolved, That all organizations of workingmen into what is known as a Trade or Labor Union should have the right to the protection of their property in like manner as the property of all other persons and societies is protected, and to accomplish this purpose we insist upon the passage of laws in the State Legislatures and in Congress for the incorporation of trade unions and similar labor organizations.

Resolved, That we are in favor of the passage of such legislative enactments as will enforce by compulsion the education of children; that if the State has the right to exact certain compliance [with] its[6] demands, then it is also the right of the [State to e]ducate its people to the proper under[standing of such] demands.

[*Resolved,* That we] are in favor of the passage of [laws in the several States] forbidding the employ[ment of children under the age] of 14 in any capacity under the penalty of fine and imprisonment.

Resolved, That necessity demands the enactment of uniform apprentice laws throughout the country; that the apprentice to a mechanical trade may be made to serve a sufficient term of apprenticeship, from three to five years, and that he be provided by his employer in his progress to maturity with proper and sufficient facility to finish him as a competent workman.

Resolved, That the "national eight-hour law" is one intended to benefit labor and to relieve it partly of its heavy burdens; that the evasion of its true spirit and intent is contrary to the best interests of the nation. We therefore demand the enforcement of said law in the spirit of its design.

Resolved, That it is hereby declared the sense of this congress that convict or prison labor as applied to the contract system in several of the States is a species of slavery in its worst form; that it pauperizes labor, demoralizes the honest manufacturer and degrades the very criminal whom it employs; that as many articles of use and consumption made in our prisons under the contract system come directly and detrimentally in competition with the products of honest labor, we demand that the laws providing for labor under the contract system herein complained [of], be repealed, so as to discontinue the manufacture of all articles which will compete with those of the honest workingman or mechanic.

Resolved, That what is known as the "truck" system of payment, instead of lawful currency as a value for labor performed, is not only a gross imposition, but a downright swindle to the honest laborer and mechanic, and calls for entire abolition; and we recommend that active measures shall be enforced to eradicate the evil by the passage of laws imposing fine and imprisonment upon all individual firms or corporations who continue to practice the same.

Resolved, That we favor the passage of such laws as will secure to the mechanic and workingman the first lien, upon property, the product of his labor, sufficient in all cases to justify his legal and just claims, and that proper provision be made for legally recording the same.

---

[6]Bracketed material supplied by the Samuel Gompers Papers editors where text of original was obliterated.

Resolved, That we demand the repeal and erasure from the statute books of all acts known as conspiracy laws, as applied to organizations of labor in the regulation of wages which shall constitute a day's work.

Resolved, That we recognize the wholesome effects of a Bureau of Labor Statistics as created in several States, and urge upon our friends in Congress the passage of an act establishing a National Bureau of Statistics, and recommend for its management the appointment of a proper person, identified with the laboring classes of the country.

Resolved, That railroad land grants forfeited by reason of nonfulfillment of contract should be immediately reclaimed by the government, and henceforth the public domain reserved exclusively as homes for actual settlers.

Resolved, That we recommend to the Congress of the United States the adoption of such laws as shall give to every American industry full protection from the cheap labor of foreign countries.

Resolved, That we demand the passage of a law by the United States Congress to prevent the importation of foreign laborers under contract.

Resolved, That we recommend to all trades and labor organizations to secure proper representation in all law-making bodies by means of the ballot, and to use all honorable measures by which this result can be accomplished.

The preamble and first and second resolutions were adopted without dispute, but the third, which related to the employment of children under 14 years of age, excited a protracted discussion. If these stories, coming from men who knew what they were talking about, and which were pathetic enough to bring tears to most eyes, could be published in full, they would form a powerful argument in favor of keeping the little ones out of the workshops and sending them to school where they belong. The resolution as it appears above was adopted unanimously.

The other resolutions were adopted with very little debate, until one was read which declared in favor of all the railroads and telegraph lines being purchased and controlled by the government. This was [dis?] approved by a number of delegates, on the ground that if the government obtained the control favored, it would make the power of the ascendant political party perpetual, by reason of the vast numbers of employees which would be placed at its mercy. President Jarrett ruled the resolution out of order, as having no relation to the objects of the congress. An appeal was taken from his decision, but the chair was sustained and the resolution left out.

The next discussion was on that plank declaring in favor of the protection of American industries. It was a fight of Pittsburgh pride against Western principles, and the debate was warm. Mr. Crawford,[7] of Chicago, thought it was a mistake to force the resolution through, as it would only cause dissension. As long as the east and west were situated as they are at present they would not agree on the subject. Therefore he was in favor of not making any reference to the tariff, promising at the same time that if the East offered no tariff resolutions, none advocating free trade would come from the West. An attempt was then made to lay the resolution on the table, but it was voted down, and after another strong argument by Mr. Jarrett in favor of the resolution it was adopted.

Saturday, November 19, 1881

Mr. Brant,[8] of Detroit, offered a series of resolutions declaring that the bill introduced in Congress in 1880, as part of the report of the Public Land Commission would have the effect, if passed, to place the bulk of the public lands at the disposal of Western cattle kings and other capitalists at a nominal figure; that those lands in a few years would be found very valuable for farming purposes, and that persons wishing to cultivate them would have to do so in the capacity of tenant farmers or hirelings in competition with Chinese labor. In view of these facts the resolutions urged that all labor assemblies pass resolutions, giving their Congressional representatives to under-

---

[7]Mark L. Crawford (1848–1932), a Chicago printer and president in 1883–84 of the International Typographical Union.

[8]Lyman A. Brant (1848–95), a printer and president of the Detroit Trade and Labor Council.

stand that if they voted for the measure, they would be punished by the political opposition of the workingmen. After a short discussion the resolutions were adopted, as were also the following, which were presented by Mr. Rodgers[9] [sic] of Pennsylvania:

Resolved, That we demand strict laws for the inspection and ventilation of mines, factories, and workshops, and sanitary supervision of all food and dwellings.

Resolved, That strict laws be enacted making employers liable for all accidents resulting from their negligence or incompetence to the injury of their employees.

The Legislative Committee will meet for organization today. It is hard to predict who will be chairman, as all are good men and equally popular. The Secretary, Mr. Foster,[10] is employed as a compositor on the Cincinnati *Enquirer,* and although a young man, is President of the Trades Assembly of Cincinnati. Mr. Gompers is organizer of the International Cigar Makers Union, of New York. Mr. Powers is General President of the Lake Seamen's Union, and is considered one of the best organizers in the West. Mr. Bergman[11] [sic] is Treasurer of the Trades Assembly of San Francisco and President of the Tailors' Union of that city. Mr. A. W. Rankin is a member of the Iron Moulders' Union of this city, and is well known. All the officers are men of more than ordinary intelligence, conservative in their disposition, and their choice gives general satisfaction to the delegates.

While the reporter for the *Gazette* speculated about the chairmanship, the new organization's predominant official was in fact the secretary, William H. Foster. Out of the five officers of the legislative committee, the executive body of the Federation, only the secretary was designated by the convention. The committee itself elected the remaining officers—the chairman (Richard Powers in 1881), first and second vice chairmen, and treasurer. Even in 1883, when the Federation changed the title "chairman" to "president," enlarged the legislative committee to nine, and provided for the designation of all officers by the convention, the constitution still specified that the election of the secretary was to take precedence. So although Samuel Gompers was a member of the committee in four of the five years that the early Federation existed (first vice chairman in 1881–82, chairman in 1882–83, first vice president in 1883–84, and president in 1885–86), he was never the leading official of this organization, as he became of its successor. Gompers played an active role throughout these years, but prior to the founding of the American Federation of Labor in 1886, the Federation was guided by its secretaries: the printers' William H. Foster (1881–83, 1885–86) and Frank K. Foster (1883–84), the carpenters' Gabriel Edmonston (1884–85), and the cigarmakers' John S. Kirchner (1886).

[9]Daniel Rogers represented the Amalgamated Association of Pittsburgh Miners and Drivers.

[10]William Henry Foster (1848?–86).

[11]Charles F. Burgman, a tailor and treasurer of the Representative Assembly of Trades and Labor Unions of San Francisco.

C. William Green: Guardian of the Middle Years*

AFL–CIO

William Green was the second president of the American Federation of Labor, serving from Samuel Gompers' death in 1924 until 1952. At the 1943 AFL convention, a commander of the American Legion exhorted labor to a greater war effort by ending strikes. Green responded as follows:

The American Federation of Labor is an open forum. We speak with frankness; we act the same way; we face all issues. We proclaim our virtues and we admit our faults.

I can with perfect propriety point out that those who seek perfection in an imperfect world are doomed to disappointment. But he who follows the pathway of logic and reason, looking beyond the inconsequential faults of a small minority, will realize that we are making a fine record in a most imperfect world.

Immediately after hearing on the radio [the news of Pearl Harbor] the American Federation of Labor did not hesitate or wait a minute. The Executive Council pledged to the president of the United States a no-strike policy for the duration of this cruel war.

That was made voluntarily, and to understand the pledge, you must understand the real value of the strike weapon . . . the mobilization of our economic strength, our last resort, the means labor uses to protect its standard of life and living. When we pledged to place that behind the door and leave it there until the war was over, labor honestly pledged itself to support the government to the bitter end.

The president of the United States, who keeps the record and studies it carefully, has spoken to us and said, "You have kept that

pledge 99.9 percent." And that pledge was kept by imperfect men. I maintain that it is an amazing record made in an imperfect world.

We hold business management in high regard. We feel that business as a whole has made a good record during the war. We do not denounce industry as a whole because of the sins committed by some managers or some directors or a minority of industry. Consequently, we do not denounce industry as a whole because some steel corporation supplied defective armorplate, because another supplied inferior wire.

Is this a world without sin? Do the members of the Church always live up to the high standards set for them? Do the fraternal organizations maintain their standards of righteousness always? Do you find perfection in family life, the most sacred organization in America?

The American Federation of Labor has never officially ordered or approved a strike of one, five, or ten men, or a hundred men since the dastardly attack was made upon us at Pearl Harbor. We have kept the faith and we are keeping the faith. We are producing the planes, the guns, the tanks, the ships, the war material so necessary in order that our brave men on the battlefields of Africa, in the Southern Pacific, in Italy, and wherever the war is being fought may be adequately supplied.

And, Mr. Commander, it might be of interest to tell you that since Pearl Harbor, while the soldiers of production have been giving their skill, their lives, their training, their genius, and their American service in the production of materials, 80,000 of them have been killed and we have buried them, many of them in unknown graves. Seven million have been injured. Does that mean that we have measured up, or have we not? I ask you to look high, look above the petty things, the human imperfections, and behold portrayed like the new day's sun before your eyes the virtues of American workers. They are the best in the entire world.

We have supported the regimentation of workers during this war in a very large way, because the winning of the war stands over and above every other consideration. But we in-

*Reprinted from AFL–CIO, *American Federationist* 88, no. 2 (February 1981), pp. 24–25.

tend to work with all like-minded people in bringing about a reconversion and a readjustment when the war ends. The children must go back to the homes and to the schools. The wife and the mother must return to her place in the home.

There are 2 million members of the AF of L in the armed services and we are planning for their return. It is our firm determination to see that the seniority rights of all these members are protected when they come back to America, and if necessary we will compel employers to give them their places back where they were before they went away.

I have spoken in response to your address, Mr. Commander, in a sincere and honest way. I have spoken to you in the kindliest manner. I want you to get our point of view. Perhaps on the morning Gabriel blows his trumpet and the dead rise from the earth, we may then construct a perfect world out of imperfect material. But until then, Mr. Commander, we must deal with the imperfections of human nature and serve as best we can. Thank you.

D. John L. Lewis and the Founding of the CIO*

AFL–CIO

John L. Lewis was a volcano.

In both action and rhetoric, he played the center stage of American labor history as president of the United Mine Workers from 1920 to 1960—and he played his role hard as well as long.

In action, John L. Lewis led one of American labor's most important events: the break with the AFL craft tradition to form the Congress of Industrial Organizations. Just as dramatically, he left the CIO presidency after just five years. He vowed in 1940 that if his candidate, Republican Wendell Wilkie, wasn't elected over President Franklin Roosevelt, he would resign. And he did.

In words, John L. Lewis was one of the most eloquent figures in American history. Yet history will perhaps best equate him with one of the few quotes in which he kept it simple. Faced with the threat of the national guard taking the place of striking miners, Lewis said: "You can't dig coal with bayonets." That has become a motto for worker reaction against government intervention and employer injunction, whether in coal or any other U.S. industry.

Lewis was born in 1880 and was a delegate to the 1901 UMW convention. Samuel Gompers hired him as an AFL field representative in 1911, but Lewis returned to the UMW in 1917 to a staff job, then became president in 1920. He retired in 1960 and died in 1969.

The following are some examples of the words which make John L. Lewis an important part of labor's centennial.

TO THE 1938 CIO CONVENTION

Our people in this movement know how hard it is to preserve their rights and their lib-

*From AFL–CIO, *American Federationist* 88, no. 5 (May 1981), pp. 22–25.

erty—even within democracy. They have battled against violence, brutality, and calumny. The forces of public order have been perverted against them. And yet our people have not faltered in their conviction that they have rights which must not be destroyed.

The agencies of public information have boiled with jeremiads against the Committee for Industrial Organization. On no other occasion of modern times has the American ideal of a free press been so sullied. The loyalty of members and friends of the CIO through these storms of falsity shows again that American people will not be misled by cynical untruths and bitter misrepresentations.

To millions, because of this movement, the word *liberty* has acquired new meaning. Often those who seek only license for their plundering, cry "liberty." In the guise of this old American ideal, men of vast economic domain would destroy what little liberty remains to those who toil.

The liberty we seek is different. It is liberty for common people—freedom from economic bondage, freedom from the oppressions of the vast bureaucracies of great corporations, freedom to regain again some human initiative, freedom that arises from economic security and human self-respect.

To the Coal Operators After Bargaining Impasse

For four weeks we have sat with you; we attended when you fixed the hour; we departed when weariness affected your pleasure.

Our effort to resolve mutual questions has been in vain; you have been intolerant of suggestions and impatient of analysis.

When we sought surcease from blood-letting, you professed indifference. When we cried aloud for the safety of our numbers you answer "Be content—'twas always thus!"

When we urged that you abate a stench you averred that your nostrils were not offended.

When we emphasized the importance of life you pleaded the priority of profits; when we spoke of little children in unkempt surroundings you said—Look to the state!

You aver that you own the mines; we suggest that, as yet, you do not own the people.

You profess annoyance at our temerity; we condemn your imbecility.

You are smug in your complacency; we are abashed by your shamelessness; you prate your respectability; we are shocked at your lack of public morality.

You scorn the toils, the abstinence, and the perils of the miner; we withhold approval of your luxurious mode of life and the nights you spend in merriment.

You invert the natural order of things and charge to the public the pleasures of your own indolence; we denounce the senseless cupidity that withholds from the miner the rewards of honorable and perilous exertion.

To cavil further is futile. We trust that time, as it shrinks your purse, may modify your niggardly and antisocial propensities.

In Defense of Free Bargaining

We believe in collective bargaining. We believe that collective bargaining is the modern device that will make it possible for Americans to live together in the years that are to follow. We do not believe that there is any other formula that can be substituted for collective bargaining that will adjust our industrial problems to the end that American industry may increase its productivity and constantly contribute toward the economic, social, and political well-being and stability of our nation to that destiny which is the heritage of all Americans.

We, with many other Americans, deprecate the tendency in recent years to substitute for collective bargaining the fiats and ukases of governmental agencies and governmental tribunals. We believe in the theory of free contract and we believe that the Constitution of our Republic protects the right of contract between its citizens. The power to contract is the difference between free men and serfs, and as one traces the history and the development of civilization, and the building of these great nations and states throughout the world, one finds that freedom began when the workman became free to contract with his employer and to have a voice in determining the conditions under which he would work and the compensation that he would receive.

Those voices throughout this land which are raised in favor of compulsory arbitration or the fixation of relations between workmen and their employers by governmental ukase are doing their country a disservice, because the destiny of Americans cannot be achieved except as free men, and our system of individual free enterprise in America cannot continue or prevail when the workers of the country are not to be free to meet their employers on a basis of equality, and to debate, if you please, in the councils provided, such differences of opinion as may exist from the standpoint of their respective interests.

IN OPPOSITION TO TAFT-HARTLEY ACT

Thou shalt not muzzle the ox that treadeth out the corn. So runs the scripture. But the Congress of the United States designated 15 million workers in this country, organized into one form or another of unions, as being cattle that treadeth out the economic corn of our country, and the Congress placed an economic muzzle on each of you. What are you going to do about it? Oh, I see. You are going to change our Constitution. God help us!

The Taft-Hartley statute is the first ugly, savage thrust of fascism in America. It came into being through an alliance between industrialists and the Republican majority in Congress, aided and abetted by those Democratic legislators who still believe in the institution of human slavery. It was bought and paid for by campaign contributions from the industrial and business interests of this country, and the Republican party and the Democratic minority made good by forging these legislative shackles for you and the men and women who pay you to intelligently represent them.

It creates an inferior class of citizens, an inferior category and a debased position politically for the men and women who toil by hand or brain for their daily subsistence and to safeguard the future for their loved ones.

Now comes the Taft-Hartley Act . . . in America, where we always believed hereto-fore that we had a free labor movement. We even presumed at times to lecture the representatives of labor in other countries and chide them because they didn't have a free labor movement.

And yet when this statute is enacted, some 73 pages in length in the printed copy, containing only two lines that say labor has the right to organize and 33 pages of other additional restrictions that dares labor to try to organize, when that comes to pass, the welkin is filled with the outcries and the lamentations of our great leaders of labor in this country calling upon high heaven to witness that all indeed is lost unless they can grovel on their bellies and come under this infamous act.

I am one of those who does not think that all is lost. I represent an organization whose members believe they pay their officers to fight for them, not to deliver them into slavery. And four weeks before this convention assembled we found our great leaders beating the drums in their own private little conclaves, trying to devise ways and means to have this convention call the Taft-Hartley Act a good act, with a minimum degree of criticism from their membership.

The question of signing the anti-Communist affidavit, which is only one small feature of the abrogations of this act, has occupied the minds of our leaders and the columns of the public press now for more than six weeks.

I suppose it is hardly necessary for me to say that I am not a Communist. I suppose it is hardly necessary for me to say that I was fighting communism in America, with the other members of my organization, before many people in this country knew what communism stood for in America and throughout the world. In the early 1920s our organization paid for the research and study of the most serious analysis and compilation of Communist activities in industrial America that has ever been gotten out before or since, and that story was published in all the metropolitan newspapers of this country in seven serial issues. That story was made a congressional document and is on files to anyone who cares to read it.

It exemplifies what I say, that the United

Mine Workers of America has been in the vanguard of our citizenship in opposing the cast iron Oriental philosophy of communism or any other damned kind of ism in this country. And we expect to remain in that position. We don't expect to change our principles too often; and we do expect some support from the American labor movement, because we think that our attitude reflects the rank and file in these great organizations of labor who work for a living and who want a country tomorrow in which their children and their grandchildren can live.

R E A D I N G 9

The Crisis in American Unionism*

Edwin E. Witte†

That there is developing a crisis in labor union-ism in this country is known to everyone. All that I shall attempt to do is to call attention to some aspects of this crisis and to do some speculating as to what may be ahead. I am not a prophet or the son of a prophet and make no claim to being an expert on the subject. I recognize that all of you know much more about it than I do. But I shall go ahead with my talk in the hope that something I say will induce some of you to correct me, if I am wrong, or to supplement what I present.

Some Manifestations of the Crisis in American Unionism

With this brief statement acknowledging my inadequacies, I shall proceed at once with my subject; and, first, let me direct your attention to some manifestations that all is not well in the house of labor.

This month the AFL–CIO—the national federation—has announced the layoff of 100 organizers, a reduction of more than one-third in its staff of organizers. This has been ascribed, and is no doubt in part due, to the decline in the Federation's revenues as a result of the expulsion of the Teamsters, the Bakers, and the Laundry Workers—unions which comprised about one eighth of its total membership. Beyond that it seems to reflect a belief or fear that the present is not a propitious time for major organizing drives.

The high hopes for gains in union membership that were entertained when the merger of the federations was effected have vanished. One—if not the major—expressed purpose of the merger was an intensification of union organizing. Plans were announced to organize still unorganized manufacturing industries, particularly the chemical industry. There was also talk of organizing the white collar and technical workers and of reinvigorating the stalled drive of the forties to organize the South.

Figures of the U.S. Bureau of Labor Statistics suggest that some gains in total union membership have occurred since the merger. In these two years the total membership of American unions is reported to have increased by approximately 500,000. Interestingly, among the unions that have made the largest gains has been the Teamsters. The next largest international, the United Automobile Workers, sustained a slight loss in total membership; while the third, the Steelworkers, had only a small growth. Until the great increase in layoffs that began in October or November 1957, organized labor, as a whole, did make modest gains—about three percent—in a two-year period. But these gains were far smaller than labor hoped for and many prophets forecast.

The recession has lessened the prospects for union growth. The upswing in union membership early in the Roosevelt administration began when the American labor movement was at its lowest point in more than 15 years. But this occurred after three years of the worst depression of all time. In all other depressions since American labor first began to organize in the early nineteenth century, union membership has declined—often drastically. There are no statistics as to what has happened to union membership in these last months, but there is every reason to believe that, with declining employment, union membership has also decreased.

*Reprinted by permission from "The Crisis in American Unionism" by Edwin E. Witte in *The Arbitrator and the Parties, Proceedings of the 11th Annual Meeting*, National Academy of Arbitrators, pp. 172–87, copyright © 1958 by The Bureau of National Affairs, Inc., Washington, D.C.

†*Edwin E. Witte served as chairman of the Department of Economics at the University of Wisconsin. He was a distinguished visiting professor at Michigan State University and served as a public member of the National War Labor Board, 1944–45, and as a member of the Wisconsin Labor Relations Board, 1937–39.*

Factors Hindering Union Growth

There are many economic and social factors that adversely affect the prospects for union growth in the near future. Perhaps the most basic among these are the changes which have been occurring in the American labor force.

Among these is the remarkable growth in the number of women workers. At the turn of the century, about one sixth of the labor force of the United States consisted of women, most of them in domestic service, agriculture, teaching, and a limited number of manufacturing industries, such as clothing manufacture and textiles. Today the percentage of the women workers in our labor force is approaching two fifths. Most of the earlier fields in which women found employment have declined, but there has occurred a phenomenal growth of women employees in clerical and sales positions plus sizable increases among the production workers in many lines of manufacture and most other industries. There has also occurred a pronounced change in the characteristics of women who are in industry. When I was a boy the women in industry were principally young girls, employed prior to marriage, and older immigrant or Negro women. Today as Dr. Henry David, Executive Director of the National Manpower Council of Columbia University, has put it: "It is no longer the young woman chiefly of immigrant origin or extraction, or the Negro woman, who is the characteristic woman wage earner. Nor is it the woman who has to work out of sheer economic necessity."[1] Sixty percent of present-day women workers are married and nearly half of all of them are over 40 years of age.

The remarkable increase in the number of women workers and the change in the characteristics of the typical women workers have confronted labor unions with a new problem which they have met only imperfectly. This is clearly indicated by the fact that, while women constitute above one third of the labor force, only one fifth of the organized workers are women. The outlook of many women workers continues to be that of short-time employees who see little need for organization. Women, moreover, are predominantly intermittent workers, only one third of them working full-time in industry throughout the year, another one third full-time for part of the year, the remaining third part-time throughout the year. Even when in the labor market, their main interest is in the home. Work by married women normally means at least two wage earners in the home and a family income which is more adequate than the husband's income alone. The "little lady" can be pretty stubborn when she makes up her mind; many women workers become very determined unionists. But most unions continue to be run by men and not along lines that appeal to the women. Women workers are not unorganizable, but labor has not solved the problems which confront it by reason of the increase in womanpower in industry and the changing character of the women workers.

Also a still largely unsolved problem has been the great growth in the white-collar, production, and technical workers. Our unions have been predominantly organizations of the manual workers. The production workers in industry are not increasing, while the white-collar workers are growing phenomenally in numbers. As automation progresses further, this trend can be expected to continue. Unions have not been completely unaware of the problems confronting them in this respect. They have made attempts to organize the engineers and a few other professional or semi-professional employees. They have sought to convince the office workers that their interests lie with the production workers. Alternately, they have permitted the office workers to have their own internationals. But these remain only small organizations and the total percentage of white-collar workers who have been "corralled" by the unions is disappointingly small, to the labor people. The trend toward more professional, technical, clerical, and other white-collar workers is one the unions are up against today and which may call for quite fundamental changes in the labor movement for its solution.

The only slightly less strong trend toward more skilled workers in industry has disturbed

---

[1]Address published in *Labor Laws and Their Administration, 1956* (Bulletin, *Bureau of Labor Standards*, No. 191), pp. 53–54.

labor somewhat less, but also is a factor affecting its growth and development. Our unions formerly were basically organizations of skilled workers. Most skilled workers are members of unions today. Not so long ago, the skilled workers had their own unions. Today they are, mainly, in the same international unions and, often, in the same locals. There are few craft unions which do not admit semi-skilled and unskilled workers. Industrial unions, in theory at least, ignore craft lines. Many unions are historical products, being industrial unions in part of their jurisdiction and craft organizations in other fields. Craft and industrial unions are now in the same tent but not too happy with each other's company. Very troublesome jurisdictional disputes have developed between building trades unions and some of the industrial unions in the mass production industries; also, disputes over representation involving attempts to carve separate bargaining units out of industrial unions. The problem of the conflict between skilled and semi-skilled and unskilled workers still troubles organized labor, although in new forms. Although not the problem that most hinders the growth of union organization, the industrial versus craft union issue nevertheless remains a perplexing one.

Also a problem faced by organized labor today is the increasing mobility of the American workers and of our entire society. This is not merely a matter of more Americans leaving their states of origin during their lifetime than earlier in our history, but of the dispersion of the plant workers through the automobile over a vast region extending many miles in every direction. This operates to make organizing other than on the premises extremely difficult and interferes greatly with union meetings and good attendance at such meetings. A problem for the unions also has developed from the dispersion of upper- and middle-income people from the central region of our cities to the suburbs. This movement has been shared by our better-paid workers. Today most workers can buy homes in the suburbs or the country, if they so desire. Once a worker moves to the suburbs he tends to take on something of the complexion and mental attitude of the suburbanites—perhaps the

most antiunion group of any large distinguishable element in our population.

Something of the same situation has been created by the rise in workers' incomes. Not all wants of American workers are being satisfied and there remains a good deal of discontent among them; but appeals addressed to the starving and oppressed are not very effective when the workers are not starving and do not feel oppressed. Prolonged, widespread unemployment also does not promote union membership, and business recession, such as we are now experiencing, has the same effect.

THE CONGRESSIONAL INVESTIGATIONS

Besides the problems posed by the sharp business decline, organized labor at this time is up against disfavor or at least low repute with the public. Organized labor is a minority group in our society and but seldom has been approved unqualifiedly by the general public. In much of American thinking, organized labor is still associated with the people who were born on the wrong side of the tracks and with the more recent immigrants and their descendants. This is less true than at an earlier date, but remains the picture many Americans have of the labor movement. To this has been added the impression of a labor leader who is a roughneck and often a crook. Many Americans have long believed that the typical labor leader is a racketeer and not infrequently a goon. To them, labor leaders and union officers seem to be men who are interested only in the dues they can collect from members and the boodle they can exact from employers.

This impression of the labor leader held by many Americans has been confirmed and strengthened by the labor scandals that have had such large space in the daily press. There have been investigations after investigations, with several, at times, going on simultaneously. Dealing only with the investigations since World War II, I mention first the investigation of Un-American Activities by the Senate Committee on Expenditures in Executive Departments, popularly known as the McCarthy Investigation. This committee is still in existence, headed by Senator Eastland, and has held a few hearings within the last year. There was for a time a parallel committee in the House of Representatives, which gave the present vice president his start to fame. The McCarthy Committee devoted some attention to communism in the ranks of labor and its proceedings made headline publicity for years. I think it is a fair statement that it discovered no Communists in labor ranks who had not previously been known to be Communists. But it gave additional publicity to the fact that Communists at one time controlled quite a few unions affiliated with the Congress of Industrial Organizations. In 1949, well before the McCarthy Committee came into existence and before the vice president was more than an obscure congressman from Southern California, the CIO expelled these Communist-dominated unions. Since then, on a few occasions obscure local union officials or representatives have "pleaded the Fifth Amendment" when questioned about their Communist connections. Labor, much more than the Congressional investigators, has gotten rid of Communists in positions of power in its ranks. Unfortunately, many Americans still believe the unions or many of them to be Moscow directed.

Then followed the investigations by a subcommittee of the Senate Committee on Labor and Public Welfare of the management or mismanagement of union health, welfare, and pension funds. This subcommittee was headed in the 83rd Congress by Senator Ives; in the 84th Congress by Senator Douglas; and in the present, 85th Congress, by Senator Kennedy. A parallel investigation was conducted by the House Committee on Education and Labor. The Senate Committee soon struck pay dirt and until this year has brought up a large quantity of muck. The disclosures have concerned such matters as excessive salaries paid to union officials running health and welfare funds, the splitting of commissions by insurance agents with the union trustees of such funds, the organization of brokerage businesses by trustees to increase their take, some direct stealing of trust monies, and the connection of notorious criminals with a few of the funds. Relative to the total number of union-managed health, welfare,

and pension funds, proof of gross mismanagement has been presented only as to a small percentage of all such funds. No similar investigations or disclosures have been made of company-managed or jointly managed health, welfare, and pension funds. The investigations in their entirety have confirmed the earlier impressions of many people that labor leaders are often crooks and thieves, stealing from their members and growing rich on the boodle. No legislation by Congress has resulted from the disclosures, but six states have provided for public disclosure of the financial operations of union health, welfare, and pension funds.

Most unfavorable has been the publicity organized labor has received from the investigations during the past year by the select committee of the Senate generally referred to as the "McClellan Committee," technically the "Select Committee on Improper Activities in the Labor or Management Field." This committee consists of four Democratic and four Republican Senators, with Senator McClellan of Arkansas as Chairman. Three of the Republican members (Goldwater, Mundt, and Curtis) have antilabor records and Chairman McClellan also was opposed by organized labor when he was last elected. One member (McNamara) is a union member; and the other three have acceptable labor records. The chief counsel, head of the Committee's staff, is Robert Kennedy, a younger brother of Senator Kennedy; but the Republican members have had their own staff, headed by John McGovern, who has been sharply criticized by Senator McNamara for statements indicating, as alleged by the senator, antilabor bias. The committee has conducted public hearings, intermittently, for more than a year and the chairman has stated that they may go on for five more years.

The most extensive hearings to date have concerned the Teamsters union; others, the Bakers, the Laundry Workers, the Distillery Workers, and the Operating Engineers. There has also been one series of hearings concerning the operations of a management consultant, Nathan Shefferman, of Chicago, doing business as the Labor Relations Associates. The committee's staff, particularly the minority staff, has also investigated the United Automobile Workers and hearings relating to the Kohler strike, encouragement of violence, and the political activities of this union have been forecast. The great majority of unions have neither been subpoenaed to appear nor have they been in any way implicated in testimony before the committee. Other than Shefferman and the management of the Sears, Roebuck store in Boston and a few smaller clients of Labor Relations Associates, management has not, to date, been brought before the committee, in spite of the fact that Shefferman testified to having served several of the largest of retailing companies and some sizable manufacturers. Until recently, organized labor indicated its support of the committee's investigations, but within this month it has charged that at least some members are out to get labor. No recommendations for legislation have come from the McClellan Committee, and none is expected in the present session.

The testimony given before the McClellan Committee has often made the headlines. Most sensational was that concerning Dave Beck, retiring president, and Jimmy Hoffa, the new president, of the International Brotherhood of Teamsters. The charges against them included diversion of large amounts of union funds for personal use, autocratic control of the union, and, in the case of Hoffa, consort with notorious criminals. Both Beck and Hoffa have been tried for violation of criminal statutes, and Beck has been convicted. The charges against James Cross, President of the Bakers' Union—a socialist—are quite similar. There has also been testimony of resort to violence by the Teamsters and some of the lesser unions investigated. Little has been added to previously disclosed facts about the mismanagement of union health, welfare, and pension funds. Surprisingly, there has been little testimony of the attempted exaction of money from employers by union officers for any purpose whatsoever. Very little, also, has been disclosed as to the rigging of union elections or the lack of democracy in unions. Less than 10 of the several hundred international unions have been disclosed to be, in any sense, corrupt or as having corrupt

officers. Aside from the men mentioned and, recently, President Maloney of the Operating Engineers, no top-name union officials have been implicated. The operations of Nathan Shefferman have been revealed as being essentially those of union busting by methods of corruption, and his list of clients represents a pretty good start toward a blue-book of American merchandising. But there has been no testimony as to the extent of similar practices in manufacturing or even a mention of the very largest corporations.

LABOR'S REACTION TO THE INVESTIGATIONS

Labor's reactions to the disclosures of corruption and other festering evils in union ranks have, to my way of thinking, been wholesome. More than a year before the McClellan Committee was organized, the AFL–CIO in its first constitution set forth as one of its principal objectives:

To protect the labor movement from any and all corrupt influences and from the undermining efforts of communist agencies and all others who are opposed to the basic principles of our democracy and free and democratic unionism (Article II, Section 10).

In this same first convention (November 1955) the AFL–CIO provided for an Ethical Practices Committee, headed by Al Hayes of the Machinists' Union, to implement this constitutional provision, through investigations on complaint or on its own initiative of all suspected corruption or communism. It set forth a procedure for the suspension until the next convention of unions found, upon investigation, to be under corrupt domination, with the further power of making recommendations for the correction of the evil conditions. It also set forth that the convention, after hearing both the accuser and the accused, was to determine whether the accused union should be expelled from the federation or allowed to resume its membership, and, if so, under what conditions.

When the investigations of the subcommittee on union health, welfare, and pension funds of the Senate Committee on Labor and Public Welfare disclosed corruption in the handling of trust funds by the Allied Industrial Workers, the Distillery Workers, the United Textile Workers, and the Laundry Workers, and by scattered local unions, the Ethical Practices Committee promptly investigated and recommended suspension of these unions, setting forth the conditions which would have to be met for reinstatement. The Executive Committee, by a well-nigh unanimous vote, sustained the recommendations and the suspensions remained in effect until the recent second AFL–CIO convention. By that time the Allied Industrial Workers had gotten rid of its officers accused of corruption and the United Textile Workers had agreed to hold a special convention supervised by a monitor and to declare its two former top officers ineligible for election. Both these unions were consequently reinstated to full membership. The suspension of the Distillery Workers was continued under a monitor, with a statement of the conditions which must be met for full reinstatement. The other unions were expelled and are today outside the Federation. The two international unions not previously so labelled which were revealed through the investigations of the McClellan Committee to have corrupt officers, the Teamsters and the Bakers, were proceeded against similarly. The Ethical Practices Committee recommended their suspension to the Executive Council; the Executive Council sustained this recommendation; and the Convention (by a five to one vote in the case of the Teamsters) changed this into expulsion from the Federation. A new Bakers' Union has been chartered, which is reported to have gained the adherence of one third of the locals of the old union. No new Teamsters' International has been organized but city centrals and state federations have been directed to expel Teamsters' locals. This is a record which seems to me to show labor's good faith in its oft-repeated expression of desire to clean its own house. On this point, note must also be taken of the creation by two international unions, the Upholsterers and the United Automobile Workers, of appeal boards composed of prominent people not connected with these unions, with authority to review and correct undemocratic actions against union members. But it remains doubtful how

much the public has been impressed. Beyond question, the labor scandals have hurt the standing of organized labor in public opinion.

PROSPECTS FOR THE FUTURE

What will be the final outcome is in the realm of speculation. Many see the most likely result to be legislation hostile to labor in the Congress and the state legislatures. Quite a few bills, which labor views with alarm, are pending in the Congress. These range from requirements for the registration of health, welfare, and pension funds, to vague proposals to make the unions subject to the antitrust laws and a more definite measure for a national right-to-work law, making it unlawful for employers and unions to contract for any form of union security. In between are the recommendations which President Eisenhower transmitted to the Congress a week ago. Many of the proposals, including some of those of the president, go beyond the correction of the evils publicized through the congressional investigations and have already drawn fire from organized labor and its supporters. What will become of them, in an election year, is pretty much anybody's guess. What seems certain is that labor this year will get nowhere in its long campaign to lighten the restrictions imposed upon it by the Taft-Hartley Act, and particularly has little chance of getting its bill enacted that would prohibit states from imposing more drastic limitations on union security agreements than those included in the national law. Further legislation placing additional restrictions upon the activities of organized labor in contests with management is more than a possibility; but I doubt whether 1958 will prove another 1947.

There is also a possibility that the labor scandals will have adverse repercussions upon labor in its contests this year over new contract provisions in many major agreements. The business recession makes 1958 a bad one for wage increases and other labor gains. The public is more than half convinced that the major cause of rising prices is the increase in wages and is in a mood to support management in resisting further increases in rates of pay or fringe benefits. There are also numerous indications that many managements this time have their backs up and seem disposed not to yield an inch. More than ever the battle is being waged in the forum of public opinion. The labor scandals have further weakened labor in this forum. At present the prospects seem to be for more and greater strikes than we have had for years, with labor in a position in which the majority of the public will regard it as a sort of "Peck's Bad Boy" or worse, a goon responsible for just about everything that is wrong. Public opinion is not always, perhaps but seldom, decisive in labor disputes, but it does count. At this time, so it seems to me, it is likely to support management in stubbornly resisting union demands. This is not predicting that labor will get nothing this year; and, of course, it will not get all that it seeks in its first demands. Only a prophet can forecast the final outcome of the 1958 contract negotiations and the strikes in which they may culminate.

On the broader question of what will be the total effects of the present crisis in labor unionism, I have little to offer that is more definite. But I call attention to the fact that this is not the first time organized labor has faced a critical situation. We now have had labor unions for more than 100 years, in all sorts of climates of public opinion and during one crisis after the other. Many of the factors in the present situation may call for changes in union tactics and may precede such changes. What is clear is that unions do not dominate our society, but they have been and are now a part of the American way of life, although theirs is a minority role. I expect them to continue as a part of the American way of life, regardless of present difficulties.

A Conditional Forecast

What I shall say from this point on is a conditional forecast, which I believe to be warranted on the basis of experience in this and other countries. It is my expectation that the major repercussions of the labor scandals may well be in the political field. Even more do I expect such a result if Congress should enact legislation which labor interprets as an attack upon its existence or effectiveness. This may also be the result of a stinging defeat, should it occur, of labor in the contract negotiations and ensuing strikes in the spring and summer. Holding the line against wage increases, particularly if unemployment continues to mount and farm prices do not improve, may well give us the most radical Congress we have had in two decades.

Interviewed, along with other public members of the former National War Labor Board after the passage of the Taft-Hartley Act, I ventured the prediction that the principal effect of this legislation, crammed down labor's throat by the 80th Congress, was likely to be increased political activity on the part of organized labor, rather than any pronounced change in the economic strength of the parties. As I look back upon that forecast, it seems to me that I was a very lucky prophet. The Taft-Hartley Act hurt labor less than it had feared and also benefited antiunion employers less than they had hoped. But the passage of the Taft-Hartley Act put labor into politics to an extent not known for many years preceding. The surprising reelection of President Truman in 1948 was ascribed by political commentators principally to a sizable switch in the farm vote, but the defeat of nearly a third of the members of the 80th Congress who had voted for the Taft-Hartley Act occurred almost entirely in industrial districts.

Organized labor has always been interested in what government is doing and to some extent has engaged in political activities. But it is most active politically when it believes that its operations in the economic sphere are being hampered or likely to be hampered. Dyed-in-the-wool unionists follow the advice of their leaders in politics when they believe their unions to be in danger. Working men generally react most violently politically when they have sustained personal loss or fear such a loss. Among situations producing such a result are unemployment, wage cuts, and defeats in strikes. It seems to me to be probable that the more the factors enumerated coincide, the more certain and the greater will be the political reaction.

There is considerable likelihood that quite a number of these factors will coincide by the elections of 1958. A heretofore little-remarked concomitant of the labor scandals has been a growing belief among ardent unionists that the investigations and exposures of the McClellan Committee have gone far enough and are motivated by a desire to weaken organized labor. A majority of the Teamsters seem to be sticking with Jimmy Hoffa. As has been noted, top AFL–CIO leaders recently met with Senator McClellan and others from his committee to warn them not to play the game of Walter Reuther's opponents. There is a distinct possiblilty that as the contract negotiations draw closer, investigations of the unions involved will strengthen this feeling among ardent unionists; and, if the negotiations prove disappointing, politicians will be blamed. Prolonged strikes resulting in defeats for labor would increase the political repercussions. These will be particularly strong should Congress enact legislation which labor deems to be designed to weaken its economic position. Every informed person also knows that a continued high level of unemployment and, still more, increased unemployment, will be hard on the "ins" in politics. It is my expectation, also, that the political reaction will not stop with party labels. It may well come to pass that the long conservative swing in American politics, manifest now for 20 years, may be reversed.

All this is in the realm of speculation, with many "ifs" about which no one can be certain. What seems clear is that the AFL–CIO merger, the jurisdictional disputes agreement, and the ethical practices codes have not solved all problems of the American unions or, more accurately, any of them. Organized labor is in a difficult situation today. Many of the factors in this difficult situation go beyond the present labor scandals and the contract negotiations, which are now in the stage of preliminary jousts in the public arena.

What this may lead to, I leave to you. I merely direct attention to the fact that not only recent developments but many others of the last quarter century have tended to make our unions far more political organizations than they were at an earlier date. American unions have always been interested in politics, but at most times not vitally so, especially when one labor federation was dominant and the principle was pretty well adhered to that each union had a definite jurisdiction which must be observed by employers and all other unions. At that time, labor-management disputes were fought out in the economic realm and public opinion mattered but little.

Today, the labor situation is very different. We again have one dominant federation, but a good many unions are outside the federation and within it there are bitter rivalries and controversies. The principle of defined jurisdiction has not been abandoned, but in many fields there are overlapping jurisdictions. More basic is the inherent conflict between defined jurisdictions and the workers' free choice of the union, which is incorporated in our national labor policy.

It may be that this policy of itself is operating to make our unions more like political organizations along European lines. In no free European country has the situation ever prevailed that one and only one national union has jurisdiction within a defined field, which goes along with the concept that all workers should belong to unions but that there is only one union to which a given worker may belong. With choice allowed between unions, politics or religion tend to become the only unifying forces in the labor movement. There has been no significant trend toward making religion a dominant factor in American unionism, but our policy of worker free choice inevitably, I believe, has some tendency toward making the unions more political. It is my thesis that this is also a likely effect of the recent developments I have noted. It is futile to talk about keeping government out of labor-management relations so long as the parties are forever turning to government for help. When they do this, not only should they expect retaliation when the almost inevitable pendular swing occurs, but they should realize that they thereby tend to make the unions more political in their objectives. Being old fashioned, I prefer our traditional American type of unionism, but I can see politically oriented unionism as a consequence of the increasing role we assign to government in labor-management relations.

PART THREE

The State of the Unions: Structure, Government, and Administration

The trade unions in the 1980s face difficult problems associated with declining membership, aging leadership, and stiff resistance to organizing in the rapid growth areas in the South and Southwest. Further complications for the labor movement arise as a result of continuing shifts in the composition of the labor force. Increasing numbers of women, youth, and white-collar workers means that the traditional blue-collar labor movement must restructure itself or face further declines in membership. The articles in this section are intended to shed some light on the current state of the unions.

The first article in this section, taken from the London *Economist*, documents the statistical fact of a declining trade union membership in the United States between 1950 and 1980. Why has this happened and how is the current crisis in the American labor movement different from that of an earlier period? An interesting array of insights in regard to these questions is provided by authors in this section. Richard B. Freeman asks the question, "Why are unions faring poorly in NLRB representation elections?" and concludes that the answer is provided, in large part, by employer opposition to unions supported by the legal framework in the United States. Michael J. Piore believes that the current crisis in American labor and the declining membership of the trade unions must be understood by examining the "growing industrial and economic malaise of our age." Piore indicates that "what is new in the current situation—and what makes it plausible to characterize it as a *crisis*—is that union power appears for the first time to be in real jeopardy in industries that have been its traditional bastions of strength."

The state of the union might also be heavily influenced by leadership and financial characteristics. Howard Banks, in an article from *Forbes*, argues that "today's trade union leaders, like yesterday's generals, are fighting the last war." Banks likens the unions today to "an army without a strategy." Neil Sheflin and Leo Troy examine the finances of American unions in the 1970s and find that the "unions' real financial wealth declined in the 1970s to the levels of the previous decade, while their real income grew at a much slower rate than during the 1960s." If the unions' assets and income decline over a period of time, this will be reflected in their ability to finance strikes and organizing activities.

In the face of the difficulties discussed in the preceding articles, what have the unions done to organize new workers? According to James T. Bennett and Manuel Johnson, "most unions have got out of the habit of organizing in the years since World War II." Bennett and Johnson believe that new union members have come about only as the result of "pushbutton unionism" in which employers deliver over workers through devices such as the union shop. James Craft and Marian Extejt claim that "new strategies and union organizing" by the AFL–CIO have not produced positive results. They examine "four strategic approaches to organizing that have been developed or re-emphasized in recent years, including the corporate power strategy, the collective bargaining strategy, community acceptance and integration strategy, and the coordinated/pool resource strategy," and they conclude that these strategies are not likely to produce major outcomes for the unions

125

In the 1980s. Andrew M. Kramer examines how trade union strategy attempts to capture more union membership. He claims that "one of the most effective organizing tools being utilized by unions today is a neutrality agreement. Neutrality agreements are agreements whereby an employer, ordinarily one that already has a number of unionized plants, agrees to remain 'neutral' in any organizing campaign conducted by the union with which it has such an agreement."

A major organizing campaign by the Amalgamated Clothing and Textile Workers Union (ACTWU) was conducted at the J. P. Stevens company over a 17-year period. This campaign in the South was thought to be a crucial one by the ACTWU and other unions, and it was commonly believed that a breakthrough by the union in J. P. Stevens would lead to widespread organization in the South. Terry Mullins and Paul Luebke examine the J. P. Stevens "victory" and conclude that "while recognizing the symbolic importance of ACTWU's victory over Stevens, the J. P. Stevens settlement is *not* a watershed for the Southern labor movement."

On a positive note, Karen S. Koziara, Patrice Insley, and Rudy Oswald provide some prescriptions for improving the position of organized labor. Koziara and Insley indicate that "organizations of working women can pave the way for unions." Their article focuses on an important development in the labor market today where various organizations of working women have developed and, apparently, Koziara and Insley believe that these groups may find a formal association with the trade unions in the future. Oswald, speaking as the AFL–CIO director of economic research, takes note of the areas where the AFL–CIO will be working with the hope of making progress in the future.

A concluding article in this section provides an excellent background for an understanding of the international trade union movement. John Windmuller provides an interesting presentation pertaining to the history and present structure of the various components of the international labor movement.

READING 10

The De-Unionisation of America*

The Economist

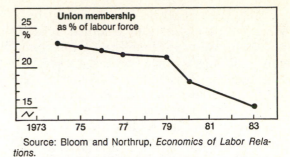

Union membership as % of labour force

Source: Bloom and Northrup, *Economics of Labor Relations.*

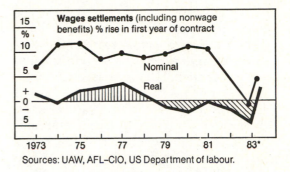

Wages settlements (including nonwage benefits) % rise in first year of contract

Nominal

Real

Sources: UAW, AFL–CIO, US Department of labour.

The retreat of American labour unions has become a rout. Between 1950 and 1980, union membership dropped from about a third of the labour force to 18 percent. Since then it has tumbled to about 15 percent. Membership of the big blue-collar unions has fallen most sharply since 1980. The memberships of the steel, carmaking, and building and transport unions have all declined by a third.

The unions have had to swallow some nasty pills. In 1980, a new era of "give-backs" (renunciation by workers of benefits already won) arrived when Chrysler workers granted the company concessions worth $600m. Since that concession by the United Auto Workers (UAW), other heavyweight unions have been reeling. The International Brotherhood of Teamsters, Chauffeurs, Warehousemen and Helpers of America, the nation's largest union, is one of these. It made (in its view) big concessions on wages and benefits, only to see the collapse of its "master freight" agreement as hundreds of transport companies negotiated new contracts at lower rates. In March, the United Steelworkers union accepted a $1.25 (equivalent to 9 percent cut in hourly wages and the loss of cost-of-living adjustments. In September, workers at Ford's Rouge steel mill accepted a 15 percent pay cut. Continental Airlines sacked its 12,000 workers after filing for Chapter 11 bankruptcy, then rehired only a third of them at half their former wages.

Public-sector unions have been cowed since 1981 when President Reagan sacked 12,000 striking air traffic controllers, smashing their union in the process. The unions' union, the American Federation of Labour–

Congress of Industrial Organisations (AFL–CIO), has failed to whip up public opposition to the Reagan administration's policies.

The long-term decline of America's unions reflects the economy's shift from manufacturing to service industries, traditionally weakly unionised, the moving of firms from the rustbowl strongholds either to the sunbelt states, or —particularly with manufacturing jobs— abroad; the emergence of union-busting law firms; and increased automation.

The short-term rout reflects increased import penetration in basic industries such as steel and cars and the deep recession from which the American economy is now emerging. In addition, the deregulation of transport industries, and the squeezing out of inflation, have made employers unwilling to give big wage rises, whose costs they are not able to pass on.

Union officials now take accountancy courses and are having the books of their employers examined to see whether their wage demands are realistic, or if givebacks are really needed to keep plants open. And they are more receptive to the idea of companies (particularly airlines and carmakers) giving workers a share of the profits in return for wage cuts.

---

*From *The Economist*, October 29, 1983, p. 71.

Workplace practices are changing, too. Workers are being asked to perform a range of tasks. This is causing problems for union negotiators. Wages cannot be tied to specific jobs; they may have to be tied to experience. But that is difficult for unions to bargain over.

Declining union membership and more assertive managers are leading some to speculate that America could soon become almost union-free. This is a conservative's pipedream because:

Not all unions are losing members. Since 1979, the biggest union representing service-industry workers, the Service Employees' International Union, has seen its membership rise by 12 percent. And the old industrial unions are fighting back: e.g., the Teamsters are trying to organize all and sundry behind their banner, from Hollywood cartoonists to pipeline diggers. The AFL–CIO is at last backing union membership drives among the salaried employees in the private sector, on whom the union movement's future depends.

The AFL–CIO's leader, Mr. Lane Kirkland, has helped persuade much of the union movement—though possibly not the rank and file—to pin its political colours to Mr. Walter Mondale, who is at present the leading contender for the Democratic party's presidential nomination in next year's elections. The unions hope for a political kickback if Mr. Mondale is eventually elected president.

The unions are responding to the charge that there is no alternative to Reaganomics. Some are unveiling a new "industrial policy"; others, supported by many academic economists, believe it makes more sense to pursue macroeconomic policies to correct the overvaluation of the dollar. They are all opposed to sporadic wage concessions in industries suffering import competition.

The AFL–CIO is trying to improve labour's bad public image by setting up a labour cable television network (it has spurned television in the past) to make programmes for national viewing.

Union weakness may not long survive economic recovery. A company such as General Motors, which this week reported a sixfold increase in profits, will find it hard to repeat recent modest pay awards. Chrysler is already giving back some of the givebacks it got from its workers last year.

And no manager can fail to notice that the collapse of union membership in the textile industry is promoting the return of sweatshops in immigrant neighbourhoods in, for example, New York. It was such exploitation of workers that made unions necessary in the first place.

READING 11

Why Are Unions Faring Poorly in NLRB Representation Elections?*

Richard B. Freeman†

Since the 1950s private sector unions have experienced a substantial decline in the number of workers organized through National Labor Relations Board (NLRB) representation elections. In the mid-1950s through the mid-1960s unions were victorious in 60 plus percent of NLRB elections, organizing from one half to three quarters of a percent of the work force annually through the election procedure (see Table 1). In the early 1980s, unions were winning a bare 45 percent of elections and engaged in so few elections that just 0.14 percent of the unorganized work force became organized via NLRB elections—a percentage below that needed for unions to maintain their share of the work force, much less to grow proportionally with the work force. The decline in union success in NLRB elections, coupled with a "natural" attrition of membership, underlies the precipitous fall in union density in the United States—a fall which contrasts sharply with increases in unionism in most other Western countries, including Canada.

What has caused the drop in union success in NLRB elections? Is lack of success due to changes in the structure of the economy, such as the rise of white-collar employment, the growth of the Sunbelt, and the increased proportion of women in the work force? Is it due to failings by the unions, who have fallen

*Reprinted with author's permission from an unpublished paper.

†Richard B. Freeman is Professor of Economics, Harvard University, and a member of the National Bureau of Economic Research.

down on the job of organizing the unorganized? Or to a decline in workers' desires for unions? Or to the increased strength and effectiveness of managerial opposition? How important is the 1970s recession in the decline?

This paper seeks to answer these questions. It offers a critical review of existing research on union success or failure in NLRB elections and presents the results of new calculations designed to cast light on the factors at work. After a brief examination of the "body" of the poor performance of unions in NLRB representation elections, the paper examines four "suspects": changes in economic structure; worker attitudes; changes in union organizing efforts; and changes in management opposition to unionism. Then it considers briefly the role of labor law in the decline in union success in NLRB elections.

THE BODY: POOR UNION PERFORMANCE IN NLRB ELECTIONS

Table 1 presents a capsule summary of the phenomenon under study. Column 1 shows the precipitous drop in the number of workers won by unions per private nonagricultural employee from 1950 to 1980, while columns 2–4 decompose the number of workers won to highlight the nature of the decline.

The decomposition in 2–4 is:

$$\frac{\text{Workers won by unions}}{\text{Private, wage, and salary workers}} = \frac{\text{Elections}}{\text{Private, non-agricultural, wage, and salary workers}} \times \frac{\text{Workers in NLRB election}}{\text{Elections}} \times \frac{\text{Workers won}}{\text{Workers in NLRB election}}$$

The first term in the decomposition measures the average size of an NLRB representation won by unions. The second term, which has received relatively little attention in popular discussion and professional analysis, represents the extent of organizing activity. The third term is the proportion of workers in elections won by unions; it has been at the center

Table 1
From NLRB Elections to New Union Representation

	Workers in Union Victories as Percent of Private Wage and Salary Workers	Elections over Private Wage and Salary Workers (000)	Workers Eligible per Election	Workers Won as Percent of Workers Eligible
1950	2.0%	.152	157	84%
1955	1.0	.108	121	73
1960	0.7	.152	76	59
1965	0.7	.161	70	61
1970	0.6	.146	75	52
1975	0.4	.136	71	38
1980	0.2	.104	54	37
Log change:				
1950–1980	− 2.30	− .38	− 1.07	− .82
1965–1980	− 1.25	− .44	− .34	− .50

Source: Private wage and salary workers from U.S. Department of Labor, *Employment and Training Report of the President*, 1981, p. 155, with private household workers excluded from the calculation. Elections, workers eligible, and workers won as percent from National Labor Relations Board, *Annual Reports*, various editions.

of many studies of declining union success in NLRB elections.

All three of the components of the decomposition equation show declines in union success: the number of elections has not kept pace with the growing work force; the average size of union victories have fallen; the proportion of workers in representation elections won by unions has fallen.

How important is each of these trends to the overall decline?

A crude decomposition is to take the logs of the principal variable workers in union victories as a percent of private wage and salary workers and the logs of the terms in the decomposition. From 1950 to 1980 the dominant terms are workers eligible per election and the win rate, workers won as a percent of workers eligible. From 1961 to 1980, which begins in a more "normal" period of unionization than 1950, all three terms have a substantial magnitude. (see the bottom part of Table 1).

Decomposing the number of workers as I have done in Table 1 treats each component as a separate entity. While for some purposes this is fruitful, it should not be taken as the last word. The three components of workers won/nonagricultural labor force are undoubtedly interrelated: when the rate in elections fall, unions are likely to cut back organizing efforts; similarly when a typical union victory

garners fewer members than in the past, the return on effort will be lower, also contributing to potentially fewer election campaigns. Ongoing research work will, hopefully, illuminate the structure of the relations between the components of union gains by NLRB elections further.[1]

From Workers Won in NLRB Elections to Union Density

Surprisingly, while there are—as we shall see—numerous studies of how unions fare in NLRB elections, there has been virtually no work relating NLRB election results to the decline in union density in the United States. Organization of members through NLRB elections is, of course, not the only determinant of unionization in the United States. Indeed, in some years, changes in union membership or in the union density have changed very differently than one would expect given members organized through NLRB elections.

Between 1960 and 1961, for example, unions won over 218,000 members through NLRB elections, but union membership fell by 746,000. Between 1967 and 1968 unions

[1]For a detailed discussion of the components of the decomposition equation see R. B. Freeman, "The Simple Economics of Changing Union Density" (NBER, forthcoming).

won 271,695 members through NLRB elections, but union membership rose by 549,000. Despite increased membership from 1967 to 1968, however, the proportion of workers organized remained virtually constant.[2] Union membership also changes because of cyclical and secular changes in employment in already organized plants; organization of workers outside of NLRB elections (as in construction, where unions organize employers by convincing them that the union represents local craftsmen and can provide the employer with skilled workers for jobs); and because of plant shutdowns. The union share of the labor force changes not only when union membership changes but also when nonunion employment changes. Because some union (as well as nonunion) plants close down every year, and new plants are "born" nonunion, there is a normal decline in membership each year, which requires a certain amount of new organization by unions simply to maintain their share of the work force.

To examine the linkage between NLRB election results and changes in density I have found the following "stock-flow" equation to be useful:

$$
\begin{aligned}
\text{Union} \\
\text{density} \\
\text{in year}
\end{aligned}
=
\begin{aligned}
&\text{Gains in Membership from} \\
&\text{NLRB elections/Work force} \\
&\text{in year} \\
&- \lambda\,[\text{Union density in} \\
&\quad \text{year } t-1]
\end{aligned}
$$

where λ is the *net* attrition rate for the union density—that is, the rate at which union density would decrease ($\lambda > 0$) or increase ($\lambda < 0$) in the absence of NLRB elections. According to this equation, the pattern of change in the union share of the work force depends on the relation between the net attrition of the union share of the work force and the rate of new organization through NLRB elections. When the rate of attrition multiplied by the existing union share exceeds the proportion of the work force newly organized by NLRB elections, the union share will fall over time.

When the rate of attrition times the share is smaller than the proportion newly organized, the union share will rise over time. When organization by NLRB elections just balances out the attrition, the union share will be constant.[3]

I have made several estimates of the magnitude of the attrition rate using variants of the "stock-flow" equation. My estimates suggest that the rate is on the order of 3 percent per year. That is, in the absence of new organization of workers through NLRB elections the union share of the work force in the United States tends to decline by roughly 3 percent a year.[4] If in one year 35 percent of the work force were organized, this proportion would decline to 34 percent [= 35 percent × $(1 - .03)$] in the following year.

With a 3 percent rate of attrition, the late-1970s–early-1980s level of new organization of workers through NLRB elections portends a disastrous decline for unionism. If unions continue to win just 0.3 percent of the work force in NLRB elections (see Table 1), the steady-state share of the work force that will be organized will fall to a bare 10 percent of the nonagricultural work force. If the union organized 0.6 percent of the work force through NLRB elections, as they did in the 1950s, the union share would stabilize at 20 percent.[5] In short, while other factors help determine union density, union success or failure in NLRB elections is an essential component in what is one of the most important changes in the U.S. labor market in recent decades: the decline in the organized proportion of private sector workers. We turn to the

---

[2]Unionization figures are from the U.S. Department of Labor, Bureau of Labor Statistics, *Handbook of Labor Statistics*, 1978, updated.

[3]For derivation and discussion of this formula see R. B. Freeman, "The Simple Economics of Declining Union Density" (NBER Working Paper, 1983).

[4]I have made several estimates of attrition using variants of the following formula: Attrition rate = (Change in union membership − Gains through NLRB elections)/ Union membership in initial period. All of our estimates range about 3 percent. See R. B. Freeman, "The Simple Economics of Declining Union Density" (NBER Working Paper, 1983).

[5]This is obtained by setting the change in membership equal to zero in the difference equation: Union share (t) = (− attrition rate) Union share $(t-1)$ + New gains in membership from NLRB elections/Work force, solving for the stable union share. In this formula t = years.

question: What factors have caused the decline in union success in NLRB representation elections?

THE FIRST SUSPECT: CHANGING ECONOMIC STRUCTURE

The first and simplest explanation of the decline in unionism is that it resulted from broad economic changes, which reduced the proportion of the work force in groups traditionally highly unionized and increased the proportion in groups traditionally nonunion. The explanation is simple because it ties the decline to the changing structure of the economy with no need to bring in changes in union or management behavior or the desires of workers for unions. It is a "technocratic" explanation, and technocratic explanations are invariably the easiest and least controversial.

To estimate the potential impact of structural changes on unionization I performed a two-part analysis. First, I estimated the impact of personal, job, and geographic factors on the probability that an individual would vote for a union in an election using data from the 1977 Quality of Employment Survey. As can be seen in the simple tabulations in Table 2, there are considerable differences in the likelihood of different workers desiring union representation. Second, I multiplied the estimated impact of being in a category by changes in the proportion of workers in that category over time to obtain the contribution

Table 2
Who Wants Unions
Percentage of private sector wage and salary *nonrepresented* employees who answered "for" to the question: "If an election were held with secret ballots, would you vote for or against having a union or employees' association represent you?"

	All Workers	Blue-Collar Workers	White-Collar Workers
All nonrepresented employees	33%	40%	28%
Sex			
Male	28	36	20
Female	41	46	38
Race			
White	29	34	26
Nonwhite	70	71	68
Age			
Under 25	40	45	36
25–39	32	41	26
40–54	29	38	24
Over 55	31	28	33
Region			
Northeast	37	38	37
North Central	26	30	24
South	36	46	26
West	35	38	29
Industry			
Agriculture, forestry, and fisheries	7	10	0
Mining	16	21	0
Construction	22	24	18
Manufacturing	36	46	21
Transportation, communication, and other public untilities	22	35	12
Wholesale and retail trade	34	45	27
Finance, insurance, and real estate	30	40	29
Business and repair services	27	23	33
Personal services	25	28	17
Entertainment and recreational services	42	51	38

Source: Data from Quality of Employment Survey, 1977. See Table 2–1 for definitions of blue- and white-collar workers.

Table 3
Estimates of the Impact of Personal, Job, and Geographic Factors on Who Would Vote for Unions in NLRB Elections

Characteristic	Relation to Vote for Unionism	Estimated Impact on Proportion Voting for Union in Election
Personal		.013
Age	Young more likely to vote for union	.003
Education	Little relation to vote	.003
Sex	Women are more likely to vote for union	.007
Race	Blacks much more likely to vote for union	.003
Job		−.030
Occupation	Blue-collar more likely to vote union	−.019
Industry	Mining *below* average desire to vote unionism	−.011
Geography	South more likely to vote for union than other regions; North Central less likely	.00
Total related changes		−.017
Total changes in proportion of eligible voters who voted in NLRB election, 19		− .22

Source: Calculated by estimating the impact of each factor over the probability of voting for a union in the 1977 Quality of Employment Survey and then applying the estimate to changes in the composition of the work force for the period 1954–1980.

of that structural shift to the percentage of workers voting union. The logic of the procedure is simple: if, for example, white-collar workers are, say, 10 percentage points less likely to vote union than other workers and if the white-collar share of the work force (and, therefore, of workers in union representation elections) rises by 5 percentage points, we would attribute .005 points [=.10(.05)] of the observed changes in the proportion voting union.[6]

The results of this analysis, summarized in Table 3, show that structural factors account for very little of the decline in the union success in NLRB elections. The reason is that while the proportion of workers in some categories likely to vote union has decreased (notably, the blue-collar workers) the proportion of workers in other categories likely to vote

union has increased (young workers, black workers). Evidence from actual representation elections also shows that black and young workers are more likely to vote "yes" than others, while women are as likely to vote "yes" as men.[7]

While structural factors contribute only marginally to the decline in the union share of votes in NLRB elections, they may contribute more to the declining number of election campaigns conducted by unions. As yet, however, I have not analyzed this possible route of impact. Barring an enormous influence of structural changes on numbers of elections (or on size of winning units, which seems a priori implausible), I conclude that structural changes in the economy are not the *prime* cause of declining union success in NLRB elections.

So what is?

[6]Formally, if B_1 is the estimated impact of the ith factor on unionization, we attribute B_1X_1 of the change to the change in X_1. Note that our analysis uses a linear probability model. More complex functional forms, such as the logistic, will yield comparable results.

[7]See Henry S. Farber and Daniel H. Saks, "Why Workers Want Unions: The Role of Relative Wages and Job Characteristics," *Journal of Political Economy*, April 1980, pp. 349–69.

Table 4
Organizing Efforts by 20 Major U.S. Unions 1953–1974

Year	Expenditures in Millions of Current Dollars	Real Expenditures Utilizing Wage Deflator	Real Expenditures per Member of These Unions	Real Expenditures per Nonunion Employee
1953	$21.1	$34.4	$3.91	$1.03
1955	22.6	34.4	3.72	1.02
1960	28.1	35.2	3.94	.95
1965	33.2	35.9	3.79	.83
1970	49.5	41.7	4.15	.81
1974	64.4	41.3	3.94	.71

Source: Paula Voos, "Labor Union Organizing Programs, 1954–1977" (Ph.D., diss., Harvard University, June 1982).

THE SECOND SUSPECT: UNION ORGANIZING EFFORTS

How have union organizing efforts changed over time? How much, if any, of the decline in private sector unionism can be attributed to a decline in union organizing activity?

Professor Paula Voos of the University of Wisconsin has analyzed these questions in some detail. She has developed estimates of the resources unions allocated to organizing activity based on the financial records of 20 different international unions. While her estimates are by no means perfect, they provide a useful indication of the trend in organizing activity. Voos' figures show that while unions have roughly maintained the same real expenditures per member for organizing, their effort has not kept pace with the growth of the work force, so that real expenditures per nonunion worker have actually declined by some 30 percent (see Table 4). To see whether this decline contributed to the falling union success rate, I made use of Voos' estimates of the impact of resources on unions' success in organizing jurisdiction. According to her econometric analysis, a 10 percent increase in dollars spent per potential union member raises the proportion for whom the union wins representation rights by 7 percent. Using this figure I estimate that the decline in union organizing effort contributed substantially to the 1950s–1970s drop in the proportion of nonagricultural workers newly organized through NLRB elections. In the early 1950s, unions organized roughly 1.0 percent of the work force annually through elections; in the early 1970s,

they organized roughly 0.3 percent of the work force annually through elections. Voos' figures suggest that the decline in organizing effort reduced the proportion of newly organized by 21 percent or 0.2 points of the 0.7 point drop.[8] While crude, these figures indicate that possibly as much as a third of the decline in union success through NLRB elections is linked to reduced organizing activity.

Another related statistic can be brought to bear on the issue of union organizing effort and electoral success. In some NLRB elections more than one union contests the right to represent workers. In this situation organizing effort is undoubtedly much higher than in elections which pit unions against management only. In 1980 the victory rate in elections with two or more unions on the ballot was 74.2 percent, compared to a rate of 47.4 percent where only one union was seeking representation rights. Prior to unification of the AFL and CIO, employers would often express a desire to work with unions associated with one rather than the other federation ("The CIO is too leftist," "The AFL is too corrupt or is too craft oriented"). After unification the number of elections with two or more unions on the ballot fell, from 23.7 percent of NLRB elections in 1953 to 6.2 percent of elections in

---

[8]My calculation of the 0.7 elasticity is based on Paula Voos, "Labor Union Organizing Programs 1954–1977" (Ph.D. diss., Harvard University, May 1982), Table 3–2, p. 20. The dollars spent for nonunion workers are from Voos, Table 1–3, pp. 87–88. To obtain the 21 percent estimate we multiply the 30 percent decline by the 0.7 estimated impact per percentage change in expenditures to obtain these figures.

1980, implying less choice for workers (and employers) among unions and less organizing activity per election.[9] All else the same, the drop of 17.5 percentage points in the proportion of elections with two or more unions on the ballot would, at 1980 rates of victory, reduce the proportion of elections won by unions by 5 percentage points or a quarter of the actual drop in the proportion of elections won by unions, an estimate surprisingly close to that obtained from Voos' analyses.[10]

All told, reduced organizing activity appears to have contributed to the decline in union representation.

MANAGERIAL OPPOSITION

While trade union organizing effort per nonunion worker has fallen, managerial opposition to unionism has increased by leaps and bounds. In the 1950s many managements did relatively little to discourage their workers from unionizing—after all, did not the law specify that the decision was for the workers to make? In ensuing decades, however, management has come to contest hotly nearly every significant NLRB election. Labor-management consultants, whose modus operandi is defeating unions in certification elections, are routinely brought in to run antiunion election campaigns. Because these consultants rarely comply with the Landrum-Griffin Act by reporting their activities to the Department of Labor, solid estimates of the number and receipts of such firms are unavailable.[11] That they have grown to become an important part of the labor relations scene is, however, incontestable.

_____

[9]*Annual Report of the National Labor Relations Board*, vols. 16 and 44, (Washington, D.C.: U.S. Government Printing Office, 1954, 1980).

[10]The differential success of unions in elections contested by several unions can be interpreted differently. It is possible that two or more unions contest an election only when workers are extremely eager to organize. Then the decline in the proportion of elections contested by unions represents a decline in worker interest, not organizing activity. As we have used the figures simply to check the plausibilty of Voos' estimates, we do not pursue the alternative interpretation here.

[11]The *AFL–CIO News* estimates about 1,500 practitioners; see *AFL–CIO News* 28, no. 2 (January 15, 1983), p. 1.

What Is the Nature of the Modern "Union-Prevention" Business?

Management opposition to union organizing drives takes three basic forms. The first, sometimes called "positive labor relations," attempts to beat unions at their own game by offering unorganized workers most of the benefits of unionism—high wages, good fringes, seniority protection, and the like—with none of the associated costs. While union leaders occasionally rant and rave against employers who practice positive labor relations, in private they do not condemn "good" nonunion employers. They believe, however, that at the first sign of economic trouble, even the most well-meaning employer will drop "positive" labor relations, and break no-layoff "promises," seniority protection, and the like.

A second employer strategy is to conduct tough legal campaigns to convince workers that their interests might be better served by voting against unions. A typical campaign might involve:

Frequent written and verbal communications with workers, particularly by their immediate supervisors.

Predictions about the possible dire effects of unionism on worker well-being.

Presentation of information about strikes designed to frighten workers that unionism will bring active conflict to the firm.

Delay of the representation election, on the (correct) assumption that the greater time between initial petitions for an election and the holding of the election, the more likely it is that union fervor will fall.

Efforts to obtain voting districts more favorable to management.

A third way to try and defeat unionism is to break the law, in particular to identify and fire leading pro-union workers.

Beginning in the 1960s the relative number of illegal activities committed by managements, after declining for years, rose at phenomenal rates (Figure 1). From 1960 to 1980 the number of *all* employer unfair labor practices charges rose fourfold; the number of charges involving a firing for union activity

Figure 1
Employer Unfair Labor Practices against Unions and Number of NLRB Representation Elections, 1950–1980

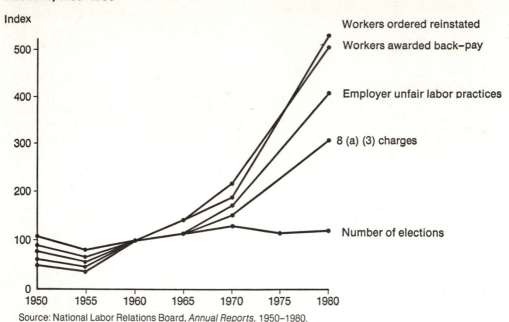

Source: National Labor Relations Board, *Annual Reports,* 1950–1980.

rose threefold; and the number of workers awarded back-pay or ordered reinstated to their jobs rose fivefold. By contrast, the number of NLRB elections barely changed in the same period. Despite increasingly sophisticated methods for disguising the cause of such firings, more employers have been judged guilty of firing workers for union activity in 1980 than ever before.[12] If one divides the number of persons fired for union activity in 1980 by the number of persons who voted for a union in elections to obtain an indication of the risk faced by workers desiring a union, one gets a remarkable result: 1 in 20 workers who favored the union got fired. Assuming that the vast bulk of union supporters are relatively inactive, the likelihood that an outspoken worker exercising his or her legal rights under the Taft-Hartley Act gets fired for union activity is, by these data, extraordinarily high.

One reason why firing workers for union activity has become increasingly popular is that the penalties for such activities are slight.

Employers who are found guilty of firing union workers are forced to reinstate the workers and to pay them limited back-pay (the wages they would have received minus whatever income they received from the alternative to the job), often several years later. In addition the employers must post a notice that they will not engage in such illegal activity again. Such notices are jocularly referred to as "hunting licenses" which, rather than convincing workers that management will forego such tactics in the future, warns them of how far management is willing to go to defeat unionism. Another reason for growing illegal management opposition is that it is an exceedingly effective way to chill an organizing campaign, as we shall see next.

HOW MUCH DOES MANAGEMENT OPPOSITION CONTRIBUTE TO UNION DECLINE?

There are a wide variety of studies of the impact of managerial opposition on NLRB elections. Some studies compare success rates across elections where management employed different tactics; others analyze the de-

[12]See Paul Weiler, "Reform of the Representation Process in American Labor Law," mimeograph, Harvard Law School, April 20, 1982, pp. 31–34 for a detailed discussion of illegal management activities.

terminants of the vote of individual workers (reported after the secret ballot election); others relate management activity in a geographic area to union organizing success in the area; while yet others study changes over time. Despite considerable differences among studies, however, virtually all tell the same story: managerial opposition to unionism, particularly illegal campaign tactics, is a major, if the major determinant of NLRB election results.

Table 5 presents a capsule summary of extant studies, divided between those focused on legal management opposition and those focused on illegal opposition. The studies of legal opposition show that:

1. The amount of company communication influences the election results, with unions winning most elections in which management opposition is light but less than half in which opposition is severe (studies 1, 2, 4, 6; also 11 and 12).
2. Union success is lower the larger the time delay between the initial petition and the actual holding of the election (studies 3 and 6).
3. Elections to which companies accede readily to the election district proposed by the union (consent elections) produce greater chances of wins than elections in which the company battles the election district until the NLRB in Washington stipulates who can or cannot vote (studies 3 and 7).

The studies of illegal company opposition show that employer discrimination against union activists, particularly firing, also has a great impact on the success rate of unions, though the magnitude of the impact varies. Two studies estimate a drop in union success in the area of 7–10 points (studies 8 and 12), while two others estimate declines in union success by 14–24 points (studies 9 and 11). Only in the rare case where a fired worker is ordered reinstated by the NLRB and actually returns to his job *before* the election does breaking the law backfire (study 9). Because of long delays before workers are ordered reinstated and because of worker fears that management will be out to get them if they go back to the job, however, relatively few return to their job before the election.

The evidence that company campaign activities affect election results is substantial and, on the face of it, compelling. Both labor and management practitioners agree that what the company does is important, and companies back this belief by spending time and money on NLRB election campaigns. Given all this, one might expect the conclusion that company opposition affects unionization significantly to go unchallenged.

It has not. In 1976 Professors Julius Getman (Yale Law School), Steven Goldberg (Northwestern Law School), and Jeanne Brett (Northwestern) published a book which argued the opposite: that even deceptive and illegal campaign tactics do not matter (see study 10). They based this conclusion on analysis of the votes of over 1,000 workers in 33 elections which indicated that while company opposition reduced the probability workers would vote union, it did not do so by what they viewed as statistically significant amounts. On the basis of their findings they recommended sweeping changes in NLRB regulation of election campaigning. In an intellectual climate favorable to deregulation this study won considerable attention, and for a period of time may have influenced NLRB policies.[13] More recent analyses of their findings indicate, however, that they reached faulty conclusions from the data. First, they erred by placing too great a stress on statistical significance as opposed to estimated effects: statistics that show company opposition *reduces* voting for a union by "insignificant" amounts do not mean that opposition does not matter, but rather that it is poorly measured or weak. Second, re-analysis of their data by Professor William Dickens of Berkeley found that some forms of company opposition do indeed have statistically significant effects and that, because many NLRB elections are decided by relatively small margins, even modest, "insignificant" effects on individual voters can accumulate to have powerful *significant* effects

---

[13] In one decision in which it decided to weaken regulation of campaigns, the board cited the Getman, Goldberg, and Herman study. *Shopping Mart Food Market, Inc.* 228 LLRB 1311 (1977).

Table 5
Studies of How Company Opposition Affects Union Success in NLRB Elections

Legal Opposition

Study	Finding	
1. *National Industrial Conference Board* study of 140 drives attempting to organized white-collar unions in 1966–1967	Percentage of wins for union depends on amount of company communication:	
	Written or no communication	85%
	Meetings with workers	51
	Meetings and written communication	39
2. *AFL–CIO* study of 495 NLRB elections in 1966–1967	Percentage of wins for union depends on extent of company opposition:	
	No opposition	97%
	Some opposition	50
	Wages increased	37
	Surveillance of union, firing	43
3. *Prosten,* analysis of probability of union win in 130,701 elections in 1962–1977	Percentage of wins falls with time delay between election and petition; is lower in stipulated than in other elections	
4. *Lawler,* study of 155 NLRB elections in 1974–1978	Percentage of election wins for union falls if company hires consultant:	
	If no consultant	71%
	If consultant	23
5. *Drotning,* 41 elections ordered void and rerun by NLRB	Nature of employer's campaign influences voting/ average number of employer communications per election:	
	Union losses	12.5
	Union wins	8.6
6. *Roomkin and Block,* study of 45,155 union representation cases in 1971–1977	Percentage of wins for union falls with delay between petition and actual election	
	Election 0–1 months	50%
	2 months	45
	3 months	41
	4–7 months	30
	8–12 months	30
7. *Seeber and Cooke* study of proportion of workers voting for union representation by state in 1970–1978	One percentage point in proportion of elections to which employers "consent" to the election district changes percentage point union success by one half	

Legal and Illegal Opposition

Study	Finding	
8. *U.S. General Accounting Office,* analysis of 400 8(a)(3) illegal firings or other discrimination for union involvement cases in 368 representation elections	Unions were more successful in campaign in which no employer discrimination occurred than in those which involved an unfair labor practice charge. Success rate:	
	No violation	45%
	Violation	38
9. *Aspin,* study of 71 NLRB elections in which reinstatements were ordered	Percentage of wins for union depends on firing, with unions doing worse unless reinstatees return to job before election:	
	All elections in region:	62%
	with 8(a)(3) firings	48
	Election held before 8(a)(3) case is settled/ discriminatee refuses to return to job:	41%
	Election held after discriminatee returns to job	67
10. *Getman, Goldberg, and Herman,* analysis of 1,293 workers in 31 elections in 1972–1973	Percentage of workers voting union reduced by 10 percent during campaign regardless of campaign tactic	
	Percentage of workers voting union reduced by sizeable, but statistically insignificant, amount by management campaign tactics	

Table 5 *(concluded)*

Legal Opposition

Study	Finding
11. *Dickens,* study of 966 workers in 31 elections in 1972–1973	Percentage of workers voting union reduced by employer activities: Legal campaign −10% Illegal campaign − 4 Employer threatening acts against pro-union workers −15 Percentage of elections unions would win in simulation model: No campaign or light campaign against 53–67 Intense campaign 22–34 Campaign with violations 4–10
12. *Catler,* study of 817 NLRB elections reported on AFL–CIO organizing reports	Company campaigning activities, unfair labor practices, and delay reduce union success, with proportion of union wins lowered by 10 points by unfair labor practice

Sources: 1. National Industrial Conference Board, *White-Collar Unionization* (New York, 1970).

2. Statement of William Kirchner, AFL–CIO Director of Organization, on *A Bill to Amend the National Labor Relations Act in Order to Increase Effectiveness of the Remedies: Hearings on 11.R.11725 Before the Special Subcomm. on Labor of the House Comm. on Education and Labor,* 90th Cong., 1st sess., 1967, 12, 15.

3. Richard Prosten, "The Largest Season Union Organizing in the Last Decade," Proceedings of the 31st meeting of the Industrial Relations Research Association (Madison, Wis., 1978), pp. 240–49.

4. John Lawler, "Labor-Management Consultants in Union Organizing Campaigns," Paper presented at the 34th annual meeting of the Industrial Relations Research Association, Washington, D.C., 1981.

5. John Drotning, "NLRB Remedies for Election Misconduct: An Analysis of Election Outcomes and their Determinants," *Journal of Business* 40, no.2 (April 1967), pp. 137–48.

6. Myron Roomkin and Richard Block, "Case Processing Time and Outcome of Elections: Some Empirical Evidence," *University of Illinois Law Review* 1 (1981), pp. 75–97. Calculated from Tables 2 and 4.

7. R. Seeber and W. Cooke, "The Decline in Union Success in NLRB Representation Elections," *Industrial Relations* 22, no.1 (Winter 1983).

8. United States General Accounting Office, *Concerns Regarding Impact of Employee Charges Against Employers for Unfair Labor Practices* (Washington, D.C.: GAO–HRD 82–80, June 21, 1982).

9. Leslie Aspin, *"A Study of Reinstatement under the National Labor Relations Act"* (Ph.D. diss., MIT, 1966).

10. Jules Getman, Steven Goldberg and Jeanne Herman, *Union Representation Elections: Law and Reality* (New York: Russell Sage Foundation, 1976).

11. William F. Dickens, *"Union Representation Elections: Campaign and Vote"* (Ph.D. diss., MIT, 1980).

12. Susan Catler, "Labor Union Representation Elections: What Determines Who Wins?" (Senior thesis, Harvard University, May 3, 1978).

on the proportion of elections won by unions (see study 12). Viewed from this perspective the Getman, Goldberg, and Herman data are consistent with, rather than inconsistent with, the other work listed in the table.

Granted that company opposition matters, how much of the decline in union electoral success can be attributed to rising management opposition?

From a quarter to a half, according to our analysis of the impact of one major indicator of illegal opposition—unfair labor practices committed by employers—on the proportion of nonagricultural workers choosing representation in NLRB elections (Table 6). Our estimates are based on three distinct studies of the relation between unfair practices and union success in elections: an analysis of success rates across states; an analysis of success rates over time; and an analysis of success rates within states over time. All of our calculations control for diverse other potential determinants of union electoral success, such as region of the country, proportion of workers who are blue-collar, and so on.

I have focused on unfair management practices not because I believe they are management's only effective antiunion weapon—the studies in Table 6 show legal opposition also has a substantial impact on union success—but, rather, because information on those practices but not on legal opposition exists over time and across states. As legal and illegal opposition have presumably grown together, we interpret the analysis as showing the effect of "total" management opposition

Table 6
Estimates of the Effect of Management Unfair Labor Practices on Percentage of Nonagricultural Work Force Newly Organized in NLRB Elections

Analysis and Data Set	Estimated Impact of 10 Percent Increase in Unfair Practices per Election on Proportion of Workers Newly Organized in NLRB Elections	Estimated Proportion of Decline in Nonagricultural Work Force Organized in NLRB Elections Due to Increased Management Unfair Labor Practices
1. Comparison of union success across states, 1950–1978	−2.5%	28%
2. Comparison of union success within states over time, 1950–1978	−3.4	38
3. Comparison of union success over time, 1950–1980	−6	49

Source: R. B. Freeman, "The Simple Economics of Declining Union Density," (NBER Working Paper, 1983). For corroborating estimates of the effect of unfair labor practices on new unionization using a different model, see David Ellwood and Glenn Fine, "Effects of Right-to-Work Laws on Union Organizing," (NBER Working Paper, 1983). We thank Ellwood and Fine for providing us with their data set for the analysis in lines 1 and 2. In lines 1 and 2, the measure of management unfair practices is all CA cases, as reported in the National Labor Relations Board," *Annual Reports*, divided by nonagricultural work force. In line 3, the measures of management unfair practices are 8(a)(3) cases, those involving employer penalization of worker for union activity, divided by workers in elections.

on union success, not of illegal opposition only.

So interpreted, the analyses show that employer opposition has a substantial and highly statistically significant depressant effect on union success rates (the first column), which goes a long way to explaining the decline in union organization of new workers in NLRB elections. For every 10 percent change in unfair labor practices per election, our estimates suggest that unionization of new workers falls from about 3 percent to 6 percent. From 1950 to 1980, when unfair labor practices per election increased sixfold, we further estimate that the rise in management opposition explains from over a quarter to nearly a half of the decline in union success organizing through NLRB elections. Put differently, had employer opposition to unionism remained at 1950 levels, our calculations suggest that unions would have organized about twice the proportion of the unorganized in 1980 as they in fact did.

The point is not that unfair practices per se have hurt unions in NLRB elections, though

they obviously have, but that opposition, broadly defined, is a major cause of the slow strangulation of private sector unionism. Analysis with other indicators of opposition (workers fired for back-pay, the decline in consent elections) show comparable results.[14]

The Role of Public Policy

In 1977 the AFL–CIO proposed a major piece of legislation, the Labor Law Reform Bill of 1977, designed to penalize more severely employers who commit unfair labor practices and thus ease the problem of organizing. Underlying this bill was a belief that if public policy toward unionization were different, so too would be union success in NLRB elections. What evidence is there, if any, that legal changes affect union organization?

There are, I believe, three pieces of evidence which suggest that the specific institu-

---

[14]The Seeber and Cooke study in Table 5 explains virtually all of the decline in union success in NLRB elections with a very different indicator, the proportion of elections which are "consent" elections.

tional mechanisms by which a country regulates unionization, and in particular allows management to fight unionization, are critical factors in unionization.

1. Canada. The principal difference between unionization in the United States and in Canada is that U.S. laws allow management to conduct lengthy, well-funded election campaigns against unions. Canadian labor law does not permit such activity. Indeed, in most provinces a union is certified without any secret ballot campaign at all: it requires 60 percent or so of workers signing authorization cards. Result: a growing unionization in Canada.

2. Right-to-Work. Under the Taft-Hartley law, states are allowed to pass so-called "right-to-work" laws which outlaw union shops (workplaces where workers must join a union or the equivalent, pay dues, within 30 days to maintain their jobs). In these states unions face serious "free rider" problems which weaken them financially and make organizing more difficult. The free rider problem is that some workers will enjoy all the benefits of unionism but not pay dues for those benefits. In right-to-work states upwards of 20 percent of workers covered by collective bargaining are not union members, compared to 10 percent elsewhere in the country. A careful analysis of unionization across states and over time by Glenn Fine and David Ellwood of Harvard University finds that new organizing in a state is reduced by about one third by passage of a right-to-work law.[15]

3. Public Sector Unionization. The great growth of public sector unionization in the United States was *preceded* by new public sector labor laws which often required municipalities to bargain with workers who had chosen to unionize. Before these laws, mu-

nicipalities could simply refuse to bargain with public sector unions; since strikes were generally illegal, workers had no easy way of "forcing" management to recognize them. Analyses of the relationship between the presence of law favorable to bargaining and unionization across states and of the relationship between the timing of union growth and passage of laws within states shows that public sector unionization was greatly enhanced by changes in the law.[16]

From these diverse alternative legal environments—Canada, right-to-work versus non-right-to-work states, U.S. public sector—I conclude that the labor law of the country does indeed influence the success of unions in representing workers. Under a different legal environment U.S. employers would behave differently, and unions might fare better in organizing the work force.

CONCLUSION

The declining rate of success of unions in NLRB representation elections is a critical factor in the fall in union density in past decades. Studies of the causes of the decline suggest that perhaps 40 percent is due to increased management opposition; perhaps 20 percent is due to reduced union organizing effort per nonunion worker, with the remainder due in part to structural changes in the economy and in part to unknown forces. As the calculations yielding these figures take the change in management opposition and the change in union organizing effort as exogenous, the figures should not be viewed as showing the "ultimate" forces at work. To some extent at least both management opposition and union organizing effort are responses to a changing economic and legal environment. What the calculations and studies underlying them do show, is that success or failure in NLRB elections, and thus the future of unionization in the United States can be traced back to specific activities by labor and management rather than to amorphous general social developments.

---

[15]Dave Ellwood and Glenn Fine, "Effect of Right-to-Work Laws on Union Organizing" (NBER Working Paper no. 1116, May 1983). See Richard Freeman and James Medoff, "New Estimates of Private Sector Unionism in the United States," *Industrial and Labor Relations Review*, Table 6, for number of workers covered by collective bargaining but who are not union members.

---

[16]Harrison Lauer, "The Effect of Police Unions" (Undergraduate thesis, Harvard University, May 1981).

READING 12

American Labor and the Industrial Crisis*

Michael J. Piore[†]

Union power is declining. Rigid ways of defining jobs and setting wages in old mass production industries are outmoded. New technologies and smaller firms require more flexible work practices.

American labor is in crisis. Its membership is on the wane, it has suffered crucial legislative defeats, and it has fallen victim to successful union-busting by the president of the United States. Labor's troubles are complex and have a number of roots in its own history, and in the growing industrial and economic malaise of our age.

DECLINE IN UNION POWER

The ebbing of union power, even in the last decade, has been very gradual. Two factors could have accounted for this: the exhaustion of the potential for new members in the mass production industries which labor had broken into in the 1930s; and the shift in the labor force toward service industries and marginal groups that were hard to organize, such as women and youth. Membership losses, moreover, were balanced in the 1960s by dramatic breakthroughs in organization and collective bargaining in the public sector, which were not fully reflected in dues-paying membership figures, and which in any case gave a feel-

*Reprinted from *Challenge*, March–April 1982, pp. 5–11. This article is reprinted with the permission of publisher, M. E. Sharpe, Inc., Armonk, New York, 10504.

†*Michael J. Piore is Professor of Economics and Mitsui Professor, Problems of Contemporary Technology, at MIT. This article is adapted from his address before the Colloque de l'Association d'Economie Politique, Université du Québec à Montréal, and is based on research financed by the German Marshall Fund of the United States. The German Marshall Fund does not necessarily endorse the views expressed here.*

ing of advance which belied the numbers. Labor's political difficulties, symbolized by the nomination of George McGovern by the Democrats in 1972, over the AFL–CIO's bitter opposition, were easily attributed to the war in Vietnam, which was, after all, not a real labor issue.

What is new in the current situation—and what makes it plausible to characterize it as a *crisis*—is that union power appears for the first time to be in real jeopardy in industries that have been its traditional bastions of strength. Throughout most of the postwar period, the labor movement thought it was operating in these industries—and in American society as a whole, to the extent that executives of those industries constituted the leadership of the American business community—under an implicit agreement. This agreement recognized the right, even the desirability, of union organization and collective bargaining, and made the protection of that right a fundamental government responsibility.

The existence of an accord between big business and big labor on this question and on the basic structure of, and goals for, American society was symbolized by the Labor-Management Committee formed by John T. Dunlop, under federal auspices and with presidential blessings, to worry about the economic crises of the 1970s. The accord may never have been quite as robust as labor had imagined. But, whatever its previous strength, it seemed suddenly to fall apart in the summer of 1978, when the AFL–CIO was defeated in an all-out effort to pass labor law reform. The defeat was generated by an extensive business lobbying campaign in which the leadership of organized industry acquiesced and which it even seemed at times actually to support. The defeat was particularly ominous because it occurred under a Democratic president and in a Congress whose key members were thought to be labor's special political allies. It forced labor to recognize belatedly a new employer shop strategy of union avoidance which had actually been developing at the plant level for some time. The key to this new strategy is an increasingly sophisticated set of techniques for forestalling union organization and managing nonunion shops in a way which seems genuinely to circumvent their employees' desire to join unions. It is still possible to find American managers who tolerate unions, but it is no longer possible—as it was in much of the postwar period—to find companies which are committed to operating in an organized environment.

A watershed in this crisis was reached in August 1981 when President Reagan dismissed the striking air traffic controllers. This was the first open attempt on the part of the federal government to break a trade union (public or private) since the 1930s. Although the president has denied that this is a general policy, his own rhetoric and that of other administration officials has essentially the same flavor as the new antiunion strategy of the private sector. It has had a chilling effect upon an already demoralized rank-and-file.

REGULATION AND THE DIVISION OF LABOR

One way of illuminating the situation of labor today is to see its crisis as part of a broader "regulatory" crisis of the economy. The word *regulatory*, as used here, does not refer to the regulation of business practices by government, but rather to the term employed in *la théorie de la régulation*, as elaborated by a group of French theorists (see the reference to Robert Boyer's work in *For Further Reading*). In that context, "regulation" is the system of institutions that keeps an economy in balance and ensures its further growth and development.

According to this theory, national economies pass through a distinct set of regulatory regimes. Each regime is embodied in a set of institutions specific to a particular period of history and peculiar to a given national content. Those institutions operate as a system to coordinate economic activities, maintain macroeconomic stability, and permit economic growth. The growth process, however, involves qualitative changes in the economic structure which eventually render a set of institutions obsolete: this means that they are less and less successful in performing their coordinating and stabilizing functions. The ensuing imbalance between the underlying structures and the institutional complex in which it is housed is the source of a regulatory crisis, which can be resolved only through the creation of a new institutional structure appropriate to the economy in its altered state.

What relationship does the decline of the labor movement have to the regulatory crisis? The key may be found in the specialization of productive resources which classical economists refer to as the division of labor. It is this division of labor, the source of apparently endless advances in productivity, that has been an essential regulatory mechanism in the industrial era. It is limited, however, by the extent of the market. Specialization makes it difficult to shift resources from one use to another. Hence, unless the market expands to absorb the increased output which specialization permits, that output is simply dissipated in supporting the resources when they become unemployed. For most of this century, the division of labor has taken the form of an increasing fragmentation of productive tasks and the assignment of those tasks to highly specialized equipment or to narrowly trained workers. This is a process known as *Taylorism*, after Frederick Taylor, who developed the principles of "scientific management" that underlie the organization of most industrial plants in the United States.

The central institution in this process has been the modern corporation. The corporation arose to *organize* the market and thereby insure the progressive extension of stable demand which would permit the realization of the economies of scale inherent in the continuous division of labor. Prior to the development of this institution in the late 19th century, the economy was primarily dependent upon the price system to coordinate individual markets and maintain macroeconomic balance more or less as envisaged in neoclassical economic theory. With the advent of the corporation, however, individual markets were increasingly controlled by the direct efforts of large enterprises. These enterprises stabilized prices, and made them instruments in the strategy of organization and control.

Mass production corporations were complemented by a set of generally smaller enterprises. These enterprises operated with much less highly specialized resources, producing goods and services in small batches for limited markets. Generally, they made specialized producers' goods, luxury consumer items, and new innovative products for which a mass market had not yet developed. They absorbed increases in the demand for mass market items which were too short-lived to sustain long-term investment in fixed capital and specialized labor.

The small-batch producers operated either as an adjunct to the planned corporate economy, moving between markets in response to fluctuations in demand, or else they competed on the basis of quality and ingenuity. They, like the larger corporations, sought to operate in an environment of stable prices.

These institutions had a particular response to macroeconomic fluctuations. When faced with weak demand, as in a recession, the large corporations preferred to manipulate the market structure in an effort to restore the demand for their own products, rather than to cut prices. The smaller, more flexible enterprises sought to shift into whatever sectors happened to remain strong. In extreme cases, both institutions tried to cut costs, particularly wages. As the corporate economy came increasingly to center in the mass consumption industries, the attempt to restore profits by cutting wages began to have a perverse effect, undermining the demand upon which recovery was ultimately dependent. This defect of macroeconomic regulation in a corporate-based economy ultimately produced the Great Depression, which can in this way be interpreted as the last fundamental regulatory crisis.

That crisis was overcome by a set of institutions put in place in the immediate postwar period. The particular institutions differed in each country, but in all countries the arrangements governing labor-management relations were crucial. In various ways, these arrangements operated to place a floor under the wage rate in an economic downturn and to insure, generally through wage-setting procedures, that national consumer purchasing power expanded at the rate required to absorb the growing output generated by further division of labor. Because this system involves a relatively rigid wage and price structure, it is dependent upon excess supplies of labor and raw materials available on call at prevailing prices. Certain subsidiary features of the postwar system insured these.

DECLINE OF DOMESTIC MARKETS

This is the regulatory structure which is now in crisis. The basic cause of the crisis is that the mass consumption industries toward which the postwar expansion was keyed have outgrown their domestic markets. The postwar institutional arrangements which were designed to insure the expansion of these domestic markets can thus no longer sustain further division of labor. In the attempt to justify these arrangements, the major industrial countries have come into direct competition for each others' markets and those of the developing world.

An obvious solution to the crisis would be to reproduce on an international scale a system analogous to that which successfully regulated the domestic economies of the industrial nations in the earlier postwar decades. Further expansion would then be based upon a continued extension of Taylorism in the same mass production industries which led earlier postwar growth. This solution is widely discussed, and one can detect, particularly in the growth and strategic development of multinational corporations, some movement in these directions. But it is not possible to detect in this movement anything like a full-fledged regulatory system.

In its absence, what seems to be developing is a shift away from mass markets to a more differentiated output produced in smaller, batch-oriented enterprises. This could be a reaction to the crisis itself: in the prevailing atmosphere of uncertainty and confusion, producers are avoiding long-term, fixed commitments by resorting to the more flexible techniques which have served as an adjunct to the corporate economy. The new microprocessor, computer-based technologies, however, seem to favor this form of production, and in these technologies, an alternative to Taylorism may be emerging.

Under these circumstances, it could be said that unions have simply become irrelevant to the country's economic health and well-being. Arrangements which were originally perceived as central to macroeconomic stability have been "marginalized." One might argue that this has permitted the natural hostility of the business community to labor to reemerge as the guiding force of their labor policies. There is undoubtedly some truth to this view, but it does not seem to explain the emergent managerial attitudes as these are manifest in conversation. These attitudes seem to be strongest among line managers, not those who must deal with national economic policy or international corporate strategy. They involve a conviction which grows out of felt experience, not ideology, and older managers describe a change which has taken place in their own attitudes over time.

Economists, especially those with little direct experience in labor-management relations, are prone to argue that the problem is the high wages which unions have imposed upon American industry. This too would be consistent with the regulatory crisis as I have diagnosed it, since high wages make it difficult for the United States to compete with other countries and that handicap would have become more severe as internationalization proceeded. But wages do not seem to be a principal concern of American businessmen when they discuss labor problems. Indeed, a number of American companies are willing to pay even higher wages, and absorb further costs by allocating specialized managerial time and attention, in order to avoid union organization. These companies—and indeed American management in general—report that their principal concern is with the restraints which unions impose upon the ability to organize production efficiently. They feel unable to design jobs, assign workers, or utilize tools and equipment in a productive way. These constrictions are seen as extreme in comparison to production in most other countries of the world, a view which is typically confirmed by foreign managers working in the United States.

There is a curious, even paradoxical, twist to complaints of this kind. American unions have a reputation for being extremely pragmatic—rooted in and organized around the enterprise (or even the shop) and strongly attached to its survival. American workers have been thought to be open to innovation and receptive to technological change. The exceptions to this openness have been craft unions, not the industrial unions around which the current debate is centered. And there is literature going back to the 1930s arguing that union-organized plants in the United States were actually more efficient than their nonunion competitors because unions promoted the best managerial practice.

This paradox suggests that perhaps it is the peculiar nature of American trade unions which is at issue, not so much in itself but relative to present trends in technology. While most postwar labor relations systems have very similar macroeconomic properties, the industrial unions which have dominated American labor relations in the postwar period have a unique mode of effectuating worker rights in the shop itself.

THE PECULIARITIES OF AMERICAN JOB CONTROL

American industrial unions have sought to control the specific details of the labor bargain for individual workers in the shop through a system of job definition. Each job is defined in very careful and elaborate detail. The union then imposes upon this detailed job structure a set of negotiated wages, actually specifying how much the employer must pay for *each* job or work task; a set of "job security" provisions which determine how those jobs (and hence the wages attached to them) are to be distributed among the workers; and a set of disciplinary standards which limit, in the light of each worker's own particular work requirements, what obligations he or she has to the employer and how a failure to meet those obligations will be sanctioned. By and large, this procedure leaves American employers free to define any set of jobs they wish, and that freedom has generally been emphasized in discussions of American industrial relations. But what is often missed in these discussions is that the freedom is conditional: the jobs must be defined; the job definitions must be stabilized over a long enough period to give them real meaning; and the employer must accept the wages, worker allocations, and disciplinary procedures which his job definitions imply.

Management complaints center around this complex of practices. The dominant strategy in the "union-avoidance" movement which developed in the last decade has been one of flexible work assignment, a system in which the precise—but also rigid—job definitions of the past are discarded in favor of one where job content varies freely with the flow and character of work. This is also the salient characteristic of the very limited union efforts to accommodate managerial concerns directly. The major union effort along these lines is the Quality of Work Life Program developed by General Motors with the United Automobile Workers. What many fail to realize, however, is that the flexible job assignments—the program's salient feature from the managerial point of view—mean an abandonment of the traditional American industrial union procedure for controlling wage determination, job security, and discipline.

No other system of union control is comparable to that in the United States. In some countries, in fact, organized labor is not present in the shop at all. Unions typically negotiate general standards at an industry (or interindustry) level which impose broad limits upon employer practices but which leave managers free to specify—and change—the precise details of work. Where unions are present in the shop and do attempt to control work practice, they operate at a very different level of decision-making. German codetermination, for example, focuses upon investment decisions and the selection of technology. French control over layoffs (which is actually exercised by government work inspectors, not unions) focuses upon employment levels and broad social categories of workers, not specific jobs. From one perspective, these foreign systems involve a degree of interference with the actual management of the enterprise which American unions abjure. To us, such control is a form of worker participation in management which borders on socialism. But it does leave the *line* manager almost complete freedom and flexibility. And that is what is lacking in organized American shops. Even foreign labor movements that have tried to exercise detailed control over actual wage payments seem to have done so in a manner which does not require rigid job definition. The Italians, for example, have sought to impose a system which pays for skill inherent in the worker, irrespective of what he does. The Japanese wage payment system tends to reflect seniority, another trait inherent in the worker, not in the work.

THE ORIGINS OF THE AMERICAN SYSTEM

How and why did the peculiar American system of job control develop? In casting around for an explanation of the American industrial system, one is struck by how readily it dovetails with "scientific management" as preached by Frederick Taylor. Taylor's central tenet was that work could be clearly defined in terms of a set of discrete tasks; that it should be broken down into those tasks, and that jobs should be built up out of a combination of them. The elements to which American unions have come to attach wages and whose distribution the job security provisions of union contracts control are the very tasks which Taylor's industrial engineers defined. And the unions have adapted, for purposes of wage determination, a set of administrative instruments which industrial engineers invented. The two most prominent of these are time-motion study and job evaluation. Thus, to a very large extent, the practice of American industrial unionism has come to rest upon, indeed to presuppose, Taylorism. And, because of this one can argue that the crisis of American unions is being aggravated—if indeed it has not actually been created—by a crisis of Taylorism. Having been built upon the principles of scientific management, American unions were pragmatic and progressive so long as scientific management was the philosophy of American management. To the extent that technical progress grew out of the implementation of these principles, unions which forced management to adopt them did make management more efficient and effective. But if technological efficiency is no longer carried by, or consonant with, Taylorism, it is easy to understand why a labor movement which presupposes that form of management should become increasingly irksome to employers.

This leads to two questions: First, how did American union practice, in contrast to that abroad, come to be closely tied to Taylorism? Second, why exactly is Taylorism in crisis?

The answer to the first question appears to be that American union practice actually grew up around Taylorism. American industrial unionism dates from the late 30s and its practices were adjusted to the patterns of technology and management prevailing in that period and during the Second World War which followed. This was a time when the principles of scientific management dominated the thinking not only of American managers but of most interpreters of industrial society. Taylor's own work had been modified, it is true, by the recognition of certain psychological components of worker behavior and motivation, but these had been essentially *added on* to the set of principles about job design which involved task specification. The trends in the composition of output, moreover—mass consumption goods before and after the war, long runs of standardized military materiel during the war itself—were most favorable to the effective and profitable application of those kinds of management principles. Finally, the controversy surrounding the original introduction of mass production technology had subsided and been forgotten. The major concerns of workers were with job insecurity and the favoritism and petty despotism of line supervision to which the extreme job scarcity of the Depression gave rise. In the subsequent war period, workers focused on the equitable distribution of wages and sacrifices in the national emergency. These concerns had very little to do with the technology which scientific management seemed to dictate. Hence unions were led to see in these managerial principles a set of neutral, even natural, instruments which could be used to preserve the ends of equitable wage administration, work distribution, and industrial discipline. Once unions adopted them for these purposes, all gains became bound up in their continued application.

Unions abroad developed very differently. First, the war constituted a much more fundamental break with the prewar union movement; in most countries, the labor movement was suppressed by the wartime regimes, and the labor relations institutions which emerged in the postwar period were new creations. Second, unions abroad were unrepresented in the shop, so that they had very little to do with the kind of micro-application of Taylorism around which American union practice developed. Thus, when practitioners of industrial relations abroad did adopt an instrument similar to those used in the United States, it did not have the same implications for shop practice. The French *système Parodi* is a system of job evaluation comparable to those characteristic in American wage determination; it was introduced at essentially the same time as American practice was developing. But the *système Parodi* is a national plan, applicable to all jobs, and imposed not by the unions but by the state. Because it had to encompass so many different jobs, it could never use the extremely narrow job definitions characteristic in the United States. And without plant level organization, it could not be applied to control shop practice in minute detail.

Shop level organization finally did emerge in much of Europe, but in the late 1960s, at a historical moment different in several important respects from the post-depression and then postwar framework in which American unions had elaborated their procedures. The 1960s were years of great economic prosperity; workers were able to concentrate upon a set of grievances connected with the conditions of work as opposed to those rooted in the scarcity of work itself. And they traced many of the work characteristics they found obnoxious to the application of Taylorism. American workers in this period also showed some of the militancy which was found in Western Europe and some of their resentment too was directed at the nature of industrial work, but that militancy never manifested itself in a full-fledged worker movement, let alone an articulated campaign against scientific management. One reason why it did not was that the union leadership clearly saw workers' gains of the last 30 years as embedded in these principles. The rank-and-file must at least have *sensed* that connection. In fact, the real changes in the United States in this period came in the organization of work in the public sector: the newly formed unions there tended to borrow the very instruments of job control which industrial unions had fashioned out of scientific management. Lastly, however, in the period when plant-level unionism was developing in Europe, Taylorism as a theory of management was already on the wane: the mass markets to which the principles of Taylorism seemed best adapted had begun to disintegrate; managers were already looking, if only very tentatively, for alternative forms of work organization. A sharp break with the older technology had not yet emerged, but the world no longer automatically accepted scientific management as synonymous with economic development, as it had in the 1930s.

TWO CRISES: TAYLORISM AND REGULATION

If the reasons are clear why the crisis of the American labor movement is related to the crisis of Taylorism, the reason for the crisis of Taylorism itself is not so obvious. A number of different indicators—the general climate of confusion and uncertainty among business decision-makers, the inability of macroeconomic models to track the economy, the deterioration in economic performance in terms of unemployment, inflation, and growth—suggest that we are in a regulatory crisis. Resolving that crisis does not necessarily mean abandoning the continued division of labor along the lines which development has followed in the past. As suggested above, it should, at least in principle, be possible to recreate on a multinational scale some analogue to the structures which insured expansion of national economies in the earlier postwar period.

The alternative of introducing more flexible production techniques to meet the demands of increasingly fragmented, specialized, and rapidly shifting markets may simply be a reaction to the crisis itself, a way of coping with the heightened confusion and uncertainty. Initially, that was precisely the case. But as the new technologies have developed, they seem to favor small-scale batch production. They clearly have a differential effect upon the cost of this form of production relative to the mass production based upon Taylorism, and hence, the advantages of organizing mass markets (or covering the cost of departing from them to create more specialized individual products) are decreasing rapidly. This has been apparent for some time in formal engineering studies. But it is now also evident in the comments of line managers. *Business Week* (August 3, 1981), for example, concludes on the basis of its interviews that computer-aided manufacturing "promises to bring automation to the batch production of goods in runs of less than 50 units," and that future factories will be producing much shorter runs. It is possible that, as this technology develops further, it will virtually eliminate the economies of scale associated with Taylorism.

Thus far, the expansion of computer-based technologies has occurred in an atmosphere of heightening international competition as well. Indeed, it has been spurred in the last several years by fears among producers that if they do not keep abreast of developments they will lose their markets to foreign competitors. But, to the extent that such techniques are actually economical in much smaller markets, countries will eventually become less dependent on expanding trade to obtain productivity advances. One can imagine a mode of regulation based on the new techniques, smaller enterprises, and a more differentiated product mix which would not require a new international economic order at all. This alternative could rest instead upon the expansion of domestic demand through industrial relations and labor market arrangements very similar in their macroeconomic properties to those which operated toward this end in the past.

Thus, it appears that there are really two alternative resolutions to the regulatory crisis. One of these would be a return to Taylorism but under a new international regulatory system. The other, which seems much more consonant with current trends, is a regulatory system based on the maintenance of domestic demand but with a new, more flexible technique of production.

Unfortunately, neither alternative will solve the problems of the American labor movement. The first alternative would permit labor to retain (or return to) its traditional forms of job control in the shop; but society would no longer depend on organized labor to maintain macroeconomic stability. In a new international division of labor, the domestic purchasing power which organized labor could assure would not be a significant factor in maintaining industrial demand. There would be no further pressure for the implicit accord with business leadership which prevailed in the earlier postwar period decades and which Dunlop's Labor-Management Committee sought to revive.

Under the second alternative, domestic purchasing power would again become critical, and this might restore the incentive for business to accommodate a labor movement as it did in earlier postwar decades. But such an arrangement would require flexibility in the technology and the job structure which is inconsistent with labor's traditional forms of job control. One way or the other, therefore, it appears that the current regulatory crisis will require a major readjustment on the part of the American labor movement if it is to survive.

FOR FURTHER READING

The following books and articles may be of interest to readers who would like to explore the topics in the article more fully.

American Labor

Aglietta, Michel. *Regulation et Crise du Capitalisme.* Paris: Calmann-Levy, 1976.

Berger, Suzanne, and Michael J. Piore. *Dualism and Discontinuity in Industrial Societies.* New York: Cambridge University Press, 1980.

Bowles, Samuel, and Herbert Gintis. *The Crisis of Liberal Democratic Capitalism: The Case of the United States.* Amherst: University of Massachusetts, Department of Economics, March 1980.

Boyer, Robert. *"La Crise Actuelle: Une Mise en Perspective Historique." Critique de l'Economie Politique,* May 1979.

Boyer, Robert. *Rapport Salarial et Analyses en Terme de Regulation.* CEPREMAP No. 8017, June 1980.

Boyer, Robert. *Les Transformations du Rapport Salarial dans la Crise: Une Interpretation de ses Aspects Sociaux et Economiques.* CEPREMAP No. 8105, February 1981.

Boyer, Robert, and J. Mistral. *Accumulation, Inflation, Crises.* Paris: P.U.F., 1978.

Chandler, Alfred D., Jr. *The Invisible Hand, the Managerial Revolution in American Business.* Cambridge, Mass.: Harvard University Press, 1977.

March, James G. and Herbert A. Simon. *Organizations.* New York: John Wiley & Sons, 1958.

Marris, Robin. *The Economics of Managerial Capitalism.* The Fici Press, 1964.

Piore, Michael J. *Birds of Passage: Migrant Labor and Industrial Societies.* New York: Cambridge University Press, 1979.

Piore, Michael J. *Convergence in Industrial Relations? The Case of France and the United States.* Cambridge, Mass.: MIT Press, Department of Economics Working Paper no. 286, July 1981(B).

Piore, Michael J. *The Theory of Macro-Economic Regulation and the Current Economic Crisis in the United States.* Cambridge, Mass.: MIT Press, Department of Economics Working Paper no. 285, July 1981(A).

Piore, Michael J. *Italian Small Business Development: Lessons for U.S. Industrial Policy.* Cambridge, Mass.: MIT Press, Department of Economics Working Paper no. 288, August 1981.

Sabel, Charles. *Work and Politics, the Industrial Division of Labor in the Age of Fordism.* New York: Cambridge University Press, 1982.

Ross, Arthur. *Trade Union Wage Policy.* Berkeley: University of California Press, 1948.

READING 13

An Army without a Strategy*

Howard Banks[†]

Today's trade union leaders, like yesterday's generals, are fighting the last war. That is why they are losing.

The list of trade union leaders who prefer to risk their members' jobs rather than accept economic reality grows longer. The leader of the airline pilots, Henry Duffy, is but the latest recruit. The list includes the United Auto Workers' Owen Bieber, the United Steelworkers' Lloyd McBride, and William Winpisinger of the International Association of Machinists.

What did they talk about at the recent AFL–CIO meeting in Hollywood, Florida? How to meet Japanese competition? How to deal with the continued shift of the United States from an industrial economy to a service economy? How to improve productivity? None of these—or at least none of these was center stage. Much of the talk was standard old-line bash-the-boss stuff. "It's all-out war," said one union official. He was talking of Continental Airlines' use of bankruptcy law to break its labor contract. The union men waxed indignant about the strikebreaking at Phelps Dodge and the production deals with foreigners in the steel and auto industries. They lamented the shrinking share of the work force with union cards, now less than 18 percent compared with 29 percent in 1970. They lamented this decline without seriously examining the reasons for it. It was a movement stuck in the 1930s and unprepared for the 1980s. One wonders what Samuel Gompers would have thought. Or John L. Lewis.

*Reprinted by permission of Forbes Magazine, October 24, 1983. © Forbes Inc. 1983, pp. 41–42.

†*Howard Banks is Manager, Washington Bureau, Forbes Magazine.*

The prevailing mood was: The recession is over and so it's time to end givebacks. A common resentment was that the companies had signed contracts and later gone to the workers or the courts to break the agreements. Shouldn't the bosses be forced to stick by the contracts they signed, the AFL–CIO men asked? They forget that the unions force the companies to sign such contracts under the threat of a business-destroying strike. And a big complaint: Union men and women are voting with their feet to cross picket lines in order to preserve their jobs.

No one asked: Why are union members themselves voting against high wages and low productivity by buying Japanese autos and TV sets? That was the question they should have asked.

Instead, the Steelworkers' union led a fight to the death at the Bunker Hill lead mining and smelting operation. Now the operation is permanently closed. At Phelps Dodge's loss-making Arizona copper refinery, that union tried again. The company fought back and kept the operation going as union people crossed over to work—at lower pay, yes, but working.

At Phelps Dodge the Steelworkers' union chose to ignore the copper industry's circumstances. U.S.-mined and refined metal has to surmount higher labor costs and a 10-cent-a-pound penalty for pollution control costs here, even though copper sells at depressed world prices. In the basic steel industry the union ignored for years the obvious trend of increasing capacity in newly industrialized nations such as South Korea, which was even competitive with Japanese industry. The result of failing to work with industry until it is too late: The proposed merger between LTV's Jones and Laughlin and Republic Steel, which will cost thousands of union jobs, as will proposed deals such as U.S. Steel's effort to buy and roll low-cost slabs from British Steel.

In the automobile industry, General Motors is working to get all its small cars from the Japanese, either as direct imports from Suzuki and Isuzu or through joint production with Toyota. If these deals go through and work, then in the next few years Ford and Chrysler could follow, substituting imports for domestically made cars. But the union leadership ignores this, saying that it wants to get back the givebacks and more in next year's negotiations.

Paradoxically, it is industries where strong unions have won the softest work rules and the fattest wage and benefit packages that are in the greatest trouble. Nowhere is this clearer than in the airline industry, where management and unions grew fat and lazy in the old protected environment. Pay for all employees in the nation's major airlines in 1982 averaged $39,400—$31,000 if the pilots' pay is excluded. Even with some givebacks, the average increased to almost $42,000 in early 1983, according to the Air Transport Association.

A sharp contrast is provided by the $22,000 average for all employees in the newer, non-unionized small airlines that have grown as a result of deregulation's competitive freedom. They provide less than five percent of the industry's total capacity, but that is sufficient to force the majors to keep fares down. For cockpit crews, pilots, copilots, and engineers, average pay at the majors is $70,000 or $100,000 with fringe benefits, and that is for what amounts to two weeks' work a month. Pilots for the smaller airlines average half that compensation.

The Machinists struck Continental earlier and lost. Enough mechanics crashed the lines to keep their $16-an-hour jobs, and there were plenty of nonunion mechanics willing to take $10 an hour to fill the gaps. Fighting their unions is costing Continental plenty. But what was the alternative? Going out of business, which, without Chapter 11, would have happened by year-end.

Now it is the pilots' turn. The position taken by Duffy, president of the Air Line Pilots Association, is that after more than $1 billion in givebacks by all the unions, the airlines are still slashing fares and almost all are losing money. "I have no intention of presiding over the dissolution of wages and conditions achieved over five decades of negotiations," he says. His attitude seems to be: Let the public pay through higher fares to keep his members in sports cars.

The saddest thing is that the unions have no policies to cope with what is happening. The best they can do is cling to some idea of a bailout, currently called "industrial policy," which boils down to federal subsidies to keep high-wage, unionized businesses alive.

Is the alternative to force Americans to work at South Korean wage levels? If it were, the unions would be right to fight. But the real alternative is better productivity—which in the long run is the only thing that can make higher wages possible. In the airlines, the non-union carriers have shown that a stewardess can sell tickets, too, and that a pilot can fly more than 55 hours a month. Throwing out the old work rules is the place to start. In the automobile industry, the medical benefits are a scandal, and union cooperation in that area could cut car costs by hundreds of dollars without touching pay levels. That might make some greedy doctors and hypochondriac workers unhappy, but it wouldn't really reduce the level of health care. Where is the new leadership that could bring the great American trade union movement into the last half of the 20th century?

READING 14

Finances of American Unions in the 1970s*

Neil Sheflin and Leo Troy†

The aggregate finances of American unions in the 1970s are examined and compared with their state in 1962. We find that unions' real financial wealth declined in the 1970s to the levels of the previous decade, while their real income grew at a much slower rate than during the 1960s. These results suggest that unions may face financial as well as operational problems in the future.

I. INTRODUCTION: ISSUES, DATA, AND SOURCES

There has been a resurgence of interest in the condition and prospects of organized labor in the United States.[1] Much of the attention has focused on the implications of structural changes in the American economy and labor force for union growth, examining such issues as the growing service orientation of the economy, the increasing representation of women and minorities in the labor force, and the migration of industry and jobs from industrial states to the Sun Belt.[2] These forces have affected the financial position of unions as well as their membership. Yet, the area of union finances has been largely ignored, even though it is clearly an important consideration in evaluating their current state and future directions. The level of unions' assets and net income provides a significant measure of their ability to finance strikes and organizational and political activities. The performance of organized labor's assets also provides information about the effectiveness of unions as managerial organizations, a subject that is likely to draw increased scholarly attention given the economic and political power of unions and the implications of the Labor-Management Reporting and Disclosure Act of 1959.

In this paper, we examine union finances in the 1970s and compare them with the 1960s. The comparison mirrors some of the forces that have affected union membership in both decades and provides insights into unions' prospects for growth in the 1980s. This paper also provides some basis for examining unions' performance as managerial and administrative organizations.

The data used in this study are from reports filed with the U.S. Department of Labor (USDL) under the requirements of the Labor-Management Reporting and Disclosure Act of 1959 and transcribed into machine-readable form by USDL. The coverage is of funds generated by unions from members and from property owned or administered by unions. Excluded are finances relating to pension and benefit plans established under collective bargaining or initiated by employers and benefits financed by employers or members and managed under trust agreements. Union members' self-financed and administered plans are included.

Adjustments were made to eliminate, as much as possible, interunion fund flows and receipts and disbursements originating from Canadian affiliates of international organizations. However, the assets and liabilities of unions were consolidated without adjustment, since interunion claims could not be distinguished and netted from the aggregates.

Some errors and discrepancies may remain in the data due to data entry errors on the part of USDL. In addition, differences in accounting treatments of various items and different reporting periods of nearly 50,000 separate organizations also introduce discrepancies when aggregated.

---

*Reprinted with permission from *Journal of Labor Research* 4, no. 2 (Spring 1983), pp. 149–57.

†*Professors Sheflin and Troy are on the faculty at Rutgers University, New Brunswick, N.J.*

[1] See, for example, the Symposium in *Executive* (1980), especially Estey (1980), Troy and Sheflin (1980), and Rosow (1980).

[2] *See* Troy and Sheflin (1980).

Deflation was done with the implicit GNP deflator. Membership figures are those used by the USDL, despite some serious doubts about the accuracy of these figures.[3]

II. Union Wealth in the 1960s and 1970s

The assets of organized labor reached new heights in the 1970s, totalling nearly $4 billion in 1976. Union wealth had doubled since 1962, and increased by approximately 50 percent since 1969. American unions continue to be the richest union movement in the free world. But in *real* terms, unions did not fare well in the 1970s—a condition probably experienced by union movements in Western countries and by many businesses. Adjusting by the GNP deflator, real total and net assets actually declined between 1969 and 1976 (see Tables 1 and 2). Real net assets per member—that is, union members' "equity"—declined even more markedly, falling by almost eight

percent. Many of the gains in the real financial position of organized labor was undone in the 1970s, with real net assets reduced to the level experienced in the mid-1960s and real net assets per member reduced below 1962 levels.[4]

Moreover, unions' financial resources slipped relative to those of corporate business. Collectively, union assets would have ranked organized labor 18th among the Fortune 500 industrial corporations in 1969, but by 1976 their ranking had slipped to 33rd. The causes of this decline include stagnation in membership growth and in real per member dues (as discussed in section III).

The decline in real wealth in the 1970s appears to have been evenly distributed among the three basic types of union organization: locals, intermediates (including federations), and nationals and internationals. The financial resources of American unions have traditionally been divided between the local unions and the national and international organizations, each with about 45 percent of total assets, with the intermediate and regional orga-

[3]USDL's membership series is derived from an annual survey of unions. As shown by Troy (1969), such self-reporting appears to lead to a rather substantial overstatement of active membership.

[4]The overstatement of membership noted in note 3 may be understating the per-member figures somewhat.

Table 1
Consolidated Balance Sheet of American Unions, 1962, 1969, 1976

	1962 (millions)	(Percent)	1969 (millions)	(Percent)	1976 (millions)	(Percent)
Assets						
Cash	$ 534	(30.2)	$ 858	(32.4)	$1,275	(32.2)
U.S. Treasury securities	406	(22.9)	478	(18.1)	335	(8.4)
Mortgage investments	134	(7.6)	168	(6.4)	195	(4.9)
Other marketable securities	275	(15.5)	547	(20.7)	964	(24.3)
Accounts and loans						
Receivable	100	(5.6)	111	(4.2)	182	(4.6)
Fixed assets	267	(15.1)	388	(14.6)	699	(17.6)
Other assets	55	(3.1)	97	(3.6)	316	(8.0)
Total	$1,771	(100.0)	$2,647	(100.0)	$3,966	(100.0)
Liabilities						
Accounts payable	19	(8.9)	44	(12.3)	70	(11.4)
Loans payable	33	(15.7)	37	(10.2)	74	(12.1)
Mortgages payable	18	(8.6)	45	(12.3)	69	(11.3)
Other liabilities	142	(66.8)	235	(65.2)	399	(65.2)
Total	$ 212	(100.0)	$ 361	(100.0)	$ 612	(100.0)
Net assets	$1,559		$2,286		$3,354	

Source: Financial data from tapes of the U.S. Department of Labor, adjusted by the authors, and from individual union reports.

Table 2
Real Assets and Liabilities

	1962	1969	1976
Total assets (in millions)	$1,771	$2,647	$3,966
Index (1962 = 100)	100.0	149.5	223.9
Deflated (1972)(in millions)	$2,510	$3,053	$2,966
Index	100.0	121.6	118.2
Deflated, per member	$ 151.2	$ 160.7	$ 151.3
Index	100.0	106.3	100.1
Liabilities (in millions)	$ 212	$ 361	$ 612
Index	100.0	170.3	288.7
Deflated (in millions)	$ 301	$ 416	$ 458
Index	100.0	138.2	152.2
Deflated, per member	$ 18.1	$ 21.9	$ 23.4
Index	100.0	121.0	129.3
Net assets (in millions)	$1,559	$2,286	$3,354
Index	100.0	146.6	215.1
Deflated (in millions)	$2,210	$2,636	$2,508
Index	100.0	119.3	113.5
Deflated, per member	$ 133.1	$ 138.7	$ 128.0
Index	100.0	104.2	96.7

Source: See Table 1. Membership figures from Department of Labor; implicit GNP deflator from *Economic Report of the President*, 1980.

nizations accounting for the remainder. In the 1970s, the distribution remained essentially unchanged (see Table 3). This distribution of assets reflects the financial autonomy of individual organizations and underlies the strength of localism in the American labor movement. In contrast, in Western European countries union structures were highly centralized. American union structure and collective bargaining practices reflect the decentralization of union financial power and, in John Dunlop's (1973) view, underlies the strong position of local unions in the American system of industrial relations.[5]

III. INCOME AND EXPENDITURES

Consolidated union income rose by almost 60 percent in the 1960s (31 percent in real terms); but between 1969 and 1976 it barely kept ahead of inflation, rising only 4 percent in real terms and less than .5 percent on a per member basis (see Table 4). American unions continued to derive their income primarily from dues in the 1970s, with over 80 percent of income coming from members in the form of dues and other charges in 1976. This signaled no real change from 1969, but it was up

[5]See Dunlop (1973, p. 5).

considerably from 1962, indicating that dues (in current values) had been substantially increased.

By 1976, dues income almost tripled over 1962 and was more than 60 percent higher than in 1969. After adjustment for inflation, real dues income was 7 percent larger in 1976 than in 1969, a far smaller rise than in the 1960s, when it increased by 28 percent. In 1976, as in the 1960s, dues income alone could not cover expenditures, although the shortfall (in real terms) was less than in earlier years. The gap between expenditures and income from members was filled by property income and income from other sources (see Table 4).

Transactions in funds that are collected and disbursed on behalf of individual members, incorporating funds for political purposes, had increased by 50 percent since 1969 (38 percent in real terms). In 1976, they comprised almost 3 percent of expenditures.[6] Significantly, property income (interest, dividends, and rents) almost doubled in current

[6]This item reflects charitable or political causes individual members may wish to support. The unions act as members' agents, since unions are prohibited by law from collecting or using funds for political purposes. The difference between receipts and disbursements reflect different accounting treatments of each item.

Table 3
Distribution of Assets

	1962 ($ millions)	(Percent)	1969 ($ millions)	(Percent)	1976 ($ millions)	(Percent)
Local unions	$ 867	(49.0)	$1,272	(48.0)	$1,988	(50.1)
Intermediate unions	94	(5.3)	139	(5.3)	232	(5.9)
Regional, national, and international	810	(45.7)	1,236	(46.7)	1,746	(44.0)
Total	$1,771	(100.0)	$2,647	(100.0)	$3,966	(100.0)

Source: Table 1.

Table 4
Consolidated Income and Expenditures, 1962, 1969, 1976

	1962 ($ millions)	(Percent)	1969 ($ millions)	(Percent)	1976 ($ millions)	(Percent)
Income						
Dues and per capita tax	$ 728	(63.4)	$1,312	(70.8)	$2,158	(72.8)
Fees, fines, assessments, and work permits	140	(12.2)	202	(10.9)	249	(8.4)
Sale of supplies	3	(.3)	3	(.2)	4	(.1)
Interest	43	(3.7)	68	(3.7)	140	(4.7)
Dividends	4	(.3)	8	(.4)	13	(.4)
Rents	9	(.8)	16	(.8)	30	(1.0)
From other sources	221	(19.3)	245	(13.2)	372	(12.6)
Total	$1,148	(100.0)	$1,854	(100.0)	$2,966	(100.0)
Expenditures						
Officers (gross)	195	(18.4)	347	(19.7)	460	(19.7)
Employees (gross)	250	(23.6)	440	(25.0)	542	(23.3)
Office and administrative	123	(11.6)	194	(11.0)	327	(14.0)
Educational and publicity	27	(2.5)	39	(2.2)	63	(2.7)
Professional fees	25	(2.4)	36	(2.0)	80	(3.4)
Benefits	179	(16.9)	321	(18.2)	459	(19.7)
Supplies	5	(.5)	3	(.2)	3	(.1)
Taxes	25	(2.4)	47	(2.7)	324	(13.9)
Other	216	(20.4)	309	(17.5)	41	(1.8)
Contributions, gifts, and grants	14	(1.3)	26	(1.5)	32	(1.4)
Total	$1,059	(100.0)	$1,762	(100.0)	$2,331	(100.0)
Net income	$ 89		$ 92		$ 635	
Memo: Receipts						
From members for disbursements on their behalf	$ 15		$ 26		$ 64	
Disbursements on behalf of individual members	$ 18		$ 31		$ 66	

Source: See Table 1.

dollars and jumped by 30 percent in real terms during the 1970s. Nevertheless, property income continues to remain a small proportion of total union income (just over six percent in 1976).

Expenditure patterns vary by level of organization. The largest expenditure item for local unions was payment of per capita to intermediate and parent organizations. National and international organizations allocate the bulk of their disbursements to salary and administrative costs.

IV. Unions' Portfolios and Investment Policies

The aggregate investment behavior of the nearly 50,000 autonomous units in organized labor has been described as passive (Troy, 1975, pp. 232–36). With more than 30 percent of union assets held as cash in 1976, roughly the same proportion as in 1962 and 1969, there has been no discernible shift in the consolidated union portfolio to take advantage of the high yields on financial assets available in the late 1960s and 1970s.

Surprisingly, mortgage investments declined as a share of total assets in 1976, as compared to 1969 and 1962. Holdings of corporate stock by unions, estimated by capitalizing dividend income using the average yield of the Standard & Poor's 500 stocks, totaled $353 million in 1976, up from $250 million in 1969 and $129 million in 1962. Yet, these holdings remain less than eight percent of total assets.[7]

The figures above refer to the consolidated assets of all unions. Investment practices differ between local and national and international organizations, and more generally between large and small organizations. National and international organizations and large unions in general have followed a more active and sophisticated asset-management path, with more assets in interest earning securities and less in cash.

The high liquidity represented by large cash holdings has often been justified by unions on the grounds that they are not profit-making organizations and that high liquidity is required in case of strike activity. Perhaps most of the funds included as cash do represent time deposits of one sort or another, but unions have taken little advantage of other opportunities to augment their income.

V. PUBLIC EMPLOYEE UNIONS

In contrast to general union trends, public employee unionism increased sharply in both the 1960s and 1970s, although it apparently tapered off near the end of the 1970s. Membership in these unions more than doubled between 1962 and 1976; but despite swift and large membership gains, public sector unions were unable to enlarge their funds as rapidly. Preliminary figures for 1976 show that public employee unions accounted for more than 10 percent of total membership but only about 3 percent of total union wealth. Dues in the public sector apparently averaged about half those charged in the private sector. Moreover, most public union funds (over 80 percent) are held by five headquarter organizations, all of which were established long before the upsurge of the 1960s and 1970s began. Postal unions are the wealthiest, and unions of other federal workers take in the largest share of receipts. Because state and local unions are exempt from federal reporting requirements, our coverage is incomplete. But we have been able to include two of the principal unions in state and local government jurisdictions, the AFT and AFSCME, and many of their affiliates.

VI. CONCLUSIONS

The 1970s witnessed an ebb in union fortunes, both in real financial measures and in real membership, that is, the share of the labor market unionized. Unions' total wealth gained sharply in nominal terms, but adjustments by the GNP deflator reduced total assets in real terms to 1960 levels. Income managed to grow in both nominal and real terms, but the gains in real terms fell well behind the gains of the 1960s. Further, there is little evidence that unions' overall investment policy has managed funds any better than the rather poor performance of the 1960s.

What do the financial figures suggest for unions in the 1980s, both in terms of membership growth and managerial performance? The service-dominated labor market is expected to continue to grow, as is the shift of goods industries from the more unionized, industrialized North to the burgeoning and predominantly nonunion Sun Belt. These structural shifts are essentially hostile to union growth. Consequently, the adverse changes in unions' financial position in the 1970s will likely make successful organizational efforts more difficult to attain in the 1980s.

With respect to unions as managerial and administrative bodies, the financial results sketched here suggest that unions have been slow to adapt to a changing environment.

---

[7]While these figures probably overstate stockholdings, their movements are of interest.

Table 5
Current and Constant Income, Expenditures, and Dues

	1962	1969	1976
Income (millions of dollars)	$1,148	$1,854	$2,966
Index (1962 = 100)	100	161.5	258.4
Deflated (millions of 1972$)	$1,627	$2,138	$2,218
Index	100	131.4	136.3
Deflated, per member (1972$)	$ 98.0	$ 112.6	$ 113.2
Index	100	114.9	115.5
Expenditures	$1,059	$1,762	$2,331
Index (1962 = 100)	100	166.4	220.1
Deflated (millions of 1972$)	$1,501	$2,032	$1,743
Index	100	135.4	116.1
Deflated, per member (1972$)	$ 90.4	$ 106.9	$ 89.0
Index	100	118.3	98.5
Net income	$ 89	$ 92	$ 635
Index (1962 = 100)	100	103.4	713.5
Deflated (millions of 1972$)	$ 126	$ 106	$ 475
Index	100.0	84.1	377
Deflated, per member (1972$)	$ 7.6	$ 5.6	$ 24.2
Index	100	73.7	318.4
Dues	$ 728	$1,312	$2,158
Index (1962 = 100)	100	180.2	296.4
Deflated (millions of 1972$)	$1,032	$1,513	$1,614
Index	100	146.6	156.4
Deflated, per member (1972$)	$ 62.2	$ 79.6	$ 82.3
Index	100	128	132.3

Source: See Table 1.

REFERENCES

Dunlop, John T. "Future Trends in Industrial Relations in the United States." Mimeographed. Third World Congress, International Industrial Relations Association, September 3–7, 1973.

Estey, Marten. "The State of the Union." *Executive*, Spring 1980, pp. 15–17.

Rosow, Jerome. "Labor's Agenda for the 1980s." *Executive*, Spring 1980, pp. 39–43.

Troy, Leo. "Trade Union Growth in a Changing Economy." *Monthly Labor Review*, September 1969, pp. 1–7.

———. "The Finances of American Unions, 1962–1969." *Explorations in Economic Research*, Spring 1975, pp. 232–51.

Troy, Leo, and Neil Sheflin. "Survival in the Service Economy." *Executive*, Spring 1980, pp. 18–21.

R E A D I N G 15

Pushbutton Unionism*

James T. Bennett and
Manuel H. Johnson[†]

Most unions have got out of the habit of organizing in the years since World War II. To the extent that they have acquired new members, outside the Civil Service and health fields, it has been primarily through union shop contracts and other kinds of "pushbutton unionism" in which the employer delivers over workers.[1]

I. INTRODUCTION

Throughout history, the potency of an idea has been measured by the number and loyalty of its adherents. Although it is widely realized that many political empires and other mass movements may control a multitude of individuals, it must also be recognized in assessing the vitality of the ideas which hold a movement together that only those who actually *believe* can be counted. The only adherents who matter are those who signify their agreement with a movement's values by voluntary choice: anything less implies the capture of bodies but not minds.

Although voluntary choice is the *sine qua non* of an idea's power to obtain the commitment of individuals, there is an organizational dimension to movements which makes mass impressment an important way to gain influence *for the organization*. Obviously, most of those whom the organization wishes to influence seldom have the time, opportunity, or, perhaps, the resources to investigate how the organization's membership divides into willing adherents versus captive passengers: the tendency, therefore, is to take membership at face value and to be suitably impressed by gross numbers. Obviously also, even captive passengers can serve organizational purposes depending upon the type and degree of coercion used to compel their association: they may be required to provide funds to the organization, to refrain from criticizing organizational policies and actions, and so forth. Therefore, mass movements tend to be expansionist organizations precisely because the extent of membership in the movement is normally taken as a prime indicator of organizational strength—even though such numbers have relatively little bearing on the vitality of the beliefs and values underlying the movement.[2] An appropriate aphorism is that movements are concerned with *adherents* while organizations care for little more than *members*.

The issue addressed in this study is the current practice of U.S. trade unions in acquiring members who are not necessarily adherents.[3] American unions began as a movement which initially attempted to win adherents through voluntary choice. Over time, however, the union movement became an organization that has changed its strategies for expansion from organizing through voluntary choice to a reliance on devices for coercing membership or support.

Section II contains a discussion of union organizing techniques to attract members and the way in which these techniques have changed over time in response to both economic and political conditions. A comparison is developed between U.S. labor unions and those in other industrialized nations in order to emphasize the role of social factors in influencing union membership. Section III documents the shift to "pushbutton unionism" and examines the techniques unions have de-

---

*Reprinted with permission; published for the Contemporary Economics and Business Association at George Mason University, Fairfax, Virginia, 1980.

†*Professors Bennett and Johnson are on the faculty of George Mason University.*

[1]A. H. Raskin, "Organizing Obstacles Are Not Just Legal," *New York Times*, July 24, 1977.

[2]See S. N. Eisenstadt, *The Political Systems of Empires* (New York: Free Press, 1963).

[3]A point may exist below which the percentage of adherents in the total membership cannot fall without the risk of the organization becoming separated from the movement. This issue of social dynamics is beyond the scope of this paper.

veloped for acquiring and retaining membership without permitting workers to vote on union representation. Section IV reviews the economic, political, and organizational implications of pushbutton unionism. The last section contains a summary and the conclusions.

The topics considered herein are both complex and controversial. To our knowledge, there are no critical studies of traditional organizing techniques, nor has any research investigated new strategies designed to expand or retain membership.[4] This study is the first attempt to analyze union organizing methods which have changed from individual choice to unionization by fiat.

II. UNION ORGANIZING: TRADITIONAL TECHNIQUES

The origins of unionism can be traced at least as far back as the European guilds of the 14th century. There are, however, some indications that there were union-like organizations performing collective protective functions in China even earlier. But the values, general objectives, and in part the organizational rationale of unions in contemporary industrial economies are a Western tradition drawn from the experiences of workers principally in the Netherlands, Italy, France, and England.[5]

In contrast to this tradition is the development of "unions" elsewhere. In the Soviet Union and Eastern Europe, as well as throughout much of the Third World, unions emerged from a combination of economic and ideological factors to be instruments of government policy. The tensions between what might simply be called the Western and Soviet Union traditions and the numerical dominance of the latter in the International Labor Organization led in 1976 to pressures from the AFL–CIO for the United States to withdraw from that agency.

These tensions are significant, not simply for their broad geopolitical or foreign policy implications but because they derive in large part from quite different concepts of the proper role of unions relative to employees, employers, and the government. It is sufficient to note that the Western tradition is based upon the conviction that unions should be independent of the government, equal and active negotiators with employers, and able representatives of the needs and aspirations of employees. These features are mutually related because each implies the other two. No Western union can hope, for example, to represent employee interests adequately if it is subservient to the government or if it merely acts in concert with employers to further management interests. Each of these features also presumes other conditions. As membership organizations, unions cannot simply proclaim themselves as self-appointed guardians of the employee; rather, they are initiated by employees, are funded by employees, and are led by employees. To achieve willing participation, union organizations in the West traditionally stressed the need to acquire as members employees who shared among themselves and with the union a belief in the objectives of the organization.

In Europe, this consonance of views was (and remains) relatively easy to obtain. Broad social, political and economic groups coalesced generations ago to create, relative to the United States, class-based societies in which individual affiliations (i.e., group memberships) became reinforcing rather than overlapping. This means that, at least up to the mid-20th century, the social forces throughout most of Europe (including Britain) consisted of a set of discrete groups, each of which shared a common heritage of language, religion, politics, culture, employment history, and so forth. Membership in each discrete social group implied a variety of characteristics shared with other members. In pluralist societies, in contrast, where there were as many or more groups, membership in one car-

---

[4]For the suggestion that unions themselves, much less academic experts in unionism, rarely understand, analyze, or research the phenomenon, see Derek C. Bok and John T. Dunlop, *Labor and the American Community* (New York: Simon & Schuster, 1979), pp. 148–49.

[5]See, for example, Sidney Webb and Beatrice Webb, *The History of Trade Unionism*, rev. ed. (New York: Longmans, Green, 1920), esp. pp. 2–21; also Barbara W. Tuchman, *A Distant Mirror: The Calamitous 14th Century* (New York: Alfred A. Knopf, 1978), pp. 38–39, 120–21.

ried no necessary implications regarding an individual's other affiliations.[6]

The employees most amenable to unionization in Europe were generally easily identifiable because they tended to be found in particular occupations, to be members of particular religions, to speak a particular language or dialect, or to have a particular economic status. All these characteristics were likely found together and, indeed, usually indicated whether a person was unionized or not. In short, rarely was a European union required to search for members; rather, workers came to unions, even perhaps to a particular union, because the union was closely linked to every other association to which the workers were also inclined. Consequently, European unions generally did not engage in organizing nor did organizing develop into a specialized activity requiring professional expertise. Moreover, few unions in Europe were very interested in amassing a large membership for the sake of numbers or interested in obtaining as members individuals who did not share the social, political, economic, and other characteristics of most existing members. Thus, European unions experienced few sudden shifts in size other than can be accounted for by parallel changes in demographics. Further, compulsory unionism (union shop, agency shop, etc.) was virtually unknown in Europe because, first, few unions there would seriously consider *forcing* someone into the organization and, second, membership was already high and stable due to the factors discussed above.[7]

However, as social groupings in Europe have become more pluralistic since the Second World War, these arrangements have also changed to some degree. In large part, this explains the quite recent pressure from British unions for governmentally protected rights to compel membership: the class structure in Britain has become considerably less rigid, over 30 percent of union members there do not support the Labor Party, and unions have experienced great difficulty in relying upon traditional appeals to "class interests."

In the United States, however, unions have not benefited from the automatic social mechanisms which in Europe caused an employee to affiliate with a union as readily as he voted for a certain political party. In this country, with numerous overlapping social groupings, employees had few affiliations which would impel them to unionism. Rather, unions had to seek out members: employees had to be confronted actively and aggressively by organizers who presented concrete reasons for joining an organization which, in a real sense, was seen as more than a little alien to the American experience. These arguments were almost exclusively economic in nature and involved individual assessment of personal benefit (or loss avoidance). Organizing became an occupation and, while much of the early rhetoric had a high ideological content, actual "field operations" of the union were intensely pragmatic.[8] Simply put, American unions had to work, and work hard, to acquire their members: major increases in size were won at great expense in time, effort, and money. Further, membership size could and often did fluctuate greatly in response to purely economic conditions as well as to the amount of effort the union expended to get or keep members.

While officials of American unions were concentrating upon organizing activities as the primary mechanism for acquiring new members, they also developed (notably in the craft unions) various "union security" devices which increasingly were given the force of law. The Wagner Act (1935) originally, for example, permitted the closed shop which is the

---

[6]Robert A. Dahl, *Democracy in the United States: Promise and Performance* 2d ed. (Skokie, Ill.: Rand McNally, 1972), pp. 343–44; see also *Ibid.*, p. 309. Bok and Dunlop, p. 48, make the same point with specific regard to industrial relations.

[7]"It was realized very early (in Europe) that people who are forced into an organization instead of joining it voluntarily are inevitably the worst and most awkward members and are bound to be a source of extra trouble. They may make the membership larger but they certainly do not make it more effective." Alexander Berenstein, "Union Security and the Scope of Collective Agreements in Switzerland," *International Labor Review*, February 1962, pp. 106–7.

[8]See J. David Greenstone, *Labor in American Politics* (New York: Alfred A. Knopf, 1969); also, Dan C. Heldman and Deborah L. Knight, *Unions & Lobbying: The Representation Function* (Washington, D.C.: Foundation for the Advancement of the Public Trust, 1979).

most compulsory of union security devices. With the closed shop outlawed by the Taft-Hartley Amendments (1947), emphasis shifted to the union shop (or post-entry closed shop). Section 14(b) of Taft-Hartley also permitted individual states to restrict all forms of union security: it did not, however, cover all forms of compulsory unionism since 14(b) left untouched exclusive representation. Since 1947, compulsory unionism has gradually lost favor according to public opinion polls (even among union members): unions have thus found it increasingly difficult to rely upon this device in the face of public hostility, a greater willingness on the part of employees to assert their rights through litigation and political action, and a growing number of judicial restrictions upon union security practices.[9]

Parallel to this decline in union security as an efficient device[10] for achieving new membership growth (it remains effective in *retaining* a union's current membership) is the phenomenon of an organizing effort which has been declining in absolute terms as well as in its ability to produce results.[11] Many features of American society are undergoing profound changes and, except for several employment areas which had been largely untapped earlier, e.g., the public sector, unions had organized by the late 60s most of the employees amenable to unionization. Remaining employees were either hostile to unionism by virtue of their work or sense of professionalism or were so distributed that an aggressive organizing campaign directed at them would entail greater costs than union officials were apparently willing to assume.[12] At the same time, employment shifts were occurring toward these difficult-to-organize fields, and employees already organized were enjoying a rising economic status which tended to make them les responsive to the traditional arguments in favor of unions.

As a consequence, American unions, with certain exceptions, not only stopped growing by the early 70s but actually began declining in membership strength—measured, for example, as a percentage of the work force. Members were lost to attrition, to labor force shifts toward nonunion employment fields, and to outright rejection of the union by previously committed (or captured) employees. With industries most amenable to unionization already saturated, with a reduced inclination or will on the part of union leaderships to engage in aggressive organizing, with a larger share of the work force moving to industries which had traditionally been unorganized, and with employees more and more acquiring what has been called a "middle class outlook" not compatible with the usual tenets of unionism, union officials were discovering that they could not, as easily as they had in the past anyway, rely upon "union security" to expand their memberships.

If membership could not be held in place or increased by traditional methods of organizing (through convincing employees that they would gain economically or through requiring union membership as a condition of employment), then clearly it would be in the collective interest of unions as organizations to develop new techniques for fostering unionization. Yet there are, in the American system of labor relations, only three points of contact through which a union can operate—employees, employers, and the government. Employees, by and large, were not a useful field for further exploration in this regard because the now-failing traditional methods had exhausted most of the possibilities. That left employers or the government as a medium through which the unions could seek to achieve their objectives. The most effective strategy would be to develop methods to induce employers to permit, approve, or encourage unionization without the union having to obtain affirmative consent from employees. Obviously, these methods would be more effective if they were embedded in a permissive structure of laws and regulations

---

[9]Indeed, according to Bloom and Northrup, the present legal situation permits at most only the "agency shop," and this of course only in the states which have not approved right-to-work laws pursuant to Taft-Hartley's 14(b): see Gordon Bloom and Herbert Northrup, *Economics of Labor Relations* (Homewood, Ill.: Richard D. Irwin, 1977), pp. 174–79.

[10]Union security is termed an *efficient* device because it attempts to achieve by legal coercion what would normally require a costly outlay of union funds and staff time.

[11]See, for example, Raskin.

[12]Bok and Dunlop, pp. 195–96.

administered by appropriately compliant government agencies.

Before considering the techniques which American unions have developed to avoid employee organizing in the face of growing public, judicial, and political rejection of "union security" methods, the importance of this new direction should be emphasized. The union movement in the United States, as it presently operates, simply cannot tolerate a period of membership decline. The significance of this assertion is fundamental. Lacking the European union's reliance upon a relatively steady flow of funds and member support derived from class affiliations, the typical American union is sensitive to psychological concerns of a social and political nature. From the social point of view, given the individual level of organizing, employees will be more reluctant to join voluntarily a movement which has acquired the image or aura of being unable to satisfy economic needs: every time a representation election is lost by a union, or a union is decertified, or membership overall drops, the union's promise of economic betterment loses some degree of credibility.[13] In the political realm, where influence is intensely psychological in origin at the outset, the union legislative effort is harmed both by reduced funding and by a perception that declining unions will be less able to marshall member-voters for or against candidates.

In both spheres there will be a time lag as knowledge of a decline and its implications spread. During this period, union leaders have an opportunity to check the decline itself, to counter the spread of the perception, or both. In particular, efforts to check the decline include the devices discussed below. Politically, the lag is somewhat longer because, first, it depends in part upon social perceptions and, second, political influence is greatly affected by forms of election support (campaign contributions and "volunteer" services) which a union may well be able to continue (or even expand as a precaution) for some time beyond severe reductions in the organization's size. The danger is that the potential social and political consequences may interact and reinforce each other. For example, reductions in political influence could make it more difficult to obtain the additional legislative protections union officials need to halt the exodus of members; similarly, employee perceptions of ineffectiveness produced initially by declining size may be exacerbated by parallel perceptions of political failures.

For a number of interrelated and compelling reasons, then, the officials of American unions have found it of vital importance to develop a variety of methods to acquire members, funds, and bargaining rights without recourse to the traditional techniques of voluntary organizing and legal compulsion. If these methods are not developed and successfully applied, American unions as organizations face the prospect of sharp reductions in their political and economic power. The union movement is still capable of launching massive organizing drives and of delaying, if not halting or reversing, the spreading rejection of "union security." The former would require an amount of money which unions heretofore have been unable or unwilling to commit to this purpose—nor is it clear that such an expenditure would ultimately have the desired effect.[14] The latter would undoubtedly stiffen the resolve of those whose purpose is to limit even further the reach of compulsory unionism. And either move would certainly require a resolve which few union leaders have shown they possess. The path ahead branches in numerous ways: while the choice is still open, the number of constraints foreclosing some of the alternatives is growing.

III. Pushbutton Unionism

As discussed above, employees have ceased to be a fruitful object of union organizational activity, both because they have become less susceptible to union inducements and because most union organizations no longer possess the expertise or the will to com-

---

[13]The union does not necessarily lose any actual ability (in an absolute sense) to win benefits; however, this will be the perception. After a while, of course, the perception increases the likelihood of self-fulfillment.

[14]Bok and Dunlop, p. 195.

mit the resources for the aggressive organizational campaigns which the remaining groups of unorganized employees would require. As one observer has noted, "The labor movement slowly but surely has lost its crusading spirit. Today, the major 'inspiration' running in labor's [sic] blood may be new ways to invest the pension funds."[15] Also recall that the second traditional method of acquiring membership, when voluntary choice has been exhausted or is ineffective, involves various forms of legal compulsion—"union security."

There is a very clear trend of opinion against compulsory unionism. Virtually all segments of the public (including union members) now reject by decisive majorities the closed, union, and agency shops; opinion seems particularly opposed to these mechanisms in the public sector.[16] Of course, if public opinion were decisive, "union security" would have disappeared years ago; instead, it is merely constrained somewhat. Effective limitations on "union security" have derived from certain changes in the judicial and legislative framework.[17]

An increasing number of states, acting under authority of Taft-Hartley's 14(b), have adopted statutes and/or constitutional provisions which make illegal all forms of union security. These "Right-to-Work" states now number 20 with the addition of Louisiana in 1976; in 1978, these states accounted for some 31 percent of the private sector work force in the United States.[18] With regard to the public sector, over 30 states currently do not permit the imposition of "union security" upon at least some segment of their public work force. This prohibition extends as well to all federal civilian employees, including those of the postal service (Executive Order 11838). The best estimate is that about 22 percent of unionized local and state employees are subject to "union security."[19] For all local and state employees for whom a "union security" legal framework may be clearly determined, approximately 48 percent are not subject (as of 1976) to such a provision by reason of a definite legal prohibition.[20]

Simultaneously, as the legislative climate has become more hostile to compulsory unionism, so has the judicial climate. As a result, in fact, of a series of court decisions, "union security" has effectively been limited (where it can exist at all) to the agency shop. No private sector employee can legally be required to become a formal member of a union; at most, some "agency fee" may be made a condition of employment (except in Right-to-Work states) and the amount of this fee might well be limited by several factors which are still the subject of extensive litigation. Roughly the same conclusions are applicable to public sector employment.

Parenthetically, it should be noted that the above summary description of the legislative and judicial status of compulsory unionism should not be interpreted to imply that the practice is now inconsequential. Clearly, as the principal back-up to voluntary membership through organizing, compulsory unionism remains a critical tool for union officials facing membership unrest and exodus. No one, including perhaps unions themselves, knows just how many employees are members of (or pay the equivalent of dues to) a union solely because the union contract under which they work has a "union security" clause. In recent years, Department of Labor analyses of "large-scale" contracts have found that upwards of 80 percent of them contain

[15]Robert Schrank, "Are Unions An Anachronism?" *Harvard Business Review* 57 (September & October 1979), p. 108.

[16]The Roper Organization, *Roper Reports*, #77-3, 1977.

[17]For an authoritative review of the law on "union security," see Thomas R. Haggard, *Compulsory Unionism, the NLRB, and the Courts* (Philadelphia: University of Pennsylvania, The Wharton School, 1977).

[18]U.S. Department of Labor, Bureau of Labor Statistics, "Employment and Earnings, May 1979," vol. 26, no. 5, pp. 72 ff.

[19]U.S. Department of Labor, Bureau of Labor Statistics, "Characteristics of Agreements in State and Local Governments, July 1, 1975," Bulletin 1947, 1977, p. 10.

[20]U.S. Department of Commerce (Bureau of the Census) and U.S. Department of Labor (Labor Management Services Administration), "Labor-Management Relations in State and Local Government, 1976," Special Studies No. 88 (April, 1978), pp. 18–32. Public sector employment totals from Ohio, Colorado, Georgia, Idaho, Tennessee, and West Virginia were excluded since, in these states, the law relating to "union security" is unclear.

such clauses[21]: unfortunately, the definitions and data sources used in these studies do not permit this 80 percent figure to be translated into employee coverage. Without a doubt, unions recognize the value of "union security," for every case challenging the practice and every attempt to extend Right-to-Work legislation are hard fought. Following an interim decision in one court action challenging the agency shop, a prominent AFL–CIO spokesman was quoted as having observed that, should the challenge be successful, the labor movement "as we know it" could be "destroyed."[22]

Nevertheless, the handwriting appears to be on the wall. The status of compulsory unionism, at best, is static, with strong indications that the practice is being gradually chipped away, restricted, and reduced to its less offensive varieties.

In the face of these parallel developments, unions have begun to look seriously at other devices to further their goal of extending unionization and increasing membership. As discussed earlier, given the nature of the American industrial relations system, whatever devices or techniques unions develop will be aimed at or accomplished through employers or the government. It must be emphasized that, at this early stage of what might be called a new phase in unionism, all observations are tentative: there is no way to know in advance which, if any, of the mechanisms described below will eventually prove viable. This is clearly a stage characterized by an active search for and experimentation with a number of techniques.

One technique which promises considerable success is direct union pressure on employers. The chances of success are great because pressuring employers is not, in itself, a new activity for unions. Indeed, unions have attempted to bypass the employee completely by directly inducing employers to accept

unionization (and "union security") from the outset. However, this technique has been newly resurrected after it had fallen into some disuse following passage of the Wagner Act. Under the Wagner Act, unions could achieve the privileged position as "exclusive representative" and could thereby force employers to bargain with them "in good faith" without any approval from or even prior contact with the employer. The Wagner Act created a system of employee elections administered by the newly created National Labor Relations Board, and triggered by a union showing of at least 30 percent support evidenced by signature cards. Simplifying considerably, a union could obtain the requisite signature cards and petition the NLRB for a board-conducted election without the knowledge of the employer. The employer might become aware of union activity only upon notice from the NLRB that an election was being requested. At this point, the employer could challenge the validity of the petition, the timing of the proposed election, the bargaining unit to be polled, and so forth.

It was, however, always possible for the employer to agree unilaterally to recognize a union with no need for an election or with a union show of only minimum employee support. Indeed, it was possible for a union to receive recognition from an employer without the knowledge of employees. Employees might be totally unaware of union activity until they were notified after the fact that a union was now "in" or that their employment was now controlled by a union contract. For a variety of reasons, these possibilities were seen in practice only infrequently, but there is now evidence that employers are being increasingly pressured to accept a union as an exclusive agent without recourse to an agent election.

Employer acceptance of a union without an election may occur when an employer is faced with persuasive evidence that, not merely 30 percent, but 50 percent or more, of the unit wants the union. The natural argument in such situations is, why go through the time and effort of an election if the outcome is certain (including a belief that nothing could be said or could happen during the pre-

---

[21]See, for example, U.S. Department of Labor, Bureau of Labor Statistics, "Characteristics of Major Collective Bargaining Agreements, July 1, 1976," Bulletin 2013, 1979, p. 13.

[22]Al Barkan, from a speech to the convention of the Illinois AFL–CIO, in the *Chicago Sun-Times*, September 13, 1978.

election period to change the minds of enough employees to affect the results)? Perhaps the employer is merely intimidated by the union when it first demands recognition; perhaps the employer chooses unilaterally to recognize one union in the face of organizing moves by another union with which he feels he cannot negotiate; perhaps the employer's decision is induced illegally through bribery or extortion; perhaps the employer does not understand that a signature card legally merely requests an election and does not necessarily mean support for the union[23]; perhaps the union has successfully misrepresented its strength. The point is that, under current labor laws, an employee could be unionized, put under a union contract, and, if the employer also agreed to a "union security" clause, forced into membership, all without ever being given a voluntary choice because all these events can lawfully occur as a result of unilateral employer accession to union demands.

Although this portion of the analysis is predicated upon the assumption that unions are developing new unionization-inducing techniques because organizing has virtually disappeared and "union security" has fallen into disrepute, it is worthwhile mentioning one technique increasingly being used which is related directly to compulsory unionism. While it is well-settled law that formal membership cannot be made a condition of employment, unions have insisted upon (and have induced employers to agree to) the continued use of contract language which, to the average reader, would seem clearly to require full membership. The business agent and the shop steward maintain that "membership is required or we'll tell the company to fire you," the company's personnel department says "membership required or the union will force us to fire you," and the contract says "union membership required within 30 days of beginning employment." If a very knowledgeable and courageous employee/applicant is sufficiently well informed to quote, say, the lan-

guage of one of many local, state, and federal court decisions, he may be simply labeled a trouble-maker and shunted aside. He may be informed that it would be quite costly to vindicate his right in court so just go ahead and join. He may be told (if judged a "hard case" likely to make an issue of it) that, well, of course, the courts have *defined* membership in terms of its "financial core" and so he doesn't have to *join*, but (since it is not a Right-to-Work state) he does have to pay union dues so why not go ahead and join anyway. Strange as it may seem (perhaps not so strange after all), many employers and their personnel departments are either unaware of fundamental employee rights or they don't really care enough in the face of possible union "trouble." It is perfectly clear that unions have every reason to continue their practice of using false and misleading contract language regarding "union security" for the practice is buttressed by general ignorance or massive indifference.

What pressures can a union bring to bear on an employer in order to win unilateral recognition without an employee involvement or to win employer acceptance of a "union security" clause (particularly one which uses the misleading language described above)? There are, obviously, a number of quite illegal pressures, the effectiveness of which depends upon ideosyncratic factors that prevent any but the broadest of generalizations. Moreover, by their nature, such pressures are hidden by all parties and rarely come to light. The assumption must be that the instances which do emerge represent only the tip of the iceberg. And, finally, examples of illegality not infrequently involve organized crime in one way or another.[24]

Unilateral recognition and/or a compulsory unionism contract clause may be achieved

---

[23]For an indication that employees themselves often do not understand (or are misled about) these cards, see *Fort-Lauderdale News and Sun-Sentinel*, January 13, 1979.

[24]For an interesting historical survey centered on one individual, see the series of articles by Seymour Hirsh in the *New York Times*, June 27–30, 1976. For a more contemporary account centered on several industries, see Jonathan Kwitney, *Vicious Circles: The Mafia in the Marketplace* (New York: W. W. Norton, 1979). Other detailed sources include John Hutchinson, *The Imperfect Union* (New York: E. P. Dutton, 1970); Joseph E. Finley, *The Corrupt Kingdom* (New York: Simon & Schuster, 1973); and Sylvester Petro, *Power Unlimited* (New York: Ronald, 1959).

through fairly straightforward bribery. The "value received" may consist of cash, kickbacks from member dues, services (e.g., expediting sales or deliveries, or a promise of "labor trouble" for competitors),[25] a "sweetheart contract,"[26] or perhaps the promise to "keep out" another union that the employer believes would be "less desirable" (ironically, this last possibility could well involve nothing more than a choice of lesser evils because the "other union" is believed corrupt, crime-controlled, radical, or possibly even a more effective bargainer). Needless to say, each of these walks a fine line between bribery and extortion: promises and threats are often just opposite sides of the same coin. A promise of "labor trouble" for one's competitor can carry the implicit threat of the same kind of trouble for oneself. Promising to "keep out" an undesired union carries the obvious threat to let it in. Direct extortion (the threat of harm) is usually the province of unions allied with or controlled by organized crime—not always, just usually, because most unions by themselves rarely possess the *organized* coercive force to threaten a company's operations.[27] The exception is a threat to do personal harm, which any union is capable of doing.[28]

There is another pressure which, being among the very newest and tentative of techniques, remains somewhat inchoate at this point: recent moves by union officials to flex their pension fund capital muscles. It has been estimated that pension funds overall control more than $.5 *trillion*, of which nearly half is to be found in funds set up and controlled at least in part by unions.[29] While such funds are often technically directed by some combination of employer and union representatives, the experience of the Teamsters Central States Fund is instructive as to the extent the employer-named directors seldom constitute an independent force.[30]

Half a trillion dollars is a *massive* source of investment capital which constitutes a massive threat should an employer be the recipient of fund capital or seeking capital from the fund. Several observers, who implicitly support such uses of pension capital for union organizational purposes, have criticized the current operation of these funds because, for example, large portions of the fund investments surveyed have gone to nonunion firms.[31] Yet this criticism seems misplaced, even granting the validity of the observer's point of view: the problem is not that an unacceptable amount of pension fund money is going to support nonunion firms but that union officials are not using this fact as a lever to accomplish their aim of transforming these firms into unionized enterprises. After all, you can't induce a firm to unionize by threatening to withdraw needed capital (capital the firm has become used to having) if it isn't already invested there. Whatever the criticisms, however, it is evident that some unions and some union activists have been vigorously exploring the limits of the pension fund "card"; they are testing various techniques for using this card in such well-orchestrated unionizing

[25]The Teamsters have developed these economic pressures to a fine art; the effort is institutionalized in something called "TEAM" (for Teamster Economic Action Mobilization). They can threaten to "shut down almost any company by cutting off truck deliveries." See *Time*, August 25, 1975, p. 54. As of 1978 (according to *Newsweek* on April 17 of that year), the general organizer for Local 1922 of the International Longshoremen's Association in Miami had been earlier convicted of extorting $124 thousand from a company in return for "labor peace."

[26]*Chicago Tribune*, April 30, 1978.

[27]With all this, there appears to be a surprising lack of desire to attack this problem. A "Justice Department prosecutor" is quoted as having declared "Organized crime . . . in labor is probably the most serious problem in the criminal field. It overrides everything else. It is frightening to the economy. I can name four national unions now in the hands of hoodlums. And Labor [Department] is not doing the job of getting at them." See *U.S. News*, January 23, 1978, pp. 62–63: also *Ibid.*, May 8, 1978, pp. 83–84.

[28]See Donald R. Cressey, *Theft of the Nation* (New York: Harper & Row, 1969), pp. 95–98.

[29]See Jeremy Rifkin and Randy Barber, *The North Will Rise Again: Pensions, Politics, and Power in the 1980s* (Boston: Beacon Press, 1978).

[30]*Time*, August 25, 1975, pp. 55–56.

[31]"Nonunion Firms Drawing Union Pension Plan Funds," *Washington Post*, August 29, 1979. The *Post* was reporting on a recent publication from the Corporate Data Exchange (New York City) in which it was estimated that "tens of billions of dollars" from union pension funds were (in 1976) invested in nonunion firms.

strategems as are now being directed at the J. P. Stevens textile company, banks, and equipment manufacturers.[32]

Another facet of employer-centered techniques of "pushbutton unionism" is a development which is more than a little difficult to understand. Several well-publicized reports have appeared in recent years regarding major employers agreeing officially either to remain strictly "neutral" or to assist actively in the organizing of their employees. It seems appropriate to suggest that even the term *neutral* is misleading since it is the functional equivalent of pleading "no contest" if charged with a crime. Speculation as to the motives and pressures standing behind such a decision would be fruitless; suffice it to say that the employer, at minimum, is agreeing to offer no defense or counter-argument to the criticisms implicit in union organizing and may indeed be called upon by the union to assist its efforts. Interestingly, these reports commonly involve new or existing plants in locations where traditional organizing has been hampered by a general suspicion regarding unions and/or where "union security" is prohibited.

The precise ways in which this is accomplished also follow the emerging pattern. General Motors has the dubious distinction of having pioneered in this area. For example, there are agreements of the "GM variety" in which the employer is induced to take no position in the event of an organizing drive.[33] The Auto Workers have been vigilant in policing this agreement and have charged General Motors on more than one occasion with, in the UAW's view, overstepping the employer's restricted role.[34] Whether this sort of strategy will be successful remains to be seen. After the neutrality agreement, the UAW succeeded

in organizing one GM plant where employees had previously rejected the automobile union's overtures. Further, most analysts of American union history have pointed to higher levels in this country than elsewhere of employer resistance to organizing as a partial explanation of our lower than average percentage of union membership.[35] The rationale behind this strategy would appear to be that neutralizing the employer eliminates a major stumbling block to unionization. That other unions share the UAW's belief in this method is indicated by its recent appearance in other industries where bargaining is industry-wide (e.g., rubber).[36]

A variation on this technique, also coincidentally emerging in the auto industry, moves the employer away from neutrality and into more active cooperation. A short while after GM agreed to the above position, the company was induced to agree that it would shape its hiring policies at new plants (particularly those in the Right-to-Work southern states) to facilitate unionization. Specifically, GM approved a controversial arrangement whereby a new plant would be staffed primarily with union members already employed by the company elsewhere but transferred on a preferential hiring basis. By thus stocking new plants at the outset with employees who were union members, the UAW would be virtually assured of winning an agent election where employees supplied locally might not be as enthusiastic about this prospect.[37]

Even more active employer support for unionization and membership acquisition can be seen in an "accretion agreement" in which the company in advance grants recognition to a union at any new facility the company may open. The plan here is that, if the

---

[32]"The UAW's $300 Million Kitty," *Forbes*, November 12, 1979, pp. 39–40; "New Weapon for Bashing Bosses," *Time*, July 23, 1979, p. 71; Debra Hauser, "The Unions' Hidden Asset," *The Nation*, February 17, 1979, pp. 171–74; and Tom Richman, "Ray Rogers Will Get You if You Don't Watch Out," *The New Englander*, September, 1978.

[33]*Business Week*, October 16, 1978, p. 50.

[34]"UAW Accuses GM of Anti-Union Drive," *Detroit News*, July, 17, 1979.

[35]See Everett Kassalow, "U.S. Labor Standards and Conditions in International Perspective," in *American Labor in a Changing World Economy*, ed. Ward Morehouse (New York: Praeger Publishers, 1978).

[36]*The Wall Street Journal*, July 17, 1979.

[37]See "Sunbelt Strategy," *Detroit News*, February 4, 1979; also, see "Athens Asks GM to Hire Locally," *Decatur (Alabama) Daily*, October 1, 1979, and "UAW Might Win Dixie in GM Pact," *The Cleveland Plain Dealer*, September 20, 1979.

employer is unionized already, any expansion of the company into new areas of the country will simply extend that status to the new location, regardless of how or from where the plant is staffed.[38] This is an obvious tactic to counter what unions have charged is a trend toward fleeing the capital-poor, high-wage, and low productivity areas of the country (most of which also happen to permit "union security") into the "Sun Belt" where compulsory unionism is generally prohibited and where local attitudes are more critical with regard to unionization. What good does it do a company to flee (assuming the flight is really from unionization, as the unions charge) if it merely carries its union along the way by prior agreement? Needless to say, if a company commits itself in this fashion and then moves into the "Sun Belt" anyway, it must be fleeing something other than unions.

The pressures described above can produce highly advantageous arrangements for union officials by aiming at employers and at the fact that these employers have it within their power unilaterally to recognize a union, sign a contract, and (where the law permits) approve a "union security" clause. Union officials and employers can almost totally ignore the wishes and needs of employees.

Thus, the overall thesis of the argument is supported by union attempts to make the employer a more or less active ally in promoting unionization as an alternative to convincing employees that union services provide workers sufficient net benefit to justify their individual decisions to vote for or to join the union. It is always preferable, however, to have additional strategies and forces available to augment union pressures on employers and, in the American industrial relations system, that added force must be the government. Unions might utilize other parties (the clergy or educators, for example) but none of these enjoys the critical and substantial role

government plays—particularly since government itself has increased its ability to affect an expanded number of social and economic activities earlier considered totally private in nature.

There are at least as many ways unions and government can join to the profit of the former as there are ways government actions impact the economy. One important category, not to be covered in great detail here, involves the areas in which government regulates union activities. For example, over the years, the NLRB has developed an enormous body of precedents regarding permissible and impermissible behavior in labor relations. Since many of these precedents affect the pace and success of unionizing, organizing, negotiating, and compelling membership or support, it should not be difficult to understand why union officials have always been interested in who makes those precedents and what these rulings might accomplish. Nor should it be any surprise that, since the NLRB's creation, there have appeared allegations that the law administered by the board and the particular ways the board's personnel have interpreted the law have tended to favor unions over employers (and employees), unionization over nonunion status, and "union security" over voluntary choice. If, in fact, there is such a disequilibrium, its import lies in the fact that, through it, union officials can avoid regular, sustained organizing and maintaining the sort of voluntary, beneficial relationship with employees which would maximize their bargaining position.

The most basic level at which this can occur is, of course, the legislation itself. The Wagner Act, in effect, declared encouragement of unionization to be the nation's public policy. In furtherance of this, as interpreted and administered by the NLRB, we may note for example such unremarked but curious situations as the fact that only a majority of employees voting in an agent election is required for the union to win, but a majority of *all* employees in the unit must vote to deauthorize a compulsory unionism contract clause. Employers may not promise or threaten employees prior to an election, but virtually no parallel prohibition is applied against union

---

[38] The *Washington Post* (September 5, 1979) reported, for example, that the newest UAW-GM agreement provides for "automatic recognition . . . at new plants without the considerable expense and risk of a representation election." See also, "Industry, Unions Watching Negotiations Between Ford and UAW on Accretion Issue," *Daily Labor Report* 152 (August 6, 1979), p. c-1.

organizations. An unfair labor practice committed by an employer can cause a union loss in an election to be not merely set aside but actually reversed into a union win, yet a union unfair labor practice seldom, if ever, has a similar result. A "union security" clause (where permitted) can be put into a contract solely by agreement between a union and an employer, but it takes a major effort involving concerted employee action in the form of a "deauthorization election" to *remove* such a clause.

Aside from labor laws, the federal government encourages (indeed, at times, almost requires) unionization in other ways through the operation of other laws. The Davis-Bacon Act has been a highly controversial example of this. As administered, Davis-Bacon sets the "prevailing wage" standard by reference to union wage rates and thus gives unionized contractors a decided edge in bidding for construction projects under the act's aegis. Also controversial is the encouragement to unionization given by minimum wage laws: the higher the minimum wage is set, the more protected is the union wage rate as employers are forced to raise the level of qualifications (experience, training, and so forth) they expect from applicants.

These, however, are relatively indirect when compared with other examples of government entering the field of organizing on behalf of unions. The Department of Housing and Urban Development administers a program of housing assistance (demonstration rehabilitation) which requires that communities desiring such funds must provide evidence to the department that they have a bargaining contract with the construction unions in the area (Section 881, 401–404, 41 Federal Register 49485–49486, 1976). In other words, to get this taxpayer-funded assistance, a public housing authority must normally already be unionized or must agree to become unionized. The Urban Mass Transportation Act (1964, and as amended thereafter) gives the Secretary of Labor the power (Section 13) to require minimum wages in accordance with Davis-Bacon and (in subsection C) "fair and equitable" labor relations standards: this power is not subject to review in any court of law.

The secretary of labor can, under this authority, condition grants of public funds for urban mass transit upon the presence and continuation of unionization and a collective bargaining contract: this is said not to infringe upon the power of the states because they are always free to refuse such federal aid.[39] As administered, however, there is evidence that the public transportation employees must not only be unionized, but also that the local contract must be acceptable to the international union. The city of Albuquerque, for example, was refused mass transit funds because the United Transportation Union (UTU) disapproved of the contract its local had signed with the city; on that basis alone, the Department of Labor refused clearance. Reportedly, one "benefit" the contract lacked was a compulsory unionism clause.[40]

Not to be outdone in this regard, the Department of Health, Education, and Welfare (Health Care Financing Administration, part of the Medicare program) has informed all health care providers that HEW regulations permit providers to be compensated by Medicare for any and all reasonable expenses related to collective bargaining (e.g., negotiations and administration of a contract) because these expenses are "related to patient care." But any expenses incurred by a provider in encouraging or discouraging unionization are "not related to patient care and, therefore, are not allowable" (i.e., Medicare will not compensate a provider for them). Should anyone miss the message (after all, not many employers in the health care field are likely to encourage unionization), the only example given of a nonallowable cost in this respect involves opposing unionization (hiring a "consultant who furnishes literature . . . or . . . training . . . to oppose employee membership in labor organizations").[41]

An interesting variation on federal legislation which encourages unionization, organiz-

---

[39]*City of Macon v. Marshall*, 439 F. supp. 1209 (M.D. Geo., 1977).

[40]*Albuquerque Journal*, editorial, January 23, 1976; see also, from the same source, articles on February 10, 1977; December 17, 1977; February 15, 1978; and July 2, 1978.

[41]Transmittal No. 218 (June, 1979), *Medicare Provider Reimbursement Manual*, in re Sections 2180–1–2.

ing, or compulsory membership is the attempt in 1977 (by way of a series of amendments to the National Labor Relations Act) to specify disproportionately harsh penalties applied against any employer deemed guilty of an "unfair labor practice" by the NLRB. The proposed "Labor Law Reform Act of 1977" (S.1883), barely defeated by a Senate filibuster, would have debarred such employers from all federal contracts for three years (Section 8). It need hardly be added that even the threat of being found guilty of an "unfair labor practice" would have created virtually intolerable pressures for an employer to conform in all important respects to the wishes of union officials with whom the company was negotiating—including their demands for recognition, exclusivity, or "union security." Obviously, should an employer have been debarred from federal contracts, the party injured most by this action would have been employees.

Closer to the frontier of experimentation is a serious push by the UAW to require "code-termination" as one of the terms set for government aid to the Chrysler Corporation. The UAW has demanded and won "shop-floor-to-boardroom" union participation in "management decisions" similar to the system ("*mit-bestimmung*") developed in Germany.[42] Clearly, union-controlled participation in a company's management places the union in the curious position of bargaining with itself.

Also at the frontier are legislative efforts to prevent plants from moving, allegedly to escape unionization. To the extent this may be true, any effort to restrict such moves must be seen as an attempt to maintain unionization when at least one of the parties (the employer) has determined that this condition is economically disadvantageous. Legislation to this effect is already on the books in Maine and has been proposed in Ohio, New Jersey, and the U.S. Congress.[43] On the federal level, the proposed legislation would have created an agency to investigate closings and transfers, have set a variety of penalties to be applied to

any firms whose plans were deemed "without adequate justification," have mandated several forms of government assistance to employees, and would have required that advance notice be given.

IV. THE IMPLICATIONS OF PUSHBUTTON UNIONISM

Pushbutton unionism has important implications for unions, employers, workers, and consumers. It is clear that unions as organizations benefit substantially from strategies which permit increases in membership without the associated costs of organizing and recruiting. Increased membership provides union officials with additional income from dues, fines, fees, and assessments that may be used to further their activities, including lobbying and the other political practices in which they have long engaged. As mentioned in the introduction, increased membership itself enhances the political power of union organizations because the strength of an organization is generally measured by total numbers. Of course, as the political influence of unions grows, it will become easier for unions to enlist government support of other practices which foster pushbutton unionism. In simple terms, pushbutton unionism increases the power of unions in the political sphere. Pushbutton unionism also enhances the bargaining strength of unions in their negotiations with employers. For example, as the number of union members grows, so do the financial resources invested in union-controlled pension funds. It is also clear that other sectors of the economy do not benefit from increases in the power of trade unions, as discussed below.

An increase in the bargaining power of unions will lead to increased demands for wages and fringe benefits beyond the competitive levels justified by productivity. To the extent that the costs of these concessions can be passed on to the consumer in the form of higher prices, inflationary pressures are exacerbated in the domestic economy. Consumers, in an attempt to avoid the higher prices of products produced by unionized firms, will then purchase lower-cost foreign imports or

[42]*Washington Post*, August 1, 1979.
[43]Richard B. McKenzie, *Restrictions on Business Mobility* (Washington, D.C.: American Enterprise Institute, 1979), p. 1.

domestic substitutes produced by nonunionized firms. If nonunion producers also raise prices to increase profits, low-cost imported goods may be the only feasible substitutes for higher-priced domestic products. In a number of highly unionized industries, e.g., leather products (40 percent union), textiles (46 percent), electrical equipment (61 percent), and primary metals (53 percent), foreign competitors have captured substantial segments of U.S. markets. Additional increases in the already alarming flood of imports would worsen the balance of payments deficit and weaken further the embattled dollar in foreign markets.

As unemployment rises due to the displacement of U.S. workers by competition from foreign firms, pressure is brought on politicians by the public, in general, and unions, in particular, for government action to stimulate demand in the economy. Historically, government spending has been increased in order to create jobs; these fiscal policy measures have typically been financed by deficit spending which results in an increase in the money supply—the primary source of inflation. Increased political power from pushbutton methods will strengthen union efforts for expansionary fiscal policies to "protect" union jobs and thereby to exacerbate inflation.

A second reaction of unions and of domestic firms to increased competition from abroad is to push for legislation that reduces foreign competition. The usual policies designed to restrict imports are quotas and tariffs. Protective tariffs affect not only the allocation of resources within the United States, but also, like most taxes, affect the personal distribution of income. Import duties tend to reduce the volume of imports and raise the domestic price of the commodity on which a tariff has been levied. On the one hand, tariffs will provide an immediate benefit to domestic producers of the good and, of course, the labor union. On the other hand, however, the public is forced to pay higher prices for the protected commodity.

The main effect of tariffs is to create a misallocation of resources by causing factors of production to be retained in protected industries rather than being transferred to their most efficient uses. Some of the resources misallocated by the effects of protective tariffs are very likely to be withheld from the production of export goods.[44] Also, by leading to a reduction in the volume of imports, protective tariffs tend to reduce foreign demand for U.S. exports. In the final analysis, then, protective tariffs tend to result in a reallocation of resources from the relatively efficient export industries to the relatively inefficient protected industries.

If employers must absorb the demands of labor unions for higher wages and fringe benefits because, for example, they are constrained from relocating, a reduction in profits and output will occur. As McKenzie has observed,

On balance . . . the country will be poorer: relocation rules cause resources to be inefficiently allocated among regions and fewer goods and services to be produced. In other words, the per capita income of the country will be restricted; that is, if it grows, it will grow by less than otherwise because of the relocation rules.[45]

Workers, even unionized employees, may not gain in an economic sense from the increased bargaining power required by union officials through "pushbutton" strategies. Both the union and the nonunion worker would be paying higher prices for products produced by unionized firms and inflation would erode the purchasing power of income. There is, it should also be noted, no guarantee that the gains made by the union workers who remain employed would be large enough to offset the effects of inflation.[46] In addition, union workers will be displaced as consumers switch to lower-cost domestic or foreign goods and services, and unionized firms respond by reducing output. Increased relative benefits for unionized workers will also result in the substitution of capital for labor. As unionized

---

[44]A complete explanation of the effects of protective tariffs can be found in Charles P. Kindleberger, *International Economics* (Homewood, Ill.: Richard D. Irwin, 1963), pp. 244–66.

[45]McKenzie, *Restrictions on Business Mobility.*

[46]For a thorough discussion of the pecuniary and nonpecuniary costs and benefits of unionization, see James T. Bennett and Manuel H. Johnson, "Free Riders in U.S. Labour Unions: Artifice of Affliction?" *British Journal of Industrial Relations* 17 (July 1979), pp. 158–72.

workers are displaced, many will attempt to find work in the nonunion sector since workers who have lost their jobs prefer working at the nonunion wage to remaining unemployed. A decline in GNP occurs as a result of displacement because unionized workers who are forced to shift to the nonunion sector generally cannot find full employment for their specialized skills. Therefore, reduced output results from lower production in the unionized sector and underemployment of labor in the nonunion sector.[47] Unionized sectors of the economy will become more capital intensive and nonunion sectors will tend to be more labor intensive. The welfare loss from displacement effects due to the increased cost of union benefits was estimated by Rees to be at least $600 million for the year 1957.[48] In a more recent study, Johnson and Mieszkowski found that the loss in aggregate welfare in 1970 due to resource misallocation caused by unionism is .33 percent of GNP, or about $6.6 billion annually for a $2 trillion economy.[49] Reynolds has pointed out, however, that this traditional measure of welfare loss underestimates the cost of increased unionization.[50] In fact, additional union earnings from pushbutton methods require the consumption of real resources. Reynolds estimated that the annual union wage advantage was at least $30 billion and that if only one half of this earnings differential represented real costs, the loss in GNP would approach $22 billion annually. Pushbutton unionism should substantially increase the displacement of workers and, therefore, the welfare loss to the economy.

It has also been shown that increased unionization has not altered the distribution or relative shares of aggregate income between labor and other factors of production. Labor's share in national income has increased over time simply because the structure of the economy has shifted toward service-oriented output which is labor intensive. Because this structural shift has little to do with union activity, investigators have traditionally adjusted for the change in labor's share due to changes in the structure of the economy. Studies of the compensation of employees as a percentage of national income have been conducted by a number of researchers who found no significant correlation between the level of union strength and changes in labor's relative share of income.[51] Marshall, Cartter, and King summarized these findings in their conclusions:

Reviewing the data from 1919 to present, and particularly the last 20 years, there seems to be no indication that trade unions in general have increased labor's share of income. Particular unions in specific industries may have done so, but if so, they have been balanced off by other unions who have been much less successful than many of the unorganized groups of workers.[52]

In addition, unionization by pushbutton techniques reduces the ability of employees to exercise free choice in determining the conditions of their work environment. For some individual workers, the pecuniary and nonpecuniary costs of unionization may be substantial, especially if the election process is avoided. Berkowitz has observed that, "Some persons would not affiliate [with the union] on a voluntary basis, even if the dues payments were negative."[53] In other words, workers who

[47]A detailed discussion of resource misallocation due to union/nonunion wage differentials and worker displacement can be found in Albert Rees, *The Economics of Work and Pay* (New York: Harper & Row, 1973), pp. 159–61.

[48]Albert Rees, "The Effects of Unions on Resource Allocation," *Journal of Law and Economics* 6 (October 1963), pp. 69–78.

[49]Harry G. Johnson and P. Mieszkowski, "The Effects of Unionization on the Distribution of Income: A General Equilibrium Approach," *Quarterly Journal of Economics* 84 (November 1970), pp. 539–61.

[50]Morgan O. Reynolds, "The Free Rider Argument for Compulsory Union Dues" (Paper presented at the conference on Economic Aspects of Union Membership: Free Riders or Paying Customers, Washington, D.C., September 15, 1978). Mimeographed.

[51]See, for example, Edward F. Denison, "Income Types and the Size Distribution," *American Economic Review* 44 (May 1954), pp. 254–69; Joseph D. Phillips, "Labor's Share and 'Wage Parity'," *Review of Economics and Statistics* 42 (May 1960), pp. 164–74; Harold M. Levinson, "Collective Bargaining and Income Distribution," *American Economic Review* 44 (May 1954), pp. 308–18; and Ray Marshall, Allen M. Cartter, and Allen G. King, *Labor Economics: Wages, Employment and Trade Unionism* 3d. ed. (Homewood, Ill.: Richard D. Irwin, 1976).

[52]Marshall et al., *Labor Economics*, pp. 374–75.

[53]Monroe Berkowitz, "The Economics of Trade Union Organization and Administration," *Industrial and Labor Relations Review* 7 (July 1954), p. 580.

are automatically unionized by pushbutton methods may become "forced riders."[54]

Increased union power through pushbutton methods is expected to bring about a more rapid unionization of Right-to-Work states and these states should be affected by rising prices due to trade union growth. In fact, Colberg has investigated the inflationary impact of greater unionization in Right-to-Work states and estimated that the cost of goods in a typical family "market basket" in these states would increase by $200.[55] Colberg assumed that the majority of union organizing efforts occur in the textile and food processing industries and that wages in these industries will increase to the level of union workers in the same region. The resulting price increases in the textile and food processing industries are 8 percent and 4.3 percent, respectively. Assuming these increases translate directly to the cost of clothing and food, a family's clothing budget would increase by $82 and the food budget by $86.[56]

V. Summary and Conclusions

In terms of obtaining and retaining membership, the source of labor union political and financial resources, American unions have operated differently from their counterparts in Western Europe. Because of social and economic factors, Western European unions have not been forced to search for members, whereas in the United States trade unions have traditionally increased membership by actively and aggressively organizing workers through an appeal to their economic self-interest. Once established, unions further increased and retained members by negotiating "union security" agreements with employers. With the passage of legislation which encouraged unionization during the Great Depression, notably the Wagner Act of 1935, unions grew rapidly in both membership and political influence. By the early 1970s, however, a number of factors influencing unionization not only caused a decline in membership, but also caused union officials to question the cost-effectiveness of organizing activity as a recruiting technique. Among these factors are the declining effectiveness of compulsory unionism, a change in the occupational structure of the work force from manufacturing to the service sector—blue-collar workers (the traditional targets of union organizers) have declined markedly relative to white-collar workers, especially in recent years—technological change which has reduced the drudgery of blue-collar work, better managers with training in "human relations" management, and more sophisticated, better-educated workers.[57]

A decline in membership poses serious problems for labor unions, for it can reduce the political effectiveness of the union and can undermine its financial support derived from dues, fees, fines, and assessments. Because the historical strongholds of labor in the blue-collar ranks have already been saturated with union activity or have declined in importance either because of the shift in occupational structure of the work force or because of competition from foreign producers, union organizing activity is both costly and likely to be ineffective. Therefore, to increase and retain members, union officials have recently changed their tactics and have elicited the assistance of employers and government in "pushbutton methods" which do not permit workers to vote on union representation.

This article documents the shift to "pushbutton unionism," surveys the techniques that have been employed, and analyzes their economic, political, and organizational implications. The methods of pushbutton unionism are new, experimental, and controversial. Direct union pressures on employers involve such techniques as the use of union pension funds as a financial weapon to obtain unilateral recognition without employee involvement and to obtain a "union security" provision in the contract; bribery, extortion, or threats may also be employed by the union to apply pressure on employers; "accretion" or "neutrality"

---

[54]See Bennett and Johnson for a complete discussion of the free rider and forced rider phenomenon.

[55]Marshall R. Colberg, *The Consumer Impact of Repeal of 14b* (Washington, D.C.: The Heritage Foundation, 1978), p. 24.

[56]*Ibid.*

---

[57]See Shrank for a discussion of these factors.

agreements have been negotiated which grant instant recognition of the union at any new facilities operated by the employer or which "pack" existing unorganized plants with union members preferentially transferred from organized plants elsewhere. Pushbutton unionism is effective because employers have the right unilaterally to recognize a union, sign a contract, and, where legal, approve a "union security" clause without consulting employees.

Unions have also gained the assistance of government in increasing membership without incurring the costs of organizing activity. The National Labor Relations Board, which oversees labor relations activity, has frequently interpreted labor legislation asymmetrically in favor of unions. For example, in an election to obtain union recognition, only a majority of those voting must be in favor of the union for the union to be installed, but, to deauthorize a union, a majority of the members of the bargaining unit must vote against the union. Minimum wage legislation and the Davis-Bacon Act help to protect union workers from nonunionized labor. Government agencies, such as the Department of Health, Education, and Welfare and the Department of Transportation, have insisted that "acceptable" union contracts exist as a condition of the receipt of federal funds. Although union bargaining and negotiating expenses are "allowable" costs to be reimbursed by federal funds for providing health care, funds expended in opposition to union activity cannot be reimbursed. Unions have also sought government assistance in restricting the mobility of firms by legislation which would create an agency to investigate plant closings, require advance notice, and penalize firms deemed to have transferred their activities without "adequate justification."

The above list of "pushbutton unionism" techniques is merely suggestive, but by no means exhaustive, for unions are actively seeking alternatives to organizing in order to recruit and retain members. One recent example is the agreement negotiated between Chrysler and the United Auto Workers which provides the union with a seat on the company's board of directors. In addition, the advocacy of the nationalization of the oil industry by the president of the International Association of Machinists can implicitly be regarded as a pushbutton unionism technique, for union political influence could be employed to aid in organizing workers throughout a nationalized industry. Variations on current methods and new techniques can be expected as unions discover through experimentation the most fruitful avenues of pushbutton unionism.

The major beneficiaries of pushbutton unionism are union officials themselves and the politicians who receive campaign contributions and support from unions. Employers, because of the increased bargaining power of unions, will experience higher costs of production and lower profits which, in the long run, will inhibit investment and reduce the capital base of the economy. Foreign competition will increase as will the prices paid by consumers for goods and services. Inflation and balance of payment problems will become more severe. Nonunion workers will be at a relative disadvantage because of decreased purchasing power as inflation erodes income and because of competition for jobs from displaced union workers. Even union members who retain their jobs may not benefit from pushbutton unionism, for it is not at all certain that the wage and fringe benefit increases obtained by individual workers will offset the effects of inflation, particularly after taking into account the payments which individuals must make to the union.

READING 16

New Strategies in Union Organizing*

James A. Craft and Marian M. Extejt

The AFL–CIO has called for new and more effective approaches in organizing. This paper reviews the classical organizing model and then identifies four strategic approaches to organizing that have been developed or re-emphasized in recent years including the corporate power strategy, the collective bargaining strategy, community acceptance and integration strategy, and the coordinated/pooled resource strategy. Factors affecting the use and success of these strategies are discussed. It is concluded that while some have promise, their limited use and mixed outcomes will probably minimize their significance in union organizing during the 1980s.

I. INTRODUCTION

Since the 1950s, the proportion of unionized workers in the American labor force has been declining. In addition, knowledgeable analysts forecast that the labor movement will likely experience continued stagnation in the 1980s (BNA, 1980), even though recent survey research suggests that a substantial proportion of currently unorganized workers would vote to join a union (Kochan, 1979). In response to this secular decline in membership, some union officials have emphasized the need for increased organizing activity and have called for more effective and creative strategies in organizing the sizeable reservoir of nonunion workers. There is, however, little analysis or systematically formulated information available about the activities unions are actually undertaking.[1]

This paper identifies and critically discusses organizing strategies that recently have been developed or re-emphasized and employed by unions. This study is based upon a thorough review of the available scholarly literature regarding union organizing, an extensive examination of union publications, labor reporting service information, newspaper accounts, and other documents describing and identifying union organizing activity, and 18 interviews with national union officials or former unionists who have particular knowledge or experience relating to current organizing strategies and approaches.

Section II presents a perspective on the classical approach to organizing and discusses ways in which this may be changing. Then, a review of emergent organizing strategies being used by some unions is given in Section III. Next, from interviews and other data, a preliminary examination is given of factors which appear to affect the use and success of these approaches to organizing. Finally, concluding comments regarding union organizing in the 1980s are developed in the last section.

II. THE CLASSICAL APPROACH

A review of the available documents, literature, and recorded experience regarding union organizing activity over the last 50 years suggests that there is not a standard body of techniques and methods that is uniformly employed in organizing campaigns.[2] The classical organizing process generally consists of various "tactics, expedients, and improvisations" developed by the individual organizers to respond to the immediate situation (Bar-

---

*Reprinted with permission by *Journal of Labor Research* 4, no. 1 (Winter 1983), pp. 19–32.

†*Professors Craft and Extejt are on the faculty of the School of Business at the University of Pittsburgh.*

[1]As far as we know, the only recent scholarly paper that focuses on this issue, but from a somewhat different perspective, is the study by Bennett and Johnson (1980). It could be read profitably in conjunction with this article.

[2]Some of the best published research regarding the classical approach to organizing includes: Bambrick and Stieglitz, 1959; Barbash, 1956; Brooks, 1937; Ginzberg, 1948; Karsh, *et al.*, 1953; McKersie and Brown, 1953; Perkel, 1957; and Strauss, 1953.

bash, 1956). There appear to be few, if any, broadly coordinated and targeted activities.

Traditionally, most unions conduct highly decentralized organizing programs with the effort directed at individual work units (e.g., offices, plants). The organizer, a person who is generally self-trained in union organizing activity and comes from the rank-and-file membership, is the key individual who has substantial control over the design and implementation of the organizing campaign. In organizing efforts, the organizer is the embodiment of the union to the prospective union members.

The emphasis in organizing activity appears to be directed heavily toward face-to-face contact with union recruits. The organizer visits homes of employees to discuss the union, develops social contacts and relationships with workers, organizes small informal meetings of prospective members, and occasionally obtains employment in the target company to have direct access to and integration with the employees. Through their contacts and effort, union organizers seek "ways to transform individual dissatisfaction into a collective condition of unrest" and "channel it into the direction of group action through the formation of a union" (Karsh, et al., 1953, pp. 33, 94). The organizer generally attempts to tailor the organizing approach to the concerns and problems of the prospective members (e.g., the special needs of women workers, skilled workers, racial and ethnic groups, white-collar workers). The organizer sells the idea of group action—that through the instrumentality of the union the employees' concerns and dissatisfactions could be addressed effectively.

Traditionally, face-to-face organizing activity is *facilitative* in nature; that is, working with and through employees to convince them of the usefulness of a union. Nevertheless, some organizing activity at the employee level includes coercive tactics as well. Some activities involve the use of group pressure, threats, or violence against union holdouts. Coercive activity has been more common, however, in the less frequent organizing efforts directed at the employer (e.g., owner or plant manager) in a "top down" organizing program. In such cases, the union generally demands recognition as bargaining agent for the employees in a proposed unit. To enforce its demand, it directly threatens or conducts a strike, slowdown, boycott, or implements organizational picketing.

This decentralized, personally oriented, and generally reactive approach to organizing appears to have been successful from the 1930s through the 1960s. Since the early 1970s, however, this approach seems to have been less fruitful as witnessed by the declining proportion of union victories in representation elections and the subsequent relative decline of union members in the work force.

III. A NEW EMPHASIS IN ORGANIZING

Leaders of the AFL–CIO have explicitly called for the development of new, more effective, and imaginative strategies and tactics to enhance organizing success (Shevis, 1980; Barry, 1980). In response to the changing environment and the encouragement of the Federation, some unions have forged new strategic thrusts and approaches to organizing that appear to transcend the classical model. Generally speaking, these approaches are oriented toward the development of coordinated and targeted activities. They seem to be characterized by union institutional planning and control rather than by delegating organizing responsibility basically to the organizer. With some of the newer strategies, increased attention appears to be directed to the employer organization (or group of employers) as a *system* rather than the decentralized orientation with emphasis on the individual plant. A few unions are employing a wider scope of pressure tactics ranging from indirect sophisticated financial pressures to coordinated direct confrontations with the employer. These unions seem increasingly willing to utilize coercive as well as facilitative tactics in organizing. Along with this, face-to-face recruiting and personal organizing activity remain important processes, but are viewed more as integral parts of a *larger program* to induce employees to join or force the employer to recognize the union.

From our review of recent organizing activity and experience, we are able to identify four basic strategic thrusts that seem to represent the "new emphasis in organizing." These include: the corporate power strategy; the collective bargaining strategy; the community acceptance and integration strategy; and the coordinated/pooled resource strategy.

IV. THE CORPORATE POWER STRATEGY

This strategy is designed to coerce a firm targeted for organizing into recognizing the union by applying financial pressures, confronting the employer, and isolating it from the business and consumer communities. Generally, careful analysis of a firm is conducted in terms of its environment and power base. Then, a multifaceted campaign is deployed focusing on the areas in which the firm appears to have the greatest vulnerability. There is a wide array of tactics and actions employed to exert pressure.

Pressure/Harass Business Associates. One significant tactic in this strategy is to prod, harass, and embarrass firms that have directorate ties or are involved in business associations with the target company. In effect, these activities are designed to bring other firms, against their will, into the labor dispute between the company undergoing the organizing drive and the union. The resulting threats of harmful publicity and possible financial loss resulting from the undesired involvement in the dispute constitute the inducement for these business associates to sever relations with the target firm or to exert pressure on it to cease resisting the organizing efforts. Such activity, it is argued, can undercut the object company's financial support and isolate it from the mainstream business community.

Illustrative of such activity was ACTWU's action to contest the board of directors elections for New York Life Insurance Company and Metropolitan Life Insurance Company—each of which had J. P. Stevens directors on its board and apparently had financial dealings with the company. The threat of adverse publicity and the cost of conducting the elections led these firms to oust the Stevens board members and exert pressures on Stevens to deal with the union. ACTWU and its allied unions have also used the threat of withdrawal of funds or severance of business relationships with firms if they retained directors from antiunion firms. Examples of this would be the 1978 threat by these unions to withdraw their assets from trust funds managed by Manufacturers Hanover to protest the membership of a Stevens official on the Hanover board. Also, Sperry Corporation received letters from numerous labor organizations protesting the membership of a Stevens official on its board and threatening to sever ties with the computer manufacturer if he were retained.

Confrontation with Owners/Management. In combination with other tactics, some unions are engaging in direct confrontations with management and stockholders of antiunion companies. The objective is to make the stockholders aware of management's behavior toward employees and unions, to create adverse publicity for the firm, and embarrass management before the owners of the company. The confrontations may take the form of mass demonstrations and picketing at a company's annual meeting. Such a tactic was used by ACTWU in launching its corporate campaign against J. P. Stevens at the 1977 annual meeting of the company in New York City. Or, the confrontations may occur in the stockholders meeting itself. For example, the union (as a stockholder attending the meeting) raises questions during the meeting regarding the company's antiunion conduct. The Teamsters union, trying to organize southern plants of PPG Industries, used such a confrontational approach in the 1980 annual meeting of the firm. The confrontation with management consumed most of the question period of the meeting.

Financial Pressures. One widely advocated tactic, designed to pressure antiunion firms by restricting their flow of investment capital, is for unions to seek increased influence over the investment of pension and welfare funds (Rifkin and Barber, 1978; Raskin, 1979; Gutchess, 1980). With greater voice in policy and decision-making, it is argued that the union can direct investment away from those companies whose behavior is deemed antiunion and which resist organizing efforts. Greater union voice and influence is gained through more assertiveness and focused objectives by labor trustees on jointly administered pension funds (e.g., negotiated multiemployer plans) and by gaining increased control and participation in other plans through collective bargaining (Greenough and King, 1976). As an example of the latter, the G. Heilman Brewing Company and the Allied Industrial Workers Local 812 recently agreed to a joint investment committee consisting of members selected by the union and the company to deal with investment of the company pension fund assets. Each side has one aggregate vote and, when the parties cannot agree, a decision is made by a neutral arbitrator.

Another aspect of the financial pressure tactic is the union threat to withdraw pension funds and other resources directly from firms whose employees it seeks to represent. For example, the Retail Clerks Union and its allies, in 1979, threatened to withdraw a reported $2 billion in deposits and pension funds from the Seattle First National Bank unless the bank recognized the union as the bargaining agent for its employees.

Product Market Pressure. As part of a corporate power strategy, unions are also employing more conventional pressure tactics to affect adversely the market position of an antiunion company and create consumer and public support for the union cause. For example, in *conjunction* with other tactics, the boycott has been used in several recent organizing campaigns. Illustrative are the United Food and Commercial Workers boycotts against Winn-Dixie and Perdue Farms, Inc., as well as ACTWU's boycott of J. P. Stevens. The success of a boycott tactic as part of the corporate power strategy is not necessarily in its economic impact on the company as much as it is in its ability to arouse the press, the public, and legislative opinion against the antiunion company.

In addition, it is to be noted that another traditional weapon, picketing, is being used in corporate campaign strategies. The Airline Pilots Association, in its short-lived campaign to organize the pilots of New York Air, picketed the airports to discourage customers from riding the airline and inform the public about the dispute.

V. COLLECTIVE BARGAINING STRATEGY

This strategic approach to organizing has been employed by unions which already have an established bargaining relationship with a company. It is an *inside* strategy whereby the union, using its bargaining leverage in the ongoing relationship, attempts to negotiate binding contractual rules that will facilitate the organization of current and planned nonunion company facilities. This strategy has been employed in multiplant firms that traditionally have been well organized but are now closing older unionized plants and opening new plants in nonunion areas. Usually, only one or two key unions represent workers in these firms and the bargaining structure is centralized.

One approach is the negotiation of a "neutrality pledge." Such a pledge, which is part of the negotiated labor agreement, requires that the company remain strictly neutral and not oppose a union organizing drive at any of the company's nonunion facilities. Neutrality pledges have been negotiated in several industries including the UAW-General Motors contracts of 1976 and 1979, the basic steel settlement agreement in 1977, and the contracts between the United Rubber Workers and most major tire manufacturers in 1979 (Craft, 1980).

Another approach implementing this strategic thrust is the negotiation of an "accretion agreement." Under such an agreement, the company emphasizes the similarities and functional integration of new facilities with existing plants. When a new plant opens, it is viewed simply as a transfer and extention of current operations—an accretion. In such circumstances, the union is granted automatic recognition as the bargaining agent for employees. Illustrative is the 1979 IUE-GM agreement in which the company agreed to recognize the IUE at new Packard and Delco plants that manufacture products similar to those where the union has representation rights. Also, the UAW has negotiated such agreements into the basic automobile industry contracts.

Finally, negotiated transfer and preferential hiring rights have also been used recently to facilitate the organization of new plants. Under the UAW-GM agreement, for example, employees have the right to transfer, with full seniority, to any new GM plant making products like those produced in plants already organized by the union. In the UAW-Budd contract, union workers laid off at the Gary, Indiana, plant are given preferential hiring rights at the new Johnson City, Tennessee, plant. These transfer and hiring rights almost insure experienced unionists in the work force of unorganized plants who may act as inside organizers during an ensuing organizing drive.

VI. COMMUNITY ACCEPTANCE AND INTEGRATION

This strategic approach is increasingly employed by unions attempting to organize workers in communities and areas of the country which have no tradition of unionization. In such communities, the union is often considered to be a "foreign force." The media, educational system, community values, and opinion leaders are frequently antiunion. In such situations, union leaders argue that building a "basis of support in the community itself" to change prevailing perceptions of the labor movement and the role of collective bargaining is a key approach to organizing workers effectively ("Union Community Role," 1978; Shevis, 1980). The objectives are to develop an acceptance of the union as a legitimate member of the community and to provide credible and acceptable channels through which the prospective union members may be approached. Implementation of this strategic approach may be direct or indirect in nature.

Using a direct approach, some unions have initiated programs to specifically address social, personal, and health needs of the people in a community. By directly focusing its efforts on meaningful problems and needs, the union develops a positive image, a more credible position, and a community acceptance from which it can begin to concentrate on organizing workers for collective bargaining. Illustrative is the South Bronx Working Center established by the ILGWU Metro Organizing Committee. Located in the heart of the Bronx, the center serves as a community "friend" providing residents with a wide range of social services and functions. In addition, it provides a union presence in an area with many nonunion shops and serves as a base for organizing drives. Also, ACTWU has recently established a program to bring health and social services to union and nonunion textile workers in 23 North Carolina communities; part of the program includes a mobile unit used for health screening purposes.

An indirect approach involves the union identification with and cooperation of the natural allies in the community that already have legitimacy and acceptance among the workers the union seeks to organize. Such organizations frequently include church groups or civil rights organizations. For example, the Retail, Wholesale, and Department Store Union (RWDSU) in organizing the predominately black work force in several Alabama food processing plants, became heavily involved in the civil rights movement in the state which laid the groundwork for its organizing achievements (Hurd, 1973). Also, Local 1199 has worked with and through the Southern Christian Leadership Conference and has used its involvement in the civil rights movement to organize hospital workers (Barbash, 1973).

VII. COORDINATED/POOLED RESOURCE STRATEGY

Through coordination and/or consolidation of organizing activity, two or more unions can reduce the resources wasted in rivalry and conduct more effective overall organizing campaigns. This strategy is used to increase organizing efficiency, enhance union power and resources, and to improve the image of labor organizations.

One classic approach which is currently being emphasized is the joint union organizing drive. Under such a program, two or more unions (usually within some common sphere of activity such as building and construction trades or the Industrial Union Department) define a particular target locale and agree to pool some resources and cooperate in organizing the employees in the area. This means that the unions would share information, identify employer targets and tactics to effectively deal with them, pool resources to sponsor newspaper and television ads to promote unionization and, to the degree possible, organizers from the various unions will work to assist one another and refer possible members to cooperating unions. In addition, such cooperation and collaboration can be used to reduce administrative costs by renting offices and halls as well as having a support staff which can be used by all cooperating unions. Illustrative of one of the recent efforts utilizing this approach was the much publicized coordinated organizing drive of the AFL–CIO Building and Construction Trades Department in Los Angeles County from 1978 to 1980. Most recently, the AFL–CIO has promoted the "Houston Project" wherein more than 30 unions are currently involved in a coordinated million-dollar project to organize the Houston area.[3]

Another traditional approach to the coordinated/pooled resource strategy is the merger of unions to, among other things, reduce rivalry and enhance organizing and bargaining clout (Janus, 1978). Illustrative is the statement by the president of ACTWU pointing out that the organizing victory over J. P. Stevens "came about because of the merger" of the Amalgamated Clothing Workers and the Textile Workers Union in 1978.[4] In addition, the United Shoe Workers merged with

ACTWU in 1979 and, currently, merger discussions are underway between ACTWU and the International Ladies' Garment Workers' Union. In the recent merger between the United Food and Commercial Workers (itself a product of the merger of the Amalgamated Meatcutters and the Retail Clerks in 1979) and the Barbers and Beauticians Union, the president of the latter union stated that their merger "will give tremendous impetus to a nationwide organizing drive among the 1,500,000 workers employed in the industry we represent."[5] Other possible mergers being discussed which could promote organizing effectiveness include the Autoworkers and the Machinists and the Service Employees International Union and the RWDSU.

VIII. Factors Affecting Use

While there has been substantial rhetoric and publicity regarding some of these strategies, our research suggests that in reality they have been employed to only a limited extent. In fact, relatively few unions appear to have used them to any significant degree and, even so, the strategies have constituted only a modest part of these unions' total organizing activity.

One key reason that such strategies have not been used more is that, AFL–CIO rhetoric aside, organizing simply does not appear to be a high-priority objective for most unions (Raskin, 1981). For those that have placed more emphasis on organizing, the generally conservative nature of unions and the typical inertia in changing from traditionally accepted activity has been important. For example, some union organizing officials who have developed and practiced classical approaches express skepticism about the utility of some of the new strategies by characterizing them as "overblown" and by questioning their cost-effectiveness. Other questions have been raised about the legality and fiduciary implications of certain activities such as the selective investment of pension funds (Northrup and Northrup, 1981). Union supporters of these approaches frequently find that the general

---

[3]For a brief but reasonably good description of the Houston Project, see 108 *LRR* 162.

[4]See BNA, *Collective Bargaining Negotiations and Contracts*, January 8, 1981, p. 4.

[5]See 103 *LRR* 399.

lack of union experience, familiarity, and understanding of certain strategies (e.g., the corporate power strategy) make it difficult to convince the leadership to invest resources in such efforts. In addition, many unions simply lack the resources to design, implement, and carry through effectively some of the newer strategies (Leftwich, 1981; Gray, 1981; Bok and Dunlop, 1970). For example, most unions do not have personnel with the requisite experience and expertise to analyze thoroughly a company in its financial and business context, carefully identify its points of vulnerability as a corporation, identify and deftly exploit significant human issues related to company policy, and guide a corporate power campaign to a successful conclusion—a process which may take several years.

Factionalism and the political nature of unions, as well as rivalries between unions, seems to have played at least some role inhibiting the implementation of certain strategies. Internally, the potential political implications of investing in unorthodox organizing activity rather than servicing existing units, the lack of clear priorities in organizing and the potentially long-term payoffs of some of these strategic approaches restrain their use (Block, 1980; Bok and Dunlop, 1970). Traditional union autonomy, rivalries, and jurisdictional disputes appear to make it more difficult to induce unions into pooled resource and cooperative strategies.

When unions have moved to implement the newer strategies, the action has often been stimulated by a serious loss of membership in a core jurisdictional area (or the growth of a large competitive nonunion sector) and the inability of the union to organize the new operations or nonunion sector using traditional methods. The strategy selection may be stimulated by some special competence or experience available to the union or a position of strength in enjoys vis-à-vis the employer. For example, the most complete example of the corporate power strategy is the ACTWU campaign against J. P. Stevens. This came after years of frustrating attempts to organize the company and obtain a meaningful foothold in the South. The special skills and expertise of ACTWU staff member Ray Rogers were in-

strumental in designing and carrying out the corporate campaign against the company. A collective bargaining strategy incorporating the neutrality pledge and accretion agreement was used by the UAW after continuing frustration employing traditional methods to organize General Motors' growing list of southern plants. The union used its considerable bargaining power to implement the strategy. In addition, the coordinated organizing drive in Los Angeles by the AFL–CIO Building and Construction Trades Department (BCTD) unions was stimulated by major defection of employers in residential construction to nonunion or "doubled breasted" status. Through cooperation and coordination of efforts, the unions were able to enhance employer targeting efforts, reduce fragmentation of activity, and recoup losses from a position of combined strength.

IX. Factors Affecting Success

From the information and data currently available, organizing outcomes resulting from the use of these strategies appear to be mixed. While a complete evaluation is not possible at this time, our findings suggest factors that seem relevant to the successful implementation and outcomes of the newer strategies.

For example, one such factor is the union's willingness to commit adequate resources to implement fully and follow through with its strategy. Some approaches such as the corporate power strategy and the community acceptance and integration strategy frequently extend over long time periods and require nontraditional expenditures (e.g., mailings to stockholders, employment of social workers). They need resources to establish and maintain appropriate visibility, maintain a significant pressure or service level, and retain special personnel to implement and conduct them. Lack of experience with such programs and various internal union political pressures can undercut the overall commitment of resources which may result in something less than maximum success. For example, the ACTWU settlement with Stevens, which was a limited success at best, appears to have been partly the result of union financial problems as well as the business problems the company was facing.

A second significant factor is the existence of a support system of other unionized employees. This is a contextual factor and refers to the extent of unionization and cooperation among unions that are complementary to those directly involved in the organizing drive. It is particularly important in developing a coordinated/pooled resource strategy. It also plays a role in community acceptance and integration strategy as well as some aspects of corporate power strategy. The effectiveness of the coordinated strategy used by the BCTD unions in Los Angeles was due significantly to the substantial unionization of support workers (e.g., truck drivers, building supply workers) in the area and their willingness to support the coordinated organizing campaign of the core building trades unions. On the other hand, lack of broad support is apparently part of the explanation for the failure of the Retail Clerks Union to force Seattle First National Bank to recognize it as the bargaining agent for workers. The threatened withdrawal of union funds never materialized at the level needed to force the bank to capitulate.

A third factor, particularly important to the collective bargaining strategy, is the ability of the parties to enforce an agreement covering a number of decentralized and diffuse operating units. For example, while the UAW has generally been quite pleased with the effectiveness of the neutrality pledge, it has found that, in some local plants, management simply does not abide by the agreement or else works through community antiunion forces to subvert union organizing activity. Where geographic distances are great, violations by management are not blatant, and operations are relatively small, it is difficult to enforce the negotiated neutrality pledge.

In addition to the above, direct management resistance and specific reactions to union strategies can certainly affect success. For example, General Electric and Goodyear have specifically refused to include a neutrality clause in their labor agreements. Some companies such as Sperry, Inc., have directly confronted and rejected union pressures to

rid their boards of managers from companies resisting union organization. Increasing numbers of employers (one knowledgeable interviewee estimated 80 percent) are using sophisticated consultants, including lawyers and psychologists, to contravene union organizing strategies and tactics to maintain a nonunion work force.

Another factor that seems to have had some impact on the success of union organizing strategies is the nature of the work force and community in which the strategy is employed. For example, the ILGWU South Bronx Working Center appears to be a strategic move to develop trust and provide a union presence in an area where there are a number of nonunion employers. Yet, the population serviced by the union is fluid and includes many immigrants (some here illegally). It is a *very slow* process to develop a relationship of confidence with the community and observe payoffs in terms of organizing breakthroughs. Also, the UAW has found that in some of the southern auto plants in which jobs were obtained on the basis of personal relationships (e.g., friends, county commissioners) promises often have been made not to vote for a union. The neutrality clause or transfer agreements offer limited possibilities in such cases.

Finally, the traditional independence of unions and the relations between them (particularly in terms of rivalries and jurisdictional disputes) can affect the success of various organizing strategies. It may be difficult to get all the appropriate unions to consider seriously a coordinated/pooled resource approach to organizing, for example. The problem is exacerbated by the fact that many unions have extended the scope of their membership to the point where they are in direct conflict with coordinate unions. Even in a cooperative organizing effort, each union carries out individual organizing activity and there are instances where a union will simply take all groups into its ranks rather than referring them to other unions which may traditionally organize such workers. Rivalries and fear of loss of independence also inhibit the prospects for merger of viable and competitive unions. However, when unions do cooperate (due to pressure or perceived mutual interest), the results seem to be beneficial. For example, the UAW and the IUE, which had directly confronted each other in the organizing campaigns in some GM southern plants, were able to reach an agreement to eliminate their competition in organizing the type of plants that had traditionally been represented by the IUE. This cooperation appears to have resulted in some organizing successes under the neutrality agreements which had evaded the unions during their rivalry. Reduction in the extent of rivalry seems to have helped the BCTD unions in coordinated organizing efforts in Los Angeles, Washington, D.C., Arizona, and elsewhere. The current showcase Houston Project, under the direction of the AFL–CIO, seems to have a commitment for at least some degree of cooperation among a diverse group of unions. The degree of cooperation and the resultant success, however, are yet to be determined in this case.

X. Concluding Comments

We have identified, reviewed, and critically evaluated strategies that recently have been developed or re-emphasized by unions to enhance organizing effectiveness. While some of these approaches appear to have possibilities and may even add new dimensions to the organizing process, we remain skeptical as to whether they will have much effect, at least in the short run, in reversing the downward trend in union membership. As we have noted, these methods generally have been rather sparsely used; even then, the results have been mixed. In addition, the prospects are not particularly bright that such strategies will be used more or with greater success in the foreseeable future. Unions have traditionally been rather unclear and imprecise on organizing priorities in terms of long-range opportunities or goals. The political realities of union leadership and the general short-term focus of decision-making militate against their increased use. It would appear that unions do little hard assessment of organizing activity to better determine how to invest resources for the biggest payoff to the union in terms of its objectives. Subsequently, it is difficult to justify substan-

tial investment in or change toward these "new strategies."

In addition, a number of external environmental factors including declining public approval of union power and union leaders (Lipset and Schneider, 1981), a sputtering economic environment with high unemployment and limited growth, and the growing sophistication of management in maintaining a "union-free environment" all work against the prospects for significant union growth over the next several years regardless of strategies employed. While there undoubtedly are other important factors to consider, our analysis of organizing strategies leads us to agree with the pessimistic forecast in the opening paragraph that unions will likely experience continued stagnation in the 1980s.

References

Bambrick, James J., Jr., and Harold Stieglitz. "White-Collar Unionization: Case Study: OEIU Organizing Campaign." In *Unions and Leadership* ed. Jack Barbash. New York: Harper & Row 1959, pp. 169–175.

Barbash, Jack. *Labor Unions in Action*. New York: Harper & Row, 1948.

_____. "The Emergence of Urban Low-Wage Unionism." *Proceedings of the Twenty-Sixth Annual Winter Meeting*. Madison, Wis.: Industrial Relations Research Association, 1973, pp. 275–83.

_____. *The Practice of Unionism*. New York: Harper & Row, 1956.

_____. *Unions and Union Leadership*. New York: Harper & Row, 1959.

Barry, John M. "New Organizing Emphasis Tied to Unity, Cooperation." *AFL–CIO News* 25 (March 1, 1980), pp. 1, 3.

Bennett James T., and Manuel H. Johnson. *Push-button Unionism*. Fairfax, Vir.: Contemporary Economics and Business Association at George Mason University, 1980.

Berenbeim, Ronald. *Labor Unions: Where are They Heading?* New York: The Conference Board, Information Bulletin No. 93, 1981.

Berkowitz, Monroe. "The Economics of Trade Union Organizing and Administration." *Industrial and Labor Relations Review* 7 (July 1954), pp. 575–92.

Bilik, Al. "Corrupt, Crusty, or Neither? The Poll-ish View of American Unions." *Labor Law Journal* 30 (June 1979), pp. 323–33.

Block, Richard N. "Union Organizing and the Allocation of Union Resources." *Industrial and Labor Relations Review* 34 (October 1980), pp. 101–113.

BNA, "Outlook on 1980s Labor Market Changes." *Labor Relations Yearbook, 1979.* Washington, D.C.: Bureau of National Affairs, 1980, p. 25.

Brooks, Robert R. R. *When Labor Organizes.* New Haven: Yale Univeristy Press, 1937.

Bok, Derek C., and John T. Dunlop. *Labor and the American Community.* New York: Simon & Schuster, 1970.

Craft, James A. "The Employer Neutrality Pledge: Issues, Implications, and Prospects." *Labor Law Journal* 31 (December 1980), pp. 753–63.

Fulmer, William E. "Step by Step through a Union Campaign." *Harvard Business Review* 59 (July–August 1981), pp. 94–102.

Ginzberg, Eli. *The Labor Leader: An Exploratory Study.* New York: MacMillan, 1948.

Gitelman, Morton. *Unionization Attempts in Small Enterprises.* Mundelein, Ill.: Callaghan, 1963.

Gray, Lois S. "Unions Implementing Managerial Techniques." *Monthly Labor Review* 104 (June 1981). pp. 3–13.

Greenough, William C., and Francis P. King. *Pension Plans and Public Policy.* New York: Columbia University Press, 1976.

Gutchess, Jocelyn. "Pension Investment: The European Model." *The AFL–CIO Federationist* 37 (June 1980), pp. 4–20.

Hurd, Richard W. "Strategies for Union Growth in Food Manufacturing and Agriculture." *Proceedings of the Twenty-Sixth Annual Winter Meeting.* Madison, Wis.: Industrial Relations Research Association, 1973, pp. 267–74.

Industrial Union Department. *A Guidebook for Union Organizers,* Industrial Union Department, AFL–CIO; Publication no. 42 (September 1961).

Janus, Charles J. "Union Mergers in the 1970s: A Look at the Reasons and Results." *Monthly Labor Review* 101 (October 1978), pp. 13–33.

Karsh, Bernard; Joel Seidman; and Daisy M. Lilienthan. "The Union Organizer and His Tactics: A Case Study." *American Journal of Sociology* 59 (September 1953), pp. 113–22.

Kochan, Thomas A. "How American Workers View Labor Unions." *Monthly Labor Review* 102 (April 1979), pp. 23–31.

Leftwich, Howard M. "Organizing in the Eighties: A Human Resources Perspective." *Labor Law Journal* 32 (August 1981), pp. 484–91.

Lipset, Seymour Martin, and William Schneider. "Organized Labor and the Public: A Troubled Union." *Public Opinion,* (August–September 1981) pp. 52–56.

McKersie, Robert B., and Montague Brown. "Non-professional Hospital Workers and a Union Organizing Drive." *Quarterly Journal of Economics* 77 (August 1963), pp. 372–404.

Mortimer, Wyndham. *Organize.* Boston: Beacon Press, 1971.

Northrup, James P. and Herbert R. Northrup. "Union Divergent Investing of Pensions: A Power Non-Employee Relations Issues." *Journal of Labor Research* 2 (Fall 1981), pp. 191–208.

Perkel, George. "The Failure of Communication in an Organizing Campaign." *Monthly Labor Review* 80 (October 1956), pp. 1200–01.

Petzinger, Thomas, Jr. "Union Official in West Wins over Few Miners in Struggle to Recruit." *The Wall Street Journal,* October 8, 1979, pp. 1, 21.

Raskin, A. H. "From Sitdowns to 'Solidarity'." Across the Board 18 (December 1981), pp. 12–32.

Raskin, A. H. "Pension Funds Could Be the Unions' Secret Weapon." *Fortune* 100 (December 31, 1979), pp. 64–67.

Rifkin, Jeremy, and Randy Barber. *The North Will Rise Again.* Boston: Beacon Press, 1978.

Seidman, Joel; Jack London; Bernard Karsh; and Daisy L. Tagliacozzo. *The Worker Views His Union.* Chicago: The University of Chicago Press, 1958.

Siedman, Joel; Jack London; and Bernard Karsh. "Why Workers Join Unions." *Annals of the American Academy of Political and Social Sciences* 274 (March 1951) pp. 75–84.

Shevis, James M. "Organizing Goals Form IUD Convention Theme." *AFL–CIO News* 25 (September 27, 1980), p. 1.

Strauss, George. "Factors in the Unionization of a Utility Company: A Case Study." *Human Organization* 12 (Fall 1953), pp. 17–25.

"Union Community Role Seen Key to Organizing." *AFL–CIO News,* December 2, 1978, p. 8.

READING 17

Labor's New Offensive: Neutrality Agreements*

Andrew M. Kramer†

INTRODUCTION

From 1960 to 1978 union membership as a percentage of the total labor force has declined from 23.6 to 19.7 percent. In each and every year since 1969, during periods of both economic growth and recession, the percentage of union membership has declined. In the more heavily unionized manufacturing industries from 1968 to 1978, unions recorded a decrease in actual membership of approximately 1.1 million members, or approximately 12 percent.[1] Both employment and union membership in the auto and tire industries have continued to decline at a dramatic pace.

Although always a goal of organized labor, increasing union membership is even more critical today because of what has been described by Solomon Barkin, former research director for the Amalgamated Clothing and Textile Workers' Union (ACTWU), as a "crisis [resulting from] the cessation of the trade union movement's expansion into new areas

and its decline in numerical strength."[2] In order to enhance its organizing efforts, labor has begun to employ new techniques. One of the most effective organizing tools being utilized by unions today is the neutrality agreement. Neutrality agreements are agreements whereby an employer, ordinarily one that already has a number of unionized plants, agrees to remain "neutral" in any organizing campaign conducted by the union with which it has such an agreement. Although the contractual language varies from agreement to agreement, a typical neutrality agreement is similar to the agreement entered into by the Goodrich Tire and Rubber Company and the United Rubber, Cork, Linoleum, and Plastic Workers (URW). The relevant portion of that agreement reads as follows:

In situations where the URW seeks to organize production and maintenance employees in a plant in which a major product is tires and which is not presently represented by a union, Goodrich management or its agents will neither discourage nor encourage the Union efforts to organize these employees, but will observe a posture of strict neutrality in these matters.[3]

Neutrality agreements are of relatively recent origin. The first union to have any major success in concluding such an agreement was the United Automobile, Aerospace, and Agricultural Implement Workers (UAW), which succeeded in having "neutrality" adopted by General Motors in 1976. This was followed in 1979 by the adoption of "neutrality" by Goodrich, Firestone, and Uniroyal in the tire industry. During the most recent negotiations between the UAW and General Motors, the UAW succeeded in extending the "neutrality" concept. While retaining "neutrality," the UAW was able to negotiate transfer rights, which further facilitate the organization of new plants, particularly in the South and Southwest. Employees were given the right to transfer with full seniority to any new General Motors plant that makes products similar to

*Reprinted with permission from Herbert R. Northrup and Richard L. Rowan, eds., *Employee Relations and Regulation in the 80s* (Philadelphia: University of Pennsylvania, Industrial Research Unit, 1982), pp. 203–21.

†*Andrew M. Kramer is a Partner of Jones, Day, Reavis, and Pogue, in Washington, D.C.* For a more detailed analysis of the issues raised by neutrality agreements, see A. Kramer, L. Miller, and L. Bierman, "Neutrality Agreements: The New Frontier in Labor Relations—Fair Play or Foul," in Boston College Law Review, *Labor Law*, Fall 1981. The author wants to thank both Lee Miller and Leonard Bierman, associates in Seyfarth, Shaw, Fairweather & Geraldson (Washington office), for their contribution to the text.

[1]United States Department of Labor, Bureau of Labor Statistics, news release, September 3, 1979.

[2]Barkin, "The Decline of the Labor Movement" quoted in *Congressional Quarterly*, July 28, 1979, p. 1507.
[3][1979] 132 Daily Lab. Rep. (BNA) D–3.

those produced at any existing UAW plants.[4] In the past, such rights have applied only when the opening of new plants resulted in layoffs at existing UAW plants.

Neutrality agreements, however, are just one part of labor's strategy to reverse the trend of declining union membership. The loss of union membership has been linked to the movement of industry to the South and Southwest and to labor's inability to wage successful organizing campaigns there. Thus, the second prong of organized labor's attempt to reverse these trends can be found in recent plant closure legislation introduced both in Congress and in several northern states. While neutrality agreements make it easier to organize plants in the South and Southwest, plant closure legislation is intended to stem the tide of industry relocation.

When viewed from a management perspective, it is difficult to see any legitimate purpose served by neutrality agreements. Such agreements offer no benefit to employers or employees and are an attempt by unions to gain an organizing foothold in the South and Southwest. They enable unions to restrict the free flow of information needed by employees in order to make an informed decision about unionization, and they are a device used by unions to circumvent the statutory protection of free speech set forth by Congress in section 8(c) of the National Labor Relations Act.

---

[4]The text of that letter agreement provides:
During the current negotiations there have been discussions between the parties regarding the transfer of operations and employees affected by the opening of new plants.
This will confirm our verbal commitment that during the term of the 1979 National Agreement any new plants opened by the Corporation in the United States to produce products similar to those now being produced at plants in which the Union is currently the bargaining representative of the production and maintenance employees will involve a 'transfer of major operations' (as historically applied by the parties) from an existing UAW-represented plant to the new plant so as to bring into play the provisions of Paragraph (96).
It is understood that the foregoing will not apply to those plants currently covered by the Preferential Consideration Procedure, nor will it apply to the current Chevrolet-Moraine, Ohio plant sites or to any new plant producing products which are similar to those produced in another existing plant where the production and maintenance employees are represented by some union other than the UAW. [1976] 237 Daily Lab. Rep (BNA) A-13-14.

Even a company with a positive relationship with its existing unions ought to consider carefully the consequences of entering into a neutrality agreement. Refusal to enter into a neutrality agreement does not mean that an employer must oppose a particular union-organizing effort. In the absence of such an agreement an employer can decide at the appropriate time what position is in its best interest and in the best interest of its employees. A company should not foreclose its option to speak out before an organizing campaign even is begun.

Employee interests are harmed when the only voice heard in an organizing campaign is that of the union. Indeed, the statutory principle of employee free choice is strengthened by having both sides set forth the respective issues so that a meaningful decision can be reached. Moreover, employers operating under a neutrality agreement will experience difficulties in organizing campaigns that otherwise they would not encounter. Public employers who ordinarily have taken no position with respect to organizing efforts have generally seen their employees vote for a union. While I believe that a campaign can be conducted by an employer under a neutrality agreement, such agreements place obvious limitations on the employer.

Because of the organizing advantages afforded by neutrality agreements, we can expect more unions to seek such agreements in the future. Because such demands might be made, it is important to look at the legal questions posed by such agreements. These include the duty to bargain about neutrality agreements, the scope of the restrictions imposed, and the application of such agreements when two rival unions are involved in an organizing campaign.

COMPATIBILITY OF NEUTRALITY AGREEMENTS WITH THE BASIC POLICIES OF THE NATIONAL LABOR RELATIONS ACT

The National Labor Relations Act was intended to protect "the exercise by workers of full freedom of association, self-organization, and designation of representatives of their own choosing."[5] The act also gives workers the right to refrain from any and all such union activity.[6] Unlike the representation system in many other countries, the National Labor Relations Act provides that the employee representative selected by the majority of employees in an appropriate unit shall be the "exclusive representative of all the employees in such unit."[7] The act prevents employers and unions from coercing or restraining employees in the exercise of their right to select a majority representative or to remain unrepresented. In enforcing these sections of the act, the National Labor Relations Board (NLRB) has emphasized the importance of maintaining "laboratory conditions"[8] to allow employees to make a "free choice"—one that is "uncoerced," "reasoned," and "thoughtful."[9] Far from contributing to free choice, neutrality agreements undermine the "laboratory conditions" sought by the board. Particularly if they are broadly drawn or construed, neutrality agreements prevent effective employer input into the election process. Such agreements cut off the flow of relevant information from the company to the employees. Employees hear only what the union wants to tell them. They are effectively cut off from the only source of information that can counterbalance union-organizing propaganda.

Neutrality agreements are analogous to contractual agreements that mandate that employees at any new stores in a retail chain automatically must become union members. In striking down such a provision, the U.S. Court of Appeals for the Ninth Circuit recently stated:

All parties proceeded on the assumption that employees of any new store should simply be accreted to the respective multi-store units in accordance with the existing contracts. This, of course, denies employees of a new store their freedom of choice, for an election is never held. New store employees are simply subsumed into the larger unit without anyone ascertaining whether they desire union representation, and if so, whether they desire to join the larger unit. The new stores' clauses were relied on to justify this practice.

The courts have frowned on this contractual usurpation of § 7 rights . . . Since contract rights cannot exist independent of the union's right to represent the unit, the new stores clause cannot bind the new employees despite the employer's acquiescence.[10]

While in the case of neutrality agreements elections are held, restriction of the free flow of information needed by the employees to make an informed decision often may, as a practical matter, make the election little more than a formality.

Neutrality agreements are subject to the same criticisms that led to the prohibitions against organizational picketing found in section 8(b)(7) of the National Labor Relations Act.[11] In describing organizational picketing, Senator McClellan, the sponsor of the 1959 Amendments to the National Labor Relations Act, stated:

Unionizing and collective bargaining are premised on the free choice of individuals who work together to join a union of their choice, and to bargain collectively; it is not based upon compulsion to join a union.

"Compulsion" is an ugly word. Decent unionism does not require it; decent unionism does not need it. Honest unionism does not need to apply that kind of tactics.

If unionism is good, if it is sound, if it is right, if it is just, we can trust in the good faith and the quality and integrity of American workers voluntarily to

---

[5]National Labor Relations Act, § 1, 29 U.S.C. § 151 (1976).

[6]*Id.*, § 7, 29 U.S.C. § 157.

[7]*Id.*, § 9(a), 29 U.S.C. § 159(a).

[8]As the board stated in *General Shoe Corp.*, 77 N.L.R.B. 124, 126(1948):
In election proceedings, it is the board's function to provide a laboratory in which an experiment may be conducted, under conditions as nearly ideal as possible, to determine the uninhibited desires of the employees. It is our duty to establish those conditions; it is also our duty to determine whether they have been fulfilled.

[9]*Sewell Mfg. Co.*, 138 N.L.R.B. 66, 70 (1962), where the board stated:
Our function, as we see it, is to conduct elections in which the employees have the opportunity to cast their ballots for or against a labor organization in an atmosphere conducive to the sober and informed exercise of the franchise, free not only from interference, restraint, or coercion violative of the act, but also from other elements which prevent or impede a reasoned choice.

[10]*NLRB v. Retail Clerks Local 588* 587 F.2d 984, 986 (9th Cir. 1978) (citations omitted).

[11]29 U.S.C. § 158(b)(7).

accept it, to desire it honestly, and to be enthusiastic to secure the benefits which flow from worthy unionism. The workers will seek to unionize. But they ought not to be compelled and hijacked to join unions whether they want to or not, when they are not given a free choice. Compulsion and hijacking are nothing in the world but top-down organization; and top-down organization has no place in American law or American institutions.[12]

Neutrality agreements share with organizational picketing many of these same characteristics. They are an attempt by organized labor to "coerce" or "buy" management silence in organizing campaigns at its unorganized plants through its bargaining strength at a company's unionized plants. Like organizational picketing, neutrality agreements are a form of top-down organizing. Unions seek to accomplish indirectly through such agreements what they are prohibited from doing directly through organizational picketing.

Such agreements clearly are a form of cooperation between labor and management that works to the detriment of employees' freedom of choice. The Supreme Court has recently inveighed against such limitations on the free flow of information in another context, stating that the first amendment presumes that "information is not in itself harmful, that people will perceive their own best interests if only they are well enough informed, and that the best means to that end is to open the channels of communication rather than to close them."[13]

In the long run, elections conducted pursuant to a neutrality agreement may result in workers feeling that they have been misled by the company's silence. The whole notion of free choice is undermined by such agreements. Moreover, the National Labor Relations Act's policy of reducing "industrial strife" and providing stability in labor relations is threatened by the use of neutrality agreements. From a policy standpoint, the value to the union of organizing a unit under

such circumstances is also dubious. The union will have to expend both time and money in organizing the unit. Ultimately, however, an unstable relationship may result in plants organized without access to all the relevant information.

DUTY TO BARGAIN ABOUT NEUTRALITY

An employer's initial concern when a union proposes a neutrality agreement is whether he has a legal obligation to bargain over such an agreement. As a practical matter, what the employer is ordinarily concerned about is whether the union can strike if he refuses to agree to "neutrality." Neither the Board nor the courts have yet had occasion to decide whether an employer must bargain about "neutrality." An analysis of the relevant statutory provisions and analogous cases, however, would suggest that he need not.

The National Labor Relations Act imposes on an employer the duty to "bargain collectively . . . [over] rates of pay, wages, hours of employment, or other conditions of employment."[14] Although the obligation to bargain "does not compel either party to agree to a proposal or require the making of a concession,"[15] if an employer is not required to bargain about a particular subject he need not even dignify the subject as a matter meriting serious discussion.

The subjects upon which an employer and a union may reach a legally binding agreement[16] are divided into two categories: mandatory subjects and permissive subjects. The parties are required to bargain in good faith about all mandatory subjects of bargaining. With respect to permissive subjects, neither side is obligated to bargain. In addition, strikes and lockouts may not be employed to support

---

[12]*Legislative History of the Labor-Management Reporting and Disclosure Act*, 1959, at 1175 (1959) (statements of Sen. McClellan).

[13]*Virginia State Bd. of Pharmacy v. Virginia Citizens Consumer Council, Inc.*, 425 U.S. 748, 770 (1976).

[14]National Labor Relations Act, §§ 8(a)(5) and 9(a), 29 U.S.C. §§ 158(a)(5) and 159(a) (1976).

[15]See generally *H. K. Porter v. NLRB*, 397 U.S. 99 (1970).

[16]Indeed, as developed *infra*, such neutrality agreements may represent a violation of section 8(a)(2) of the act and thus be an "illegal" subject of bargaining. For a general discussion of the "illegal" bargaining category, see R. Gorman, "Unionization and Collective Bargaining," in *Basic Text on Labor Law*, 528-31 (1976).

a proposal concerning a permissive subject of bargaining.[17]

The National Labor Relations Act does not specifically enumerate the items that are mandatory subjects of collective bargaining. As the Supreme Court made clear in *Allied Chemical and Alkali Workers v. Pittsburgh Plate Glass Co.*,[18] however, sections 8(d) and 9(a) of the act fix definitively the outer limits of the class. As stated by the Supreme Court:

> Together, these provisions establish the obligation of the employer to bargain collectively "with respect to wages, hours and other terms and conditions of employment" with "the representatives of his employees" designated or selected by the majority "in a unit appropriate for such purposes." *This obligation extends only to the "terms and conditions of employment" of the employer's "employees" in the "unit appropriate for such purposes" that the union represents.*[19]

In *Pittsburgh Plate Glass*, the Court determined that benefits for retirees did not satisfy the prerequisites of a mandatory subject of bargaining because retirees are not "employees" within the meaning of section 2(3) of the act. Moreover, irrespective of their status as employees, they were not and could not be members of the bargaining unit represented by the union. Accordingly, retiree benefits could only be a mandatory subject on the basis of their impact on active bargaining unit employees. The Court then established the test for whether such items could be considered mandatory subjects of bargaining based on their impact on members of the bargaining units. "[I]n each case the question is not whether the third-party concern is antagonistic to or compatible with the interests of bargaining-unit employees, but whether it *vitally affects* the 'terms and conditions' of their employment."[20] Applying this test, it concluded that the retiree benefits were not a mandatory subject of bargaining because "the benefits that active workers may reap by including re-

tired employees under the same health insurance contract are speculative and insubstantial at best."[21]

Applying the Supreme Court's analysis in *Pittsburgh Plate Glass* to neutrality agreements would yield the same result. The essential principle of *Pittsburgh Plate Glass* is that the obligation to bargain extends only to terms and conditions of employment of bargaining unit employees. A neutrality agreement binds the employer not to oppose the union's organizational efforts in other bargaining units. In pressing for a neutrality agreement, the union is not advancing the working conditions of bargaining unit employees, but is using its status as their bargaining representative as leverage for its own organizational objectives completely outside the bargaining unit. The union's nonunit organizational efforts at best only tangentially affect the conditions of employment of bargaining unit employees.

Borg-Warner is also instructive on this issue. In *Borg-Warner*, the employer insisted on the inclusion in the agreement of a "ballot" clause calling for the employer's last bargaining offer in all future negotiations to be put to a vote of unit employees before a strike could be called.[22] The Court held that the ballot clause was not a mandatory subject of bargaining. The decision rested in part on the fact that the clause dealt only with the relation between the employees and their unions, rather than employer-employee relations. It was also based on the Court's judgment that the clause undermined the independence of the union as the employee's representative by enabling the employer to bargain directly with the employees. Thus, the Court held that, although such a clause was not illegal, it could not be the subject of mandatory bargaining.

Similarly, the United States Court of Appeals for the Tenth Circuit has held that an "application of the contract" clause is not a mandatory subject of bargaining.[23] An "appli-

---

[17]*NLRB v. Wooster Div. of Borg-Warner Corp.*, 356 U.S. 342 (1958).

[18]404 U.S. 157 (1971).

[19]*Id.* at 164 (emphasis added).

[20]*Id.* at 179 (emphasis added).

[21]*Id.* at 180.

[22]*Supra* note 17.

[23]*Lone Star Steel Co. v. NLRB*, 104 L.R.R.M. 3134 (10th Cir. 1980).

cation of the contract" clause requires that an employer apply the terms of a collective bargaining agreement to any new operations acquired during the life of that agreement once the contracting union is recognized as the bargaining representative of a majority of the employees at the new facility. In a hearing before the board, an administrative law judge (ALJ) found that such a clause did not relate to the terms and conditions of current employees and was therefore not a mandatory subject of bargaining. Moreover, he stated that "'the principal purpose for the . . . clause is [as] an organizing device,' and was therefore not a mandatory subject of bargaining." The board disagreed and held that such a clause did constitute a mandatory subject. The Tenth Circuit reversed the board, however, adopting the ALJ's reasoning.

If an "application of the contract" clause does not properly constitute a mandatory subject of bargaining because it is primarily an organizing device, clearly a neutrality agreement would suffer from the same shortcoming. Moreover, a neutrality agreement, like a "ballot" clause, relates primarily to the relationship between the union and the employees. It has virtually no direct impact on the terms and conditions of employment in the bargaining unit covered by the agreement. Therefore, it would seem that neutrality agreements should, at most, properly be classified as permissive subjects of bargaining. Thus, employers would be free to refuse even to bargain with unions about "neutrality" proposals.

IMPACT OF NEUTRALITY AGREEMENTS ON MANAGEMENT

The obvious purpose of a neutrality agreement is to prevent an employer from taking an active part in union organizational drives and elections. As such, neutrality agreements restrict an employer's right to express an opinion about a particular union or about unionism in general. The extent of the restriction will depend on the drafting of the specific neutrality agreement.

Unions generally maintain that "neutrality" requires management to refrain from making any statements concerning a union's organizing campaign. According to the president of one of the major unions to conclude a neutrality agreement, "neutrality" creates a zone of corporate silence. The typical neutrality agreement, however, should not be read so broadly.

Although a neutrality agreement would constitute a waiver by a company of its right of free speech, such a waiver probably does not extend so far as to prohibit management entirely from making statements regarding a union-organizing campaign. A strong argument can be made that a company retains its right to issue "neutral" remarks about unionization and the differences between union and nonunion plants, especially the effects these differences have on employees.

In this regard, it must be remembered that the union has the burden of establishing a waiver of a statutory or constitutional right.[24] Even if statutory or constitutional rights were not involved, the burden of proving a breach of contract would fall upon the union. "If a written contract is ambiguous, or open to different constructions, then it must be construed most strongly against the party who prepared it."[25] Since a neutrality agreement will ordinarily be prepared by the union or included at its insistence, a court or the board should read any ambiguities in the agreement in the light most favorable to the employer.

In determining the scope of the restrictions imposed by neutrality agreements, some guidance can be garnered from the Railway Labor Act.[26] Unlike the National Labor Relations Act, which guarantees the employer freedom of speech, the Railway Labor Act provides that "representatives . . . shall be designated by the respective parties without *interference, influence,* or coercion by either

---

[24]See, e.g., Gary Hobart Water Corp., 210 N.L.R.B. 742(1974), affd, 511 F.2nd 284 (7th Cir.), cert. denied, 423 U.S. 925 (1975), where the board stated: "While statutory rights may be waived, the board and the courts have repeatedly emphasized that such waivers will not be readily inferred, and there must be a clear and unmistakable showing that waiver occurred." 210 N.L.R.B. at 744.

[25]*Miravalle Supply Co. v. El Campo Rice Milling Co.,* 181 F.2d 679, 683 (8th Cir.), cert. denied, 340 U.S. 822 (1950).

[26]45 U.S.C. § 151 et seq. (1926).

party over the designation of representatives by the other; and neither party shall in any way *interfere with, influence,* or coerce the other in its choice of representatives."[27] In interpreting this proscription, the United States Supreme Court has stated:

The intent of Congress is clear with respect to the sort of conduct that is prohibited. "Interference" with freedom of action and "coercion" refer to well-understood concepts of the law. The meaning of the word "influence" in this clause may be gathered from the context ... The use of the word is not to be taken as interdicting the normal relations and innocent communications which are a part of all friendly intercourse, albeit between employer and employee. "Influence" in this context plainly means pressure, the use of the authority or power of either party to induce action by the other in derogation of what the statute calls "self-organization." The phrase covers the abuse of relation or opportunity so as to corrupt or override the will, and it is no more difficult to appraise conduct of this sort in connection with the selection of representatives for the purposes of this act than in relation to well-known applications of the law with respect to fraud, duress, and undue influence.[28]

In more recent cases, the courts have interpreted the prohibitions against "influencing" elections of employee representatives even less restrictively.[29] The exact parameters of acceptable company conduct under a neutrality agreement cannot be determined with certainty. In light of the lack of any benefit to employers and their employees resulting from neutrality agreements, it is best to avoid entering into such agreements in the first place. If such agreements are entered into, however, one thing that is certain is that management cannot state that it opposes the union's organizing effort. As discussed above, it would seem that the company retains the right to give employees factual information concerning the company and the union. So long as the information given to employees is couched in a straightforward, unbiased, and frank manner, without the interjection of the employer's opinions, it would appear to come within the parameters of being "neutral."[30] Providing such information would constitute neither employer discouragement nor encouragement of the union efforts to organize its employees.

Often the right to provide factual information is set forth specifically in the neutrality agreement. For instance, the UAW agreement with Dana Corporation provides:

Our Corporate position regarding union representation is as follows:

We believe that our employees should exercise free choice and decide for themselves by voting on whether or not they wish to be represented by the UAW or any other labor organization.

We have no objection to the UAW becoming the bargaining representative of our people as a result of such an election.

Where the UAW becomes involved in organizing our employees, we intend to continue our commitment of maintaining a neutral position on this matter. The Company and/or its representatives will communicate with our employees, not in an anti-UAW manner, but in a positive pro-Dana manner.

If a majority of our employees indicate a desire to be represented by the UAW, we will cooperate with all parties involved to expedite an NLRB election.

In addition, we reserve the right to speak out in any manner appropriate when undue provocation is evident in an organizing campaign.[31]

Nevertheless, even when an employer such as Dana has negotiated as part of a neutrality agreement explicit provisions allowing it to speak out in order to set the record straight, such explicit provisions may still not be sufficient. For example, in the first arbitration case involving a neutrality agreement, which involved Dana and the UAW, an arbi-

---

[27]*Id.* § 152 (emphasis added).

[28]*Texas & N.O.R. Co. v. Brotherhood of Railway & Steamship Clerks,* 281 U.S. 548, 568 (1930) (citations omitted). *See also* Virginian Railway Co. v. System Federation No. 40, 300 U.S. 515 (1937).

[29]*Adams v. Federal Express Corp.,* 470 F. Supp. 1356 (W.D. Tenn. 1979); *Brotherhood of Railway & Steamship Clerks v. Philadelphia, Bethlehem & New England Railroad Co.,* 428 F. Supp. 1308 (E.D. Pa. 1977); *Teamsters v. Braniff Airways, Inc.,* 70 L.R.R.M. 3333 (D.D.C. 1969). *Contra, Brotherhood of Railroad Trainmen v. Richmond, Fredericksburg and Potomac Railroad Co.,* 69 L.R.R.M. 2884 (E.D. Va. 1968).

[30]*Webster's Third New International Dictionary* (1971 ed.) defines "neutral" as "not engaged on either side; not siding with or assisting either; lending no active assistance to either or any belligerent."

[31]Letter of Neutrality Agreement between Dana Corporation and the UAW (December 7, 1979).

trator found that Dana had violated its agreement by speaking out against the union in response to union misrepresentations regarding the rate of pay of other unionized employees, Dana hourly employees, and Dana executives.[32]

The arbitrator held that numerous union misrepresentations did not represent "undue provocation" by the union of the kind which permitted the company to speak out against the union. The arbitrator also, in an extraordinary move, awarded $10,000 in damages to the union because of the company's contractual breach, even though the union did not seek such monetary relief.

The Dana arbitration case makes it clear that the only way that an employer can be certain to protect its rights of free speech is by refusing to agree to a neutrality provision in the first place. Even when a neutrality clause expressly reserves the employer's right to speak out under certain conditions, that right may construe narrowly in subsequent arbitrations.

The Dana arbitration case was preceded by a court case in which the UAW successfully obtained a temporary restraining order prohibiting Dana, or persons acting on its behalf, "from making antiunion or anti-UAW oral or written statements or other communications to its employees at its Gastonia facility or otherwise departing from a position of neutrality with regard to [an] upcoming National Labor Relations Board election at that facility."[33] Then, based on a speech by the company president to employees of the Gastonia facility that followed, Dana was found in contempt. Judge Young ordered that Dana purge itself of contempt by:

1.[S]ending a written communication, in form satisfactory to the plaintiff, to all employees of . . . [the] Corporation repudiating both the written and oral statements of . . . [the Company President], promising to abide by the contents of its neutrality agreement, and indicating its neutrality in any forthcoming National Labor Relations Board election;

2.[P]rovid[ing] access to each plant of . . . [the] Corporation in which . . . [the Company President] addressed assembled workers, for a representative of the plaintiff to address each shift of workers, assembled, for the length of time that . . . [the President] addressed such shift, and . . . [the President] shall be and remain present throughout the giving of each such address;

3.[C]lear[ing] all the specially colored bulletin boards throughout the . . . Corporation plants of any and all antiunion materials, refrain[ing] from posting such material on any bulletin boards in the future, reserv[ing] no less than half the space upon said bulletin boards for the use of plaintiff to affix communications, and giv[ing] a representative of the plaintiff daily access to each such bulletin board for posting and for reviewing posted materials until a National Labor Relations Board election shall be held.[34]

The decision in this case, which represented a clear instance of judicial prior restraint of speech, is currently being appealed.[35]

The Dana case, in particular, suggests that neutrality agreements are likely to involve employers in costly court litigation over any statements they make which could be construed as unfavorable toward unions. Neutrality agreements in this way provide unions with another weapon with which to enhance their organizing efforts. Throughout a campaign, a union can hold out the threat of litigation to inhibit an employer from communicating with his employees. If an employer does speak out and the union does not like the substance of management's comments, it can go to court in an attempt to gag the employer. At the very least, the act of litigating itself may assist the union by creating additional propaganda suggesting that the company cannot be trusted to keep its word.

As previously discussed, neutrality agreements facilitate union organizing by eliminating the primary source of informed opposition to the union's efforts—the employer. Moreover, some agreements extend beyond neutrality and provide an even greater organizing advantage to a union. Thus, the UAW's extension of its 1976 neutrality agreement with General Motors to guarantee employees

---

[32]Decision of arbitrator in application of neutrality letter involving Wix Corporation and UAW, *printed in* [1981] 41 *Daily Lab. Rep.* (BNA) E-1.

[33]*UAW v. Dana Corporation*, 104 L.R.R.M. 2687 (1980), *appeal docketed*, No. 80-3548 (6th Cir. 1981).

[34]*Id.*
[35]*Id.*

the right to transfer with full seniority to new plants opened by the company greatly aids the union's ability to organize these new plants. The UAW's comments on this new agreement are revealing.

Few challenges to labor are as critical as the organizing of new plants or runaway shops, especially those dotting the traditionally antilabor areas of the Sun Belt and South.

For GM workers, that challenge has focused on the fact that the corporation has opened or plans to open several new plants, many of which are in areas where workers have had limited contact with unions in the past and business and right-wing resistance to unions remains high.

[This agreement is a] major breakthrough . . . [which] is expected to build a more positive climate, especially in the South, for the UAW and for other unions.[36]

These developments in the use of neutrality agreements to enhance union ability to organize in the South and Southwest come at the same time that organized labor is seeking to maintain its membership in the North through legislation restricting a company's ability to close or relocate its plants. For example, at the time of the present Congress, H.R. 1037, a bill introduced on January 22, 1981, by Congressman Gaydos, would severely restrict the ability of businesses to relocate operations and shift capital as they see fit. A number of similar bills, including H.R. 5040, S. 1609, and S. 2400, were introduced in the previous Congress. The general scheme contemplated by these bills is to impose lengthy notice provisions and penalties in order to inhibit businesses from relocating their operations.

Under H.R. 1037, which is currently being considered by Congress, for instance, businesses generally must give at least two years prior written notice before closing an establishment or transferring operations. After such notice is given, the Department of Labor then investigates the "merits" of the business' decision. If the Department of Labor determines that the closing or transfer of operations is not "justified" or is otherwise improper, the business will then become ineligible under the Internal Revenue Code for: (1) investment cred-

its, (2) accelerated depreciation, (3) foreign tax credits, (4) deferral of tax on income earned outside the United States, and (5) ordinary and necessary business expense deductions for expenses related to the transfer of operations. Such businesses will also not be entitled to derive benefits from the industrial development bond provisions of the Internal Revenue Code.[37] The entire act will be supervised by a new bureaucracy known as the National Employment Relocation Administration. Such proposed plant closure legislation represents an attempt by government to inhibit plant movement from the North to the South and Southwest, thereby protecting union membership.

Coupled with organized labor's efforts to enact plant closure legislation, unions are increasingly seeking to raise that issue at the bargaining table as well. The Oil Chemical and Atomic Workers (OCAW), for instance, intends to make plant closures a major issue in its 1982 negotiations.[38] From labor's perspective, however, legislation like H.R. 1037 is preferable, since enactment of legislation like H.R. 1037 would impose, by statutory mandate, restrictions on the transfer of capital of a kind which could not realistically be achieved through collective bargaining.

LEGALITY OF NEUTRALITY AGREEMENTS UNDER SECTION 8(a)(2) OF THE NATIONAL LABOR RELATIONS ACT

Section 8(a)(2) of the National Labor Relations Act provides, in part, that it is an unfair labor practice for an employer "to dominate or interfere with the formation or administration of any labor organization or contribute financial or other support to it."[39] The question thus arises whether an agreement between an employer and a union providing that the employer will be "neutral" with respect to future organizational efforts by that union presents the kind of employer support that poses a violation of section 8(a)(2).

---

[36][1979] 183 *Daily Lab. Rep.* (BNA).

[37]H.R. 1037, 97th Cong., 1st Sess., § 2701 (1981).
[38]*See* [1981] 95 *Daily Lab. Rep.* (BNA) A-3.
[39]29 U.S.C. § 158(a)(2)(1976).

In a sense, an employer remaining officially "neutral" when a union attempts to organize additional employees represents an expression of a point of view by the employer. The employer is simply saying that he has no real opinion one way or the other as to whether the employees should vote to have the union represent them or not. The law clearly allows employers the right to express that sort of opinion.[40] Indeed, the National Labor Relations Act explicitly protects that right.[41]

Thus, there is nothing wrong with an employer expressing its views on the representation of his employees by a particular union. An employer's simple statement that it feels it is in the best interest of its employees to be represented by a union does not constitute the kind of support for that union that violates section 8(a)(2) of the act. Furthermore, the right of employer free speech extends even to the situation where more than one union is competing to represent the bargaining unit. An employer's noncoercive declaration of a preference for one union over another does not constitute a violation of section 8(a)(2).[42]

Consequently, if neutrality agreements are read, from the point of view of the employer, as merely being an expression of its views toward unionization, such agreements seem to pose no real problems in terms of section 8(a)(2) of the act. The problem, however, is that it is unrealistic to view such agreements as having no more force than a mere public statement by the employer setting forth his views with respect to unionization. Neutrality agreements are binding contracts to assist, albeit through their silence, a union.

Neutrality agreements go beyond merely voluntarily refraining from taking a position against a particular union. Under a neutrality agreement, an employer contractually agrees, for the period of that contract, not to oppose the organizational efforts of the union with which the agreement was reached. The very fact of having reached such an agreement enhances the union's stature in the eyes of the employees. It goes beyond mere neutrality and borders on active assistance.

Overall, neutrality agreements clearly seem to violate the spirit, if not the precise language, of section 8(a)(2), which was enacted by Congress to guarantee employees "complete and unfettered freedom of choice."[43] The kind of "support" and "assistance" employers, by way of neutrality agreements, give unions tends to hamper employee free choice and should, as matter of policy, be found to violate section 8(a)(2) of the National Labor Relations Act.[44]

Whether or not neutrality agreements will, in fact, be found by the NLRB to violate section 8(a)(2) of the National Labor Relations Act is questionable. The NLRB has exhibited a distinct predilection toward upholding contractual commitments between unions and employers, even when such agreements tend to directly impinge on the rights of individual employees.

For example, the board, under its *Briggs Indiana*[45] doctrine, has upheld agreements under which the union agrees, for the term of the contract, not to represent certain groups of employees. The board, in upholding such agreements, has flatly rejected assertions that such agreements work most unfairly to disenfranchise certain groups of employees.[46]

Similarly, the board has upheld agreements which allow a union's majority status for pur-

---

[40]See *NLRB v. Virginia Electric Power Co.*, 314 U.S. 469 (1941).

[41]National Labor Relations Act, § 8(c), 29 U.S.C. § 158(c)(1976).

[42]Rold Gold of California, Inc., 123 N.L.R.B. 285 (1959). See also Alley Construction Co., 210 N.L.R.B. 999, 1004 (1974); Stewart-Warner Corp., 102 N.L.R.B. 1153 (1953).

[43]*NLRB v. Link-Belt Co.*, 311 U.S. 584, 588 (1941).

[44]The United States Supreme Court had made clear that an employer need not intend to unlawfully aid a union for a § 8(a)(2) violation to be found. As long as the result of the employer's actions is to unlawfully aid the union and hamper employee free choice, a § 8(a)(2) unfair labor practice action will exist. *ILGWU v. NLRB (Bernhard-Altman Texas Corp.)*, 366 U.S. 731, 739 (1961).

Furthermore, employees' subjective reactions to employer support of a union need not be proved for a § 8(a)(2) action to lie. What is of primary consequence is the tendency of the employer's assistance to the union to coerce employees in the exercise of their rights. *NLRB v. Vernitron Electrical Components, Inc.*, 548 F.2d 24, 26 (1st Cir. 1977).

[45]See Briggs Indiana Corp., 63 N.L.R.B. 1270 (1945).

[46]See Allis-Chalmers Manufacturing Co., 179 N.L.R.B. 1 (1969).

poses of recognition to be determined by methods other than a secret ballot election.[47] Such agreements are upheld despite the recognized questionable validity of those methods, and despite their seemingly obvious disadvantages in terms of encouraging uncoerced employee free choice.

Ultimately the protection of individual employee rights and the policies favoring "free" elections which underlie the National Labor Relations Act and which are threatened by neutrality agreements probably lies with the courts. The Supreme Court, particularly in the recent case of *Connell Construction Co. v. Plumbers Local 100*,[48] has shown a marked willingness to protect individual employee rights, even if it is necessary to read deeply into the National Labor Relations Act's underlying policy considerations to do so.

In *Connell*, despite seemingly clear language in section 8(e) of the National Labor Relations Act permitting such arrangements, the Court struck down an agreement between a construction industry employer and a union whereby the employer agreed to use only unionized subcontractors. The Court, in reaching its decision, displayed a willingness to look behind the specific statutory language to the policy considerations underlying the act. Focusing in part on how such agreements thwart the desires of individual employees, the Court held that such "top-down" organizing violated the National Labor Relations Act.[49]

Thus, while it seems rather unlikely that the National Labor Relations Board will strike down neutrality agreements, the courts may be sympathetic to the erosion of individual employee rights which such agreements produce. The courts may view neutrality agreements as representing much more than simply an employer's expression of opinion regarding unionization. Thus, they may find that neutrality agreements are inherently destructive of the right to free elections guaranteed by the National Labor Relations Act and that such agreements constitute improper aid to the unions with which they are concluded.

CONCLUSION

Even a brief examination of the trends in organizational activity in the 1980s makes clear that unions intend to use their "friends" in the business community and the legislatures to maintain and increase their membership. As union membership continues to decline, through the loss of jobs in the heavily organized industries in the North and through labor's continued inability to successfully organize in the South and Southwest, we can expect increased pressure on business and on Congress to come to the aid of organized labor. The International Union of Electrical Workers (IUE) has already vowed to make neutrality a key issue in its upcoming negotiations with General Electric and Westinghouse.

To date, however, the developments discussed above remain in an embryonic stage. Only a few unions have had any notable success in concluding neutrality agreements. Plant-closure legislation has yet to be enacted by Congress and has only been enacted in a limited form in two states.

Employers should resist entering into neutrality agreements. They should insist on allowing their employees the freedom to make an informed choice based on all the relevant information. In addition, industry should oppose the proposed plant-closure legislation. It must expose this legislation for what it really is—an attempt to restrict the flow of capital to its most productive uses. Industry must act instead of react. It must stand up to such unwarranted legislative interference with business that, in the long run, will reduce productivity and employment. It must stand up for the rights of its employees to determine, based on all the relevant data, whether they wish to be represented by a particular union. For if the business community will not, there is no one else who will.

---

[47]See Snow & Sons, 134 N.L.R.B. 709 (1961), *enfd*, 308 F.2d 687 (9th Cir. 1962).

[48]421 U.S. 616 (1975).

[49]*Id.* at 632, n.11.

READING 18

Symbolic Victory and Political Reality in the Southern Textile Industry: The Meaning of the J. P. Stevens Settlement for Southern Labor Relations*

Terry W. Mullins and Paul Luebke†

In October 1980, J. P. Stevens & Company ended a long, bitter labor-management battle by signing a contract with the Amalgamated Clothing and Textile Workers Union (ACTWU). Labor hailed the victory as its long-delayed breakthrough for workers in the traditionally non-union, low-wage industries of the South. This paper assesses the importance of the Stevens/ACTWU settlement for Stevens, the textile industry, and the changing Southern economy. When the ACTWU victory is examined in this light, it becomes clear that the impact of the settlement is far more limited than is generally believed.

I. INTRODUCTION

In October 1980, one of the longest and most bitter labor-management struggles in recent times culminated in a signed contract between J. P. Stevens & Company and the Amalgamated Clothing and Textile Workers Union (ACTWU). In the course of the 17-year

*Reprinted with permission by the *Journal of Labor Research* 3, no. 1 (Winter 1982), pp. 81–88.

†Professors Mullins and Luebke are on the faculty of the University of North Carolina at Greensboro.

struggle to prevent unionization of its workers, Stevens acquired the dubious distinction of violating labor laws more than any other company in the 46-year history of the National Labor Relations Act. For its part, ACTWU proclaimed its agreement as "historic" for workers in the southern United States. This paper examines the productivity and profitability of Stevens, other textile firms, and non-textile, capital-intensive industries in the South. In addition, it considers the changing political attitudes of southern managers in capital-intensive firms, which are increasingly resistant to unionization. While recognizing the symbolic importance of ACTWU's victory over Stevens, which is detailed below, this paper concludes that the J. P. Stevens settlement is *not* a watershed for the southern labor movement.

II. HISTORY OF THE CONFLICT

The current drive to organize southern textile workers began in 1963 when the Textile Workers Union of America (TWUA) selected Stevens as its organizing target. Stevens, the country's second largest textile firm, employs more than 39,000 hourly workers in approximately 80 factories located primarily in the southern United States. After targeting Stevens, the small, weak TWUA sought and obtained money and manpower from the Industrial Organizing Department of the AFL–CIO to wage its prolonged unionization campaign. During the early years of the struggle, the company successfully resisted all organizing efforts. However, the tide turned toward the union during the 1970s when the union's standard organizing tactics were supplemented by a three-pronged effort consisting of legal charges of unfair labor practices, a consumer boycott of Stevens' products, and a corporate campaign designed to isolate Stevens from the rest of the business and financial community.

Organizing Efforts. The organizing efforts of the TWUA can be characterized as a series of disappointing and frustrating defeats. From 1963 to 1975, the union lost 11 of 12 elections held in Stevens facilities. The only victory during those years was the 1974 election at seven Stevens plants in Roanoke Rapids, North Carolina. Even there the victory was precarious: The union won by a slim margin of 237 votes out of 3,205 cast. The company pointed to the union's lack of success as proof that the workers were uninterested in "outside interference" from unions. The union argued that it lost elections because the company systematically intimidated workers by firing those suspected of pro-union activities or sympathies. In the face of these difficulties, the union gained strength in 1976 when the 140,000 member TWUA merged with the 360,000 member Amalgamated Clothing Workers Union to form the ACTWU.

The tangible results of these numerous organizing efforts were meager. About 3,000 workers were covered by the Roanoke Rapids election. In addition, the National Labor Relations Board (NLRB) granted the union representation rights for about 1,550 more workers at several plants in North Carolina and Alabama where the company had been found guilty of unfair labor practices during organizing campaigns or elections. In all, ACTWU can claim representation rights for approximately 10 percent of Stevens workers.

The Legal Conflict. The National Labor Relations Act establishes workers rights in the area of collective bargaining, and the NLRB has the responsibility to oversee the act. Very early in the struggle to unionize Stevens, the union charged that the company was systematically violating the rights of workers to join unions and bargain collectively. While the union cited a variety of unfair labor practices, the most common complaint was that the company was intimidating workers and firing employees engaged in unionizing activities. The court record between 1963 and 1980 supports the union charges. The NLRB found Stevens guilty of unfair labor practices in 22 of 23 separate cases (*Business Week*, June 9, 1980). Each case usually contained dozens of specific charges of unfair labor practices. By 1976 the NLRB had found Stevens guilty of il-

legally firing or discriminating against 289 workers for union activities (Somplatsky-Jarman, 1978).

Apparently unwilling to abide by NLRB findings, Stevens ignored most of the NLRB decrees issued between 1963 and 1976. As the decrees were ignored, the NLRB petitioned the Federal Circuit Court of Appeals in an effort to force compliance. At various levels of review, Stevens was a consistent loser. By 1978, 16 cases had been appealed. Of these, 3 were overturned, 13 were upheld, with 3 resulting in contempt citations. As the union's position was supported not only by the NLRB but upheld by the courts, Stevens began to control its first-line supervisors more carefully, and the number of unfair labor practices charges decreased.

Even in plants where the union had won representation elections, little progress was made in negotiating contracts. After over two years of negotiation at Roanoke Rapids without any substantive progress toward a contract, ACTWU charged the company with bargaining in bad faith. In December 1977, an NLRB administrative law judge agreed, stating that Stevens "approached these negotiations with all the tractability and openmindedness of Sherman at the outskirts of Atlanta" (239, NLRB, p. 769).

The Consumer Boycott. The consumer boycott of J. P. Stevens products, patterned after the successful boycott of table grapes led by Caesar Chavez, was begun in late 1976. Consumers were asked to boycott Stevens products until the company signed a contract with ACTWU. The union won the support of the National Council of Churches and three major Protestant denominations for the boycott. While the boycott was successful in focusing public attention on the conflict between Stevens and the union, it was not a particularly effective economic tool. There was no discernable impact on the company's sales or profits attributable to the boycott, for two major reasons. First, many of Stevens' products are sold to other manufacturers as raw material for finished goods. Second, Stevens' products sold directly to consumers are rather inconspicuously labeled and are sold under a variety of labels.

The Corporate Campaign. The corporate campaign, brainchild of ACTWU's Ray Rogers, was instituted in 1977 to isolate Stevens from the business and financial community. The primary tactic was to force resignations of outside directors from the Stevens board of directors by putting pressure on the companies employing the outside directors. Two types of pressure were applied. First, companies supportive of Stevens were threatened by loss of business from unions and union members if their support continued. Second, pressure was applied by highly publicized letter writing and telegram campaigns directed at companies whose officers were serving as outside directors to Stevens. The goal was not to change Stevens' industrial relations policies by changing the make-up of the board of directors. Rather the goal was to polarize the business community and alienate Stevens from its normal supportive relationships. At the same time, similar efforts were made to force Stevens officers to resign from the boards of other companies.

These efforts met with considerable success. In March 1978, James Finley, Stevens CEO at the time, declined to stand for reelection as a director of Manufacturers Hanover Trust, a large New York bank with significant financial ties to Stevens. His decision was reached after various unions threatened to withdraw their assets from the bank. Since the assets of the unions, union members, and union pension funds on deposit with the bank were estimated at approximately $1 billion, this represented a formidable threat indeed. David Mitchell, Chairman of Avon Products, Inc., resigned from the boards of both Stevens and Manufacturers Hanover Trust in March, 1978. Later that same year Finley resigned from the board of New York Life Insurance Company. At the same time, R. Manning Brown, Jr., Chairman of New York Life, resigned from the Stevens board. As in the case with Manufacturers Hanover Trust, New York Life had significant financial ties to Stevens (*Business Week*, June 9, 1980). In early summer 1980, Rogers was threatening to attempt to oust Finley from the Sperry Corporation board unless a contract could be negotiated.

III. THE SETTLEMENT

On October 20, 1980, J. P. Stevens & Company announced its willingness to sign a contract with the ACTWU. The subsequent ratification of the contract signaled the end of one of the longest labor-management disputes since collective bargaining was institutionalized in the United States in the 1930s. The contract was a two-and-a-half year pact covering approximately 4,500 hourly workers at 10 plants. While the member-ratified contract was fairly simple and straightforward, both sides made significant concessions to reach an agreement. Management made the following concessions:

1. In light of Stevens' vow "never" to sign a contract, the first concession was the simple willingness to negotiate and sign a contract.
2. Stevens agreed to a "check-off" provision, which allowed union dues to be deducted directly from the employee's paycheck.
3. The company agreed to accept arbitration of workplace conditions.
4. Stevens agreed to pay employees of their Roanoke Rapids, North Carolina, plants about $3 million in withheld pay raises. This amount is equivalent to the 8.5 percent raise given other Stevens workers in July 1979. Each worker will receive about $1,000 (*The Wall Street Journal*, 21 October 1980).

The ACTWU made the following concessions:

1. The union agreed to end both its boycott of J. P. Stevens products and the corporate campaign against the company.
2. The union agreed to limit its organizing efforts at Stevens' nonunion facilities for 18 months. Specifically, the union has agreed to refrain from using the parking lots, rest areas, canteens, or the plants themselves for organizing activities (*The Wall Street Journal*, 21 October 1980).

Although 10 plants are now unionized with a signed contract, a somewhat diminished battle for the other plants remains. The ACTWU agreed to limit its activities at these other plants, but it vowed to continue using all methods of organizing not specifically prohibited by the new contract. Likewise, the company vowed to use every means at its disposal to keep the remaining plants union-free.

IV. THE MEANING OF THE J. P. STEVENS SETTLEMENT

The settlement has significance not only for J. P. Stevens but for the entire textile industry and the South's other employers. The implications of the settlement for each of these is discussed below.

For J. P. Stevens. J. P. Stevens has made every effort to convince the public and perhaps itself that the settlement with ACTWU will have a minimal impact on the company and its industrial relations. As Whitney Stevens observed the day of the settlement, "We haven't succumbed in any way, and I doubt that this agreement will be the first step toward any further unionization," (*The Wall Street Journal*, 21 October 1980). To emphasize this point, he went on to say that the new contract didn't give the unionized workers either better wages or benefits than other Stevens' workers.

Despite these disclaimers, much has changed at J. P. Stevens. The union is no longer the dreaded outsider attempting to storm the barricades; it is now the intimate enemy. Before signing the settlement management could regard the union as a hostile interloper, unwanted by workers and management alike. Now management will have to deal with the union on a day-to-day basis. Both sides will have to abide by a commonly agreed upon document governing wages, working conditions, and benefits. Dealing with the countervailing power of ACTWU in a grievance system is far different from dealing with an individual worker who can be fired for disagreeing with management's definition of the situation.

Under the contract an orderly grievance procedure culminates in binding arbitration, and the mere threat by ACTWU of submitting important issues to an arbitrator will have two extremely important results. First, both sides will try to devise work rules that they can tolerate. This will be a major departure for Stevens, where work rules until now have been solely at the discretion of management. Second, when worker grievances are filed, Stevens' management will seek to settle the issue without submitting to arbitration. This is because Stevens management regards the National Labor Relations Board (NLRB), which oversees arbitration, with as much misgiving as it does the union.

Besides the grievance procedures, Stevens must also tolerate periodic negotiations with ACTWU in the organized factories. As each contract draws to an end, it will be necessary for management and union representatives to consider jointly the issues of wages, working conditions, and fringe benefits. Over a period of years it is likely that collective bargaining will improve wages, benefits, and working conditions in unionized plants. If this happens, Stevens will find it necessary to make comparable improvements in its nonunion operations as well. Failure to do so would be likely to lead to unionization of its other plants. While only 10 percent of Stevens workers are currently unionized, this unionization will result almost inevitably in the monetary benefits of unionization being spread to the remainder of its workers. In fact, Stevens may find it necessary to provide its nonunion workers with better conditions of employment than its unionized workers.

For the Textile Industry. The ACTWU-Stevens settlement put the industry on notice that unionism cannot be resisted by sheer obstinance on the part of management. If Stevens cannot forever delay signing a contract, then no company in the industry can safely ignore unionization efforts. On the other hand, a floodtide of unionization is not likely to sweep the southern textile industry, because the companies in the industry are diverse, and the industrial relations policies pursued by the individual companies vary significantly.

Stevens' flagrant violation of NLRB regulations led the NLRB to grant ACTWU unprecedented access to Stevens' plants and enable ACTWU to pressure other major corporations to sever their ties to Stevens. Most textile firms recognize that the Stevens approach is not the only strategy open to employers wishing to avoid unionization.

One strategy is to provide workers with most of the things that unions traditionally promise to deliver. These can include better wages, working conditions, and fringe benefits than the industry at large. The world's largest textile firm, Burlington Industries, with only 10 percent of its workers unionized in the United States, has successfully pursued this strategy. Some companies, such as medium-sized Cone Mills, have tolerated weak unions at some of its plants while keeping others union-free. A primary tactic has been to refuse to grant dues check-off. This could be considered a containment strategy. A number of companies, among them, Guilford Mills (Greensboro, North Carolina) meet the union head-on by training supervisors to handle situations which can lead to organizing efforts. Among the training tools used are mock organizing campaigns in which the supervisors have opportunities to role-play the parts of both organizers and supervisors. These programs are designed to train supervisors in labor law, organizational policies, and in defusing potentially volatile confrontations between workers and management that otherwise fuel unionization campaigns.

Regardless of approach to antiunionism, all textiles companies will be very tough negotiators concerning wages if their workers should vote in a union. It is notable that the Stevens settlement did not contain a wage increase. It will be difficult for ACTWU to deliver higher wages because the industry is labor-intensive, has narrow profit margins, and faces stiff competition from foreign competitors. These industry characteristics are among the major factors keeping wages lower in the textile industry regardless of the degree of unionization.

For the South. The ACTWU-Stevens settlement will have a relatively small impact on the southern region as a whole. The industry of the region is segmented into relatively high-paying and relatively low-paying groups. Which group an industry falls into is governed largely by the degree to which it is capital-intensive or labor-intensive. In general, capital-intensive industries have paid the highest wages, while the labor-intensive industries have not.

In response to unionization efforts in the South, capital-intensive industries are more likely to find a relatively easy accommodation with the unions. In addition to textiles, other labor-intensive industries, furniture and apparel for example, can be expected to resist unionization efforts strongly. This difference in approach results largely from the relative impact that union-won wage increases would have on costs and profits. For example, labor-intensive J. P. Stevens had only $1,100 profit per employee in 1979. The profit per employee for major textile firms was $1,700 in 1979. During that same year Stevens had about $23,700 in assets per employee, while the industry average was about $24,700 (*Forbes*, May 26, 1980). This contrasts sharply with the capital-intensive brewing industry where a company such as Anheuser-Busch earned more than $8,000 in profit per employee and had over $100,000 in assets per employee in 1979. In textiles, payroll constitutes 53 percent of value added, but it is only 13 percent of the value added in the brewing industry (*1977 Census of Manufacturers, 1978*). This means that a pay raise of a given percentage has four times the impact on costs in the textile industry as it does in brewing. Further, stiff foreign competition faced by the textile industry makes it difficult to pass along wage increases to U.S. consumers through higher prices.

A further political reality is that even capital-intensive, high-wage firms in the South are often resistant to unionization. For example, Michelin built a major tire plant in 1974 near Greenville, South Carolina, because both the firm and the Greenville Chamber of Commerce wanted to maintain a "union-free environment," (Sloan and Hall, 1979). Libby-Owens-Ford formed a wholly owned subsidiary when it constructed a new factory in

Laurinburg, North Carolina, which removed the new plant for the national collective-bargaining agreement it had previously signed with the United Glass and Ceramic Workers. General Motors, ostensibly "neutral" when the United Auto Workers (UAW) sought to organize a new steering gear plant in Athens, Alabama, during 1980 and 1981, alerted employees to the "threat" of UAW workers with accrued seniority at shut-down Northern plants resettling in Athens, thereby taking jobs from local workers. Placed on the defensive by this issue, the UAW lost the NLRB representation election in January 1981 by 721 to 659 (Moberg, 1981).

In Gastonia, North Carolina, best known for business leaders' repression of a communist-led textile strike in 1929 (Pope, 1941), the UAW and the Ohio-based Dana Corporation were locked during 1981 in a bitter battle over unionization of the Wix auto filter workers at a factory recently acquired by Dana. The UAW had assumed that Dana's management would acquiesce in the unionization of the Gastonia plant, since Dana has 8,000 workers under UAW contract in the Midwest. But Dana has endorsed the long-standing anti-unionism of Gastonia's businessmen, stating publicly that "we don't think third-party representation is essential for [our workers] to get their rights" (McInnis, 1981).

To be sure, management in the high-wage sector does not always avoid unionization. At Tenneco-owned Newport News Shipbuilding and Drydock Co., Virginia's largest employer (16,500 employees), the United Steelworkers won a representation election in January 1978, had the election upheld at the NLRB and the U.S. Court of Appeals, and signed a 42-month contract in March 1980 (*Steel Labor*, 1980).

Overall, efforts by economic development offices in southern state governments in recent years have focused on recruiting firms from traditionally high-wage industries (Luebke, McMahon, Risberg, 1979). Such recruiting efforts will reduce the relative importance of textile employment throughout the region. Over time, organizing at Stevens and other textile firms will become less important than labor organizing in the high-wage sector.

Thus, the ACTWU-Stevens settlement, far from a "labor breakthrough," is almost limited in its impact to the single case. The contract was a great symbolic victory for ACTWU since Stevens had said "never," but substantively the union-management battle will be fought individually at each plant in the South, within the context of the particular industrial sector and management attitudes at each company.

REFERENCES

U.S. Department of Commerce. Bureau of the Census. *1977 Census of Manufacturers*. Washington, D.C.: U.S. Government Printing Office, 1978.

"How the Textile Union Finally Wins Contracts at J. P. Stevens." *The Wall Street Journal*, October 21, 1980, sec. 1, pp. A-1, A-24.

"Is the J. P. Stevens War Over?" *Business Week*, June 9, 1980, pp. 85–87.

"Local 888: The Story of Sunbelt Struggle." *Steel Labor* 45 (April 1980), pp. 7–10.

Luebke, Paul; Robert McMahon; and Jeffrey Risberg. "Selective Industrial Recruitment in North Carolina." *Working Papers for a New Society* 6 (March–April 1979), pp. 17–20.

McInnis, Douglas. "UAW Fights for a Place in the Sun(belt)." *The News and Observer* (Raleigh, N.C.), April 12, 1981, sec. IV, p. D-1.

Moberg, David. "Three Strikes for the UAW at GM's Biggest Nonunion Plant." *In These Times* 5 (February 4–10, 1981), p. 7.

Pope, Liston. *Millhands and Preachers*. New Haven: Yale University Press, 1941.

U.S. Department of Labor. National Labor Relations Board. *Decisions and Orders of the NLRB* 239, October 13, 1978–January 19, 1979, "J. P. Stevens & Company and the Amalgamated Clothing and Textile Workers Union, AFL–CIO," pp. 738–75.

"A Scorecard on Capital and Labor." *Forbes*, May 26, 1980, pp. 137–43.

Sloan, Clifford, and Robert Hall. "It's Good to Be Home in Greenville." *Southern Exposure* 7 (Spring 1979), pp. 83, 89–90.

Somplatsky-Jarman, Bill. "The Company That Disdains the Law." *Business and Society Review* no. 24 (Winter 1977–1978), pp. 50–54.

READING 19

Labor Looks at the American Economy*

Rudy Oswald[†]

The struggle of the Polish workers to establish a democratic free trade union rekindled the recognition of the role of trade unions in a free and democratic society. That struggle was instructive of the inherent desire of workers to form their own democratic institutions to deal with employers concerning the basic conditions of the workplace and with the government as its policies interrelate with the concerns of workers.

However, many people who have been inspired by the struggle of the Polish workers have failed to understand the struggle of American workers and of the role of trade unions in the American economic and political environment.

Unions in the United States, as in Poland, rose out of the struggle of workers to achieve a measure of democracy on the job.

The continued dynamics of workers is reflected in recent headlines that dealt with the football strike or the Detroit teachers strike or with the Chrysler workers rejecting the proposed new contract. However, the true perspective of where that struggle is in the United States is that most negotiations result in a settlement without a strike—some 98 percent of all negotiations and thus the strike headline is the unusual rather than the usual.

Another headline grabber is the "givebacks" of labor. True, a number of unions have made contract adjustments in light of the

*Reprinted with permission from the National Council for the Social Studies, *Social Education*, January 1983, pp. 22–24.

†*Rudy Oswald is Director of the Department of Economic Research, AFL–CIO, Washington, D.C.*

particular circumstances of their industrial situation, but the common element in contracts negotiated in 1982 was continued improvements. Contracts negotiated in the first half of 1982, (outside of trucking and auto) averaged first year wage gains of 7 percent. But it has not been these wage gains that have beset U.S. international competitiveness, but rather the effect of high interest rates in raising the value of the dollar. Since the first of 1982, the dollar rose by 25 percent against the Japanese yen, making Japanese goods that much less expensive in the United States, and American goods that much more expensive in Japan.

Today, some 22 million American workers belong to trade unions, and I include in that figure those associations that act like unions, and engage in collective bargaining. Unions represent some 20 percent of the work force, but I think a more accurate description is 30 percent of those workers who are eligible to join unions because they are working as wage or salary employees in nonsupervisory jobs.

A number of movies recently have described some of the early struggles of trade unions in this country. Perhaps the best description of that struggle was reflected in the recent hit, *Norma Rae*, where it described the meaning of that struggle in a particular textile plant. But that struggle goes on against the growing array of lawbreakers who abrogate the basic right guaranteed to workers under the National Labor Relations Act to be able to form and join unions for collective bargaining purposes. The Polish workers did not achieve the legal protection of that right, but legal protection of that right in the United States is being eroded by the actions of a new group of so-called labor-management consultants whose sole purpose is to deny workers their right to form and join unions. These consultants would paint unions as a relic of a time past, rather than as an essential part of the free democratic process of determining the wages and conditions of employment. That democratic element is as important today as it was 20 or 50 years ago. The trade union movement will overcome these attacks as it had the attacks of physical goons employed to destroy unions in earlier eras.

Changing Labor Movement

The trade union movement is a movement that continually changes and grows to reflect the shifts that are taking place in the economy in which it exists. As old industries decline, new industries look toward unionism as a means of protecting their interest. As the work force becomes more white-collar, more female, more minorities, younger, so too the labor movement becomes more reflective of those sectors of the economy. But it is the economy overall that has a profound effect upon the collective bargaining situation and the elements related thereto.

As an essential part of the fabric of democratic society, organized labor has not limited its energies to collective bargaining. Its historic mission has been to improve the lot of the poor, the exploited, and the victims of discrimination. No other organization in society has concerned itself with as wide-ranging a program for social improvement. Labor's support for free public education, for instance, goes way back to 1837. Labor was the first organized group to fight for a minimum wage for women and children. Although almost all union members make more than the federal minimum wage, organized labor continues to press for legislation that will assure that the minimum wage will not fall behind the level of inflation. Unions have been in the forefront of the fight for equal employment opportunities, voting rights, civil rights, workers' compensation, unemployment compensation, better housing, public health programs, and adequate and equitable tax structures.

Today that fight is more important than ever. The Reagan administration economic policies are undoing the gains in economic and social rights that have been achieved over a half century. His policies have cut education and training programs and weakened the enforcement of basic civil rights statutes and regulations. His economic policies have rewarded the wealthy at the expense of the middle class and poor. The huge tax cuts and shifts to defense spending have been paid for by social program cuts and high federal deficits. The economy has been pushed into the deepest and longest recession since the depression, by the administration-supported tight money policies and its tax and budget policies. Thus, a crucial element for all working men and women is the overall economic and social climate within which they live. This climate of recession and repression of social progress impinges on the basic need for jobs and social progress.

To deal with these issues, labor must extend its actions into the political arena where these basic decisions are made.

Rise in Unemployment

Recently, the Labor Department reported that unemployment in the country soared to 10.8 percent, more than 11 million men and women without jobs.

In 15 months, the Reagan tight monetary policies, big defense boosts coupled with tax cuts for the wealthy, and budget cuts in social programs resulted in unemployment rising by more than 3 million.

We in the AFL–CIO together with millions of other concerned Americans will press the Congress for a major correction in the national economic course and a change in tax policy, budget cuts, deregulation, and high interest rates.

We will work for a restructured tax system and for the restoration of those budget cuts which deprive the old and the needy of vital services. We will seek enough regulation of our giant industries to ensure protections for workers and consumers. We urge policies that will return interest rates not just to 10 percent to make the money lenders richer, but to the 4, 5, and 6 percent rates that built this nation.

We will fight to overcome Reaganomics and set America right again. David Stockman let the cat out of the bag in November 1981 when he told the truth—admitting that the Kemp-Roth supply-side tax magic was never anything more than a "Trojan Horse" to get the top tax rates down. Ever since then, Americans have had a better understanding of which end of the horse was making economic policy.

We will continue to defend our unions and defend collective bargaining as the only sure route to a worker voice in his or her destiny. I think we've proved again in 1981 and 1982 that collective bargaining is a responsible, dynamic, and adaptable system that produces industrial democracy in the best sense of that term.

In recent years, collective bargaining agreements have put a lot more safety nets under American cities and American industries than President Reagan has put under the people his administration has been throwing out of work.

And American unions have been a lot more reasonable to friend and foe alike than President Reagan was to the air traffic controllers when he used the might and majesty of U.S. government to crush their union and their aspirations, at a cost of billions to taxpayers.

We trade unionists will continue to seek and find employers who agree with us that a good contract with a good union is good business.

As we bargain our contracts and as we gain legislatively, we continue to raise the floor under the American workers, union and non-union alike.

And you know, we have to stop every once in a while and note that the news is not all bad.

As hard as the past months have been, we ought to note that the great sweep of conservatism that was going to cover the nation just hasn't made it.

Some 20 months ago, the Smart Money had it that the New Right would sweep the Congress in November 1982.

We haven't won a lot of resounding victories in the Congress in the year past, but neither has the New Right.

They promised they would bury this labor movement in legislative restrictions, and we're still alive and well. Thanks.

They said they would pass a national Right-to-Work law, and we've blocked them.

They said they would gut the Brown Lung protections for textile workers, and we beat them in the courts.

They said they would shatter the prevailing wage rates for government construction. When they couldn't win that legislatively, the executive branch did it administratively. And again, thanks to the courts, that effort has been beaten back.

They said they would roll back the child labor protections and make more subminimum workers available for the fast food chains, and we beat them back—with the period for public comment extended, a euphemism for backing away from the heat.

Our involvement in those issues shows the clear necessity of reliance on all three branches of government—legislative, executive, and judicial. Organized labor has come to that strategy from recognition that we can lose in the legislative halls what we won at the bargaining table.

POLITICAL ACTION

Political activities are important extensions of labor's role in collective bargaining, and they have immeasurably enriched American life. Only to the extent that labor is able to be successful at the collective bargaining table are these efforts possible. Efforts to limit or destroy collective bargaining weaken democracy. Conversely, whatever strengthens the process of free collective bargaining strengthens democracy and freedom.

The role of American trade unions as free trade unions everywhere in the world must act as the bastion of freedom both in the workplace and in the legislative arena. The American trade union movement is proud of the role it has been able to play in this regard and is ready to meet the challenge of today and tomorrow.

In the proud, 101-year history of American labor as a united national federation, we did not quit in the beginning when President McKinley and various governors called out both federal and state troops to break what they called the conspiracy of trade unionism.

We did not quit in the 1930s when the nation's unfettered, laissez-faire economics brought us the worst depression in our history. We survived that as a great president, Franklin Roosevelt, gave us the Wagner Act, which recognized the right of individual Americans to band together in unions so they didn't have to face the boss alone.

We did not quit in the 1970s, when Richard Nixon tried to brush us aside and tried to corrupt this nation's administration. Indeed, we were the first national organization to call for his impeachment.

And we're certainly not going to quit today when President Reagan brings us the worst of all possible worlds. He's trying to revive the economic policies of McKinley, kill the life-saving social services of Franklin Roosevelt, and turn back the clock on worker progress with a callousness that would make Calvin Coolidge blush.

The president has destroyed the economy, but he and the New Right have surely learned they can't bust this labor movement.

We view organized labor's role in society as the nation's main enduring, private force for progress and for human and economic rights. We are and remain the nation's single most powerful voice fighting for decency, for progress, and for democracy and all that it implies.

We have a long history and we have long memories. We have persevered before, and we progressed before, and the combining link is simply that we will not quit.

R E A D I N G 20

Organizations of Working Women Can Pave the Way for Unions*

Karen S. Koziara and
Patrice J. Insley†

Almost two thirds of all women who work full-time are in white-collar occupations. Relatively few of them (about 13 percent) belong to unions.[1] During the last few years, however, a number of organizations have formed outside the traditional labor movement to address working women's problems.

Between 15 and 20 major organizations of working women formed in urban areas during the last decade. About 12 of them are linked nationally. The others are local and autonomous. All are still relatively small, given the size of their potential constituencies. Few have more than a thousand members. Those members work for a number of employers in a given area, and any one firm may employ only a few members.[2] The general overarching goal of these organizations is improving employment conditions faced by working women, particularly women in low-income white-collar jobs. This goal has two related dimensions. The first involves economic or "bread and butter" issues, including low wages, employment discrimination, and lack of promotional opportunities. The second dimension involves the right to be treated with dignity and to have one's work be seen as meaningful and serious and includes problems such as sexual harassment and arbitrary and demeaning treatment by supervisors. A related goal is building a firm organizational base. This involves continued organizing efforts designed to introduce working women to the idea of working together to solve shared problems.

Organizations of working women generally focus on resolving immediate problems as a way of achieving goals. The tactics used vary enormously and are tailored to the specific problem being addressed. These tactics can be classified into four general categories: information gathering, conciliation, direct action, and education.

Information gathering is both an important first step in becoming established and also an important ongoing activity for these organizations. Initially, surveys conducted among selected populations of working women help identify particular employment problems and problem employers. This information serves as a basis for program planning and as a way of letting people know of the organization's existence. Employment problems are handled on a case-by-case basis. Examples of the issues handled are failure of a firm to live up to an affirmative action plan, specific incidents of sexual harassment, low wages, and employer failure to post promotional opportunities.

Conciliation involves approaching the employer or governmental agency in an effort to resolve an identified problem. In some instances, the problem can be resolved through discussion sessions; in other instances, the employer or concerned agency is unwilling to meet with representatives of the organization or is unwilling to make any concessions. If efforts at conciliation through discussion are unsuccessful, then direct action can be used.

Direct action can take many forms. Not enough members work for any one employer

*From U.S. Department of Labor, *Monthly Labor Review* 105, no. 6 (June 1982), pp. 53–54.

†*Karen S. Koziara is chairperson and a professor in the Industrial Relations and Organizational Behavior Department, Temple University, and Patrice J. Insley is a graduate student at the university.* The title of their full IRRA paper is "Organizing Low-Income Women in New Ways: Who, Where, and Why."

[1]Linda H. LeGrande, "Women in Labor Organizations: Their Ranks Are Increasing," *Monthly Labor Review,* August 1978, p. 9.

[2]Information in this report comes primarily from interviews with officers and directors of Working Women, Women Employed, and Interfaith Women's Alliance for Working Women conducted by the authors during 1980 and 1981.

to make effective use of strikes and strike threats; therefore, most forms of direct action are designed to bring the involved employer unfavorable publicity. Examples of such activities include public awards, such as a Christmas "Scrooge of the Year" award and a "Pettiest Office Procedure" award. These have the combined impact of making the organization visible, while at the same time putting pressure on the involved employer. Other forms of direct action include presentation of signed petitions, picketing, and even sit-ins.

Also government agencies can be used to pressure employers to live up to their legal obligations. This is most frequently used when the issue is affirmative action, equal employment opportunity, or age discrimination. Banks have been a major focus of this type of action because of the large numbers of low-income women employed in banking. Efforts have been made by organizations of working women to have the U.S. Department of Labor's Office of Federal Contract Compliance Programs monitor affirmative action programs in the banking industry, and a number of administrative complaints have resulted. These tactics have had some success: a number of banks have made back-pay settlements, four banks in Baltimore raised wages of low-level bank employees, several banks and insurance companies have agreed to job-posting programs, and at least one bank has instituted a major training program for clerical employees.[3]

Education and outreach are extremely important activities for working women's organizations. They are accomplished through programs, seminars, and publications and serve two major functions. First, they are a way to get visibility and to reach potential members. Getting people involved in educational programs is also an important way of increasing member commitment. It is also a service that encourages people to maintain their membership, perhaps even after a specific employer-based problem has been resolved.

The second major function performed by educational activities is to help women understand and develop ways of handling problems at work. Examples of typical subjects include skills assessment, conflict management in an office setting, equal employment opportunity law, retirement planning, assertiveness training, and career planning. Additionally, some educational programs are more general and aim at developing an understanding of common problems and solutions.

Currently, organizations of working women do not perform the functions performed by unions. They do not press for certified bargaining rights, they negotiate with employers only over limited issues, and they do not sign collective bargaining contracts. Additionally, they have relatively little contact with the labor movement.

A major reason for their independence from the labor movement is the belief that the organizing model used by unions is ineffective in organizing women in clerical occupations. There are several explanations for the labor movement's inability to effectively organize these workers. One explanation is that the labor movement has not been willing to expend the resources or develop the tactics necessary to organize successfully in these areas. A second explanation is that female clerical and service workers have not been ready to join unions.[4]

Both explanations are consistent with the emergence of working women's organizations which provide a new model for organizing female clerical workers. Some observers have described this model as "preorganizing," or creating the conditions that make union organizing viable.

In theory, the potential exists for innovative and cooperative arrangements between working women's organizations and the labor movement. There are mutual interests. Many unions are interested in organizing in new areas, and organizations of working women do not provide as broad employment protections

---

[3]Working Women, *Report from Working Women*, April 1980.

[4]Roberta Lynch, "Women in the Work Force," *The Progressive*, October 1979, p. 29.

as do collective bargaining contracts. In fact, members of one affiliate, Nine to Five in Boston, formed a local union, which joined the Service Employees International Union as Local 925.[5]

_____
[5]Nancy Seifer and Barbara Wertheimer, "New Approaches to Collective Power," in *Women Organizing: An Anthology*, eds., Bernice Cummings and Victoria Schuck.

This indicates that innovative arrangements can be developed. However, the essence of innovation is doing things differently than before, and that type of organizational change is often difficult to achieve because of institutional barriers facing it.

READING 21

The International Trade Union Movement*

John P. Windmuller†

I. HISTORICAL OVERVIEW

A. To 1914

Trade unions are preeminently national institutions. They pursue their primary tasks of defending and improving the conditions of life and work of their members within the confines of national systems of industrial relations. Yet for well over a century trade unions have also had international interests and commitments which they have expressed through international trade union organisations.

Two different types of international trade union organisations established themselves securely in the last decade of the 19th century and the first decade of the 20th. One was based on an identity of interests among individual national unions for specific crafts, trades, and industries in various countries and resulted in the formation of so-called International Trade Secretariats. The other type was of a broader character, for its members consisted of the central federations of trade unions, also called national centres.

International Trade Secretariats (often abbreviated as Secretariats or ITSs) first became established in 1889 with the creation of the International Federation of Boot and Shoe Operatives. Its constituent bodies were unions of workers engaged in boot and shoe manufacturing in several European countries. Organisations composed of unions in other trades and industries followed the example in the next few years, including those for miners (1890), clothing workers (1893), typographers (1893), metal workers (1890), textile workers (1894), transport workers (1896), and many others. By 1914 close to 30 ITSs existed. While acknowledging their support of long-range socialist aims, their efforts were devoted to such practical tasks as disseminating trade information, helping travelling journeymen, and discouraging the international transport of strikebreakers.

The second type of international trade union organisation, composed of central trade union federations, emerged from conferences in Copenhagen (1901), Stuttgart (1902), and Dublin (1903). First known as the International Secretariat of Trade Union Centers, the organisation called itself the International Federation of Trade Unions (IFTU) from 1913 on. Before the outbreak of war put an end to its activities, it claimed as affiliates about 20 central trade union federations with some 7,700,000 individual members, mostly from Europe, but also including the American Federation of Labor (AFL).

B. From 1914 to 1939

After the war the IFTU reorganised itself in 1919 under a new constitution at a meeting held in Amsterdam, while many ITSs, too, reestablished their organisations. Another important development at this time was the establishment of two new organisations: the Red International of Labor Unions (RILU) and the International Federation of Christian Trade Unions (French initials: CISC). The RILU came into existence in 1921 when the leaders of the Communist Party and the Soviet Union decided to create a separate worldwide trade union international, often also called the Prof-intern. The formation of the so-called Popular Front in 1935 put an end to the activities of the RILU. At that time Communist parties and trade unions throughout the

*Reprinted with permission from Roger Blanpain ed., *Comparative Labour Law and Industrial Relations* (Deventer, The Netherlands: Kluwer, 1983).

†John P. Windmuller is Martin P. Catherwood Professor of Industrial and Labor Relations at the New York State School of Industrial and Labor Relations, Cornell University.

world were ordered by Moscow to cooperate with and join democratic political and trade union organisations to stem the advance of Nazi and fascist movements. The formal dissolution of the RILU, however, occurred only in 1943 when the Comintern was disbanded.

The creation of a separate Christian trade union international (CISC) in 1921 was the culmination of many years of organisational work among Christian workers in several European nations, particularly Germany, Italy, France, and the Low Countries. First organised at local or regional and then at national levels, the Christian trade unions offered an organisational and philosophical alternative to those believing Catholic and Protestant workers for whom membership in socialist unions, with their anticlerical and even antireligious sentiments, was unacceptable.

Of the three prewar international federations—IFTU, RILU, and CISC—the IFTU was the largest and certainly the most representative one, even though its membership fluctuated from a peak of well over 20 million in the immediate post-World War I period to fewer than 10 million after the destruction of the German unions by the Nazi regime. When World War II broke out in 1939, the IFTU's affiliates claimed a total of about 14 million members, which included the AFL.

C. After 1939

World War II did more than merely disrupt the functioning of international trade union organisations. It also created the opportunity to reconsider fundamentally the international trade union structure. For many organisations, post-war labour unity in place of prewar division became a key objective. A world labor conference that met in London in February 1945 decided to disband the IFTU and establish a new and all-encompassing world labor organisation, the World Federation of Trade Unions (WFTU). Its principal initiators were the British TUC, the Soviet AUCCTU, and the American CIO. The founding congress was held in Paris in October 1945. The most important absentee was the American Federation of Labor which as a matter of principle refused to be associated with unions controlled by governments or political parties, specifically with unions in Communist countries and more generally with Communist-dominated unions anywhere.

Other organisations that declined to join the WFTU were the constituents of the Christian international labour federation (CISC). That rather small body reorganised itself after the war on an even smaller scale than before 1939, due to the loss of important affiliates in Germany, Austria, and Italy where the post-war drive for labour unity had led to the formation of unitary trade unions. In the 1960s the CISC gradually abandoned its ties to the Church and adopted a secular programme. In 1968 it chose the new name of World Confederation of Labour (WCL).

The peaceful coexistence inside the WFTU of entirely different conceptions of the role of trade unions in society was of relatively short duration. Disagreements over support for the Marshall Plan and other important political and trade union issues led most affiliated unions from Western countries to sever their ties in 1949. Before the end of the year a new organisation had been launched: the International Confederation of Free Trade Unions (ICFTU). In this endeavor the unions disaffiliating from the WFTU, headed by the British TUC and the American CIO, were now for the first time since 1945 joined by the AFL.

Thus, as of 1949 there existed—and there still exist currently—three international trade union federations: the ICFTU, the WFTU, and the WCL. Given their worldwide scope, these three organisations may be referred to as global internationals. In addition, there exist quite a few additional, independently formed, international trade unions of a regional or industrial character, including some of considerable importance. Clearly the world of international labour, specialized though it may be, does not suffer from a shortage of organisations. The structures and the relationships between the various parts are complex, and if possible one of the main objectives of the account which follows should be to present an intricate situation in terms that create at least a superficial impression of order and clarity, even if the reality is very different.

II. THE INTERNATIONAL CONFEDERATION OF FREE TRADE UNIONS

By any measure except size the ICFTU is the most representative of the three global trade union internationals, especially since the American AFL–CIO decided to rejoin it in 1981 after an absence of 12 years. Not only are the ICFTU's affiliates the largest trade union organisations in almost every Western European country as well as in North America and Australasia, but the ICFTU also has sizable followings in Asia and Latin America. Only in Africa, for reasons to be explained, is it sparsely represented. Of course in the Communist countries of Eastern Europe and elsewhere (Cuba, Vietnam, North Korea, the PR of China) it has no members at all. Ideologically the ICFTU is open to trade unions of various views—socialist, social-democratic, pragmatic. The only stipulation is reasonable freedom from domination by governments, political parties, or other external forces. Similarly wide is the range of members in terms of their countries' level of economic development: the ranks of the ICFTU consist of unions both from the world's most highly industrialized and from some of the least developed areas.

A. Aims and Activities

1. Overall Goals. Because of the diversity of its membership the ICFTU has always taken care to formulate its basic aims in terms that are likely to be broadly acceptable to a wide-ranging membership, regardless of political orientation. Consequently the ICFTU avoids taking sides on certain ideological issues, such as the nationalisation of industries or the transformation of capitalism to socialism, and instead emphasises the beliefs and values shared by virtually all constituents, notably a

rejection of totalitarian regimes, a devotion to democratic principles of government, support for efforts to safeguard world peace, the struggle for social justice, and the fair distribution of wealth and incomes at national and international levels. Subsumed under these basic aims is a set of more specific objectives whose formulation and priority are to some extent subject to changing circumstances and opportunities. For example, the pursuit of the goal of full employment, though of permanent concern to the ICFTU, is bound to receive more programmatic emphasis in periods of severe economic crisis than in times when job opportunities are plentiful.

2. Representational Work and Services. Most ICFTU activities can be fitted into one of three categories: representation, organisation, and services. Representational work consists of the use of public forums, reports, resolutions, and similar means to express concerns and protests on a wide range of issues, from restrictions on freedom of association to the plight of migrant workers. In its representational capacity the ICFTU thus acts as a kind of international labour conscience, calling attention to injustices committed by governments or employers and appealing to the international community to exert its moral authority and pressure on behalf of a particular cause, an organisation, or sometimes even an incarcerated trade union leader.

The organisational work of the ICFTU is directed chiefly to the promotion and strengthening of trade unionism in areas where unions are weak and vulnerable, thus mostly in countries of the third World. The object is to strengthen those organisations which share the philosophy of trade unionism represented by the ICFTU. Assistance may include training programmes for union officials, direct financial subsidies although this is now usually avoided, gifts of equipment, or study trips for selected leaders. Although the organisational work is a key activity, it is limited by available resources and must be coordinated with parallel activities conducted by certain national trade union federations, including the American AFL–CIO, the German DGB, the Swedish LO, and several others.

The third set of ICFTU tasks, the provision of services, is closely linked to its representational and organising work. It includes not only conventional types of educational, research, informational, and public relations programmes, but has expanded in recent years into so-called extra-budgetary development projects among which vocational training, medical and health care, employment promotion, and the development of workers' cooperatives are particularly prominent.

B. Structure and Government

1. Membership and Finances. In the main the ICFTU is composed of national trade union centres, and as a rule only one centre from one country. There are, however, exceptions. In some instances two national centres of similar scope but separated by political or philosophical differences have been accepted into membership. Italy (CISL and UIL) and India (INTUC and HMS) are apt examples. In other instances dual affiliation stems from the existence of separate organisations for blue-collar and white-collar workers, as in the case of Sweden (LO and TCO) and Denmark (LO and FTF). Individual unions are not generally eligible for membership, but some exceptions have been made both for independents (the United Mine Workers in the United States) and for individual unions whose national centre does not belong to the ICFTU (Sohyo in Japan).

ICFTU membership figures are best regarded as rough estimates, since they are likely to be somewhat inflated by the claims of affiliates in countries where such data are usually unreliable. Figures for 1983 showed a total of 134 affiliates in 94 countries with an overall individual membership of about 85 million.[1]

---

[1] ICFTU *Report on Activities, 1979–1982* (Brussels, 1983), p. 31.

Europe has always been in first place in the geographic distribution of ICFTU membership, followed at some distance by North America, Asia, and Latin America (including the Caribbean). Africa and the Middle East are only weakly represented. Most governments in these two areas discourage or prohibit affiliation.

To support its core activities the ICFTU until fairly recently depended essentially on two sources of income: regular affiliation fees from all members and voluntary contributions from the more affluent ones. Regular affiliation fees make up about two thirds of the total, roughly $3 million out of $4.5 million, based on a rate that in 1983 was about $80 per 1,000 members annually. This meant that an organisation with about 10 million members, for example the British TUC, would by paying $800,000 in annual contributions. It is possible, however, to negotiate reductions where justified by special circumstances, such as unfavourable exchange rates, low levels of local dues, or restrictions on foreign currency transfers. In fact, a substantial number of affiliates, mostly in less-developed countries, pay at substantially lower rates. In recent years voluntary payments into the International Solidarity Fund have totalled about $1.2 million per year.

In the last decade a new source of income has become available which has greatly improved the ICFTU's financial position: the so-called extra-budgetary funds. These represent to some extent grants made by private organisations such as foundations, as well as intergovernmental agencies such as the ILO, but to a much larger extent they consist of indirect allocations provided by various national governments. The development agencies or ministries of these governments—which include among others the Netherlands, the Scandinavian countries, and Canada—support jointly agreed ICFTU development programmes either by direct funding or indirectly through allocations to their central trade union federations which, in turn, pass on all or part of the amount to the ICFTU. (In several instances, extra-budgetary funds have also been made available to support the development work of the International Trade Secretariats, discussed below.) In the first few years of the 1980s, the ICFTU's income from extra-budgetary funds averaged $3.5 million annually, a very sizable amount by comparison with the income from normal dues. In fact, because the availability of such relatively large sums may create a variety of problems and because the sources themselves may be a problem, the ICFTU has adopted a special set of rules to govern the acceptance and use of extra-budgetary funds.[2]

2. Governing Bodies and Secretariat. Policy-making responsibilities in the ICFTU are divided between several bodies. The supreme authority is vested in a congress which meets every four years. Because of their relatively large size and the long intervals between meetings, the congresses cannot be the key decision-making bodies. That role belongs to the Executive Board and particularly to certain committees of the board. Its current elected membership consists of 37 titular representatives and an equal number of first and second substitutes, all chosen so as to ensure the widest possible geographic distribution. The general secretary is a board member ex officio, and the International Trade Secretariats are entitled to be represented by four nonvoting members. Normally the full board meets only twice a year. Urgent matters arising between board sessions are placed before a subcommittee of about 10 members. A special position is held by another subcommittee: the Finance and General Purposes Committee, whose voting members head up the ICFTU's most important affiliates in Europe, North America, and Asia. It has a broad mandate for allocating ICFTU resources, which is of course a key item of decision making.

Day-to-day activities are the responsibility of a secretariat headed by a general secretary who is elected by the congress. (Currently the position is held by Jan Vanderveken, a Belgian national, who has been associated with the ICFTU since 1951.) Of the five general secretaries who have held that office since 1949, four have been nationals of the Low Countries. This is not unusual. Citizens of the smaller countries tend to be regarded as neutral in the contest for influence that sometimes develops between the larger constituents. Smaller countries also seem to be represented in disproportionately large numbers in other staff positions in the ICFTU, the International Trade Secretariats, and similar international trade union groupings.

3. Regional Organisations. The ICFTU was the first international trade union body to foster the formation of regional organisations. This innovative idea was designed both to create a mechanism through which trade unions could join forces to cope with problems specific to their part of the world and also to avoid an excessive concentration of authority at ICFTU headquarters. The implementation of the idea, however, has been anything but uniform. The two regional organisations in Asia and the Western Hemisphere—designated respectively as ARO and ORIT—have become reasonably self-starting organisations, due largely to the presence in their areas of important national trade union federations able to provide leadership, direction, and financial support. But their efforts to develop an independent regional role have not always proceeded smoothly. Their claims to a large measure of regional autonomy have from time to time clashed with the central body's insistence on its own ultimate authority. This is probably an inevitable problem and surely a sensitive one, for it involves conflicting prerogatives, ambitions, and interests. For example, in the late 1970s the ICFTU Executive Board refused to endorse a new constitution adopted by ORIT, the ICFTU's regional organization for the Inter-American region, because practically all references to ORIT's status as an ICFTU regional body had been dropped, as well as the references to the ulti-

---

[2]See the statement on "Handling, Purposes, and Manpower Implications of Projects Financed by Extrabudgetary Means," approved by the 12th ICFTU Congress in Madrid, November 1979.

mate authority of the ICFTU Executive Board. A revised and more acceptable version was ultimately approved.[3] Similar examples could be cited with regard to the relationship between ARO, the ICFTU's Asian body, and ICFTU headquarters.

In Africa the experience with building a regional organisation has been entirely different. The African Regional Organisation (AFRO) has never developed sufficient momentum, nor has it had the resources, to become a self-starting body. An important obstacle to its growth has been the opposition of most African governments to a regional trade union organisation with international links, one whose material and moral resources would be provided largely from outside the African area. They fear that such a body might be able to strengthen the defensive and claims-making role of trade unions well beyond the point most African governments are willing to tolerate at this time.

Europe presents yet another case. Although the European Regional Organisation (ERO) was the first ICFTU regional and easily had the potential for becoming an important, even a powerful, body at European level, its constituents eventually decided to promote the establishment of an even more widely based European trade union federation, one that would be open to both ICFTU affiliates and nonaffiliates, but therefore necessarily separate from the ICFTU. As a result of this decision, ERO was disbanded and a nearly all-inclusive European Trade Union Confederation (ETUC) founded. Because of its independent character the ETUC will be reviewed in a separate section.

III. THE WORLD FEDERATION OF TRADE UNIONS

Ever since the split in 1949 the principal constituents of the World Federation of Trade Unions (WFTU) have been the labour organisations in countries governed by Communist parties and allied to the Soviet Union. In addition the WFTU contains a substantial number of labour organisations in non-Communist countries, although most of them are of only secondary importance. One may, therefore, characterise the WFTU as chiefly but not entirely the international trade union body of the Soviet Bloc.

A. Aims and Activities

Under the terms of its constitution the WFTU's overall aim is "to improve the living and working conditions of the people of all lands." This is to be achieved by the organisation and unity of the world's working class, assistance to unions in less-developed countries, opposition to war, and an unremitting struggle against fascism. Although that is a very broad mandate, the denial of an adversary role for trade unions in Communist countries has severely circumscribed the field of action of the WFTU inside the Bloc. That also explains why the WFTU agenda is concerned to a large degree only with events occurring outside the Soviet orbit.

A foremost WFTU concern has always been firm support for the foreign policy goals of the Soviet Union. The lone and almost inexplicable exception was the secretariat's rebuke of the 1968 invasion of Czechoslovakia by the Warsaw Pact powers, but that deviation was quickly redressed and those responsible for it removed from their positions. More characteristic are the uniformly optimistic accounts of working conditions and trade union activities in the Soviet Union and allied Communist countries, coupled with exposures of brutal violations of trade union freedoms and human rights in Western countries and a picked group of Third World countries. Another important activity, conducted in cooperation with WFTU affiliates, consists of training programmes for trade union leaders and activists in less-developed countries, both in schools inside the Soviet Bloc and in the field. Considerable importance is also attached to a WFTU presence at the United Nations and its specialised agencies, especially the International Labour Organisation (ILO).

[3]*Report of the ICFTU 12th World Congress, 1979* (Brussels, 1979), p. 196.

B. Structure and Government

1. Membership and Finances. Although the WFTU has not published a list of affiliates and their membership figures since 1949, its claim to being the largest international labour federation is not open to argument. In 1978 its 73 affiliates contained, according to their own count, a total of 190 million members, while the number claimed to be represented by the 810 participants at the 1982 Congress in Havana was 269 million. The Soviet labour federation (AUCCTU) accounts for over half of the total. It must be noted, however, that union membership in Communist countries is usually close to the total nonagricultural labour force because social benefits and entitlements (access to vacation resorts, social insurance, etc.) are often administered by the unions, which means that membership confers important advantages.

Not all unions in Communist-led countries are WFTU members. The Yugoslav unions were expelled in 1950 after that country rejected Soviet hegemony. They were later invited to return but declined, although they do send observers to WFTU congresses. The unions in China and Albania departed in the mid-1960s, after the break between their countries and the USSR became irreparable. The most recent nonaffiliate was Poland's now-suppressed trade union, Solidarity. Also absent, but in a different category, are the Italian trade union federation (CGIL) and the Spanish CCOO. Both are under Communist leadership, but closely linked to political parties whose political position may be described as Eurocommunism. The CGIL disaffiliated from the WFTU in 1978 after over 30 years of membership. The French labour federation (CGT) also briefly considered disaffiliation but decided against it when the French Communist party ended a brief period of liberalisation.

Very little is known about the WFTU's finances. It appears that its income stems mostly from ordinary affiliation fees and voluntary contributions, but the amounts involved and the rates on which they are based are not available. The regular budget figure for 1976 was very exceptionally made public and apparently amounted to $1.6 million.

2. Governing Bodies and Secretariats. In its internal government the WFTU follows the usual pattern of most international trade union bodies. Supreme authority is vested in a congress which recently has been meeting at four-year intervals. In order to foster an image of being a widely representative organisation, the WFTU encourages attendance and even participation in the formal decisions of its congresses by nonmember organisations. Second in line is the General Council, a smaller version of the congress. The Executive Bureau has a membership of about 30 from the major affiliates. The secretariat consists of a general secretary (currently Ibrahim Zakaria, a national of the Sudan), and five secretaries, including one from the Soviet Union.

3. Trade Unions International. To serve the industrial interests of its membership the WFTU contains 11 Trade Unions International (TUI) for individual economic sectors such as mining, metals, transport, etc. Whether the TUIs actually perform industrial functions is questionable, for in countries governed by Communist parties the tasks assigned to trade unions are mostly production-oriented and only secondarily concerned with protection and claims-making. The evidently tenuous industrial role of the TUIs was recently acknowledged by the head of the TUI for the textile industry in the WFTU's own journal. He wrote:

The question of the relationship between the political and trade interests of the TUIs is often the subject of study. Various discussions are underway to see if the political problems and general resolutions are not predominant in the work of the TUIs, with matters relating to the particular branches of industry relegated to a back-seat position.[4]

TUI policies and activities are determined, at least in a general sense, by the WFTU, for

---

[4] *World Trade Union Movement*, no. 11 (1981), p. 4 (emphasis added).

the TUIs are not autonomous decision-making bodies. Moreover, their expenses are financed by allocations from the WFTU rather than by dues collected directly from their own member unions.

IV. THE WORLD CONFEDERATION OF LABOUR

A. Membership

When the World Confederation of Labour (WCL) abandoned its Christian identity in the mid-1960s, it adopted a militant secular programme based on humanist, socialist, and syndicalist ideas. It also sought to alter the balance of its programme and the composition of its membership by enlarging its activities in the less-developed countries. At the time these decisions were made, the core of the WCL dues-paying membership consisted of a few affiliates in Belgium, the Netherlands (two organisations), and France. Other affiliated organisations were scattered mostly among Third World countries where they usually lagged far behind the affiliates of the ICFTU and the WFTU in terms of membership.

In the last few years, the small nucleus of dues-paying European organizations has shrunk even further, and no compensatory growth has occurred in the outlying regions. The French CFDT, an important trade union federation in its own country, left the ranks in 1978. The Dutch Catholic federation (NKV) departed two years later. Both had been unsuccessfully urging the WCL to engage in serious merger negotiations with the ICFTU.

The adverse financial consequences of their departure were substantially erased, however, by the Dutch government's foreign economic aid subsidy to the WCL, at least for the time being. The WCL was thus able to add a sizable amount of "extra-budgetary funds" to its income—about $600,000 in 1982 from the former NKV alone—to help finance its programmes. This income, together with funds contributed by the Dutch Protestant CNV, the Belgian CSC, and German Catholic organisations, goes far to explain the remarkable survival of what is, all things considered, an exceedingly weak organisation. But some share of the reasons for survival must also be attributed to the leadership's profound belief in the WCL's mission and their unwillingness to make common cause with the much larger and ideologically much more diffuse ICFTU.

B. Aims and Activities

Since its transformation in the 1950s the WCL has sought to emphasise its status as an ideological alternative both to the Marxist-Leninist materialism of the WFTU and the social-democratic pragmatism of the ICFTU. It rejects the model of Soviet society almost as resolutely as it opposes "international capitalism." In their place it propagates a system based on democratic planning, participation in decision-making, and trade union independence from any form of external control. According to its vision of the future, "real democracy" and "true socialism" will ultimately become the earmarks of a genuinely egalitarian society, although nowhere in the WCL's programmatic statements have "true socialism" and "real democracy" ever been defined in concrete terms.

WCL activities focus on educational and social programs in the less-developed countries. It attends ILO meetings but has not been strong enough to gain even a single seat among the worker delegates on the governing body. Its few remaining European affiliates participate in the work of the relevant EEC agencies and in European trade union bodies, including the ETUC, which are undoubtedly far more important to their daily business than the WCL.

C. Organisation and Structure

The WCL's arrangements for internal government are grouped around a conventional four-tiered structure: a congress, a council, a confederal board, and an executive committee. The first three are composed of elected delegates from affiliated organisations, while the executive committee is made up mainly of full-time WCL officials: the general secretary and five assistant general secretaries.

Regional WCL organisations currently exist for Latin America (CLAT) and Asia (BATU). CLAT is militantly anti-establishment, anti-capitalist, and anti-American and has concentrated its efforts particularly among peasants and agricultural workers. The European regional body (EO) was dissolved in 1974 when the WCL's European affiliates joined the new European trade union—ETUC. In the same year, the WCL's African organisation (PAWC) dissolved itself under pressure from African governments but continues to lead a shadowy existence as FOPADESC.

V. INDEPENDENT REGIONAL FEDERATIONS AND RELATED BODIES

The three international confederations reviewed in the preceding sections seek out eligible members in most parts of the world. A more limited geographic territory is claimed by an increasing number of regional and sub-regional trade union bodies, not as affiliates of one of the global organisations but as independent entities. Of special importance are the European Trade Union Confederation (ETUC), the Organisation of African Trade Union Unity (OATUU), the Trade Union Advisory Committee to the Organisation for Economic Cooperation and Development (TUAC—OECD), and the Council of Nordic Trade Unions. But even this is not a complete list. Mention should also be made of the International Confederation of Arab Trade Unions (ICATU), an essentially political rather than a trade union body, the Commonwealth Trade Union Council, and the ASEAN Council of Trade Unions.

Regional organisations owe their existence to a multiplicity of reasons. Some were founded to express, in the domain of labour, the hegemonic aspirations of a particular country or ruler, or to propagate a particular ideology. Others came into existence mainly to represent the joint economic interests of trade unions in a particular region or met a need for bringing the special concerns of workers to the attention of a regional intergovernmental agency. In sum, both political and economic factors have played a role, with political considerations generally dominant in the less-developed areas and economic considerations more important in industrialised areas.

A. The European Trade Union Confederation

Currently by far the most important trade union body at European regional level is the European Trade Union Confederation (ETUC). It came into being in 1973 but had several forerunners which cannot be reviewed here.[5] There are now well over 30 ETUC affiliates with a total membership of over 40 million. Headquarters are in Brussels where most European agencies of concern to the ETUC have their central office.

The ETUC is an entirely independent body organisationally and financially. Its membership includes almost all trade union federations in Western European countries (with a few exceptions noted below), and most of its activities are centered on the defense of joint trade union interests in the European Economic Community and other European-wide bodies.

The policies of the ETUC closely reflect the common concerns of its members. At present these are converging, above all, on the struggle against unemployment and the adoption by governments of employment-oriented economic policies. Insofar as the Common Market countries coordinate their economic and social policies, the ETUC seeks to ensure that labour's priorities are taken into account. The ETUC thus acts as a regional lobby in the context of a supranational agency, supplementing and to a certain extent harmonising the separate national efforts of its member organisations. Other areas of recent concern to the ETUC have included the extension of industrial democracy throughout the Common Market, the adoption of integrated energy

---

[5]See John P. Windmuller, "European Regionalism: A New Factor in International Labour," *Industrial Relations Journal* 7, no. 2 (Summer 1976), pp. 35–48.

policies, proposals to improve the work environment, and efforts to eliminate discriminatory treatment of the weaker segments of the labour force (women, young workers, migrants, the handicapped, etc.).

Political issues have generally been of secondary importance in ETUC activities, though the organisation regularly adopts resolutions expressing its support of political freedom, democratic forms of government, strict observance of human and trade union rights, peaceful coexistence, and negotiated steps toward disarmament. Where differences on some of these issues exist, they tend to be matters of emphasis rather than principle and can often be overcome by judicious formulations.

More difficult has been the question of eligibility for ETUC membership by Communist-led trade union organisations in Italy, France, Spain, and Portugal. Here the views of several key ETUC affiliates have diverged quite sharply. One group, led by the British TUC, has generally favoured their admission, while another group, headed by the German DGB, has opposed it. The outcome so far has been mixed. The Italian CGIL has been taken in, but the Communist-led organisations in France, Spain, and Portugal have had their requests denied or deferred. Every time the issue has been raised it has created a major controversy.

To complete its structure the ETUC has promoted the establishment of industry committees to represent the European-wide interests of workers and their unions in particular economic sectors, until now especially in metals, mining, agriculture, and communications. The industry committees act as lobbies and pressure groups, but may someday seek to become bargaining agents within a European-wide system of industrial relations. The most substantial one among them, the European Metalworkers' Federation (EMF), has recently mounted a major effort to assist its affiliated national metalworkers unions in attempts to reduce the inflow of Japanese automobiles and other metal products.

The relationship of the European industry committees to the International Trade Secretariats is a problem area that may be difficult to resolve. Some industry committees operate chiefly under ETUC auspices, while others are linked more closely to the ITSs in their economic sector. The conflicting pulls and competitive lines of authority have been a source of great tension in some situations.

B. The Organisation of African Trade Union Unity

Although trade unionism in most African countries is of relatively recent origin, several regional organisations have already appeared and then disappeared—some oriented toward Western conceptions of trade unionism, others more compatible with the WFTU trade union model. Most African governments have shown little tolerance for trade union pluralism or for trade unions independent of government control. With support from many African governments, the Organisation of African Unity (CAU) established a regional trade union organisation in 1973—the Organisation of African Trade Union Unity (OATUU)—intended as the all-inclusive and singular regional trade union body for Africa. But in recent years the OATUU's attempt to achieve a regional monopoly has received several setbacks, and an increasing number of African central trade union bodies have affiliated with the ICFTU or WFTU, depending on their ideological orientation.

Nevertheless, the OATUU maintains relations with the ICFTU, WFTU, and WCL and cooperates with them in activities that are of a trade union character, such as labour education programmes. But it also hews closely to the general political and international positions adopted by the OAU. Consequently it emphasises its support for "positive neutrality" in world affairs and proclaims itself to be an anti-capitalist, anti-imperialist, anti-colonialist, and anti-Zionist organisation. Major targets of its criticism are forces external to the region, in particular multinational corporations and their governments in Western countries. African governments and their sometimes very harsh labour and social policies are treated with much circumspection, although the governments are commonly the largest single employers in their countries, as well as the principal industrial rule-makers. Of the obscure financial arrangements in the OATUU it can be said with confidence only that it is not supported solely or even chiefly by contributions from its own affiliates and that government subsidies from Libya and elsewhere are of considerable importance.

C. The Trade Union Advisory Committee to the OECD (TUAC-OECD)

When the Marshall Plan for European economic recovery from the ravages of World War II neared completion in the early 1960s, the participating governments in Europe and North America decided to maintain certain supranational structures that had played a key role in the administration of the programme. That decision accounts for the existence of the Organisation for Economic Cooperation and Development (OECD) and its trade union "satellite," the Trade Union Advisory Committee (TUAC-OECD).

TUAC represents trade union interests at the OECD in about the same way as the ETUC represents trade union interests in the Common Market agencies. Its constituents are some 40 trade union federations from over 20 OECD member countries in the European area, North America, and Japan. Virtually all TUAC members are affiliates of the ICFTU or the WCL, but no affiliates or former affiliates of the WFTU have been admitted to membership.

Because the OECD is basically a research-oriented, idea-producing, and consensus-seeking organisation rather than an action agency, TUAC's foremost objective is to ensure that adequate consideration is given to trade union viewpoints in the preparation of OECD reports, studies, and policy recommendations to member governments. In recent years OECD items of chief interest to TUAC have included employment-creation policies, manpower and human resource development programmes, trade and tariff issues, and especially the development and su-

pervision of international guidelines for the conduct of multinational companies—an area in which the OECD has done some pioneering work.[6]

D. Subregional Bodies

Regional coalitions of countries seem to lead, sooner or later, to the emergence of parallel coalitions of trade unions. That tendency holds not only for genuine regional alliances, as in Europe, but also for interregional and subregional groupings. For example, the Commonwealth (formerly called the British Commonwealth of Nations), which is a loose association of states based chiefly on a common historical attachment to the former British Empire, has recently (1980) spawned a Commonwealth Trade Union Council whose declared purpose it is to ensure that "trade union views are taken into account by Commonwealth governments and institutions." A similar instance is the ASEAN Council of Trade Unions, a recently formed alliance of trade union federations in the five member countries of the Association of South East Asian Nations.

A flourishing group of this kind is the Council of Nordic Trade Unions, a subregional association of trade union federations in the five Nordic countries (Sweden, Norway, Denmark, Finland, and Iceland), founded in 1972, whose membership is expressly limited to organisations affiliated both with the ICFTU and ETUC. That rule intentionally excludes federations representing the interests of professional and managerial employees. With a budget of about $600,000 and a full-time staff of seven professionals, the Nordic Council coordinates the policies of its member organisations on socio-economic and labour market issues of concern to the Nordic governments, such as free labour mobility, social welfare, social insurance, and international trade; prepares research papers and policy positions on these matters; and serves as a device

---

[6]See Duncan C. Campbell and Richard L. Rowan, *Multinational Enterprises and the OECD Industrial Relations Guidelines* (Philadelphia: University of Pennsylvania, The Wharton School, 1983).

for reaching unified Nordic trade union positions in international labour bodies. By voting as a bloc in the ICFTU, ETUC, TUAC, ILO, and similar organisations, the unions of the Nordic countries can increase their weight by a considerable margin. Their joint views also carry greater force in bilateral contacts with organisations such as the British, German, and American labour federations.

VI. International Trade Secretariats

The organisations to be examined in this section, the International Trade Secretariats (ITSs), are composed of individual national unions in particular sectors of industry. They focus on developments and problems in particular industries or occupational categories, and their mandate is therefore primarily an economic or industrial rather than a political one. Consequently they are sometimes referred to as the industrial internationals.

A. Organisation and Structure

1. Relations with Global Internationals. The ITSs are autonomous and self-governing organisations. Their relationship to the ICFTU is based on the so-called Milan Agreement of 1951 (revised in 1969) under which the ITSs agreed to follow the ICFTU's lead on broad policy issues, while the ICFTU recognised the General Conference of the ITSs as the collective representative of ITS interests and granted to the ITSs a nonvoting presence in all ICFTU governing organs. The agreement does not preclude individual ITSs from maintaining separate bilateral relations with the ICFTU or even from deciding to have no relations with the ICFTU at all.

The principle of autonomy determines not only the relations between the ITSs and the ICFTU but also among the ITSs themselves. Their formal link is a General Conference, a loosely structured body which meets about once a year for a review of common problems and interests. Informal contacts are, of course, far more extensive, both among leading ITS officials and between them and the ICFTU leadership. They are, after all, parts of the same general labour movement, sharing identical or at least very similar values and conceptions about the position of trade unions in society.

2. Membership and Finances. There are currently 14 ITSs. The total has diminished over the years, mostly due to mergers. On the other hand, mergers plus successful recruitment have considerably increased the size of almost all ITSs in recent decades. The largest organisation by far is the International Metalworkers' Federation with about 140 affiliated organisations distributed among some 70 countries and numbering in their ranks about 14 million workers. Other ITSs with at least 4 million members include the Commercial and Clerical Workers, Public Service Employees, Chemical Workers, Textile Workers, and Transport Workers. Although Western Europe and North America furnish the largest number of ITS affiliates (with the obvious exception of the Plantation Workers ITS), most ITSs contain affiliates from all parts of the world except the Communist-ruled countries.

In order to be truly independent, trade unions must be financially self-reliant. The ITSs generally meet that condition except for the Plantation Workers Secretariat which depends in large part on subsidies from the ICFTU. Each ITS has its own structure of dues. The average current dues figure is probably about $0.50 per individual member per year. For some ITSs engaged in particularly extensive activities in the Third World, special levies and outside funding constitute important sources of extra income. Special funds, particularly for educational and union-building programmes, have been obtained from the ILO and the foreign aid budgets of European and North American governments. Some ITSs, however, have declined external support to avoid jeopardising their independence.

3. Governing Bodies and Trade Groups. Although each ITS has devised its own governing arrangements, a fairly common pattern prevails. It usually includes a general assembly or congress, an executive board, and the elected officers and staff. To keep expenses down, the intervals between congresses have become increasingly longer in the last few decades and now average three to four years. Congresses, although not of great decision-making importance, are useful occasions to cement the ties between the organisation and its affiliates, particularly affiliates which are not large and important enough to occupy a seat on the executive board. A key role in the decision-making process is played by the top full-time official, the general secretary. Indeed, so important is his role that the calibre of the general secretary is probably the main determinant of ITS performance.

When the ITSs were first established, many covered only a single occupation or industrial sector. That is no longer the case. Mergers and the rise of new industries have transformed most ITSs into multi-industrial or multi-occupational bodies whose individual components sometimes face entirely different challenges in their spheres of activity. The diversification has led the ITSs to establish separate industrial sectors. The Metalworkers ITS, for example, whose industrial jurisdiction includes automobile manufacturing, basic steel, electrical and electronic products, shipbuilding and several other sectors, has established a number of trade groups to meet the varying needs of its affiliated unions, especially in countries where the structure of unionism is relatively fragmented and specialised, as in Britain and the United States.

B. Aims and Activities

Advancing the joint interests of their constituents, and particularly their economic interests, has always been the principal aim of the ITSs. It still constitutes their chief *raison d'etre*. On a different plane they do, of course, support vigorously the search for a more just social order, the protection of human and trade union rights, the extension of democratic forms of government, and the maintenance of peace with freedom. But their orientation and make-up leads them to stress practical trade union work, and this they perform in a variety of ways.

1. Solidarity and Organisational Work. Mobilising international support on behalf of an affiliated organisation involved in a major domestic conflict is one such activity. Support may be expressed in various forms: moral encouragement, appeals to member organisations to extend financial assistance (the ITSs usually do not maintain strike funds), coordination of international boycott actions against employers, or public condemnation of a government for particularly harsh anti-union measures.[7]

A major portion of ITS activities since the early 1950s has been the organisational work in Third World countries. The aim is the establishment or reinforcement of individual unions to the point where they can effectively represent the interests of their members and at the same time contribute to the development and modernisation of their societies.

2. Information and Research. Disseminating information about economic conditions and terms of employment in particular industrial sectors has long been one of the most useful services which the ITSs provide to their members. Some of the larger ITSs have recently begun to compile and computerise specific data on the financial condition and terms of employment of large individual firms, particularly multinational firms, so as to be able to make this information fairly readily available to affiliates for use in collective bargaining. Some ITSs have initiated research on the long-term economic outlook for the industries in which they operate, with special attention to prospective changes in the volume of employment. Increasingly, too, several ITSs are

---

[7]For an ITS engaged in an unusually broad range of activities on behalf of employee interests, see Herbert R. Northrup and Richard L. Rowan, *The International Transport Workers and Flag of Convenience Shipping* (Philadelphia: University of Pennsylvania, The Wharton School, 1983).

attending to problems of occupational health and safety in their sectors.

3. Multinational Companies. As long as collective bargaining remains primarily a national rather than an international activity, the contribution which the ITSs make to the outcome will be a relatively modest one. However, the expansion of multinational companies during the past two or three decades and the adoption by the OECD and other international bodies of international codes of conduct create the possibility that international bargaining structures may eventually emerge in which the ITSs could then be a key factor on the union side. Some initial steps in that direction have already been taken. The Metalworkers' ITS, for instance, has established several so-called corporation councils covering a substantial number of multinationals (General Motors, Ford, etc.) to facilitate bargaining coordination among unions in different countries whose members are employed in the subsidiaries of these corporations. Although the process of creating an all-encompassing united front on the union side is likely to be extremely slow, attempts to achieve regional cooperation as a first step may yield results more quickly, especially at the European level.

Coordinated international union action may also result from appointments of leading ITS officials to membership on corporate boards of directors under national codetermination laws. This has been happening on a modest scale in the FR of Germany, where a few industrial unions have named top ITS officials to board seats reserved by law for employee representatives. (German law does not require board members to be German citizens.) A few board seats may not make much difference, especially not when the firms involved are subsidiaries of multinationals headquartered in other countries. But if the German pattern of codetermination is in some form extended to all Common Market countries, as has been proposed, the presence of ITS officials on corporate boards could become a significant factor in the internationalization of industrial relations.

VII. CONCLUDING OBSERVATIONS

Although trade unions generally operate within national economic, social, political, and legal contexts, they have also established a complex but fragmented network of international associations. To some extent the fragmentation is caused by functional distinctions between the broad policy concerns of national trade union federations and the industrial concerns of individual national unions. But that is only a partial explanation. In recent decades ideological and regional attachments have become even more important determining factors causing proliferation.

Ideological differences of a fundamental nature separate the international bodies of trade unions in democratic countries with chiefly market-oriented economies from labour organisations in planned economies under Communist party leadership. These fundamental divisions are likely to persist, for they are bound up with transcending differences over the organisation of society and the principles that should govern the relations between individuals, institutions, and the state.

An increasingly important deconcentrating factor is regionalism. It extends, as we have seen, not only to the countries of the Third World, but has also spread to the older regions, as shown by the emergence of the European Trade Union Confederation and the Nordic Council of Trade Unions, both active and independent organisations strongly supported by their affiliates. Regionalism is likely to remain a decisive factor shaping the structure of international trade unionism.

There is no need to inflate the importance of international trade union bodies. They are auxiliaries and agents rather than principals. Those among them which are bona fide organisations will continue to play a constructive role in promoting the extension of trade union and human rights, supporting as far as their means permit the growth of trade unions in developing areas, representing the viewpoints and interests of workers before international agencies, and coordinating trade union efforts to establish an international system of industrial relations. It is not spectacular work, but it is useful and deserves more attention than it usually receives.

REFERENCES

Lorwin, Lewis L. *The International Labor Movement: History, Policies, Outlook.* New York: Harper & Row, 1953.

Miotto, Roberto. *Les Syndicats Multinationaux.* Rome: Instituto per l'Economia Europa, 1976.

Neuhaus, Rolf. *International Trade Secretariats: Objectives, Organization, Activities.* Bonn: Friedrich-Ebert-Stiftung, 1982.

Piehl, Ernst. *Multinationale Konzerne und Internationale Gewerkschaftsbewegung.* Frankfurt: Europäische Verlaganstalt, 1974.

Rowan, Richard L.; Herbert R. Northrup; and Rae Ann O'Brien. *Multinational Union Organisations in the Manufacturing Industries.* Philadelphia: University of Pennsylvania, The Wharton School, Industrial Research Unit, 1980.

Windmuller, John P. *The International Trade Union Movement.* Deventer, The Netherlands: Kluwer, 1980.

PART FOUR
Collective Bargaining

A. Structure and Strategy in Collective Bargaining

Collective bargaining has become an institutionalized and legally protected mechanism for determining wages, hours, and working conditions in the United States since the passage of the Wagner Act in 1935. Essentially a two-party process involving labor unions and management, collective bargaining has an interesting origin, and its development has experienced interesting structural changes.

The first two articles in this section deal with the structure of collective bargaining and a perceived need to reform the system. John Dunlop discusses the major characteristics and framework of the collective bargaining system as it existed in the 1970s, and Quinn Mills calls for a reform of the system in the 1980s. Mills believes that "collective bargaining procedures and relationships between labor and management must reflect less conflict, more cooperation as the nation's economy struggles to meet international competition and domestic needs."

The third article in this section is written by an industrial relations practitioner, Douglas H. Soutar, who believes that we are now living in an age of major challenges to the collective bargaining process. In spite of challenges to the system, Soutar remains a strong adherent of the collective bargaining process. He believes that collective bargaining remains an experimental system and one that is struggling to achieve its ultimate maturity.

In the early 1980s, a wave of wage concessions emanated from the bargaining tables in America's major industries. "Concession bargaining" developed quickly and some have indicated that it may have a major effect on labor-management relations in the United States. Robert McKersie and Peter Cappelli analyze the concept of concession bargaining and discuss the dilemma that it creates for trade union leaders.

R E A D I N G 22

Structure of Collective Bargaining*

John T. Dunlop[†]

DISTINCTIVE FEATURES OF U.S. COLLECTIVE BARGAINING

Collective bargaining is carried on within a framework of law, custom, and institutional structure that varies considerably from one country to another. The framework of bargaining in the United States has certain characteristics that sharply distinguish it from that of most other industrial democracies.

Perhaps the most significant characteristic of the American collective bargaining system is that it is highly decentralized. There are approximately 150,000 separate union-management agreements now in force in the United States. A majority of union members work under contracts negotiated by their union with a single employer or for a single plant. Only 40 percent of employees covered by collective agreements involve multi-employer negotiations, and the great bulk of these negotiations are confined to single metropolitan areas.

In the United States, unlike most countries in Western Europe, one union serves as the sole representative for all the employees in a plant or other appropriate bargaining unit. This practice conforms to the American political custom of electing single representatives by majority vote. It can also be traced back to the tradition of conflict among the

*From Gerald S. Somers, ed., *The Next Twenty-Five Years of Industrial Relations*, Industrial Relations Research Association,© 1973, pp. 10–18. Adapted and excerpted from Derek C. Bok and John T. Dunlop, *Labor and the American Community* (New York: Simon & Schuster, 1970), chaps. 7 and 8. A final section reports briefly on the application of the analysis to recent problems of the construction industry.

†John T. Dunlop is Lamont University Professor at Harvard University.

autonomous international unions. To restrain such conflict, the American Federation of Labor—as far back as the 1880s—developed the concept of exclusive jurisdiction. Under this principle, only one union was authorized to represent employees in a particular occupation, a group of jobs, or occasionally, an industry. Employers generally accepted exclusivity since it stabilized labor relations by diminishing disputes among competing unions. It was natural, therefore, for the principle to be embodied in public policy when the government began to develop detailed regulation over collective bargaining. Thus, during World War I and under the Railway Labor Act of 1926, a system of elections was adopted to enable groups of employees to select a single representative by majority vote. The same procedures were subsequently carried forward on a broader scale in the National Labor Relations Act of 1935 and its subsequent amendments.

Under almost any system, collective bargaining leaves room for a degree of individual negotiation over certain terms and conditions of employment. Even in the United States, the law explicitly provides that an employee can discuss individual grievances with representatives of management. And in a few fields—for example, the performing arts—agreements typically leave employees free to bargain individually for salaries above the minimum. For the most part, however, collective agreements in the United States specify the actual wages and terms of employment which in fact govern the workers in the bargaining unit, and individual employees do not negotiate different terms on their own behalf.

The absence of any authority in law to extend a collective bargaining contract to others who have not accepted the agreement is rooted in the structure of the American industrial relations systems. It is comparatively easy to extend a contract containing a few minimum terms and conditions, particularly when the contract has been negotiated by an association representing a large and representative group of firms. In the United States, however, where rival unions may coexist in a single industry, where contract terms set actual rather than minimum requirements, and where provisions are highly complex and often vary from one firm to another, it would be very difficult to find a single set of terms that would be suitable for all firms in the industry.

In another respect, the structure of bargaining in this country has caused the law to play a more ambitious role in collective negotiations than it does abroad. Although we rely less heavily on legislation to fix the substantive terms of employment, there is much more regulation in the United States over the tactics and procedures of bargaining. Thus, law in the United States defines the subjects that must be bargained about. It requires the parties to "bargain in good faith" and clothes this obligation with detailed rules proscribing stalling tactics, withholding of relevant information, and other forms of behavior that are considered unfair. The net result is a complex of regulations that greatly exceeds anything to be found in other industrialized countries.

THE PARTIES AND THE STRUCTURE OF BARGAINING

These special characteristics help to define the framework of the American system of collective bargaining. Within these contours, several types of negotiation go on. The most familiar aspect of bargaining involves the discussions between the parties over the terms and conditions of employment for the workers involved. But a vital part of the bargaining process has to do with determining the structure and the procedures through which these discussions will take place.

One question of structure has to do with the level at which different issues should be resolved. This problem is particularly significant in any negotiation that affects more than one place of work. In a situation of this kind, the parties must decide which issues should be agreed upon at the negotiating table and incorporated into a master agreement and which should be left for labor and management representatives to settle at the company, plant, or departmental level. Agreements made at these subsidiary levels are called local supplements. Sometimes the interdependence between the two settlements creates problems. Is one settlement contingent upon the other, and is a failure to conclude one a ba-

sis for a strike or lockout in all units? Which settlement will be made first?

These questions are often difficult to resolve. In a multiplant company, for instance, such matters as the amount of time allowed for wash-up before the end of a shift or the allocation of parking facilities might be best handled at the plant level. But it is also clear that policies or precedents on these matters at one plant may influence decisions elsewhere. Considerations of bargaining power and market competition may also influence the level at which particular issues are treated. As technological and market changes take place, it may be necessary to alter these arrangements and provide for more centralization on some issues, as with the introduction of containers in the East Coast longshore industry, and greater decentralization in other instances, such as the determination of the number of trainmen in a crew on the railroads. Since conditions vary widely from one plant or industry to another, there is little uniformity among collective bargaining relationships in the pattern of centralization and decentralization in negotiations.

A second problem in arranging negotiation procedures concerns the range of jobs, territory, and employees to be governed by the ensuing agreement. Several illustrations may be helpful. The basic steel companies took major strikes in 1946 in part to achieve separate negotiations for their fabricating facilities from their basic steel operations. As a result, separate agreements with different expiration dates and different wage scales now are negotiated at different times, reflecting the different competitive conditions that affect these two types of operations. In view of differing market conditions for the different products involved, the major rubber companies have on occasion insisted on differential wage increases for tire plants and those plants making rubber shoes and other rubber products. Conversely, 26 cooperating international unions sustained an eight-month strike in the copper negotiations of 1967–68 in an effort to obtain collective bargaining agreements with the same expiration dates and identical wage increases for all employees of a company.

A third set of structural problems has to do

with the relations among different craft unions bargaining with a common employer. In recent years, the newspaper printing industry, the West Coast shipbuilding industry, and the construction industry have suffered many strikes growing out of disagreements over the wage pattern or sequence of settlements among a group of interrelated crafts agreements. For example, the 114-day New York newspaper strike of 1962–63 was fought by Bertram Powers, president of Local 6 of the International Typographical Union, largely to change a system of bargaining which had existed since the early 1950s. Under the prior agreement, wage settlements had been made with the Newspaper Guild and then extended to other newspaper unions. As a result of the strike, contract expiration dates were negotiated which removed the five-week lead the Guild has previously held and thus eliminated its ability to impose an industry wide pattern on the other unions before they ever got to the bargaining table. Thus, the strike enabled Powers to put an end to a follow-the-leader pattern that had deprived his union of any real power to negotiate its own wage agreements.

Serious questions may arise also in deciding which subjects should be encompassed within the scope of collective bargaining. The subjects that are dealt with vary widely, reflecting in each contract the problems of the relevant workplace and industry. Some maritime agreements specify the quality of meals and even the number of bars of soap, towels, and sheets that management is to furnish to the crew. Such provisions are natural subjects for negotiation, since they are vital to men at sea, but they would make no sense in a normal manufacturing agreement. In some contracts in the ladies' garment industry, companies agree to be efficient and to allow a union industrial engineer to make studies of company performance. These provisions would be regarded as ludicrous in the automobile industry. Detailed procedures respecting control over hiring are central to collective bargaining in industries with casual employment, where employees shift continually from one employer to another, as in construction and stevedoring; but in factory and office employment,

new hiring typically is left to the discretion of management. In this fashion, the topics raised in collective bargaining tend to reflect the problems of the particular workplace and industry.

The law also plays a part in deciding the subjects for negotiation, since the National Labor Relations Act (Section 9a) requires the parties to bargain in good faith over "rates of pay, wages, hours of employment, or other conditions of employment." Pursuant to this act, the National Labor Relations Board and the courts have decided which subjects are mandatory topics for collective bargaining and which are optional. In some instances, particular subjects or bargaining proposals have been held to be improper or illegal and hence nonnegotiable, such as a union's insistence on a closed shop or an employer's demand that the union bargain through a particular form of negotiating committee or take a secret ballot prior to calling a strike. On the whole, however, the board and the courts have steadily broadened the scope of mandatory bargaining to include Christmas bonuses, pensions, information on plant shutdowns, subcontracting, provisions for checkoff of union dues, and many other topics.

The provisions of the National Labor Relations Act would appear to make legal rulings decisive as to the scope of bargaining. And on a few issues, such as pension plans, litigation undoubtedly played a significant role. In the main, however, although the law may help to define the outer limits of bargaining, the actual scope of negotiations is largely decided by the parties themselves.

DISPUTE SETTLEMENTS AND THE STRUCTURE OF BARGAINING

In disputes over the terms of an agreement, there are three elements that may shape the procedures, beyond ordinary mediation, to be used for settling differences.[1] The first involves the *substantive terms* in dispute—wages, pensions, technological dis-

[1] While no scheme is ideal for all purposes, practitioners will readily recognize the types of disputes which follow. These do not, of course, constitute an exhaustive list. In fact, disputes seldom occur in the pure forms here cited, since actual cases typically involve mixtures.

placement, crew size, incentive systems, job evaluation, promotion criteria, and the like. Some subjects are more complex than others; some issues treat all employees equally, while the essence of others is that they involve differential treatment among groups of employees. Some questions are easily compromised; others arise from differences of principle or involve matters that virtually affect the institutional security and well-being of one or both of the parties.

The second critical feature of a dispute has to do with the *relations between the particular labor and management organizations*. The character of the negotiation may differ enormously between the first contract and, say, the fifteenth to be negotiated by the parties. One or both parties may be afflicted with intense internal leadership rivalry; expectations among constituents may be very high with respect to the results of negotiations, thereby complicating agreement-making and ratification; the preceding contract period may have been most difficult to administer, with the consequence of a large backlog of unresolved grievances that shape attitudes in the negotiations.

A third feature, present in some disputes is the determination of one side to change the *structure of bargaining*. Such disputes involve a change in the design of collective bargaining negotiations themselves—the scope of employees to be covered by the agreement, the timing of expiration dates of various agreements, the selection of a leader among a group of unions—as much as disagreement over wages, hours, and working conditions. Two subtypes are especially significant: (a) disputes involving relationships of two or more unions, typically craft unions, bargaining with the same management or an association of employers, and (b) controversies over the range of plants or companies or employees to be included, formally or informally, within the scope of the negotiations. In cases of rivalry among unions, managements are often seeking to expand the scope of bargaining with a group of craft unions. In coalition bargaining it is typically the union which seeks to expand the effective coverage of the agreement and enlarge the scope of possible future strikes.

Disputes arising from attempts to change the structure of bargaining no doubt involve the most difficult negotiations, with the most serious and longest work stoppages. A list of the disputes and stoppages that have attracted the greatest public attention in the private sector in recent years would include the following cases where the structure of bargaining was a major issue.

Stoppage	Years	Time
New York City newspapers	1962–63	114 days
East coast longshore industry	1964–65	60 days
Cleveland construction industry	1965	39 days
Maritime industry, East and Gulf coasts	1965	78 days
Pacific Shipbuilding Association, electricians	1966	5 months
New York plumbers	1966–67	6 months
Railroad shop crafts	1967	1 day
San Diego shipbuilding	1967–68	4 months
Copper industry	1967–68	8 months
East coast longshore industry	1968–69	2 months

Disputes over bargaining structure often lead to prolonged work stoppages and substantial money settlements without ultimately resolving the underlying structural issue. Since adjustments in bargaining structure are not readily negotiated, higher money settlements are simply a rough compromise to postpone the ultimate day of reckoning. As a result, disputes over bargaining structure can persist over many years, with an accommodation in bargaining arrangements being made bit by bit through negotiations that are often characterized by prolonged stoppages.

RECENT APPLICATIONS OF THE ANALYSIS TO CONSTRUCTION

The collective bargaining structure in construction was, in my view, a major contributing factor to the high level of work stoppages over the terms of agreements and to the rapid rate of inflation of wage rates and benefits in the late 1960s and early 1970s.[2] The level of effective demand or the degree of monopoly power of labor organizations or their control

[2]For a discussion see Daniel Quinn Mills, *Industrial Relations and Manpower in Construction* (Cambridge, Mass.: MIT Press, 1972), chap. 3.

over hiring, often alleged to be the operative factors, do not provide a very convincing explanation nor do they provide much of a reason why such results had not taken place earlier in periods of strong demand. Moreover, they do not provide much of an understanding of the accelerating inflationary process as it spread throughout large segments of the industry and diffused geographically in the period prior to the imposition of wage controls in this industry alone on March 29, 1971. By early 1971 first year settlements were running 16–18 percent a year and one out of three expiring agreements resulted in a work stoppage.

The collective bargaining structure in many regions of the country, particularly in the East,[3] and in many branches of the industry had become increasingly obsolete as contractors and workers had increased the range of their movement with the highway system, as the pension, health and welfare, and other benefit funds were less appropriate to a single locality, and as union contractors in various branches of the industry confronted quite different forms of competition. In many areas the role of the strike or lockout ceased to be a means to encourage conventional collective bargaining as many contractors and workers continued to work in nearby areas and as national agreements tended in many cases to undermine local negotiations.

The Construction Industry Stabilization Committee from the outset sought to encourage reforms in the structure of collective bargaining in the industry as a long-run contribution to stabilization "in furtherance of effective collective bargaining in the industry," to use the language of the executive order. The tripartite Committee, working through the national union and association leaders, developed the following program to improve the structure of collective bargaining.

a. Each branch of the industry should develop a bipartite national craft board to play an active role in the settlement of local disputes over terms of agreements.
b. The geographical scope of agreements was reviewed by the national organizations, and in many cases agreements were consolidated with appropriate adjustments in the local union and contractor organizations for collective bargaining purposes. Special attention was directed to the need for several wage zones in many enlarged agreements in order not to adversely affect union contractors in rural regions.
c. Separate and lower wage schedules were developed by many crafts for some branches of the industry, such as residential construction.
d. The geographical scope of funded benefits were reviewed to reduce in many cases the administrative costs of benefits in small locals and contractor groups.
e. The work rules in agreements should be reviewed both to secure greater uniformity and to encourage productivity.
f. The Committee itself has been concerned with the timing of the expiration of agreements among related crafts in a locality.

While not all crafts and employer organizations have been equally interested in promoting a structure of collective bargaining which is less prone to strife and to inflation, the operations of the Committee and the craft boards have made a significant contribution in these directions. Indeed, these larger and longer-run objectives of national leaders of both sides have made it possible to achieve the shorter-run purposes of stabilization and significant retardation in the rate of inflation.

---

[3]For a careful study see the report of the Construction Industry Collective Bargaining Commission on the geographical bargaining structure of New York State, 1970.

READING 23

Reforming the U.S. System of Collective Bargaining*

D. Quinn Mills[†]

Collective bargaining procedures and relationships between labor and management must reflect less conflict, more cooperation as the nation's economy struggles to meet international competition and domestic needs

Can collective bargaining in the United States meet the challenge of the 1980s by tempering traditional confrontation with new cooperative approaches? Can management and labor modify their adversarial, rule-making relationship by exploring and recognizing mutual needs? This article examines some recent events that suggest affirmative answers to both of these questions.

Labor unions developed in the United States within a generally hostile business and legal environment. As early as 1806, unions in major eastern cities were being prosecuted in court as "combinations in restraint of trade." During the economically turbulent 1870s, industrial workers seeking better pay and conditions of work attempted strikes and public protests, only to be dispersed by police. In 1877, railway strikers throughout the country were repulsed by federal troops. During the depression of the 1890s, martial law was declared to break strikes in the western mines. And the federal government intervened at the railroads' request to defeat the 1894 strike by the American Railway Union against the Pullman Company; to further assist the company, a federal court enjoined the railway workers from interfering with interstate commerce.

Following World War I, strong opposition by employer associations and further unfavorable court decisions contributed to a dramatic decline in the labor movement. Revitalization of the unions occurred during the 1930s, but only after lengthy strikes, and the enactment of federal legislation—the Norris-Laguardia Act (1932) and the Wagner Act (1935)—favorable to the organizing rights of workers.[1]

Born in turmoil, and victorious over adamant employer opposition, U.S. unions view themselves essentially as adversaries to management, a role which their legislative successes during the 1930s appeared to legitimize. And during organizing campaigns in recent decades, employers have tended to force unions ever more strongly into an overall anti-management posture. The turbulence of labor relations in the construction and textile industries exemplifies this phenomenon.

AMBIGUOUS NATIONAL LABOR POLICY

Some have argued that the purpose of our system of collective bargaining no longer commands a national consensus. When the Wagner Act was passed, it included a statement endorsing collective bargaining and the right of workers to join unions as being in the national interest. It appeared that the United States was committed to incorporating unions among the institutions of its pluralist democracy and to making its economic system work by and through their addition. But with passage of the Taft-Hartley Act in 1947, the mood of the Congress and of the public seems to have shifted somewhat: the right of employees not to join unions in effect became enshrined with their right to join unions. When, by decisions of the courts in subsequent years, employers were permitted to attempt to persuade employees not to join unions, the national policy had come full circle. For all prac-

---

*From U.S. Department of Labor, *Monthly Labor Review* 106, no. 3 (March 1983), pp. 18–22.

†D. Quinn Mills is Albert J. Weatherhead, Jr., Professor of Business Administration at Harvard University. This article is an adaptation of a paper presented at the National Labor-Management Conference in Washington, D.C., in the fall 1982.

[1]For an interesting discussion of the history of U.S. labor relations, see *A Brief History of the American Labor Movement, 1970 Edition,* BLS Bulletin 1000 (Bureau of Labor Statistics, 1970), and the 1976 supplement to that bulletin (also BLS Bulletin 1000).

tical and legal purposes, government has ceased to favor a specific industrial relations policy, and seeks rather to serve as an unbiased umpire in the choice which employees make as to union affiliation.

The result of this apparent shift in public policy is, as might be expected, that labor relations in the United States is now best described as a series of disconnected events. There is no overall pattern or purpose. The national policy is one of free choice for individual employees, and the choices vary considerably among individuals and over time. The energies of business and labor are channeled into the struggle over union recognition rather than into making collective bargaining an institution which contributes to national economic objectives. Within this environment, which might best be termed "benign neglect" by government, collective bargaining has stagnated.

In practice, then, collective bargaining in the United States involves open economic conflict over the rights of employees, unions, and management in the workplace. Under U.S. law, employees who strike for better wages and benefits, or to preserve existing levels of wages and benefits, are gambling with their jobs. Managers are free to replace the strikers either on a temporary or permanent basis. Thus it is that economic strikes by long-established unions in our country often quickly become struggles over the continued existence of the union.

THE RESULT: A LAW OF THE SHOP

Some management and union representatives have described collective bargaining in our country in terms of a fistfight: the question is which side will be knocked down, or out, first. Given such a relationship, it is not surprising that there is little trust between the two sides. Where there is little trust, conflicts over the terms of the employment relationship are resolved not through mutual understanding but with specific, written contractual arrangements which the Congress has chosen to make legally enforceable.

The American collective bargaining agreement consequently reflects the importation of much of the adversarial system of U.S. law into the workplace. The agreement sets forth rules which are legally binding on the parties and establishes a grievance procedure as the mechanism by which the rules are enforced. The union and management take the roles of contending parties, as in a lawsuit, whenever there is a dispute in the plant. And increasingly, the parties bring attorneys into the grievance procedure to conduct what is virtually, though not yet entirely, a formal court proceeding to resolve their differences.

Many of the requirements of due process in our legal system have been incorporated directly into the contract grievance procedure. (The major exception is that the strict rules of evidence do not apply.) Thus, the grievance procedure involves several steps with appeals to higher levels, ending in a quasi-judicial proceeding before an arbitrator. To ensure that a disciplinary action will survive the oversight of an arbitrator, the employer must have established clear rules of conduct in the workplace; have communicated them to employees; and have documented transgressions. At some plants, for example, groups of managers (for arbitrators insist that there be more than one witness of an employee's infraction of a company rule) assemble to watch workers punch out at the timeclock at the end of the workday. Employees seen punching out early or punching more than one card are subject to disciplinary action by management.

Due process is a treasured right of U.S. citizens and is not to be disparaged. But its incorporation in the industrial relations world has given us a "law of the shop" that has become more and more burdensome to our economic enterprises. For, like U.S. law generally, collective bargaining agreements have grown increasingly complex. What began as one-page documents establishing that the union and the company would deal with each other have become contracts, hundreds of pages long, specifying in minute detail rules for the operation of economic enterprises. In some agreements, for example, many pages of rules are devoted solely to the question of how management is to make temporary assignments of employees to cover for other workers who are absent. But, because neither managers nor union officials really know what all the rules mean in certain instances, each noncustomary assignment made by the company tends to find its way into the grievance procedure.

RULES AS A PRODUCTIVITY DRAIN

Rules alone cannot ensure that an organization will perform well. They may keep it from dissolving into self-defeating open warfare, but often do not permit it to achieve its potential. An organization which depends upon adherence to a myriad of rules will always be vulnerable to competition from other organizations which operate in a more consensual and cooperative fashion, even when the latter have fewer resources. And, although an organization of rules may sometimes pull itself together to respond to an emergency, this need not necessarily occur.

It follows, then, that primary dependence on establishing and enforcing rules is a very poor way to run an economic enterprise. The existence of a multitude of rules, many of which attempt to "stretch the work" to maintain jobs in ways reminiscent of depression-era tactics, constrains productivity and raises costs. For example, maintenance classifications may prohibit an employee from doing incidental work outside the strict limits of his or her trade; multiple job classifications may exist even where a person in a single combined classification could do the work effectively, without undue effort and stress; and, job classifications may be perpetuated although technological change has rendered the incumbents' work trivial. Other restrictions may limit the amount of work a person may be assigned, such as permitting a mechanic to open only two flanges. The location of materials and inventory may be restricted by contract or past practice to retain jobs in now-inefficient areas of the plant. In some cases, rules may prohibit employees being assigned work during breaks, and simultaneously prohibit supervisors from doing the employees' work, so that emergencies occurring at coffee breaks or lunchtime cannot be legally handled under the agreement.

Over time, rules tend to become increasingly costly and constraining as technology,

materials, products, and other aspects of production change. Even rules which made great sense at first become out-of-date under changing conditions. But the rules are difficult to change, and particular employees may be further benefited the more outdated the rules become. Sometimes a company can pay a high price and "buy the rules out," or a union can persuade some workers to give up favored positions for the good of the membership as a group. But often, change cannot be accomplished without a bitter struggle between management and labor.

Furthermore, the rule-making process promotes a set of attitudes which are inimical to successful enterprise. The existence of the rulebook encourages both management and labor to assert their rights under the contract, rather than to attempt to work out problems. It gives rise to "shop-floor lawyers," rather than problemsolvers. It fosters conflict and controversy. It undermines trust.

To a large degree, it seems that unions have become captives of their origins. Born in adversity and conflict, they continued to act as opponents of management even when their strength had become much greater. In some instances, unions have created thickets of rules in which to immobilize management, just as spiders build webs to ensnare prey. But when the thickets of rules have crippled productivity, the unions have discovered themselves to be caught alongside management in the trap. Plants have declined in competitiveness, and jobs have been lost. The unions have discovered too late that a snare is no less a snare because they have set it themselves.

A PRESCRIPTION FOR CHANGE

In a recent survey conducted by the Harris organization, a majority of the general public professed the belief that unions contribute less than they once did to the growth and efficiency of business. Not surprisingly, only 15 percent of union leaders agreed with this judgment.[2] The need for unions to assist companies in the light of increased foreign compe-

[2]Louis Harris, quoted in *Daily Labor Report* (Washington, D.C.: Bureau of National Affairs, June 3, 1981), pp. A14–A16.

tition is apparent to the public. To the inhabitants of the Snow Belt, it is similarly evident that unions should cooperate with local business to stem the outflow of industry and jobs to the South and West. Public perceptions of a productivity problem are suppported by Bureau of Labor Statistics estimates, which show particularly sluggish growth in output per labor hour after 1973.[3]

Collective bargaining practiced primarily as rule-making has become self-defeating for both unions and management. It interferes with management's efficient operation of the enterprise, and ensnares employees with legitimate grievances in a web of red tape. It also contributes to the vehemence of employer attempts to resist union organization drives. Study after study of U.S. managers has shown that managers fear the imposition of restrictive work practices far more than the higher wages and benefits which unionization may bring. Companies' efforts to make competitive operations out of older plants often fail because changes in current work rules take the form of additional complex rules which do not provide the flexibility needed to turn a facility around. What management really needs is fewer rules altogether, and willing cooperation from the work force. The union, for its side, needs a management sensitive to the needs of people. Both are very difficult to obtain in the U.S. labor relations environment.

There are, of course, many reasons for this. The unions cite a long list of management actions and inactions which they feel justify an emphasis on protected rules and challenges to management action. Among the accusations frequently leveled at management are its failure to update the equipment in union plants; its location of new and more profitable products in nonunion facilities; and its burdening of unionized facilities with unfairly heavy overhead charges. Such actions call into question the good faith that management would show in any more cooperative relationship.

Managers have also helped to shore up the archaic labor relations system. American management has often proved unsympathe-

tic to the problems of workers. For example, U.S. firms are quick to turn to layoffs during business downturns in an effort to maintain profit levels. (In contrast, many firms abroad and some few U.S. firms attempt to preserve employment at the cost of short-term fluctuations in profits.) It should be acknowledged, however, that U.S. unions often contribute to the problem by insisting upon layoffs by seniority in preference to worksharing among employees during business declines, and that the U.S. unemployment insurance system encourages this preference by generally denying benefits to workers on short workweeks due to economic conditions.

Because of the substantial inefficiencies created by outdated rules, and the risk of resulting job losses, managers and union officials should always have at the top of their agenda the minimizing of rule-making and the broadening of cooperation and consensus. This is the only method by which the flexibility needed to meet changing conditions and the ability to call forth the full potential of people can be obtained. In some instances, the relaxation of restrictive rules will cause employees to lose jobs, or to be assigned to less desirable jobs. But it is an illusion in most situations to think that jobs can be preserved in the long term by restrictive practices. Instead of preserving the few jobs at risk, high costs imperil the jobs of all persons in a plant.

Collective bargaining should be more than a fistfight, more than rule-making. It must be more than merely adversarial. And there is ample evidence that it can be.

A great irony of history may serve as an example. At the end of World War II, the U.S. occupation authorities, under General Douglas MacArthur, reorganized the Japanese economy. The great trading companies, or *zaibatsu*, were broken up. Trade unions were established to add a dimension of social responsibility to Japanese political life. But the occupation authorities did not simply copy the U.S. industrial relations system. Instead, they imposed what they thought would be a better system, of which company-specific unions were to be the building blocks. And in West Germany, British occupation authorities

---

[3]See *Productivity and the Economy: A Chartbook*, BLS Bulletin 2084 (Bureau of Labor Statistics, 1981), p. 4.

with similar purposes in mind reorganized German industrial relations. In the British zone of occupation they introduced three major reforms: elected work councils, union representation on the boards of directors of companies (initially in the coal and steel industries only), and a few national industrial unions to bargain at the industry level with companies on behalf of the workers. In later years, a reunited Western Germany adopted the British innovations on a nationwide basis. In Japan, MacArthur avoided the adversarial and rule-making obsession of U.S. labor relations. In Germany, the British avoided the multiplicity of trade union organizations that contributes to decentralized and disorderly industrial relations in Great Britain.

The reforms in Germany and Japan were largely a dramatic break with pre-war institutions in both countries. Such substantial change was made possible by the virtually total devastation which war had imposed on the industrial and social fabric of both nations. But over the years since the war, managers and unions in Japan and Germany have, by and large, built successfully upon the reforms instituted by occupation authorities. Many observers believe that these reforms in industrial relations have had as much to do with the economic success of the two nations as did any material assistance they were given in the post-war period.

The irony is that neither the United States nor Britain has been able to implement domestically the sorts of reforms in industrial relations practices that were imposed on the defeated powers. The result is that both Germany and Japan today have systems of collective bargaining which are much better suited to the needs of a competitive international economy than that of Britain or the United States. We in the United States apparently have known for many years the direction in which we should move, but we do not know how to get there from here.

Of course, there is no "clean slate" in this country as there was in the defeated powers at the end of World War II. We are not in a position to abandon collective bargaining as rule-making, or simply to dispense with the adversarial element of our collective bargaining process. But we must move beyond these obsessions in substantial ways if a major new contribution to U.S. economic performance is to be made. Rule-making may be replaced by a greater degree of employee participation and commitment in the workplace, but unless the adversarial posture also changes, increased participation may be of no use. Instead of resolving production problems, participatory schemes may simply add delays to management decision-making. And if the parties insist on treating earlier participatory decisions as precedents for further matters, the problem-solving mechanism may itself become yet another source of conflict and rigidity in the bargaining relationship.

Fortunately, a concept of collective bargaining that goes beyond rule-making has deep roots in the U.S. labor movement. Before the 1930s, unions ordinarily envisioned themselves becoming involved in a broad range of problems associated not only with the difficulties of employees on the job, but also with the performance of the business enterprise. In union meetings, skilled trades workers debated what we would today call management issues. The dividing line between prerogatives of management and those of labor was far less well defined than it is now.

It is time to draw on this older tradition of the U.S. labor movement, and leave behind the concept of collective bargaining as primarily a rule-making process. This should be accomplished by putting far more flexibility into the collective bargaining agreement—making provisions less detailed, reorganizing work arrangements, and designing different incentives for both management and labor. Some rule-making and the legal enforceability of contracts are not to be abandoned. But they must take a back seat to attempts to move the collective bargaining process beyond continual confrontation and into a more constructive mode.

A commitment to enhancing productivity is not easily made by the U.S. unionist. Too often, past attempts to boost productivity have simply meant speeding up the pace at which managers require employees to work. But there is far more to improving productivity than speed-ups; and the failure to seek productivity improvement in a company threatens the continued existence of jobs that the company provides. Unions must become more sophisticated in their response to management efforts to improve productivity. Some efforts, perhaps, should be opposed, but others must be supported. And the goal of improving productivity should be accepted.

Today, the United States is full of experimental efforts to extend collective bargaining beyond the concepts of the 1930s—to increase the participation of the worker in his or her job and to help preserve jobs by keeping business viable. These efforts extend across many industries and various sectors of the economy, and take many forms, including quality circles, Scanlon plans, and job enrichment programs. They cannot yet be described as successes, although many have shown promise. These endeavors are of great significance for the future—they are steps that are being taken today to meet tomorrow's needs. If successful, these innovations may provide the basis for a new system of collective bargaining which will help preserve jobs, increase the number of U.S. businesses that successfully meet the challenge of foreign competitors, and enhance the contribution and satisfaction of employees in the American workplace.

The economic revitalization of the United States in the 1980s is getting off to a start, though slow and uneven. With recent tax legislation, the government has provided certain economic incentives which may help to restore the U.S. goods-producing sector to long-term viability, although much remains to be done in the important area of job creation for the next decade.

Within this broad economic context, both business and labor have their separate obligations. Business should be prepared to assist our work force in adjusting to the substantial production and employment changes which the 1980s are going to bring, both by providing workers with more advance notice of planned innovations, and by implementing changes in ways that minimize adverse effects on employees. The unions, for their part, should be ready to work with management toward a broader concept of collective bargaining than has been common in recent decades—one which is based on the participation of employees and union officials in the business process and which includes their commitment to the success of the individual enterprise.

The transition to a new cooperative mode of collective bargaining will be a difficult one, given the traditionally antagonistic atmosphere of U.S. labor-management relations and the fact that the change will probably have to be accomplished within a generally unfavorable business environment. But the alternative is a degree of economic and social unrest which cannot be in the best interests of management, workers, or, indeed, of the nation as a whole.

READING 24

An Era of Challenge for Collective Bargaining*

Douglas H. Soutar†

The past 2 1/2 years have been ones of challenge to collective bargaining. I find nothing particularly unusual in this nor do I believe that collective bargaining is in a crisis stage or at a crossroad. After over 40 years in this business, my impression is that we are experiencing only one more cycle in the evolution of the process and I suggest it has a long way to go before reaching full maturity. As in all periods of challenge, there are various ways to approach the problems involved and observers have various solutions.

One of the reasons for different perceptions of the status of the process lies in the changing nature of the observers during a given period, i.e., periodically, we have new labor union representatives as well as new faces in the media, in government, and in management. At any given time, therefore, we find the collective bargaining wheel being reinvented.

As a strong adherent of collective bargaining for some decades, I have found no reason to lose my enthusiasm, and have so stated for the record on numerous occasions. Variations on its theme seem to be almost infinite and we need only try to match our imaginations to the current problems facing us to eventually resolve them. The literature is replete with examples of these efforts, and successes or defeats, but it is obviously more difficult to predict where we go from here.

Rather than attempt to dwell on any one point, other than the viability of collective bargaining, I will try to identify different areas and factors which make up the kinds of problems and challenges facing collective bargaining during the balance of this century.

The first of these is the now rather shopworn one of the role of "concessions" in bargaining during a recession. After over a quarter of a century of very rewarding participation in the economic redistribution of the nation's wealth, organized labor, in its post-World War II generational mode, has for the first time since the Great Depression faced the necessity for taking "less" rather than "more" a la Sam Gompers. Union leaders have differed in their reactions to this crisis usually, but not always, in direct relation to the severity of the employer's financial situation.

Union leaders turned statesmen frequently find their chances for later success at the polls severely diminished but we have seen some, like Doug Fraser and Lloyd McBride, rise to the challenge (but they aren't up for reelection). Others have been opposed to concessions and have, at least thus far, toughed it out within their industries. Of course, some of the "concessions" may be illusory where there is recoupment of losses during the life of the contract—or in a relatively short period thereafter, or there have been quid pro quos, which some observers say only mortgage the long-term financial security of the enterprise in favor of short-time respite. Only the years to come will reveal the extent to which this may be the case.

The reasons behind the need for concessions are, by now, familiar to all. Without belaboring them in detail, they include pricing ourselves out of international markets as in autos, agricultural implements, metals, electronics, and others, particularly in the basic smokestack-type industries, even where they are not particularly labor intensive. While wage-push inflation probably has had more to do with this situation than any other factor, we must include energy and commodity prices, transportation, taxes, and loss of productivity. These factors are interrelated but the thread of excessive labor cost and its rip-

*An address presented at Georgia State University, May 5, 1983.

†Douglas H. Soutar is senior vice president of Industrial Relations and Personnel, ASARCO, Inc.

ple effect is undeniable, although I am sure my co-panelists will promptly deny it. I can only refer them to the experiences of the United Kingdom, Sweden, or more recent references, such as the *New York Times* editorial of October 15, 1982, entitled "The Chrysler Dilemma," which said, in part: "but the hard truth is that if the workers extract more pay now there probably won't be any later. Chrysler's survival—and perhaps the survival of the American auto industry—depends on wage restraint." "It was union bargaining power that made the auto workers affluent. Now that they have lost some of that power, they were bound to lose some of their wage advantage." "For 30 years the domestic auto companies could afford big wage settlements because they were the only sellers around. Now they must reckon with fierce competition from Japan . . . but if Chrysler, and General Motors, and Ford are to hold their own against Nissan and Toyota, their workers will have to accept less pay . . . it may not be easy to live on $9.55 an hour (direct wages) . . . it would be even harder to live without any job at all."

And last month Paul Volcker, Chairman of the Federal Reserve Board, said in commenting on the recent Eastern Airlines settlement, "but a tendency toward generalization of cost-increasing wage bargains would clearly impair longer-term inflationary prospects and ultimately the sustainability of recovery." We could pursue this issue for the rest of the day, but I abandon it quickly considering my role of Daniel in the lion's den!

As our basic industries have lost their competitive position worldwide, the impact on our economy has, in turn, put pressure on legions of other employers to pursue concessions in bargaining, or to unilaterally make adjustments where no union is involved. Thus almost all of our wage and salary earners have suffered in some degree but many of us now think we see a little light at the end of the tunnel.

Last week, we enjoyed a phenomenon which may bear fruit in hastening our economic recovery, namely the crossing of the curves of annual rates of productivity and in-

flation for the first time since the Eisenhower years. Efforts such as Thatcher's and Reagan's may have had much to do with this, and, if the hoped-for capital regeneration and deployment occurs according to supply-side theories, unemployment should begin to decrease and interest rates moderate or at least maintain a holding pattern. However, as profits begin to appear once again or improve, it is quite likely that union demands in collective bargaining, as well as the expectations of the other 80 percent of American workers, will once again dictate employer concessions based upon rising demand and prices.

During the spring of 1981, in a speech at Notre Dame on trends foreseen for collective bargaining, I said that inflation during the balance of the 1980s would continue in the range of 7.5 to 14 percent and average out around 9 percent. Although the current annual rate is about half of the latter, my mind is unchanged in view of those latent forces at work in the economy which provide the pressures behind collective bargaining positions over the long term.

Although the current experiences with so-called concession bargaining may largely disappear in better economic times, I do anticipate that some of the ameliorations of the traditional adversarial postures in collective bargaining will continue to affect it for the better. For collective bargaining to work properly, its adversarial nature must continue. A strike-free society is no more probable nor desirable than the risk-free environment so devoutly desired by the environmentalists. But, within the confines of collective bargaining as a legislative process, there is a great deal of room for problem-solving through those various joint labor-management devices to be found working within a variety of industries. I suspect this continuum will be found even in those relationships which have been the most adversarial in the past.

While we will continue to see successes among those employers who prefer and can reasonably attain and sustain nonunion status, there is emerging an increasingly larger middle-ground class of employers who, while still embracing traditional adversarial collective bargaining, find more room for joint problem-solving. And, there will continue to be a so-called more progressive group that is willing to attempt to work out almost all employer-employee relationships with minimal recourse to adversarial collective bargaining. Whether the latter group's efforts can adequately protect the interests of employees, stockholders, and the consuming public remains to be seen. There are some of us who do not easily forget the fruits of settlements too easily arrived at in earlier years which forced prices up at the expense of a voiceless and nonparticipating consumer market. When I say too easily arrived at, we should hasten to observe the role of union power in bringing about some of these overly expensive settlements.

The role of collective bargaining, through joint labor-management dialogue at national levels, can also be enhanced through such mechanisms as the present Labor-Management Group chaired by John Dunlop and consisting of top representatives of labor and management, which is a nongovernmental successor to earlier panels convened by presidential executive order. We will also shortly see reconstitution of a national forum (The Institute of Collective Bargaining and Group Relations, Inc.) for more direct discussion and furtherance of collective bargaining per se. This group will be chaired by Doug Fraser and include top representatives of labor and management.

As the cost of living decreases, or at least remains constant, and productivity and employment increase, the need for any future "incomes policy" will decrease. Since most of us would prefer not to see such measures as wage-price controls, this is a decided plus, for such policies would inhibit collective bargaining and its own solution of problems in the years to come, just as it has seemed to have solved many of our problems during the last two and one half years. If the Reagan administration cannot accomplish all this, then in the next one, be it Democrat or Republican, the risk of such measures will most assuredly increase, bringing once again the types of Wage-Price Board challenges of the early 1940s,

1950s, and 1970s to collective bargaining. These can include, lest we forget, binding arbitration, and increased use of government intervention.

In this same vein, we may again see a reemergence of the "emergency disputes" syndrome (which has received relatively little attention during the past decade except in the public employee domain) where union power is such that disputes impact sufficiently on the public to provoke the now well-known charges of "failure of collective bargaining," and "something has to be done." Nothing could be more damaging to collective bargaining than overkill in this area, so all parties should strive to avoid any such trend.

It has been popular of late to talk about alleged long-term changes in the structure of bargaining, said to be shifting from the so-called multiple forms and pattern bargaining to unit-by-unit bargaining geared to individual plant and company economic situations. While much of American industry bargains that way now, to its great advantage, I do not foresee the disintegration to any great extent of the companywide, industrywide, areawide models that now exist. Conversely, by the end of the century, I would anticipate an even more full-blown version of such bargaining up to and including broad national agreements, and quite probably some international forms thereof. From a current employer's point of view, this is not a rosy prospect but the straws are in the wind. If anyone doubts the international challenge, they need only turn to the current Vredeling proposal within the European Economic Community, and the guidelines and codes of conduct adopted and proposed by such bodies as the ILO, the OECD, and the UN.

The semantics of my earlier reference to joint problem-solving obviously could include "worker participation" in its various forms. Europe, Latin America, and Japan, among others, have utilized such procedures either under legislation or through practice, or both. Our U.S. labor leaders have not embraced these concepts to the same degree, limiting their experience to the labor-management efforts which have attained popularity during the last few years in the form of QWL, and joint labor-management committees of various sorts. Of course, this country has a long history of productivity-sharing programs and joint labor-management committees, particularly during World War II, but their staying power has been limited.

The importation of "worker participation" schemes into the United States, in the European sense of codetermination, may be like carrying coals to New Castle, as I have suggested on other occasions. Our U.S. model of contract administration, with its detailed grievance and arbitration procedures, not to mention the additional forceful hand of government through such bodies as the War Labor Board, Wage Stabilization Board, Pay Board, and the vast array of regulatory bodies, may be more effectively accomplishing approximately the same end without the more undesirable means.

In unionized companies I anticipate that our system of contract administration, which seems to be working well under all the circumstances, will become increasingly effective. No obvious substitute is in view, even over the horizon of the 90s. There will be much attention paid to improvements in the handling of grievances, in mediation and its various forms, and in a variety of experiments with arbitration, all too numerous to mention.

In the broader world of nonunion workers, the equivalent of grievance procedures are increasingly found, permitting recourse to higher levels of authority and providing employee problem-solving mechanisms which tend to dull the appeal of the collective bargaining model. Nevertheless, the impact of the one on the other is crystal clear, and the nonunion employer who stumbles will find himself joining the other club.

Despite the incursions of government regulation into the areas historically reserved for collective bargaining, it is interesting to note that the National Labor Relations Board and the courts have increasingly rendered decisions which clearly appear to strengthen collective bargaining and have avoided creation of new remedies and causes of action, all presumably to the end that collective bargaining will continue to serve the parties and find solutions to common problems. The now familiar technological explosion (some call it Second Industrial Revolution) seems to be an important factor in producing these kinds of decisions, and I must say they are refreshing. For a more detailed discussion of this process, I refer you to an article by Messrs. Stephen Tallent and Burton J. Fishman prepared for the Edward F. Carlough Labor Law Conference at Hofstra Law School on June 9, 1982.

On the other hand, some well-qualified observers have lamented decisions which weaken the finality of arbitration, or fail to honor it entirely, as in certain NLRB decisions. Since arbitration is increasingly turned to as an efficient substitute for other litigious proceedings—in an increasingly litigious society—any substantial weakening of the process also damages, in turn, the workings of contract administration under the umbrella of collective bargaining.

It has also been suggested that where arbitration is not fully utilized in contract administration, for financial reasons or because of the above-mentioned legal restraints, union members will increasingly turn to the so-called "duty of fair representation" suits, further clogging the courts. Another rapidly emerging source of litigation is the rash of "termination at will" cases, which of course are not limited to unionized sources.

Touching on the challenge of the technological explosion, a number of interesting facets appear, e.g., the prospect of an increasing number of employees in new companies to be organized. Only last month Jackie Presser, new president of the Teamsters, said that one of his organization targets would be "Silicon Valley." Whether organized labor has the specialized and logistical abilities to adapt to such rapid technological challenge remains to be seen. There are a number of experts who question whether its present resources are adequate for the task. If not, labor's representation of the American work force may not come up to its current expectations.

Two other areas for unionization in coming years, among others, are public employees and the South. Labor seems to be better structured to make progress on the former front than the latter. Some critics observe that the AFL–CIO will continue to have problems in retaining its membership if it does not devote more attention and appeal to minorities and women, and raise its level of militancy in general. The extent to which any rapid progress on these fronts would unstabilize collective bargaining, I leave to your own imagination.

A common theme affecting administration of the work place in recent years, from management's point of view, is the tendency or shift away from traditional concepts of authority. We see and hear this on all sides and it is obviously not just limited to the labor-management relations area but affects all of our institutions. A variety of new gimmicks are suggested and developing which circumvent or put down the role of authority in the work place and the enterprise. Just where do we draw the line in future years to accommodate these conflicting interests? Certainly one way to accommodation is through collective bargaining as in the past. Where collective bargaining does not exist an employer will have to emulate the best of his peers to stay ahead of the union organizer in order to satisfy the needs of the restless and stress-oriented employee. On the other hand, "running a ship by committee" has never been a very practical modus operandi.

It has been a long time between the recession of the 30s and the current one, with the result that many of the present generation of workers do not carry the scar tissue of an unemployment experience, at least until now. Thus the new generation will insist that job security measures, including plant closings and transfers, increasingly be the subject of collective bargaining, thereby creating new challenges and additional costs for employers. I anticipate that much intellectual effort will be expended on the development of new devices in this area and that, hopefully, the consumer and the nation can afford such plans.

We can expect more attention to what might be called alternative work patterns such as permanent part-time, phased retirements, job sharing, the rehiring of retirees, use of sabbaticals and other methods to meet the indi-

vidual needs of employees and the production needs of their employers. While most of such progress to date has been in nonunion plants, it is probable that there will be more of such experiments in future collective bargaining.

Another shift could be in the payment of salaries to hourly employees—a development which for some reason has had little sex appeal for labor to date but is obviously a cornerstone of the nonunion sector of American employment.

Considering the problems that our unions have had with decreasing membership and decreasing political clout, it is very understandable that they wish to improve the latter as well as their legislative activities. Despite these good intentions, the recent "Alliance for Progress," which, in addition to representatives from a variety of liberal organizations, included such union heads as Doug Fraser, Glenn Watts, and Bill Winpisinger, never really got off the ground for reasons that are not clearly understood. I assume we will see new, and probably more successful efforts, in the years ahead.

Again, the kind of tripartite approaches envisioned by the "National Labor Accord," so highly touted by Lane Kirkland in the spring of 1980 as one of the great events in labor's domestic history, have also strangely disappeared. And national planning of the Humphrey-Hawkins Bill type has seemingly made little progress even though such a strong advocate as Bill Winpisinger of the IAM has hammered on it at every turn. Considering the alleged successes of this approach in other countries, I anticipate that we will hear more about it and slowly drift in this direction.

Summing up, it seems to me that management and labor have adjusted quite well to the challenges of changing economic and social forces of our times, despite an oversupply of critics who appear to be driven more by "art for art's sake" rather than by observed basic deficiencies in the collective bargaining process.

From management's perspective, if there has been any overriding problem through the years, it has been with an unnecessary use of power by unions at the bargaining table—a power which derives from many sources, but which has been tempered by strong counterforces in our domestic society and worldwide, in the short term.

As it faces the future labor should be judicious and cautious in use of its power, adjusting to the most important need to meet its perceived opponents at least half way. At the same time, management has matured during recent years and is, on the whole, quite willing to adjust, *provided* the rights of the individual are observed in the process.

Quoting from the concluding sentence of a recent article of mine in the *New York Times,* opposite Bill Winpisinger, I said: "It is suggested that we are all in the same boat, eventually headed for the same egalitarian results within the confines of our system, and that labor will work with us to this end."

READING 25

Concession Bargaining*

Robert B. McKersie and
Peter Cappelli†

How to Distinguish the Species Called Concession Bargaining

We are in a period of very intense and widespread economic change. Concession bargaining is a development that has come to the fore as the pace of economic change has accelerated. Certainly, the modern industrial era has witnessed change on a continuing basis, what Schumpeter has called the "creative destruction" of capital. In other words, there is a continuous process of disinvestment and reinvestment of capital.

For a variety of reasons, the current period has taken on the character of a *convulsion* rather than steady change that can be "taken in stride." Another term which characterizes the change and one that is a favorite of economists, is *discontinuity*; an abrupt change from one rate of capital redeployment to a different rate of redeployment.

The current situation can be understood more clearly if we consider the role that expectations play in the changes. Employment, like life itself, contains inherent risks. Workers estimate their chances of keeping a job based on experience in the industry and their sense of the labor market as to what is happening in comparable situations. While these expectations change over time, they are reasonably stable and provide the backdrop against which decisions about wages and other matters are taken. For example, labor leaders and

union members as they press for better contracts are aware that over the long run the firm may respond by mechanizing and finding other ways to use less of the higher-priced labor. Also, if a company announces that it is shutting down a facility, the response of the workers to this prospect will depend upon what they see as their alternatives for finding other work.

When a discontinuity or shock of severe proportions hit, then "all bets are off," and expectations previously formed no longer accurately represent the situation and must be reshaped, a type of agonizing reappraisal. This appears to be the situation in many industries today.

Factors Precipitating the Convulsion or the Onset of Extensive Restructuring

Since concession bargaining is just one adaptive mechanism to these convulsions it is useful to enumerate some of the forces and factors that have given rise to the extensive amount of economic change that is taking place across the world.

One view is that we have reached the end of a long wave, a period of innovation and growth that has characterized many industries since World War II. Students of the Kontrief Cycle point out that such turning points are inevitable given the way in which innovation occurs, capital is accumulated, markets expand, and then there is a shift of economic activity to the "new shoots."

Whether or not we subscribe to this mechanistic view of economic development, it is clear that there are fundamental changes occurring in many industries across the world. The transformations in production and employment are triggered by a variety of developments. In some cases, the trigger comes from new products, for example—radial tires; in some cases, from new manufacturing processes—like robots. In other cases, the fundamental change is organizational, for example, the rise of mini-mills in steel and new methods of killing and processing meat in the meatpacking industry. Certainly, the move to deregulate several industries such as airlines and

*Reprinted with permission from Working Paper 1322–82, Alfred P. Sloan School of Management, MIT, June 1982.

†*Robert B. McKersie is a professor of industrial relations at MIT and Peter Cappelli is a professor at the University of Illinois.*

Chart 1
Alternate Strategies for Managing Economic Dislocation

Problem definition	Prospect of a large-scale worker displacement	→ Decision to close →	Plant shutdown
Coping strategies			
A. Public	Bailout employment subsidies	Industry restructuring programs	Economic development Community task force Income support Labor market programs: retraining, relocation
B. Private	Productivity bargaining Alternate plans Worker ownership	Enterprise continuity of employment programs (e.g., IBM)	Advance notice Counselling, training by employer of last repose Severance pay
Overall orientation	Preventing job loss	Staging the change (protecting the workers, not the jobs)	Cushioning the impact
Moderating factors affecting the success of a strategy	E.g., voluntary attrition rate, induced attrition rate (e.g., early retirement), local labor market alternatives and mobility of labor force, size of the organization, magnitude of the phase-out (i.e., partial or complete shutdown).		

over-the-road trucking in the United States must be seen as a basic organizational change that has set significant forces for economic change in motion.

Superimposed on these technical and organizational changes is the development of world markets and world trade. In effect, we see a type of rationalization of industrialized economies that represents a type of a world division of labor. We cannot understand the pressures in the automobile, steel, and tire industries without reference to the development of worldwide markets.

For other industries, there has been a drop in the worldwide demand for their products. This certainly characterizes shipbuilding and the steel industry. Whether these changes are temporary (cyclical) or more permanent (secular), it is too early to tell.

Finally, the worldwide recession (bordering on what some people would call a depression) is also an important force in the overall picture. We are therefore witnessing a conjugation of developments and forces that together provide the biggest shock to expectations concerning employment security since the 1930s.

Alternate Strategies for Dealing with Economic Dislocation

At this point, it may be helpful to use a chart (see Chart 1) to illustrate the various mechanisms that are used in different countries for dealing with the prospect of economic dislocation: for the private and public sectors, for the stages of preventing job loss, staging the job loss, or cushioning the job loss. The advantage of using this chart is that it puts concession and productivity bargaining in the context of other strategies.

One of the major points to be explained is why there is so much more concession bargaining taking place in the United States while the response to economic change in other countries has been in the other cells of the diagram.

A few general comments about the patterns may help our understanding of concession bargaining in the United States. Early on in the adjustment cycle, as the forces for economic change start to gather, there is not very much concession bargaining in any country. In the United States, this period was characterized by plant shutdowns; in Germany and Japan, the approach was industry restructuring and efforts to redeploy the affected workers in a variety of human resource planning techniques. In Britain and to some extent in Canada, there was outright opposition to plant shutdowns, and in Britain especially, efforts to prevent the job loss by a variety of government support programs.

As the crisis deepens and the reach of economic change goes deeper and wider into the fabric of the economy, the question then is: how do the parties respond? There are no easy generalizations. It is clear at this stage that there is considerable resistance to additional plant shutdowns. They cannot be justified on the basis of excess capacity. It is clear that the core of the economy is under threat in some cases. In some countries, unions and workers may respond to such situations in political terms. They demand that the industry not be dismantled, and solidarity prevents any consideration of concessions that would weaken the established wage and benefit scale. How a union and its members respond is a function of the ideology of the union (class solidarity versus business pragmatism) and the extent of bargaining power inherent in the situation. Unions in the United States do not enjoy as much bargaining power even in the industries where they have been traditionally strong in terms of the percent of the work force organized. In the rubber industry, for example, approximately 20 percent of tire production is now done in nonunion plants, and in the steel industry the development of the mini-mills is making the steel workers' position vulnerable. The automobile industry is of particular interest because the UAW still enjoys a very strong position. Here, the choice for the union is between advocating a very strong protectionist position versus engaging in concession bargaining in an effort to beat the competition in the marketplace. It is remarkable in terms of international comparisons of labor movement philosophy and outlook that the UAW has not done more than urge Congress to pass special legislation and to visit Japan to secure voluntary export agreements. Of course, the UAW is aware that the political climate in the United States, at least presently, has not been conducive to legislation that would protect industries like automobiles that are under the brunt of increasing imports.

CONCESSION BARGAINING IN THE TIRE AND AIRLINE INDUSTRIES

Now, let us take a closer look at the process of concession bargaining. From the union's point of view, one might think of it as bargaining to save jobs; management is saying that they need lower labor costs in order to maintain employment, and they are asking the union either to do something about it or face unemployment. The key question for the union is whether management is accurately presenting their true situation.

It may be helpful to look in detail at the experience of two industries, tire manufacturing and air transport, which in many ways span the range of experience with concession bargaining. The tire industry represents old-line manufacturing, while air transport represents a relatively new, service industry. Both have experienced shocks that have led their firms to threaten the security of current employment levels.

The Tire Industry

The story in tire manufacture is one of excess capacity in multiplant operations. Plants and local unions compete against each other to stay open, and they do that through concession bargaining. The crisis was brought about by two developments which paralleled those in auto. First, there was a fall in the demand for domestic tires. Consumers responded to OPEC price increases by driving less. When they bought cars, they bought lighter, fuel-efficient cars. Both developments cut down on tire wear and replacements. More importantly, the cars they bought tended to be imports, equipped with imported tires. Fewer original equipment tires were needed (see Chart 2). The second change, which began

Chart 2
Consumption of Automotive Tires in the United States

	(Million Units)		Tires on Imported Cars
Year	Production	Tire Imports	
1973	223	15	13
1976	190	16	14
1977	237	17	15
1978	230	17	17
1979	215	20	16
1980	168	18	16

about 1970, was a shift in demand away from bias to radial tires. Radials have superior handling characteristics, and cars equipped with them get better gas mileage. In addition, most of the imported cars came equipped with radials; owners were likely to replace them with radials, too.

The industry responded to these developments beginning with the shift to radials. American manufacturers needed new equipment to manufacture radial tires, and they were faced with a choice of converting existing plants or constructing new ones. Certain areas in the United States were offering tax incentives for new plant construction (mainly in the South). This seemed to tilt the balance for tire manufacturers, and they constructed new radial plants almost entirely in the South (Chart 3). Meanwhile, the North was left with the existing bias plants which continued to operate. The shift in demand toward radials continued; they increased from 2 percent of the tire market in 1970 to 55 percent in 1980. One result of this shift away from bias tires was the creation of substantial excess capacity in the northern plants.

These changes were accentuated by the OPEC price increases, particularly those in 1979. The subsequent decline in driving, the recession that followed the price increases, and the "radial effect" (the fact that radials need replacing about one third as often and were coming to constitute the bulk of the market) produced a general decline in the demand for tires. The decline in the demand for bias tires was precipitous, and the resulting excess capacity in bias plants meant that some would have to close.

Which plants should close? An obvious answer was to close the high-cost plants. At

Chart 3
New Tire Plants

	Tires per Day (000)
Firestone: Decatur, Illinois	26.3
Goodyear: Union City, Tennessee	47.0
Goodrich: Miami, Oklahoma	11.0
Goodyear: Lawton, Oklahoma (nonunion)	22.0
General: Waco, Texas	20.6
Goodyear: Gadsden, Alabama	52.5
Firestone: Wilson, North Carolina (nonunion)	20.0
Uniroyal: Admore, Oklahoma (nonunion)	36.0
Total	235.8

Note: Industry capacity between 1960 and 1980 was approximately 600,000–800,000 tires per day.

a plant level, local management and local unions had an incentive to lower costs in order to keep their plants from closing. There is some indication that higher-level management left the plants free to compete with each other to stay open. They competed by secur-

Chart 4
Tire Industry Concessions

Year 1978	Location	Status after Concession
10/3/77	Firestone: Akron	Closed
1/11/78	Goodyear: Akron (Plant 1)	Closed
1/24/78	Goodyear: Gadsden, Alabama	Open
3/29/78	Goodrich: Akron	Closed
5/18/78	Seiberling: Barberton, Ohio	Closed
11/14/78	Mohawk: Akron	Closed
11/16/78	Mansfield: Mansfield, Ohio	Closed
1979		
4/16/79	General: Akron	Closed
5/?/79	Goodyear: Akron (Plant 2)	Closed
6/11/79	Mohawk: West Helena, Arkansas	Closed
1980		
2/4/80	Goodyear: Los Angeles	Closed
2/10/80	Uniroyal: Detroit	Closed
6/27/80	General: Peru, Indiana	Open
7/7/90	Uniroyal: Chicopee Falls, Massachusetts	Closed
10/30/80	Firestone: Middlesville, Indiana	Closed
1981		
2/22/81	Cooper: Texarkana	Open
3/27/81	General: Akron	Closing 1982
4/2/81	Mercer: Newark	Closed
5/19/81	Firestone: Memphis	Open
7/16/81	Goodyear: Topeka	Open
8/13/81	Firestone: Akron	Closed

ing concessions at the plant level. It is an indication of the excess capacity that virtually all of these plants closed eventually (Chart 4). The plants that closed were all bias plants, and they were almost all in the North. There are no more tires being made in Akron, once the center of the industry.

The Air Transport Industry

This is a very different case—price competition following deregulation forced revenue in some carriers below costs and brought them near bankruptcy. Before 1978, government regulations restricted entry and made it difficult to compete on prices and routes. After deregulation in 1978, new carriers were free to enter the market; the number rose from 38 to 80 between 1978 and 1981. Charter and intrastate carriers were able to compete with the main airlines on trunk routes. As a result, price competition increased substantially, especially on the well-traveled routes.

The new carriers (and the charter and intrastate carriers) had substantially lower labor costs. Most were nonunion, with lower salary scales. All had younger crews with lower seniority pay. And they got more work out of their crews through tougher work rules. Southwest Airlines, for example, even though it is unionized, gets 50 percent more flight time from its crews than do many of the main carriers. Their labor costs are less than half; labor costs at smaller, regional carriers like Midway are two-thirds less. The older, established carriers still retained some cost advantages, particularly on longer flights where their larger planes cut average costs.

The situation changed in 1979 when OPEC price increases doubled fuel costs (then about 30 percent of total costs). Because the demand for air transport is very sensitive to the business cycle, the recession that followed the OPEC increases led to a substantial fall in demand. The situation got so bad in 1980–81 that the demand for air travel declined absolutely for the first time since World War II.

With all of this competition in the industry and with the absolute demand for transport declining, the market produced tremendous

Chart 5
Airline Concessions
($ Millions)

Profits	Carrier	Concession
−31.4	Braniff	10 percent pay cut and variable earnings plan through 1983; contractual wage increases continue.
−360	Pan Am	10 percent pay cut through 1982; contractual increases suspended; work rule changes.
−66	Western	10 percent pay cut for six months, now in jeopardy as Teamsters have rejected it—other groups may follow; pilots may agree to reduce labor costs to 1982 level through productivity.
−24.5	Republic	10 percent pay cut for clerical staff; one-month pay deferral for pilots—repaid by August; 10 percent pay cut for flight attendants may be extended to 1982—currently in court.
−43.5	Continental	10 percent pay cut from pilots.
−49.9	Eastern	Variable earnings plan—employees contribute to offset losses up to a certain percentage.
−148	United	Productivity concessions from pilots; two-man crews on 727s.
+86.5	Delta	No concessions.
+72.2	American	No concessions.

excess capacity (one estimate put the excess capacity on the North Atlantic route equal to 50 jumbo jets per day). The excess capacity led to price cutting on many runs and price levels often below costs. 1981 was the worst financial year in aviation history; fourth-quarter losses for the industry were $294.9 million. 1980 was the next worst year, and 1982 is expected to be about as bad.

Many of the carriers had loaded up on debt just before this period, and the recent rise in interest rates particularly hurt those with short-term debt (Chart 5). The following airlines are in the worst position: Republic and Pan Am took on substantial short-term debt to finance mergers; Braniff also took on short-term debt to finance expansion; Western and Continental borrowed to fund new equipment. These airlines are all in danger of being unable to fund their current debts and of being reorganized or simply going under.

Concessions in the airline industry will not make up the cost advantage that the new carriers have on shorter flights. Prices are not closely related to average costs on individual routes. So concessions do not help a carrier compete on the market; they are designed to free resources to service debts and meet capital requirements. This is clearly a different situation than in the tire industry.

The pattern of concessions is straightforward. They have occurred this year because conditions now are the worst in history. Some carriers are doing rather well, some are near the brink, and most are somewhere in the middle. Although most are trying for concessions, those able to secure them are carriers who are worst off, who are actually in financial danger.

As with any other negotiation, concession bargaining can take place both at local and national levels. Bargaining at local levels requires that the firm have autonomous units—the case in multiplant industries such as rubber, not the case in air transport. Although one hears more about negotiations at the national level, there is much more concession bargaining at the local level.

It is natural to wonder why there are so many concessions now and why they are happening where they are. The short answer is not simply because of the recession but because of the structural change in the economy. The industries undergoing concession bargaining have experienced several years of severe structural change. Many industries have suffered excess capacity because of a permanent fall in demand (as in tires and auto). Some have seen the entry of large numbers of low-cost competitors because of deregulation (trucking and airlines). Others are damaged by low-cost foreign competition (steel and autos). These problems have led to a fall in the demand for the industry's product and a subsequent fall in the demand for labor; current levels of employment cannot be maintained at current cost levels because of the shift in demand. These problems have been building in many cases throughout the 1970s; the recession simply made them worse.

What does management ask for in concession bargaining? They want to reduce labor costs but there may be many ways to do that, not all of them equally easy. Certain items are more visible from the union's point of view and may also require more levels of approval. Management usually asks for work rules, scheduling changes, grading adjustments, wage and fringe freezes, and wage and fringe cuts—in that order. The first items are less visible and can usually be negotiated locally. The latter ones are more difficult to secure but cut costs faster.

In general, will the unions agree to concessions? The different levels within a union may have different interests in concessions. The Local should be particularly concerned with employment consequences when concession bargaining takes place at the plant. The International may be more concerned with the effect of concessions there on the pattern, on them spreading to other plants, and less concerned with the employment risk. Whether the union agrees to the concessions may, therefore, depend on which level makes the decision. And that differs with the issue—work rules, for example, are usually left to the local level. It also differs with the union—some may allow more autonomy at the local level.

The key question for the union is whether management is serious in its threats. The Local and the International may have different information and perceptions regarding the truth of management's arguments. It may be the case that the International actually has to convince the Locals to take management's claims seriously.

Alternative employment prospects also influence decisions. There may be cases where skilled workers are willing to see a shop close rather than make any concessions because they are reasonably certain of finding jobs with equal compensation elsewhere.

In the tire industry, there have been cases where the Locals have not granted concessions. In this recent period, they appear to have always granted them. The reason would seem to be that the union believes management to be serious in its threats, a conclusion reinforced by recent experience, and that alternative employment prospects in the industry and in the region are dismal. In airlines, for example, the picture is not so clear. American, for example, could not get concessions from anyone because it did not appear to be in bad enough straights. On the other hand, even the machinist's union, which has a policy of opposing all concessions in principle, made an exception for Braniff because it was so obviously in trouble. One finds similar variance in other industries. Chrysler got concessions first, perhaps because they were in the worst shape; General Motors got them last (and apparently got least) because they appeared to be in the best financial position. Yet even at Chrysler, workers in the more successful plants were reluctant to go along with the concessions because they felt that their plants would continue to operate, perhaps under a different owner.

Are the unions getting anything in return for the concessions? Sometimes they are, and this may be what is new about concession bargaining. But concessions are designed to cut labor costs, and it would be irrational for management to give back items that increase labor costs, such as work rules or wage and fringe improvements. Yet these are the traditional union goals. The real challenge here is for unions to look for improvements in other areas, such as union security arrangements, job security, future wage and benefit improvements, some say in management decisions, etc.—in short, move into areas traditionally considered management's prerogative.

How much management is willing to give for the concessions obviously depends on how badly they want them. If they are simply rearranging production between plants, and the unemployment threat comes from that, management may not care that much about concessions. If the company is threatening to go out of business, however, they may want them quite badly. In the rubber industry, it was clear that many plants had to close, and there was little reason to believe that the com-

panies cared which ones were shut down. In these local concessions, the union received virtually nothing in return. But in national bargaining with Uniroyal, where the company was threatening to go out of business, the union secured a number of improvements, including the right to audit company books in return for wage concessions.

In the air transport industry, the unions won a number of improvements in return for concessions, largely because the companies were actually threatening to close and desperately needed the concessions. Pilots at Western and United won no-layoff clauses; workers at Pan Am and Western gained profit sharing; Republic employees took a stock swap as a concession.

Where concession bargaining takes place, one might expect it to permanently alter industrial relations. First, labor costs and employment security will be more closely linked. Second, negotiations will increasingly include plant and firm characteristics, contributing to the break-up of contract patterns within and between industries. Finally, bargaining may extend into areas of traditional management prerogative as the price for union concessions.

Evaluation of Concession Bargaining

Since the dust has not settled on this period of intense activity, it is not possible to discern what the net effect of these bargains will be. There is the cynical view that the whole business is a plot by management to gain the upper hand and to drive down the social wage. The other view, and the one to which we are more prone to subscribe, is that we are witnessing a period of inevitable economic adjustment. Consider the automobile industry in the United States. Rather than sticking strictly with a protectionist position, the union has been willing to join the issue and to put operations in the United States on a more competitive basis. A very valuable lesson about maintaining economic viability on a worldwide basis has been driven home to many automobile workers. If the result (and this is a big *if*) is to stem the tide of foreign imports and to not only protect existing jobs but to regain some lost employment, then this will promote a very strong reinforcement within the thinking of the U.S. labor movement. At a minimum, the willingness to mark time on cost of living and to give up the annual improvement factor and other gains means that the labor cost picture will be more favorable in the United States for Japanese manufacturers who might be contemplating *making* rather than *shipping* automobiles into the United States. In other words, from the union's point of view, there is the need to keep wage scales at a point where foreign companies are motivated to contemplate the possibility of producing their products in the United States. Of course, the union faces the challenge of organizing these workers, but the UAW is one union that has a good record of organizing new facilities that are brought on line in their industry.

Returning to the main theme of positive adjustment, from a public policy point of view, it certainly is preferable for workers to make adjustments that reduce labor costs rather than holding firm and forcing companies to shut down additional plants. From the viewpoint of future generations, a plant shutdown is a continuing loss. Workers who are willing to work longer hours and to work for less are making a contribution to the job viability of a community for the future.

The important conceptual distinction is between viewing concession bargaining as an element of distributive bargaining, that is, whatever the workers give up is a direct gain to management (in this case, increased profits) versus some form of integrated or mixed bargaining, where both sides gain more than they give up. This latter case, of course, depends upon the elasticity of employment. If the concessions are sufficient to increase the volume of activity and to pull back into the economy work that has been exported to other countries, then the concession bargaining is indeed a case where both sides gain.

Of course, there are situations where concessions have no possibility of increasing revenue, in the public sector for example. It is not surprising that in the face of financial cutbacks, unions in the public sector are not engaging in concession bargaining and are forcing management to lay workers off and to bargain through the changes on a distributive basis.

The situations where there is the greatest chance of mutual gain are those where there is competition from the nonunion sector or from abroad. Thus, tires, trucking, airlines, meatpacking, and autos all contain the possibility that concession bargaining may help the employment prospects in the unionized sector.

Yet, even in these industries there are a number of examples where concession bargaining has taken place and it has not brought about the desired improvement in job security. This is because either the plant in question was so antiquated that it eventually needed to close and the concession bargaining was just buying time, or because a long-run overcapacity existed in the industry where some plants needed to be closed. The concessions did not move the particular plant in question far enough up the league tables to prevent a shutdown. Bridgeport Brass, for example, closed a plant in the fall of 1980 three years after the union involved agreed to a cut in wages and benefits of almost $1.30 an hour.

Is There Anything New This Time Around with Concession Bargaining?

A number of analysts, such as John Dunlop, maintain that what we are witnessing today is just a rerunning of an old movie. I think these commentators are right with respect to the side of the bargain that the company gains, namely wage reductions, work rule changes, increased time on the job. However, it is on the other side of the bargain, what workers gain, where there is some new ground, what might be called the latest frontier or what unions mean by "more." Let me enumerate these dimensions and make a few comments about what we see as interesting trends.

1. A Look at the Books. In a number of agreements management has said that it will show the union important financial data. For example, in the settlement last year between Armour and the Food and Commercial Workers' Union, the company agreed to provide a five-year plan of capital expenditures and each January to provide a summary, plant-by-plant, of investment activities. In the Ford settlement, there will be meetings in which the company shares information about investment plans as they affect employment on a worldwide basis. In the case of one of the large airlines, information will be provided so that the Pilots' Union can be sure that the productivity improvements that have been realized as a result of their concessions do not result in the layoffs of any pilots. (The company gave the guarantee that pilots not needed as a result of productivity improvements would be kept on board until attrition took effect.)

2. Union Security.
In a number of agreements, unions have obtained important institutional gains. For example, Armour agreed to recognize the union in any new plant based on a check of authorization cards rather than forcing the issue to a representation election. In trucking, there are some limitations on the establishment of nonunion subsidiaries—in other words, a deterrent to further development of the double-breasted trucker.

3. Job-Investment Bargaining.
One of the most interesting developments has been the coupling of employment security with investment behavior on the part of the corporation. In a number of significant situations, such as in the paper industry, at General Electric's Erie operations, Goodyear in Topeka, Timken for its Canton plant, a commitment has been made convening investment dollars as part of the concession deal. Perhaps the word *bargaining* is too strong a term to describe the deal because the unions are not writing into the contract any information about a company's decision to modernize its facilities. Rather, it is a linkage, a type of coordination across the employment and investment themes. It is somewhat analogous to what happens when a community goes all out to attract a new facility of a company. The community makes tax concessions or provides some

other inducements—with the promise by the company to put new jobs in the locality. Nothing is legally binding but it is understood that the coordination will take place because it is in the interest of both sides to go through with the understanding. Similarly, we see a development of this sort in the context of concession bargaining. Whether U.S. unions will push it to the next step of filing complaints through arbitration or through the courts if they feel a company has reneged on its side of the bargain remains to be seen. But in any event, we appear to be moving into a new era where unions are much more interested and sensitive about the investment decisions that companies are making.

4. Enhanced Job Security.
Given the prominence of this subject in negotiations in the U.S. automobile industry, this is clearly one of the significant dimensions of concession bargaining. It is rather complicated and a number of points need to be made. First, even if the job security is not made explicit, it certainly is involved implicitly in any concession bargaining because the presumption is that by lowering labor costs, then more business will be attracted and jobs will be made more secure. A number of important assurances have been given by companies with respect to job security. In terms of the diagram used earlier, a number of them have been willing to move to the staging category rather than continuing the abrupt process of shutdowns on short notice. Thus, several companies have said they will not shut any additional plants down for one or two years and if they do they will give at least six months advance notice. Ford has gone further and has said that if there are excess workers it will endeavor to handle the problem through attrition.

The other dimension of job security is a guarantee against layoffs. Ford will experiment with this for two plants where 80 percent of the workers will be kept on regardless of production levels. Similarly, United Airlines has agreed to not lay off any of its pilots (in exchange for major changes in availability of pilot time). These assurances go a long way in the direction of what has come to be known as the Japanese method of career employment—also practiced by a number of high-tech firms such as IBM and Hewlett Packard.

There are several questions concerning this trend. How far can a company go in guaranteeing no layoffs when it is not in control of its market position or the demand for its product? Ford can achieve no-layoff for several plants but it may be at the expense of moving work into those plants from other places, thereby having a secondary effect on job security of other workers. While a company can use human resource techniques to even out the ups and downs and to avoid layoffs that are part of the cyclical activity of the industry, it cannot go so far as to avoid layoffs if the demand is not there for the product. The second major question has to do with the preference of the workers who are in the industries we have just cited.What preference do they put on stability of employment as contrasted from earlier patterns of work interrupted by periods of idleness? It is not clear that such a pattern of work alternated by leisure leads to lowered productivity by itself. What does lead to such behavior is fear of *permanent* job loss, and as we were saying above, assurances against that are things that most companies cannot give. The in-between category and where commitments about no layoffs do make sense is where technology has changed and companies initiate discretionary adjustments, such as major reorganizations. This is where there can be considerable resistance to change, and by using human resource planning techniques, phasing in the changes, and not laying workers off, there is a much greater likelihood that these changes will be introduced, accepted, and incorporated more readily, helping the competitive position of the company.

5. New Values. It is clear that the designers of a number of the concession agreements are attempting to set in place the new values of *openness, equality of sacrifice,* and *egalitarianism.* Whether these values will "take" or are just the expressions of the philosophy of the people at the top remains to be seen. In the work by Athos and Pascale it is estimated that to change the values of an organization in a radically different direction takes a minimum of 10 years. But in any event, some forces have been set in motion that may move some companies and some industries in the direction of what has been called in the literature, Theory Z.

The Dilemma for Labor Leaders

The economic crisis and the possibility of concession bargaining pose incredibly difficult dilemmas and decisions for union leaders. They find themselves in a type of no-win situation.

This may be called the predicament of participation. Helping shape business decisions presents an acute problem for union leaders and worker representatives. They find themselves in a dilemma with sharply drawn disadvantages on each side. On the one hand, if they become involved, they may be viewed by the rank-and-file as having been coopted by management and thereby suffer the stigma associated with business demise. These fears are well illustrated by the experience of some of the unions in British Steel who have been blamed by rank-and-file members and community representatives for having gone along with the decisions that have dismantled a large part of the steel-making capacity. Worker Directors who have been "associated" with the decisions have been treated as strangers in their home territories.

On the other hand, if union leaders do not get involved to challenge the business decision, they may also be condemned; an illustration comes from the United States. The United Automobile Workers represented approximately 1,000 workers at a Dana Corporation plant in Wisconsin making front-end axles. In a survey conducted among the workers about a year after the plant closed down, the workers expressed many more negative feelings about the union than about management. The workers viewed management as having made an inevitable decision to close the plant down in the face of a drop in demand that hit the vehicle industry. However, the workers felt that the union should have done more to force the company to transfer other work into the plant or to have put pressure on the company to close another plant. Union representatives were seen as having failed in their tasks, since it is their responsibility to make job security a number one objective. If job security is not pressed, then there can be a substantial backlash against union leaders.

During the early stages of the adjustment cycle, labor leaders may be able to "look the other way" in hopes that the problem will go away, or if local rank-and-file people enter into adjustments on their own, then they can ignore the impact at the national scale. This is the approach that the Teamsters had taken until recently.

When the crisis becomes severe enough that national leaders have to move into the picture, they must gauge how much of the crisis is cyclical and how much is permanent (unless some changes are made in labor costs). This is very much a judgment and puts them in the impossibly difficult position of trying to estimate the future fortunes of a given company, industry, and economy.

In the short run there is no easy solution. Over the long run, the only way for union leaders to get out of the bind that such a defensive position always poses for them is to take the initiative on a countrywide or indeed on an international basis to organize the market and to take the wage rate out of competition. Thus, after this crisis is over, we can expect to see much more activity across industrialized countries by the international trade union confederations. Our view is that they are biding their time on the question of multinational bargaining and that once economies begin to pick up strength, unions will be moving to avoid a repetition of the present situation by standardizing wage rates and conditions as much as possible.

The Next Time Around

Of course, efforts to establish a labor standard may prevent wholesale concession bargaining, but ultimately pressure will come from some sector, if not from an underdeveloped economy then from a new industry with a better idea and a lower-cost product. The interaction between achieving wage gains and wage adjustments is dynamic. In some respects, concession bargaining has been more intense in those industries that have enjoyed stability as a result of the union scale and collective bargaining. The workers have been immunized from concern about labor costs because the seniority principle enabled most workers in the industry to count on continuing employment. Certainly, the recent pressure in collective bargaining for cost-of-living clauses must be seen as having been otherwise. In unorganized industries where everyone is at risk, there may be more interest in keeping the operation competitive.

By contrast, in industries that have *not* been as strongly organized, such as garments and textiles, concession bargaining has not been as necessary precisely because the threat on a continuing basis of nonunion products has kept wages and benefits in line with competitive conditions. It is true that wages have been kept on the low side. But from a long-run view, it would seem that accommodation has occurred on a more gradual basis—rather than a long period of stability followed by a crisis and a very tough shake-out of the sort that is happening in a number of industries today. George Shultz uses the example of the dam and the buildup of water to illustrate this change. One can have a gradual runoff or one can hold back the pressure for an extended period of time only to have a complete breakdown and a flood where everyone "runs for cover."

Another fact of life is that where wages have been taken out of competition, management also goes "asleep" and stops scanning the horizon for information about what is going on elsewhere in the industry. Both sides become overly complacent.

The trick is to achieve a balance of stability and change—neither extreme is functional. In collective bargaining we have the concept of the *living document*, a term first used by the UAW in the early 1950s. Both the employment relationship and the competitive position of the business need to subscribe to this dialectic of continuity and change.

B. Management Organization for Collective Bargaining

The employment relationship is basically an economic one. As competition increases and profit margins narrow, business decisions must be based more closely upon economic grounds if the business is to survive. A great deal of attention is currently being given to the management organization for collective bargaining, and the industrial relations/personnel function has been upgraded considerably within the total context of the corporation. In the first article in this section, Audrey Freedman discusses "management objectives in bargaining," and "evaluating labor relations performance." A second article discusses management's right to operate during a strike. The right to strike is a fundamental part of the collective bargaining process; however, the right of an employer to utilize temporary or permanent replacements for workers engaged in an economic strike in order to continue operation is also clearly recognized under law. Perry discusses several cases where this right has been used by management.

Managing Labor Relations*

Audrey Freedman†

MANAGEMENT OBJECTIVES IN BARGAINING

For unionized companies, bargaining—the actual negotiation of a contract—is a crucial event. And while union security, management rights, and other institutional arrangements may once have been major issues, today the wage and benefit package gets the spotlight. Company managements usually negotiate with a specific wage and benefit objective and a set of objectives on nonwage items. Past history and development of the union contract in the individual company is the baseline for analysis of current objectives. The pivot point is where the individual company is, immediately prior to bargaining.

Meaning and Subtleties of Target Setting

For unionized companies, wage targets and nonwage goals specify the best deal the company expects to get. Not just a list of what management wants, they are actually an evaluation of what, given the situation, will occur when management's trade-off schedule meets the union's agenda. This interpretation suggests that attaining a target represents a realistic optimum exchange from management's point of view.

Thus, target setting includes the use of good judgment about the union's ultimate settlement point and trade-offs—and the costs to each party of various strategies and maneuvers, including strikes and lockouts.

*Reprinted with permission from The Conference Board, Report No. 765, pp. 35–46, 71–75.

†Audrey Freedman is senior research associate at The Conference Board.

These judgments temper "what management would ideally prefer" and produce what can be called a realistically planned outcome.

Patterns in Management's Criteria for Wage Setting

Local labor market comparisons are the primary wage criterion in nonunion companies (see Chart 1), and also in situations where the employer is the dominant party in collective bargaining (see Table 1). In the absence of unions, or where unions are weak, employers are free to offer wages only in the amount necessary to draw and retain the desired quality and quantity of workers from the local labor market. Companies in this position are also likely to give more weight to criteria specific to the firm, such as financial ability, and to internal comparisons of wages in the firm.

Where unions are present and strong, it becomes necessary for management to add criteria that reflect the union's "demands." The influence of strong unions creates the effect of an industrywide wage level (as opposed to localized wages). One of the ways unions seek to "take wages out of competition" is to induce management to emphasize industry comparisons or "patterns," and to put less weight on differentiated local wage levels. Thus, in unionized firms, *industry patterns* are given priority over local wage levels as a wage-targetting criterion (see Chart 1). This priority is even stronger in situations where the union is particularly "powerful" because of high unionization, a multiplant (or even companywide) bargaining structure, or where the costs of a strike are severe. The more powerful the union is relative to the firm, the more weight given to the union-preferred wage criteria and the less weight given to local labor market and firm-specific criteria.

To be more specific, within the unionized group of responding companies, those that gave greater weight to *local labor market conditions* were found to be (1) smaller; (2) in single-plant bargaining structures; (3) less unionized; (4) independent of any "pattern bargaining"; and (5) manufacturing firms in industries with higher labor-to-total-cost ratios. Conversely, firms that assigned greater

Chart 1
Scale of Company Considerations In Setting Wage and Benefit Targets

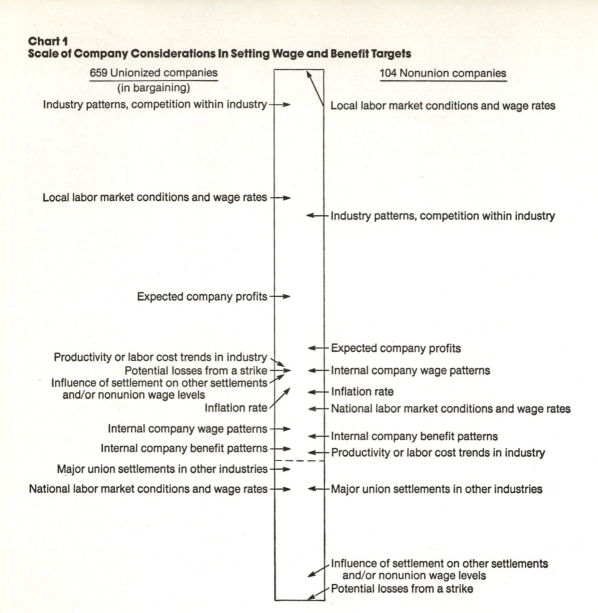

weight to *industry comparisons* were (1) larger; (2) in more centralized bargaining structures; (3) in pattern bargaining relationships; (4) more likely to be found in the transportation, communications or public utilities industries; and (5) in industries with lower labor-to-total-cost ratios (see Table 2).

Nevertheless, where unionization is present, an overall high priority was accorded to industrywide or bargaining-related criteria as opposed to local or firm-specific factors. This suggests that the majority of the firms have accommodated their wage policies to the "re-

alities" of union agenda in collective bargaining. And, even in union-free companies, as Chart 1 shows, the industry comparison has secondary importance.

Wage-Targetting Criteria in Detail

Among the surveyed companies, as a whole, the wage criteria given priority are: industry patterns and competition; local labor market conditions and wage rates; and expected profits. However, after these top three, a variety of other points were considered. These are all

"Keeping Pace" on Wages

"The general problem of wage inflation involves *many* settlements, as well as innumerable wage-setting situations not even involving a settlement.

"It comes down to the nature of the present inflation: Its dominant characteristic is that it has great inertia. That is not a terribly scientific word in economic circles. And I have found that business people often accept it and understand it more readily than textbook economists. Most simply, it describes a situation in which average wages rise about, say, seven percent this year because they rose about seven percent last year—with the current state of the labor market or the strength of demand for products having a relatively small effect in shifting the average a little higher or lower in any particular year.

"What causes this inertia? Many economists cite inflationary expectations. I believe that the process is more backward-looking (or, perhaps, sideward-looking) than that term implies. That is, firm A grants seven percent for its workers because that is what firm B did. In a world with long-term relationships between firms and their workers giving rise to what Arthur Okun has analyzed as a world of implicit contracts, fairness is important and keeping pace with other wages is an acceptable definition of what is fair. A cousin to this effect is pattern-setting in union bargaining. The verdict is not yet in on how important this is in the aggregate, but it clearly plays a part in settlements that are traditionally related. Another channel through which inertia is maintained is through the effect of price inflation back onto wages. Most prices move up with wages and some wages are, in turn, responsive to prices."[1]

shown on Chart 1, a ratio scale that depicts their respective importance.

Very few companies gave "national" labor markets first (or even second or third) mention. However, a very small but noticeable group of companies placed high importance on major union settlements in other industries. On closer examination, these companies are not "all of a kind," nor are they all major national companies with companywide bargaining units. Nine, in fact, are companies bargaining plant by plant, and four are single-plant companies.

Companies were also asked to indicate the factors considered in setting wage and benefit targets for their *largest bargaining unit* so that this could be compared with companywide factor rankings. Divergent rankings would suggest a degree of union power in major units (but only in major units) that forces the company to shift considerations. It could also imply that management purposely makes exceptional policy for its biggest unionized group. The two sets of rankings, however, were almost completely parallel. At the major bargaining unit, there is slightly more relative weight given to the productivity or labor-cost factor—perhaps because it is more susceptible of exact quantification in a particular unit such as one plant.

Nonunion Companies Rank the Considerations

The most noticeable aspect of the nonunion companies' considerations is much more diffusion among the criteria that are taken into account in wage setting. The nonunion respondents cited such items as "internal company wage patterns" more often, and also national labor market conditions and wage rates. The citation of consumer price inflation suggests that, even without union pressure,

[1]George L. Perry, in *Wage, Price, and Credit Controls in America: Pros, Cons and Prospects.* The Conference Board, Information Bulletin No. 58, May 1979.

managements incorporate some concepts of real-wage maintenance into their wage policies.

Without union pressure, nonunion companies more freely stress those comparisons that are particularly important to their individual situations. Withal, nonunion companies are most likely to base their wages on local area wage rates, as already noted.

Bargaining Structure and Wage Target Factors

The unionized company's emphasis on industry patterns is even stronger in companies with a centralized, multiplant bargaining structure. Decentralized, plant-by-plant bargainers are somewhat more able to use local wage rates as a primary criterion (see Table 1). In this respect, plant-by-plant bargainers are more like nonunion companies.

The effect of master contract bargaining units is particularly noticeable in the rating of local wage levels as *"not considered"* by one fifth or more of the multiplant bargainers. These master contract companies are most clearly dealing with an "industry rate." However, there is no commensurately heavy downgrading of industry patterns by the single-plant bargainers. This is why industry patterns receive the highest rating for the unionized companies taken as an undifferentiated group.

Industry Choice of Factors

Industry rankings of factors show less pattern than the grouping by bargaining structure. Great emphasis on industry pattern is reported by utilities—which also have centralized bargaining structures because they are "systems" rather than plants, and are highly unionized. However, retail and wholesale trade also emphasizes industry patterns—yet it is an industry with localized firms.

Local labor markets and wage rates are particularly stressed in durable goods manufacturing, but also are given substantial importance in retail and wholesale trade. They are given little or no consideration by utilities, communications, and transportation indus-

tries—the "systemwide" wage companies. Of these three industries, transportation is the only one to give major importance to potential losses from a strike in developing its bargaining targets. Communications companies cite two considerations that were seldom mentioned by others: major union settlements in other industries, and national labor market conditions and wage rates. Detailed industry responses are presented in Table 2.

Nonwage Goals

Companies often have "policies"—longstanding, companywide positions or traditions with respect to their unionized employee groups. On occasion, these may be specified as *bargaining objectives for a particular contract* negotiation. This could occur, for example, during negotiation of a first contract for a newly organized unit: Management might choose to initiate a policy stance on, for example, union security clauses. Another occasion when "policy" could become an objective or goal in a specific negotiation might occur if the company bargainers expected a union demand on an item that has long been implicit company policy or tradition. Historical examples in actual bargaining are numerous, covering subjects such as union security, cost-of-living clauses, supplemental unemployment benefits, companywide bargaining units, or other structure changes. Thus, a union drive to change some contract term that is *also* fundamental company policy, will very likely cause the company to identify the item as an "objective" in negotiations. In this case, the objective would be to maintain the status quo—the company policy—intact.

Bargaining goals or objectives outside the wage area will also include items that, while not part of company policy, complete management's agenda at each bargaining round. Eighty-seven percent of the companies in The Conference Board survey had a set of nonwage goals in their latest negotiation, in their largest bargaining unit. In terms of specific nonwage goals, companies reported objectives in eight to nine subjects per company, with the most frequent mentions: (1) paid time off; (2) flexibility on assignment of em-

Table 1
Most Important Influences on Wage and Benefit Targets, by Predominant Bargaining Structure in the Company, Multiplant Companies[1]

Factor	Plant by Plant	Multiplant, Master Contract	Multiplant Master, with Local Supplements	Multiemployer Contract
	Percent of Companies in Each Bargaining Structure Ranking Factor			
Industry patterns, competition within industry				
Ranked first	33	51	63	45
Second–third	36	32	27	27
Not considered	3	4	1	3
Local labor market conditions and wage rates				
Ranked first	36	15	11	27
Second–third	32	32	16	18
Not considered	4	20	22	30
Expected company profits				
Ranked first	16	17	10	6
Second–third	24	18	34	18
Not considered	10	12	7	18
Productivity or labor-cost trends in industry				
Ranked first	7	10	3	15
Second–third	16	23	29	24
Not considered	15	6	11	9
Potential losses from a strike				
Ranked first	5	8	4	18
Second–third	20	19	26	15
Not considered	11	19	11	12
Influence of settlement on other settlements and/or nonunion wage level				
Ranked first	3	6	1	9
Second–third	28	23	14	6
Not considered	12	17	18	18
Inflation rate				
Ranked first	2	4	3	3
Second–third	18	27	11	27
Not considered	12	10	21	9
Internal company wage patterns				
Ranked first	3	7	—	12
Second–third	14	19	7	21
Not considered	16	14	29	42
Internal company benefit patterns				
Ranked first	2	5	—	6
Second–third	12	12	5	15
Not considered	15	13	29	42
Major union settlements in other industries				
Ranked first	2	5	7	6
Second–third	10	17	18	33
Not considered	37	32	29	9
National labor market conditions and wage rates				
Ranked first	1	1	1	3
Second–third	11	16	12	15
Not considered	35	30	29	27

[1]Structure of "all or most" bargaining situations.
[2]Percentages in vertical columns add to more than 100 percent because respondents cited more than one factor in a particular rank.

Table 2
Industry Breakdown of Most Important Influences on Company Wage and Benefit Targets[1]

	Durable Goods Mfg. N = 271	Nondurable Goods Mfg. N = 194	Misc. Mfg. N = 16	Transportation N = 25	Communication N = 14	Utilities N = 70	Retail and Wholesale Trade N = 49	Construction N = 16
Industry patterns, competition within industry								
Ranked first	86	84	2	10	5	42	25	4
Second–third	90	68	4	6	4	24	12	11
Not considered	10	3	2	2	1	1	5	—
Local labor market conditions and wage rates								
Ranked first	94	47	4	3	—	9	16	10
Second–third	81	49	10	3	1	29	15	3
Not considered	22	19	—	12	1	6	2	1
Expected company profits								
Ranked first	52	26	5	1	2	10	5	—
Second–third	69	51	2	4	2	12	9	6
Not considered	21	19	2	4	2	14	11	2
Productivity or laborcost trends in industry								
Ranked first	22	9	—	2	—	5	1	3
Second–third	52	39	3	9	1	8	10	2
Not considered	32	26	2	—	—	6	11	3
Potential losses from a strike								
Ranked first	13	15	1	6	—	1	—	—
Second–third	56	49	3	3	—	5	13	4
Not considered	19	25	4	2	2	27	7	1
Influence of settlement on other settlements and/or nonunion wage level								
Ranked first	10	7	2	2	—	3	3	2
Second–third	62	48	4	7	2	14	10	7
Not considered	40	20	4	7	1	15	9	1
Inflation rate								
Ranked first	5	4	—	1	—	5	1	—
Second–third	42	31	3	8	6	27	5	3
Not considered	34	29	2	2	—	5	10	4
Internal company wage patterns								
Ranked first	11	4	2	—	—	2	—	2
Second–third	35	26	3	4	1	16	12	2
Not considered	53	30	4	11	2	8	11	7
Internal company benefit patterns								
Ranked first	5	6	—	—	—	2	—	1
Second–third	31	17	2	2	—	8	8	2
Not considered	51	23	2	11	2	9	12	8
Major union settlements in other industries								
Ranked first	7	6	1	3	5	1	—	1
Second–third	38	22	1	6	3	11	5	3
Not considered	90	72	4	3	1	23	27	4

Table 2 *(concluded)*

	Durable Goods Mfg. N=271	Nondurable Goods Mfg. N=194	Misc. Mfg. N=16	Transportation N=25	Communication N=14	Utilities N=70	Retail and Wholesale Trade N=49	Construction N=16
National labor market conditions and wage rates								
Ranked first	4	—	—	1	1	—	—	1
Second–third	34	19	1	6	6	11	1	2
Not considered	90	74	6	1	2	19	29	5

[1]Some companies gave more than one factor a "first", "second", or "third" ranking.

ployees; (3) pensions; and (4) health benefits (see Chart 2).

The list derives from two sources: expected union initiatives as well as company goals. Respondents were asked to identify areas where (1) management expected a union initiative and its goal was *to keep the status quo;* (2) management had a goal of making the existing provision *more favorable to the company* by tightening or otherwise improving it; and (3) management was prepared *to give something in exchange* for, or in trade for, something else. Thus, a lack of "mentions" in Chart 2 represents a lack of activity in that subject area—not necessarily any absence of the subject in the contracts, letters of agreement, or past practices of the employer. Even in the least frequently mentioned subjects—income security bargaining and union security arrangements—over half of the companies had a bargaining objective.

The frequency of mentions suggests relative "heat" in the subject area. *The source of the initiative,* however, is significant. For example, pension bargaining objectives were specified by more than four out of five companies. But the management plan was to tighten or take back some pension element in less than a tenth of the companies. Chart 3 depicts the company's planned position on each subject for the 568 companies identifying goals and goal achievement. The results show that, in 61 percent of the 4,939 citations, the company expected a union demand and had specified its goal as maintaining the status quo. On average, companies expected to resist about five such union initiatives. On the other hand, companies were prepared to make favorable-to-the-union offers in over

one fifth (21 percent) of all goal citations—nearly two per company. Lastly, a little over one sixth (18 percent) of the goals involved tightening up or obtaining an agreement that would be more favorable to the management.

The overall picture of company bargaining objectives in the mid-1970s is one of status quo or "stand pat" positions on the part of management. Newspaper stories about "take backs" characterizing management's stance in 1978 seem to have overemphasized a few situations. The survey data show management anticipating union demands in many areas, willing to trade on a limited number of subjects (chiefly on funded benefits), and seeking favorable exchanges from the union in one subject area: flexibility in assignment of employees.

Company Objectives

Management negotiators are guided by company objectives that have been developed in advance. These objectives reflect (1) the reality of the company's current financial position; (2) the union's agenda and power; and (3) a variety of external trends and pressures that—to some extent—"pattern" the anticipations and analyses of both bargaining parties.

When analyzed by a yardstick internal to each company individually, bargaining over *benefit items* contains a substantial potential for exchange: Companies planned to "give" almost as many times as they planned to "hold the line." On the other hand, company positions on those nonwage items that clearly might be called institutional relationships, and/or affect supervision of the work force,

Chart 2
Management Nonwage Goals (percent of 568 responding companies with a goal in area)

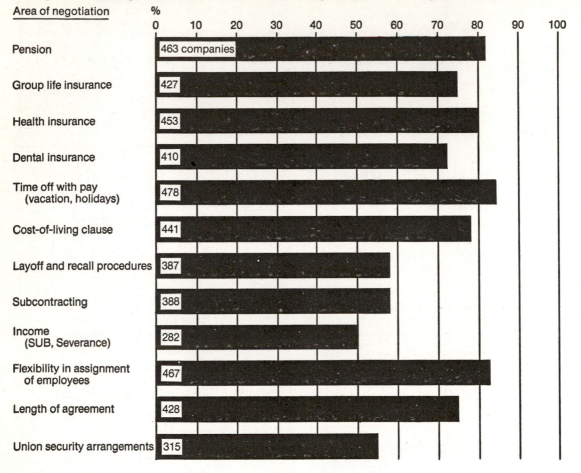

Area of negotiation

Area of negotiation	
Pension	463 companies
Group life insurance	427
Health insurance	453
Dental insurance	410
Time off with pay (vacation, holidays)	478
Cost-of-living clause	441
Layoff and recall procedures	387
Subcontracting	388
Income (SUB, Severance)	282
Flexibility in assignment of employees	467
Length of agreement	428
Union security arrangements	315

ranged from "stand pat" to "take back." There was little room for exchange in this territory. The fairly clear distinction between trading and nontrading territories may bear a very light touch of rationale:

The nontrading territory is more associated with incalculable (but potentially major) costs; with productivity-altering outcomes; with institutionalizing the union as a participant in work force direction. The trading territory, on the other hand, is simply "money."

The itemized nonwage objectives shown in Chart 3 are discussed in detail below.

Funded Benefits. A high proportion of all companies had specific bargaining goals in this area, many of them planning to offer benefit liberalization, or entirely new benefit items, in exchange for another goal that management was seeking. This was particularly true in the pension area, where 38 percent of responding companies planned to liberalize the program. In some cases, where bringing the plan into compliance with the Employee Retirement and Income Security Act (ERISA) may have required changes, the high response for "give" on this item may include some such liberalizations that were treated as bargaining chips for exchange in union negotiations.

Health benefits was a second area of "give." A third of the companies reported plans to use added health benefits in exchange for some other item, and 30 percent planned to use life insurance in this way. The elements for trading may have been wage or other items and union demands in the benefit area.

Chart 3
Management Nonwage Goals (nature of the objective)

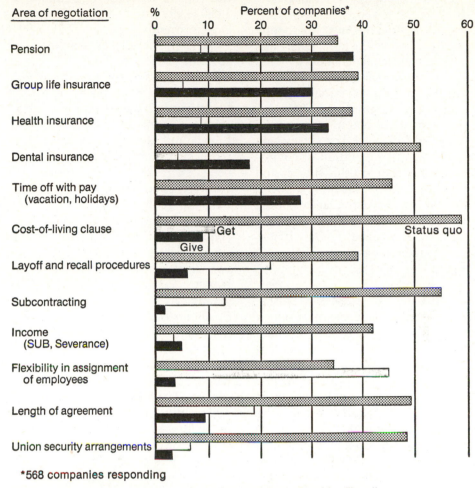

*568 companies responding

▨ Goal was to keep the status quo in face of union pressure to add or liberalize.
☐ Goal was to tighten existing provision or get a more favorable one.
■ Goal was to offer a specific element in trade for something else.

It seems less likely that the trading plan extended outside of the wage-benefit area, into other parts of the list in Chart 3.

For each of the four benefit areas identified, less than 10 percent of the companies indicated an objective of tightening, or "getting back" something previously negotiated. Thus, within the benefit area the trading may be primarily a company-anticipated union demand for benefit liberalization A; to be resisted by the company, which planned to offer liberalization of Type B (or Type A–1) instead.

Company interviews, and the survey pretest, suggested the great sense of risk felt by management about its benefit programs. To some extent, the price of a health-benefit package, once negotiated, is out of management's control. In the pension area, the risks are seen as even greater—particularly by companies that expect less growth in their work forces in the future. One respondent flatly stated: "We plan and monitor the bargaining on benefits even more than on wages." Another company observed that benefit changes are pattern changes (because of companywide programs) *and* they are long-term commitments that are never rescinded. Therefore, even though that company bargains plant-by-plant, its bargaining objectives on benefits are set and reviewed at corporate headquarters.

Time Off with Pay. The most frequently mentioned goals involved paid-time-off practices such as vacations and holidays. Some union leaders have identified the reduction of work time as the major union initiative of the late 1970s, giving as the primary rationale an increase in employment and in membership that was expected to follow.[2] The survey data show that the highest proportion of companies expected to bargain on this subject and had a goal (Chart 2). About half (46 percent) planned to hold the line in the face of union pressure; but 28 percent had an offer they were prepared to make (Chart 3). Only 10 percent planned to reduce paid time off in some specific respect.

Cost-of-Living Clauses. "Escalator clauses" were once considered the concern of only a few industries and unions. But, by the late 1970s, they were the subject of specific bargaining objectives in nearly four out of five (78 percent) responding companies. Hold-the-line strategy is clearly very strong: Three out of five companies had a firm goal of keeping the status quo; that is, fending it off if they have no cost-of-living clause; and not enriching its formula if they already have COLA. A little over one third (37 percent) of the largest bargaining units already had COLA clauses.

Inflation, coupled with increasing duration of union contracts, has been accompanied by growth of COLA to its present level of 43 percent of *major* bargaining agreements (a Bureau of Labor Statistics grouping of contracts covering 1,000 workers or more).[3] However,

escalators were present in only 38 percent of the smaller of these agreements (covering 1,000–4,999 workers), while 78 percent of the large contracts covering 50,000–99,999 had COLA, and it was present in *all* contracts covering 100,000 or more.[4] The median number of workers in the largest bargaining unit in companies surveyed by The Conference Board was 852, the average was 3,045.

Layoff and Recall Procedures. Layoff and recall clauses in union contracts may have been "exercised" in depth during the 1974–1975 recession, the deepest since the 1930s. Bargaining objectives on layoff and recall terms in the contract were specified by 68 percent of the companies. Two out of five (39 percent) expected union demands for a more favorable clause, and planned to resist change. Nearly a quarter of all companies (23 percent) planned to tighten their existing provisions, or obtain one more favorable (to the company.) Thus, this subject was the second most likely to have a "take-back" goal. It is closely related to flexibility in assignment of employees—the subject most likely to have a management "take-back" objective.

The role of seniority in layoff and recall procedures is central, and the scope and arrangement of seniority units in the company or plant affect the efficiency with which a work force reduction can be accomplished—and the remaining workers be reassigned for maximum productivity. In a 1972 Bureau of Labor Statistics study analyzing the layoff and recall provisions of 364 contracts, all but one assigned seniority a part in governing the order of layoff.[5] The weight given seniority relative to other factors, the order and timing of successive displacements downward in the job scale ("bumping"), and other aspects of job-placement (and replacement) moves probably represent the bulk of bargaining substance on this subject.

Subcontracting. Layoff insecurities raised by the recession also caused some union de-

[2]"Stimulating new job opportunities while increasing job security and providing workers with more leisure are the aims. We expect that thousands of additional workers will be put on the payroll" from page 1 of a United Auto Workers news release, October 2, 1977. See also "Slowing the Decline in the Auto Work Force," *Business Week*, October 25, 1976, p. 114.

[3]See U.S. Bureau of Labor Statistics, *Characteristics of Major Collective Bargaining Contracts*, July 1, 1976, Bulletin No. 2013, Table 1.4; also Victor Sheifer, "Collective Bargaining and the CPI: Escalation versus Catch-Up," *Proceedings of the 31st annual meeting*, Industrial Relations Research Association, August 29–31, 1978, p. 260.

[4]Sheifer, "Collective Bargaining," *Proceedings*, p. 259.

[5]Bureau of Labor Statistics, *Layoff, Recall, and Work-sharing Procedures*, Bulletin No. 1425-13, p. 31.

mands for more restrictions on subcontracting, "to keep more work for our members." Companies, expecting this, had specific goals of maintaining existing contract clauses in 55 percent of the bargaining cases. This was the second highest "stand pat" position, after that on cost-of-living clauses. Subcontracting restrictions appear in about half (52 percent) of major contracts (those covering 1,000 or more workers).[6] If their incidence is the same or lower among The Conference Board respondents, then a large part of the bargaining goals in this group was avoidance of any *introduction* of restrictions on subcontracting.[7]

Income Security. Half of the responding companies had an agenda on the subjects of severance pay, supplemental unemployment benefits, and similar income-security plans. This was the least often mentioned subject area for planned objectives.

A great majority of companies with objectives on this subject expected union demands for liberalizing benefits, and planned to retain the status quo. Some five percent of companies planned to liberalize—a course that was taken recently in the auto and steel industries.[8]

Flexibility in Assignment of Employees. *This was the subject on which management planned to make gains.* Eighty-two percent of all companies had a specific goal. In most cases, it was to obtain more favorable contract terms. This was the sole area in which management had a clearly positive stance: In all other subjects, management's position was preservation of the status quo. The nature of the subject area ("flexibility in assignment of employees") is relatively broad and unspecific (as opposed to, e.g., COLA). However, it would cover much of what in bargainers'

shorthand would be called "management rights terms." Thus, the objective of getting more favorable terms may be interpreted as getting back management latitude and freedom that was eroded in earlier bargains, or by arbitration. It is also possible that, just as the 1974–75 recession sharpened union awareness of some contract job protections, it also sharpened the pressure on management to adjust and readjust work assignments, schedules, work force arrangements, and the like, in ways and at speeds precluded by existing union agreements. There are data strongly suggesting that flexibility in directing the work force is *not* being sought for the purpose of removing *barriers to new technology*: major problems in that area are not reported.

Length of Agreement. Half of the companies (49 percent) planned to hold the line in the face of a specific union demand on this subject. In the early 1960s, the proportion of major agreements of three years' duration or more was two out of five.[9] It is 70 percent at present.[10] The long-term trend toward lengthened contract terms may have been encouraged by NLRB rules that prevent replacement of existing union representation during contract terms of up to three years. Cost-of-living clauses have also helped, by making long-term wage contracts responsive to inflation and thus less susceptible to bad guessing. Finally, the cost of bargaining and the attendant risks may have made short-term contracts unappealing to both parties. This mixture of causes and incentives to lengthen contract terms has not recently been interrupted by rapid inflation and the form of wage and price controls instituted in late 1978. In the first quarter of 1979, renegotiated contracts "had an average duration of 31.8 months, compared with 30.5 months when the same parties previously bargained."[11]

[6]*Characteristics of Major Collective Bargaining Agreements,* July 1, 1976, Table 7.3.

[7]An assumption that would best fit the smaller, plant-by-plant bargaining structure in the surveyed group.

[8]A fuller discussion of recent bargaining on this subject can be found in Audrey Freedman, *Security Bargains Reconsidered: SUB Severance Pay Guaranteed Work,* The Conference Board, Report No. 736, 1978.

[9]Marvin Friedman, "Discussion," *Proceedings* of the 31st annual meeting, Industrial Relations Research Association, August 1978, p. 278.

[10]*Characteristics of Major Collective Bargaining Agreements,* July 1, 1976, Table 1.4.

[11]U.S. Department of Labor, news release, April 27, 1979, p. 2.

Union Security. In addition to recognizing the union as exclusive bargaining agent for the covered employee group, employers have been asked by unions to negotiate various forms of "union security" arrangements in the contract. Essentially, these clauses promote union membership either by requiring it, or by creating strong incentives to join and remain a member. Very generally, "union shop" clauses require all employees to join within a specified time after employment—and to remain members. "Agency shop" clauses require payment of agency fees to the union, by all those who choose to remain nonmembers. "Maintenance of membership" clauses, less stringent, essentially restrict withdrawal from membership to a specified time period.

This subject was a battleground a generation ago, but by now union shop clauses are prevalent except for those 20 "right to work" states where they are prohibited. Some 71 percent of major contracts have varieties of union shop clauses, and another 7 percent have "agency" shops. Three percent have maintenance of membership and 18 percent have no specified union security other than recognition.[12]

Just under half (48 percent) of the companies had a goal of maintaining the status quo in the face of a union demand on this subject. Given the broad coverage of some kind of union security, it seems most likely that the demands expected were in the nature of a "tighter" security clause—perhaps reducing the time that a new employee can postpone joining to its legal minimum of 30 days.

EVALUATING LABOR RELATIONS PERFORMANCE

What is expected of labor relations executives and managers? How does the company measure success in managing the labor relations environment? Of course, there are punctuation-marks in the process—specific events, like negotiations, have measurable

outcomes. But the situation and trend (good or bad) of labor relations in a company comprises a process more inclusive than bargaining.

Managing labor relations, then, is directing the process and environment toward one most comfortable for the corporation. During the interview portion of the study, respondents had the most difficulty with questions directed toward this subject: What are labor relations executives trying to foster? What outcome is sought? Is there any specific objective in this company? Finally: How are you, the Corporate Vice President of Labor Relations, evaluated?

"Keeping things under control" and "making sure that there are *no surprises*" were frequent responses. Beyond this, however, there emerged a list of priority considerations on which a chief executive would judge his company's labor relations performance. *In nearly every interview the considerations were cited tentatively; and were mixed with comments that the factors could not be precisely measured; and that no one function in the corporation could be held entirely accountable for any of them.*

This sharing of accountability goes in both directions. One vice president, after citing the cost of a settlement as the major factor the CEO uses in evaluating his performance, observed: "Of course, it is the CEO's final decision on bargaining that determines this cost." Then he mused: "Well, that decision itself is taken in the context of the union's power to shut us down." After some more thought, he observed: "Of course, the actual wage cost per unit of output depends on the plant manager's adeptness in handling the labor force."

Using the evaluation considerations developed in interviews, the mail survey asked (1) *if* the company evaluates the performance of the labor relations function, and (2) on what specific criteria the evaluation is based. This series of questions was based on two judgments derived from extensive pre-test interviews. First, it appeared that one of the measures of the *importance* of the labor relations function is the extent to which it is formally or

---

[12]*Characteristics of Major Collective Bargaining Agreements,* July 1, 1976, Table 2.1.

Chart 4
Evaluation of Labor Relations Performance

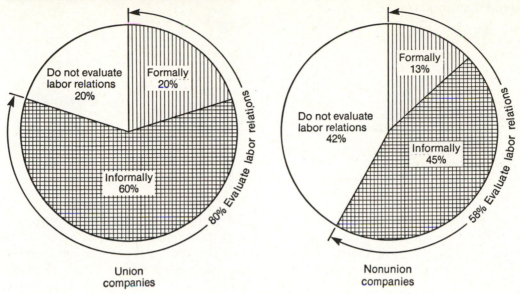

Union
companies

Nonunion
companies

informally evaluated by corporate executives. Second, the criteria or dimensions on which this judgment is based represent *an agenda of priorities that may suggest company policy* or value systems. In direct terms, the evaluation issue can be described this way: How do you know when you are doing well? And how do different kinds of companies define "doing well"? Finally, what does this suggest about the purposes of labor relations in U.S. companies at the end of the 1970s?

The results of this analysis, like much of the other material in this study, indicate that the Wild West imagery of labor relations is no longer appropriate. Management does not have a simple cowboys-and-Indians scorecard, in which the aim is only to vanquish a known adversary—the union. Labor relations now occupies a much more complex world of economic production function. The labor relations agenda resembles a more general management agenda of focusing on *economic costs* and arranging work force systems to minimize those costs per unit of output.

Not only is labor relations more complex and "economic"—it also must take account of the subtle political and social aspects of em-

ployee grouping. Employers deal with individuals, with unions, with government, with interest groups, community groups, and others—each concerned with some aspect of the workplace and the work relationship.

Extent of Evaluation

Unionized companies were more likely to evaluate their labor relations function than nonunion companies (see Chart 4). This suggests that labor relations may be more important in companies where unions already represent some workers. However, it is possible that many nonunion companies do not use the term *labor relations* or may identify the subject in personnel terms. Thus, some nonunion companies that evaluate performance may have responded negatively—but do, in fact, carefully appraise their performance in this area.

Among the companies that evaluate the function, about one quarter conduct *formal* appraisals. This proportion is the same for both union and nonunion companies that make such appraisals. While the itemization of "formality" was not developed in the sur-

Table 3
Priority of Factors Used in Evaluating Labor Relations Performance in Unionized Companies

	Number of Times Item Was Ranked				
	First	Second	Third	Fourth or Lower	Not Considered
Effect of negotiations on labor cost	281	104	53	76	9
Size of settlement compared with industry settlement	92	148	69	160	54
Employee attitudes and morale	72	101	133	200	17
Cooperative relations with union	31	71	120	273	27
New union organizing	50	57	52	257	107
Unexpected strikes during negotiations	21	39	45	299	119
Wildcat strikes during contract	5	12	28	315	163

vey, interviews suggest that it includes: (1) specification of measurements, (2) the regularity of review, and (3) possibly the level and type of executive involved in the evaluation.

Major Evaluation Factors Are Economic

For union companies, evaluation factors given greatest importance were the economic ones: (1) effects of negotiations on labor cost and (2) size of settlement compared with industry settlement.

These two criteria for judging labor relations performance clearly stood out above others, and might be said to constitute the main appraisal standards for labor relations executives and staff in the modern corporation (see Table 3). They relate directly to *contract bargaining*, and specify its *measurable economic outcome* as the most important aspect of the negotiation. So, in spite of large amounts of day-to-day labor relations handled in the company, wage rate outcomes in bargaining are a make-or-break item in judging the effectiveness of the labor relations function.

Distinctions between the Two Top Economic Factors

The difference between the two top factors, both economic, is the frame of reference. "Effects of negotiations on labor cost" has a very definite individual-company competitive orientation, while "size of settlement com-

pared with industry settlement" suggests a concern with group pattern. Cost consciousness is perhaps a sharp-pencil bargainer's criterion, while the bargainer who looks to being within an industry pattern has an implied "reasonable" limit.

The companies ranking industry wage comparisons highest were likely to be larger, paying higher wages, with greater profit-rate increases, greater bargaining-unit centralization, and a record of fewer strikes.

Comments by respondents added another element to the economic cost judgment: Labor relations is also evaluated on the *enhancement of management flexibility* achieved through its efforts. In a sense, the extent of management freedom represents the obverse of the labor union contract's provisions. *Whatever is pledged in the union contract is a restriction on management freedom.* Thus, a simple goal of maximizing management freedom would logically imply operating without a contract or a grievance procedure—in fact, a return to nonunion status. A few companies indicated that their evaluation of labor relations includes this element, but the language they used was more limited: "preservation of management rights," "absence of restrictive operating provisions," and so on. The tone of these entries suggests more of a line-holding position than aggressive dismantling of all prior accommodations to the union.

Some other entries suggest the "no surprises" desire of top management, particularly in the cost aspects of settlements: "results versus plan," "absence of problems for the Presi-

Table 4
The Effect of Labor Relations Priority on Evaluation Factors for Labor Relations Performance, in Multiplant, Unionized Companies

	Percentage of Bargainers, and of Union Containers Ranking Factor			
	First	*Second*	*Third*	*Not Considered*
Effect of negotiations on labor cost				
Bargainers[1]	60	20	8	1
Union containers[2]	45	22	14	3
Size of settlement compared with industry				
Bargainers	23	36	11	8
Union Containers	13	23	21	19
Employee attitudes				
Bargainers	11	19	28	4
Union containers	20	22	22	1
Cooperative relations with the union				
Bargainers	6	14	27	2
Union containers	6	14	18	12
New union organizing				
Bargainers,	4	7	11	37
Union containers	26	23	15	8
Unexpected strikes during negotiations				
Bargainers	5	11	12	28
Union containers	5	8	10	33
Wildcat strikes				
Bargainers	2	4	9	41
Union containers	1	2	5	56

[1]Bargainers: Companies stating that "achieving the most favorable bargain possible" was a more important labor relations function than "keeping as much of the company non-union as possible."
[2]Union containers: Companies selecting the latter over the former.

dent," and "total concessions compared with industry settlement."

The Employee Climate

A major element in evaluating labor relations performance—just below economic criteria in overall importance—is employee attitudes and morale. The emphasis is on individual workers, not on the institution of the union. So the labor relations function of corporations is expected to perform more than *union* relations—it is judged in employee relations terms as well. In fact, "employee attitudes and morale" is cited as of primary or secondary importance 173 times, while "cooperative relations with the union" receives only 102 such mentions. Companies that empha-

size union containment over bargaining optimization—the companies that are less unionized—are somewhat more likely to give employee attitudes a major role in their evaluation of labor relations performance (see Table 4).

Organization and Strikes

New union organizing is cited as a major or secondary evaluation factor 107 times—but is also rated irrelevant 107 times. There is a close correlation between the forced-choice priority on union prevention and the company's use of new union organizing as a factor in evaluating labor relations (see Table 4). For both questions, the extent of existing unionization is a major determinant of the importance that management places on union prevention. Even among companies stressing union containment, however, the economic criterion of labor cost is the preeminent evaluation factor.

Strikes are generally less important criteria for evaluation, even when they are unanticipated. As between the unexpected strike during contract negotiations and the wildcat strike, however, there is clearly a heavier emphasis on the negotiations strike. Possibly a negotiations strike is a signal to top management that the union's position or its determination has been misjudged by the labor relations executive and staff. If so, about one tenth of the responding companies judge their labor relations performance primarily in terms of foreknowledge and control in the negotiations process.

Nonunion Companies

In nonunion companies, the list of possible evaluation factors is shortened by the absence of any that relate to negotiation and wage bargaining. It would, however, be inaccurate to ascribe lack of concern for economic (wage) outcomes to nonunion companies. Their wage-setting practices operate in a different sphere—perhaps within the financial and compensation management framework.

Similarly, the possibility of strikes is nearly nonexistent, as is "cooperative relations with the union." So, it is not surprising that nonunion firms stressed *employee morale* as the major factor, and *new union organizing* as a secondary factor, in evaluating labor relations.

Overall Evaluation Factors

The list of evaluation factors in Table 3 has the interesting characteristic that complete "success" in one of them can lead to a poor record in one or more of the others. Selecting the most important performance criterion requires hard choices, but a priority may be necessary for guidance in situations where conflict develops. For example, a particularly good employee morale program might cool a cooperative union relationship, if the union becomes threatened by management-initiated communication and change. Another example: An all-out effort to cut labor costs can lead to negotiations strikes, or to wildcatting over an incompletely accepted change in "atmosphere."

Thus, when choice or priority becomes necessary, Table 3 shows that economic performance takes some precedence over employee morale. And these two take a clear precedence over institutional relations with unions.

Having recognized the potential *conflict* among items in Table 3, it is also important to see their interrelationships. That is, neglect of any of these areas of concern is likely to cause other areas to disintegrate. For example, exclusive focus on cooperative union relations could, over a period of time, lead to high-cost bargains and to poor employee morale.

The answer from interviewed companies, and from the data as a whole is: "Labor relations is responsible for *all of these*, but we judge its performance primarily by economic results."

READING 27

Plant Operation during Strikes*

Charles R. Perry†

Collective bargaining is, in the final analysis, a process of economic power accommodation. The foundation of this process is the right of unions to strike and the right of companies to take a strike in the event of an honest impasse over mandatory subjects for good faith bargaining. One potentially significant power asset available to companies in collective bargaining is their right to continue to do business by operating production facilities during a strike using nonstriking personnel. In theory, this option could play an important role in determining the basic balance of bargaining power in union-management relations in this country. In practice, however, it has not done so, because the right to operate has been little used and less discussed, at least in polite company, as a management option to augment the economic power inherent in its right to take a strike. This situation, however, seems to be changing judging by a growing number of widely publicized instances of plant operation in such firms as The Washington Post and Newport News Shipyard and such industries as the West Coast paper and San Francisco hotel industries, where operation during a strike seemed unthinkable. Thus, the time has come to bring plant operation out of the closet where it has been for the last 20 years since the prestigious Independent Study Group on the Public Interest in National Labor Policy last addressed the issue in polite company.

Plant operation is not an easy subject for dispassionate discussion and analysis. Any new power asset, whether plant operation, coalition bargaining, or mutual aid, that threatens to change significantly the balance of power already established in bargaining relationships is far more likely to be the subject of a holy war rather than of heavenly understanding. At the risk of becoming a hostage in just such a holy war, I propose to discuss and analyze the legal, philosophical, technological, and institutional considerations surrounding exercise of management's right to operate, based on the results of a study of the experience of firms that have exercised the right. This study was conducted under the auspices of the Wharton School's Industrial Research Unit and was published in 1983 under the title "Operating During Strikes."

THE RIGHT TO OPERATE

The basic right of an employer to continue to do business in the face of a strike by operating production facilities has been clearly recognized by the courts and endorsed by the Independent Study Group, which stated that "as a matter of law, we stand without compromise for the employer's right to operate his plant and the right of individuals to enter that plant despite a strike."[1] The right of an employer to utilize temporary or permanent replacements for workers engaged in an economic strike in order to continue operation is also clearly recognized under law. That right extends to the use of temporary, but not permanent, replacements for workers subject to an offensive lockout.

The right to operate and to utilize replacement workers is not absolute. It is qualified by an extensive set of federal, state, and, in some cases, local regulations governing various aspects of bargaining and employment relationships. A detailed account of all such regulations is virtually impossible given varying state and local laws. It is, however, possible to identify a limited number of basic types of le-

*Reprinted with permission from Herbert R. Northrup and Richard L. Rowan, eds., *Employee Relations and Regulation in the 80s* (Philadelphia: University of Pennsylvania, Industrial Research Unit, 1982), pp. 193–202.

†*Charles R. Perry is Associate Professor of Management and Industrial Relations at The Wharton School, University of Pennsylvania.*

[1]Committee for Economic Development, *The Public Interest in National Labor Policy* (New York: Committee for Economic Development, 1961), p. 88.

gal constraints that may impede the successful exercise of the right to operate. With no pretense of technical legal expertise, I suggest that the following are potential legal problem areas.

Federal Regulations

The basic obligation of an employer to bargain in good faith up to and beyond the point of an honest impasse is no different for an employer who operates during a strike than for one who does not. Most of the firms studied, however, indicated that they felt compelled to be particularly scrupulous in meeting this obligation in order to protect themselves from what they felt was a higher than average probability that charges would be filed by the union and pursued by the National Labor Relations Board (NLRB) because of plant operation. Two other areas in which firms felt it was advisable to be extremely careful were: (1) imposition of discipline for picket line activity; and (2) inducement of workers or replacement workers to cross the picket line.

A second area of federal regulation of concern to employers who operate during strikes is compliance with the Fair Labor Standards Act (FLSA). Companies who operate using managerial, professional, technical, supervisory, and clerical personnel as temporary replacements must determine who among those personnel is exempt and nonexempt under the FLSA and how their status may be changed by assignment to production jobs on a full-time or part-time basis for varying periods of time. The fact that most plants that operate do so using extended shifts and workweeks can create some complex legal problems and expensive overtime pay obligations that few employers wish to violate, if only to maintain morale among replacement workers.

A third area of concern to employers who operate during strikes is the Occupational Safety and Health Administration (OSHA) and, to a lesser extent, the Equal Employment Opportunity Commission (EEOC). Compliance with the requirements of those agencies regarding working conditions and work force composition may be difficult to maintain when operating with replacement personnel. Thus far, none of the firms studied has encountered serious legal challenges to continued operation during a strike from either OSHA or the EEOC, but there is apprehension that those two agencies could cause problems in the future should they choose, as OSHA is alleged to have done at Newport News by becoming actively involved on a partisan basis in a strike situation. For the most part, however, OSHA and the EEOC seem to constitute more of a bother than a barrier in plant operation for the foreseeable future, particularly in light of the outcome of OSHA's efforts at Newport News.

State Regulations

There are three areas in which firms that have operated during strikes have encountered real or potential problems under state law in some states—unemployment compensation, licensing requirements, and antistrike-breaking laws. None of these problems has represented an insurmountable barrier to operation, but all have necessitated some accommodation in method of operation at some locations.

The eligibility for unemployment compensation of workers who are unemployed due to a labor dispute in the form of either a strike or a lockout is both a complex and an emotional issue in its own right—one which need not be discussed here. The issue is further complicated by plant operation in those states that have adopted a "stoppage of work" approach to eligibility for unemployment compensation. In these states, eligibility for benefits is based on a two-step analysis beginning with a determination of whether a labor dispute exists and proceeding to a determination of whether a labor dispute has resulted in a stoppage of work at the employer's place of business. If a labor dispute results in a stoppage of work, employees are not eligible for benefits; if it does not, employees are eligible for benefits. Courts in different states have arrived at different conclusions regarding what constitutes a stoppage of work, but as a general rule, a decrease in total output of less than 20 percent in a plant operation situation may not be considered a stoppage of work for purposes of determining benefit eligibility.

State licensing laws may profoundly affect the ability of a company to operate successfully during a strike. The operation of most production facilities requires certain technical skills. Nearly all states license individuals who practice such trades as electrician, boiler operator, or, closer to home, dealers in casinos. Thus, the ability to recruit an adequate supply of fully qualified and licensed replacement personnel for such skilled jobs is crucial to successful operation during a strike without legal liability for violation of state law.

Both the federal government and certain states restrict the hiring of replacements for striking workers. The intent of both federal and state laws in this area is to prevent the use of professional strikebreakers. The relevant laws are not onerous, and most state laws may be meaningless by virtue of federal preemption of the field. Nonetheless, such laws, federal and state alike, continue to be a source of concern to employers who operate during strikes. None of the employers studied, however, yet had encountered any significant problem under those statutes.

THE DECISION TO OPERATE

There are two basic constraints on management in utilizing its right to operate during strikes. The first is the "fear of confrontation" arising out of the potential union and public relations problems that can result from plant operation during strikes. The second is the "fear of failure" arising out of the practical problems anticipated in staffing and operating a struck production facility. In combination, these institutional and technological constraints have deterred most, but not all, managements from exercising their legal right to operate during a strike. There is, however, a growing minority of managements that have overcome the fear of confrontation and failure. The obvious question is why and how.

The Commitment to Operation

Plant operation may be either an offensive or a defensive weapon for management in its relationship with a union. Historically, plant operation has tended to be viewed primarily as an offensive weapon, most likely to be used in the context of what has been termed a "conflict" relationship in which management "strongly opposes the very existence of the union" and "does more or less everything it can to prevent or eliminate unionism."[2] More recently, plant operation has been admitted to the slightly more polite company of a "power bargaining" relationship in which management "concludes that the union is there to stay, and ceases open attempts to destroy it" but "will try to keep the union weak and defensive." The invitation of plant operation to join the truly polite company of "accommodation bargaining" relationships as an acceptable management alternative to "simply closing down production when a strike is called" remains to be seen.

It is difficult to discern the blend of offensive (philosophical) and defensive (pragmatic) considerations that leads firms to pursue their option to operate during strikes. It is possible, however, to gain some insight into the question of motivation by investigating the circumstances that surround the emergence and evolution of corporate commitments to plant operation as a bargaining tactic. On the basis of such an investigation, I would offer three general observations.

Firstly, the decision to risk confrontation through plant operation generally has some pragmatic foundation. Changes in corporate policy and practice with respect to plant operation have tended to come at discrete intervals over the past 20 years—around 1960, 1970, and 1980. Each of these changes came at a time of adjustment to change in basic economic and competitive conditions which served to increase management's potential strike costs in terms of losses of both sales and customers. At a more micro level, a number of the firms studied cited a particularly painful strike situation, either immediately past or imminently prospective, as a major factor in their initial decision to attempt plant operation.

[2]E. Edward Herman and Alfred Kuhn, *Collective Bargaining and Labor Relations* (Englewood Cliffs, N.J.: Prentice-Hall, 1981), p. 79.

Secondly, the decision to risk confrontation through plant operation rarely is motivated by purely economic considerations—institutional factors also play or come to play a major role. Two of the periods of expanded use of the plant operation option—1960 and 1980—coincided with growing general management resistance to unionism and the third—1970—came at a time of growing union pressure on management. Again, at a more micro level, several of the firms studied openly admitted that their commitment to plant operation was part of a more basic change in labor relations philosophy and posture designed to shift relations from accommodation to power bargaining in an effort to regain or maintain the offensive in dealing with unions. In some cases, that change came about as a result of changes in top management and, in others, as a result of changes in union tactics—most notably, coalition bargaining.

Thirdly, plant operation, despite its offensive roots and potential, generally is not perceived or practiced as a weapon to be used to eliminate unionism. The breadth and depth of the commitment of most firms to plant operation as an offensive as well as a defensive weapon tends to grow over time, but seems to stop well short of using operation to break, rather than take, a strike. Specifically, most firms perceive the offensive limits of the plant operation to be a question of relative power, not absolute survival, and therefore avoid such measures as hiring permanent replacements or encouraging back-to-work movements that "challenge the union's status as exclusive bargaining agent . . . and thereby transform the strike from an incident in a long-term bargaining relationship to a war for survival."[3]

The Logistics of Operation

There are three basic problems confronting management in implementing a decision to operate during a strike. The first, obviously, is the recruitment of an adequate supply of

[3]Committee for Economic Development, *Public Interest*, p. 88.

qualified replacement personnel to man production operations. The second is the establishment and maintenance of ingress and egress to the plant not only for replacement personnel, but for the transport of materials and the product. The third is the protection of the security of the replacement personnel and the production facility.

These problems are rarely solved easily and are never solved well without extensive planning and detailed preparation, which is now a routine part of preparations for negotiations in firms committed to plant operation as a possible response to strike action. Such operating plans and preparations vary from company to company and plant to plant. There is, however, a fairly consistent pattern among such plans in their approach to manning, access, and security which supports the following generalizations.

The basic source of replacement labor for plant operation is nonunion personnel regularly employed within the company, including managerial, professional, technical, supervisory, and, in some cases, clerical employees. Most firms have found this pool of potential replacement personnel adequate to meet their needs, although most have had to reach beyond the struck facility to meet their needs for skilled labor, particularly in the maintenance area and in jobs requiring licenses. A few have had to do the same for unskilled labor in some of their more labor-intensive operations. Where firms have found it necessary by virtue of the scale or duration of operation to augment their own personnel by hiring from the outside, they typically have done so on a temporary basis. The hiring of permanent replacements generally is not perceived as an option to be used except in unusual circumstances.

The problem of establishing and maintaining ingress and egress is a real one and may be sufficiently troublesome to deter operation in some locations. Mass picketing, with its attendant harassment, intimidation, and, possibly, violence is not uncommon in plant operation situations. Most firms choose not to confront such activity directly by forcing the picket line. Instead, they elect to operate the plant under siege until such time as they can secure the assistance of the courts and law enforcement agencies in limiting and controlling picket activity—a choice that necessitates stockpiling of raw materials and providing for the housing and feeding in the plant of company personnel. The disruption of deliveries and shipments by truck, rail, or water may not end with effective control over mass picketing, but generally has been overcome by reliance on carrier supervisory personnel, utilization of nonunion carriers, and, in a few cases, specially trained company personnel.

The problems of harassment, intimidation, and violence are not confined to the picket line, where they can be most easily observed, documented, and, with outside assistance, controlled by management. Such activity can extend both inward and outward from the picket line and be directed at either the plant or personnel. The possibility of attempts to interrupt operation by acts of violence directed at company facilities and/or personnel on or off the plant site is a real concern of any management that chooses to operate during a strike and succeeds in doing so. Such acts are not uncommon in plant operation situations, but they rarely, if ever, reach epidemic proportions. Most vulnerable are off-site facilities, such as utility connections and pipelines, and the homes of local company personnel which are not under the security control of management. For the most part, firms have been able to rely on local police for control of violence and harassment, but in a few cases they have felt it necessary to augment such protection by extended security measures off-site as well as on-site.

The Results of Operation

Plant operation during strikes clearly is not an easy or inexpensive option to pursue, which raises the obvious question of whether it is indeed a worthwhile option. Judging by the enthusiasm of most companies which are committed to plant operation, the answer to that question is most definitely yes. That answer raises a second question regarding both the nature and the magnitude of the benefits of plant operation. Unfortunately, those benefits are difficult, if not impossible, to measure,

but they are not beyond the realm of informed speculation. On that basis, I would offer the following observations.

In the short run, plant operation serves primarily to cut losses, not to make a profit either in the marketplace or at the bargaining table, which, in effect, makes it more a defensive than an offensive tactic. Plant operation should serve to reduce the sales and revenue losses associated with a strike and limit the concessions made by management to avoid or curtail those losses. The magnitude of those benefits, not surprisingly, tends to be roughly proportional to the level of normal production attempted and achieved during strike operation . . . a level which varied among the companies studied from simply finishing work in progress to operation at close to normal capacity. Even firms at the upper end of this range, however, were reluctant to claim that their "savings" outweighed their "costs" on a short-term basis.

In the long run, plant operation during strikes appears to offer more substantial benefits in terms of both customer and union relations. Plant operation generally is felt to have beneficial long-term effects on customer retention and confidence. Similarly, plant operation also is felt to have a positive effect on union militancy, at least in the short term. In addition, firms reported that successful operation of a plant had a noticeable effect on the militancy of unions at other plants and even on the militancy of the union at the plant beyond the next one or two sets of contract negotiations. That phenomenon reflects basic union and worker skepticism regarding management's ability to operate—skepticism which seems to persist for a considerable period of time even in the face of successful operation during a strike and to reappear at varying intervals depending on degree of operating success.

Perhaps the most significant result of plant operation has been its impact on management attitudes. Success in operating plants during strikes has led many companies to be more aggressive in testing the institutional limits of their willingness to operate and the technological limits of their ability to operate. The result in most cases has been a clear lessening of both the fear of confrontation and the fear of failure with respect to specific situations and to general policies. Thus, there has been a tendency for nonoperation rather than operation to become the selective option among firms that have substantial experience in operating plants during strikes, to the point that operation is an accepted fact of life in some collective bargaining relationships.

CONCLUSIONS

The right to operate during a strike provides management with a potentially powerful weapon with which to give new meaning, and some would argue life, to its right to take a strike. Despite that fact, it is a right that has not been widely exercised by management, which has regarded plant operation as neither a popular nor an easy option to pursue. Thus, plant operation is not an integral element in our system of collective bargaining.

The fact that plant operation has not been an easy or a popular option does not mean that it has no role to play in the future of collective bargaining. Operation of struck facilities using salaried personnel has become an integral part of collective bargaining in at least two high-technology industries—telephone and oil refining—and has begun to work its way into collective bargaining in other industries such as chemicals, paper, and printing. The long-term trend toward less labor-intensive operations in most industries coupled with the growing ratio of salaried (white-collar) to hourly (blue-collar) workers in most companies suggests that plant operation may be, or may become, less difficult than has been perceived by management. That clearly has been the case for most firms that have exercised their right to operate.

Growing technological feasibility and/or management confidence in the ability to operate suggest that willingness, rather than ability, to operate will become even more important as a basic constraint on the exercise of the right to operate during strikes. Undoubtedly, the institutional costs of plant operation—short-run violence and long-run bitterness—continue to constitute a serious constraint on use of the option to operate. The desire for labor peace which underlies that constraint, however, now appears to be weakening in the management community at the same time that the costs of nonoperation during strikes seem to be increasing as a consequence of growing foreign and domestic nonunion competition.

The potential for expanded use of plant operation during strikes as a device to enhance management ability to take a strike has not gone unnoticed by the labor movement. Plant operation threatens to undermine the basic weapon used by unions in the process of economic power accommodation called collective bargaining—and it is unlikely that unions will accept this prospect passively, Thus, it is logical to expect unions to respond to any clear expansion in the use of plant operation by management with efforts to inhibit successful use of the option. The nature of such efforts remains to be seen, but several possibilities may be worth noting. One possibility is government intervention, either directly through legislation or indirectly through existing regulations. A second possibility is self-help measures such as sabotage, boycotts, and the organization of supervisory personnel.

There are few more perilous adventures than attempting to predict the future in labor relations, particularly when those in the field cannot agree as to whether the 1980s will be a decade of accommodation or of confrontation. Nonetheless, it appears that legally, economically, technologically, and, yes, philosophically, conditions in the early 1980s are favorable for expanded use of plant operation during strikes as a management power asset. What the result of these conditions will be remains to be seen and rests in your hands and the hands of the other practitioners of the arcane art of collective bargaining.

C. Collective Bargaining in the Public Sector

The determination of working conditions through collective bargaining is a growing activity among employees in the public sector. There has been much discussion pertaining to the adaptability of private sector bargaining and industrial relations techniques in the public sector, the right to strike by public employees, and the development of public policy applicable to public employee labor relations.

Wellington and Winter distinguish between the public and private sector in terms of the labor-management environment. Their article is written around the major premise that "the public sector is *not* the private, and its labor problems *are* different, very different indeed."

In the summer of 1981, President Reagan moved to fire members of the Professional Air Traffic Controllers Organization (PATCO) who had gone on strike. Air controllers, who belonged to PATCO, were employed by the federal government and, as such, they did not have the right to strike. Herbert R. Northrup discusses the strike and its significance for employee relations in the public sector.

READING 28

The Limits of Collective Bargaining in Public Employment*

Harry H. Wellington and
Ralph K. Winter†

Writing in the March 1969 issue of the *Michigan Law Review*, Mr. Theodore Kheel, the distinguished mediator and arbitrator, placed the weight of his considerable authority behind what is fast becoming the conventional wisdom. In the public sector, as in the private, Mr. Kheel argues, "the most effective technique to produce acceptable terms to resolve disputes is voluntary agreement of the parties, and the best system we have for producing agreements between groups is collective bargaining—even though it involves conflict and the possibility of a work disruption."[1] Clearly for Kheel, as for others, the insistence upon a full extension of collective bargaining—including strikes—to public employment stems from a deep commitment to that way of ordering labor-management affairs in private employment. While such a commitment may not be necessary, a minimal acceptance of collective bargaining is a condition precedent to the Kheel view. Those skeptical of the value of collective bargaining in private employment will hardly press its extension. But even if one accepts collective bargaining in the private sector . . . the claims that support it there do not, in any self-evident way, make the case for its full transplant. The public sector is *not* the private, and its labor problems *are* different, very different indeed.

---

*Reprinted from *The Unions and the Cities*, © The Brookings Institution, 1971, pp. 7–32.

†*Members of the Brookings' associated staff in Economic Studies and professors at the Yale Law School.*

[1]"Strikes and Public Employment," 67 *Michigan Law Review* 931, 942 (1969).

THE CLAIM FOR COLLECTIVE BARGAINING IN THE PRIVATE SECTOR

Four claims are made for private-sector collective bargaining. First, it is said to be a way to achieve industrial peace. The point was put as early as 1902 by the federal Industrial Commission:

The chief advantage which comes from the practice of periodically determining the conditions of labor by collective bargaining directly between employers and employees is that thereby each side obtains a better understanding of the actual state of the industry, of the conditions which confront the other side, and of the motives which influence it. Most strikes and lockouts would not occur if each party understood exactly the position of the other.[2]

Second, collective bargaining is a way of achieving industrial democracy, that is, participation by workers in their own governance. It is the industrial counterpart of the contemporary demand for community participation.[3]

Third, unions that bargain collectively with employers represent workers in the political arena as well. And political representation through interest groups is one of the most important types of political representation that the individual can have. Government at all levels acts in large part in response to the demands made upon it by the groups to which its citizens belong.[4]

Fourth, and most important, as a result of a belief in the unequal bargaining power of employers and employees, collective bargaining is claimed to be a needed substitute for individual bargaining.[5] Monopsony—a buyer's

---

[2]*Final Report of the Industrial Commission* (Washington, D.C.: U.S. Government Printing Office, 1902), p. 844.

[3]See, for example, testimony of Louis D. Brandeis before the Commission on Industrial Relations, January 23, 1915, in *Industrial Relations*, Final Report and Testimony Submitted to Congress by the Commission on Industrial Relations, S.Doc. 415, 64 Cong. 1 sess. (1916), 8, 7657–81.

[4]See, generally, H. Wellington, *Labor and the Legal Process* (New Haven, Conn.: Yale University Press, 1968), pp. 215–38.

[5]See, for example, *Final Report of the Industrial Commission*, p. 800: It is quite generally recognized that the growth of great aggregations of capital under the control of single groups of men, which is so prominent a feature

monopoly,[6] in this case a buyer of labor—is alleged to exist in many situations and to create unfair contracts of labor as a result of individual bargaining. While this, in turn, may not mean that workers as a class and over time get significantly less than they should—because monopsony is surely not a general condition but is alleged to exist only in a number of particular circumstances[7]—it may mean that the terms and conditions of employment for an individual or group of workers at a given period of time and in given circumstances may be unfair. What tends to insure fairness in the aggregate and over the long run is the discipline of the market.[8] But monopsony, if it exists, can work substantial injustice to individuals. Governmental support of collective bargaining represents the nation's response to a belief that such injustice occurs. Fairness between employee and employer in wages, hours, and terms and conditions of employment is thought more likely to be ensured where private ordering takes the collective form.[9]

There are, however, generally recognized social costs resulting from this resort to collectivism.[10] In the private sector these costs are primarily economic, and the question is, given the benefits of collective bargaining as an institution, what is the nature of the economic costs? Economists who have turned their attention to this question are legion, and disagreement among them monumental.[11] The principal concerns are of two intertwined sorts. One is summarized by Professor Albert Rees of Princeton:

If the union is viewed solely in terms of its effect on the economy, it must in my opinion be considered an obstacle to the optimum performance of our economic system. It alters the wage structure in a way that impedes the growth of employment in sectors of the economy where productivity and income are naturally high and that leaves too much labor in low-income sectors of the economy like southern agriculture and the least skilled service trades. It benefits most those workers who would in any case be relatively well off, and while some of this gain may be at the expense of the owners of capital, most of it must be at the expense of consumers and the lower-paid workers. Unions interfere blatantly with the use of the most productive techniques in some industries, and this effect is

---

of the economic development of recent years, necessitates a corresponding aggregation of workingmen into unions, which may be able also to act as units. It is readily perceived that the position of the single workman, face to face with one of our great modern combinations, such as the United States Steel Corporation, is a position of very great weakness. The workman has one thing to sell—his labor. He has perhaps devoted years to the acquirement of a skill which gives his labor power a relatively high value, so long as he is able to put it to use in combination with certain materials and machinery. A single legal person has, to a very great extent, the control of such machinery, and in particular of such materials. Under such conditions there is little competition for the workman's labor. Control of the means of production gives power to dictate to the workingman upon what terms he shall make use of them.

[6] The use of the term *monopsony* is not intended to suggest a labor market with a single employer. Rather, we mean any market condition in which the terms and conditions of employment are generally below those that would exist under perfect competition.

[7] There is by no means agreement that monopsony is a significant factor. For a theoretical discussion, see F. Machlup, *The Political Economy of Monopoly: Business, Labor and Government Policies* (Baltimore: The Johns Hopkins Press, 1952), pp. 333–79; for an empirical study, see R. Bunting, *Employer Concentration in Local Labor Markets* (University of North Carolina Press, 1962).

[8] See L. Reynolds, *Labor Economics and Labor Relations*, 3d ed. (Englewood Cliffs, N.J.: Prentice-Hall, 1961), pp. 18–19. To the extent that monopsonistic conditions exist at any particular time one would expect them to be transitory. For even if we assume a high degree of labor immobility, a low wage level in a labor market will attract outside employers. Over time, therefore, the benefits of monopsony seem to carry with them the seeds of its destruction. But the time may seem very long in the life of any individual worker.

[9] See *Labor Management Relations Act*, § 1, 29 U.S.C. § 151 (1964).

[10] The monopsony justification views collective bargaining as a system of countervailing power—that is, the collective power of the workers countervails the bargaining power of employers. See J. Galbraith, *American Capitalism: The Concept of Countervailing Power* (Boston: Houghton Mifflin, 1952), pp. 121 ff. Even if the entire line of argument up to this point is accepted, collective bargaining nevertheless seems a crude device for meeting the monopsony problem, since there is no particular reason to think that collective bargaining will be instituted where there is monopsony (or that it is more likely to be instituted there). In some circumstances collective bargaining may even raise wages above a "competitive" level. On the other hand, the collective bargaining approach is no cruder than the law's general response to perceived unfairness in the application of the freedom of contract doctrine. See Wellington, *Labor and the Legal Process*, pp. 26–38.

[11] Compare, e.g., H. Simons, "Some Reflections on Syndicalism," *Journal of Political Economy*, 1–25 (1944), with R. Lester, "Reflections on the Labor Monopoly Issue," *Journal of Political Economy* 55 (1947), p. 513.

probably not offset by the stimulus to higher productivity furnished by some other unions.[12]

The other concern is stated in the 1967 Report of the Council of Economic Advisers:

Vigorous competition is essential to price stability in a high-employment economy. But competitive forces do not and cannot operate with equal strength in every sector of the economy. In industries where the number of competitors is limited, business firms have a substantial measure of discretion in setting prices. In many sectors of the labor market, unions and managements together have a substantial measure of discretion in setting wages. The responsible exercise of discretionary power over wages and prices can help to maintain general stability. Its irresponsible use can make full employment and price stability incompatible.[13]

And the claim is that this "discretionary power" too often is exercised "irresponsibly."[14]

Disagreement among economists extends to the quantity as well as to the fact of economic malfunctioning that properly is attributable to collective bargaining.[15] But there is no disagreement that at some point the market disciplines or delimits union power. As we shall see in more detail below, union power is frequently constrained by the fact that consumers react to a relative increase in the price of a product by purchasing less of it. As a result any significant real financial benefit, beyond that justified by an increase in productivity, that accrues to workers through collective bargaining may well cause significant unemployment among union members. Because of this employment-benefit relationship, the economic costs imposed by collective bargaining as it presently exists in the private sector seem inherently limited.[16]

THE CLAIMS FOR COLLECTIVE BARGAINING IN THE PUBLIC SECTOR

In the area of public employment the claims upon public policy made by the need for industrial peace, industrial democracy, and effective political representation point toward collective bargaining. This is to say that three of the four arguments that support bargaining in the private sector—to some extent, at least—press for similar arrangements in the public sector.

Government is a growth industry, particularly state and municipal government. While federal employment between 1963 and 1970 increased from 2.5 million to 2.9 million, state and local employment rose from 7.2 to 10.1

---

[12]A. Rees, *The Economics of Trade Unions* (Chicago: University of Chicago Press, 1962), pp. 194–95. Also see H. Johnson and P. Mieszkowski, "The Effects of Unionization on the Distribution of Income: A General Equilibrium Approach," *Quarterly Journal of Economics* 84 (1970), p. 539.

[13]*Economic Report of the President together with the Annual Report of the Council of Economic Advisers*, January 1967, p. 119.

[14]Ibid., pp. 119–34. See generally J. Sheahan, *The Wage-Price Guideposts* (Washington, D.C.: Brookings Institution, 1967).

[15]See H. Lewis, *Unionism and Relative Wages in the United States: An Empirical Inquiry* (Chicago: University of Chicago Press, 1963), and earlier studies discussed therein.

[16]See generally J. Dunlop, *Wage Determination under Trade Unions* (New York: Macmillan, 1944), pp. 28–44; M. Friedman, "Some Comments on the Significance of Labor Unions for Economic Policy," in *The Impact of the Union*, ed. D. White (New York: Harcourt Brace Jovanovich, 1951), p. 204; Rees, *The Economics of the Trade Unions*, p. 50–60.

In A. Ross, *Trade Union Wage Policy* (University of California, 1948), the argument is made that the employment effect of a wage bargain is not taken into account by either employers or unions (pp. 76–93). One reason given in support of this conclusion is the difficulty of knowing what effect a particular wage bargain will have on employment. But the forecasting difficulty interferes in any pricing decision, whether it is raising the price of automobiles or of labor, and it certainly does not render the effect of an increase on the volume purchased an irrelevant consideration. Uncertainty as to the impact of a wage decision on employment does not allow union leaders to be indifferent to the fact that there is an impact. If it did, they would all demand rates of $100 per hour.

Ross's second argument is that there is only a loose connection between wage rates and the volume of employment. It is not clear what he means by this assertion. It may be a rephrasing of the uncertainty argument. Presumably he is not asserting that the demand curve for labor is absolutely vertical; although proof of that phenomenon would entitle him to the professional immortality promised by Professor Stigler (see G. Stigler, *The Theory of Price*, 3d ed. [New York: Macmillan, 1966], p. 24), the unsupported assertion hardly merits serious consideration. But if the curve is not vertical, then there is a "close connection" since the volume of employment is by hypothesis affected at every point on a declining curve. Probably he means simply that the curve is relatively inelastic, but that conclusion is neither self-evident, supported by his text, nor a proposition generally accepted on the basis of established studies.

million,[17] and the increase continues apace. With size comes bureaucracy, and with bureaucracy comes the sense of isolation of the individual workers. His manhood, like that of his industrial counterpart, seems threatened. Lengthening chains of command necessarily depersonalize the employment relationship and contribute to a sense of powerlessness on the part of the worker. If he is to share in the governance of his employment relationship as he does in the private sector, it must be through the device of representation, which means unionization.[18] Accordingly, just as the increase in the size of economic units in private industry fostered unionism, so the enlarging of governmental bureaucracy has encouraged public employees to look to collective action for a sense of control over their employment destiny. The number of government employees, moreover, makes it plain that those employees are members of an interest group that can organize for political representation as well as for job participation.[19]

The pressures thus generated by size and bureaucracy lead inescapably to disruption—to labor unrest—unless these pressures are recognized and unless existing decision-making procedures are accommodated to them. Peace in government employment too, the argument runs, can best be established by making union recognition and collective bargaining accepted public policy.[20]

Much less clearly analogous to the private model, however, is the unequal bargaining power argument. In the private sector that argument really has two aspects. The first, just adumbrated, is affirmative in nature. Monopsony is believed sometimes to result in unfair individual contracts of employment. The unfairness may be reflected in wages, which are less than they would be if the market were more nearly perfect, or in working arrangements that may lodge arbitrary power in a foreman, that is, power to hire, fire, promote, assign, or discipline without respect to substantive or procedural rules. A persistent assertion, generating much heat, relates to the arbitrary exercise of managerial power in individual cases. This assertion goes far to explain the insistence of unions on the establishment in the labor contract of rules, with an accompanying adjudicatory procedure, to govern industrial life.[21]

Judgments about the fairness of the financial terms of the public employee's individual contract of employment are even harder to make than for private-sector workers. The case for the existence of private employer monopsony, disputed as it is, asserts only that some private-sector employers in some circumstances have too much bargaining power. In the public sector, the case to be proved is that the governmental employer ever has such power. But even if this case could be proved, market norms are at best attenuated guides to questions of fairness. In employment as in all other areas, governmental decisions are properly political decisions, and economic considerations are but one criterion among many. Questions of fairness do not centrally relate to how much imperfection one sees in the market, but more to how much imperfection one sees in the political process. "Low" pay for teachers may be merely a decision—right or wrong, resulting from the pressure of special interests or from a desire to promote the general welfare—to exchange a reduction in the quality or quantity of teachers for higher welfare payments, a domed stadium, and so on. And the ability to make informed judgments about such political decisions is limited because of the understandable but unfortunate fact that the science of politics has failed to supply either as elegant or as reliable a theoretical model as has its sister discipline.

Nevertheless, employment benefits in the public sector may have improved relatively more slowly than in the private sector during

---

[17]U.S. Bureau of the Census, *Public Employment in 1970* (1971), Table 1, and Bureau of the Census, *State Distribution of Public Employment in 1963* (1964), Table 1.

[18]See *Final Report of the Industrial Commission*, p. 805; C. Summers, "American Legislation for Union Democracy," 25 *Mod. L. Rev.* 273, 275 (1962).

[19]For the "early" history, see S. Spero, *Government as Employer* (Remsen, 1948).

[20]See, for example, *Governor's Committee on Public Employee Relations, Final Report* (State of New York, 1966), pp. 9–14.

[21]See N. Chamberlain, *The Union Challenge to Management Control* (New York: Harper & Row, 1948), p. 94.

the last three decades. An economy with a persistent inflationary bias probably works to the disadvantage of those who must rely on legislation for wage adjustments.[22] Moreover, while public employment was once attractive for the greater job security and retirement benefits it provided, quite similar protection is now available in many areas of the private sector.[23] On the other hand, to the extent that civil service, or merit, systems exist in public employment and these laws are obeyed, the arbitrary exercise of managerial power is substantially reduced. Where it is reduced, a labor policy that relies on individual employment contracts must seem less unacceptable.

The second, or negative, aspect of the unequal bargaining power argument relates to the social costs of collective bargaining. As has been seen, the social costs of collective bargaining in the private sector are principally economic and seem inherently limited by market forces. In the public sector, however, the costs seem economic only in a very narrow sense and are on the whole political. It further seems that, to the extent union power is delimited by market or other forces in the public sector, these constraints do not come into play nearly as quickly as in the private. An understanding of why this is so requires further comparison between collective bargaining in the two sectors.

THE PRIVATE-SECTOR MODEL

Although the private sector is, of course, extraordinarily diverse, the paradigm is an industry that produces a product that is not particularly essential to those who buy it and for which dissimilar products can be substituted. Within the market or markets for this product, most—but not all—of the producers must bargain with a union representing their employees, and this union is generally the same throughout the industry. A price rise of this product relative to others will result in a decrease in the number of units of the product sold. This in turn will result in a cutback in employment. And an increase in price would be dictated by an increase in labor cost relative to output, at least in most situations.[24] Thus, the union is faced with some sort of rough trade-off between, on the one hand, larger benefits for some employees and unemployment for others, and on the other hand, smaller benefits and more employment. Because unions are political organizations, with a legal duty to represent all employees fairly,[25] and with a treasury that comes from per capita dues, there is pressure on the union to avoid the road that leads to unemployment.[26]

This picture of the restraints that the market imposes on collective bargaining settlements undergoes change as the variables change. On the one hand, to the extent that there are nonunion firms within a product market, the impact of union pressure will be diminished by the ability of consumers to purchase identical products from nonunion and, presumably, less expensive sources. On the other hand, to the extent that union organization of competitors within the product market is complete, there will be no such restraint and the principal barriers to union bargaining goals will be the ability of a number of consumers to react to a price change by turning to dissimilar but nevertheless substitutable products.

Two additional variables must be noted. First, where the demand for an industry's product is rather insensitive to price—that is, relatively inelastic—and where all the firms in a product market are organized, the union need fear less for employment-benefit trade-

---

[22]This is surely one reason that might explain the widely assumed fact that public employees have fallen behind their private sector counterparts. See J. Stieber, "Collective Bargaining in the Public Sector," in *Challenges to Collective Bargaining*, ed. L. Ulman (Englewood Cliffs, N.J.: Prentice-Hall, 1967), pp. 65, 69.

[23]See G. Taylor, "Public Employment: Strikes or Procedures?" 20 *Industrial and Labor Relations Review* (1967), pp. 617, 623–25.

[24]The cost increase may, of course, take some time to work through and appear as a price increase. See Rees, *The Economics of Trade Unions*, pp. 107–9. In some oligopolistic situations the firm may be able to raise prices after a wage increase without suffering a significant decrease in sales.

[25]*Steele v. Louisville & Nashville Railroad Co.*, 323 U.S. 192 (1944).

[26]The pressure is sometimes resisted. Indeed, the United Mine Workers has chosen more benefits for less employment. See generally M. Baratz, *The Union and the Coal Industry* (New Haven, Conn.: Yale University Press, 1955).

off, for the employer is less concerned about raising prices in response to increased costs. By hypothesis, a price rise affects unit sales of such an employer only minimally. Second, in an expanding industry, wage settlements that exceed increases in productivity may not reduce union employment. They will reduce expansion, hence the employment effect will be experienced only by workers who do not belong to the union. This means that in the short run the politics of the employment-benefit trade-off do not restrain the union in its bargaining demands.

In both of these cases, however, there are at least two restraints on the union. One is the employer's increased incentive to substitute machines for labor, a factor present in the paradigm and all other cases as well. The other restraint stems from the fact that large sections of the nation are unorganized and highly resistant to unionization.[27] Accordingly, capital wil seek nonunion labor, and in this way the market will discipline the organized sector.

The employer, in the paradigm and in all variations of it, is motivated primarily by the necessity to maximize profits (and this is so no matter how political a corporation may seem to be). He therefore is not inclined (absent an increase in demand for his product) to raise prices and thereby suffer a loss in profits, and he is organized to transmit and represent the market pressures described above. Generally he will resist, and resist hard, union demands that exceed increases in productivity, for if he accepts such demands he may be forced to raise prices. Should he be unsuccessful in his resistance too often, and should it or the bargain cost him too much, he can be expected to put his money and energy elsewhere.[28]

What all this means is that the social costs imposed by collective bargaining are economic costs; that usually they are limited by powerful market restraints; and that these restraints are visible to anyone who is able to see the forest for the trees.[29]

THE PUBLIC-SECTOR MODEL: MONETARY ISSUES

The paradigm in the public sector is a municipality with an elected city council and an elected mayor who bargains (through others) with unions representing the employees of the city. He bargains also, of course, with other permanent and ad hoc interest groups making claims upon government (business groups, save-the-park committees, neighborhood groups, and so forth). Indeed, the decisions that are made may be thought of roughly as a result of interactions and accommodations among these interest groups, as influenced by perceptions about the attitudes of the electorate and by the goals and programs of the mayor and his city council.[30]

Decisions that cost the city money are generally paid for from taxes and, less often, by borrowing. Not only are there many types of taxes but also there are several layers of government that may make tax revenue available to the city; federal and state as well as local funds may be employed for some purpose. Formal allocation of money for particular uses is made through the city's budget, which may have within it considerable room for adjustments.[31] Thus, a union will bargain hard for as large a share of the budget as it thinks it possibly can obtain, and even try to force a tax increase if it deems that possible.

[27]See H. Cohany, "Trends and Changes in Union Membership," 89 *Monthly Lab. Rev.* (1966), pp. 510–13; I. Bernstein, "The Growth of American Unions, 1945–1960," *Labor History* 2 (1961), pp. 131–57.

[28]And the law would protect him in this. Indeed, it would protect him if he were moved by an antiunion animus as well as by valid economic considerations. See *Textile Workers Union of America v. Darlington Manufacturing Co.*, 380 U.S. 263 (1965).

Of course, where fixed costs are large relative to variable costs, it may be difficult for an employer to extricate himself.

[29]This does not mean that collective bargaining in the private sector is free of social costs. It means only that the costs are necessarily limited by the discipline of the market.

[30]See generally R. Dahl, *Who Governs? Democracy and Power in an American City* (New Haven, Conn.: Yale University Press, 1961). On interest group theory generally, see D. Truman, *The Government Process: Political Interests and Public Opinion*, 3d printing, (New York: Alfred A. Knopf, 1955).

[31]See, for example, W. Sayre and H. Kaufman, *Governing New York City: Politics in the Metropolis* (New York: Russell Sage Foundation, 1960), pp. 366–72.

In the public sector, too, the market operates. In the long run, the supply of labor is a function of the price paid for labor by the public employer relative to what workers earn elsewhere.[32] This is some assurance that public employees in the aggregate—with or without collective bargaining—are not paid too little. The case for employer monopsony, moreover may be much weaker in the public sector than it is in the private. First, to the extent that most public employees work in urban areas, as they probably do, there may often be a number of substitutable and competing private and public employers in the labor market. When that is the case, there can be little monopsony power.[33] Second, even if public employers occasionally have monopsony power, governmental policy is determined only in part by economic criteria, and there is no assurance, as there is in the private sector where the profit motive prevails, that the power will be exploited.

As noted, market-imposed unemployment is an important restraint on unions in the private sector. In the public sector, the trade-off between benefits and employment seems much less important. Government does not generally sell a product the demand for which is closely related to price. There usually are not close substitutes for the products and services provided by government and the demand for them is relatively inelastic. Such market conditions are favorable to unions in the private sector because they permit the acquisition of benefits without the penalty of unemployment, subject to the restraint of nonunion competitors, actual or potential. But no such restraint limits the demands of public employee unions. Because much government activity is, and must be, a monopoly, product competition, nonunion or otherwise, does not exert a downward pressure on prices and wages. Nor will the existence of a pool of labor ready to work for a wage below union scale attract new capital and create a new, and competitively less expensive, governmental enterprise.

The fear of unemployment, however, can serve as something of a restraining force in two situations. First, if the cost of labor increases, the city may reduce the quality of the service it furnishes by reducing employment. For example, if teachers' salaries are increased, it may decrease the number of teachers and increase class size. However, the ability of city government to accomplish such a change is limited not only by union pressure but also by the pressure of other affected interested groups in the community.[34] Political considerations, therefore, may cause either no reduction in employment or services, or a reduction in an area other than that in which the union members work. Both the political power exerted by the beneficiaries of the services, who are also voters, and the power of the public employee union as a labor organization then combine to create great pressure on political leaders either to seek new funds or to reduce municipal services of another kind. Second, if labor costs increase, the city, like a private employer, may seek to replace labor with machines. The absence of a profit motive, and a political concern for unemployment, however, may be deterrents in addition to the deterrent of union resistance. The public employer that decides it must limit employment because of unit labor costs will likely find that the politically easiest decision is to restrict new hirings rather than to lay off current employees.

Where pensions are concerned, moreover, major concessions may be politically tempting since there is no immediate impact on the taxpayer or the city budget. Whereas actuarial soundness would be insisted on by a profit-

---

[32]See M. Moskow, *Teachers and Unions* (Philadelphia: University of Pennsylvania, Wharton School of Finance and Commerce, Industrial Research Unit, 1966), pp. 79–86.

[33]This is based on the reasonable but not unchallengeable assumption that the number of significant employers in a labor market is related to the existence of monopsony. See R. Bunting, *Employer Concentration in Local Labor Markets*, pp. 3–14. The greater the number of such employers in a labor market, the greater the departure from the classic case of the monopsony of a single employer. The number of employers would clearly seem to affect their ability to make and enforce a collusive wage agreement

[34]Organized parent groups, for example. Compare the unsuccessful attempt of the New York City Board of Education to reduce the employment of substitute teachers in the public schools in March 1971. *New York Times*, March 11, 1971, p. 1.

seeking entity like a firm, it may be a secondary concern to politicians whose conduct is determined by relatively short-run considerations. The impact of failing to adhere to actuarial principles will frequently fall upon a different mayor and a different city council. In those circumstances, concessions that condemn a city to future impoverishment may not seem intolerable.

Even if a close relationship between increased economic benefits and unemployment does not exist as a significant deterrent to unions in the public sector, might not the argument be made that in some sense the taxpayer is the public sector's functional equivalent of the consumer? If taxes become too high the taxpayer can move to another community. While it is generally much easier for a consumer to substitute products than for a taxpayer to substitute communities, is it not fair to say that, at the point at which a tax increase will cause so many taxpayers to move that it will produce less total revenue, the market disciplines or restrains union and public employer in the same way and for the same reasons that the market disciplines parties in the private sector? Moreover, does not the analogy of the private sector suggest that it is legitimate in an economic sense for unions to push government to the point of substitutability?

Several factors suggest that the answer to this latter question is at best indeterminate, and that the question of legitimacy must be judged not by economic but by political criteria.

In the first place, there is not theoretical reason—economic or political—to suppose that it is desirable for a governmental entity to liquidate its taxing power, to tax up to the point where another tax increase will produce less revenue because of the number of people it drives to different communities. In the private area, profit maximization is a complex concept, but its approximation generally is both a legal requirement and socially useful as a means of allocating resources.[35] The liquidation of taxing power seems neither imperative nor useful.

Second, consider the complexity of the tax structure and the way in which different kinds of taxes (property, sales, income) fall differently upon a given population. Consider, moreover, that the taxing authority of a particular governmental entity may be limited (a municipality may not have the power to impose an income tax). What is necessarily involved, then, is principally the redistribution of income by government rather than resource allocation,[36] and questions of income redistribution surely are essentially political questions.[37]

For his part, the mayor in our paradigm will be disciplined not by a desire to maximize profits but by a desire—in some cases at least—to do a good job (to implement his programs), and in virtually all cases by a wish either to be reelected or to move to a better elective office. What he gives to the union must be taken from some other interest group or from taxpayers. His is the job of coordinating these competing claims while remaining politically viable. And that coordination will be governed by the relative power of the competing interest groups. Coordination, moreover, is not limited to issues involving the level of taxes and the way in which tax moneys are spent. Nonfinancial issues also require coordination, and here too the outcome turns upon the relative power of interest groups. And relative power is affected importantly by the scope of collective bargaining.

THE PUBLIC-SECTOR MODEL: NONMONETARY ISSUES

In the private sector, unions have pushed to expand the scope of bargaining in response to the desires of their members for a variety of

---

[35]See generally R. Dorfman, *Prices and Markets* (Englewood Cliffs, N.J.: Prentice-Hall, 1967).

[36]In the private sector what is involved is principally resource allocation rather than income redistribution. Income redistribution occurs to the extent that unions are able to increase wages at the expense of profits, but the extent to which this actually happens would seem to be limited. It also occurs if unions, by limiting employment in the union sector through maintenance of wages above a competitive level, increase the supply of labor in the nonunion sector and thereby depress wages there.

[37]In the private sector the political question was answered when the National Labor Relations Act was passed: The benefits of collective bargaining (with the strike) outweigh the social costs.

new benefits (pension rights, supplementary unemployment payments, merit increases). These benefits generally impose a monetary cost on the employer. And because employers are restrained by the market, an expanded bargaining agenda means that, if a union negotiates an agreement over more subjects, it generally trades off more of less for less of more.

From the consumer's point of view this in turn means that the price of the product he purchases is not significantly related to the scope of bargaining. And since unions rarely bargain about the nature of the product produced,[38] the consumer can be relatively indifferent as to how many or how few subjects are covered in any collective agreement.[39] Nor need the consumer be concerned about union demands that would not impose a financial cost on the employer, for example, the design of a grievance procedure. While such demands are not subject to the same kind of trade-off as are financial demands, they are unlikely, if granted, to have any impact on the consumer. Their effect is on the quality of life of the parties to the agreement.

In the public sector the cluster of problems that surround the scope of bargaining are much more troublesome than they are in the private sector. The problems have several dimensions.

---

[38]The fact that American unions and management are generally economically oriented is a source of great freedom to us all. If either the unions or management decided to make decisions about the nature of services provided or products manufactured on the basis of their own ideological convictions, we would all, as consumers, be less free. Although unions may misallocate resources, consumers are still generally able to satisfy strong desires for particular products by paying more for them and sacrificing less valued items. This is because unions and management generally make no attempt to adjust to anything but economic considerations. Were it otherwise, and the unions—or management—insisted that no products of a certain kind be manufactured, consumers would have much less choice.

[39]The major qualification to these generalizations is that sometimes unions can generate more support from the membership for certain demands than for others (more for the size of the work crew, less for wage increases). Just how extensive this phenomenon is, and how it balances out over time, is difficult to say; however, it would not seem to be of great importance in the overall picture.

First, the trade-off between subjects of bargaining in the public sector is less of a protection to the consumer (public) than it is in the private. Where political leaders view the costs of union demands as essentially budgetary, a trade-off can occur. Thus, a demand for higher teacher salaries and a demand for reduced class size may be treated as part of one package. But where a demand, although it has a budgetary effect, is viewed as involving essentially political costs, trade-offs are more difficult. Our paradigmatic mayor, for example, may be under great pressure to make a large monetary settlement with a teachers' union whether or not it is joined to demands for special training programs for disadvantaged children. Interest groups tend to exert pressure against union demands only when they are directly affected. Otherwise, they are apt to join that large constituency (the general public) that wants to avoid labor trouble. Trade-offs can occur only when several demands are resisted by roughly the same groups. Thus, pure budgetary demands can be traded off when they are opposed by taxpayers. But when the identity of the resisting group changes with each demand, political leaders may find it expedient to strike a balance on each issue individually, rather than as part of a total package, by measuring the political power of each interest group involved against the political power of the constituency pressing for labor peace. To put it another way, as important as financial factors are to a mayor, political factors may be even more important. The market allows the businessman no such discretionary choice.

Where a union demand—such as increasing the disciplinary power of teachers—does not have budgetary consequences, some trade-offs may occur. Granting the demand will impose a political cost on the mayor because it may anger another interest group. But because the resisting group may change with each issue, each issue is apt to be treated individually and not as a part of a total package. And this may not protect the public. Differing from the private sector, nonmonetary demands of public-sector unions do have effects that go beyond the parties to the agreement. All of us have a stake in how school children are disciplined. Expansion of the subjects of bargaining in the public sector, therefore, may increase the total quantum of union power in the political process.

Second, public employees do not generally produce a product. They perform a service. The way in which a service is performed may become a subject of bargaining. As a result, the nature of that service may be changed. Some of these services—police protection, teaching, health care—involve questions that are politically, socially, or ideologically sensitive. In part this is because government is involved, and alternatives to governmentally provided services are relatively dear. In part, government is involved because of society's need for it. This suggests that decisions affecting the nature of a governmentally provided service are much more likely to be challenged and are more urgent than generally is the case with services that are offered privately.

Third, some of the services government provides are performed by professionals—teachers, social workers, and so forth—who are keenly interested in the underlying philosophy that informs their work. To them, theirs is not merely a job to be done for a salary. They may be educators or other "change agents" of society. And this may mean that these employees are concerned with more than incrementally altering a governmental service or its method of delivery. They may be advocates of bold departures that will radically transform the service itself.

The issue is not a threshold one of whether professional public employees should participate in decisions about the nature of the services they provide. Any properly run governmental agency should be interested in, and heavily reliant upon, the judgment of its professional staff. The issue rather is the method of that participation.

Conclusions about this issue as well as the larger issue of a full transplant of collective bargaining to the public sector may be facilitated by addressing some aspects of the governmental decision-making process—particularly at the municipal level—and the impact of collective bargaining on that process.

PUBLIC EMPLOYEE UNIONS AND THE POLITICAL PROCESS

Although the market does not discipline the union in the public sector to the extent that it does in the private, the municipal employment paradigm, nevertheless, would seem to be consistent with what Robert A. Dahl has called the "'normal' American political process," which is "one in which there is a high probability that an active and legitimate group in the population can make itself heard effectively at some crucial stage in the process of decision," for the union may be seen as little more than an "active and legitimate group in the population."[40] With elections in the background to perform, as Mr. Dahl notes, "the critical role . . . in maximizing political equality and popular sovereignty,"[41] all seems well, at least theoretically, with collective bargaining and public employment.

But there is trouble even in the house of theory if collective bargaining in the public sector means what it does in the private. The trouble is that if unions are able to withhold labor—to strike—as well as to employ the usual methods of political pressure, they may possess a disproportionate share of effective power in the process of decision. Collective bargaining would then be so effective a pressure as to skew the results of the "'normal' American political process."

One should straightaway make plain that the strike issue is not simply the importance of public services as contrasted with services or products produced in the private sector. This is only part of the issue, and in the past the partial truth has beclouded analysis.[42] The services performed by a private transit authority are neither less nor more important to the public than those that would be performed if the transit authority were owned by a municipality. A railroad or a dock strike may be more damaging to a community than "job action" by police. This is not to say that gov-

---

[40]R. Dahl, *A Preface to Democratic Theory* (Chicago: University of Chicago Press, 1956), p. 145.

[41]Ibid., pp. 124–25.

[42]See, for example, Spero, *Government as Employer*, pp. 1–15.

ernmental services are not important. They are, both because the demand for them is inelastic and because their disruption may seriously injure a city's economy and occasionally impair the physical welfare of its citizens. Nevertheless, the importance of governmental services is only a necessary part of, rather than a complete answer to, the question: Why be more concerned about strikes in public employment than in private?

The answer to the question is simply that, because strikes in public employment disrupt important services, a large part of a mayor's political constituency will, in many cases, press for a quick end to the strike with little concern for the cost of settlement. This is particularly so where the cost of settlement is borne by a different and larger political constituency, the citizens of the state or nation. Since interest groups other than public employees, with conflicting claims on municipal government, do not, as a general proposition, have anything approaching the effectiveness of the strike—or at least cannot maintain that relative degree of power over the long run—they may be put at a significant competitive disadvantage in the political process.

The private-sector strike is designed to exert economic pressure on the employer by depriving him of revenues. The public employee strike is fundamentally different: Its sole purpose is to exert political pressure on municipal officials. They are deprived, not of revenues but of the political support of those who are inconvenienced by a disruption of municipal services. But precisely because the private strike is an economic weapon, it is disciplined by the market and the benefit-unemployment trade-off that imposes. And because the public employee strike is a political weapon, it is subject only to the restraints imposed by the political process and they are on the whole less limiting and less disciplinary than those of the market. If this is the case, it must be said that the political process will be radically altered by wholesale importation of the strike weapon. And because of the deceptive simplicity of the analogy to collective bargaining in the private sector, the alteration may take place without anyone realizing what has happened.

Nor is it an answer that, in some municipalities, interest groups other than unions now have a disproportionate share of political power. This is inescapably true, and we do not condone that situation. Indeed, we would be among the first to advocate reform. However, reform cannot be accomplished by giving another interest group disproportionate power, for the losers would be the weakest groups in the community. In most municipalities, the weakest groups are composed of citizens who many believe are most in need of more power.

Therefore, while the purpose and effect of strikes by public employees may seem in the beginning designed merely to establish collective bargaining or to "catch up" with wages and fringe benefits in the private sector, in the long run strikes may become too effective a means for redistributing income; so effective, indeed, that one might see them as an institutionalized means of obtaining and maintaining a subsidy for union members.[43]

As is often the case when one generalizes, this picture may be considered overdrawn. In order to refine analysis, it will be helpful to distinguish between strikes that occur over monetary issues and strikes involving nonmonetary issues. The generalized picture sketched above is mainly concerned with the former. Because there is usually no substitute for governmental services, the citizen-consumer faced with a strike of teachers, or garbage men, or social workers is likely to be seriously inconvenienced. This in turn places enormous pressure on the mayor, who is apt to find it difficult to look to the long-run balance sheet of the municipality. Most citizens are directly affected by a strike of sanitation workers. Few, however, can decipher a municipal budget or trace the relationship between today's labor settlement and next year's increase in the mill rate. Thus, in the typical case the impact of a settlement is less visible—or can more often be concealed—than the impact of a disruption of services. Moreover, the cost of settlement may fall upon a constituency much larger—the whole state or nation—than that represented by the mayor.

---

[43]Strikes in some areas of the private sector may have this effect, too.

And revenue-sharing schemes that involve unrestricted funds may further lessen public resistance to generous settlements. It follows that the mayor usually will look to the electorate that is clamoring for a settlement, and in these circumstances the union's fear of a long strike, a major check on its power in the private sector, is not a consideration.[44] In the face of all of these factors other interest groups with priorities different from the union's are apt to be much less successful in their pursuit of scarce tax dollars than is the union with power to withhold services.[45]

With respect to strikes over some nonmonetary issues—decentralization of the governance of schools might be an example—the intensity of concern on the part of well-organized interest groups opposed to the union's position would support the mayor in his resistance to union demands. But even here, if the union rank-and-file back their leadership, pressures for settlement from the general public, which may be largely indifferent as to the underlying issue, might in time become irresistible.[46]

The strike and its threat, moreover, exacerbate the problems associated with the scope of bargaining in public employment. This seems clear if one attends in slightly more detail to techniques of municipal decision making.

Few students of our cities would object to Herbert Kaufman's observation that:

> Decisions of the municipal government emanate from no single source, but from many centers; conflicts and clashes are referred to no single authority, but are settled at many levels and at many points in the system: no single group can guarantee the success of any proposal it supports, the defeat of every idea it objects to. Not even the central governmental organs of the city—the Mayor, the Board of Estimate, the Council—individually or in combination, even approach mastery in this sense.

> Each separate decision center consists of a cluster of interested contestants, with a "core group" in the middle, invested by the rules with the formal authority to legitimize decisions (that is to promulgate them in binding form) and a constellation of related "satellite groups" seeking to influence the authoritative issuances of the core group.[47]

Nor would many disagree with Nelson W. Polsby when, in discussing community decision making that is concerned with an alternative to a "current state of affairs," he argues that the alternative "must be politically palatable and relatively easy to accomplish; otherwise great amounts of influence have to be brought to bear with great skill and efficiency in order to secure its adoption."[48]

It seems probable that such potential subjects of bargaining as school decentralization and a civilian police review board are, where they do not exist, alternatives to the "current state of affairs," which are not "politically palatable and relatively easy to accomplish." If a teachers' union or a police union were to bargain with the municipal employer over these questions, and were able to use the strike to insist that the proposals not be adopted, how much "skill and efficiency" on the part of the proposals' advocates would be necessary to effect a change? And, to put the shoe on the other foot, if a teachers' union were to insist through collective bargaining (with the strike or its threat) upon major changes in school curriculum, would not that union have to be considerably less skillful and efficient in the normal political process than other advocates

---

[44]Contrast the situation in the private sector: "Management cannot normally win the short strike. Management can only win the long strike. Also management frequently tends, in fact, to win the long strike. As a strike lengthens, it commonly bears more heavily on the union and the employees than on management. Strike relief is no substitute for a job. Even regular strike benefits, which few unions can afford, and which usually exhaust the union treasury quite rapidly (with some exceptions), are no substitute for a job." E. Livernash, "The Relation of Power to the Structure and Process of Collective Bargaining," *Journal of Law & Economics* 6 (October 1963), pp. 10, 15.

[45]A vivid example was provided by an experience in New Jersey. After a 12-hour strike by Newark firefighters on July 11, 1969, state urban aid funds, originally authorized for helping the poor, were diverted to salary increases for firemen and police. See *New York Times*, August, 7, 1969, p. 25. Moreover, government decision makers other than the mayor (for example, the governor) may have interests different from those of the mayor, interests that manifest themselves in pressures for settlement.

[46]Consider also the effect of such strikes on the fabric of society. See, for example, M. Mayer, *The Teachers Strike: New York, 1968* (New York: Harper & Row, 1969).

[47]"Metropolitan Leadership," quoted in N. Polsby, *Community Power and Political Theory* (New Haven, Conn.: Yale University Press, 1963), pp. 127–28.

[48]Ibid., p. 135.

of community change? The point is that with respect to some subjects, collective bargaining may be too powerful a lever on municipal decision making, too effective a technique for changing or preventing the change of one small but important part of the "current state of affairs."

Unfortunately, in this area the problem is not merely the strike threat and the strike. In a system where impasse procedures involving third parties are established in order to reduce work stoppages—and this is common in those states that have passed public employment bargaining statutes—third-party intervention must be partly responsive to union demands. If the scope of bargaining is open-ended, the neutral party, to be effective, will have to work out accommodations that inevitably advance some of the union's claims some of the time. And the neutral, with his eyes fixed on achieving a settlement, can hardly be concerned with balancing all the items on the community agenda or reflecting the interests of all relevant groups.

THE THEORY SUMMARIZED

Collective bargaining in public employment, then, seems distinguishable from that in the private sector. To begin with, it imposes on society more than a potential misallocation of resources through restrictions on economic output, the principal cost imposed by private-sector unions. Collective bargaining by public employees and the political process cannot be separated. The costs of such bargaining, therefore, cannot be fully measured without taking into account the impact on the allocation of political power in the typical municipality. If one assumes, as here, that municipal political processes should be structured to ensure "a high probability that an active and legitimate group in the population can make itself heard effectively at some crucial stage in the process of decision,"[49] then the issue is how powerful unions will be in the typical municipal political process if a full transplant of collective bargaining is carried out.

The conclusion is that such a transplant would, in many cases, institutionalize the power of public employee unions in a way that would leave competing groups in the political process at a permanent and substantial disadvantage. There are three reasons for this, and each is related to the type of services typically performed by public employees.

First, some of these services are such that any prolonged disruption would entail an actual danger to health and safety.

Second, the demand for numerous governmental services is relatively inelastic, that is, relatively insensitive to changes in price. Indeed, the lack of close substitutes is typical of many governmental endeavors.[50] And, since at least the time of Marshall's *Principles of Economics*, the elasticity of demand for the final service or product has been considered a major determinant of union power.[51] Because the demand for labor is derived from the demand for the product, inelasticity on the product side tends to reduce the employment-benefit trade-off unions face. This is as much the case in the private as in the public sector. But in the private sector, product inelasticity is not typical. Moreover, there is the further restraint on union power created by the real possibility of nonunion entrants into the product market. In the public sector, inelasticity of demand seems more the rule than the exception, and nonunion rivals are not generally a serious problem.

Consider education. A strike by teachers may never create an immediate danger to public health and welfare. Nevertheless, because the demand for education is relatively inelastic, teachers rarely need fear unemployment as a result of union-induced wage increases, and the threat of an important nonunion rival (competitive private schools) is not to be taken seriously as long as potential consumers of private education must pay taxes to support the public school system.

---

[49]Dahl, *Preface to Democratic Theory*, p. 145.

[50]Sometimes this is so because of the nature of the endeavor—national defense, for example—and sometimes because the existence of the governmental operation necessarily inhibits entry by private entities, as in the case of elementary education.

[51]A. Marshall, *Principles of Economics*, 8th ed. (New York: Macmillan, 1920), pp. 383–86.

The final reason for fearing a full transplant is the extent to which the disruption of a government service inconveniences municipal voters. A teachers' strike may not endanger public health or welfare. It may, however, seriously inconvenience parents and other citizens who, as voters, have the power to punish one of the parties—and always the same party, the political leadership—to the dispute. How can anyone any longer doubt the vulnerability of a municipal employer to this sort of pressure? Was it simply a matter of indifference to Mayor Lindsay in September 1969 whether another teachers' strike occurred on the eve of a municipal election? Did the size and the speed of the settlement with the United Federation of Teachers (UFT) suggest nothing about one first-rate politician's estimate of his vulnerability? And are the chickens now coming home to roost because of extravagant concessions on pensions for employees of New York City the result only of mistaken actuarial calculations? Or do they reflect the irrelevance of long-run considerations to politicians vulnerable to the strike and compelled to think in terms of short-run political impact?

Those who disagree on this latter point rely principally on their conviction that anticipation of increased taxes as the result of a large labor settlement will countervail the felt inconvenience of a strike, and that municipalities are not, therefore, overly vulnerable to strikes by public employees. The argument made here, however—that governmental budgets in large cities are so complex that generally the effect of any particular labor settlement on the typical municipal budget is a matter of very low visibility—seems adequately convincing. Concern over possible taxes will not, as a general proposition, significantly deter voters who are inconvenienced by a strike from compelling political leaders to settle quickly. Moreover, municipalities are often subsidized by other political entities—the nation or state—and the cost of a strike settlement may not be borne by those demanding an end to the strike.

All this may seem to suggest that it is the strike weapon—whether the issue be monetary or nonmonetary—that cannot be transplanted to the public sector. This is an oversimplification, however. It is the combination of the strike and the typical municipal political process including the usual methods for raising revenue. One solution, of course, might well be a ban on strikes, if it could be made effective. But that is not the sole alternative, for there may be ways in which municipal political structures can be changed so as to make cities less vulnerable to strikes and to reduce the potential power of public employee unions to tolerable levels.

All this may also seem to suggest a sharper distinction between the public and private sectors than actually exists. The discussion here has dealt with models, one for private collective bargaining, the other for public. Each model is located at the core of its sector. But the difference in the impact of collective bargaining in the two sectors should be seen as a continuum. Thus, for example, it may be that market restraints do not sufficiently discipline strike settlements in some regulated industries or in industries that rely mainly on government contracts. Indeed, collective bargaining in such industries has been under steady and insistent attack.

In the public sector, it may be that in any given municipality—but particularly a small one—at any given time, taxpayer resistance or the determination of municipal government, or both, will substantially offset union power even under existing political structures. These plainly are exceptions, however. They do not invalidate the public-private distinction as an analytical tool, for that distinction rests on the very real differences that exist in the vast bulk of situations, situations exemplified by these models. On the other hand, in part because of a recognition that there are exceptions that in particular cases make the models invalid, we shall argue that the law regulating municipal bargaining must be flexible and tailored to the real needs of a particular municipality. The flexibility issue will be addressed directly, and in some detail, after consideration of the contemporary setting in which public bargaining is now developing.

READING 29

The Rise and Demise of PATCO*

Herbert R. Northrup†

This paper examines the Professional Air Traffic Controllers Organization (PATCO) strike of 1981 and assesses its impact on labor relations in the federal sector. The author finds the root causes of the stoppage in the history of PATCO's relations with the Federal Aviation Administration, the equivocal manner in which the federal government had dealt with previous PATCO strikes, and the ineptness of PATCO's leaders. He argues that PATCO's basic goal was to gain the right to bargain under private sector rules, and that the union would have made considerable progress toward that goal if it had accepted the government's last offer in 1981. The author also describes the international aspects of the strike, including the strong steps taken by the Reagan administration to maintain transoceanic service.

The strike by the Professional Air Traffic Controllers Organization (PATCO), which began in August 1981 and resulted in the dissolution of the union, was undoubtedly a watershed event in governmental labor relations. It is the thesis of this article, however, that the strike was the inevitable result of PATCO's long-term drive to "privatize" its relations with the Federal Aviation Administration (FAA), its public sector employer; of the weak response thereto by the federal government until the later years of the Carter administration; and of the failure of PATCO's new lead-

*Reprinted, with permission, from the *Industrial and Labor Relations Review*, 37, no. 2 (January 1984), pp. 167–84. © 1984 by Cornell University. All rights reserved.

†*The author is Professor of Industry and Director of the Industrial Research Unit (IRU) at the Wharton School, University of Pennsylvania.* The research was underwritten by generous grants from the J. Howard Pew Freedom Trust in support of the IRU's Labor Relations and Public Policy Series. Charles Bender assisted in checking legal citations.

ership to understand the greatly altered political and economic environment of 1981. In order to understand the strike and its aftermath, it is therefore necessary to summarize the federal government's labor relations policy, PATCO's 13-year struggle with the FAA, and PATCO policies that were designed to develop a special framework for its bargaining.

THE BARGAINING ENVIRONMENT

As federal government employees, controllers' salaries are set by Congress, pursuant to the civil service system. FAA management does not control wages, benefits, the length of the workday or workweek, or key personnel practices. The FAA does have a major voice in such matters as work schedules, hours, holiday and overtime pay, merit promotions, and personnel relations on the job.

Controller-FAA relations take place within the federal employee relations system, which was set on its current course by Executive Order 10988, issued by President John F. Kennedy on January 17, 1962; modified on October 29, 1969, by Executive Order 11491 issued by President Richard M. Nixon; and since 1978, governed by the Civil Service Reform Act (CSRA),[1] Title VII of which superseded the executive orders but maintained their basic policies. A three-member Federal Labor Relations Authority (FLRA), modeled after the National Labor Relations Board (NLRB), administers regulations like those in the Taft-Hartley Act concerning unfair labor practices and union representation. Like the NLRB, the FLRA has an independent general counsel, and its orders are subject to judicial review. The CSRA forbids strikes, and it also outlaws compulsory unionism by protecting an individual's right to join or not to join a union.

Matters in the purview of Congress are excluded from the grievance procedure. Unsettled grievances must be submitted to arbitration. Either party may ask the FLRA to review an arbitration award. Impasses in negotiation are referred first to the Federal Mediation and

[1]Pub. L. No. 95-454, 92 Stat. 1111, effective January 11, 1979.

Conciliation Service and, if not settled, to the Federal Service Impasses Panel (FSIP) created by Executive Order 11491. The FSIP has wide latitude to effectuate a settlement, including the right to "take whatever action may be necessary," which includes binding arbitration. Strikes are an unfair labor practice, and penalties for a union that promotes or encourages a strike include decertification.[2]

Policy Development at the FAA. The FAA grew up with the aviation industry, and for many years it was a small, paternalistic organization operated with a tinge of military flavor.[3] Following the tragic two-plane collision over the Grand Canyon in the late 1950s, Congress authorized greater expenditures on air traffic control, which resulted in the purchase of new equipment and the rapid expansion of the air traffic controller labor force. At the same time, the FAA embarked upon a program to upgrade controllers' status and pay. Its emphasis upon the stress and responsibility of controllers was later adopted by PATCO as the rationale for its economic program of higher wages, shorter hours, and special considerations for controllers who claimed disability.

Initially, the FAA was ill-prepared for collective bargaining as initiated under Executive Order 10988 and was especially unprepared for the type of militancy that PATCO exhibited at an early date. Committees appointed as early as 1969 and as late as 1982

criticized the FAA's relations with its employees, although pointing out that PATCO leadership was heavily to blame.[4] The FAA has attempted to address these issues with varying success and has stationed labor relations personnel in each of its several regional offices. Policy determinations in personnel and labor relations matters, however, as in operations, are made at the national level.[5]

PATCO'S TUMULTUOUS CAREER: 1968–1980

The strike that ended PATCO's bargaining days was just one of many during its tumultuous career. Almost from its inception, its history was marked by confrontations, as its officials fought not only for improvements in salary and working conditions but actually for superior rewards in these areas—and did so both by political and by direct action. Moreover, the entire PATCO history featured a determination to escape from the constraints of civil service labor relations, so that wages could be bargained and strikes legalized.

PATCO's Pre-1981 Strikes

From its organization by a group of New York City controllers in January 1968 until its 1981 strike, PATCO was involved in no fewer than six serious disruptions of air transport services. In July 1968, under the leadership of F. Lee Bailey, its lawyer/executive director, PATCO sponsored a month-long slowdown that seriously disrupted key airports.[6] The

---

[2]Under Title VII of the CSRA, the FLRA can issue cease-and-desist orders, require negotiations, or in case of strike, decertify the striking union and "take any other appropriate disciplinary action." Strikes are also forbidden by other laws, such as 5 U.S.C. 73, which states that "an individual may not accept or hold a position in the Government of the United States or the Government of the District of Columbia if he participates in a strike . . . against the Government of the United States or the Government of the District of Columbia." The definition of "strike" as set forth in the National Labor Relations (Taft-Hartley) Act includes a slowdown or "other concerted interruption of operations by employees." Stating that "at common law, no employee, whether public or private, had a constitutional right to strike in concert with his fellow workers," the U.S. Supreme Court upheld the constitutionality of this provision. See *U.S. Federation of Postal Clerks v. Blount*, 404 U.S. 802 (1971).

[3]This comment is based on the recollection of longtime FAA employees interviewed in Washington, D.C., in February 1982.

[4]For the early Corson Committee report, see *The Career of the Air Traffic Controller—A Cause of Action* (Washington, D.C.: U.S. Department of Transportation, 1970); for the recent "Jones" report, see *Management and Employee Relationships within the Federal Aviation Administration*, Contract No. DTG A01-82-C-30006 (Washington, D.C.: FAA, 1982), 2 vols.

[5]M. J. Fox, Jr. and E. G. Lambert, "Air Traffic Controllers: Struggle for Recognition and Second Careers," *Public Personnel Management* 3, no. 2 (May–June 1974), pp. 199–200. The author has confirmed that central control of labor relations still exists and, given the nature of the operations and bargaining arrangements, seems to be required.

[6]Widespread publicity on this stoppage appeared in all the general and industry newspapers and labor relations services. See, for example, *Aviation Daily*, throughout the month-long period.

FAA and the federal government were in a "state of shock" and did nothing.[7]

One year later, a three-day slowdown induced the then-secretary of transportation to appoint a committee to look into FAA-PATCO relationships. The resultant "Corson Report" criticized both parties and recommended changes in FAA policies.[8] In addition, the FAA suspended 80 controllers for up to 15 days for their participation in the job action.[9]

In March 1970, PATCO instituted a "sick-out" that lasted 20 days and was the most disruptive job action to that date, as 2,200 controllers at key major airports called in sick. This time, the Air Transport Association (ATA), the airlines association whose members had lost millions of dollars because of PATCO's tactics, was prepared for action. It won an order directing that the stoppage be ended and that individual defendant controllers return to work.[10] The FAA won similar orders in Minneosta[11] and Alaska.[12] When PATCO and striking controllers ignored those orders, the U.S. District Court, Eastern District of New York, found them in contempt of court and levied fines on a daily basis for each day lost. The district court in Alaska also issued fines for contempt. An additional complaint filed by the ATA in New York sought collective damages in excess of $50 million. Individual controllers, fearful that their homes and life savings could be lost, pressed for settlement. Negotiations between PATCO and ATA lawyers resulted in a September 9, 1970, stipulation of settlement, under which the ATA waived its damage claims and PATCO agreed to a permanent injunction, issued by the U.S. District Court, which stated:

PATCO, its officers, agents, employees, and members, its successors or assigns, and any other person acting in concern with it or them, is permanently prohibited and enjoined from, in any manner, calling, causing, authorizing, encouraging, inducing, continuing, or engaging in any strike (including any concerted stoppage, slowdown, or refusal to report to work) by air traffic controllers employed by an agency of the United States, or any other concerted, unlawful interference with or obstruction to the movement or operation of aircraft or the orderly operation of any air traffic control facilities by any agency of the United States.[13]

The stipulation-order also provided that if PATCO engaged in any action that violated its terms, then the union would be required to pay the ATA or its assignees $25,000 per day for each day during which the violation occurred and that this obligation was "in addition to and without prejudice to any other rights" of the plaintiffs, but that PATCO could ask the court to vacate or to revise this judgment if Congress made PATCO strikes lawful. The ATA thus had a weapon that it could, and would, bring to bear in the future.

The FAA also discharged 67 controllers for their participation in the 1970 sick-out. Twenty-seven of the controllers were later reinstated by civil service appeals, and then, in February 1972, Secretary of Transportation John Volpe ordered the rehiring of the remaining ones. His action was probably influenced by the facts that 1972 was an election year, the Nixon administration was then negotiating with the maritime unions over their threats to refuse to transport the Soviet Union's new grain purchases, and PATCO had recently affiliated with the Marine Engineers Beneficial Associ-

---

[7]As characterized by an FAA employee, personal interview, February 1982.

[8]See footnote 4.

[9]See, for example, *Government Employee Relations Report*, No. 306 (July 21, 1969), p. A-5; and *Aviation Daily*, October 24, 1969, p. 353.

[10]The material on this slowdown is taken from the extensive litigation and various briefs pertaining thereto. See, in particular, *Air Transport Association v. Professional Air Traffic Controllers Organization* 313 F.Supp. 181 (E.D. N.Y. 1970), *rev'd in part sub nom. United States v. PATCO*, 438 F.2d 79 (1971), *cert. denied*, 402 U.S. 915 (1971).

[11]*United States v. Professional Air Traffic Controllers Organization*, 312 F.Supp. 189 (D. Minn. 1970).

[12]This order was affirmed in *United States v. Robinson*, 449 F. 2d 925 (9th Cir. 1971).

[13]The terms of the agreed-upon order were upheld in *Air Transport Association v. Professional Air Traffic Controllers Organization*, 453 F.Supp. 1287 (E.D. N.Y. 1978), *aff'd*, 594 F. 2d 851 (1978), *cert. denied*, 441 U.S. 944 (1979).

ation (MEBA), a small but politically significant AFL–CIO maritime union.[14]

The 1970 strike also resulted in the end of Bailey's tenure as executive director of PATCO, the abolishment of his job, and the election of John F. Leyden as president, a position he held until his ouster 10 years later. In addition, PATCO was disqualified as a bargaining agent for 126 days by Assistant Secretary of Labor W. J. Usery, pursuant to Executive Order 11491. After the union was reinstated by Usery, it won an exclusive bargaining-rights election in 1972 and its first agreement with the FAA in March 1973.[15]

Peace reigned until 1976. In July and August of that year, after the Civil Service Commission refused to reclassify controllers to higher salary grades, PATCO staged slowdowns for five days at the nation's busiest airports,[16] just before the Republican National Convention scheduled for Kansas City. PATCO rescinded slowdowns before the ATA could secure an injunction, but the action was successful. On January 13, 1977, the Commission reversed itself and increased most controllers' wages after PATCO threatened another stoppage.

Two years later came another disruption. Controllers the world over have often claimed that they should be entitled to "familiarization flights," so that they can observe how flight controls work aboard airplanes.[17] When the U.S. international airlines abolished such free rides, PATCO called a "spontaneous" slowdown on May 25–26 and June 6–7, 1978, at major airports. This resulted in the second

judicial rebuff of such tactics when the ATA asked for a contempt citation pursuant to the permanent injunction the parties had agreed to in September 1970.

PATCO claimed that the 1970 injunction did not apply because it applied to a "sick-out" and the understaffing of facilities, whereas the 1978 actions pertained to familiarization flights. The District Court, Eastern District of New York, found this argument specious, concluding that the "injunction is still in full force and . . . effect." Since, therefore, PATCO had disobeyed the injunction on four days, the court ordered "PACTO to pay the plaintiff Air Transport Association of America the sum of $100,000, i.e., $25,000 for each daily violation of the 1970 injunction, as provided for in that injunction." In his comments, Judge Thomas G. Platt also expressed dismay that the U.S. Department of Justice did not join the issue, declaring, "It is . . . the sworn duty of the attorney general to enforce . . . [the laws prohibiting strikes by federal employees] but for reasons not fathomable to this court, they have yet to initiate any investigative or enforcement proceedings."[18]

The final disruption before 1981 occurred at Chicago's O'Hare International on August 15, 1980. Following the FAA's refusal of a PATCO demand for an annual tax-free bonus of $7,500 to compensate for the alleged greater stress on the job at that busy airport, PATCO members there initiated a slowdown that caused 616 delays of 30 minutes or more and cost the airlines more than one million dollars in wasted fuel. This time the FAA sought a court order from the District Court, Northern District of Illinois, but this action was dismissed on the ground that the enactment of the CSRA had deprived district courts of jurisdiction in such matters and that relief could now be obtained only pursuant to the CSRA on application of the FLRA's general counsel, after an FLRA complaint had been issued. Although this decision greatly emboldened the strike advocates in PATCO, it was later re-

---

[14]See *Aviation Daily*, February 9, 1972, p. 221, for strike details.

[15]See Fox and Lambert, "Air Traffic Controllers," pp. 201–203; *PATCO Newsletter*, July 23, 1972, p. 1, and May 3, 1973, pp. 1–5. Prior to this time, PATCO bargained only for its members; Executive Order 11491 was the first to provide for exclusive representation.

[16]The press noted that the slowdown had varying effects but was most noticeable in New York, Chicago, and Washington, D.C.

[17]*The Controller*, the official publication of the International Federation of Air Traffic Controllers Associations (IFATCA), makes frequent reference to the "need" for such flights, as does the *PATCO Newsletter*.

[18]The case is cited in footnote 13.

versed and never concurred in by other district or appellate courts.[19]

The Strike Fund and Other PATCO Policies

In 1977, PATCO established a thinly disguised strike fund known as the National Controller Subsistence Fund, to which was allocated 15 percent of the membership dues received by the national organization. By August 1981, over $3 million was in this fund, and three controllers who had been discharged for strike activity were receiving payments from the fund equal to their full salaries.[20] The FAA filed a complaint with the FLRA charging that the fund violated the no-strike provisions of Title VII of the CSRA, and a second one when PATCO established regulations to administer the fund. The FLRA dismissed both, reasoning that preparing for a strike was a legal activity, provided that no strike ever occurred![21]

Under Leyden's leadership, PATCO had as an objective the establishment of a separate FAA corporation, modeled on the U.S. Postal Service, but providing for PATCO and other union participation on the board of directors and for the right to strike for its employees. PATCO hired a consultant to draw up this proposal, and a bill incorporating the idea was introduced in Congress. The objective, of course, was wage determination on a private sector model.[22]

Making good use of claims that controllers were subject to extraordinary stress, PATCO also won an extraordinarily liberal retirement and disability program.[23] In 1972, President Nixon signed the Air Traffic Controllers Career Program Act (Public Law 92–297),[24] which authorizes controllers to retire at age 50 if they have 20 years of active service. (In contrast, the normal age of voluntary retirement for federal employees, which in turn is more liberal than that under the social security system, is 55 afer 30 years of service or age 60 after 20 years.) The Controllers Program Act also stipulates very liberal disability retirement provisions, plus a "second careers" program: up to two years training at government expense at full salary for controllers who have to leave traffic control work because of a medical or proficiency disqualification.

In 1974, Congress greatly liberalized the Federal Employees' Compensation Act, providing a means for generous retirement allowance to federal employees who suffer slight disabilities.[25] Thereafter, both disability claims by controllers and "system errors"[26] committed by them suddenly rose signifi-

[19]See *United States v. PATCO*, 504 F.Supp. 432 (N.D. Ill. 1980); *rev'd*, 653 F.2d 1134, 107 LRRM 3057, No. 80-2854 (7th Cir., 1981); *cert. denied*, 454 U.S. 1083 (1981).

[20]Deposition of Robert E. Poli, then president of PATCO, August 12, 1981, vol. I., pp. 34–80, and of Robert E. Meyer, then executive vice president, August 13, 1981, vol. I, pp. 34–68—both in *In the Matter of Air Transport Association v. Professional Air Traffic Controllers Association*, Civil Docket No. 70, Cir. 400 (U.S.D.C., E.D. N.Y.).

[21]Re: *Professional Air Traffic Controllers Organization*, Case No. 22-09583 (CO). Decision letter to Edward V. Curran, director of labor relations, FAA, from Alexander T. Graham, regional director, Washington Regional Office, FLRA, April 30, 1979; and Re: *Professional Air Traffic Controllers Organization*, Case 3-CO-50. Decision letter to Edward V. Curran, director of labor relations, FAA, from Bruce D. Rosenstein, acting regional director, FLRA, November 30, 1980.

[22]The report of the consultant is summarized in the *PATCO Journal*, November–December 1975, pp. 21–24.

See also a reprint of the article, "Controllers Seek Divorce from Federal Government," *PATCO Newsletter*, August 1979, pp. 11–12; a story by United Press International based upon interviews with PATCO officials, released July 13, 1981; a statement by Leyden, *PATCO Newsletter*, June 1979, p. 2; and Robert E. Poli, "Maybe It's Time to Dismiss the FAA," *New York Times*, August 16,1981, p. E-19. This last article appeared two weeks after the "definitive strike" began. Representative William Clay reintroduced the idea in 1981 in a bill (H.R. 1576) that would also have given PATCO all of its economic demands. Ironically, some smaller airports hired controllers from the private sector after the strike began; those airports had lost their FAA controllers, who were reassigned to larger flight centers at least until the impact of the strike lessened. See Brenton R. Schlender, "Some Small Airports Hiring Firms to Provide Air Traffic Controllers," *The Wall Street Journal*, March 14, 1982, p. 29.

[23]See Fox and Lambert, "Air Traffic Controllers," for a good summary of the development of Public Law 92-297.

[24]86 Stat. 141 (1972).

[25]For criticisms of the loose construction of this law and its equally loose administration by the U.S. Department of Labor, see several reports of the U.S. Comptroller General and a popular version, Fern Schumer, "I'm Not All Right, Jack," *Forbes*, June 25, 1979, p. 78. See also *Daily Labor Report* 140 (July 22, 1981). E pages, and 62 (March 31, 1982), E pages.

[26]Systems errors are defined as situations in which planes being monitored by a controller violate separation standards.

cantly. A careful academic study found a significant correlation between the increase in system errors and controller disability applications during this period.[27] An error could be used as proof that a controller's job performance was declining and would therefore aid his disability application. In addition, it could be claimed that the error resulted in such stress that it disabled the controller, and doctors' testimony could be used to support such claims. Indeed, one Atlanta psychiatrist "diagnosed as totally disabled 154 air traffic controllers."[28] In 1978, following a report of the U.S. Comptroller General, Congress ended the funding of the "second careers" program authorized by Public Law 92–297, and controller disability claims dropped steadily, although they still remained numerous.[29] One of PATCO's demands in the 1981 negotiations was reinstitution of this program.

A third endeavor of the Leyden administration was to bring PATCO within the mainstream of organized labor. The affiliaton with MEBA aided this, as did Leyden's courting of the Air Line Pilots' Association (ALPA) and his strong personal bond with John J. O'Donnell, then ALPA president.[30] Leyden also sought international support for his union, initially from the International Federation of Air Traffic Controllers' Associations (IFATCA). Founded in 1961, IFATCA is a combination of an international trade union secretariat and a semiprofessional organization that affiliates national controllers' organizations throughout the world. PATCO had affiliated with it in

1971 and, by reason of the size of the U.S. air transport industry, PATCO was the largest IFATCA affiliate and the largest financial contributor; in fact, it was larger than all other affiliates combined. During this period, the IFATCA stressed its role as a professional, rather than union, organization. Since PATCO leaders were more interested in mutual support activities than in other aspects of IFATCA's activities and were unhappy about contributing so much more financial support than other IFATCA affiliates, PATCO disaffiliated in 1976.[31] Between 1974 and 1980, PATCO, through MEBA, was also affiliated with the International Transport Workers' Federation (ITF), an international trade union secretariat that affiliates unions in all transportation industries.[32]

PATCO also became especially close to and admiring of the Canadian Air Traffic Control Association (CATCA), which has waged a number of successful strikes and which, as later events would demonstrate, controlled the key North Atlantic route through which most flights between Europe and North America pass. Regular visits of CATCA and PATCO officials began in 1968, and joint briefings were an obvious and a regular feature of those visits.[33]

A final objective of the PATCO program during these years was the unionization of noncontroller employees of the FAA under PATCO's aegis and control and then expansion to other "elite" groups of government employees. To that end, PATCO sponsored and financed the growth of three organiza-

---

[27]Michael E. Staten and John Umbeck, "Information Costs and Incentives to Shirk: Disability Compensation of Air Traffic Controllers," *American Economic Review* 72, no. 5 (December 1982), pp. 1023–37.

[28]Sam Hopkins, "Psychiatrist Facing Trial in Controller Stress Suit," *Atlanta Constitution*, August 29, 1981, pp. 1-A and 6-A. The *PATCO Newsletter*, April 9, 1976, pp.7 and 14–15, contained excerpts from an article by this doctor stating that air traffic controllers had "a very special type of personality structure," and that because of inadequate equipment, controllers could not "follow any type of medical regimen aimed at alleviating their medical conditions," which he ascribed to them. This doctor has been the subject of litigation brought by insurance companies.

[29]Data are from the source cited in footnote 27.

[30]See, for example *PATCO Journal*, November–December 1975, pp. 29–35, for one of the frequent stories on O'Donnell and favorable mention of the ALPA.

[31]See *PATCO Newsletter*, October 24, 1973, p. 15; Christmas 1973, p. 17; April 1, 1974, p. 11; July 5, 1974, p. 8; Christmas 1974, p. 4; and June 1980, p. 3; *PATCO Journal*, May 1975, p. 43; and the *Controller*, December 1971; no. 2 (no month), 1978, pp. 3–5; and no 4, 1980, p. 17.

[32]Reference to the ITF affiliation is found in *PATCO Newsletter*, November 11, 1974, p. 2; and August 5, 1972, p. 16. For a discussion of ITF policies in ocean and air transport, see Herbert R. Northrup and Richard L. Rowan, *Multinational Collective Bargaining Attempts*, Multinational Industrial Relations Series, no. 6 (Philadelphia: Industrial Research Unit, The Wharton School, University of Pennsylvania, 1979), pp. 473–520.

[33]The depositions of Poli and Meyer contain numerous references to CATCA meetings, and correspondence and telegrams in the author's possession confirm this. Such meetings on earlier occasions occurred frequently and are repeatedly mentioned in the *PATCO Newsletter*.

tions: the Professional Airway Systems Specialists (PASS), which on December 31, 1981, defeated an incumbent union to win bargaining rights for 8,500 FAA electronics technicians; the National Association of Flight Standard Employees (NAFSE), which was certified to represent the 200 employees stationed in Oklahoma City who check airline performance in flight; and the Professional Aeronautical Center Employees (PACE), which represents instructors at the FAA's Oklahoma City instructional facility for controllers. All three had been expected to affiliate with PATCO just before its demise, and to pave the way for PATCO to recruit elsewhere in the federal service among technical and professional employees.[34] The final strike, however, came before this program could be completed.

THE COUP AND STRIKE PREPARATIONS

PATCO entered the 1980s in a seemingly very strong position. Its membership, as a group, was among the highest-paid government employees, averaging $33,000 annually by mid-1981.[35] Controllers' fringe benefits, including the already noted disability and pension provision, were superior to those of other government employees, which in turn are generally superior to those in private industry.[36] Although controllers in several busy metropolitan airports certainly worked under stressful conditions, others in the less-traveled areas could claim no such pressure. Moreover, as was later made clear by the 1981 strike, there was considerable evidence of overstaffing in the system.

In the political arena, PATCO had won the support of many U.S. congressmen and senators, both conservative and liberal. The union distributed political funds carefully but generously and, as described above, was able to gain support for laws that met many of PATCO's

aspirations. Moreover, the FLRA's decisions were often supportive of the union. With a checkoff dues income of approximately $5.5 million per year, cash balances in excess of $3.5 million, and almost an equal amount in its thinly disguised strike or "subsistence" fund, PATCO in 1981 was clearly an economically sound and effective organization of approximately 15,000 members.

There were, however, some elements of disquiet. The strikes involving familiarization flights and the O'Hare bonus convinced Langhorne M. Bond, the FAA administrator appointed by President Carter, of the need to devise an effective antistrike mechanism. Deciding that the FLRA had "an antimanagement record" and that it was "almost impossible for management to achieve a fair result under the FLRA," Bond was determined to develop a program to deal with strikes in collaboration with the Department of Justice and to use the courts for relief. He also developed a detailed strike plan, which called for operation of air traffic facilities during a strike and for the federal courts to enjoin and to punish strikers.[37] To emphasize his determination, in 1980, Bond published his strike contingency plan in the Federal Register.[38]

The Coup

The most serious problem facing PATCO, however, was dissension at the top. In January 1980, before the expiration of Leyden's term of office, the PATCO executive board forced his resignation and replaced him with Robert Poli, the executive vice president who had quietly won control of the board. The coup was legitimized in June 1980, when Poli was elected president after Leyden did not contest the election.[39] Poli then placed his own

[34]Poli deposition, pp. 229–41; and *PATCO Newsletter*, January 30, 1978, p. 3, and November 1978, p.10. PASS affiliated with MEBA in June 1983.

[35]The data are from the FAA.

[36]See Gordon F. Bloom and Herbert R. Northrup, *Economics of Labor Relations*, 9th ed. (Homewood, Ill.: Richard D. Irwin, 1981), chap. 22, for a comparison of fringe benefits in government and in private industry.

[37]Don Francke, 'The FAA's Finest Hour... An Interview with Langhorne M. Bond," *The Journal of Air Traffic Control* 24 (January–March 1982), pp. 6–11.

[38]See 45 Fed. Reg. 221, November 13, 1980, DOT/FAA, 14 CFR, Part 91; 46 Fed.Reg. 43, March 5, 1981; and 46 Fed. Reg. 149, August 4, 1981, 14 CFR Part 91, for what was originally termed the FAA "Job Action Contingency Plan," and later the "National Air Traffic Control Contingency Plan."

[39]There was some opposition to Poli at the 1980 convention of PATCO, but the failure of Leyden to go to the

supporters in key positions and employed new staff and attorneys.

The coup, however, caused PATCO to lose significant support. Discharged employees in the national office filed charges of unfair labor practices—charges that the National Labor Relations Board sustained.[40] Officials of other unions rallied to Leyden's defense, and the ALPA temporarily put him on its payroll. Then, the AFL–CIO Public Employee Department, with which Leyden had worked as PATCO's delegate, appointed him its executive director, a position he still holds today. Poli had been PATCO's "inside man" during his 10 years as executive vice president, and he was relatively unknown among the labor establishment, except among the public employee unions; apparently, he did not court his fellow union officials or seek their advice. As a key union official told the author in confidence, "Few of us knew him and he did not consult us." Rather, Poli concentrated his efforts on preparing for what he described as "our most difficult challenge . . . which will test our union as it has never been tested,"[41] namely, the "definitive strike" aimed at achieving PATCO's basic aims of inducing Congress to establish an independent FAA, permitting wage bargaining, and legitimizing strikes.[42]

Poli and his associates did solidify one union relationship that Leyden had neglected, namely, the international one. Robert E. Meyer, long a vice president for PATCO's Great Lakes region, was appointed executive vice president after the coup. He was a close friend of H. Harri Henschler, formerly vice president of the Canadian Air Traffic Control Association, who had become president of IFATCA. Meyer had been a vice president of IFATCA, and soon after the coup, PATCO reaffiliated and Meyer again became one of IFATCA's officers. By then, IFATCA had assumed a much more militant union stance, as is described below.[43]

Strike Preparations

After winning election to office in June 1980, the Poli administration moved rapidly in its strike preparations. The message carried to the field was direct: 1981 was to be the year in which the definitive strike would win PATCO its goals. Since FAA negotiators had no authority to grant wage or other key demands and since Congress might be reluctant to do so, PATCO's reasoning was that Congress would act only if a strike paralyzed air traffic. The Poli administration assumed that both Congress and the Reagan administration would then support lesislation granting PATCO both substantially improved economic conditions and its basic objective, bargaining freedom under an independent FAA.

The unions' plan called for very high initial demands, such as $10,000 per year salary increases, a 32-hour workweek, increased pension and disability benefits, and a liberal number of familiarization flights. If, as expected, no agreement were reached by the contract expiration date in June, and if membership support for a strike were less than overwhelming (less than 80 percent), the plan was to have the union negotiating committee agree to a tentative contract and Poli to persuade the media that membership ratification was likely—but then to have the tentative agreement overwhelmingly repudiated by the executive board and, it was hoped, by the membership as a result of an "education campaign."

---

membership and the care of Poli and his group to avoid overt action before the convention both demoralized and softened the opposition. Confidential discussions with several sources suggest that Leyden was wholly surprised by the coup and had expected the January 1980 executive board meeting to be a routine one. Instead, it lasted all night. Both Leyden and Poli resigned, but the executive board, probably as planned, accepted Leyden's resignation, which it had demanded, but refused to accept Poli's and then designated him president.

[40]Professional Air Traffic Controllers and PATCO Employees' Union, 261 NLRB no. 132 (May 14,1982); *White-Collar Report*, no. 1304 (January 21, 1982), pp. A-3–4. A group of those discharged by Poli sent a letter to the membership on August 4, 1980, detailing the discharges and resignations and explaining why the employees of PATCO had formed a union (a copy is in the author's possession).

[41]See Poli's letter in the *PATCO Newsletter*, January 1981, p. 3.

[42]The term *definitive strike* shows up in various places, but was most widely used in the PATCO call-in telephone recordings described below.

[43]See *PATCO Newsletter*, June 1980, p. 3; and the *Controller*, no. 1, 1980, p.17.

This action, in turn, would provide the necessary strike rationale: the members were presumably too militant to be controlled by the reasonable union negotiators. To gain support for this plan, controllers were assured that any members disciplined for striking would receive their salary and benefits from PATCO until reinstatement was obtained through political pressures.

Poli and other union officers were extraordinarily explicit in communicating this plan. It was described in call-in telephone recordings and at "cluster" meetings (geographic groups of local union representatives brought together to hear the plan explained by national officers), and it was clearly hinted at in public comments.[44] A group called the "choir boys" was recruited to insure that tight discipline from the top was maintained,[45] and detailed financial plans to cover legal costs were made.[46] On the political front, PATCO leaders, sharply critical of FAA Administrator Bond in the Carter administration, endorsed Ronald Reagan for President in October 1980—receiving in return a letter endorsing an efficient control system and fairly compensated controllers, but making no mention of strike support.[47]

The PATCO leadership seemed to ignore in its staging of the strike one key group: the federal managers. Former Secretary of Transportation Drew Lewis and former FAA Administrator Lynn Helms, both of whom came to their positions with experience in labor matters, had Bond's strike contingency plan updated and strengthened and, as discussed below, established good relationships with their foreign counterparts. Most important, they gave their subordinates full support, kept the White House fully informed, and in turn received the president's full backing in their negotiations and policies.[48]

Negotiations and Strike Votes

Upon its ascendency in January 1981, the Reagan administration faced the possibility of not one, but two strikes affecting the airline industry. In addition to PATCO, the ALPA had threatened to strike on March 1, 1981, unless new two-engine planes were operated with three-member cockpit crews. But the ALPA leadership persuaded the president to appoint a study commission, which recommended against its demand, and ALPA acquiesced and defused the issue among its members.[49]

Whereas the ALPA leadership had concentrated on overcoming strike sentiment, the opposite occurred within PATCO. On many

---

[44]Several of the telephone recordings are in the author's possession, as are the minutes of the Sacramento, California, cluster meeting, April 30, 1981, in which the PATCO stategy is very explicitly set forth and it is noted that the same message was being given all around the industry at similar union meetings. (Copies of these documents, and of others cited in this article that are not publicly available, will be provided, within reason, by the author, provided anyone requesting copies pays the full cost of reproduction and mailing.)

Poli's strike threats were widely reported in the press prior to the June 22 deadline. Repeatedly he declared, "The only illegal strike is one that fails." See, for example, William M. Carley, "Rough Flying: Air Traffic Controllers Put Reagan on Spot with Threat to Strike," *The Wall Street Journal*, June 17, 1981, p. 1.

[45]David Trick, director of organization under Poli and third man in the PATCO hierarchy, termed choir boys "educators and organizers" in his deposition, p. 45, in the New York district court case (see footnote 20 for citation). It was quite probably, however, that choir boys (and one "choir girl") were selected for their physical size, aggressiveness, and loyalty to Poli and his policies. I believe that they were, in fact, enforcers, having been described in the minutes of the Sacramento cluster meeting as "responsible for building a strike force which is ready to go when necessary." (See footnote 44.) This belief is also based upon my discussion with several sources whose identity must remain confidential. As pointed out below, the government's extensive preparation for and sharp reaction to the strike kept violence to a minimum, and the role of the choir boys apparently did not develop as planned.

[46]Additional monies were tansferred to the strike ("subsistence") fund; bank loans of $650,000 were obtained; $100,000 cash was given to PATCO's lawyers, prior to the strike; and $300,000 in cash was withdrawn from a safe-deposit box. See depositions of Poli, pp. 38–98, and of Meyer, vol. I, pp. 36–77 and vol. II, pp. 161–177. At the

Sacramento cluster meeting, reference was also made to a large fund in a California bank that was never explained in the depositions or elsewhere that I have found.

[47]A copy of the Reagan letter of October 20, 1980, was reproduced in a *New York Times* advertisement, August 16, 1981, p. 69.

[48]This was attested throughout my FAA interviews and is clearly reflected in subsequent events, as described below.

[49]For this and other ALPA policies, see my article, "The New Employee Relations Climate in the Airline Industry," *Industrial and Labor Relations Review* 36, no. 2 (January 1983), pp. 167–81.

occasions, Poli told the media that a strike would occur, and he continued such belligerent talk down to the June 22, 1981 deadline.[50] But when that day arrived, he agreed to a generous contract offer that provided that the Reagan administration would seek congressional approval to grant all controllers an immediate pay raise in excess of $2,000; pay at overtime rates after 36 hours per week instead of after 40; an increase in the night-shift differential from 10 to 15 percent; 14 weeks' severance pay to experienced controllers who left work for medical reasons; and a greater voice to PATCO in establishing operation and safety policies. These pay and benefit increases, which averaged 6.6 percent, were to be in addition to a salary increase of 4.8 percent due in October 1981 for all federal employees. Thus, if Congress had approved this final offer, controllers would have gained pay increases in excess of 11 percent, or more than twice that gained by other federal employees, [51] and PATCO would, in effect, have negotiated wages and major working conditions—subjects presumably reserved to Congress.

If PATCO had stopped here, accepted the contract, and joined the administration in seeking congressional approval for its effectuation, the union would not only be alive and well today, but it would also have made considerable progress in its drive to negotiate wages—a subject Congress had retained as its prerogative. The administration, anxious to avoid a strike, apparently convinced that controllers deserved an increase higher than the general one for other government employees, and conscious that if a strike came, the administration's position would be strengthened by an offer that was clearly discerned as "fair,"[52] came as close to wage negotiatons on the private model as it is possible for an administration to do with civil service employees. Previous administrations had reacted similarly to the demands of the controllers, as in the 1974 negotiations preceding the controllers' retirement and disability legislation, but the negotiations in 1981 came closer than any other to the private sector model. If the union had accepted the administrations' offer, it could have established a precedent that might have altered all labor relations in the federal service, contrary to the desire of the administration, and probably to that of Congress as well.

In spite of this opportunity, Poli's apparent acceptance of the government's final offer merely followed the script that already had been laid out in the cluster meetings. A strike-authorization vote taken before the June 22, 1981 deadline was claimed to have won support from 70 percent of the membership who voted. PATCO maintained that its "long-standing policy" was to order a strike only after an 80 percent endorsement vote.[53]

Although Poli told reporters just after the June 22 settlement that he "felt good" about the contract, the PATCO executive board met on July 2 and recommended unanimous rejection of the contract negotiated by their president and the several other board members who sat on the executive committee. The membership then voted by mail to reject the contract, 13,495 (95.3 percent) to 616 (4.7 percent), on ballots that carried their names. Poli immediately set a new strike deadline for 7 A.M. August 3, 1981, and raised PATCO's demands to an amount that the FAA claimed would add $38,914 to the airlines' cost per controller. Secretary Lewis told Poli that his "union proposals are excessive and an affront to the American public. We cannot yield to, or even entertain such demands."[54] Meanwhile, strike sentiment was whipped up by Poli and his central staff with press conferences, pub-

---

[50]See footnote 44.

[51]A copy of the contract offer is in my possession.

[52]This point was made clearly by Secretary Lewis in several press conferences immediately after the strike.

[53]According to David Trick, Director of Organization, PATCO called off the strike set for June 22 because it "lacked the 80 percent membership support required for a strike." Joann S. Lublin, "Air Traffic Union Lacked 80 Percent Vote It Needed to Strike," *The Wall Street Journal*, June 24, 1981, p. 12. This author has found no record of a strike vote prior to the first six PATCO strikes, but he does have a copy of a PATCO policy statement, released by a member of the O'Hare cluster, that contains the 80-percent "policy."

[54]"Statement of Secretary of Transportation Drew Lewis," news release, U.S. Department of Transportation, August 1, 1981. The FAA calculated the total costs of these demands at $681 million in 1982, exclusive of the costs of a 32-hour week.

licity statements, and other propaganda by his adherents in the field.[55]

Negotiations with the government resumed but were fruitless, as Poli remained uncompromising. As the new strike deadline drew near, he refused to extend it despite requests by Lewis, the speaker of the House of Representatives, and the director of the Federal Mediation and Conciliation Service. Poli also ignored a very explicit warning drafted by a majority of the Senate and several congressmen that PATCO would receive no strike support from them.[56] The PATCO strike plan moved inexorably toward its goal, despite yet other warnings from the president and several cabinet members that there would be no amnesty for strikers and no talks with PATCO during a strike and despite clear indications that the FAA would institute its plan to keep the air transport system moving at whatever capacity was possible.[57]

There is no evidence that PATCO officials conducted a secret-ballot strike vote. Although Executive Vice President Meyer later claimed that 82 percent of the membership favored a strike, he could give no details under questioning regarding how or when that figure was computed.[58]

THE STRIKE AND THE DEMISE

PATCO's long-planned strike began on schedule at 7 A.M. on August 3, 1981. The FAA was ready with its strike plan. All flights were controlled by the central flow operation, so that none was cleared locally until a signal was given at the national level; this served to prevent overcrowding any locations by not permitting flights until the receiving airport control staff could accept them. At first, about 50 percent of all flights were cleared; then, the number was raised to 70 percent about 10 days later; and gradually, the number was increased as new controllers were trained. The towers and stations were staffed by controllers who refused to strike, military personnel lent by the U.S. Department of Defense, retirees called back, and supervisors. Some smaller airports were denied controllers who were needed elsewhere, and it was readily apparent—as is often the case when a company operates during a strike[59]—that the system had been overstaffed. It was also soon obvious that PATCO had failed to shut down the air traffic system as its officials had believed it would and that airline executives and the general public were neither panic-stricken by nor sympathetic to PATCO's action. Gradually, the system has moved toward full capacity while employing about one-fifth fewer personnel (13,000 in place of 16,395). The last military controllers who were assisting the FAA returned to the armed services in June 1983.[60]

Of course, the strike was damaging. Many potential customers undoubtedly hesitated to fly until they were assured about their safety. On that point, Secretary Lewis, FAA personnel, the ALPA, and individual pilots all reassured the public.[61] No accident occurred that could have been attributed directly to oper-

[55]A clipping file collected for this article shows this "whipping up" of strike sentiment throughout the country.

[56]The July 28, 1981, letter from 55 senators and 19 congressmen advised Poli that "any illegal action by PATCO and its members will be viewed with extreme disfavor in the Congress." A copy is in the author's possession.

[57]See, for example Richard Witkin, "Air Control Union is Warned by United States as a Strike Looms," New York Times, August 3, 1981, pp. A-1, A-12, in which Secretary Lewis is quoted as saying that if PATCO struck, there would be "no amnesty" and "no negotiations while a strike persisted." He further stated that these warnings "come directly from President Reagan." The same article quoted the secretary of defense as willing to provide 600 to 700 controllers if there were a strike, and the attorney general as stating that anyone who violated the ban on strikes by federal employees would be prosecuted "to the fullest extent permitted by law."

[58]Meyer deposition, vol. I, pp. 182–204.

[59]For general experience, see Charles R. Perry, Andrew M. Kramer, and Thomas J. Schneider, Operating During Strikes, Labor Relations and Public Policy Series no. 23 (Philadelphia: Industrial Research Unit, The Wharton School, University of Pennsylvania, 1982).

[60]The data are from the FAA.

[61]Secretary Lewis was the chief spokesman for the Reagan administration, and he repeatedly gave interviews, spoke on television, and generally communicated the concern for safety. Then-president of ALPA J. J. O'Donnell and numerous individual pilots countered claims of danger and disregard of safety made by Poli and other PATCO spokesmen on many occasions. See, for example, the New York Times and The Wall Street Journal throughout August and September 1981, especially August 3 through 15.

ations during the strike, although one crash has raised questions.[62] The public was soon satisfied that the airways were safe, despite the continued unsupported claims to the contrary by PATCO spokesmen and, as noted below, by its international allies. Nevertheless, the airlines were badly hurt by the strike. Already staggering from recession, they were forced to cut back key flights, and they lost much-needed revenues while spending millions on costly delays.[63]

The Administration's Counterattack

Besides its carefully executed plan to maintain operations, the Reagan administration moved swiftly to punish PATCO, its officials,

---

[62]Three major crashes occurred during the 1981–82 strike period. In the first, involving World Airways at Boston, a plane skidded into the harbor, killing two persons. The National Transportation Board ruled that the primary cause of the crash was the failure of the FAA to provide adequate information on runway ice conditions—as had happened in several pre-strike accidents. Controller failure was not considered a factor. New computer equipment, now authorized, should greatly remedy this lack of information. See National Transportation Safety Board, *Aircraft Accident Report, World Airways, Inc., Flight 30H . . . Boston Logan International Airport, January 23, 1982*, Report No. NTSB/AAR-82-15 (Washington, D.C.: NTSB, December 15, 1982).

The second crash was that of an Air Florida plane into a Potomac River bridge in January 1982, killing 78 people. The principal cause appears to have been ice on the wings. In turn, this was the result of inadequate de-icing; poor communications between American Airlines maintenance personnel who did the de-icing and Air Florida pilots; the relative inexperience of Air Florida pilots in such weather; or increased separation of flights mandated by the shortage of experienced controllers, which caused ice to form on wings of planes while they awaited take-off; or some combination of the above. Since no other plane taking off just before the ill-fated one had the same problem, the fourth possible cause—increased separation of flights—does not seem likely. See National Transportation Safety Board, *Aircraft Accident Report, Air Florida, Inc. . . . Near Washington National Airport, January 13, 1982*, Report No. NTSB/AAR-82-8 (Washington, D.C.: NTSB, August 10, 1982).

The final crash, that of a Pan American plane at New Orleans after take-off, killing 153 persons, was attributed to a wind shift, which the weather experts acknowledge they know too little about. A new drive is now underway to accumulate knowledge about this problem. No controller error was apparently involved. See National Transportation Safety Board, *Aircraft Accident Report, Pan American World Airways, Inc. . . . New Orleans International Airport, July 9, 1982*, Report No. NTSB/AAR-83-102 (Washington, D.C.: NTSB, March 21, 1983).

[63]See the citation in footnote 49, for many details of the airlines' problems during this period.

and striking members for their illegal action. A flood of injunctions, criminal actions, and contempt actions poured forth, brought both by the government and the ATA. PATCO's strike fund was sequestered to pay for fines of several million dollars per day assessed by courts against the union.[64]

Four hours after the strike began, President Reagan personally announced that any striker who was not back on the job within 48 hours would be discharged and could not be reemployed by any federal agency. This policy was effectuated. About one fourth of the controllers—4,199—had not heeded the strike call and continued to work. Another 875 returned to work before the president's deadline expired, leaving 11,310 who remained on strike and were discharged.[65] For replacements, the FAA expanded its Air Traffic Service Academy training program, and by late 1983, the air traffic control system was fully staffed.

The FAA promptly moved before the FLRA to decertify PATCO, according to the requirements of the Civil Service Reform Act. After some rather extraordinary administrative behavior, for which the Court of Appeals, District of Columbia, sharply criticized the FLRA, PATCO was decertified, and this action was later affirmed by the same court.[66]

The Union Response in the United States

As noted, Poli had made little effort to seek support from other unions before the strike, nor had he realistically assessed the exent to which organized labor could render direct as-

---

[64]Data on legal actions are from FAA files. See also various issues of *Daily Labor Report*, from August 5 through September 30, 1981.

[65]Data provided by the FAA's labor relations office.

[66]*Professional Air Traffic Controllers Organization v. Federal Aviation Administration*, FLRA Case No. 3-CO-105, October 22, 1981; aff'd 685 F. 2d 547 (D.C. Cir. 1982); *Daily Labor Report* no. 104 (October 22, 1981), pp. E-1–9. The decision process of the FLRA included negotiations among members, discussions with interested labor officials, public criticism of one board member by another, and other actions indicating that the FLRA may well require a thorough restructuring and new administrative and operating rules.

sistance without undergoing several legal penalties.[67] Once the strike began, the president's
resolve became obvious, the airlines achieved
a 70 percent capability to schedule flights, and
it became clear to experienced labor officials
that, barring an unexpected development or
an emotionally charged accident attributable
to controller error, PATCO had embarked on
a doomed course. Finally, PATCO's exorbi-
tant demands in light of the already high salaries of its members aroused little sympathy
among organized labor's largely blue-collar
rank-and-file.

As a consequence and with few exceptions,
the union establishment's support of PATCO
was largely confined to issuing statements, a
symbolic court case which was quickly dismissed,[68] equally symbolic walking on picket
lines, contributions to a relief fund for the discharged strikers, a limited boycott of the airlines, and pressure on Congress and the president to lift the prohibition against rehiring
PATCO strikers.[69] The president in part defused the last effort by issuing an order providing that controllers not convicted of wrongdo-
ing during the strike could be employed by
the federal government in jobs other than

controller or related ones.[70] This order neither satisfied organized labor nor provided
jobs for many strikers. Attempts by some
members of the House of Representatives to
pressure the Reagan administration to rehire
the strikers were both rebuffed by the administration and set back by a poll, conducted by
congressmen who favored reinstating the
strikers, which demonstrated that most controllers who stayed on the job were opposed to
permitting strikers to return or to working
with them.[71]

A fundamental failure of PATCO's approach was its total lack of success in gaining
any support whatsoever from the ALPA, the
leaders of which had been completely es-
tranged by Poli's coup and who were also completely opposed to a strike that was believed to
endanger pilot jobs. ALPA president O'Donnell and individual pilots repeatedly countered claims by PATCO spokespersons that
the airways were not safe after the strike com-
menced, and they cited the excellent cooperation that they were receiving from working
controllers. These statements did much to re-
assure the public and to lighten the task of the
administration and the FAA. At the same
time, however, the ALPA did join organized
labor in urban amnesty for the strikers.[72]

---

[67]Since the private sector airline unions are within the
jurisdiction of the Railway Labor Act, and since strikes in
violation of contracts thereunder are clearly enjoinable
and striking unions are subject to damage suits, airline
unions could not easily support the strike. See *Brotherhood of Railroad Trainmen v. Chicago River and Indiana
Railroad Co.*, 353 U.S. 30 (1957); and *Flight Engineers International Association v. American Airlines, Inc.*, 303 F.
2d 5 (5th Cir. 1962).

[68]A group of union officials, Ralph Nader, and others
filed suit to force the government to rehire the strikers.
The suit was dismissed for failure to exhaust administrative remedies and no appeal was taken. *Douglas Fraser v.
Lewis* (D.D.C., Cir. No. 81-2729, December 21, 1981).
The union officials also filed a request with the FAA and
with other agencies to change rules and rehire the strikers. This was denied as was a request for reconsideration.

[69]For a good summary of the situation, see "Unions
Wary of Legal Risks in Honoring PATCO Picket Lines,"
Daily Labor Report, no. 152 (August 7, 1981), pp. A-10–11.
See also "AFL–CIO Sets Up Fund to Aid Air Control-
lers," *Daily Labor Report*, no. 162 (August 21, 1981), p. A-
1. The airlines boycott was largely ignored by the time of
the November 1981 AFL–CIO convention, and it also did
not ground the executive fleet of the Teamsters, the
IAM, and other unions that own such appurtenances.
See "Many Union Officials Traveled by Plane," *New York
Times*, November 20, 1981, p. A-21, which reported on
the diminishing air travel boycott.

[70]The president's statement and memorandum are
found in *Daily Labor Report*, no. 236 (December 9, 1981),
p. E-1. See also Jeff Sommer, "Despite Amnesty, No Ex-
Controllers Get Federal Jobs," *Philadelphia Inquirer*,
March 20, 1982, p. 4-A.

[71]The Roper Organization was retained by the Subcommittee on Investigations and Oversight of the Committee on Public Works and Transportation, U.S. House
of Representatives, after the FAA and PATCO differed
on whether nonstrikers objected to strikers returning. In
February 1982, Roper sent carefully constructed questions to a randomly selected 20 percent of the working
controllers at their home addresses. "An almost unprecedented response for a mail survey that employed no fol-
low-up mailing and . . . no . . . incentive for responding"
resulted in an 82-percent return. Fifty-eight percent were
against the return of the strikers under any condition, 31
percent would permit them back under certain conditions, and only 10 percent felt that they should be hired
unconditionally. See *Aviation Safety, Air Traffic Control
(PATCO Walkout), Hearings before the Subcommittee on
Investigations and Oversight of the Committee on Public
Works and Transportation*, House of Representatives,
97th Cong., 1st and 2d sess. (Washington, D.C.: U.S. Government Printing Office, 1982), pp. 741–88.

[72]Initially, O'Donnell suggested that the former Director of the Federal Mediation and Conciliation Service

Despite their serious reservations about PATCO's course and tactics, the leaders of other unions were certainly concerned about the effect of PATCO's crushing loss. In particular, officials of public employee unions feared that the administration's actions would become a precedent for other governmental bodies. Moreover, the president's hard line, and the support it won from the public, could encourage a similar employer reaction to strikes in private industry.[73]

International Union Response

Since unions in one country seldom support strikes by those in another,[74] it is rather astonishing that PATCO's strongest support came from the Canadian Air Traffic Controllers Association (CATCA) and other affiliates of IFATCA, which by this time was determined to assume a more active role in industrial disputes. A few days after PATCO struck, the IFATCA executive board invoked its Resolution A5, which reads in part:

(a) . . . Member Associations will not clear aircraft into airspace under the jurisdiction of substituted services [i.e., those taking the place of striking controllers], and in addition . . .
(b) . . . [they should] consider refusing [air traffic control] service to U.S. Registered Aircraft.[75]

(FMCS), W. J. Usery, be hired as a special mediator; he and other ALPA officials also joined in approving a resolution at the AFL–CIO convention asking that the controllers be rehired. See Richard Witkin, "Judge Orders Fine: Head of Air Pilots' Union Suggests Mediator as Deadlock Persists," *New York Times*, August 5, 1981, pp. A-1 and A-14; and Warren Brown, "AFL–CIO's Executive Council Votes to Raise Dues $14.6 Million by '83," *Washington Post*, November 15, 1981, p. A12. O'Donnell's most important act, however, was to call a press conference on August 19, 1981, in order to declare that the airways were safe and specifically to refute Poli's claims to the contrary. See "Pilot Union Chief Calls Airways 'Safe', Says Near-Misses Are below a Year Ago," *The Wall Street Journal*, August 20, 1981, p. 8.

[73]See, for example, William Serrin, "Unionists Anxious Over PATCO Strike," *New York Times*, October 21, 1981, p. A24.

[74]Northrup and Rowan, *Multinational Collective Bargaining Attempts*, reviews the claims of transnational support of strikes and finds little evidence to support any such claims.

[75]IFATCA, "The Federation: Past–Present–Future," IFATCA conference document, 21st annual conference, Amsterdam, the Netherlands, May 3–8, 1982, Agenda Item A. 1. 6., pp. 1–2.

The overt rationale for such action was, of course, that the airways were not safe when a dispute involving IFATCA affiliates existed. Even before the IFATCA communication was sent out, controllers in New Zealand,[76] Norway,[77] France,[78] and later those in Portugal,[79] began delaying or refusing clearance to U.S.-flag or U.S.-bound aircraft. It was the Canadians, however, who inflicted the most damage. For two days, August 10 and 11, 1981, CATCA refused to clear any planes to or from the United States. The result was a virtual shutdown of traffic on the busy North Atlantic route, causing massive inconvenience during the height of the summer travel and costing the airlines millions of dollars. CATCA officials claimed that this action was necessary because of innumerable near-accidents, a list of which they had furnished to Canadian flight control authorities.[80]

This action by Canadian controllers proved to be the high watermark of PATCO and IFATCA efforts to shut down the U.S. air system. They failed because the U.S. authorities had prepared their foreign counterparts with

---

[76]New Zealand controllers first denied clearance to United States-bound aircraft, then delayed them. Effectiveness was limited by lack of cooperation from Australian controllers who were not affiliated with IFATCA. (IFATCA, "Annual Report of the Regional Vice President, Pacific Region," IFATCA conference document, 21st annual conference, Amsterdam, the Netherlands, May 3–8, 1982.) A strong message from Secretary Lewis to the New Zealand transportation minister aided in ending the disruption. (A copy of this message is in the author's possession.)

[77]The head of the Norwegian controllers was a leader of the pro-boycott faction in IFATCA, but obstructions in Norway were few and short-lived.

[78]French controllers issued many statements supporting PATCO, but after a few days of intermittent boycotts and slow clearance tactics, they yielded to pressure from their government and ceased interference.

[79]After several postponed announcements of boycott, the Portuguese controllers at the key Azores station began a 48-hour boycott on August 16. Transatlantic carriers rerouted their flights with only very minor problems. See Robert D. McFadden, "Controllers in Azores Set Boycott but Atlantic Flights are Rerouted," *New York Times*, August 16, 1981, pp. 1 and 37.

[80]Some Air Routes to Europe Shut for Hours as Strikers Get Canadian Group's Help," *New York Times*, August 11, 1981, pp. A-1 and B-7-9; "European Flights Slashed amid Big Delays as Canada Fails to Halt Union Backers," *New York Times*, August 12, 1981, pp. A-1 and A-22. Similar stories can be found in many Canadian and U.S. newspapers published during this period.

information about the dispute and the likelihood of IFATCA-sponsored action. Both Dutch and Danish authorities visited U.S. facilities and pronounced them safely and expertly handled.[81] The Director of Air Traffic Services, Transport Canada, investigated each of 22 alleged hazardous incidents reported by CATCA and found them either nonexistent or routine. In a telegram to CATCA on August 11, he gave the facts on each occurrence and commented:

More accurate information in your report of alleged incidents would be appreciated. We have not found any occurrence that required "evasive action" or "action to avoid collision." The irregularities were minor in nature and have occurred in the past when the U.S. air traffic control system was manned in a normal manner. I hope. . . . that you will publicly correct some erroneous statements that you have made in recent days.[82]

According to J. Lynn Helms, then FAA administrator, a "vital element" in ending the CATCA boycott was the commitment of the United States to open up and, if necessary, maintain air traffic control over transoceanic routes. Helms reported:

When the Canadian controllers started their initial efforts to exclude U.S. traffic across the North Atlantic, I went to ICAO [International Civil Aviation Organization] and obtained agreement that under the Chicago Accords if Canada was not able to fulfill its obligations to handle international air traffic then the airspace control should be assigned to the United States. Obviously, this was clearly coordinated with my Canadian counterpart, Mr. Walt McLeish. During his negotiations with the Canadian controllers, they rejected the possibility.

In the key conversation with Mr. McLeish, I outlined my plan and intent to use AWACS airplanes and missile cruisers, all with FAA controllers aboard, and that we definitely *would* open up the North Atlantic, and Azores, and the North Pacific routes. Based on this, he returned to the negotiations, advised them he now knew how we planned to do it, and agreed it could be done. Therefore, they would permanently forfeit their jobs. They

returned to work, and this broke the back of the foreign support so the French and Portuguese accepted the finality of it within 24 hours. At no subsequent time did I face major concerns from foreign controllers and the American labor movement accepted that position as final.[83]

Threatened by dismissals and other sanctions, the Canadians called off their boycott on August 13.[84] IFATCA held three emergency meetings to seek support for PATCO, but found that a majority of affiliates were unwilling to risk penalties at home in order to support a strike abroad.[85] Moreover, the claims of safety violations in the United States were becoming more obviously hollow as the system continued to function, as air traffic directors from various countries reported otherwise, and as pilots affirmed their satisfaction.[86]

---

[83]Letter from J. Lynn Helms, FAA administrator, to the author, July 26, 1983. The ultimatum from the ICAO to Canada's air traffic control authorities was confirmed in my interviews with officials of Transport Canada in August 1983.

The Chicago Accords to which Helms refers are the international agreements that allocate international air space to the air traffic control organizations of various countries. The accords require each country to provide the control services agreed on; failure to do so permits the ICAO to delegate a country's control authority to others.

[84]See Joann S. Lublin and Frederick Rose, "Atlantic Flights Begin Resuming Normal Service," *The Wall Street Journal*, August 13, 1981, p. 3. The Canadian authorities suspended 154 controllers for their refusal to handle planes from the United States, but an attempt to charge controllers with contempt of court in the matter was dismissed ("Canada to Suspend 154 Air Controllers," *Financial Times*, October 7, 1981, p. 3; and "Canadian Order Dismissed," *New York Times*, September 17, 1982, p. A-19).

[85]See Richard L. Hudson, "Foreign Air Controllers Postpone Plans for Boycott, but Industry Remains Wary," *The Wall Street Journal*, August 14, 1981, p. 3; John Tagliabul, "World Controllers Say They Back Strike but Avoid Immediate Move," *New York Times*, August 24, 1981, p. A-1; and a confidential report to the FAA on the IFATCA meeting, Rome, November 13–14, 1981, in the author's possession.

[86]In the *Monthly News Bulletin* of the International Federation of Air Line Pilots' Association (IFALPA), September 1981, p. 2 appeared this statement:

No reports of incidents in USA airspace had been received by IFALPA, the first six weeks of the strike. A number of individual pilots, including principal officers and regional vice presidents [of the IFALPA] had reported that they were satisfied that their own flights in USA airspace had been as safe as flights were before the USA Air Traffic Controllers dispute began.

---

[81]Reports of the Dutch and Danish inspectors are in the author's possession.

[82]The communication was sent to PATCO Executive Vice President Meyer by W. J. Robertson, president of CATCA, who had received it on August 11, the second day of the Canadian boycott.

PATCO's Demise

Decertified and overwhelmed by debts, PATCO first tried reorganization. Poli, Meyer, and Trick all resigned.[87] That did not alter anything. Bankruptcy and finally dissolution followed.[88] A new organization, the United States Air Traffic Controllers' Organization (USATCO), rose from the ashes, headed by Garry Eads, a former PATCO vice president and Poli's successor as PATCO president, but it has had little success in enrolling working controllers.[89] Meanwhile, many of the striking controllers have risked more of their life savings for legal fees on thus far quite unsuccessful efforts through civil service procedures to win reinstatement. It now appears that fewer than five percent are likely to succeed in this endeavor.[90]

---

[87]Poli Resigns Post with Controllers," *New York Times*, January 1, 1982, p. 7.

[88]"'The Union is Gone' PATCO Says; Organization Files for Bankruptcy," *White-Collar Report*, no. 131 (July 9, 1982), pp. A-9–A-10. PATCO had requested Chapter 11 status on November 26, 1981; this permitted it to operate with court protection against creditor lawsuits while it attempted to work out a plan for paying the enormous debts assessed against it for contempt on numerous counts. On July 2, 1982, PATCO bankruptcy was converted to a Chapter 7 proceeding, which involves no possibility of a viable reorganizing action.

[89]James Crawford, "New Organization Hopes to Unionize Controllers," *Federal Times*, April 4, 1983, pp. 4 and 15; and "New Air Traffic Controllers' Union Being Built by Veterans from PATCO," *Daily Labor Report*, no. 90 (May 9, 1983), pp. A-2–A-5.

[90]See Gregory Jaynes, "Lawyers at Odds on Tactics to Aid Striking Controllers," *New York Times*, February 21, 1982, p. 26; and Sara Schwaider, "Air Controllers: Paying the Price," *Philadelphia Inquirer*, February 8, 1982, p. 1. The success rate for reinstatement has been very low, whether the striker is represented by counsel or not. Thus, as of May 18, 1983, of 12,015 appeals filed, only 351 were initially granted a reversal of their discharges by the initial hearing officer, and some of these could be reversed on appeal (data from the FAA). Precedent-setting legal action has gone decisively against the attempts of controllers to gain reinstatement. See *United States v. Gary Greene et al.,*—F. 2d—(5th Cir., January 31, 1983); *Ketcham v. Department of Transportation, FAA, Merit Systems Protection Board,* no. DAO 75281 F0713, March 16, 1982; *Brown v. Federal Aviation Administration, Merit Systems Protection Board,* no. NVO 75281 F457, May 19, 1983; and *Schapansky v. Department of Transportation, FAA, Merit Systems Protection Board,* no. DAO 75282 F1130, October 28, 1982.

Concluding Observations

The PATCO strike did more than inconvenience air travelers, inflict great economic damage on airlines, cost 11,000 controllers their jobs, and destroy a union. The strike also raised serious questions about employee relations in the public service and about whether the whole matter could have been handled differently. It both affected and reflected labor relations in this era.

Federal-Employee Bargaining

Unions in the federal service have always found their main role to be political lobbying. The fact that wages and basic conditions of work are set by Congress makes this inevitable. Formerly under the Kennedy and Nixon orders, and now pursuant to the CSRA, unions have a greater bargaining role than they did before the 1960s, but it is still quite limited. The result is often twofold: union officials' frustration over their inability to negotiate basic wages and benefits, and their search for issues that will enhance their standing with the rank-and-file. This, in the words of a careful student of the problem, "causes relatively unimportant and even frivolous issues to clutter negotiations, and [to] tend to linger on the table because not much is accomplished by disposing of them."[91] Moreover, because strikes are illegal, the pressure to settle on the part of unions and management is considerably lessened, and preparation for bargaining by both parties is frequently poor.[92]

From its inception, PATCO strove to operate outside these constraints by using the strike weapon. To be sure, PATCO followed the model of the federal civil service union by effective lobbying and by support of its congressional friends. Nonetheless, until Langhorne Bond, FAA administrator under Presi-

---

[91]Douglas M. McCabe, "Problems in Federal Sector Labor-Management Relations under Title VII of the Civil Service Reform Act of 1978," Industrial Relations Research Association, proceedings of the 1982 spring meeting, *Labor Law Journal* 33, no. 8 (August 1982), p. 560.

[92]Ibid.

dent Carter, initiated a turnabout in FAA philosophy and approach and the Reagan administration, unlike all its predecessors, had the will when tested to meet the challenge, PATCO had also been very successful in operating an aggressive private sector bargaining policy in a public setting. The willingness of the Reagan administration to bargain over wages, and to recommend substantial wage increases, not only brought PATCO close to its goal but could well have altered the whole course of federal labor relations, if PATCO's leadership had not risked everything by its 1981 strike.

Unquestionably, if PATCO had succeeded in that strike, the right to bargain for wages and to strike in the public sector would, in effect, have been granted. It is important to note that to prevent this from occurring once PATCO had struck, the Reagan administration needed not only the will but the political muscle to accomplish its objective. Even in the face of the strong public support of the president's actions, PATCO's congressional supporters, in a vain effort to obtain a deal for reinstatement of the strikers, were able to prevent the payment of salary increases to working controllers until late 1982.[93]

In the past, the government's reaction to illegal strikes by controllers was equivocal at best, and more strikes occurred despite the sweeping injunction won by the ATA in 1970. These government policies encouraged Poli and his supporters to believe that such a procedure would be repeated, and thus contributed to the 1981 strike. If the 1981 strikers were to be reinstated, the federal government would again signal indecision about its belief in the traditional strike proscription in the federal service.[94] Yet such reinstatement has

been advocated in 1983 by one congressional committee, although opposed by another.[95] The cost of reinstatement, in terms of possible future service disruption and wage escalation, would be high, and also the investment in defeating PATCO's challenge to the rules could be lost. On the other hand, if the present stance is maintained, then it should be clear that federal sector labor relations are considerably different from those in the private sector.

Another Approach?

The success of the Reagan-Lewis approach of discharging the strikers and of maintaining the federal service bans on strikes has been criticized by some as a case of overkill. For example, Ronald W. Haughton, former chairman and now a member of the FLRA, suggested in 1982 that the case could have been referred to the Federal Services Impasses Panel (FSIP), a public hearing held, pressure put on PATCO to conform to legal procedures, and, if necessary, arbitration required to the issues in dispute.[96] Haughton even proposed that instead of decertifying the union, the government should levy no penalty against PATCO if the strikers returned to work.[97]

---

[93]Democratic Representative William D. Ford of Michigan, a strong supporter of PATCO and chairman of the U.S. House of Representatives Post Office and Civil Service Committee, bottled up the increase for this period, but his proposed bill providing amnesty for the discharged controllers lost on the House floor in 1982.

[94]In 1978, for example, Representative Ford successfully pressured the Postal Service to grant re-employment rights to postal employees who had struck two major facilities in New Jersey. "Settlement of Postal Strike Suit Gives Strikers Chance for Rehire," *Daily Labor Report*, no. 116 (June 16, 1982), pp. A-1–A-2.

[95]The report of the U.S. House of Representatives, Committee on Appropriations, *Department of Transportation and Related Appropriation Bill, 1984*, Report no. 98-246, 98th Cong., 1st sess. (Washington, D.C.: U.S. Government Printing Office, 1983), p. A-27, states: "the Committee urges the FAA to consider certain previously dismissed air traffic controllers eligible for reinstatement . . . and placed on the 'reinstatement eligibles' lists." On the other hand, the Committee on Appropriations of the U.S. Senate opposed this recommendation as "a serious mistake that could result in grave consequences . . . inconsistent . . . extremely disruptive to the air traffic system [and] . . . a severe blow to the morale of controllers who stayed on the job and worked diligently and efficiently during the rebuilding period." U.S. Senate, *Department of Transportation and Related Agencies Appropriation Bill, 1984*, Report no. 98-000 (draft), 98th Cong., 1st sess. (Washington, D.C.: U.S. Government Printing Office, 1983), pp. 30–31.

[96]See the testimony of Mr. Haughton before the U.S. House of Representatives, Subcommittee on Investigations, Committee on Post Office and Civil Service, February 24, 1981, 97th Cong., 2d sess. mimeographed.

[97]Haughton at first dissented to the FLRA decertification order, but when PATCO did not return to work, he later concurred.

This suggestion clearly represents a far different approach to federal sector strike prohibition than that of the Reagan administration; it follows the soft line of the FLRA, which refused to see the creation of a strike fund by a union forbidden to strike as an unfair labor practice. It is always possible that the Haughton proposals could have ended the strike. Yet, given PATCO's record and the government's historically ambivalent approach to the previous strikes, it seems likely that if the strike had ended without severe penalties, including discharges, fines, and decertification, the PATCO leadership, having come so close to achieving unrestrained wage bargaining and the de facto right to strike, would again have created a crisis to gain their goals.

PATCO and the Current Scene

It is difficult to assess the general effect of the PATCO strike, except to note its undoubted effect on other unions' propensity to initiate a strike in the federal sector. The strike occurred during a period of economic recession while a conservative administration was attempting to curtail excessive government spending, to restrain the upward march of federal transfer payments, and to reduce government regulation of enterprise. In such a period, union power is certain to be diminished, and this trend has been exacerbated by the problems of key industries in which union strength has been concentrated, such as automobiles, steel, trucking, air transport, and farm equipment. Furthermore, the PATCO strike was a decided setback for organized labor in government employment—unionism's major, if not only, growing sector. It also marks a defeat in organized labor's long-term and still basically unsuccessful attempt to organize the salaried and service sectors. Finally, the Reagan administration's handling of the dispute probably stiffened government bargaining at the municipal and state levels, but to what extent cannot be quantified.

Whatever the broader implications of the strike, one thing is certain: the PATCO leaders committed about every strategic blunder in the bargaining book. They overestimated their ability to shut down the airline system; they underestimated their ability to hold their members in line; they overestimated their support from their political friends, the public, and other unions; they had a great victory and a giant step toward their goal of private sector wage bargaining but threw it away; and worst of all, they ignored management's preparations to resist the strike and President Reagan's determination to break with the past and to enforce the law. Rarely has such an amateurish performance by a union been displayed so publicly or dealt with so decisively.

PART FIVE
Labor Market Issues

This section presents several articles that pertain to labor market issues.

Equal employment opportunity remains an important issue in the field of labor and industrial relations. In the first article, Barbara B. Reagan discusses the problem of occupational segregation by sex. The author reviews the labor market situation of women and explains what she believes are the major causes of job segregation. She concludes that "economic forces will be a major determinant of the future opportunities for women." This article provides a background for a consideration of the very important and much discussed topic of comparable worth. Some have speculated that comparable worth is the equal employment opportunity issue for the 1980s. George Milkovich discusses "the emerging debate" pertaining to the comparable worth issue. His article "serves to introduce principle issues related to equal pay, comparable worth, and the earnings gap." A second article pertaining to comparable worth is presented by Thomas Mahoney who takes it as his task to "explore the issue of comparable worth in terms of traditional market explanations of wage determination." He attempts to "outline the argument for reliance upon wage determination and the challenges to that argument by advocates of the comparable worth concept."

Employers in the United States have operated for many years under a doctrine known as employment-at-will. This doctrine has been taken to mean that the employment relationship can be terminated by either party with or without notice or cause. Challenges to the doctrine have been brought to the courts and the continued use of the doctrine is now being questioned. Jack Stieber discusses various issues that arise under the employment-at-will doctrine in his article, "Employment-At-Will: An Issue for the 1980s," and he concludes "that all employees deserve statutory protection against unjust discharge." A brief note by Charles Bakaly and Joel Grossman takes exception to some of the conclusions reached by Jack Stieber. Bakaly and Grossman believe that the employer's right to eliminate employment should be protected.

Basic industries such as steel, automobiles, and rubber have been undergoing profound structural changes in the past two years. Plant closings has become a central issue in the field of industrial relations. Kovach and Millspaugh analyze the plant-closing issue within the context of collective bargaining. They find that "because the courts and the legislatures have failed to respond, the collective bargaining arena is showing activity" in regard to plant-closing matters.

A concluding article in this section by Sar Levitan and Richard Belous present some insights into "Working Wives and Mothers: What Happens to Family Life?" Articles in this book have indicated the major role that women play in the labor market. Levitan and Belous raise interesting questions: "What is the effect of these occurrences on the institution of the family?" and "Does the economic independence of working women influence their decisions to either begin or end a marriage or to rear children?"

READING 30

De Facto Job Segregation*

Barbara B. Reagan†

I. IDENTIFICATION OF THE PROBLEM

Occupational segregation by sex exists when individual women are unable to make career choices freely, unfettered by subtle or implicit societal barriers. Such career choices include whether to work in unpaid production at home or in the workplace. Occupational segregation by sex also exists when employers have fixed perceptions of the role potential of women that give priority to women's sexual attractiveness or their motherhood or wifehood roles. As a result, employers treat all women working for pay as if they are secondary workers, weakly attached to the market, who only qualify for positions of lower status that are subordinate to those held by men.

The results of sexism in occupational segregation are fourfold. First, women tend to be segregated and crowded into certain "female" occupations such as primary and secondary teachers, nurses, secretaries, typists, office clerical workers, retail sales clerks, health technologists, waitresses, sewers, assemblers, and manufacturing checkers. Women are excluded or discouraged from going into some other occupations, particularly positions involving administration or supervision of men, top leadership, and power. Second, within a given occupation, women tend to be concentrated in the lower levels. Third, women's work is less highly valued than men's. Fourth, the total economic product of society is lower

*Reprinted with the author's permission. This article was prepared for testimony before the Joint Economic Committee and published by the U.S. Government Printing Office; it is contained in *Women in the U.S. Labor Force* (New York: Praeger Publishers, 1979), pp. 90–102.

†*Professor of Economics, Southern Methodist University, Dallas, Texas.*

than it otherwise would be if women with skills and ability were permitted to produce up to the limits of their capabilities.

In short, occupational segregation by sex currently results in the overrepresentation of women in the less favorable occupations. Even if equal pay for equal work is achieved, equality of opportunity will not occur simultaneously. This paper does not deal with the problems of attaining equal pay for equal work.

Before World War II and even as late as 1950, the world of work sharply segregated women into jobs that were "helping" positions for men, nurturing children, the ill, or the disadvantaged, or working in other people's homes. Women were expected to stay in the labor force only a short time or to be part-time or part-year workers. Jobs thought to be suitable for women were often extremely specific in job content, with little or no possibility of promotion and that could be filled by intermittent workers. Continuous job service and career development were not expected. Even fathers who aspired to college educations for their daughters talked about the value of young women getting some kind of skill certification as insurance against the possibility that something might happen to their future husbands.

II. MAJOR CHANGES IN THE WORKPLACE

Since World War II and particularly since 1960, we have become aware of two major changes in the workplace related to women and their employment. These changes have had ripple effects throughout society, but many rigidities in the world of work have remained.

The increased number of women in the American civilian labor force, which has been well documented,[1] is clearly one of the most far-reaching transformations of our history. From 1950 to 1975, the number of female workers has more than doubled. Since 1940, the number nearly tripled. Fifty-six percent of all women in the United States aged 18 to 64

[1]"Employment and Training Report of the President" (Washington, D.C.: U.S. Government Printing Office, 1976), pp. 143, 213, and 228.

years are now in the civilian labor force. The recent increase in the number of mothers with children under six who are working in the marketplace is particularly sharp.[2] It is difficult to imagine what the level of gross national product would be in the absence of the current rates of labor force participation of women, even allowing for alternate sources of labor supply, such as younger workers.

There are those, even today, who like to think of women workers as a residual labor force, to be called upon when needed on a temporary basis and sent back to the kitchen and the nursery when not needed. Such a view does not fit the modern aspirations of a work force with many women who see themselves as developing careers and working for much, if not all, of their adult lives.

The young woman of today is concerned about how she is going to develop as a whole person; whether she should marry and have children; how and whether she and her husband are going to fit together marriage, children, and two careers; how much she should invest in her own education, and what is the likely pay-off of such an investment. She has little doubt, however, that at some time in her life she will be interested in the opportunities available for paid employment.[3] She then wonders what her chance to contribute to her family and to society will be. Will she find a society receptive to her making a contribution in a meaningful way that will permit her to maximize her potential? Even though she is questioning, her expectations of the marketplace are far greater than were those of her older sisters and her mother and aunts. The increase in women's labor market expecta-

tions is also a major transformation in our history.

The more education a woman has, the more likely she is to want to work. The increase in women's expectations is shown by the proportion of women going to college, the proportion of women who are college graduates, and the shifts in majors of women currently in college. In 1974, the proportion of women 18 to 19 years of age going to college was 33 percent, after a steady rise from about 15 percent in the early 1950s. In 1974, the proportion of men 18 to 19 years of age going to college was also 33 percent, but that represented a fall from the peak of 44 percent in 1969. The drop in college enrollment by men occurred after 1969 because the labor market took a downward turn during this period after more than 10 years of steady, substantial growth. Many young men decided to seek alternative career paths in the depressed labor market; in contrast, young women were not deterred from their desire for upward mobility by means of a college education, despite the depressed labor market.[4]

Rising expectations of young women are also shown in the changes in freshman career plans, in spite of declining labor markets. Increasing numbers of women, upon entering college, plan to major in fields that have been atypical for women. The proportion of first-year college women who planned to be business majors increased from 3.3 percent in 1966 to 8.5 percent in 1974. Similarly those young college women who said they planned to become lawyers increased from 0.7 percent

---

[2] The labor force participation rate of wives who had children under 6 years old doubled from 18 percent in 1960 to 37.4 percent in 1976: at the same time the labor force participation rate of all women aged 20 to 24 increased from 45 to 65 percent. U.S. Department of Labor, Bureau of Labor Statistics, January 12, 1977, unpublished data; U.S. Department of Commerce, Bureau of the Census, *Current Population Reports*, Series P-50, no. 29 (Washington, D.C.: U.S. Government Printing Office).

[3] The worklife expectancy at birth for a female was 22.9 years in 1970, compared with 40.1 years for the male. Howard N. Fullerton, Jr., and James J. Byrne, "Length of Working Life for Men and Women, 1970," *Monthly Labor Review*, February 1976, p. 32. (U.S. Department of Labor, Bureau of Labor Statistics.)

[4] The data are quoted from current population surveys of the U.S. Bureau of the Census by Dr. Richard Freeman in "The Overeducated Americans" (New York: Academic Press, 1976), pp. 33–38. He uses the data as part of the evidence he quotes to show that the work world is becoming better for women. I suggest this evidence better supports a finding that young women in the early 1970s have rising expectations that the work world will be open to permitting them to make maximum contributions in it.

It also should be noted that the proportion of college graduates who are women is slowly moving upward. It was 40.2 percent in 1963–64 and 44.4 percent in 1973–74. For the increase over the 10-year period, see table 237 in "Statistical Abstract of the United States, 1975" (Washington, D.C.: U.S. Department of Commerce, Bureau of the Census) and "Earned Degrees Conferred, 1972–73 and 1973–74, Summary Data," NCES 76–105 (Washington, D.C.: U.S. Department of Health, Education, and Welfare), p. 21.

of all women entering college in 1966 to 2.3 percent in 1974. The percentage of these women hoping to become doctors increased from 1.7 percent to 3.5 percent. The big changes were (a) the decrease in the proportion of young women planning to become elementary or secondary teachers, 34.1 percent in 1966 but only 11.9 percent in 1974 (a realistic view of the expected fall in demand for teachers); (b) the increase in the proportion planning to go into health services (including nursing but excluding doctors) from 11.9 percent in 1966 to 22.7 percent in 1974; and (c) the increase in the undecided group, from 3.6 percent in 1966 to 12.6 percent in 1974.[5]

Young women who realize that the market for teachers is depressed and likely to remain so for some time apparently are moving in large numbers to health service professions, other than doctors. At least, this is their first idea. This is not surprising, given the ideas of many of their parents, teachers, and counselors that the realistic vocational interest of young women should be in supportive roles and in occupations requiring lower investment in human capital; nor is it surprising, given previously increasing societal needs for workers in health areas.[6] Health professions other than doctors are a traditional area for employment of women; 93 percent of the nurses, dieticians, and therapists in 1974 were women. Movement from teaching to nursing or other health professions (excluding doc-

tors) therefore does little to break down barriers to occupational segregation by sex.

The desire of women to move into law, medicine, and management does knock on those barriers.

III. Documenting Job Segregation

Given the sharp increase in numbers and proportion of women now employed outside the home and given the rising aspirations of women, the question then is whether there have been important shifts in the occupational distribution by sex. (1) Are women still crowded into the same "female" occupations? Yes. Sex typing of jobs is still dominant. (2) Is there movement of women into male-dominated fields? Yes, a little. (3) Do women have vertical mobility; have they moved into top-level positions of a given occupation and thus been able to demonstrate their ability to supervise men and to assume leadership roles? No, there is not much vertical mobility. One must therefore conclude, based on the above three factors, that occupational segregation is still very much present, in spite of legislation calling for an end to discrimination based on sex. As a result, only a limited number of jobs are available to women, and college-trained women tend to be seriously underemployed.

The 57 occupations in which at least 100,000 women were employed in 1973 are shown in Table 1. About 75 percent of all women workers were employed in these occupations. The 10 largest occupations in which more than 40 percent of all women workers were concentrated were secretary, retail trade salesworker, bookkeeper, private household worker, elementary schoolteacher, waitress, typist, cashier, sewer and stitcher, and registered nurse. Of the 10 largest, women comprised 83 to 99 percent of the workers in the particular occupation, except for retail trade salesworkers, where women comprised 69 percent. Of the 57 largest, women made up more than 75 percent of the employees in 31 (or more than half) of the occupations. Male employment showed much less occupational concentration. The 10 largest occupations for men employed less than 20 percent of all men workers, compared with the 40 percent noted

[5]Data from the American Council on Education quoted by Freeman, "Overeducated Americans," p. 40. The proportion of women enrolled in medical school increased from 6 percent in 1960 to 18 percent in 1974, with the proportion of women in the first-year class in 1974 up to 22 percent. The proportion of women enrolled in law schools increased from 4 percent in 1960 to 19 percent in 1974, with the proportion of women in the first-year class in 1974 up to 23 percent. See John B. Parrish, "Women in Professional Training—An Update," *Monthly Labor Review,* November 1975, p. 50.

[6]The expanding room for women in health service occupations may be diminished in the late 1970s by health policy developments which will result in a slowdown in hospital expansion and an improvement in wages and working conditions which will make health service jobs more attractive to white males. See Rashi Fein and Christine Bishop, "Employment Impacts of Health Policy Developments," forthcoming in a special report of the National Commission on Manpower Policy, Washington, D.C.

Table 1
Women Employed in Selected Occupations, 1973 Annual Averages

Occupation	Number (000)	Percent Distribution of Women	Women as Percent of Total Employment
Total	32,446	100.0	38.4
White-collar workers	19,681	60.7	48.7
Professional, technical workers	4,711	14.5	40.0
Accountants	162	.5	21.6
Librarians, archivists, and curators	133	.4	82.1
Personnel and labor relations workers	104	.3	33.7
Registered nurses	805	2.5	97.8
Health technologists and technicians	236	.7	71.5
Social workers	161	.5	60.8
Teachers, college and university	133	.4	27.1
Teachers, except college and university	2,038	6.3	69.9
Elementary school teachers	1,094	3.4	84.5
Kindergarten and prekindergarten teachers	185	.6	97.9
Secondary school teachers	565	1.7	49.5
Writers, artists, and entertainers	313	1.0	33.7
Managers, administrators	1,590	4.9	18.4
Restaurant, cafeteria, and bar managers	160	.5	32.4
Sales workers	2,240	6.9	41.4
Hucksters and peddlers	169	.5	77.2
Real estate agents and brokers	142	.4	36.4
Sales clerks (retail trade)	1,561	4.8	69.0
Clerical workers	11,140	34.3	76.6
Bank tellers	293	.5	89.9
Billing clerks	137	.4	83.0
Bookkeepers	1,466	4.5	88.3
Cashiers	909	2.8	86.7
Counter clerks (except food)	266	.8	76.2
Estimators and investigators (n.e.c.)	164	.5	49.5
File clerks	245	.8	86.3
Keypunch operators	230	.7	90.9
Payroll and timekeeping clerks	143	.4	72.2
Receptionists	431	1.3	96.9
Secretaries	3,037	9.4	99.1
Statistical clerks	204	.6	68.5
Stock clerks and storekeepers	120	.4	25.3
Teacher aides (except school monitors)	207	.6	90.4
Telephone operators	372	1.1	95.9
Typists	999	3.1	96.6
Blue-collar workers	5,244	16.2	17.6
Craft and kindred workers	463	1.4	4.1
Blue-collar supervisors	109	.3	7.5
Operatives	4,482	13.8	31.4
Assemblers	600	1.8	49.7
Checkers, examiners, and inspectors (manufacturing)	377	1.2	49.5
Clothing ironers and pressers	118	.4	77.1
Dressmakers and seamstresses (except factory)	131	.4	96.3
Laundry and dry cleaning operators (n.e.c.)	112	.3	63.3
Packers and wrappers (n.e.c.)	420	1.3	61.5
Sewers and stitchers	891	2.7	95.5
Textile operatives	240	.7	56.9
Nonfarm laborers	299	.9	6.9
Stockhandlers	130	.4	17.3
Service workers	7,008	21.6	63.0
Private household workers	1,330	4.1	98.3
Child-care workers	532	1.6	98.3
Private household cleaners and servants	631	1.9	98.3
Service workers (except private household)	5,678	17.5	58.1
Cleaning service workers	707	2.2	34.1
Building interior cleaners	358	1.1	54.2
Lodging quarters cleaners	196	.6	96.6
Janitors and sextons	153	.5	12.6

Table 1 (concluded)

Occupation	Number (000)	Percent Distribution of Women	Women as Percent of Total Employment
Food service workers	2,370	7.3	69.7
Cooks	555	1.7	59.8
Food counter and fountain workers	254	.8	80.9
Waiters, waitresses, and helpers	1,082	3.3	82.9
Health service workers	1,398	4.3	87.6
Dental assistants	112	.3	98.2
Health aides and trainees (excluding nursing)	150	.5	82.4
Nursing aides, orderlies, and attendants	790	2.4	83.9
Practical nurses	345	1.1	96.4
Personal service workers	1,140	3.5	73.9
Child-care workers	342	1.1	95.5
Hairdressers and cosmetologists	458	1.4	91.8
Farm workers	514	1.6	17.0

Source: Based on U.S. Department of Labor, *1975 Handbook on Women Workers*, Bulletin 297 (Washington, D.C.: U.S. Government Printing Office, 1976), pp. 89–91.

above for the 10 occupations employing the most women. The 57 occupations with the largest number of men employed covered 52 percent of all men workers; whereas the 57 largest occupations for women, as noted above, employed about 75 percent of the women.[7]

The above statistics show that women are concentrated in selected occupations much more than men are. The concentration of women into these few selected occupations has resulted in these occupations being relatively crowded, as evidenced by the relatively low wages paid in them. There is a reserve pool of qualified women outside the labor force who would be willing to work in these female jobs if the wages were increased or conditions of work improved.

Another facet of this question is the growing concentration of women in "female" jobs during the last 15 years. The 10 occupations in which most women were employed in 1973 are listed in Table 2. In some cases, summary data for a broader occupational group is also given in order to permit comparisons when the detail is not available. Because the data in this table are from different sources with slightly different definitions and are based on samples which are subject to normal sampling error, general comparisons should be made, rather than specific ones. (Dashes are used

[7]*1975 Handbook on Women Workers*, pp. 89–92.

when data are not available.) Trends may be meaningful even though differences between the selected years are small.

As the proportion of women increased among all occupations in the last 15 years, the most numerous jobs for women remained largely female jobs. Many of these female jobs have become even more concentrated with women as the market expanded, as in the case of retail sales clerking, bookkeeping, cashiering, secretarial and typing work, and food service work including that of waiter. In a declining labor market, private household jobs became more highly concentrated with women. Registered nursing and elementary school teaching positions showed little change, remaining highly concentrated with women. Most of the increase in women in the labor force has been absorbed through expansion of clerical and service worker jobs, which traditionally are "female" jobs.

A. Slow Movement into Male-Dominated Fields

Another aspect of recent changes in occupational segregation is whether women now are being employed in fields long considered male preserves; that is, higher-paid professional and managerial jobs. The question arises as to what proportion is suitable to be selected as the norm for women's participation in an occupation—50 percent, the same

Table 2
Proportion of Employed Workers Who Were Women in Each of the Selected Occupations for Selected Years since 1960

Occupation	1975*	1974†	1973‡	1970§	1960§
All occupations	39.0	38.9	38.4	37.7	32.8
Nurses, dieticians, therapists	—	93.1	—	94.4	96.0
Registered nurses	—	98.0	97.8	97.3	97.5
Teachers, except college	70.6	¹69.2	69.9	70.2	72.6
Elementary school teachers	—	84.3	84.5	83.6	85.8
Salesworkers, retail trade	61.6	¹60.9	—	—	—
Sales clerks, retail trade	—	69.4	69.0	64.6	63.3
Bookkeepers	—	89.2	88.3	82.0	83.4
Cashiers	—	87.7	86.7	83.5	76.9
Secretaries, typists, and stenographers	98.4	¹98.4	—	96.6	96.5
Secretaries	—	—	99.1	97.6	97.1
Typists	—	—	96.6	94.2	95.1
Operatives except transport	39.5	¹40.4	39.2	37.9	35.5
Sewers and stitchers	—	—	95.5	93.7	94.0
Food service workers	74.6	¹74.7	69.7	68.0	67.6
Waiters	—	—	82.9	88.8	86.6
Private household workers	98.0	¹98.2	98.3	96.6	96.4

*U.S. Department of Labor, Bureau of Labor Statistics, "Employment and Earnings" (Washington, D.C.: U.S. Government Printing Office, January 1976), table 18, p. 146. Employed persons 20 years and over; annual averages of monthly data.

†Unless otherwise specified, 1974 data are from U.S. Department of Labor, Bureau of Labor Statistics, "Employment and Earnings" (Washington, D.C.: U.S. Government Printing Office, June 1975), table 1, p. 7; annual average of monthly data.

‡U.S. Department of Labor, 1975 Handbook on Women Workers (Washington, D.C.: U.S. Government Printing Office, 1976), pp. 89–91; annual averages of monthly data.

§U.S. Department of Commerce, Bureau of the Census, 1970 Census of Population, "Detailed Characteristics of the Population, U.S. Summary" (Washington, D.C.: U.S. Government Printing Office, 1973), table 221. Employed persons 14 yrs. old and over, pp. 718ff.

proportion women have of all jobs (41 percent in 1976), or a looser definition based on free choice without barriers. As long as women are in low proportions in some fields, all we need to say is that barriers should be removed so that more women who wish to do so may move into the male-dominated fields. As long as the major direction for policy is clearly "more," we need not stop now to worry about how much more.[8]

Women are beginning to move slowly into male-dominated professions as shown in Table 3.

The proportion of women in the total for all professional fields is highly influenced by the concentration of women in the high-employment areas of primary school teachers and nurses. In the specific professional areas that traditionally have been male-dominated, more women are being employed as accountants in 1974 than in 1960. Similarly, the pro-

portion of women employed as college and university teachers has increased. Smaller gains have been made in law and medicine since 1960. Extremely small gains have been made in engineering, with possible regression since 1970.

The proportion of all women college graduates working in professional occupations fell from 81 percent in 1969 to 69 percent in 1974. This drop was related to the reduced chance of getting a teaching job in secondary or elementary schools; this reduced chance fell from 49 percent in 1969 to 43 percent in 1974.[9]

Women have also been moving slowly in the last 15 years into management positions, but there is still a long way to go, as shown in Table 4. Interpretation of the data on women in management is clouded by the fact that a higher proportion of women than men counted in the management category serve as supervisors, rather than true managers. Furthermore, the earnings and promotion possibilities of

[8]Kenneth E. Boulding and Barbara B. Reagan, "Guidelines To Obviate Role Prejudice and Sex Discrimination," American Economic Review, December 1973, p. 1050.

[9]Freeman, "Overeducated Americans," p. 171.

Table 3
Proportion of Employed Workers Who Were Women in Specified Male-Dominated Professions for Selected Years since 1960

Occupation	1974*	1973†	1970‡	1960‡
All occupations	38.9	38.4	37.7	32.8
All professional, technical	40.5	40.0	39.8	38.4
Accountants	23.7	21.6	26.0	16.4
Architects	—	—	3.5	2.0
Computer specialists	19.0	19.5	19.6	29.8
Engineers	1.3	—	1.6	.8
Engineering and science technicians	—	10.2	10.9	9.0
Lawyers and judges	7.0	—	4.8	3.4
Physicians, dentists	9.3	—	8.5	5.9
Religious workers	10.1	—	10.3	16.5
Clergymen	—	—	2.9	2.3
Teachers, college and university	30.9	27.1	28.4	23.7

*U.S. Department of Labor, Bureau of Labor Statistics, "Employment and Earnings" (Washington, D.C.: U.S. Government Printing Office, June 1975), table 1, p. 7; annual average of monthly data.

†U.S. Department of Labor, *1975 Handbook on Women Workers,* Bulletin 297 (Washington, D.C.: U.S. Government Printing Office, 1976), pp. 89–91; annual averages of monthly data.

‡U.S. Department of Commerce, Bureau of the Census, 1970 Census of Population, "Detailed Characteristics of the Population, U.S. Summary" (Washington D.C.: U.S. Government Printing Office, 1970), table 221. Employed persons 14 year old and over, pp. 718 ff.

Table 4
Percent of Employed Persons Who Are Women in Selected Manager Jobs by Years

Occupation	1974*	1973†	1970‡	1960‡
All occupations	38.9	38.4	37.7	32.8
Managers and administrators except farm	18.5	18.4	16.5	14.7
Bank officials, financial managers	21.4	19.4	17.6	8.7
Buyers and purchasing agents	24.9	25.1	—	—
Buyers, wholesale and retail trade	36.3	—	29.5	35.5
Health administrators	—	—	44.6	75.1
Officials, administrators; public administration; n.e.c.	20.8	—	19.1	17.4
Restaurant, cafeteria, bar managers	33.9	32.4	34.1	32.5
Sales managers, department heads, retail trade	32.4	28.9	23.8	23.4
Sales managers except retail trade	—	—	3.5	<.1
School administrators	27.8	29.0	26.5	25.6
College	—	—	23.5	30.7
Elementary and secondary	—	—	27.1	25.0

*U.S. Department of Labor, Bureau of Labor Statistics, "Employment and Earnings" (Washington, D.C.: U.S. Government Printing Office, June 1975), table 1, p. 7; annual average of monthly data.

†U.S. Department of Labor, *1975 Handbook on Women Workers,* Bulletin 297 (Washington, D.C.: U.S. Government Printing Office, 1976), pp. 89–91; annual averages of monthly data.

‡U.S. Department of Commerce, Bureau of the Census, 1970 Census of Population, "Detailed Characteristics of the Population, U.S. Summary" (Washington D.C.: U.S. Government Printing Office, 1970), table 221. Employed persons 14 years old and over, pp. 718 ff.

managers are related to the size and market power of their firms. Women managers may be less likely than men to be with the larger, more powerful firms. Sharp increases have been made in the employment of women in such positions as bank officials and financial managers. The market has expanded from about 24,000 such jobs in 1960 to over 300,000 in 1970 and to over 500,000 in 1974, an increase that is related to the growth in branch banking. The growth of women's proportion of such employment from about 9 percent in 1960 to 21 percent in 1974 is one of the sharpest changes observed. Women also gained in positions such as sales manager and department head in retail trade as the number of such jobs grew.

Health administration is another occupa-

Table 5
Women in Corporate Boards

	Number of Women Directors	Number of Corporations	Number of Directors Positions
Total	207	237	26
Women on more than 1 board	36	—	91
Women with family affiliation to founder or president	37	34	38
Boards with 2 to 4 women directors	—	21	46
Boards with 1 or more women who do not have family affiliation to founder or president	—	203	—
Women on 1 or more boards and who do not have family affiliation to founder or president	170	—	—

Source: With thanks to Dr. Alva Clutts, School of Business Administration, Southern Methodist University, for making these counts from the directory listing in *Business and Society Review* (Winter 1975–76), and bringing them to my attention.

tional group with tremendous growth from 1960 to 1970; the number of jobs grew from about 7,000 to 84,000. In this group of jobs, however, men were employed in such large numbers that the proportion of women managers decreased from 75 percent of the health administrators to 45 percent in the 10-year period. Women also lost ground from 1960 to 1974 as buyers in wholesale and retail trade, as well as college administrators from 1960 to 1970.

Although not considered a separate occupational category, the number of women who are on the boards of large corporations is related to women's role in management. Data on the relative number of board positions held by women is incomplete. A listing of the women members of the boards of directors of 237 corporations in the United States was made by *Business and Society Review* in the winter issue of 1975–76.[10] It was noted that appointment of women to boards of directors was just a trickle in 1972 and prior years, but increased more rapidly thereafter. Eighty of the women listed were appointed in 1975. Over the years, a few women were appointed to corporate boards because of family relationships to the men who founded or owned the businesses. Now additional women are being asked to serve because of their own accomplishments and knowledge. As company leaders begin to think about adding women as directors, they

have a tendency to select women who already sit on another board, as indicated in Table 5.

Of the 237 corporations who have at least one woman director, only 203 have women who are not related to the founder or president and only 170 women hold these positions. Obviously there should be more opportunity in the board rooms of many corporations for women with skills and experience to make a contribution.

B. Vertical Mobility

Once a woman has trained for a male-dominated field and obtained employment in an entry-level position, occupational segregation by sex still exists unless women have vertical mobility comparable to that of men. In part, this is a function of on-job-training opportunities. Employers with limited perceptions as to women employees' promotability will be reluctant to make on-job-training opportunities available to them. Women may be excluded from informal networks. Sex discrimination can take many subtle forms that slow or deter women's progress up the professional or managerial ladder.

It is not enough for counselors to urge a young woman to feel free to train for entry into a male-dominated field if her interests lie in that field. Active support systems, and attitudinal changes must also be made available if she is to have equal opportunity in the male-dominated profession or occupation.

---

[10]"Who Are the Women in the Board Rooms," a survey, *Business and Society Review* 16 (Winter 1975–76), p. 5.

Many of the "female" occupations have extremely limited channels for promotion. Many occupations have been fragmented into specific tasks requiring pre-employment training. Specific training for clerical or service tasks leads to permanent typecasting. Licensing and accreditation keep work groups separated and without promotional possibilities. For example, nurses' aides do not learn on the job how to be nurses; they have to attend school to do so.

About two thirds of all jobs in New York City municipal hospitals do not have educational or training requirements for entry, but neither do they have promotional possibilities.

Even in industries where promotional ladders are common, certain jobs were traditionally isolated. An example of particular interest involves telephone operators. The American Telephone and Telegraph Company, in agreeing to affirmative action for enhancing equal employment opportunity, now provides for exit from this job by removing sex as a barrier to horizontal or vertical mobility. Since the plan cannot, however, create experience linkages between the operator job and other jobs, the company has to train the operators who move into craft jobs as if they were newly hired.

The point is important because it illustrates how closely the conditions for market protection are related to jobs rather than to the people who fill them. Equal opportunity as a strategy tends to increase the pool of eligibles in competition for the better jobs, but it does not make good jobs out of poor ones.[11]

A study of labor market changes between 1960 and 1970, from which the above quotation was excerpted, arrives at the following conclusion: Among 270 labor market segments in the occupational-industry matrix, only 38 had a considerable proportion of their jobs so organized as to make possible promotion based on on-job training. The 38 occupation-industry segments were composed primarily of managers and sales people in finance, insurance, and real estate; professional, technical, and craft workers in public administration; professional workers in manufacturing and trade; managers in wholesale manufacturing, construction, agriculture, retailing, other consumer services, education, health, restaurants, and utilities; and craft workers in manufacturing, transportation, utilities, and other consumer services. These occupation-industry groups were among the higher-paying groups. They provided only 11 percent of all jobs in 1960 but expanded to cover 16 percent of all jobs in 1970. The increase occurred primarily in public administration. Manufacturing and utilities had relatively declining employment from 1960 to 1970. These 38 segments with strong internal promotion ladders were not occupation-industry groups with many women employees.[12]

If the occupational groups in the above study were divided into categories based on average annual earnings, women would be concentrated in three of the four lowest-paid categories, as of 1970. The proportion of women falling in the three lowest-paid categories ranged from 65 to 76 percent. The earnings ratios for these low-paid groups ranged from 43 to 78 percent of the average earnings of all the groups. Perhaps most discouraging of all, the dominance of women in these three low-paid categories had increased from 1960 to 1970. The occupations in these groups were primarily office and nonoffice clerical work in manufacturing, nondurable retailing, finance, insurance, real estate, and some service industries; technical work in health and product services; sales work in nondurable retailing; and service work in education, restaurants, and other consumer service industries.[13]

Women are subjected to typecasting in the labor market. They have limited occupational mobility, either horizontal or vertical. Consciousness of their occupational segregation is being raised, but barriers to their progress still exist.

IV. CAUSES OF JOB SEGREGATION

Why does occupational segregation by sex persist? Why are women continuing to enter traditional jobs for women instead of being

---

[11]Marcia Fredman, "Labor Markets: Segments and Shelters," *Landmark Studies* (Montclair, N.J.: Allenheld, Orman, 1976), pp. 42–43.

[12]Ibid., pp. 42 and 72.
[13]Ibid., pp. 21, 71–73.

hired in nontraditional jobs? Clearly, more women entering into traditional jobs makes it even more difficult to reduce barriers to employment of women in nontraditional jobs because of the continually larger numbers involved. Until sizable numbers of women throughout the economy—in business, universities, and government—hold leadership and executive positions with policymaking responsibilities, occupational segregation by sex and sex discrimination will not be eliminated. The total economy and the society as a whole will be the loser, as well as the women and families involved. White men gain when they can restrict entry to their jobs, but women lose more than white men gain; thus society suffers a net loss.

Part of the explanation for discrimination must lie outside the field of economics; some employers continue to discriminate against women, even when it is in their economic interest to hire women for nontraditional positions. Some employers will not hire women in top-level positions even when women are "good buys"—that is, a woman who is currently underemployed in relation to her training and experience could be hired and her work upgraded with only a reasonable increase in pay. Economic incentives to the employer have not been enough to open up opportunities to more than a few highly qualified women.

Recent new laws against sex discrimination in employment are now on the books. However, lack of enforcement, slowness of judicial processes, subtle but strong retaliation against people who raise individual discrimination cases for discussion and judgment, the attitude of those in power that these issues are not serious all have tended to negate the effectiveness of antidiscrimination legislation. Only the persistent pressure of women activists has kept antidiscrimination measures alive. Recent efforts to end university obligation to enforce anti-sex discrimination measures represent a case in point of continuing pressure to undo even limited progress—a negative precedent if these efforts were to prevail.

Until our society finds ways to show that sex discrimination will not be tolerated, and powerful political leaders do more than make token appointments of a few women, the waste of occupational segregation will persist.

There are many reinforcing and interlocking factors causing occupational segregation by sex to persist. First, there is the cumulative effect of past discrimination. There is outright discrimination against individual women of skill and ability. There is also backlash, particularly today, from men who feel very insecure when women in the work world are in positions that are not subordinate to them. Most important numerically is the narrow perception that many men in positions of power have of the potential of women in the work world. Such men never think of women for management, executive, and leadership positions. These narrow attitudes are supported by institutions throughout our culture which have long and deep historical roots.[14] They are based on attitudes that (1) woman's primary role is in the home, (2) her attachment to the labor force is temporary or secondary to the home, (3) she is interested only in intermittent work to meet rising costs in periods of inflation, or to earn just "pin money." The recent expectations of women who have been entering the labor force attest to the opposite view. Many women are serious about their careers and their work role potential. They are interested in making the greatest possible economic contribution to their families[15] as well as to the productivity of society. Women are dismayed at the negative attitudes,[16] the institutional barriers, the waste involved when they are not permitted to develop their careers fully after investing in their human capital.

Many top male executives are completely blind to the sex discrimination involved in occupational segregation. They are so imbued with the rightness of the view that men should be in all the top positions that underutilization of women employees is beyond

[14]For detailed analysis, see Martha Blaxall and Barbara B. Reagan, eds., Women in the Workplace, the Implications of Occupational Segregation (Chicago: University of Chicago Press, 1976).

[15]This is not a new attitude for women. It is just that the means have changed.

[16]A male colleague of mine quips that the reason occupational segregation by sex persists is simple—the cost of a sex modification operation is so high.

their current understanding. Even calling the issue to their attention may not result in immediate awareness. It takes repeated efforts and often personal involvement through wives and daughters before real insight occurs. This blindness is not limited to older men, nor to business leaders. Some political leaders, even relatively young ones, also lack insight, despite the fact that politicians should be particularly sensitive to current trends in women's role potential. Recently, a business executive was quoted in the press as saying that he asked his secretary if she felt discriminated against because of her sex. She said, "Of course not." As a form of proof, this is analogous to the Southern planter in the early 1930s who asked his black sharecropper if he liked his position. The answer was, "Yes, sir, Boss, and I appreciate it."

The increased awareness of many men in power positions of the moral wrong and economic inefficiencies in racial discrimination has provided a strong basis for extending and widening their view of the role potential of women. The surprise to women is the slow rate at which employers' views have changed and sex discrimination has ended. Women are also surprised at the strength of the backlash against women moving into higher positions, even though the movement is so infinitesimal.

Male executives today often fear "reverse discrimination" when in fact women really are not going anywhere in the top echelons. Examination of a business, government agency, or university may reveal this. Unless a male superior supports and pushes a female so as to open opportunities for her, she does not go very far up the ladder. Men think nothing of a male executive supporting and pushing a male protege. But when the protege is a woman of talent and skill, many men see this as undue favoritism, instead of a simple normal protege situation.

Some of the resistance against opening opportunities for women to move up the executive ladder in the world of work comes from men who themselves feel insecure and indeed are inadequate as managers. Unfortunately, in our culture there are still men who are unable to deal with women at work in positions other than subordinate ones. They are not willing to see women move into positions where in the future they might conceivably compete with them or their close male colleagues.

In the world of work, efficiency ratings are common place. It is time, in my opinion, to rate an executive on his ability to work with women and his willingness to open opportunities for them at top levels. If he is unable to handle this, his management ability should be appropriately downgraded. As with racial discrimination at work, inner feelings do not have to be monitored; actions do!

V. CONCLUSION: ECONOMIC FORCES AFFECT SEGREGATION

The future effect of efforts to end sex discrimination and reduce sex role stereotypes in the workplace may well depend on the general health of the economy and its growth rate, as well as on the strength of agents of change. Merely opening entry-level positions in atypical fields for women, although useful, will not solve the problem. The policy of using women only when the economy needs them, and the blindness to role potential of women can easily block advancement of new entrants. Concurrent movement of women in top-level executive positions and into the corporate board rooms is also necessary. At this point, the potential competition of women with men for top-level jobs is very threatening to men. It is particularly threatening if the growth of the economy and thus the increase in the number of executive-level jobs is low. Differing growth rates for the overall economy suggest different scenarios.

If labor markets expand through the second half of the 1970s, the rising expectations of women and the movement of women into the labor market may well shift former patterns and reduce barriers to women in the workplace. On the other hand, if labor markets remain depressed through the second half of the 1970s, the rising expectations of women workers may well come into sharp conflict with the realities of occupational segregation and the barriers to their occupational mobility. At least two alternate outcomes are possible with depressed labor markets. The ensuing conflict between women's expectations and the barriers to their occupational mobility may be enough to change the previously established equilibrium and to open greater opportunities for women. Such movement may be small. Nevertheless, a small amount of movement may be large enough to ease social tensions, even though full productivity gains are not realized.

An even more likely scenario in a slow economy with relatively high unemployment rates would be increased rigidities in occupational segregation by sex and decreased opportunities for women. This could be a reaffirmation of the old view that women are secondary workers in the labor market and male heads of families receive priority in employment. Economic forces will be a major determinant of the future opportunities for women.

READING 31

Comparable Worth: The Emerging Debate*

George T. Milkovich[†]

A significant national debate over the pay differences between men and women and the systems used to determine wage rates has emerged.[1] While all the questions have yet to crystallize, two basic issues seem to underlie the controversy. The first is whether the currently accepted standard, equal pay for equal work, is discriminatory, and if so, should it be replaced with another standard, equal pay for work of comparable worth. Underlying this issue is whether wage differences observed in labor markets should continue to serve as a factor in the determination of the relative value of work. The challenge to the equal pay for equal work standard also questions whether current compensation systems, specifically job evaluation and market surveys, simply perpetuate the discriminatory practices alleged to be reflected in the market.[‡]

A second, perhaps more basic issue in the debate, involves the persistent gap between the earnings of men and those of women. The oft-quoted data, "The average earnings of fully employed women in 1978 ($8,583) is 58 percent of the fully employed male average earnings ($14,790)" is used in the popular press to highlight the issue. Some assert that this earnings gap is proof of discriminatory compensation practices, the implication being that if average earnings of both sexes were equal, society would have achieved employment relations free of sex discrimination. The focus is on differences in rates for jobs traditionally dominated by women (e.g., office and clerical) versus rates for male-dominated jobs (e.g., managerial and crafts). The underlying question, therefore, is whether the relatively lower average wages paid for clerical, office, and operatives jobs is attributable to work-related factors, such as the job's relative contributions to the production of goods and services, the degree of unionization, and employer and industry characteristics? Or are the differences in wages principally a result of discriminatory traditions that "crowd" women into traditional jobs, which in turn depress the wage rates for those jobs?

The potential resolution of these issues will have far-reaching consequences. Society in the 1980s, through governmental and judicial interpretation of existing legislation and through possible additional legislation, faces at least two basic policy options. One is to reduce the earnings gap between men and women by requiring employers and unions to raise the rates for relatively lower-paid jobs (in which larger proportions of women have traditionally been employed) to match rates for higher-paid "male-dominated" jobs. The other is to avoid tampering with the vast array of wage structures and wage determination systems found in the economy and, instead, rely upon the removal of discriminatory barriers that have historically hindered women's entry into the higher-paid jobs, through vigoroous enforcement of equal employment and affirmative action practices.

This paper will serve to introduce the issues in this debate. It will examine the differing standards of equal work versus comparable worth and the implications for contemporary pay practices. Also, it will analyze the "earnings gap" and the models and research that underlie much of our information about this "gap." Subsequent papers in this study examine specific aspects of these issues and other related issues in greater detail.

*Reprinted with permission from E. Robert Livernash, ed. *Comparable Worth: Issues and Alternatives*, Washington, D.C.: Copyright © 1980 by the Equal Employment Advisory Council, 1980, pp. 24–47. Reprinted with permission of the publisher.

†*George T. Milkovich is a professor of human resources at the Center for Human Resources Research in the School of Management at the State University of New York at Buffalo.*

[1]Pay in this chapter refers to all payments, direct and indirect.

‡Comments of Jerry Newman, Frank Krzystofiak, and the other authors of the study on an earlier draft of this chapter are greatly appreciated.

Figure 1
Compensation System: Basic Concepts, Components, and Objectives

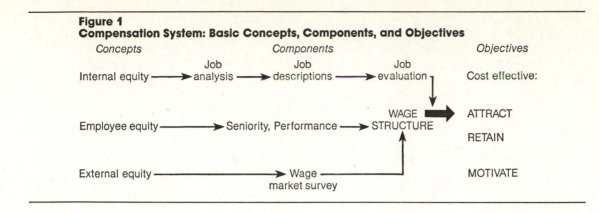

I. EQUAL PAY: FOR EQUAL WORK OR FOR WORK OF COMPARABLE WORTH?

Equal work and work of comparable worth represent very different standards on which to base pay. Equal work, a standard underlying contemporary compensation systems, has a reasonably well-accepted interpretation in labor-management relations, within the judicial system, and among compensation experts. By contrast, the notion of comparable worth does not have as clear a definition, and perhaps therein lies some of the confusion and concern. Comparable worth appears to take on different meanings to different people. It seems to have become a rallying cry for those who perceive the "earnings gap" as an example of the social injustice present in the U.S. society. For others, comparable worth is a behavioral or social science construct, akin to "organization climate" or "quality of working life," for which researchers may attempt to develop measures and conduct investigations. This section of the paper examines equal work and comparable worth, their respective definitions, and their implications for pay decisions.

A. Equal Work

Equal work is work of similar content, requiring that similar work behaviors and tasks be performed under similar working conditions, and requiring similar responsibilities, efforts, and abilities. The entire focus of equal work is job-related. Within contemporary compensation systems, the objective is to pay jobs of equal work content equally and, just as importantly, to pay jobs with different work content differently, based upon the relative value of the work to the organization's objectives.

At this point, some background in contemporary compensation practice is necessary to appreciate more fully the role of the equal work standard in the process of the determination of pay.[2] Most compensation systems have multiple objectives; for example, those listed in Fig. 1, "to influence employee decisions to join, to remain, and to work efficiently in a cost-effective manner" are commonly found in corporate compensation policy manuals.

While compensation systems have multiple objectives, these objectives may differ among employers generally, or even within the same employer at different locations or at different times. Some organizations, for example, may not try to influence work force productivity with pay for performance or with incentive pay systems, but will emphasize the attraction and retention of a competent work force as the principal objectives. Still other organizations may simply focus on minimizing costs, and thus set as low a wage as possible.

1. Internal Equity. To achieve these objectives, compensation systems are designed to

---

[2]Entire textbooks examine compensation systems in considerable detail. The interested reader is urged to refer to these more detailed treatments. David W. Belcher's *Compensation Administration* (Englewood Cliffs, N.J.: Prentice-Hall, 1974) is acknowledged as a classic.

balance at least three concepts of equity in setting pay rates; internal, external, and employee equity. Internal equity refers to the relationships of different jobs within an organization. How, for example, does the work of the key punch operator compare to the work of the computer operator to the programmer to the systems analyst? The relationships among jobs yield the job structure or the levels of work found in an organization. They reflect the fact that the content of one set of tasks and behaviors (a job) is either equal to or different from another set of tasks and behaviors. Furthermore, the relative value of the contributions of these jobs is based on their work content and its contribution to the accomplishment of the organization goals. For example, the contribution to the organization of a systems analyst who designs a new inventory or production control system is greater than the contribution of the job that programs the system or that key punches the program. Thus, internal equity, or the relationships among jobs within the organization, has two aspects: (1) the relative similarities and differences in work content of jobs, and (2) the relative value or contribution of the work to the organization's goals.

Internal equity is operationalized in compensation systems through a sequence of processes. The first of these is job analysis, which is the systematic collection of information about the tasks performed, the abilities and behaviors required to perform them, and the environment under which they are performed.[3] The results of job analysis are summarized in job descriptions or work descriptions, which usually consist of a one- or two-page summary of the job.

Job evaluation, the third process in the sequence for determining internal equity, is the systematic evaluation of job descriptions (summaries of job content) to determine a job structure based upon the contributions or value of the jobs to the organization's goals. Through these procedures, internal equity is translated into a structure of jobs based upon the work performed and the value of this work to the organization.

Job evaluation has received special attention in the debate over equal work and comparable worth, as evidenced by the National Academy of Sciences' contract with the Equal Employment Opportunity Commission.[4] The other two processes, job analysis and preparation of job descriptions, have received less attention in the debate, though it can be argued that both are crucial. It is only through proper job analysis that the job-relatedness of most pay decisions, and for that matter, most human resource decisions, can be justified.

As the following list indicates, perceptions of job evaluation seem as diverse as the blind men viewing the elephant:

1. Aids in determining the essential similarities and differences in job duties, tasks, and action.
2. Within a job family or occupation, determines the relative contribution or value of jobs to an organization.
3. Aims at providing a systematic-objective basis for the comparison of job contents.
4. Is a method which helps to establish a justified rank order of jobs—it is only one of the starting points for establishing the relative differentiation of wage rates.
5. Is to establish a mutually acceptable criterion of equity.
6. Aim is to establish on an agreed logical basis the relative values of different jobs in a given plant or industry. Job evaluation does not, of course, take the place of established procedure for bargaining between employers and workers, but use of a system of job evaluation may facilitate the development and maintenance of an equitable relationship among different jobs.

---

[3]While internal equity, through job analysis, job descriptions, and job evaluation, focus on the job and not on the individual employee, it is incorrect to assume that employee skills and abilities do not enter into the design and tailoring of work. The notion that people are somehow fixed and matched to jobs as pegs to holes is antiquated. Jobs are designed and tailored to fit work force capabilities and employees seek out education and are trained to match job requirements. It is a dynamic interplay between job content and employee qualifications.

[4]See Donald J. Treiman, "Job Evaluation: An Analytical Review," Interim Report to the Equal Employment Opportunity Commission (Washington, D.C.: National Academy of Sciences, 1979).

7. Is an attempt to determine and compare the demands which the normal performance of particular jobs make on normal workers without taking account of the individual's abilities or performance of the work concerned.[5]

Two basic aspects of job evaluation emerge from these views:

1. A *measurement aspect:* That job evaluation, properly developed and administered, is a relatively objective, systematic, analytical process which assesses both the similarities and differences in the *content of work,* and the *relative value of the work* to the organization.
2. A "rules of the game" or *process aspect:* That job evaluation, properly administered, provides procedures through which various interested parties interact and exchange views pertinent to the content of work and its relative value.

Under the former view, the premise is that the two key constructs, work content and relative value of the content, can be assessed in some acceptable, objective manner. The view is not new; in the 1930s and 1940s, industrial engineers, psychologists, and management scientists worked toward developing job evaluation as a relatively objective approach to measuring the content of work and its relative value.[6] Renewed interest in the measurement aspects of job evaluation again appeared in the 1970s, and Schwab's chapter in this volume reflects this interest.[7]

There is a need to distinguish between a job evaluation plan as originally developed and the plan as it is applied and used over the years. At the time of its development, a job evaluation plan is designed to model the existing pay structure. In so doing, the plan is intended to incorporate the external economic forces as well as the existing customs and conventions of the work environment. Over time the pay differences may change as well as the norms and relationships of job content. Several studies have found that the weights and factors originally developed to mirror the prevailing pay structures had been modified through the application of the plan.[8]

The other characteristic of job evaluation, the process to achieve a consensus on differences in pay, emphasizes the nonmeasurement, "rules of the game." In this view, Livernash observed that "Job evaluation is not a rigid, objective analytical procedure. Neither is it a meaningless process of rationalization. Job evaluation must produce acceptable results. The results may be judged from two bases: wage relationships among key jobs or relationships within clusters. Job evaluation is tested by the degree of correlation achieved between points of key jobs and acceptable wage relationships."[9] He further points out that historically job evaluation was developed to bring some order and acceptance to the hodgepodge of unrelated wage rates that existed in the 1930s and 1940s.

To gain acceptance of pay differences, the job evaluation process involves the various parties concerned about pay differences. In some situations this includes union and management representatives; in others it involves compensation committee representatives

[5]For these and other views on job evaluation, see *Job Evaluation* (Geneva: International Labour Organisation, 1960).

[6]For example, see Jay L. Otis and Richard H. Leukart, *Job Evaluation,* 2d ed. (Englewood Cliffs, N.J.: Prentice-Hall, 1954); C. H. Lawshe, Jr. and R. F. Wilson, "Studies in Job Evaluation: 6. The Reliability of Two-Point Rating Systems," *Journal of Applied Psychology* 31 (1947), pp. 355–65.

[7]The U.S. Civil Service Commission recently completed an extensive revision of their classification systems. The techniques and research designs used reflected the state of the art in measurement. For example, see J. M. Mådden, *An Application to Job Evaluation of a Policy-Capturing Model for Analyzing Individual and Group Judgment,* Technical Report PRL—TDR—63—15, AD—417—273, Lackland Air Force Base, Texas (1963); R. C. Mecham and E. J. McCormick, *The Use in Job Evaluation of Job Elements and Job Dimensions,* Lafayette,

Ind.: Purdue University, Occupational Research Center 1969); David D. Robinson et al., "Comparison of Job Evaluation Methods," *Journal of Applied Psychology* 59 (1974), pp. 633–37; L. R. Gomez-Mejia, R. C. Page, and W. W. Tornow, *Traditional versus Statistical Job Evaluation* (Minneapolis: Control Data Corporation, Research Report 169–79, 1979).

[8]W. M. Fox, "Purpose and Validity in Job Evaluation," *Personnel Journal,* October 1962, pp. 432–37.

[9]E. Robert Livernash, "The Internal Wage Structure," in G. W. Taylor and F. C. Pierson eds, *New Concepts in Wage Determination* (New York: McGraw-Hill, 1957), pp. 140–72.

from various functions or divisions of management to higgle over the appropriate slotting of jobs into a pay structure. To effectively achieve acceptance of pay differentials, the job evaluation process must be relatively open to the participation of all relevant parties. Perhaps current and future plans must include wider participation of various employee groups. However, the prospect of wider participation raises such issues as which employee groups to include, how to insure fair representation, etc.

2. External Equity. The second aspect of equity shown in Figure 1, external equity, refers to the relationships among jobs among employers in the external labor market. The basic issues to be answered in external equity are how do other relevant employers pay for equal work, and how do we wish to pay for it? External equity is established by determining the going rate for similar work in relevant external labor markets. These rates for jobs are usually established through a process of surveying the practices of other employers, yet the process is more involved than it may seem. It requires that the following sequence of decisions be faced:

1. Which employers should be included in the survey?
2. Is the work content of the jobs described by surveyed employers equal?
3. How is "pay" to be defined?
4. Which wage policy is consistent with the organization objectives?[10]

The question of which employers to include in the survey process is a critical decision in the wage determination process. Should all those employers who use the jobs under question be included, regardless of size, industry, and geographic location? A partial answer involves the definition of the relevant labor markets for each specific job for each employer. These labor markets are based in part on the product/service markets in which the employer competes, as well as the type of skills

and abilities the job requires. It is of some interest to note that the process for establishing the relevant external labor markets, and the relevant employers to survey has not been raised in the debate over equal work versus comparable worth; nor, it would seem, has the process been systematically researched by wage and salary experts.[11]

Another decision which must be faced in the determination of the going rate is whether the content of the jobs to be surveyed are similar to those under analysis. For example, does the work content of a programmer position in one organization require knowledge of only the BASIC language, whereas the job in the employer surveyed require proficiency in a range of languages including BASIC, COBOL, and PL 1? In the latter case the two "programmer" jobs are dissimilar and should not be matched in the survey.

Other decisions, such as determining precise definitions of "pay" and statements of wage policy, are also critical in the process of establishing going rates. The need to define pay is apparent if one realizes that actual rates paid for work may differ from pay ranges, that total or gross pay (including the opportunity to accumulate overtime pay) differs from base pay, and that some employers offer superior benefit packages and less "pay" than others. The concern in establishing the going rate is to ensure comparison of "apples to apples."

The wage policy issue refers to the decision to set wage rates at a rate that matches, leads, or follows the going rate established in the market. While the rationale underlying each policy is beyond the scope of this paper, it is relevant to note that employers differ in their approach to the market. For example, some employers adopt a "wage leader" policy; that is, they set their rates above going rates for equal work in the market to insure that a highly qualified and efficient workforce will apply for their job opportunities. These differences in approaches to the labor markets reflect the high degree of decentralization and unique-

---

[10]For greater detail on the survey process, see David W. Belcher, *Compensation Administration* (Englewood Cliffs, N.J.: Prentice-Hall, 1974).

[11]It should also be noted that other compensation decisions, such as the process of establishing pay grades, ranges, and progression schedules, require additional analysis.

ness that exist in wage determination procedures.

3. Employee Equity. Employee equity is the third aspect of equity incorporated in compensation systems. Employee equity focuses on the relationships among individual employees employed in similar work within an employer. For example, should one programmer be paid differently from another if one has greater seniority and/or superior performance, or should all programmers receive the same pay? This aspect of equity focuses directly on the individual employees in relationship to the work performed. Merit or "pay for performance" and seniority or "automatic progression" are common practices designed to recognize work-related differences among individuals performing equal work.

The standard of equal pay for equal work is a factor in all three aspects of equity. Internal equity focuses on the assessment of equal and different work through the operations of job analysis, job description, and job evaluation. The concerns for matching specific work content, "apples to apples," in the wage and salary survey process insures that equal work is being compared across employers when the "going rates" in the relevant labor markets are determined. Finally, the equal work standard is seen in the use of performance and seniority or experience to determine pay differences. Such systems recognize that differences in performance and/or experience within equal jobs can be recognized with pay. Thus, the equal work standard is a critical factor in the wage determination process.

The previous discussion was intended to provide a brief overview of contemporary compensation systems. The danger is that a reader will conclude that a simple, uniform set of practices exists. In a society and economy as diverse as the United States, compensation practices and wage decisions are equally diverse and complex. These may include the absence of any formal system, or job analysis plans, multiple job evaluation systems, multiple wage surveys, differential geographic allowances, group and individual incentive and bonus arrangements, lump sum awards,

seniority, merit, COLA increments, international arrangements, varying wage policies, and arrangements in which employees participate in a variety of compensation committees.

The above list includes only some of the direct compensation systems; indirect compensation or benefit systems are equally diverse. Furthermore, the influence of unions has not been discussed; obviously, they play a critical role in the determination of wage settlements, establishing wage patterns, and even influencing, in some cases, the details included in job analysis, job descriptions, and evaluation.

B. Equal Work among Occupations

In the current debate over equal work and comparable worth, it is important to consider the process by which occupational pay differences evolve. For example, what are the bases for wage differences between key punch operators versus programmers, or typists and secretaries versus electronic component assemblers versus plumbers or electricians? One criticism of the equal work standard is that while processes such as job evaluation, job analysis, performance evaluation, and incentive pay may perform a reasonable function within job families or groups of jobs related in work content, they are not as useful in the establishment of wage rates among jobs with diverse work content. The fact that some organizations use multiple job evaluation systems, e.g., one for office and clerical jobs, another for manufacturing, and still another for managerial jobs, seems consistent with this argument. A possible explanation lies in the fact that different types of work possess different factors which contribute to the organization goals.[12]

The problem is to develop measures, com-

---

[12]Research using quantitative job analysis, which seeks to identify basic elements of work and workers' abilities and behaviors in dissimilar jobs, may be applicable here. See, for example, F. Krzystofiak, J. Newman, and G. Anderson, "A Quantified Approach to Measurement of Job Content," *Personnel Psychology* 32, no. 2 (Summer 1979), pp. 341–57; and M. D. Dunnette, "Task and Job Taxonomies as a Basis for Evaluating Employment Qualifications," *Human Resources Planning Journal* 1, no. 1 (1977).

mon denominators, that permit or facilitate comparison across the diverse types of work found in the U.S. economy. It is the problem of comparing the value or contribution of apples versus oranges to one's health, or of comparing a ton of copper with a ton of steel in the wealth of a nation's natural resources; a common yardstick is required. In contemporary compensation systems, that yardstick has been found in the wage rates generated in the marketplace (external equity)—by the interactions of the employers' demand for labor expressed as job opportunities, and the workers' willingness to fill these opportunities under the terms and conditions offered. Adam Smith observed:

There may be more labour in an hour's hard work than in two hours's easy business; or in an hour's application to a trade which cost 10 years' labour to learn, than in a month's industry at an ordinary and obvious employment. But it is not easy to find any accurate measure either of hardship or ingenuity. In exchanging indeed the different productions of different sorts of labour for another, some allowance is commonly made for both; it is adjusted, however, not by an accurate measure, but by the higgling and bargaining of the market, according to that sort of rough equality which though not exact, is yet sufficient for carrying on the business of common life.[13]

Yet it is precisely the wage rates generated in the market, this common denominator, that advocates of the comparable worth notion maintain are inherently biased against women and minorities. The market, its imperfections, and its role in the wage determination process are discussed in a later section.

C. Equal Work: A Brief History

The debate between equal pay for equal work and equal pay for work of comparable worth is embedded in legislative history and court decisions on the Equal Pay Act and Title VII of the Civil Rights Act of 1964. A brief overview helps understand the debate.

1. Equal Pay Act. Both statutes have the same fundamental objective of remedying discriminatory compensation. Generally, the Equal Pay Act requires that women and men receive "equal pay for equal work" and states:[14]

No employer having employees subject to any provisions of this section shall discriminate, within any establishment in which such employees are employed, between employees on the basis of sex by paying wages to employees in such establishment at a rate less than the rate at which he pays wages to employees of the opposite sex in such establishment for equal work on jobs the performance of which requires equal skill, effort, and responsibility, and which are performed under similar working conditions, except where such payment is made pursuant to (*i*) a seniority system; (*ii*) a merit system; (*iii*) a system which measures earnings by quantity or quality of production; or (*iv*) a differential based on any other factor other than sex: Provided, That an employer who is paying a wage rate differential in violation of this subsection shall not, in order to comply with the provisions of this subsection, reduce the wage rate of any employee.

Thus, the "equal work" standard under this act establishes quite specific standards to judge whether employers paying differing wages to men and women are illegally discriminating. The standards include:

Within the same establishment;

Jobs the performance of which require similar skills, efforts, and responsibility; and

Performed under similar working conditions.

Four exceptions (affirmative defenses) were provided that permit inequalities in pay. Thus, inequalities are permitted if they are caused by:

A seniority system;

A merit system;

A system which increases earnings by quality or quantity of production; or

Some factor other than sex.

Under judicial interpretation of the Equal Pay Act, the work content of jobs does not have to be equal but only "substantially

[13]Adam Smith, *The Wealth of Nations* (London: Book 1, C.V. 1776).

[14]29 U.S.C. § 206(d).

equal." Furthermore, the courts' findings have emphasized first, the actual job behaviors, tasks, and work content performed, instead of simply job titles and second, the skills and abilities required to perform the job content, rather than the skills possessed by the employee. Thus, equal pay for equal work has been translated into equal pay for performance of substantially equal job content requiring substantially equal skills within the same establishment.

2. Title VII. Title VII, a much broader law, also deals with inequalities in pay and, specifically, with its relationship to the Equal Pay Act. The amendment to 703(h) of Title VII, known as the Bennett Amendment, provides:

It shall not be an unlawful employment practice under this title for any employer to differentiate upon the basis of sex in determining the amount of wages or compensation paid or to be paid to employees of such employer if such differentiation is authorized by the provisions of section 6(d) of the Fair Labor Standards Act of 1938, as amended (29 U.S.C. 206(d)) (i.e., the Equal Pay Act).

A key issue in the equal work/comparable worth debate is the precise interpretation of the Bennett Amendment. The debate centers around whether both features of the Equal Pay Act—(1) four affirmative defenses permitting inequalities in pay and (2) the substantially equal work standard—are included in Title VII. On the one hand, the Bennett Amendment can be construed as including both features in the Civil Rights Act. Alternatively, it can be interpreted as including only the four affirmative defenses and not the equal work standard. This is a vital difference. If the equal work standard is not included in the Civil Rights Act, then another may be used. The most likely substitute is the standard of comparable worth—that jobs of comparable worth must be paid equally.

D. Comparable Worth

"Comparable worth is the most difficult issue that has arisen under Title VII and, ultimately, it could have the same impact on the nation as school desegregation did in the 1950s," EEOC Chair Norton is reported telling a recent conference.[15] The notion of comparable worth, for which no operational, practical definition seems to exist, holds that whole groups of jobs, such as those in clerical and nursing work, are traditionally underpaid because they are held by women, and that these lower wage rates amount to sex discrimination under Title VII. Proponents of substituting "comparable worth" as the standard for wage determination maintain:

Women have historically been "crowded" into certain occupations through discriminatory practices in society;

The labor market reflects this crowding and thus the employment discrimination that caused the crowding; and

If the labor market is discriminatory, so too are pay systems based on it.

Thus, existing pay systems based on the labor market mirror present and past discrimination. The following excerpt perhaps reflects the basic position of comparable worth proponents:

Additionally, the practice of setting wages according to job families (occupation) is a sure way of producing sex-biased results. It is clear that the marketplace is biased against women; therefore to use the marketplace as a basis for paying clerical workers less than maintenance workers, for example, is to perpetuate discrimination.[16]

Proponents of comparable worth, also see an immediate need to eliminate the external labor market's influence in wage setting. "To the extent bias does exist in the marketplace, and as long as it remains uncorrected, many women are involuntarily contributing each paid day to maintaining the high salaries which exist in predominantly male jobs."[17]

Even if such bias were empirically verified, the absence of a workable definition of com-

---

[15]"Fair Employment Practices: Summary of Latest Developments," no. 383 (Washington, D.C.: Bureau of National Affairs, November 8, 1979). A more recent speech seems to suggest a modified position.

[16]H. Remick, "Strategies for Creating Sound, Bias-Free Job Evaluation Plans," *Job Evaluation and EEO: The Emerging Issues* (New York: Industrial Relations Counselors, 1978), p. 91.

[17]Remick, "Strategies for Creating," p. 122.

parable worth is particularly troublesome. Without a workable process akin to collective bargaining or to job analysis, evaluation and wage surveys, it is unclear how employers, unions, courts, and agencies can apply comparable worth.

Some may suggest that employers' hiring, selection, and upgrading procedures have undergone modification under Title VII. These modifications were also "particularly troublesome." Why not similar modification of equal pay for equal work? In the former case, work-related procedures were available, test validation procedures and nondiscriminatory programs were already developed and in use by many employers. Thus far, no workable procedures exist to translate comparable worth into practice.

How is one to determine the difference between comparable worth versus noncomparable worth? What factors and measurement procedures are to be used? Some have suggested that quantitative job evaluation and job analysis, properly conducted, might provide the answer.[18] In fact, proponents of comparable worth see job evaluation in two veins:

1. As a potential tool to determine comparable worth within organizations, thereby solving a major limitation of the concept; or
2. As another example of administrative rules and procedures steeped in the traditions and customs of the workplace, mirroring the pay inequalities in the external market, and simply perpetuating the historic discrimination found in the employment relationship.

On the one hand, if job evaluation can operationalize the concept of comparable worth, it has potential for ferreting out current biased pay inequalities; on the other hand, if job evaluation does nothing more than mirror the past, it may itself be a source of discrimination. As discussed earlier in this chapter and as later chapters in this volume will demonstrate, job evaluation is only one of several processes involved in wage determination systems. It is highly unlikely to be useful as a measure of comparable worth.[19]

Job analysis, as discussed earlier, has yet to be examined as a possible answer to the current inability to operationalize comparable worth. Quantitative job analysis analyzes jobs in terms of basic behaviors and tasks required to perform a job.[20] The notion of comparable worth implies that the job content and/or the qualifications required to perform the work establish value. Under the comparable worth theory, the content of diverse types of jobs must somehow be judged in terms of "comparability." Consider, for example, how one could compare the content of specific jobs such as electricians, registered nurses, elementary school teachers, plumbers, foundry workers, bus drivers, systems analysts, tellers, and employment recruiters, across a variety of employers, in various geographic locations, in different industries, under different union situations. Perhaps job analysis approaches can identify dimensions of work content and behaviors which are universal across all jobs; considerably more research is required to evaluate this option—to date it seems unlikely.[21]

Lost in the debate over a workable definition of comparable worth is the more basic issue of whether the current standard, equal pay for equal work, should be replaced with comparable worth. Even if quantitative research in job evaluation and analysis would yield a universal taxonomy or a set of guidelines for determining comparable worth, the basic issue confronting society is a value judgment. The absence of a clear meaning of comparable worth tends to obscure the debate over the possible consequences of discarding the equal pay for equal work standard.

---

[18]Donald J. Trieman, "Job Evaluation: An Analytical Review," Interim Report to the Equal Employment Opportunity Commission (Washington, D.C.: National Academy of Sciences, 1979).

[19]See, for example, the paper by Donald P. Schwab in *Comparable Worth: Issues and Alternatives*, ed. E. Robert Livernash (Washington, D.C.: Equal Employment Advisory Council, 1980), p. 49.

[20]See footnotes 7 and 12.

[21]Perhaps an answer can be found in developing a process that can be applied. Existing taxonomies, such as those found in Functional Job Analysis or derived from the Position Analysis Questionnaire, could be considered, though this author's experience with PAQ suggests it lacks the specificity required for compensation decisions, and the FJA lacks the rigor that should be required in contemporary compensation systems.

Table 1
Median 1972 Earnings of Full-Time Year-Round Workers by Occupation and Sex Group

	Median Earnings		Women's Median Income as Percent of Men's
	Women	Men	
Professional and technical workers	$8,796	$13,029	67.5%
Managers and administrators (except farm)	7,306	13,741	53.2
Sales workers	4,575	11,356	40.3
Clerical workers	6,039	9,656	62.5
Craftsmen and kindred workers	5,731	10,429	55.0
Operatives (including transport)	5,021	8,702	57.7
Service workers (except private household)	4,606	7,762	59.3
Private household workers	2,365	—	—
Nonfarm laborers	4,755	7,535	63.1

Source: U.S. Department of Commerce, Bureau of the Census, *Current Population Reports*, Series P–60, no. 90, 1973.

II. THE DIFFERENCES IN MEN'S AND WOMEN'S PAY

The force underlying the emerging debate over pay determination seems to be the disparity in male/female earnings: the "earnings gap." As reflected in Table 1, the median earnings of women are substantially less than men's, across occupations.

The very existence of this "gap" is considered by some to be evidence that society and contemporary compensation systems discriminate against women. Further, the "gap" may be growing; women's median full-time earnings in 1955 were 64 percent of men's, yet by 1973 women's median earnings were only 57 percent of men's earnings.[22] During the last decade a number of research studies have begun to investigate the factors which may be related to the earnings gap. While a detailed review of all the academic work is well beyond this paper's intent, some background in the work is vital to understanding more fully what is and is not known about the "earnings gap," and more importantly, how much of the gap is attributable to discrimination. The plan for this section is to discuss briefly the general model used to investigate pay differences and then examine some of the complexities involved in the measurement of discrimination in male and female pay differences.[23]

[22]"The Earnings Gap Between Women and Men," Women's Bureau. Employment Standards Administration (Washington, D.C.: U.S. Department of Labor, 1975).

[23]For an excellent treatment of pay differences from an economic and sociological perspective as well as cross-

A. General Model: The Earnings Gap and the Role of Discrimination

The general approach for determining the degree of discrimination in the wage determination process is deceptively simple. The portion of the male/female differential attributable to discrimination is determined by:

1. Estimating the portion of the difference that is attributable to work-productivity related factors;
2. Inferring the remaining, unexplained portion of the differential to be wage and employment discrimination.

An illustration may aid in the explanation of this "residuals" approach. Assume the following information:

	Average Wage	Average Education
Males	$10,000	12 years
Females	$ 5,800	9 years

Also assume that the following empirical model has been derived based on data for males.

Male Wage = $1,000 + ($750 × Education)

It is clear that not all of the gap between the male and female average wage is attributable to discrimination. Part of the difference

cultural, see H. Phelps Brown, *The Inequality of Pay* (Berkely: University of California Press, 1972).

may be attributed to the lower average education of women, and the remainder would be inferred to be discrimination. If women were paid as if they were men, under this approach they would receive $1,000 plus $750 for each of their nine years of experience, for a total of $7,750. The difference between men's actual earnings ($10,000) and women's *expected* earnings, had they been compensated as if they were males ($7,750) reflects a nondiscriminatory productivity difference ($2,250 = (12 years − 9 years) × $750 per year). The difference between women's expected earnings ($7,750) and their actual earnings ($5,800) reflects that difference which is not explained by differences in education and thus, is assumed under this approach to be the result of sex discrimination ($7,750 − $5,800 = $1,950).[24]

Review of studies that use this general model conclude that the portion of the earnings gap not attributed to work-productivity factors (i.e., attributed to discrimination) ranges between 12 percent and 70 percent.[25]

---

[24]The most common technique used in the study of male/female pay differentials is regression analysis which takes the following general form:

$$Y_i = B_{0+} \sum_{j=1}^{n} B_j X_{ji} + U_i$$

where Y_i is the level of wages or earnings; $X_{li}, \ldots X_{ni}$ are the n work-productivity factors used to explain Y.

To compare two groups such as male/female wages, the usual approach is to estimate this equation for each group:

Males: $Y_i^m = B_o^m + \sum_{j=1}^{n} B_j^m X_{ji}^m + U_i^m$

Females: $Y_i^f = B_o^f + \sum_{j=1}^{n} B_j^f X_{ji}^f + U_i^f$

A detailed discussion on the use of these formulas appears in A. S. Blinder, "Wage Discrimination: Reduced Form and Structural Estimates," *Journal of Human Resources* 8 (1973), pp. 436–55. The process is to compare the portion of the male/female differential explained by the productivity-related factors and the constants; the residual is attributed to discrimination. An additional step in the analysis is to examine the work-productivity-related variables associated with females and value them as if they were male factors. The difference between the wages females would *expect* if their work-productivity attributes were valued as if they were males and the *actual* wages paid to females is treated as discrimination.

[25]See, for example, Kahne and Kohen, "Economic Perspective on the Role of Women in the American Economy," *Journal of Economic Literature* 13 (1975), pp. 1249–

These differences in results may be accounted for by differences in the samples, time periods, methods, and sources of data used. In general, however, the more factors considered to be related to work-productivity, the smaller the "residual" portion of the earnings gap and the smaller the role inferred to discrimination.

One factor, differences in the occupation in which males and females are employed, is often the most significant factor in explaining the male/female earnings gap. Some argue that to include a person's occupation in the model ignores the effects of employment discrimination. Bergmann and Oaxaca, for example, assert that women and men have unequal access to occupations caused by the traditional sex-role stereotyping of occupations, traditional barriers to educational opportunities, and the discriminatory employment practices of employers and unions.[26] Unequal access contributes to the "overcrowding" of women into certain occupations, which itself tends to dampen pressures for wage increases. Thus, the effects of including occupation affiliation in any model of the earnings gap is to mask effects of occupational discrimination, and hence, to ignore the alleged role that discriminatory hiring and promotion practices may play in the determination of wage differences.

Conversely, to exclude the job in which a person is employed from any model of wage differentials is to argue that differences in occupations are not related to wage differences! The unresolved dilemma facing researchers is how to separate that portion of differences in occupations that may be related to productivity and thus, wage differences, from the portion that is the product of discriminatory employment practices. Translated to a somewhat more practical level, this dilemma surfaces in litigation over wage discrimination. The issue boils down to which factors are permitted in a

---

74; and I. V. Sawhill, "The Economics of Discrimination Against Women: Some New Findings," *Journal of Human Resources* 8 (1973), pp. 383–95.

[26]B. R. Bergmann, "Occupational Segregation, Wages, and Profits When Employers Discriminate by Race or Sex," *Eastern Economic Journal*, 1974, pp. 103–10; R. L. Oaxaca, "Sex Discrimination in Wages," in *Discrimination in Labor Markets*, ed. A. Ashenfelter and A. Rees (Princeton, N.J.: Princeton University Press, 1973).

model of the wage determination process. Plaintiffs advocating the comparable worth theory tend to argue that to include occupational affiliation factors, such as job and the level of the job in an organization, simply masks the discriminatory effects of the hiring and upgrading practices. Defendants would be expected to argue that jobs and the level of jobs in the organization are productivity-related and must be included in any model of the wage determination process.[27]

B. Complexities Related to the Measurement of the Wage Determination Process and Discrimination

Several troublesome issues confront the "residuals" approach to assessing the role discrimination may play in the wage determination process. To begin, four issues must be addressed.

1. The Models Underlying the Analysis. Discrimination under the "residuals" approach is inferred. To do this with any degree of confidence requires that the model include all other significant work-productivity related factors. Omitting any of these factors will incorrectly inflate the unexplained residual and, thus, the role discrimination is assumed to play. Fig. 2 lists some of the factors that must be considered in any model of wage determination. These include:

1. Work-related differences in male/female characteristics (e.g., seniority, skills, and abilities);
2. Differences in employee work behaviors (e.g., performance, absenteeism, turnover);
3. Differences in the content of the work performed (e.g., budgetary responsibilities and skills required);
4. Differences in union membership and union characteristics (e.g., belonging to a relatively powerful pattern leader);

---

[27]See e.g., *Presseisen v. Swarthmore College*, 14 FEP Cases 1312 (E.D. Pa. 1976), 15 FEP Cases 1466 (E.D. Pa. 1977); *James v. Stockham Values & Fittings Co.*, 559 F.2d 310, 15 FEP Cases 827 (5th Cir. 1977).

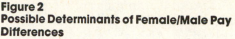

Figure 2
Possible Determinants of Female/Male Pay Differences

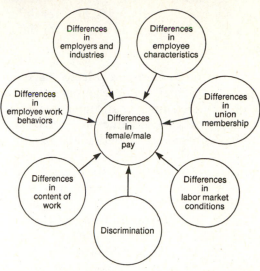

5. Differences in employers and in industries (e.g., profits, size, willingness to pay, capital/labor intensive);
6. Differences in labor market conditions (e.g., vacancies by ability/skill level.)

While many of the recent studies of male/female wage differences include some of these factors, *none* of the published studies include all of them. This is not because researchers are not aware of these factors; the omissions are due in large part to two problems. First, there is a lack of adequate, publicly available data, and second, proxies are often used which, on their face, seem to include most factors, but on closer examination reveal that much of the information is too abstract. For example, few studies include differences in job performance because the data are difficult to obtain. Yet many compensation systems pay different wages for differences in performance. Data for other employee work behaviors such as absenteeism and turnover are equally difficult to obtain and typically are excluded. Differences in "content of the work" is another troublesome factor. Most studies attempt to account for differences in work content by including the "occupation" in which the job is classified. However, the occupational codes used, such as clerical, sales, managerial, professional, crafts, operatives, etc., are so broad that they do not account for differences among the types of work within each occupation. All managerial jobs are not alike, nor are all crafts, sales, etc. Yet differences in work content do account for differences in wages.

2. Most Models Assume a "Macro" Perspective.

While actual pay decisions are made at the level of the employer and union, with few exceptions most economic analyses of the earnings gap are conducted at the national, market, or perhaps industry level. It is simply incorrect to assume that all the critical factors which go into wage determination in all establishments across the United States, are reflected in such aggregate analysis. Unfortunately, aggregate models often do not adequately include such "micro" factors as differences in employee work behaviors; in the education, skills, and abilities to perform specific jobs; in the specific content of the work; in the interaction or match between employee skills and abilities and the work; in the employer's wage policies; or, in union objectives and relationship to employers. Research and modelling of the compensation process and the role of discrimination in it must be performed at the level of the establishment, the department, and the job. Inferring and evaluating employer-union behavior from existing aggregate data is inadequate and perhaps misleading.

3. Measurement of Factors Included in the Models.

Table 2 lists some of the factors and the typical approach used to measure these factors. It is important to examine closely the measurement of each factor, since it is the measure that is actually used in the model. For example, training is an aspect of "Employee Qualifications," and differences in "training" seem to be an important factor to consider in the study of male and female pay differences. Note that, if included, training is usually considered to be vocational training, and is measured as a dummy variable—yes or no—and hence, ignores the field of vocational training, the years of training, the quality of training and, finally, whether the training was

even required for the job in which the person is employed!

The models also omit the interaction between an individual's qualification and the job in which she or he is employed. Consider for example, education; every published study of male and female wage differentials includes this variable as a productivity-related factor. Education, as a concept, conjures up thoughts of levels of education (high school, college, vocational school) and fields of education (content of course work, and training), yet the most common measure of education used is years of schooling. Hence, it may omit differences in fields of education, and more importantly, whether the education obtained has any relationship to the job. The fact that the author has a Ph.D. doesn't mean that the qualification is required in my job. The mere fact of possession of a qualification does not mean it is work-related. Examples of cab drivers, typists, locomotive engineers, painters, etc. with college degrees are numerous.

Finally, most studies revert to the use of "proxies" for factors which cannot be measured directly. Thus, for example, years of education serves as a proxy for all the differences in a person's skills and abilities, or performance is measured by absenteeism, or the content of the work by major occupational classifications, or differences among employers by major industrial classifications. The use of proxies simply abstracts much of the detailed, work-relatedness found in contemporary systems of wage determination that may account for differences in wages.

4. Lack of Publicly Available Data.

The point has already been made that publicly available data tends to be useful for only aggregate economy, industry, or occupation-wide analysis. This level of analysis misses the diversity and complexity of wage decisions made at the employee/employer level. Most data banks generated by public agencies such as the Michigan Survey Research Center's "Panel Study of Income Dynamics," or the Census Bureau's "Summary of Economic Opportunity" lack the specificity required. Measures of employee qualifications, job content,

Table 2
Possible Determinants of Male/Female Pay Differences: Commonly Employed Measures

Determinants	Common Measures Employed in the Models
Employee qualifications	
Seniority/Experience	Time spent in Civilian Labor Force, frequently omitting seniority within job or employer
Skills/Abilities	Omitted
Education/Training	Years of education, vocational training coded 0, 1; omitting worker relatedness
Health	Some work limitations
Employee work behaviors	
Performance	Usually omitted, occasionally proxies such as absenteeism
Absenteeism	Usually omitted
Turnover	Usually omitted
Part-time/Full-time	Usually included, coded 0, 1
Hours worked	Usually included as hour/week
Union membership	Usually coded 0, 1; union characteristics omitted
Content of work performed	Usually coded as major occupational categories; Managers, Professional, Clerical, Sales, Crafts, etc.
Tasks/Behaviors required	Omitted
Employer/Industries	Usually coded by major industrial classifications such as Agriculture, Mining, Construction, Durable/Nondurable Manufacturing, Finance, Communications, etc.
Profits/Size/Wage policy	Specific employer characteristics are typically omitted.
Market/Region	
Market conditions	Typically coded as high/low unemployment and high/low wages; more detailed aspects of market typically included in employer market surveys are omitted
Regions	Typically coded as Northwest, South, West, etc.
Other factors	Macroeconomic studies may include such factors as marital status, family background, whether or not a person has migrated once since age 16, and age.

Sources: R. Oaxaca, "Sex Discrimination in Wages," in *Discrimination in Labor Markets*, ed. A. Ashenfelter and A. Rees (Princeton, N.J.: Princeton University Press, 1973); A. S. Blinder, "Wage Discrimination: Reduced Form and Structural Estimates," *Journal of Human Resources* 8, no. 4 (1973), pp. 436–55; Francine Blau, *Equal Pay in the Office* (Lexington, Mass.: Lexington Books, 1977); I. V. Sawhill, "The Economics of Discrimination against Women: Some New Findings," *Journal of Human Resources* 8 (1973), pp. 383–95; H. Sanborn, "Pay Differences between Men and Women," *Industrial and Labor Relations Review* 17 (1964), pp. 532–50; R. Oaxaca, "Male-Female Differentials in the Telephone Industry," in *Equal Employment Opportunity and the AT&T Case*, ed. P. A. Wallace (Cambridge, Mass.: MIT Press, 1976); J. E. Buckley, "Pay Differences between Men and Women in the Same Job," *Monthly Labor Review* 94 (1971), pp. 36–39.

and employer and union characteristics are not included. Hence, also lacking is the capacity to relate precise differences in qualifications, job requirements, employers, and labor markets to wage differences.

Thus, existing empirical formulations and methodologies have not adequately modelled the wage determination process and hence do not adequately account for the role of discrimination. This is principally due to: (1) the omission of significant work-related factors in most models; (2) the lack of focus on the employer—union and individual job interaction as the level of analysis; (3) the absence of adequate measures for the factors; and (4) the lack of micro, publicly available data to perform such analysis.

III. CONCLUDING OBSERVATIONS

The present chapter serves to introduce the principal issues related to equal pay, comparable worth, and the earnings gap. The debate over substituting comparable worth for equal work as the standard for wage discrimination hinges on two issues: (1) the current lack of a workable definition of comparable worth, and (2) more basically, the lack of any systematic analysis of the possible consequences of its application. What, for example, are the consequences of raising the wages paid for those jobs dominated by women to correspond to some "national average" of the rates paid jobs dominated by men? Is it analogous to an OPEC increase in oil prices, which passes through all stages of the economy and is reflected in increased costs of living? Will those currently employed in higher-paid occupations perceive their wages to be unfairly low, and will future workers be less likely to invest in the training and education required for some of these jobs? How important are wage differentials in the allocation of the labor force? How will changing the occupational wage differentials affect individual decisions to choose one job over another, one career over another, or one employer over another? These and other questions related to the possible consequences of abandoning the equal work standard must be thoroughly examined if the solutions are to be arrived at on other than emotional grounds. On the other hand, the formulation and application of alternative policy options should not be held up until these questions are examined. An example of this is that women will remain concentrated in the lower-paid occupations without the vigorous application of equal opportunity and affirmative action practices by employers.

This paper also addresses the problems faced in modelling the wage determination process, and in isolating the role of discrimination in it. These problems include the lack of a well-developed and tested model of the wage determination process at the level of the employer/union, the need to refine the process for identifying and measuring productivity-related factors, the need to parcel out the effects of employment or occupational discrimination from the analysis without ignoring the productivity effects of job differences, and the need to make job, employee, and employer data publicly available. Of these, the major missing piece is the lack of a well-developed model of the employer wage determination process. This is particularly unfortunate, since the public debate focuses on issues that can be most effectively addressed through such a model.

Finally, the hope is that the debate over equal work/comparable worth will help generate the much needed research into the wage determination process. Many of the concepts and techniques used in contemporary compensation systems were developed and refined in the 1930s and 1940s. It is time to reexamine them; perhaps the challenges to current practices will rebuild the links between practice, policy, and research in the field.

R E A D I N G 32

Market Wages and Comparable Worth*

Thomas A. Mahoney[†]

My task in this essay is to explore the issue of comparable worth in terms of traditional market explanations of wage determination.[1] Advocates of comparable worth are challenging existing wage differentials and rationalizations of those differentials. I will try here, in abbreviated form, to outline the argument for reliance upon market wage determination and the challenges to that argument by advocates of the comparable worth concept.

What is termed the *issue of comparable worth* relates to the continuing gap between earnings of male and female wage earners: females, on average, earn 60 percent of what males earn. Much of this earnings gap can be attributed to the different distributions of male and female employment among different occupations and jobs. Male employment is concentrated in higher-paying occupations and female employment is concentrated in lower-paying occupations. Observation of this fact, however, does not explain why predominantly female occupations pay lower wages than predominantly male occupations. Comparable worth advocates argue that female earnings are depressed below male earnings for a variety of reasons, including wage discrimination. Some criterion of job worth is sought such that male and female occupations of comparable worth can be identified. Differences in wages for occupations of comparable worth might then be attributed to wage discrimination.

While originating in the context of male-female earnings differentials, the issue of comparable worth pervades examination of every kind of wage differentials. Basically, the issue of comparable worth relates to the determination of relative worth of any two jobs or occupations, and not merely the relative worth of male- or female-dominated occupations. Hence, any criterion of job worth for the comparison of male and female occupations also ought to be applicable to comparison of any other occupations.

Note that the criterion of comparable worth thus advanced is enunciated as separable from wages. Wage rates are established in various ways including employer specification, collective bargaining, and legislative action. Advocates of the comparable worth concept argue that the resulting wage rates need not (and often do not) reflect comparable worth of jobs. Some measure of comparable worth is sought as a criterion for evaluating wage rate comparisons. Wage differentials reflective of job worth differentials would presumably be acceptable, while wage differentials associated with gender and not reflective of job worth differentials would be judged to be discriminatory.

Several approaches to the assessment of job worth have been advanced, including the concept of market determination of wage rates. An alternative approach involves some form of job evaluation more or less independent of market wage determination. While aspects of both approaches appear in current wage determination practices, our primary concern in this essay is the concept of market wage determination.

THE MARKET WAGE RATIONALE

The rationale for market wage as a criterion of job worth is derived from traditional (neoclassical) economics. Briefly, it is argued that the determination of worth of anything is individual and relative. It is individual in that tastes, desires, and values differ among individuals, resulting in different assessments of worth of any object of exchange. Were this

*Reprinted with permission from ILR Report, Spring, 1982, *Comparable Worth*, the New York State School of Industrial and Labor Relations, Cornell University, pp. 15–20.

†*Thomas A. Mahoney is editor of Academy of Management Journal, Owen Graduate School of Management, Vanderbilt University.*

[1]This essay benefited considerably from the suggestions of Sara Rynes.

not so, no exchange of goods or services would occur; the purchaser in any exchange must judge the object of exchange as worth more than does the supplier of the object. (Observe, for example, any garage sale). Judgments of worth also are relative; they reflect comparison between the anticipated outcomes of one exchange and the most attractive alternative to that exchange. This alternative, which must be foregone if the exchange is carried out, represents the opportunity cost of the exchange. Thus judgments of worth of any exchange vary among individuals as a function of tastes, and vary over time within a single individual as attractive alternatives and opportunity costs change.

How then can we talk of a common measure of worth? The market concept as elaborated in economic theory provides a potential mechanism for identifying some common measure of value of exchanges. Individual buyers and sellers seek out beneficial exchanges, and the various rates of exchange observed in the market influence the valuations of opportunity cost of both buyers and sellers. Alternative rates of exchange available in the market represent to both buyers and sellers an element of what is foregone when entering into any specific exchange. Another major element of opportunity cost is the valuation of nonmarket uses such as work in the home or leisure. Both alternative wage rates in the labor market and personal valuation of time spent homemaking or skiing influence the opportunity cost to the worker of accepting a specific wage and employment offer.

In the competitive market assumed by market theorists, the actions of both buyers and sellers seeking their personal advantage tend to converge upon a single rate of exchange, a market rate at which all who wish to buy and sell are accommodated. In a similar manner, it is argued, a market wage is generated through the actions of buyers and sellers in a competitive labor market. Each employer and employee considers alternatives and the opportunity cost associated with each, and enters into exchanges of work and wages which are considered worthwhile. Alterna-

tives available to the employer include hiring other persons with greater or lesser potential productivity, losing production and sales, subcontracting to other employers, and making technological substitutions for labor. Alternatives available to the employee include other job opportunities, investment in education and training, nonmarket work in the home, and consumption or leisure. Only exchanges judged worthwhile by both parties are consummated, and the rates of exchange converge upon a common market wage rate through competitive action. Thus, it is argued, the market wage rate is the best available measure of job worth, reflecting as it does the collective valuations of worth by employers and employees.

In theory, a market wage is associated with each job or occupation, and the wage differential between any two occupations reflects the collective judgments of relative worth of these occupations by employers and employees. One occupation is paid more than another as necessary to attract the desired number of applicants and to the extent that it is viewed as more productive of value to the employer. It is this structure of wage differentials obtained in a competitive labor market that reflects the relative worth of different occupations. Furthermore, the structure of wage differentials can be expected to change as labor demands and supplies change as a result of employers and employees altering their valuations of different jobs.

Advocates for market wage determination of relative occupational worth also would argue that no other approach to wage determination is feasible. Any arbitrarily imposed structure of relative wage rates that is inconsistent with what would be obtained through competitive market bidding will result in market imbalances of supply and demand. Over time, employers will find ways to subvert the arbitrarily imposed structure through the use of side payments of one form or another, and a structure of total payments reflective of market forces will emerge. Evidence of such behavior can be noted during periods of wage controls in different societies and, particularly, in the experience of job evaluation in the Netherlands following World War II.[2]

LIMITATIONS OF THE MARKET WAGE CRITERION

The competitive market model provides an appealing means of identifying the worth of any object of exchange. In practice, however, the characteristics of the competitive market model are infrequently realized. Most markets, and particularly the labor market, are imperfect, with the consequence that observed rates of exchange may differ considerably from that rate which might have emerged in a perfectly competitive market. Critics of the market wage rationale point up these imperfections when calling for a substitute criterion of job worth.

Literal operationalization of the market wage criterion of job worth would require removal of all social and institutional constraints upon wage determination since, by definition, market wage is that wage rate which emerges from the competitive actions of individual employers and employees seeking their own self-interests. In fact, both wage determination and the employment processes of the labor market are constrained by regulations, collective agreements, traditions, and customs which many argue render the concept of a competitive market wage inoperative and infeasible.

Moreover, both parties to the employment contract, employers and employees, seek to avoid the uncertainties of spot bidding markets assumed in the competitive market model. A variety of institutions have developed over time to buffer both employers and employees from the rigors of the competitive model. Contracting for future exchange, whether in the form of a collective agreement or implicit contracts of indefinite term enunciated in employer policies, is a common way of stabilizing the employment exchange. Rather than relying upon day-to-day contract-ing, both employers and employees seek attachments of indefinite tenure such that individuals will remain with a firm over time and advance through training and experience to occupy more responsible positions in the firm. Insofar as possible, both parties seek to restrict recruiting into the firm's labor force to entry jobs and to fill other jobs through promotion from within. Increasingly, the model of an internal labor market through which employees attached to the firm are allocated to different jobs has replaced the model of a labor market external to the firm from which employees are recruited to fill openings. Wage rates for jobs other than entry jobs thus are less subject to supply and demand uncertainties.[3]

Employee attachments to employers also constrain mobility and the consequent market pressure upon wage rates, particularly wage rates for more highly skilled jobs in the promotional or career hierarchy. Instead of a single market rate prevailing for many of these jobs, variability of wage rates has become the norm. As Arthur Ross observed 25 years ago, "the single rate is a reliable token of combination rather than competition at work."[4] Wage rates for other than entry jobs are more subject to what might be termed *social influences* of the labor force attached to the firm; the wage structure must be perceived as socially acceptable if it is to elicit the continuing attachment and cooperation of that work force.[5]

Judgments about the equity of wage differentials within an organization take the form of comparisons and can be illustrated in terms of social comparison models. Individuals compare their rates of exchange of occupational

---

[2]Martin P. Oettinger, "Nationwide Job Evaluation in the Netherlands," *Industrial Relations* 4 (1964), 45–59, describes this experience.

[3]For a general discussion of internal labor market concepts, see Peter B. Doeringer, "Determinants of the Structure of Industrial-Type Internal Labor Markets," *Industrial and Labor Relations Review* 20 (1967), pp. 206–20.

[4]Arthur M. Ross, "The External Wage Structure," in *New Concepts in Wage Determination*, George W. Taylor and Frank C. Pierson ed. (New York: McGraw-Hill, 1957), p. 189.

[5]See Lester Thurow, *Generating Inequality: Mechanisms of Distribution in the U.S. Economy* (New York: Basic Books, 1975), for elaboration of this formulation.

inputs for outcomes with similar rates of exchange realized by others. Rates of exchange which are perceived to be unequal are judged to be inequitable, thus discouraging further exchange.[6] In practice, a wage structure in an organization which is perceived as inequitable gives rise to grievances, turnover, and an unwillingness to accept certain job assignments.

While the relative importance attached to different work outcomes is individualistic, most attention typically focuses upon the wage rate, usually the most visible and obvious symbol of outcome. Concepts of inputs to the job also may vary, but the most common tend to be either what one brings to the job in terms of past training and experience or what one expends on the job in terms of energy and effort. Finally, the choice of appropriate comparison job or person also varies, but typically focuses upon another job and incumbent closely related in terms of work process or physical proximity.

The importance of social comparison in the determination of wage structures in an organization was recognized years ago in the conceptualization of job clusters by John Dunlop and Robert Livernash.[7] Job clusters are "job groups within which internal comparison is most significant."[8] The role of social comparison and job clusters in wage determination can be observed in the differentiation between wage structures for plant and office jobs, the selection of so-called key jobs representing different job clusters in job evaluation, and the institutionalization of tandem relationships for wage adjustment in collective bargaining. Social comparison norms institutionalized into custom and tradition thus tend to dominate wage determination within internal labor markets. The external labor market primarily influences wage rates for entry jobs rather than jobs filled through promotion, with the consequent problem of wage and salary compression noted in many organizations. For the occasional job that is particularly sensitive to market rates because of occupational hiring, as distinct from promotion from within, "red circle" rates are often tolerated; that is, higher rates are tolerated as long as required by competitive pressure, but are not to be incorporated into the socially accepted wage structure of the organization.

So-called internal labor markets are illustrative of a more general problem in the application of market concepts to the assessment of job worth. That problem relates to market segmentation.[9] Instead of a single, general labor market where employers and employees compete in the exchange of labor, we have numerous labor markets, markets which are segmented by barriers to mobility. For various reasons, workers and employers are constrained from crossing these barriers, and wage rates in each segmented market are more or less independent of wage rates in other segmented markets. Some of these barriers take the form of licensing and certification requirements, skill, education and experience requirements, or the expenses of geographic relocation. Other barriers may take the form of hiring and placement constraints reflecting social beliefs and customs regarding the appropriateness of women entering certain occupations. These beliefs and customs may constrain employers and workers as much as licensing requirements from actions they might otherwise take in a competitive market.

An initial consequence of market segmentation may be the crowding of labor supplies in one market and a scarcity of supplies in a related market, with consequent wage differentials between the two market segments. Thus, for example, market segmentation by sex might result in the channeling of female graduates in English into teaching occupations and male graduates in English into journalism and advertising. Wage differentials between teaching and advertising become established and accepted in normative social values. Once established, such differentials are particularly resistant to change. Evidence of such persistent differentials was cited as

[6]J. Stacy Adams, "Inequity in Social Exchange," in *Advances in Experimental and Social Psychology*, vol. 2 ed. L. Berkowitz (New York: Academic Press, 1965).

[7]John T. Dunlop, "The Task of Contemporary Wage Theory," and E. Robert Livernash, "The Internal Wage Structure," in Taylor and Pierson, *New Concepts.*

[8]Livernash, *ibid.*, p. 148.

[9]See, for example, Arne L. Kalleberg and Aage B. Sorenson, "The Sociology of Labor Markets," *Annual Review of Sociology,* 1979.

wage contours by John Dunlop 25 years ago, and these differentials persist to this day.[10] Just as a structure of wage differentials for different jobs becomes accepted as the social norm in a plant, so also are occupational wage differentials accepted as the norm in a broader society. Relative occupational wage rates for 1970 in the United States, for example, were basically unchanged from the 1960 structure of relative occupational wages despite significant changes in labor market conditions during that period.[11]

For these reasons, critics of the market wage criterion of occupational worth argue that occupational wages are in fact determined by influences other than those rationalized in the theory of competitive markets. Occupational wages need not reflect occupational worth, and a criterion of worth is sought which is independent of market wage.

SOME OVERLOOKED ISSUES

Note that the hypothetical wage differential between male English majors in advertising and female English majors in teaching mentioned above reflected differences in both jobs and industries of employment but not differences in education and training qualifications. Job or occupational differences and differences in qualifications or human capital are considered as potential justifications for wage differentials in discussions of comparable worth; industry differences of employment have not been accorded the same treatment. Industry considerations may have been ignored in part because many occupations are virtually unique to an industry of employment, e.g., bricklayers are concentrated in construction, aeronautical engineers are concentrated in aerospace, and copy editors are concentrated in publishing. Yet, as Dunlop observed, wage contours essentially reflect industry and product market differences and not occupational differences (truck drivers in Boston are paid differently in different industries). Industry wage differentials typically are explained in terms of "ability to pay"

variations, that is, differences in the elasticity of product demand, the proportion of labor costs to total cost, and overall levels of productivity. While the specific tasks of brewery truck drivers in Boston undoubtedly differ from the tasks of laundry truck drivers, the primary difference is industry of employment and ability to pay of the employers. To the extent that there is segmentation of industry labor markets according to sex (whether by custom or other constraints), industry wage differentials will appear as differential pay for comparable qualifications and even comparable occupations. Market rates in segmented industry markets will differ one from another reflecting product market influences rather than job or qualification influences.

The distinctions among personal qualifications, job requirements, and industry of employment raised above are central to concerns for comparable worth and to the issue of applicability of market wage concepts as a criterion of worth. Examinations of both comparable worth issues and market wage concepts often tend to confuse personal qualifications for employment and job requirements. This confusion is compounded when job or occupation and industry of employment are related, making it difficult to disentangle occupational *requirements* from industry *characteristics*. Both occupation and industry characterize labor demand while employee qualifications characterize labor supply, and it is not clear either in the concepts of comparable worth or market wage whether personal characteristics or job requirements are more appropriately viewed as the basis for comparability. In theory we can conceive of a one-to-one correspondence between labor supply characteristics (employee qualifications) and labor demand characteristics (occupation and industry), yet we have difficulty in developing operational measures to demonstrate this correspondence. Decades of research into employee selection demonstrate the variability of associations between employee characteristics and job or task characteristics (e.g., employees with different qualifications often are equally successful in satisfying job requirements for performance). Lacking a close correspondence between employee and job char-

[10]Dunlop, "Task of Contemporary Wage Theory."
[11]Thurow, *Generating Inequality*.

acteristics, it is not clear whether the concept of market wage is more appropriately associated with job or personal characteristics. Contributing to the confusion, the advocates of comparable worth often pose the issue in terms of people with equal qualifications working on different jobs and receiving different wages. Both the advocates of comparable worth and a market wage concept must address the distinction between employee and job characteristics in the development of their arguments.

One last consideration in the examination of the market wage concept as a criterion of job worth must be mentioned. This is the implication that the market wage criterion is best implemented through decentralization of wage determination to individual organizations without requiring any standardization of wage determination process or occupational worth criteria. The concept of market wage is rationalized as a measure of worth on the basis of assumptions about independent, competitive behaviors of individuals in the labor market. Thus wage rates derived within individual employing organizations and which are acceptable to both the employer and employees might be accepted as reflective of worth regardless of comparability with wages paid by other employers or some other criterion of worth.

Measures of market wage rates across segmented markets are unlikely to demonstrate much convergence and would, in practice, be unreliable guides to wage determination. The convergence of wage rates around a single market rate anticipated in competitive market models assumes standardized units of labor demand and supply in addition to the usual assumptions of competition. Observed wage rates will display variation as jobs vary among employers and as job performance varies among individuals, even within a single occupation. Thus decentralization of wage rate setting to individual organizations probably is more likely to produce wage rates reflecting economic worth than are prescriptions of worth based upon wage surveys.

Interestingly, social norms regarding wage differentials and job worth also are likely to display greatest agreement within segmented social groups. Employees in a single organization will more likely achieve consensus regarding appropriate wage differentials in that organization than all workers in the Midwest will concur regarding appropriate wage differentials. Whether market wage or social comparison concepts are employed in the assessment of job worth, a decentralized approach appears more feasible and defensible than an approach seeking a single, standardized criterion for job worth applicable to the entire U.S. work force. Market wage concepts thus may well have more validity in the assessment of occupational worth when operationalized as a decentralized process of decision making than when operationalized as wage survey measures of worth.

READING 33

Employment-at-Will: An Issue for the 1980s*

Jack Stieber†

Each year private sector employers terminate about 3 million employees for noneconomic reasons.[1] In the United States such terminations are called "discharge for cause." While there are no reliable comparative figures, it is clear from the literature and discussions with scholars and practitioners in other countries that discharge for cause occurs much more frequently in the United States than in other industrialized nations.[2] The reasons for this are not entirely clear, though there is little doubt that among the contributing factors are the greater concern with job security in other countries, the generally higher unemployment rate in the United States which makes it easier for employers to replace discharged workers, a strong dedication to individualism and property rights in the United States, and the existence of laws prohibiting unjust discharge in other countries.

There is no such general statutory prohibition in the United States. Protection against unjust discharge in this country is provided to a minority of all employees through collective bargaining, antidiscrimination laws, civil service, and teacher tenure laws.[3]

By far the best protection against unjust discharge is afforded by the grievance and arbitration procedures which are found in over 95 percent of all collective bargaining agreements.[4] The 22 million American workers covered by such agreements have better protection against being disciplined or discharged without just cause than workers in any other country. Thousands of discharge cases are appealed to arbitration each year, of which about 50 percent result in reinstatement of the employee with full, partial, or no back-pay because of a finding that the discharge was without just cause.[5]

Statutory protection is also provided by federal and state laws making it unlawful to discharge employees for union activity or to discriminate in employment on grounds of race, sex, religion, national origin, physical handicap, or age. Most government employees are protected against unjust discharge by civil service and teacher tenure laws.[6]

All other employees—the 60 million private sector employees not covered by collective bargaining, and statutorily protected employees who cannot demonstrate prohibited discrimination—are subject to the employment-at-will doctrine. This common law doctrine holds that an employment having no specific term may be terminated by either party with or without notice or cause. As one court put it 100 years ago: employment relationships of an indefinite duration may be terminated at any time without notice "for good

---

*Presidential address to Industrial Relations Research Association, 37th annual meeting, December 29, 1983, San Francisco, California. Reprinted with permission.

†Jack Stieber is dean of the School of Labor and Industrial Relations, Michigan State University.

[1]Derived from *Monthly Labor Review* 77 (1954), p. 86, table B-1; J. Medoff, "Layoffs and Alternatives under Trade Unions in U.S. Manufacturing," *American Economic Review* 69 (1979), pp. 380, 389; J. Stieber and R. Block, *Discharged Workers and the Labor Market*, U.S. Department of Labor, Employment, and Training Administration, Grant no. 21-26-80-11 (1983).

[2]J. Stieber and J. Blackburn, eds., *Protecting Unorganized Employees Against Unjust Discharge* East Lansing: Michigan State University, School of Labor and Industrial Relations, (1980), pp. 46–80, 135–68.

[3]Title VII of the Civil Rights Act of 1964, 42 U.S.C. par. 621–34 (1976; Supp. II 1978 and Supp. III 1979); Employment Opportunities for Handicapped Individuals Act, 29 U.S.C. par. 795–95j (Supp. II 1979).

[4]*Collective Bargaining Negotiations and Contracts*, Bureau of National Affairs 51, no. 5 (1979); *Daily Labor Report*, no. 206, October 25, 1982, p. A-8, BNA.

[5]G. Adams, "Grievance Arbitration of Discharge Cases," *The Arbitration Journal* 41 (1978); K. Jennings and R. Wolters, "Discharge Cases Reconsidered," *The Arbitration Journal* 31 (1976), pp. 164–80; F. Holly, "The Arbitration of Discharge Cases: A Case Study," *National Academy of Arbitrators Proceedings* 10 (1957); pp. 1–16; D. Jones, "Ramifications of Back-Pay Awards in Suspension and Discharge Cases," *National Academy of Arbitrators Proceedings* 22 (1957), pp. 163–74.

[6]See note 3 above.

cause, for no cause, or even for cause morally wrong."[7]

In recent years an avalanche of articles analyzing and generally criticizing the employment-at-will doctrine has appeared in law school reviews and industrial relations journals.[8] Interlaced with these articles have been an increasing number of state court decisions finding exceptions to the employment-at-will doctrine.[9]

Newspapers, business and trade magazines, and columnists, titillated by a few astronomical jury awards to wrongfully discharged employees, played up these decisions in a way that led many discharged employees to believe that they had a viable court suit, and convinced employers that they were in imminent danger of being saddled for life with incompetent employees. Lawyers and consultants came to the rescue with schemes to protect the sacred right of employers to fire employees with or without a reason.

EXCEPTIONS TO EMPLOYMENT-AT-WILL

What are these court exceptions to employment-at-will that have aroused so much concern among employers and encouraged false hopes of winning large jury awards among discharged employees? The three theories most commonly advanced in support of wrongful discharge suits have been based on claims of violation of public policy, the existence of an implied contract, and the covenant of good faith and fair dealing.

The Public Policy Exception

The most widely accepted common law limitation to the employment-at-will doctrine has been the public policy exception, which argues that an employer may not fire an employee for reasons that contravene fundamental principles of public policy. Some 20 states have recognized this exception in cases in which an employee was fired for refusing to commit an unlawful act, for performing an important public obligation, or for exercising a statutory right or privilege.[10] Typical cases involved firing an employee for refusing to give false testimony at a trial or administrative hearing, serving on a jury, reporting illegal conduct by an employer (i.e., "whistle-blowing"), refusing to violate a professional code of ethics, filing a worker's compensation claim, or refusing to take a polygraph test.

Here are a few examples of such cases: In one of the earliest cases the California appellate court ruled in 1959 that it was against public policy for the Teamster's Union to discharge a business agent for refusing to give false testimony before a legislative committee. Such action rendered the union liable for damages to the business agent.[11]

In 1978 the Michigan Appeals Court held that an employee stated a valid cause for relief when he alleged that he was discharged for refusing to manipulate and adjust sampling results in pollution control reports which were required by law.[12]

In a 1981 Illinois case, the employee alleged that he was fired for offering information to the police about possible criminal behavior on the job by another employee and for agreeing to assist in the investigation. The court held that there is a clear public policy favoring investigation and prosecution of criminal offenses.[13]

[7]*Payne v. Western & Atlantic R.R.*, 81 Tenn. 507, 519–20 (1884).

[8]L. Blades, "Employment-at-Will versus Individual Freedom: On Limiting the Abusive Exercise of Employer Power" *Columbia Law Review* 67 (1967), p. 1404; C. Summers, "Individual Protection against Unjust Dismissal: Timed for a Statute," *Virginia Law Review* (1976), pp. 481–533; J. Blackburn, "Restricted Employer Discharged Rights: A Changing Concept of Employment-at-Will," *American Business Law Journal* 17 (1980), p. 467; A. Blumrosen, "Strangers No More: All Workers Entitled to Just Cause Protection Under Title VI," *Industrial Relations Law Journal* 2 (1978), p. 519; C. Peck, "Unjust Discharges from Employment: A Necessary Change in the Law," *Ohio State Law Journal* 40 (1979), p. 1; J. Stieber, "The Case for Protection of Unorganized Employers against Unjust Discharge," *Industrial Relations Reserach Association Proceedings* 32 (1980), p. 155; R. Howlett, "Due Process for Nonunionized Employees: A Practical Proposal," *IRRA Proceedings* 32 (1980), p. 171.

[9]*The Employment-at-Will Issue*, A BNA Special Report (1982).

[10]Ibid., p. 8.

[11]*Peterman v. International Brotherhood of Teamsters, Local 396*, 174 C.A. 2d 184, 344 P. 2d 25 (1959).

[12]*Trombetta v. Detroit, Toledo and Ironton R. Co.*, 81 Mich. App. 489, 265 N.W. 2d 385 (1978).

[13]*Palmeteer v. International Harvester Co.*, 85 Ill. 2d 124, 421 N.E. 2d 876 (1981).

The Implied Contract Exception

The implied contract exception, which is recognized in 13 states, has found an implied promise of job tenure for employees with records of satisfactory performance, in employee handbooks, personnel manuals, or oral statements made during employment interviews.[14]

Examples of such cases include: The Michigan Supreme Court held in 1980 that an employer who has a written policy or has made an oral statement that an employee would not be discharged without just cause must adhere to such policy.[15]

The California Court of Appeals, in a 1981 decision, found that evidence supported the claim that an implied promise was made to the employee based on the 32-year duration of his employment, his promotions and commendations, assurances he received, and the employer's personnel policies. The employee claimed that he was discharged for refusing to participate in negotiations with a union because of a purported "sweetheart agreement" which enabled the company to pay women lower wages than male employees.[16]

In another 1981 case originating in New York, the employee signed an application stating that employment would be subject to the company's Employee Handbook, which said that dismissal would occur only for just and sufficient cause. He also received oral assurances of job security. The New York Court of Appeals held that there was sufficient evidence of a contract and a breach of contract to sustain a cause for action.[17]

The Good Faith and Fair Dealing Exception

This exception, which has been clearly recognized in only three states, California, Massachusetts, and Montana, holds that no matter what an employer says or does to make it clear that employment is at-will and that an employee may be dismissed without cause, he must deal with the employee fairly and in good faith.

In 1977, the Massachusetts court ignored an explicit written contract that reserved to the employer the right to fire an employee for any reason. The employee, a 61-year-old salesman with 40 years of service, claimed that he was fired to avoid paying him sales commissions on a multimillion dollar order. The court held it was for a jury to decide if the employer's motive in firing him was suspect. If it so found, then the discharge was wrongful because the law imposed a covenant of good faith and fair dealing on every contract.[18]

In a 1980 California case, the court found that an employee could sue for wrongful discharge in both contract and tort, in the case of an employee with 18 years of satisfactory service with an employer which had violated its own specific procedures for adjudicating employee disputes. The court further held that, if a jury found that the employer had acted in bad faith, the company could be held responsible for pain and suffering and be assessed punitive damages.[19]

In 1983, the Montana Supreme Court approved a jury award of $50,000 to a cashier who alleged that she was discharged without warning and was forced to sign a letter of resignation. The employer claimed she was fired for carelessness, incompetency, and insubordination. The court said that there was sufficient evidence for the jury to find fraud, oppression, or malice and held that an employer's breach of good faith and fair dealing is a tort for which punitive damages may be imposed.[20]

To nonlawyers, which most of us are, the above principles and decisions may not appear surprising or unreasonable. They merely support what most people would regard as fair and decent behavior on the part of employers toward employees: that employers should not

---

[14]*The Employment-at-Will Issue*, p. 8.

[15]*Toussant v. Blue Cross and Blue Shield of Michigan*, 408 Mich. 579, 292 N.W. 2d 880 (1980).

[16]*Pugh v. See Candies, Inc.*, 116 Cal. App. 3d 311, 171 Cal. Rptr. 917 (1981).

[17]*Weiner v. McGraw-Hill*, 83 A.D. 2d 810, 442 N.Y.S. 2d 11 (1st Dept. 1981).

[18]*Fortune v. National Cash Register*, 373 Mass. 96, 364 N.E. 2d 1251 (1977).

[19]*Cleary v. American Airlines, Inc.*, 111 Cal. App. 3d 443. 168 Cal. Rptr. 722 (1980).

[20]*Gates v. Life of Montana Insurance Co.*, Mont. Sup. Ct. no. 82–468, August 5, 1983.

penalize employees for refusing to commit unlawful acts, for exercising their lawful rights, or for behaving as good citizens; that employers should not take advantage of employees by virtue of the power they have over their economic welfare; and that they should treat employees fairly. It may, therefore, come as a surprise to learn that most courts do not look at it this way; that they interpret the public policy exception so narrowly as to give it only very limited application; that they do not regard written or oral policy statements as binding on employers; and that they do not hold that employers must behave fairly and in good faith toward their employees.

Consider, for example, the following court rulings: The District of Columbia Court of Appeals in 1981 rejected a public policy exception in a case in which an employee claimed that his employer had required that he testify in an administrative proceeding, and then fired him in retaliation for testifying truthfully against the employer's interests.[21]

In another 1981 case, the Indiana Appeals Court held that an at-will employee, who reported alleged misconduct by his superiors and questioned the safety of drugs marketed by the company, failed to state a claim for wrongful discharge because he was not exercising a statutory right or complying with a statutory duty.[22]

In 1980 a New York court ruled that a bank employee, who alleged that he had been discharged because he had uncovered evidence of illegal foreign currency manipulation, was terminable at-will because he had no written employment contract.[23] This employee's termination was only a minor episode in a major case in which the Securities and Exchange Commission declined to bring civil action against the company, despite staff findings that Citicorp, the largest foreign exchange dealer in the world, had violated the tax and

currency laws of seven countries. SEC officials argued that because Citicorp had never represented to stockholders and investors that its senior management had "honesty and integrity," it had no legal duty to disclose breaches of these basic norms. Furthermore, these officials noted that Citicorp's pursuit of profits it knew to be probably unlawful was "reasonable and standard business judgment."[24] The SEC decision not to prosecute Citicorp fits very well with the earlier court ruling that the bank could, with impunity, fire the employee who complained about the currency manipulations to the board of directors. Both decisions are a sad commentary on what passes for acceptable business behavior in the eyes of the law.

The increasing frequency of court rulings on exceptions to the employment-at-will doctrine has led to the exaggerated notion that the doctrine is all but dead in the United States. Thus, attorney William Isaacson has said: "The employment-at-will doctrine is tottering in most jurisdictions and, in some, has for all practical purposes, already fallen. It would be ironic if unrepresented employees under state law developed more rights in the workplace than employees represented by unions."[25]

A business view was presented in *Fortune* magazine:

Your average progressive commentator, not understanding the centrality of firing to our economic system, which would otherwise collapse under the deadweight of goof-offs, opposes at-willism and yearns to counter it with the so-called implied contract doctrine. The latter . . . protects employees against dismissal so long as their performance is adequate.[26]

Unfortunately, and contrary to these assertions, the employment-at-will doctrine is alive and well in most states. As noted earlier, only a minority of state courts have granted public policy or implied contract exceptions, and only three have explicitly recognized that all employment relationships are subject to the

[21]*Ivy v. Army Times Publishing Co.*, 428 A. 2d 831 (D.C. 1981).

[22]*Campbell v. Eli Lilly & Co.*, 413 N.E. 21d 1054 Ind. App. 1980), affirmed 421 N.E. 2d 1099 (1981).

[23]*Edwards v. Citibank*, 100 Misc 2d 59, 418 N.Y.S. 269 (Sup. Ct. N.N. Co. 1979), affirmed 74 A.D. 2d 553, 425 N.Y.S. 327 (1st Dept. Appeal dismissed), 51 N.Y. 2d 875, 433 N.Y.S. 2d 1020 (1980).

[24]*New York Times* (February 18, 1982), pp. 1, 30.

[25]Speech to American Arbitration Association, *Daily Labor Report*, no. 100 (May 23, 1983), BNA.

[26]*Fortune*, May 30, 1983.

covenant of good faith and fair dealing. The majority of states still adhere to the undiluted employment-at-will doctrine for employees not covered by collective bargaining agreements or protected by specific statutes.

LIMITATIONS TO EXCEPTIONS TO EMPLOYMENT-AT-WILL

Even under the most liberal interpretation of the employment-at-will doctrine, the recognized exceptions apply to only a minute proportion of the 3 million employees who are discharged each year. The overwhelming majority of discharged employees are fired for such everyday occurrences as: excessive absenteeism or tardiness, sleeping on the job, fighting in the workplace, horseplay, insubordination, using abusive or profane language, falsifying company records or application forms, dishonesty, theft, disloyalty to their employer, negligence, incompetence, refusal to accept a job assignment, refusal to work overtime, possession or use of intoxicants or drugs, etc.[27] In more than half of the discharges for the above-noted reasons, arbitrators selected under union-management agreements have found insufficient evidence to support the discharge penalty and have reinstated the employee with full, partial, or no back-pay depending on the circumstances in each case.[28] Yet none of these discharges would qualify as an exception to the employment-at-will doctrine if they occurred in a nonunionized company.

Another limitation to the applicability of the public policy and implied contract exceptions to the employment-at-will doctrine is that it is used almost exclusively by executives, managerial, and higher-level employees, who constitute only a small minority of all employees. One study of 92 wrongful discharge cases found only 8 which involved so-called secondary market employees.[29] Typical job titles of plaintiffs in wrongful discharge cases

are: company vice president, sales manager, marketing director, foreman, physician, sales representative, pharmacist, department manager, etc.

The rarity of hourly and lower-level salaried employees among wrongful discharge plaintiffs is due to several factors. Such employees are less likely to consult attorneys than higher-level employees. Even when they do consult attorneys, they are less likely to pursue their claims because they and their lawyers have lower expectations concerning their rights in general and their rights to job security in particular. The contingent fee system, under which most wrongful discharge suits are taken, discourages attorneys from representing low-income employees because they can expect smaller returns from such cases.

A second explanation for underrepresentation of low-income employees in court cases is the inherent bias in the nature of the public policy and implied contract exceptions. The opportunities for low-income employees to be fired for refusing to commit unlawful acts, such as testifying falsely at a hearing or trial or falsifying company records, are small because these employees do not usually have access to information relevant to such acts. Similarly, discharge for performing an important public obligation or "blowing the whistle" on illegal conduct by an employer is more likely to occur among upper-level, technical, or professional employees because they are in a better position to detect dangerous or illegal practices. There is also a greater willingness by such employees to question decisions of their employers.

The implied contract exception has little relevance to lower-level employees because they are rarely in a position to inquire about future job security when they apply for a job. Nor are they likely to read carefully an employee handbook which may give rise to an implied contract obligation. Even if they were aware of such a handbook provision, most employees would not realize that it could be used to bring a court suit for wrongful discharge.

The only category of exception which might be considered equally applicable to both lower- and upper-level employees is that

[27]F. Elkouri and E. Elkouri, *How Arbitration Works*, 3d ed. (BNA, 1973), pp. 652–66.

[28]See note 5 above.

[29]"Protecting Employees at Will against Wrongful Discharge: The Public Policy Exception," *Harvard Law Review* 96, no. 8 (June 1983), p. 1941.

based on a statutory right or privilege, such as being fired for filing a worker's compensation claim.[30]

ALTERNATIVE COURSES OF ACTION

In principle there is widespread agreement that the employment-at-will doctrine has no economic or moral justification in a modern industrialized nation. The idea that there is equity in a rule under which the individual employee and the employer have the same right to terminate an employment relationship at will is obviously fictional in a society in which most workers are dependent upon employers for their livelihood. Recognizing the problem is, however, more difficult than finding an acceptable solution.

By far the best solution would be unionization. The best protection against unjust discharge is afforded by a collective bargaining agreement containing a grievance and arbitration procedure. Put in its simplest form, one answer to the employment-at-will problem is: Let those who want protection against unjust discharge join a union.

But this is both an oversimplification and an illusory solution. Many workers who join unions do not receive the benefits of unionization because they represent a minority of the bargaining unit in which they are employed. Thus, under the National Labor Relations Act, if less than 50 percent of the employees vote to unionize, 100 percent remain unprotected against unjust discharge. In 1981 unions won only 43 percent of NLRB certification elections, the lowest proportion in 25 years.[31] This indicates that joining a union does not guarantee protection against unjust discharge. In addition, protection of the right to organize does not apply to several million supervisory employees under the National Labor Relations Act.

The illusory nature of unionization as a solution to the employment-at-will doctrine is even more evident from the fact that the percentage of organized employees has decreased from 35 percent of the nonagricultural labor force in 1955 to 23 percent in 1980.[32] Thus, the tide of unionization has been receding rather than advancing, leaving an ever increasing number of employees without protection against unjust discharge. There is no evidence that this trend is likely to be reversed in the foreseeable future.

Voluntary employer action to provide due process, including impartial arbitration, for discharged employees, has been proposed by the American Arbitration Association and is supported by progressive employer representatives as the best way to deal with the employment-at-will issue.[33] As in other fields of human behavior, voluntarism is always preferable to compulsion in labor-management relations. Unfortunately the record provides little basis for optimism that voluntary employer action is the key to the employment-at-will problem. Only a handful of employers—all of them very large—have adopted voluntary arbitration for their nonunion employees. Most nonunion employers, who have recognized that employees should have an outlet for their grievances, have instituted systems wherein some higher level of management reviews and has the final word on employee discharges.

Voluntary systems, though laudable, do not begin to approach the magnitude of the problem posed by employment-at-will. Few employers will voluntarily adopt impartial arbitration, and those most in need of outside review are least likely to provide it. According to a Conference Board study, nonunion complaint systems enjoy little credibility among employees and terminations are rarely appealed through such systems.[34]

A third solution, which finds support among many lawyers, would place its faith in the judiciary to circumvent the anachronistic

[30]Ibid., pp. 1942–47.

[31]Speech by K. Moffett, *Daily Labor Report*, no. 12, September 7, 1983.

[32]*U.S. Bureau of Labor Statistics News*, September 3, 1979; *BLS Earnings and Other Characteristics of Organized Workers*, May 1981.

[33]Stieber and Blackburn, *Protecting Unorganized Employees*, pp. 4–20; J. Schauer, discussion of "Due Proceeds for Nonunionized Employees," *IRRA Proceedings* (1979), pp. 180–2.

[34]The Conference Board, *Nonunion Complaint Systems: A Corporate Appraisal* (1980); "Policies for Unorganized Employees," *PPF Survey no. 125* (April 1979), BNA.

employment-at-will doctrine. Those who support this approach point to court decisions over the last decade as evidence that the courts can and will find a way to protect employees generally against capricious and arbitrary discharge.

I have previously noted the inadequacy of the public policy and implied contract exceptions to the employment-at-will doctrine insofar as hourly workers and lower-level salaried employees are concerned. It is among these employees that the problem of unjust discharge is most serious, as indicated by the 50 percent reversal rate in cases appealed to arbitration. With respect to the larger issue of protection against unjust discharge for all employees, Professor Theodore St. Antoine has noted:

There is no case in this country where the court has clearly held as a matter of common law that discharge must be justified. I see no chance of getting the courts to adopt full-scale just cause protection.[35]

Indeed the courts themselves have begun to draw back from some of their earlier decisions in wrongful discharge cases in favor of the view that it is up to the legislature to explicitly strike down the employment-at-will doctrine. Thus, the New York Court of Appeals has allayed concerns among employers resulting from its 1982 decision upholding the right of an employee to sue his employer for wrongful discharge. In a 1983 case the Court barred a complaint of wrongful discharge by an employee of 23 years who claimed that he was fired in reprisal for disclosing top management accounting improprieties. The Court said:

If the rule of nonliability for termination of at-will employment is to be tempered, it should be accomplished through a principled statutory scheme, adopted after opportunity for public ventilation, rather than in consequence of judicial resolution of the partisan arguments of individual adversarial litigants. In sum, under New York law as it now stands, absent a constitutionally impermissible purpose, a statutory proscription, or an express limitation in the individual contract of employment, an employer's right at any time to terminate an employment at will remains unimpaired.[36]

THE STATUTORY APPROACH

The above failings in the unionization, voluntary employer action, and judiciary approaches to doing away with the employment-at-will doctrine leads to a consideration of federal or state legislative action. As noted above, legislative bodies are much better equipped than the courts to deal with the myriad problems that must be dealt with in devising a workable solution to protect employees against unjust discharge. I and others have elsewhere set forth proposals to deal with such issues as: Federal versus state action, definition of just cause, employer coverage, employee eligibility, conciliation before adjudication, remedies for unjust discharge, cost, employee representation, and the composition of the tribunal.[37] I do not intend to discuss the content of legislation on this occasion.

I recognize that some of the issues that must be dealt with in legislation do not have perfect answers. But the failure to find the ideal solution to every problem should not be used as an excuse to do nothing. The injustice done by the employment-at-will doctrine to thousands of discharged employees is too great to allow it to continue for want of a perfect substitute. The application of such a standard to other laws would have resulted in no action to prohibit discrimination in employment on grounds of race, sex, or national origin, to provide protection against occupational hazards in the workplace, and to guarantee that employees receive the benefits to which they are entitled in pension plans. Most of us would agree that on balance these laws have served a useful purpose despite many problems in their implementation. I am confident that a law to protect employees

---

[35]*The Employment-at-Will Issue*, p. 23.

[36]*Murphy v. American Home Products Corp.*, N.Y. Ct. App. no. 35, March 29, 1983.

[37]J. Stieber and M. Murray, "Protection Against Unjust Discharge: The Need for a Federal Statute," *Journal of Law Reform* 16, no. 2 (Winter 1983), pp. 336–41; Summers, "Individual Protection Against Unjust Dismissal."

against unjust discharge would yield equally desirable results.

Legislative action to protect employees against unjust discharge would have to surmount major obstacles. Bills do not get adopted in Congress or in state legislatures merely because they are in the public interest. Without the support of major pressure groups, such bills die in committee or never even reach the hearing stage.

It is understandable that there is no pressure group to lobby for a bill to protect employees against unjust discharge. No political action committee representing discharged employees exists to contribute campaign funds to legislators. Employees who are discharged for cause do not advertise their situation, even when they believe they have been treated unfairly. They are more likely to hide the fact that they were fired from their last job in order to enhance their prospects for future employment.

In the field of labor-management relations, few bills become law without the endorsement and active support of employer organizations or unions, or preferably both groups. Employers strongly oppose dilution of the employment-at-will rule.[38] Even unionized employers, who have lived with grievance procedures and arbitration for many years, want to retain the right to discharge their nonunion employees without having to prove just cause to an impartial tribunal.

Unions are often depicted as being harmed by legislation protecting nonunionized workers against unjust discharge, on the supposition that it would make organization more difficult. This view has been put forth by academicians, employers, and government representatives.[39] They argue that such legislation as OSHA, Title VII of the Civil Rights Act, ERISA, and even the Fair Labor Standards Act, has made union organization more difficult by substituting government regulation for protection through collective bargaining.

Curiously, unions do not appear to share these views. Though it is not a priority item on labor's legislative agenda, union representatives have indicated support for legislation to protect nonunionized workers against unjust discharge.[40]

In view of the obstacles to legislation to do away with the pernicious employment-at-will doctrine, one can hardly be optimistic about the prospects for statutory protection against unjust discharge in the next few years. Yet the 60 million employees who presently do not enjoy such protection can draw some hope from the words of a man who has earned a well-deserved reputation as a pretty good prognosticator on both economic and political matters. In *The General Theory of Employment, Interest, and Money* John Maynard Keynes wrote,

Is the fulfillment of these ideas a visionary hope? Have they insufficient roots in the motives which govern the evolution of political society? Are the interests which they will thwart stronger and more obvious than those which they will serve? I am sure that the power of vested interests is vastly exaggerated compared with the gradual encroachment of ideas. Soon or late, it is ideas, not vested interests, which are dangerous for good or evil.[41]

The ideas espoused by Lord Keynes in *The General Theory* were certainly more revolutionary in the 1930s than the simple notion that I have put forward here today.

Keynes's ideas were proved sound in less than a decade. I trust that the much more modest proposal that all employees deserve statutory protection against unjust discharge will be tested and proved equally sound during the decade of the 1980s.

---

[38]*The Employment-at-Will Issue*, pp. 13–15.

[39]P. Wallace and J. Driscoll, "Social Issues in Collective Bargaining," *U.S. Industrial Relations 1950–1980; A Critical Assessment*, ed. J. Stieber, R. McKersie and Q. Mills (Madison, Wis.: IRRA, 1981), pp. 252–53; M. Lovell, "A Reagan Official Views a Changing Labor-Management Relationship," *IRRA Proceedings* (1982), pp. 271–78; *The Employment-at-Will Issue*, pp. 20–21.

[40]D. Wilson, discussion of "Due Process for Nonunionized Employees," *IRRA Proceedings* (1970), pp. 180–82; *The Employment-at-Will Issue*, p. 18; H. Epstein, comment on "Arbitration of Job Security and Other Employment-Related Issues for the Nonorganized Workers," *National Academy of Arbitrators Proceedings* 34 (1981), pp. 62–67.

[41]J. M. Keynes, *The General Theory of Employment, Interest and Money* (New York: Harcourt Brace Jovanovich, (1936), pp. 383–84.

READING 34

Does First Amendment Let Employees Thwart the Boss?*

Charles G. Bakaly, Jr. and
Joel M. Grossman†

Until recent years, employees working for an indefinite term, and not under a collective bargaining agreement, could be terminated at any time with or without cause. This principle, known as the employment-at-will doctrine, has been recognized in all states for more than 100 years. Recently, however, this doctrine has been substantially limited by the courts.

One way in which courts have limited the at-will doctrine has been by holding that employees otherwise terminable for any reason could not be terminated for a reason that contravened public policy. In the first of the so-called public policy cases, a California court held that a union official couldn't be fired for refusing to commit perjury before an investigatory commission. Subsequent cases held that employees could not be fired for refusing to engage in price fixing, for reporting another employee's criminal activities, or for exposing illegal banking practices.

Recently, a federal court of appeals, interpreting Pennsylvania law, has taken the public policy exception to the employment-at-will doctrine into the area of the First Amendment to the Constitution. The First Amendment, of course, provides that the government will not deprive its citizens of free speech. This protection previously had been extended, with narrowly tailored exceptions, to public employees while on the job. Now, in *Novosel v. Nationwide Insurance Co.*, the appellate court has held that *private companies* cannot terminate employees for exercising their First Amendment rights.

According to the plaintiff's complaint, Nationwide asked its employees to help it lobby the Pennsylvania House of Representatives for a no-fault insurance bill. Specifically, the company instructed them to obtain signatures to be forwarded to state legislators.

Mr. Novosel disagreed with the company's position. He refused to participate in the lobbying effort, and he privately criticized it. For this reason, he alleged, he was fired. Claiming that his firing was contrary to public policy, he brought a lawsuit for wrongful discharge.

Nationwide sought and obtained a summary dismissal of the complaint from the trial court. The company convinced the lower court that even if Pennsylvania recognized a public policy exception to the employment-at-will doctrine, it would not extend to these facts. However, the appellate court found that if Mr. Novosel could prove that he was terminated for failing to lobby the legislature for no-fault reform, then Nationwide had fired Mr. Novosel for his "political beliefs" and had committed a tort. The case was sent back to the district court for trial.

The Novosel decision raises significant questions in an area of the law already of concern to employers. In Novosel, unlike the earlier public policy cases, the employer had done nothing illegal or immoral. It simply engaged in a legitimate attempt to persuade the legislature to enact a no-fault insurance law that would be of economic benefit to the company. Mr. Novosel was not a "whistle-blower," exposing corporate corruption or illegality. Nor had he been asked to violate any law. He simply disagreed with company policy, and refused to carry it out.

The Novosel decision is at least as troubling for what it did not say as it is for what it said. The court didn't limit its holding to the case of an employee terminated for failing to act in furtherance of the employer's political beliefs. By invoking the very broad protection of the First Amendment, and by applying that

*Reprinted with permission from Richard D. Irwin, Inc., and Dow Jones, Inc., *The Wall Street Journal*, December 8, 1983.

†Messrs. Bakaly and Grossman are lawyers with the Los Angeles-based firm of O'Melveny & Myers. They are co-authors of "Modern Law of Employment Contracts," published by Law & Business/Harcourt Brace Jovanovich.

protection to employees in private industry, the court's decision could be extended in disturbing ways.

Because the Novosel decision was not expressly limited to the facts of the case, it leaves room for future courts to hold that any limitation on an employee's freedom of speech or association would be contrary to public policy. In order to improve the company's image in the community, or to create the opportunity for potentially profitable business relationships, a company might ask an employee to join the local Chamber of Commerce, Lions Club, or Kiwanis Club. The employee, for reasons of his own, might refuse to do so. Under the Novosel rationale, should an employee be fired for failing to join one of these groups, he could bring a lawsuit for wrongful termination.

Other potential implications of Novosel are even more troubling. If an employee cannot be fired for exercising his right to free speech, then presumably the law would protect acts of blatant disloyalty. A Zenith engineer could announce that, in his opinion, RCA made better television sets, and couldn't be fired for it. A J. C. Penney salesman could recommend to customers that they go across the mall to Sears where, in his opinion, the merchandise is better, and couldn't be fired for it. By the same token, an employee's First Amendment rights would include telling his boss exactly what he thought of him, or creating disharmony at company meetings. Perhaps most troubling, an employee who feared that his job was in jeopardy could begin to make critical statements about the company, in an effort to protect his position.

It is time for the courts to remember that employment law has two sides: The employer, too, has rights that must be protected. An employee owes a duty of loyalty to the company that pays him. Quite simply, he is paid to do his job, and the company has the right to tell him what that job is. If the employee doesn't like it, or if it violates his own personal code of ethics, he is free to quit. But as long as the employer does not order him to commit perjury, fix prices or the like, the employee must either carry out his duties or be subject to termination.

A more reasonable approach to the public policy exception was adopted in the 1980 New Jersey case of *Pierce v. Ortho Pharmaceutical Corp.* A doctor doing research for a drug company objected to the use of saccharin in a particular drug. She felt that saccharin was hazardous, and that she could not work on the project for moral and ethical reasons. When the company ordered her to continue to work on the project, she quit. She then sued, asserting that for all practical purposes she had been fired for protesting the use of saccharin. Such a termination, she claimed, was contrary to public policy.

The New Jersey Supreme Court rejected her claim. It held that only the New Jersey Legislature could declare what the public policy of the state is. The employee's personal code of ethics does not constitute public policy: laws passed by the state legislature do.

This approach to the public policy exception should be followed. It is now time for the courts to remember that employers also deserve protection from disloyal employees, or employees who do not perform the work they are asked to do. In the end, nothing could be more contrary to public policy than providing judicially imposed job tenure for those who least deserve it.

READING 35

The Plant-Closing Issue Arrives at the Bargaining Table*

Kenneth A. Kovach and
Peter E. Millspaught†

During the first three years of the 1980s, the United States has watched its economy undergo immense dislocations. Technological obsolescence, declining competitiveness in world markets, a severe recession, and other factors have combined to force drastic structural changes in many sectors, particularly in the heavy industries. Steel, automobiles, machine tools, textiles, and rubber have provided a strong foundation for the American economy for over half a century, but now they find their very survival is at stake. Associated with these industries' efforts to adjust is the movement of capital in pursuit of new priorities and the consequent economic disruption associated with plant closings.

I. THE CENTRAL ISSUES

Traditionally, organized labor and management in the United States have perceived their interests in relation to plant closings to be in opposition. Viewing plant shutdowns as a threat to job security, union membership, union territorial prerogatives, and wage and benefit achievements, organized labor has vigorously pressed for a voice in the closing decision. Management has just as vigorously resisted, contending that such decisions are management's prerogative and are necessary to the effective operation of a profitable business enterprise.

*Reprinted with permission from *Journal of Labor Research* 4, no. 4 (Fall 1983), pp. 367–74.

†*Professors Kovach and Millspaugh are on the faculty of George Mason University, Fairfax, Virginia.*

In recent years, a public interest dimension has been introduced into the plant-closing debate. Greater recognition that the injury from a shutdown can readily move beyond the worker and touch his family, the small businesses dependent on the plant, the economic and social fiber of the community, and the viability of local government is now being strongly promoted by a number of public interest groups.[1] Also gaining currency is the public interest thesis of corporate accountability, which would place the responsibility for plant closings at the corporation doorstep.[2]

II. THE INSTITUTIONAL SETTINGS

The plant-closing combatants are waging their struggle primarily within the framework of three institutions: the courts, the legislatures, and the collective bargaining process. The federal judiciary has been engaged in the plant-closing debate primarily through labor's contention that the terms of the National Labor Relations Act (NLRA) bring management shutdown decisions within the ambit of mandatory bargaining.[3] Although the National Labor Relations Board appears to favor this interpretation, the courts have been considerably more cautious.[4] Through a small number of recent opinions, the Supreme Court has provided a degree of protection against mandatory decision bargaining in plant-closing

[1] B. Bluestone and B. Harrison, *Capital and Communities* (Washington, D.C.: The Progressive Alliance, April 9, 1980); M. Green, J. Bernstein, V. Kamber, and A. Teper-Marlin, *The Case for a Corporate Democracy Act of 1980* (Washington, D.C.: Americans Concerned about Corporate Power, December 1, 1979).

[2] R. Nadar, *Taming the Giant Corporation* (New York: W. W. Norton, 1979); M. Green et al., *The Case for Corporate Democracy Act.*

[3] This is based most frequently on the argument that the plant-closing decision is a "term" or "condition" of employment by the act's definition. See 29 U.S.C. ss158 (d) which characterizes collective bargaining as "the performance of the mutual obligation of the employer and the representative of the employees to . . . confer in good faith with respect to wages, hours, and other *terms and conditions of employment.*" (emphasis added).

[4] The difference between the National Labor Relations Board and the courts in this area has been apparent for some time. See analysis in T. Schwartz, "Plant Relocation or Partial Termination: The Duty to Decision-Bargain," *Fordham Law Review* 39 (1970), pp. 81, 86.

situations.[5] The Court's inclinations were reaffirmed last summer in its ruling that management had no duty to bargain over an economically motivated decision to partially terminate a business.[6]

Sensitive to entrepreneurial freedom, the courts generally have given little indication that decision bargaining requirements with respect to plant closings will be enlarged under NLRA interpretations in the foreseeable future. A partial judicial success can be reserved for labor, however, as the requirement for "effects" bargaining in plant-closing situations under the amended NLRA appears now to be firmly in place.[7]

Over the years, judicial initiative in plant-closing situations has been solicited on other grounds as well. For a brief interlude, the courts seemed to be on the verge of accepting job protection from a shutdown based on the theory that seniority rights established in a labor contract were "vested," thereby surviving termination of the agreement and following the job to a subsequent facility.[8]

The courts have also been asked to use interpretation of the terms of labor contracts to find an unwritten intent that worker job entitlements would continue beyond a plant closing.[9] Theories favoring the perception of a job

as a legally protectable property interest rather than a mere contract right have also been advanced.[10] Even the public interest arguments of the corporate accountability lobby have appeared in the courtroom in opposition to plant closings.[11] One conclusion, however, is inescapable: None of these or other theories has succeeded in securing any significant judicial intervention in plant-closing situations.[12]

What, then, can be anticipated from the second institutional arena in which plant-closing issues are being played out, i.e., the legislatures? In recent years, certain segments of organized labor along with various public interest groups have taken their case for plant-closing relief to both the state legislatures and the Congress.[13] Campaigning since the mid-1970s, these groups have prompted the introduction of plant-closing legislation in some 21 states as well as the U.S. House of Representatives and the Senate.[14]

Although the legislative proposals at the state level vary widely, requirements for prenotification, severance benefits, and the establishment of a community action fund are

---

[5]Although the Court has required bargaining on a decision to subcontract work previously being done by union employees in *Fibreboard Paper Products Corp. v. N.L.R.B.*, 379 U.S. 203 (1964), the decision to terminate an entire business for whatever reason has been protected from bargaining in *Textile Workers Union v. Darlington Manufacturing Co.*, 380 U.S. 263 (1965), as has an economically motivated decision to partially terminate in *First National Maintenance v. N.L.R.B.* 452 U.S. 666 (1981).

[6]*First National Maintenance v. N.L.R.B.*, 452 U.S. 666 (1981).

[7]*N.L.R.B. v. Adams Dairy, Inc.*, 350 F. 2d 108 (CA8, 1965), *cert denied*, 382 U.S. 1011 (1965). Acknowledged in *First National Maintenance*, "Effects" bargaining, as the term implies, requires the parties to bargain in good faith over the effects of a management decision; in this case, the decision to shut down.

[8]*Zdanok v. Glidden Co.*, 288 F.2d 99 (2nd Cir, 1961). This ruling was extremely controversial, little followed, and eventually overruled. For a critical analysis of the case see Aaron, "Reflections on the Legal Nature and Enforceability of Seniority Rights," *Harvard Law Review* 75 (1962), p. 1532; *contra* see Blumrosen, "Seniority Rights and Industrial Change: Zdanok v. Glidden Co.," *Minnesota Law Review* 47 (1962), p. 505.

[9]The *Zdanok* holding again provides an excellent example of the application of broad interpretation of the

terms of a bargaining agreement to achieve this purpose. It has been argued that broader "contextual" interpretations are warranted because the workers of today "are caught up in a system of industrial relations that transcend the immediate contracting situation." See Blumrosen, "Seniority Rights," p. 528.

[10]The perception of a job as a legally protectable property interest has had its advocates in this country for many years. See for example P. Drucker, "The Job as Property Right," *The Wall Street Journal*, March 4, 1980. This concept was explored recently in the major plant closing case of *United Steel Workers v. U.S. Steel Corp.* 492, F. Supp. 1 (1980).

[11]*United Steel Workers v. U.S. Steel Corp.* 492 F. Supp. 1 (1980), Brief *Amici Curiae*.

[12]P. Millspaugh, "Plant Closings and the Prospects for a Judicial Response," *Journal of Corporation Law* (Spring 1983).

[13]See description of these efforts in Bluestone and Harrison, *Capital and Communities*, note 1; Labor Union Study Tour Participants, *Economic Dislocation; Plant Closings, Plant Relocation, and Plant Conversion* (Washington, D.C.: UAW, USA, IAM, May 1, 1979), a report on plant closing laws in Sweden, West Germany, and Great Britain with recommendations for similar laws in the United States.

[14]B. Bolle, "Overview of Plant Closings and Industrial Migration Issues in the United States," Economics Division, Congressional Research Services of the Library of Congress, May 15, 1980; P. Millspaugh, "The Campaign for Plant-Closing Laws in the United States: An Assessment," *The Corporation Law Review* (Fall 1982).

the most universal.[15] A major stumbling block to the passage of such state proposals is the fear that such laws would create a strong disincentive to state economic and industrial development efforts.

Sweeping plant-closing relief proposals have appeared at the federal level, generating considerable fact-finding activity through public hearings.[16] Ambitious requirements for governmental intervention before and after the closing decision, along with other controversial features, have thus far prevented federal proposals from gaining the support necessary for enactment. In addition, in light of a generally unfavorable political climate, the prognosis for a legislative response in the near term is not encouraging.

III. COLLECTIVE BARGAINING DEVELOPMENTS

In contrast to the lack of responsiveness within the courts and legislatures, plant-closing issues are gaining stature within the collective bargaining process. It can be argued that because the courts and the legislatures have failed to respond, the collective bargaining arena is showing activity. Whatever its cause, the emergence of plant-closing issues in the bargaining process could be a driving force shaping labor/management relations in the 1980s. This development is not, however, without its ironies.

For half a century or more, management has resisted union involvement in plant-closing decisions. Although required to "effects" bargain, management's discretion to close in the first instance has been practiced by the business community and has been largely protected by the courts.[17] Hard pressed to survive the forces of a new economic order, manage-

ment has necessarily intensified its interest in plant shutdown bargaining. Ironically, the management that is now more willing to bargain over the ultimate job security question is less able to guarantee the jobs in question. There is also evidence that although plant-closing considerations are appearing at the bargaining table with increased frequency, it is not at the pleasure of either party. As a result of such bargaining, labor must often sacrifice major "givebacks,"[18] while management surrenders a degree of entrepreneurial control and often must guarantee against future shutdowns.

The precise extent to which plant-closing considerations have invaded the collective bargaining process can only be a matter of conjecture. Some indication of the extent to which they have penetrated specific industries in recent years, however, is reflected in Table 1.

Over recent months, plant-closing bargaining has become evident in many industrial sectors. In the meatpacking and processing industries, for example, plant-closing considerations became a major component in recent labor contracts.[19] A similar outcome was experienced in the tire industry's pacts with the

---

[15]The content of the legislative proposals, both state and federal, are examined in Millspaugh, "The Campaign for Plant-Closing Laws."

[16]Most of the public hearings on plant-closing legislative proposals in recent years have been conducted outside of Washington, D.C. in areas experiencing plant shutdowns. They have been held under the auspices of the Senate Committee on Education, Labor, and Human Resources, and the House Committee on Education and Labor, or a respective subcommittee.

[17]Various clauses in labor agreements giving manage-

ment specific rights to shutdown decisions have become quite standard, such as:

1. Without intending by the language of this section to limit the functions and prerogatives of management or to define all of such functions and prerogatives, it is agreed that the following are the exclusive functions of the employers . . . *the right to decide the number and location of its plants*, the creation of new departments and the elimination of existing departments in a plant.
2. The union recognizes other rights and responsibilities belonging solely to the company, prominent among which is the *right to decide the number and location of plants*.
3. *It shall be the sole right of the company to diminish operations in whole or part or to remove a plant for operation or business of same or any part thereof, to any location as circumstances may require* (emphasis added).

See "Major Collective Bargaining Agreements, Management Rights, and Union-Management Cooperation," *Bureau of Labor Statistics Bulletin,* 1425–5, pp. 15–16.

[18]A term that connotes a union bargaining concession in the form of "giving-back" to management contract rights previously secured.

[19]Especially noteworthy was the United Food and Commerical Workers pact with Armour Meats. In return for security against unannounced future shutdowns, the union agreed to a production line speed-up and a wage and cost-of-living freeze through 1985.

Table 1
Plant Movement Limitations by Industry[a]

	Total Studied		Agreements Having Plant Movement Limitations	
	Agreements	Workers (000)	Agreements	Workers (000)
Total, all unions	1,823	7,339.2	392	2,873.1
Total, 9 unions	764	3,654.9	271	2,277.3
Autoworkers	118	995.2	39	738.2
Clothing workers	19	165.3	12	143.3
Electrical workers	110	295.8	16	29.0
Garment workers	42	257.0	36	242.8
Machinists	89	285.7	16	76.0
Meat cutters	50	142.8	19	66.7
Retail clerks	48	137.0	18	64.0
Steelworkers	120	587.8	42	430.7
Teamsters	168	748.4	73	486.6
Other	1,059	3,724.3	121	595.8

[a]Because of rounding, sums of individual items may not equal totals.
Source: "Characteristics of Major Collective Bargaining Agreements," *Bureau of Labor Statistics Bulletin,* 2065, 1980. [Note that these figures reflect only "plant movement" limitations. This should be distinguished from an agreement pertaining to a plant shutdown where no relocation is contemplated.]

United Rubber Workers.[20] Other industries are following suit. Nowhere, however, has the issue gained the prominence it experienced in the beleaguered auto industry.

IV. THE AUTOMOBILE MANUFACTURING INDUSTRY

Perhaps hardest hit of the major industries, the automakers have initiated large-scale, industrywide plant closings. With management working for company survival[21] and unions fighting for job preservation, plant-closing bargaining has been suddenly stripped of its previous forms of gamesmanship. What is emerging is a negotiating process dominated by the plant-closing issue which now presents a credible and practical problem on both sides of the bargaining table.

An explicit plant-closing component first appeared in the auto industries' labor/management arrangements in connection with

the loan guarantee measures taken by the federal government to assist the Chrysler Corporation in 1974. At the government's insistence both the union and the company were required to make concessions designed ultimately to keep the doors open at Chrysler plants. The United Auto Workers ratified an enormous $1.068 billion giveback in the form of direct wages and various economic supplements in return for a seat on the Chrysler Board of Directors for UAW president Douglas Frazier and a voice in layoff decisions.[22]

The agreement contained such radical concessions by both sides in comparison with other recent industry agreements that it was perceived initially as merely a temporary aberration. Union givebacks of such magnitude and the unprecedented codetermination concessions[23] by Chrysler management could

---

[20]Under the fear of eminent shutdowns, the union agreed to $9.9 million in wage concessions, representing a 13 percent increase in labor costs over the life of the contract in its pact with Uniroyal.

[21]In the case of General Motors, its automaking subsidiaries.

[22]The company also agreed to establish a profit-sharing plan for its blue-collar workers and to allow access to the company books by union auditors as part of the total arrangement.

[23]Codetermination connotes the sharing of decision-making authority between labor and management. It is representative of a growing trend in the United States, much of which seems patterned after the European model. For a further discussion of codetermination in general

only be attributed to governmental third-party pressure and the unique circumstances surrounding the pact. This generalization, however, proved to be premature.

In 1981, some 10 months before the union contracts were to expire, both the General Motors Corporation and Ford Motor Company approached the UAW to begin negotiations on new agreements. Talks were begun first with General Motors where it soon became apparent that plant-closing considerations could not be ignored and, indeed, would be a significant factor in shaping any agreement. Although talks subsequently broke down, it now appears that they centered primarily on marketing strategy considerations in an effort to minimize the necessity of anticipated plant closings. For example, the concept of tying union economic givebacks to reduced auto prices was seriously explored for the first time in recent memory in the auto industry.[24]

With the union and General Motors at an impasse, talks with Ford began. In time these talks could enter the annals of United States labor negotiations as the most innovative ever undertaken in a major industry. In a sweeping agreement concluded in February 1982 and subsequently ratified by local unions and the UAW bargaining committee, the parties culminated a prodigious good faith effort to restructure their relationship as it pertained to job preservation. One need look no further than the basic terms of this agreement to appreciate the extent to which plant-closing considerations permeated the bargaining. Union givebacks included a three percent annual improvement factor, cost-of-living allowances for nine months, and considerable reductions in the 26 personal and 43 general worker holidays over the three-year contract.

In return, Ford granted the union a form of profit sharing for its members along with both "decision" and "effects" bargaining rights in connection with any future plant closings. The company guaranteed the union against plant closings for two years, that work force reductions would be accomplished through normal attrition, and that laid-off workers with over 15 years seniority would receive a severance benefit equal to 50 percent of their present salary until reaching retirement age.

The major significance of the 1982 Ford-UAW contract may be found in its precedent-setting impact within the industry. General Motors' announced intention in late February 1982 to close seven more plants, coupled with the success of the Ford negotiations, sent General Motors and the UAW back to the bargaining table. The parties reached agreement on a pact comparable to the Ford contract in breadth and basic structure. The Chrysler pact cleared the local union ratification process by a bare 52 percent margin. In return for a company pledge not to close the seven plants, the union conceded some fundamental gains in improvement factors and cost-of-living adjustments in the wage package.

V. CONCLUSIONS

Unable to obtain legislative and judicial support for the increasingly serious problems of plant closings, labor unions are bringing the issue to the bargaining table. The influence of plant-closing considerations on the collective bargaining process may be shown to correlate with the business conditions under which the bargaining is conducted. Certainly the potency of plant-closing considerations has been evident in the recent round of negotiations in the ailing automobile industry.

As a matter of national labor policy, the desirability of addressing plant-closing problems exclusively within the collective bargaining process will surely be debated in the years ahead. There are those who contend that the bargaining process called for under the NLRA as interpreted by the courts provides the appropriate mechanism for resolving such an issue. They will point to the recent plant-closing bargaining developments to support their position. Others will hold to the view that the

and the Chrysler agreement in particular, see Kenneth A. Kovach, Ben Sands, and William Brooks, "Is Co-Determination a Workable Idea For U.S. Labor-Management Relations?" *MSU Business Topics* (Winter 1979).

[24]It was announced that for every $1 per hour giveback in labor costs a $150 per car production savings could be realized and that this would in turn equate to a $250–$300 reduction in the retail price. Dealers were to be asked for concessions also.

existing bargaining structure is weighted against union interests and will continue to seek legislative or judicial intervention to right the imbalance. However appropriate, adequate, or inadequate this bargaining response, it would appear that labor and management, within the limits of their own resources, have begun to grapple with the problem.

The advent of spreading plant shutdown bargaining raises related questions that only time can answer. The extent to which this development marks a watershed in the history of U.S. labor/management bargaining is uncertain. It is tempting to conclude that the contract innovations reflected in the recent auto pacts will usher in a new era of labor-management relations and that the former relationship has been irreversibly altered. To conclude that future relations will soon embrace principles of codetermination and abandon their adversarial moorings would be unrealistic. It would be more prudent to suggest that some residue of the good faith and cooperation forced on the parties by today's distressed conditions may survive the return to better times.

READING 36

Working Wives and Mothers: What Happens to Family Life*

Sar A. Levitan and Richard S. Belous†

The changing work role of women has caused much concern about the survival of the family; most women can mix work with marriage and motherhood and handle or better share the resulting household responsibilities

American families seem to be besieged from all sides. Divorce rates are climbing; marriage is being postponed, if not rejected; fertility rates are falling; increasing numbers of children are being raised only by their mothers, either because of divorce or because their parents were never married; and wives and mothers in record numbers are rushing out of the home into the labor market. What is the effect of these occurrences on the institution of the family? Does the "economic independence" of working women influence their decisions to either begin or end a marriage or to rear children? Too frequently, the changing work patterns of women are confused with causing the deterioration of family life. Careful analysis of family-related data show that although American families are changing, they are not eroding.

The fact that women are working in record numbers is not a new phenomenon. What has changed are the conditions and places in which they work. Many tasks which were once performed inside the home are now the source of jobs held by women outside the home. World War II stands as a major breaking point in female work patterns. The war effort's high demand for labor and patriotic fervor induced many women to join the labor force, boosting the size of the female work force by 57 percent during the war. Some analysts predicted that after the war family work patterns would return to the previous norm. They reasoned that rising productivity and economic growth would continue to boost the income earned by husbands, thus reducing the need for another check and inducing wives to return to their homes. This, of course, did not happen, as economists failed to consider the nonpecuniary attractions of work and the appetite for more income.

Since World War II, American households have shown a strong propensity to increase their consumption of goods and services. Many wives joined the work force to finance these upward consumption patterns. Like the mechanical rabbit leading the greyhounds around the racetrack, these aspirations have consistently stayed ahead of rising productivity, often requiring another paycheck in the chase for the "good life." With inflationary pressures and slow growth in productivity during the 1970s and early 1980s leading to sluggish gains and even occasional declines in real earnings, another check became necessary to maintain the standard of living, or growing consumption expectations, to which the families had become accustomed. By 1980, three of five families had at least two household members in the labor force—in most cases, the husband and the wife.

Work, Marriage, and Motherhood

Some futurologists have assumed that the vast upsurge of women in the work force may portend a rejection of marriage. Many women, according to this hypothesis, would rather work than marry. This "independence effect" would reduce the probability that women would marry as they are better able to support themselves. The converse of this concern is that the prospects of becoming a multipaycheck household could encourage marriages. Data show that economic downturns tend to

*Reprinted from U.S. Department of Labor, *Monthly Labor Review* 104, no. 9 (September 1981), pp. 26–30.

†Sar A. Levitan is director of the Center for Social Policy Studies, George Washington University, and Richard S. Belous is executive director of the National Council on Employment Policy. This article is adapted from their book, *What's Happening to the American Family?* to be published by The Johns Hopkins University Press, Fall 1981.

postpone marriage because the parties cannot afford to establish a family or are concerned about rainy days ahead. As the economy rebounds and prospects improve for employment, financial security, and advancement, the number of marriages also rises. In the past, only the earnings and financial prospects of the man counted in this part of the marriage decision. Now, however, the earnings ability of a woman can make her more attractive as a marriage partner—a modern version of the old-fashioned dowry.

Coincident with the increase in women working outside the home is the increase in divorce rates. Yet, it may be wrong to jump to any simple cause-and-effect conclusions. The impact of a wife's work on divorce is no less cloudy than its impact on marriage decisions. The realization that she can be a good provider may increase the chances that a working wife will choose divorce over an unsatisfactory marriage. But the reverse is equally plausible. Tensions grounded in financial problems often play a key role in ending a marriage. Given high unemployment, inflationary problems, and slow growth in real earnings, a working wife can increase household income and relieve some of these pressing financial burdens. By raising a family's standard of living, a working wife may bolster her family's financial and emotional stability.

Psychological factors also should be considered. For example, a wife blocked from a career outside the home may feel caged or shackled to the house—a situation some have dramatically likened to a pressure cooker with no safety valve to release the steam. She may view her only choice as seeking a divorce. On the other hand, if she can find fulfillment through work outside the home, work and marriage can go together to create a stronger and more stable union.

Also, a major part of women's inequality in marriage has been due to the fact that, in most cases, men have remained the main breadwinners. With higher earnings capacity and status occupations outside of the home comes the capacity to wield power within the family. A working wife may rob a husband of being the master of the house. Depending upon how the couple reacts to these new conditions, it could create a stronger equal partnership or it could create new insecurities.

Given these conflicting and diverse factors that may have bearing on divorce, statistical demonstration showing a direct positive relationship between divorce and a wife working is unattainable. Often studies have reached the conclusion that families in which the wife is working are no more likely to separate or divorce than households in which only the husband is in the labor force.

The relationship between the expanding female work force and reduced fertility rates appears to be clearer. With advances in family planning, a majority of wives have managed to combine motherhood with work. The entry of women in the work force has not led to a vast increase in childlessness among married couples, but has led to a lower fertility rate among working wives when other social and economic factors are taken into consideration. Yet some reservation may be appropriate. In West Germany, for example, fertility rates of the native population during the 1970s have declined even more than in the United States, but with a smaller increase in female labor force participation.

Coping with Family-Related Duties. The wife's responsibilities outside the home have not filtered back into a major reallocation of responsibilities within the family. With the rising costs of household help, the option to pay another person to do the housework is beyond the means of the vast majority. Also, there are limits as to the chores that can be passed on to the friendly neighborhood supermarket clerk or appliance seller. Even more than in the office or factory, too many household chores cannot be mechanized. Worksharing by other members of the family remains largely a hope. The working wife and mother is, therefore, left to her devices to cope as wage or salary earner and unpaid houseworker.

When the number of hours a working wife labors outside the home are added to the time spent on household chores, some studies have concluded that most working wives wind up laboring more hours per week than their husbands. Rough estimates based on data from the late 1960s and early 1970s indicated that a wife may average 65 hours on her combined jobs inside and outside the home (assuming that she holds a full-time job in the labor market). This exceeds the average time husbands spent working on the job and in the home by about eight hours per week. However, a more recent study based on data from the mid-1970s indicates that married women labored about the same total hours in their combined jobs as men—roughly 60 hours per week. There has been only a very small increase in the hours of housework done by married men (still under three hours per week, or one sixth the time spent by working wives).[1] It is difficult to make accurate estimates of time use by men and women, but it appears that there still exists a significant sexual division of labor even if total hours worked may be becoming equal for many married men and women.

Just as pathologies within labor markets—such as sexual discrimination—have been slow in changing, so will home adjustments to the new realities of both husband and wife working outside. For example, while most men are just starting to become involved in household responsibilities, this trend soon may be the single largest impact on families associated with wives entering the labor force. In the absence of social upheavals, the slow evolution is toward family work roles based more on equality and less on sexual stereotypes. Many working wives appear to be assuming a larger role in making major family-related decisions than nonworking wives with no earnings, but again, change has been slow. Yet, there seem to have been some changes in sharing responsibility and authority.

No Turning Back

If the survival of the family depends on women returning to the home to become full-time housewives and mothers, the institution's future existence is indeed fragile. There has been no decline in the career aspirations

of women, and continued progress in family planning, bedroom technology, and household management will let more women become both wives and mothers as well as workers outside of the home. As the potential rewards and work opportunities for women expand, the psychic and economic attractions in the marketplace are likely to exert even greater pull.

With inflationary pressures and slow growth in productivity leading to sluggish gains and even occasional declines in real earnings, more families will depend on two wage earners just to make ends meet or to finance a higher standard of living. Women in the work force, including the majority of married women, are in the labor force to stay, and this is not a new phenomenon. It was only with the rise of the industrial revolution—and then only when it was in full swing and immigrants supplied adequate and cheap labor—that wives were viewed as full-time mothers. The current American family has a long way to go before it fully adjusts to these new and shifting work patterns. The greatest changes will be the reallocation of work responsibilities within households. A decrease of chores allocated along traditional sexist lines coupled with women sharing more effectively in the family decision process are the primary adjustments that will be made. These changes—unlike fads which come and go—will probably have some of the deepest and most lasting effects on the family institution and on American society. Instead of dissolution, they offer real opportunities for improved, more stable, and richer lives within families.

Going It Alone

It appears that female-headed families will remain a significant phenomenon on the American scene. Such families, despite feminist advances, are still more likely to be poor and to experience sustained economic hardship. Trying to be family head, mother, and full-time member of the labor force has been a difficult challenge for most women. Working women who head households are at an even more disadvantage than other women.

Single-parent families tend, however, to be

[1]Sandra L. Hofferth and Kristin A. Moore, "Women's Employment and Marriage," in *The Subtle Revolution*, ed. Ralph W. Smith (Washington, D.C.: The Urban Institute, 1979), pp. 113–15; and Frank P. Stafford, "Women's Use of Time Converging with Men's," *Monthly Labor Review*, December 1980, pp. 57–58.

a temporary phenomenon. Data on the gross flows of women who become family heads indicate that this condition is for many women only a way station, as they later marry or remarry. Still, the conditions experienced by these women and their children present serious problems covering a wide range of social issues from welfare to labor market discrimination. Many have found it impossible to pull families out of poverty without government help.

At the start of the 1970s, nearly 1 of 10 families was headed by a woman; this ratio rose to 1 of 7 families a decade later, when more than 8 million women headed families. Altogether, these families accounted for 26 million persons, including 12 million children. Today, 17 percent of all American children are being raised in a family headed by a woman, compared with 10 percent in 1970.

Black children are far more likely than white youngsters to live in a home maintained by a woman. In 1980, half of all black children were being raised in such a household, compared with 12 percent of all white children. A Hispanic youngster had about a 20-percent chance of living in this type of household.

The reasons families had a female head also changed during the 1970s. Historically, widows have represented the largest proportion of women who headed families. At the start of the 1970s, roughly 43 percent of female family heads were widows, twice the proportion who were divorced. By the end of the decade, divorced women accounted for 34 percent of all women who headed families, while widows represented 29 percent of the total. The relative rate of women who had never married and were heading a family had doubled during this period.

However, the rising incidence of families headed by women is not due exclusively to increasing marital instability or illegitimacy. Families headed by women increased by nearly 2 million between 1940 and 1970. About two fifths of the increase is attributed to the propensity of women to form separate households rather than share housing with relatives. This pattern continued during the 1970s, when more than half of the households with a female head were formed for this reason. Income-support programs also may have boosted the growing ranks of women who head families, as did more out-of-wedlock births and, of course, general population increase.

Economic Realities

Of the major differences that exist between households headed by women and those of married couples, distinctions based on income are easiest to quantify. Poverty haunts only 1 of 19 husband-wife families and 1 of 9 families maintained by men; but about 1 of 3 families headed by women live in destitution.

Beyond the higher prevalence of poverty, the entire income distribution of families headed by women is lower than that of other kinds of families. In 1979, about 4 of 5 families headed by women had earned incomes under $15,000, compared with 3 of 10 of all husband-wife families and 1 of 3 families headed by men.

The median income of the families women head is less than half that of husband-wife households. Where dependent children are involved, the median drops to one third. If a female family head has a child under six years, her family income on average is only two fifths of that for a household headed by a woman with no youngsters.

Coupled with this factor are the younger ages of the women who are heading families. About four of seven of the children who live in a household headed by a woman have a mother who is under 35 years. These younger women, who have a greater chance of having a child, represented 28 percent of all families headed by women in 1970. By 1979, this younger group had grown to represent 37 percent of the families headed by women.

National longitudinal data, which have followed female cohorts for several years, have increased our knowledge about families women head. Data tracking the same women—as they go through a dissolution of husband-wife family and then try making it on their own—give a clearer picture of this dynamic process than information based on cross-sectional estimates. The national longitudinal surveys at Ohio State University included interviews with a nationally representative sample of more than 5,000 women under 25 years and 30 to 44 years at the time of the first interview (1967 and 1968, respectively). These women were interviewed annually or biennially, and the data provided a time path of their experiences over 10 years. Some of the most important features indicated by longitudinal data concerning families women head are:[2]

Temporary Status. There is a large flow of women who move into and out of being heads of families, and few women remain in this condition for an extended period. Over the first five years, the surveys found that as many as 16 percent of all adult women sampled were heading a household. However, only 9 percent were household heads during the entire period: 6 percent of the white women and 21 percent of black women.

Economic Problems. The transition from a husband-wife family to head of a household often creates dire economic problems which the women who head the new households often cannot solve without outside aid. For the older age cohort, the average household income for white families that experienced this disruption declined by 49 percent over the survey period. While the average income of black families fell by only 38 percent, their income prior to disruption of the family was only about two thirds of the average for the white households. This same condition is also true for women in the younger age cohort.

Employment Patterns. Labor force patterns of women who experience marital disruption is quite different for whites and blacks for both the younger and older women. When their marriages ended, the older cohort of white wives increased their labor force participation rate from 58 percent to 70 percent. For black women, just the opposite happened: their rate fell from more than 80 percent to 69 percent. Transition patterns also differ for black and white women concerning their seeking occupational training. When they be-

came family heads, the number of the older women who obtained training increased by more than 40 percent for whites but fell by 37 percent for blacks. For younger white women, the labor force participation rate climbed from 51 percent to 68 percent after the disruption. Younger black women, unlike their older counterparts, experienced a decline in participation rates after divorce, but it rose much less than that for the young white women—from 46 percent to 53 percent. For younger white women after divorce, the chances of resorting to training increased by 23 percent, while for younger black women it fell by 13 percent.

Even if a female family head lands a job, her earnings are not likely to make up for the income lost because a husband has left. Average per capital income will decline by 20 percent for white families and 13 percent for black families.[3]

Transfer Payments. Families headed by women depend on transfer payments as a major source of income. About 16 percent of all white female heads and 48 percent of black female heads receive public welfare payments. More than 23 percent of the white women who headed families, and 19 percent of the black women received social security or disability payments. One third of the poor white female heads and more than 50 percent of poor black female heads received at least half of their household income from public income transfer programs. On average, earnings by a female head provided only about one third of household income for families living in poverty and about three fifths for those above the poverty line.[4]

Thus, whatever other advantages a woman perceives in single parenthood over a bad marriage, most families headed by women find the going very rough economically. Even when they combine work with welfare and

[2]Frank L. Mott, *The Socioeconomic Status of Households Headed by Women* (Washington, D.C.: U.S. Government Printing Office, 1979), pp. 10, 29, 45, and 52.

[3]Frank L. Mott and Sylvia F. Moore, "The Causes and Consequences of Marital Breakdown," in *Women, Work, and Family*, ed. Frank L. Mott (Lexington, Mass., Lexington Books, 1978), pp. 123–24.

[4]Liz B. Shaw, *Economic Consequences of Marital Disruption* (Columbus: Ohio State University, Center for Human Resource Research, 1978), pp. 16 and 19.

other transfer payments, many female heads of households can barely lift their families out of poverty—and a significant number live below the poverty threshold.

The word *family*, at one time, evoked a picture of a husband, a wife, and their children living together in one household. Now, a variety of cameos surround the central picture. None of the cameos, however, portray the extended family that many analysts had anticipated because they believed a separated woman would return to her parents' or grandparents' household, taking her children with her. An increasing percentage of never-married or formerly married mothers are heading their own households instead of living as a subfamily unit in someone else's household, emphasizing the precarious status of families headed by women. In extended families, a divorced, separated, or never-married mother could count on the financial and social support of other adult family members to help provide for basic needs and ease such problems as child care. Today, if a woman decides, or is forced by circumstances, to separate or divorce, the chances are that she will have to head her own household.

There are some indications that the increase in the single-parent household will not be as swift in the 1980s as it was in the 1960s and 1970s. The view that the woman should seek liberation outside a husband-wife family is not shared by the vast majority of female family heads. Nor is it correct to conclude that those women who remain family heads do so by choice. When questioned, long-term female family heads most often indicated that their current household structure is not their first choice.[5]

Policy Changes Needed

Social policies can have a significant impact on the work and living decisions of households, even those that are well above the poverty threshold. The federal income tax codes are a prime example: in 1979, the estimated tax liability of 16 million couples exceeded $8 billion, solely because they were married. Even couples with a relatively low family income pay a marriage tax penalty if there are several wage earners in the household. The marriage tax penalty in 1980 for a couple with a combined income of $40,000 was $1,900 (assuming standard deductions), while for a $10,000-a-year couple, the extra tax liability was more than $200. Whatever its equity and costs, there is little evidence that the marriage tax has had a statistically significant impact on marriage, but it may affect work decisions.

Other laws (including social security) affecting family income and work decisions are based on the assumption that the husband would work while the wife became a full-time housewife. Social security laws also assume that, once married, the couples would stay together. One problem with the social security system is that a wife's earnings result in higher total family benefits only if her entitlement exceeds 50 percent of her spouse's benefits. In most cases, the two-earner couple pays far more into the system that a one-earner couple, but receives only a marginal increase in benefits.

Many other social policies are based on family-related assumptions which existed in a bygone age. But American households have become highly pluralistic, and government programs will have to be attuned to the different needs and problems of various types of families. A comprehensive family policy has been impossible to fashion because interested parties cannot agree on even the basic goals. While one policy may seem more dramatic, incremental reform of the already existing system may be the most realistic approach to help families during this rough period of transition.

Shifting work roles are altering family life, and changes in living arrangements are having a feedback effect on labor markets. Whether the family is better off because of the changes depends, in large measure, on personal value judgments. Public policies can ease the transition, but such policies should consider that there is no longer one dominant family type. Despite problems, the family remains a resilient institution. Most Americans live in families, and will continue to do so.

[5]Christopher Lasch, *Haven in a Heartless World: The Family Besieged* (New York: Basic Books, 1977), p. 162.

P A R T   S I X

Technology and Human Resource Policy

Some have argued that the United States is presently in the midst of a technological revolution that will have a major impact on the labor force. In the first article, Robert T. Lund presents some testimony before the U.S. House Committee on Science and Technology pertinent to manufacturing technology and human resource policy. Lund's testimony is based on a study that was conducted at MIT on "(1) emerging manufacturing technologies that will be important during the next decade and (2) the issues that will be raised by these technologies." Fourteen major U.S. firms supported the study and "their interest in sponsoring the study was to learn how their human resources would be affected by new technologies." The second article, "The Low-Skill Future of High Tech," by Henry Levin and Russell Runberger, indicates that "high technology will not ease our unemployment problems or upgrade workers' skills. Students, therefore, would benefit most from a strong general education rather than a specialized technical one." Levin and Rumberger challenge the general assumption that increasing levels of automation require an increase in skills.

What role will robots play in American industry? What problems does the introduction of robots create for workers, unions, and management? These questions are dealt with in three articles in this section. Sar Levitan and Clifford Johnson believe that there is "little liklihood that the worker will become obsolete in the forseeable future" as a result of the introduction of robots. These authors discuss "The Future of Work: Does It Belong to Us or to the Robots?"

The introduction of robots in the workplace has created problems for workers. Ichiro Saga indicates that "robots have been portrayed as mechanical wonders that actually increase job opportunities. But the strains produced by large-scale automation are beginning to affect the style and substance of Japanese labor-management relations." Saga states that "automation is subtly transforming the structure of employment in the auto industry and is adversely affecting the lives of workers, young and old." Along the same lines, Dale Buss analyzes the promises and problems that high technology is bringing to the automobile industry. In an article titled "Retraining of Workers for Automated Plants Gets off to Slow Start," he discusses the challenge to the unions created by automation. According to Buss, "autoworkers believe that their unions should do more to shield them from the effects of automation." The union position in regard to the issue is presented by Joseph Konowe in his article, "Robotics and Their Effect on the Work Force."

The concluding article in this section discusses the implications of robotics technology for collective bargaining and labor law. Terry Leap and Allayne Pizzolatto believe that "changes in collective bargaining and labor law are possible as robotics technology grows in the United States."

READING 37

Manufacturing Technology and Human Resource Policy*

Robert T. Lund†

America is heavily dependent on technology for its production of goods and services. We rely on machines and know-how to sustain the torrent of products from our factories. We count on technological innovation to provide new products and to improve our production systems. To construct a picture of the future of jobs in industry, then, we must first have a clear idea of where technology is going. During this next decade, changes in technology will have a profound effect on the nature of work and on the structure of the workplace. Strategic plans and policies regarding people and jobs will be useful only if they are made within the context of the new technologies.

Dr. John Hansen and I, both members of the Center for Policy Alternatives at MIT, have just concluded a study of (1) emerging manufacturing technologies that will be important during the next decade and (2) the issues that will be raised by these technologies. This is the first public disclosure of the results of that investigation. The study was performed under the sponsorship of 14 major U.S. firms, all leaders in their industries. Eleven of the 14 were manufacturing firms, whose

*From statement before joint hearings of the House Committee on Science and Technology, Science, Research, and Technology Subcommittee, and the House Budget Committee, Task Force on Education and Employment, Washington, D.C., June 9, 1983.

†Robert T. Lund is assistant director, Center for Policy Alternatives, MIT. The opinions expressed in this article are those of the author and do not necessarily represent those of the Massachusetts Institute of Technology or of any of the sponsors of the research reported herein.

combined annual output was approximately $110 billion. Their interest in sponsoring the study was to learn how their human resources would be affected by new technologies.

A time horizon of 10 years for the application of manufacturing technology is about as far as one can go in making a reasonably safe forecast. Anything having a major impact within that time span will already be known either in actual application or in development. Conversely, a time horizon of 10 years for human resources policy setting and implementation is about as short a time interval as will permit adjustment of skills, jobs, attitudes, and size of work force to the new technologies.

I will first briefly summarize our findings relative to new technologies, then describe the major human resource issues we see resulting from the application of these technologies, and finally suggest areas of strategic response to these issues, both for private and public policymakers.

Megatechnologies of the Next Decade

If we consider every different manufacturing process (such as laser cutting of microelectronic chips) as a specific technology, then there are thousands of technologies in use in manufacturing, and the job of locating the significant ones is immense. If we look, instead, at the basic principles or devices underlying the specific process (coherent light or the laser, for example), then we find there are only about a dozen relatively new techniques that are the basis for virtually all of the emerging manufacturing technologies. This short list includes acoustics, computers, electron beams and plasmas, holography, lasers, materials substitutions, pattern recognition, robots, superconductors, telecommunications, and a small group of technologies lumped under the heading of biotechnologies (enzymes, genetic manipulation, etc.).

Of these dozen or so technologies there are only two that will have truly enormous impact on industry during the next decade. These two—computers and telecommunications— will be so pervasive and have such profound consequences that they deserve the attention of all concerned with industrial policy.

Each of the other techniques we examined in our study had important applications in a few industires, but each was relatively inconsequential as compared to the very great impacts to be expected from computers and telecommunications. Indeed, in many cases the value of these other technologies was found to be highly dependent on either computer or communications technology, as in the case of computer support to electron beam, acoustics, pattern recognition, or superconductivity applications.

Biotechnologies appear to have potential for very great long-run influence, but that influence is seen to be more than a decade away. Until the mid-1990s the real sources of hope and concern will be found in the industrial applications of the two "megatechnologies," computers and communications. Let us examine the reasons for their importance. They are summed up in three words: *integration, pervasiveness,* and *convergence.*

Integration. Both technologies have the unusual capability of linking many separate functions and coordinating them in ways that are beyond human capability, in speed, volume, accuracy, or endurance.

For many years mini- and microcomputers have managed individual machine operations. In some continuous process industries, such as chemical manufacturing or oil refining, computers have managed complete systems consisting of multiple operations. The past decade has demonstrated the capability of the computer to integrate a number of machine tools, transport devices (including robots), and inspection and test functions into flexible, efficient, manufacturing units. Such manufacturing systems are capable of producing a variety of finished parts or products in a small fraction (on the order of 1/100) of the time required by conventional technology. During the coming decade we will see this form of computer-based integration advancing rapidly in the batch production segments of the metalworking industry and we will see continued advances of computer applications in continuous process manufacturing such as

steel, textiles, paper, glass, etc. and in high-volume discrete product manufacture such as automobiles and appliances.

In similar fashion, communications technology is also becoming integrative, as is exemplified by the local area network concept, in which all information generated within a firm or plant is available for use by people, machines, or computers quickly, inexpensively, and accurately. These systems, using a coaxial cable or optical fiber bus as its spinal cord, are analogous to the human nervous system, in that many different functions can be carried out simultaneously. In addition to the spread or these integrating communications networks, the trend is also to link these networks through microwave and fiber optic channels across the country and the world.

Pervasiveness. Most technologies tend to be limited to only a few industrial sectors. A solvent extraction process may be useful in the manufacture of only a few chemicals; an electron beam process may be used only to weld certain metal parts. The great difference between such typical manufacturing technologies and the megatechnologies is that the megatechnologies apply equally well across *all* industries. Furthermore, they can be applied to *existing* process equipment as well as to new forms of machinery such as robots. Microprocessor controls can be added to existing machines to upgrade their performance. New communications systems can link existing sources of intelligence as well as new forms of remote sensing or voice command systems.

Not only are these technologies spreading throughout all manufacturing, but their pervasiveness is felt within the firm from the factory floor to the boardroom. In a sense, the diffusion of these technologies is very similar to the introduciton of electrical motors into manufacturing late in the 19th century.

Convergence. Perhaps the most significant fact relative to computer and telecommunications, the element that holds out the greatest economic promise for the future, is that these megatechnologies are converging. New products and processes are being created that combine the power of the computer and of modern communications technology. The results can be seen in telephones that look like television screens and act like computers. The myriad product innovations that will spring out of the union of these two technologies is impossible to forecast. The opportunities for production and sale of new industrial, commercial, and consumer products provides a reassuring prospect in what could be a rather difficult period of economic adjustment.

At the same time, however, the application of these integrative, converging technologies in manufacturing will have serious consequences for the work force. We will examine these next.

Expected Impact on the Work Force

If computer and communications technologies are to be dominant sources of technological change in the near future, what can we expect the consequences to be for those employed in manufacturing? Several of the more important issues are discussed here. Our forthcoming report[1] develops these ideas and others more thoroughly.

The word *expected* is critical to this discussion. Our projections are based on current industrial practices and policies. While there are execeptions among firms, there is a general tendency to treat human resources and technology as independent subjects that are handled by separate groups of specialists. Prevailing practices and policies reflect this dichotomy. The issues we describe will arise if this approach continues.

Industrial policies can be changed, however. The relationships between people and technology are not necessarily fixed. We frequently see technology being bent to the needs of people. If organizations such as those that sponsored our research become active in meeting the new megatechnologies with fresh policies, the consequences could be substantially altered. I will discuss later what some of those new policies might be. First, let

us examine the expected outcomes if there are no policy changes.

Displacement. Industrial employment levels are dependent on many factors other than manufacturing technology. These factors include:

1. The extent of international competition for product markets.
2. The stability of national and international economic and political conditions.
3. Product innovation and diffusion that stimulates new demand.
4. Labor-price differentials or other cost advantages that encourage the flight of jobs to other countries.
5. The extent to which employment is shared through shorter workweeks, early retirement, or other approaches.

Because the factors such as these can mask the employment effects of technology, we have not attempted to forecast its influence on future employment levels. It seems evident, however, that employment cannot be sustained at past levels in many industrial sectors.

What we do know is there will be widespread *displacement*. People will be forced to move within the firm or between firms, from one job to another, from one skill to another, from one location to another, from one social group to another. This displacement is likely to be accompanied by at least temporary unemployment for some workers. The new computer-aided technologies in design, engineering, and manufacturing are enormously productive. Computer-integrated manufacturing systems reduce labor requirements by factors ranging from 3:1 to 20:1 or greater. This is one of the reasons for believing there will be shrinking work forces in certain sectors. The effects of these levels of productivity increase simply cannot be compensated by market growth of comparable magnitudes. White-collar job holders will also experience displacement. Jobs that have consisted primarily of gathering or passing on information are likely to disappear as these functions are taken over by computer/communications sys-

[1]John A. Hansen and Robert T. Lund, *Connected Machines, Disconnected Jobs,* in press.

tems. As is explained later under infrastructure changes, staff specialist jobs are also likely to shrink or disappear.

Skill Changes. The nature of jobs will change. Instead of a direct physical involvement with the product or with the machine producing the product, the worker becomes a monitor, a parts loader or unloader, a troubleshooter, or an overseer of a process in which computer intelligence directs machines through their paces. As has already occurred in chemical manfacture and some parts of steel and papermaking, the worker may be removed to a control room, physically separated from the sight, sound, feel, or smell of the process. He or she is required to judge whether the process is proceeding correctly by observing machine conditions reported by meters, digital readouts, and cathode ray tube displays. The new skills required to perform this kind of work include:

1. Conceptual thinking—ability to reason in abstract terms.
2. Visualization—ability to manipulate mental patterns.
3. Understanding of manufacturing processes.
4. Statistical inference.
5. Verbal communication.

In addition, a monitoring role demands a high level of attentiveness to the task. In at least one firm the criterion of "responsible behavior" was used in selecting operators for automated systems. These skills and attributes are substantially different from the strength and motor skills (agility, dexterity, hand-eye coordination) that are being eliminated. It remains to be seen whether training or retraining can accomplish the kinds of skills adjustments required, particularly for more senior workers.

The role of production supervisor will also require new skills. In addition to being able to understand and manage a sophisticated technology, the supervisor must be able to integrate information and make decisions on an array of topics. As individual workers come to control entire systems of machines, collegial relationships between supervisor and worker will be more appropriate than formal boss-subordinate roles. Changes of this kind involve not only aptitudes but also the basic personalities of supervisors and managers. Here, too, is a formidable challenge to training and organizational development experts.

Integration of the Infrastructure. Conventional manufacturing organizations have had complex infrastructures of specialist groups responsible for such functions as quality control, inventory control, production scheduling, dispatching, expediting, materials handling, maintenance, or time standards. Computer-integrated manufacturing systems are so tightly coupled in time that decisions regarding an aberration in the process (faulty material, a machine out of control, a change in a customer's order) cannot be handled through channels that take specialists hours or days to work out. A new kind of production manager is likely to emerge who will be able to make decisions in minutes and still consider all the factors previously handled by specialists. New combinations of computer and communications technologies will make it possible for one person to recieve and to coordinate all of the necessary information quickly and easily. This "control room executive" must be able to deal with a broader range of issues, use a greater amount of information, and operate in a shorter time horizon than the current functional manager. He or she will also be operating much more alone, because fewer specialists will be needed, and there will be less need for data gatherers and sifters.

Gaps in Skill Levels Progression. It has been traditional in American industry for workers entering at low-level unskilled jobs to work their way up through a succession of jobs to more highly skilled, better-paying positions. This traditional progression may be blocked by the effects of computer-based automation. The jobs that are the chief targets for elimination through the application of computers to production processes are the moderately skilled machine operators, welders, inspectors, assemblers, painters, platers, etc., that constitute a large bulk of the mid-range blue-collar jobs. Jobs at either the high or low end of the skills spectrum are less likely to disappear.

If the mid-range jobs disappear, it is clear that there will be gaps or bottlenecks in the normal promotion process from lower- to higher-skill jobs. The inability to progress through transitional promotions is likely to cause frustration, anger, and resentment among workers.

We believe similar gaps may begin to show up between the first-level operating management that is making very short-term operating decisions and a top-level management that handles strategic planning and decision making. In this case, the gap will result from the thinning out of middle managers and staff specialists whose jobs have been either taken over by integrative computer/communications systems or eliminated because of reductions in the number of people requiring supervision.

Loss of Management Status. Even if a manager or supervisor becomes comfortable with the increased technical content of the job (and many will not), the shift from managing people to managing machines may be perceived as a loss of status. The importance of a managerial job is, at present, often gauged by the number of people under his or her jurisdiction. Until new standards replace present conventional thinking, managers may find the transition uncomfortable.

Organizational Restructuring. Three factors point to the need for significant restructuring of the organization of manufacturing firms: (1) the emergence of the control room executive who replaces the staff specialist, (2) more responsive and complete networks of information easily accessible companywide, and (3) greater facility in the use of computer/communications systems for analysis and planning by top levels in the firm's management. These factors point to a thinning of the ranks of middle managers and functional specialists. Responsibility for operating decisions will be increasingly delegated downward; strategic plans and decisions will become the province of top management.

The implication is an organizational shift in two directions, a "recentralization" of strategic decision making at top levels and and a significant increase in delegated authority to first-level management. There would be much less in the middle levels. One might visualize such an organization as having a wasp-waisted pyramid structure.

Resistance to Change. It becomes clear that every level of the firm will be impacted by the megatechnologies. For many, these impacts will have negative connotations with respect to employment, income, job location, skills, social relationships, status, opportunity for growth, and job satisfaction. In the face of such adverse conditions, the tendency is for people to resist change. Resistance can take overt forms of refusal or retaliation, or it can become subtle interference with or undermining of the purposes of the change.

Suggested Action

If these are the issues that will be increasingly important during the coming decade, what needs to be done to make the transitions as beneficial as possible for Americans? I suggest that the actions undertaken by any sector of our society concerned with these problems—government, industry, labor, universities—should have the objective of developing an environment that:

1. Promotes the positive aspects of change for the individual and the organization.
2. Provides maximum personal security during periods of transition.
3. Creates increased teamwork among government, industry, labor, and academic organizations in solving the human problems imposed by the megatechnologies.

Keeping in mind these objectives, we can suggest possible actions to deal with some of the issues. These are summarized only briefly.

They obviously require much more detailed development.

Displacement. Our first priority is to recognize displacement as a national problem. It has been largely hidden by the recession. Both public and private policymakers must realize that failure to deal with the problems of displacement will mean high and protracted unemployment levels. Specific policy recommendations for dealing with displacement include:

1. Increased corporate responsibility for continuity of employment of the individual, although not necessarily with the same firm.
2. National laws requiring portability of pension, seniority, and group insurance rights.
3. Improved training and retraining resources more closely coupled to future industrial needs.
4. National and regional employment networks using the computer/communications technologies now available.
5. Closer cooperation among industrial firms, community service organizations (including schools), and labor organizations in the areas of job counseling, relocation assistance, and employment experiments.

Plant Conversion Dislocation. This is a subsidiary issue to the displacement problem. If companies are to rejuvenate their facilities in order to provide continuing employment opportunities in a specific community, there may be extensive temporary lay-offs during the renovation process. The objective during this time would be to maintain incomes while preparing the work force to handle new jobs competently. One policy suggestion is the establishment of local or regional cooperative assistance programs that would provide (1) temporary employment during the transition and (2) training in new skills.

Job Progression Gaps. Here, too, recognition that there is a problem is the first prerequisite. Second is an awareness that technology is not immutable, that it can be tailored to

fit human needs, and that people need not be forced to adapt to technology. Given these conditions the following policies are recommended:

1. Greater technical literacy among human resource and organizational development people in industrial firms, and management recognition that human resource people must participate in technology planning.
2. Increased emphasis on job design, in which technology is purposefully arranged to provide humans with both meaningful work and opportunity for advancement.
3. Redefinition of job evaluation criteria to conform to the new skills requirements of technologically impacted jobs.

Organizational Restructuring. There is opportunity in this area for academic support to industry in providing people with the new managerial and technical competencies demanded. This involves the revamping of curricula to include subjects on manufacturing technology, job design, quality systems, and integrative manufacturing problemsolving. Curtailment of professional jobs because of shrinkage of middle management and of manufacturing infrastructure will place additional demands on educational institutions for retraining of executives and staff people for new careers, and for job placement activity.

Exploitation of Opportunities. All these efforts would be of little purpose if there were no benefits to be gained from solving the problems. The benefits of these megatechnologies, however, are substantial and crucially important to our economic welfare. We see three major areas of opportunity:

1. Prevention of further deterioration of our industrial competitiveness in international markets.
2. Industrial growth through products that exploit the new technologies.
3. Repatriation of product manufacture to America where the reduced labor content in the product makes labor-cost differen-

tials unimportant and thereby eliminates the comparative advantage of foreign countries.

4. Improvement in the quality of worklife, including the elimination of hazardous or demeaning work.
5. A higher general standard of living.

These opportunities are worth a concerted effort by all sectors of our society. Government must play an active role in removing barriers to technological change, providing general economic stability, deciding problems of equity, and, on occasion, being the early buyer. Although the roles for government may be difficult and controversial, failure to provide the environment in which these opportunities can be grasped will put government policymakers in the even more difficult role of having to devise equitable sharing of a declining amount of work and income among its citizens.

REMANUFACTURING

Remanufacturing is a widespread but little-recognized industrial activity in the United States. It has the unique capability of prolonging the lives of durable goods well beyond their normal economic lifetimes. In so doing, remanufacturing is able to conserve materials and energy, provide employment, improve our standard of living, reduce waste, and yield profits for those operating these businesses. For a variety of reasons remanufacturing deserves to be considered a weapon to combat the effects of recession and a part of our future way of life.

Remanufacturing involves collecting worn-out or discarded products of the same kind, disassembling them under factory conditions, refurbishing all reusable parts, replacing unrepairable parts, and reassembling the parts into products having at least the equivalent performance of the products when new. In some cases, the products are upgraded in the process by substituting parts less likely to fail or by introducing new controls or other features made possible by newer technology. Such products carry a warranty comparable to that of a new product and are as reliable and durable as the original product. The price of a remanufactured product is typically between 40 percent and 70 percent of a new item.

The remanufactured products most familiar to the average American citizen are replacement automotive components, such as starter motors, alternators, clutch assemblies, water pumps, or engines. Many other products, however, are also remanufactured. The list includes telephone headsets, computers, machine tools, pumps, valves, robots, and even diesel locomotives. The military services also have remanufacturing facilities where equipment such as tanks and helicopters are restored to first-class condition.

In studies of remanufacturing conducted at the MIT Center for Policy Alternatives we have found there were fairly well-defined criteria for what can be profitably remanufactured. From a physical standpoint the product must be durable, that is, it is not dissipated during use. It must be capable of disassembly, and a majority of its component parts must be repairable. From an economic point of view, the product should have a high value added. In other words, the labor, energy, and capital equipment cost embodied in the product should be a high percentage of the product price. The nonfunctioning or wornout unit (called a "core" in the trade) should have a low market or trade-in price as compared to its real economic worth. There must be a continuing supply of cores of reasonable quality.

The market for remanufactured products should consist of knowledgeable buyers who can evaluate the product and appreciate its worth. This criterion tends to restrict remanufacturing to commercial and industrial items, because most consumers at present are incapable of judging intrinsic product worth or are biased against used or older products. As remanufacturing becomes more prevalent, this restriction may change.

We have identified an impressive list of benefits to society provided by remanufacturers. Several of these benefits are especially pertinent to the search for new ways to solve the country's economic problems. I will describe those benefits briefly and then suggest ways in which remanufacturing could be put to work to assist the economy.

Resource Conservation

An outstanding contribution of remanufacturing is its conservation of energy and materials. Remanufacturing is one of those rare instances of an industrial activity whose products embody more energy than is used by the activity to produce them. Our studies indicate that for every kilowatt hour of energy used in remanufacturing from five to six kilowatt hours of equivalent energy are recaptured in the salvaged products. In a sense, remanufacturing can almost be said to be creating energy.

Materials conservation figures are even more impressive. For every pound of new material required to replace parts that cannot be reused, approximately eight pounds of valuable metals, plastics, and other materials are conserved. Conservation of materials in the form of usable parts is a much more economic approach than is the recovery of materials through recycling processes where the only value saved is the raw material itself.

Favorable Pricing

Because prices can be significantly lower for remanufactured products than for new products, such items become attractive alternatives to users who must husband their cash. By offering lower-priced options, remanufacturers broaden the market. They provide goods that can compete favorably with lower-priced, foreign-made products, and they provide a stimulus to competitive pricing in markets that may be dominated by a few firms.

Employment Opportunities

Remanufacturing is a labor-intensive, portable industry. It can be located anywhere that is convenient for the collection of cores. Capital equipment investment is low relative to that of the original manufacturing process, and the labor skills required include a good many jobs at low levels. Remanufacturing thus is a prime candidate for introduction into areas of high unemployment and economic distress.

Profitable Business

Despite the low prices for their products, remanufacturers are profitable businesses. Increasing numbers of original equipment manufacturers are turning to remanufacturing their own products as a means of adding to their revenues. In recent years, some of these firms have found remanufacturing to be a major (even sole) source of profits. Remanufacturing is not only a source of employment and resource conservation, it is also a source of tax revenue.

Policy Suggestions Relative to Economic Recovery

This enumeration of benefits makes it fairly evident how remanufacturing can help American economic recovery. As a matter of fact, it is clear that remanufacturing is already making a substantial contribution, and one of the most sensible public policies would be to avoid doing anything that would interfere with its growth and development.

There are some special possibilities, however, that should be considered:

1. Remanufacturing can be used to upgrade existing manufacturing and service technology. Many older machines can not only be restored to like-new performance but they can be upgraded by the addition of electronic sensors and controls to match the sophistication of new machines. Remanufacturing can make an important contribution to reindustrialization.

2. Areas especially hard hit by plant closings should consider using the abandoned plants and work forces as bases for remanufacturing. In some instances, the product remanufactured might even be the product originally produced in that plant.

3. Remanufactured items produced by reputable American firms may find acceptance in other countries. This would be especially true for industrial machinery, transport vehicles, and replacement components.

Many countries have had bad experience with used equipment "deals" from the United States, so they are wary of buying items that are not new. Warranted goods from an established remanufacturer could have a better reception, however.

Public Involvement

There is one strong factor in favor of remanufacturing: its jobs do not move overseas. Remanufacturing is very much an American form of enterprise. It is a highly beneficial activity that should be encouraged.

What can the government do relative to remanufacturing? It can act as a source or a catalyst for standards for the industry, so a remanufactured item is recognized as conforming to certain quality and performance requirements. It can act to advocate the purchase of remanufactured goods through example, using the purchasing policies of government agencies to demonstrate support. Finally, it can act to encourage the establishment and growth of remanufacturing activities by favorable tax, capital assistance, employment, and export policies.

Because of the diversity of their products, remanufacturers are not represented as an industry in Washington. Few congressmen have ever heard of the activity. There is a need for advocacy, both in the industry and in the government. It is expected that a clearer recognition of the advantages of remanufacturing will stimulate action on its behalf.

R E A D I N G 38

The Low-Skill Future of High Tech*

Henry Levin and Russell Rumberger†

High technology has become the nation's latest white knight, heralded as a means of creating many new jobs at home and restoring our economic supremacy abroad. Politicians and editorial writers even look to high technology as a way of upgrading the skills of the American labor force and increasing worker satisfaction.

To fulfill this promise, policymakers have proposed vast changes in our educational system. The New England Board of Higher Education recently endorsed an ambitious proposal from three high-tech consultants that calls upon government and industry to raise $1 billion for high-technology education. The House of Representatives has already passed a bill that would provide $425 million to upgrade math and science education at the elementary, secondary, and college levels. Although most of the funds would be spent on improving the quality of teaching, $20 million is slated to recruit and train faculty in high-technology fields at junior and community colleges. The bill also provides at least $15 million to help develop programs in computer education. Other proposed federal legislation would provide tax credits to manufacturers who donate computers to schools; California already provides such credits on state taxes. Many states are also independently pursuing ways to increase the number of science, math, and computer courses required of all high-school graduates.

*Technology Review, August–September 1983. Reprinted with permission from Technology Review, copyright 1983.

†Henry Levin is professor at the School of Education and Department of Economics and director of the Institute for Research on Educational Finance and Governance at Stanford University. Russell Rumberger is senior research associate and economist at the Institute.

These proposed changes are based on two assumptions. First, future job growth in the United States will favor professional and technical jobs that require considerable education and training in computer-related areas. Second, high technology will require upgraded skills because workers will be using computers and other technical equipment.

Unfortunately, these assumptions are dead wrong. The expansion of the lowest-skilled jobs in the American economy will vastly outstrip the growth of high-technology jobs. And the proliferation of high-technology industries and their products is far more likely to reduce the skill requirements of jobs in the U.S. economy than to upgrade them. Therefore, America's policymakers should revise their educational priorities and place greater emphasis on a strong general education rather than a narrow specialized one.

SKILLED WORKERS NEED NOT APPLY

The Department of Labor has projected a faster rate of growth for high-tech jobs than for jobs in other occupations in the 1980s. While total employment is expected to increase 22 percent between 1978 and 1990, employment in data processing, machine maintenance, and computer programming are projected to grow between 70 and 148 percent (see Figure 1).

But such percentage changes are misleading. The total number of new jobs generated in these and other high-technology occupations will be vastly outweighed by the number of jobs generated in other areas. For instance, the five occupations expected to produce the most new jobs in the 1980s are all in low-skilled areas: janitors, nurses' aides, sales clerks, cashiers, and waiters and waitresses. No high-tech occupation even makes the "top 20" in terms of total numbers of jobs added to the U.S. economy. While employment for engineers, computer specialists, and other high-technology professionals will grow almost three times as fast as employment overall, these occupations will generate only about seven percent of all new jobs during the rest of this decade.

Statistics on specific occupations reinforce

Figure 1

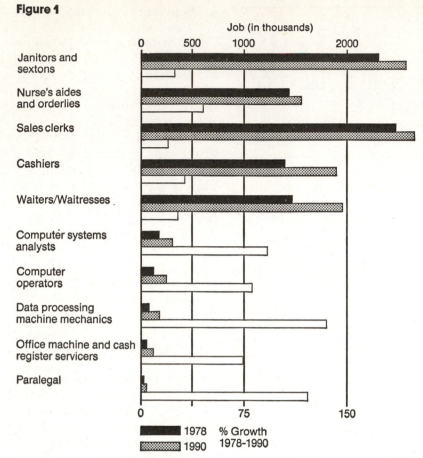

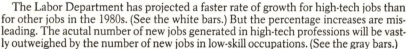

The Labor Department has projected a faster rate of growth for high-tech jobs than for other jobs in the 1980s. (See the white bars.) But the percentage increases are misleading. The acutal number of new jobs generated in high-tech professions will be vastly outweighed by the number of new jobs in low-skill occupations. (See the gray bars.)

this picture. Employment for computer-systems analysts will increase by over 100 percent between 1978 and 1990, yet only 200,000 new jobs will actually be created. And while there will be 150,000 new jobs for computer programmers, some 1.3 million new jobs are projected for janitors, nurses' aides, and orderlies. Indeed, in each of these categories alone, there will be nine unskilled jobs for every computer programmer.

As a whole, employment growth in the United States will favor the low- and middle-level occupations, according to the Labor Department. By 1990, jobs in all professional and managerial occupations will account for only 28 percent of all employment growth, less than in either of the previous two decades. In contrast, clerical and service occupations will account for 40 percent of total employment growth in the 1980s.

These estimates suggest that most job expansion will occur in areas that require little or no training beyond high school. Even if the number of high-tech jobs doubles or triples in the next decade, they will hardly make a ripple in the overall job market in America.

THE MINUTE DIVISION OF LABOR

Job projections aside, there is no question that high technology will have a profound effect on many American jobs. Vast segments of the labor force will find their jobs altered by sophisticated computer technologies. Secretaries will trade their typewriters for word-processing equipment, bookkeepers will use computerized financial spread sheets, purchase and inventory employees will keep records on computerized systems, mechanics will use diagnostic systems employing micro-computers, and telephone operators will rely on computerized directories. But will the use of these new technologies require workers with more sophisticated skills?

Based on past experience, the answer seems to be no. Throughout the history of industrial production in this country, management has endeavored to divide and subdivide work into repetitive, routine tasks for which unskilled and low-paid workers can be used. This approach was first advocated by Adam Smith in *The Wealth of Nations* and later refined by Charles Babbage, who argued that it was cheaper to hire many workers capable of performing dissociated tasks than to hire a single worker capable of doing them all.

Technology has generally been used to aid and abet this division of labor. More than 20 years ago, James Bright, a professor at the Harvard Business School, examined the effects of automation on job-skill requirements in industries such as metalworking, food, and chemicals. The general assumption then, as today, was that increasing levels of automation required increasing skills. However, Bright observed that the skill requirements of jobs first increased and then decreased sharply as the degree of mechanization grew. He found that in the long run, automated machinery tends to require less operator skill. Once operators master their particular machines, "Many so-called key skilled jobs, currently requiring long experience and training, will be reduced to easily learned, machine-tending jobs."

Our recent analysis of job-skill requirements in the U.S. supports Bright's conclusion. We compared Department of Labor data on job-skill training requirements for specific occupations in 1960 with those in 1976. We found that in spite of continuing advances in technology and the widespread shift toward automation, job-skill requirements have changed very little over the last two decades (see Figure 2).

Figure 2

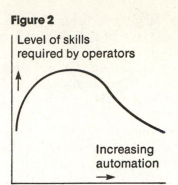

Level of skills required by operators

Increasing automation

More than 20 years ago, James Bright, a Harvard Business School professor, examined the effects of automation on job-skill requirements in the metalworking, food, and chemical industries. Bright found that skill requirements first increased and then decreased sharply as the degree of automation grew.

The impact of more recent technologies only reinforces this conclusion. Many of the jobs in the printing industry, for instance—typesetting, layout, and photoengraving—have historically required highly complex craft skills. But over the last 10 years, technological advances have enabled many of these operations to be performed by machines. The introduction of teletypesetting machines have eliminated many manual typesetting operations. Tasks that once required handling and proofing of metal plates and castings can now be done with paper—and soon by computer. Many manual operations involved in reproducing photographs have been automated. Complete layouts can be duplicated and transmitted to distant presses with a high degree of precision. Taken together, these advances have sharply reduced the skill required of workers who remain in the composing room.

DANGER SIGNS OF HIGH TECH

Computers, which are at the very heart of the high-technology revolution, provide another textbook example. Early computers were not only large and expensive by today's standards; they required programmers and operators with fairly complex skills. But as computer languages become more "user-friendly," the level of skills needed to operate computers declines.

The new generation of office computers is specifically designed so that workers can use computers for a wide variety of tasks without any knowledge of computer languages. In the office, computers now perform many of the tasks formerly done by secretaries. Word processors can correct typing errors automatically by the use of electronic dictionaries, so letter-perfect typing and strong spelling skills are no longer required. In addition, each operator's performance can be monitored by the computer so that supervisors can instantaneously compare productivity among workers.

Ironically, high technology could be used to enhance the quality of working life and increase the level of worker skills. At General Motors, for instance, managers and workers meet regularly to discuss new assembly-line technology and analyze how it can be applied to give workers a greater sense of responsibility on the job. But whether these meetings will actually accomplish anything remains to be seen. Judging from the past, we have every reason to believe that future technologies will continue to simplify and routinize work tasks, making it more difficult for workers to express their individuality and judgment.

The danger signs are already evident in places such as Silicon Valley. Although some executives, programmers, and engineers are stimulated by their jobs, most workers in the valley are employed as office workers, assembly workers, and low-level technicians. Many are overeducated for their jobs and find little challenge from high tech. That may be why, according to a recent front-page story in the *San Jose Mercury*, a third of all workers in the valley take drugs and drink on the job. According to local narcotics agents quoted in the article, drug users in these plants are believed to be largely responsible for thefts on the job as well as accidents.

Just as ominous is the possibility that high tech will eliminate more jobs than it creates. Researchers at the Robotics Institute at Carnegie-Mellon University estimate that in the next 20 years, robotics could replace up to 3 million manufacturing positions involving operating machinery, and potentially eliminate all 8 million of these positions by the year 2025. The widespread use of computer-aided design may virtually eliminate the occupation of drafter in the not-too-distant future, a potential loss of 300,000 skilled positions. A recent study from the Upjohn Institute estimates that robots could eliminate three times as many jobs as they will create, and the Director of Advanced Products and Manufacturing at General Motors predicts that the "factory of the future" will employ 30 percent fewer workers per car because of robotics. Even if laid-off production workers are retrained for high-tech positions, they may not be able to achieve a comparable income level. Placement counselors in Michigan found that laid-off steel or iron workers retrained for high-tech positions and lucky enough to find jobs typically received wages at half their previous level.

Another danger from high tech is that it may facilitate the transfer of production overseas, further reducing the number of jobs available in the United States. Much high-tech assembly requires no more than a primary education, and many countries in the world can provide workers with such qualifications at less than $1 an hour. Atari's recent announcement that it was shifting most of its manufacturing facilities to Taiwan and Hong Kong illustrates this danger. As a result of this move, some 1,700 workers in Silicon Valley—middle managers as well as production workers—will be laid off.

Whereas past technical innovations primarily displaced physical labor, future technologies, rooted in the microelectronics revolution, threaten to displace mental labor. Entire classes of skilled or semiskilled workers can be made obsolete by sophisticated software packages.

ADAPTING TO A HIGH-TECH WORLD

Obviously high technology is not going to be a cure-all for our nation's economic woes. And its potential impact on the workplace and society in general could be a lot more disturbing than we'd like to think. What, then, are its implications for education?

To begin with, an excessive emphasis on specialized schooling will not prepare workers for the future. Although many workers will need to acquire new knowledge to adjust to technological change, they will probably have to learn different, rather than more demanding, skills. Most of these new skills can best be acquired on the job and through short training courses rather than through expanded science, math, and computer-programming studies.

In fact, in a recent survey of industrial employers in Los Angeles conducted for the local chamber of commerce, Wellford Wilms, professor of education at UCLA, found that they prefer employees with a sound education and good work habits to those with narrow vocational skills. A similar survey of British companies seems to confirm employer preference for workers with a good attitude and a sound education.

In the future, technological advances will come at an increasingly fast pace. Specialized job skills will be more rapidly rendered obsolete and the once-familiar work environment will change at a bewildering rate. We believe that the best possible preparation for adapting to this lifetime of change will be a strong general education. By that we mean a knowledge of different political, economic, social, and cultural tenets as well as the acquisition of strong analytical, communicative, and computational skills. These are essential for understanding the currents of change in society and for adapting to such change constructively.

This approach should also fulfill the need to provide a common educational background for all students that will best serve the democratic interests of our society. A democratic society requires that citizens be qualified to understand the major issues of the day, discuss them, and take appropriate action. Early specialization not only deprives students of the general knowledge and skills needed to adapt to a changing labor market; it also fails to provide the basis for democratic participation.

In a high-tech future, a solid basic education will become more, not less, important. The challenge of the schools will be to upgrade the overall quality of instruction by attracting the best talent society has to offer. This will require major curriculum improvements, competitive professional salaries, and a much greater commitment to educational quality on the part of teachers, parents, policymakers, and society in general.

FURTHER READING

Braverman, Harry. *Labor and Monopoly Capital.* New York: Monthly Review Press, 1974.

Bright, James R. "Does Automation Raise Skill Requirements?" *Harvard Business Review* 104 (August 1981), pp. 42–55.

Carey, Mark L. "Occupational Employment Growth Through 1990." *Monthly Review* 104 (August 1981), pp. 42–55.

Cooley, Mike. *Architect or Bee?* Boston: South End Press, 1983.

Greenbaum, Joan M. *In the Name of Efficiency: Management Theory and Shopfloor Practice in Data Processing Work.* Philadelphia: Temple University Press, 1979.

Hunt, H. Allan, and Timothy L. Hunt. *Human Resource Implications of Robotics.* Kalamazoo: W. E. Upjohn Institute for Employment Research, 1983.

Rumberger, Russell W. *Overeducation in the U.S. Labor Market.* New York: Praeger Publishers, 1981.

Scientific American, September 1982.

Zimbalist, Andrew, ed. *Case Studies in the Labor Process.* New York: Monthly Review Press, 1979.

The Future of Work: Does It Belong to Us or to the Robots?*

Sar A. Levitan and
Clifford M. Johnson†

As the silicon chip helps chip away many factory and office functions, prospects are bright for both robots and microprocessors, but investment and other constraints seem to assure no revolutionary loss of employment

Today, futurists are discussing the onset of a sweeping technological revolution, one which would rival or surpass the Industrial Revolution of the 19th century in importance. This envisioned social order has been given many names—"postindustrial," "technetronic," or "information" society. At the center of this flurry of interest in technological change is the microprocessor. While computerized automation has been theoretically feasible for more than a decade, large and expensive computer systems could produce cost savings only in the most massive industrial settings, and automated machinery could not be easily adapted to serve various production functions. Now, with the development of the microprocessor, these obstacles have been overcome and the potential uses of computerized machinery at the workplace have dramatically increased.

Microprocessor technology is best symbolized by the silicon chip, a miniaturized system of integrated circuits which can direct electrical current and, thereby, generate vast com-

†Sar A. Levitan is professor of economics and director of the Center for Social Policy Studies, The George Washington University, Washington, D.C., and Clifford M. Johnson is a research associate at the center. This article is adapted from their book, Second Thoughts on Work (Kalamazoo, Mich: W.E. Upjohn Institute, 1982).

*From U.S. Department of Labor, Monthly Labor Review 105, no. 9 (September 1982), pp. 10–13.

putational power. A silicon chip the size of one square centimeter can perform millions of multiplications per second, and has the capacity to store the texts of the Declaration of Independence, the Constitution, and a few chapters of the Federalist Papers. Technological advances are expected to result in at least a fourfold expansion of these capabilities within a decade, so that the microprocessors of the future will be extremely powerful computers on a single silicon chip or combination of chips. The reduction in size is astounding—today's hand-held programmable calculators have more computational power than the first full-scale computers built during World War II, computers which could have been "hand held" only by juggling 18,000 different vacuum tubes.

This miniaturization of computer technology is particularly important because it has been accompanied by dramatic cost reductions, making microprocessors economically competitive in a wide range of industrial applications. Once designed, silicon chips can be mass produced at a very low cost, and even further price declines are anticipated as volumes rise. As a result, a calculation which cost 80 cents to perform in the early 1950s costs less than one cent today, after adjusting for inflation. The combined reductions in size and cost of microprocessor technology have triggered renewed interest in prospects for automation and in the broader possibility of a wholesale transformation of modern society driven by these new technological capabilities.

The silicon chip is particularly important to economical automation because it provides the basis for fully integrating computer and machine. In industrial settings, the microprocessor makes possible the development of manufacturing machinery with unique adaptability. The great majority—at least 75 percent—of all manufactured goods fall into the category of shorter, lower-volume production runs, with only the most basic industries continuing to fit the mass-production stereotype. Technological advances in microelectronics, therefore, were an essential precondition to widespread automation, and the expanding use of reprogrammable machinery has triggered today's intense debate regarding the future of industrialized societies.

The potential impact of microprocessors is heightened by their seemingly endless number of applications. This new technology promises to alter not only the factory, but the office as well. Sophisticated word processors and computerized information storage and retrieval systems are becoming increasingly cost-effective, and because this new technology does not require knowledge of specialized computer languages, their growing use may raise traditionally low productivity among office workers. These office innovations are considered qualitatively different from previous office equipment which "mechanized" or "automated" routine tasks. While memory typewriters made an office worker's tasks easier, emerging computer technologies may change the means by which information is transcribed and made available to others. Again, only with the silicon chip has this decentralized use of computer technology at an affordable cost become possible.

'Robot Revolution' Coming

The use of the microprocessor to automate production functions is epitomized by the development of the robot. Prior to the last decade, robots were confined to the domain of children's stories and science fiction—their practical and efficient application in work settings was virtually inconceivable given the state of computer technology. The silicon chip has thrust robots from fantasy to reality, and the technology is being pursued with remarkable speed and vigor. A number of top computer companies are now considering entry into the robot market, and several large U.S. corporations have made commitments to purchase robots which are already available. The use of robots in manufacturing has nearly quadrupled between 1979 and 1981, and most analysts expect the sales curve to shoot higher during the next few years.[1] Most importantly, microprocessors seem to be in a prime posi-

tion for the implementation of "learning curve pricing" strategies in which firms lower prices in anticipation of rising volumes and declining unit costs. The entry of large computer companies into the robot market could ensure this aggressive marketing stance and trigger a sharp rise in robot sales by 1990.

Today's robots bear little resemblance to the creations of screenplay writers and science fiction authors. Rather than some form of mechanical humanoid, industrial robots are characterized by mechanical arms linked to reprogrammable computers. An exact definition of a robot, as distinct from other automated machinery, eludes even industry representatives. The Robot Institute of America, an industrial trade group, stresses that it is the "reprogrammable and multifunctional" character of robots which is unique, allowing them to perform a variety of tasks.[2] And the emerging versions of robots are varied—the more extravagant include a "bureaucratic robot" which stamps signatures on letters, a robot "nurse" to assist handicapped persons in wheelchairs, a robot "janitor and guard dog" for the home, and "talking robots" which would advertise products or give job training to illiterates. Microprocessors are revolutionizing design methods for the development of new manufactured goods, and have become an integral part of nearly all modern research equipment so as to expedite lengthy data analysis.[3] Innovations such as voice-sensitive computers which can directly transcribe dictation into written text may be marketable within just a few years. It is this diversity of applications for microprocessor technology which distinguishes it from less significant innovations, and which has led futurists to predict a societal transformation "comparable with the agricultural revolution that began about 10,000 years ago, and with the industrial revolution."[4]

[1]"Robots Join the Labor Force," *Business Week*, June 9, 1980, p. 62; and Joann S. Lublin, "As Robot Age Arrives . . . ," *The Wall Street Journal*, October 26, 1981, p. 1.

[2]Otto Friedrich, "The Robot Revolution," *Time*, December 8, 1980, p. 75.

[3]Gene Bylinsky, "A New Industrial Revolution is on the Way," *Fortune*, October 5, 1981, pp. 106–14; and Barnaby J. Feder, "The Automated Research Lab," *New York Times*, October 27, 1981, p. D1.

[4]Herman Kahn, William Brown, and Leon Martel, *The Next 200 Years* (New York: Morrow, 1976), pp. 8, 20–24.

How Far . . .

There is little consensus as to where the "robot revolution" is heading and how far it will go. The technology itself may be refined to such an extent that most factory work could be carried out by robots and automated machinery. For example, a study conducted at Carnegie-Mellon University asserts that the current generation of robots has the technical capability to perform nearly 7 million existing factory jobs—one third of all manufacturing employment—and that sometime after 1990, it will become technically possible to replace all manufacturing operatives in the automotive, electrical-equipment, machinery, and fabricated-metals industries.[5] Yet these theoretical estimates of the potential for automation, which reach as high as 65 to 75 percent of the factory work force, do not reflect the rate at which the new technology will actually be introduced to the workplace. The pace of innovation will depend on the relative costs of labor and computerized technologies, as well as on broader levels of supply and demand for goods and services. Predictions of this nature are infinitely more difficult than abstract assessments of future technological capabilities.

The automobile industry offers an interesting case study, because it is probably the first manufacturing industry to aggressively pursue the use of robots in automated processes. The push toward automation in the auto industry is a response to both rising labor costs and growing concerns for quality control and competitiveness in international markets. Auto manufacturers already find it possible to operate robots for $6 per hour, well below the $20 per hour required for the pay and benefits of a skilled worker in 1981.[6] General Motors, aware of the growing use of robots by Japanese auto makers, predicts that by 1987, 90 percent of all its new capital investments will be in computer-controlled machines.[7] A 1980 survey conducted by the American Society of Manufacturing Engineers predicted that robots will replace 20 percent of existing jobs in the auto industry by 1985, and that 50 percent of automobile assembly will be done by automated machines (including robots) by 1995.[8] Even the United Auto Workers anticipates a 20-percent decline in membership by 1990 and has successfully obtained advance notice and retraining rights from auto manufacturers in a growing effort to gain protection from sweeping automation. Yet, few of these estimates include any consideration of the extent to which capital shortages confronting robot manufacturers and purchasers may limit the speed with which the new technology is adopted.

Projections of the impact of microprocessors on office employment are even more problematic, with analysts more frequently predicting the number of office jobs "affected" rather than eliminated by automation. The Carnegie-Mellon study argued that 38 million of 50 million existing white-collar jobs would eventually be affected by automation, while a vice president for strategic planning for Xerox Corporation offered the more conservative guess of 20 to 30 million jobs affected by 1990.[9] There is a general agreement that office technologies will be changing rapidly, but little indication of whether the result will be reduced office employment, shifts in future employment growth, or simply higher levels of productivity in white-collar settings.

A 1982 study prepared for the International Labour Office found that microelectronic technology has not caused widespread displacement of office workers, but perhaps only because of the impact of poor economic conditions on the rate of diffusion of the new technology in office settings. Selected case studies of the banking and insurance industries suggested that new job opportunities were being created, but the skills made redundant by new technologies were generally inappropriate for those emerging opportunities. The report stressed that this trend poses special threats to employment prospects for

---

[5]Lublin, "As Robot Age Arrives . . . ,"; and "The Speedup in Automation," *Business Week*, August 3, 1981, p. 62.

[6]*Congressional Record* (daily edition), December 10, 1981, p. S14908.

[7]Harley Shaiken, "Detroit Downsizes U.S. Jobs," *The Nation*, October 11, 1980.

[8]Fred Reed, "The Robots Are Coming, The Robots Are Coming," *Next*, May–June 1980, p. 32.

[9]"The Speedup in Automation."

women, and called for additional education and training efforts to close the "skill gap" caused by the use of microprocessors in office jobs.[10]

Perhaps the greatest fears that automation will lead to widespread unemployment have been voiced, not in the United States, but in Western Europe. For example, two British authors have predicted nothing short of the collapse of work as a social institution in an era of microprocessors:[11]

It is impossible to overdramatize the forthcoming crisis as it potentially strikes a blow at the very core of industrialized societies—the work ethic. We have based our social structures on this ethic and now it would appear that it is to become redundant along with millions of other people.

In West Germany, studies of the impact of automation on future employment levels commissioned by the Bonn government projected that the number of jobs in 1990 will at best be marginally above 1977 levels—a pessimistic view in light of anticipated population growth. The issue of technologically induced unemployment increasingly is capturing the attention of West European leaders, and unions in Italy, Germany, and elsewhere are responding with demands for shorter workweeks to protect employment levels. Perennial fears that machines would replace workers have never been fulfilled, but European futurists insist that it will be different this time.

. . . and How Fast?

While the impact of automation in the past has been offset by the emergence of new industries and by growth in the service sector of the economy, these avenues for employment growth may indeed be less open in an era of microprocessors. The electronics industry, which supports this computerized technology, certainly will experience rapid growth in the coming decade, but a 1979 survey of the world electronics industry prepared for the Organization for Economic Cooperation and Development revealed that the internal use of its own technology will keep employment growth in this sector to a minimum.[12] It is this "reproductive" potential of computerized technology—the prospect of robots building robots—which challenges traditional patterns of employment growth through new industries. And to the extent that the microprocessor will affect service as well as manufacturing industries, even the recent trend of expanding service employment may fail to provide jobs.

In spite of these relatively unique characteristics of microprocessor applications, predictions of immediate and massive job losses tend to ignore the market forces which slow the pace of technological change. As stressed in recent research by the Bureau of Labor Statistics, many factors limit the speed of diffusion of technological change and thereby mitigate possible employment implications. The size of required investment, the rate of capacity utilization, and the institutional arrangements within industries all can act as "economic governors" which slow the adoption of automated technologies.[13]

Virtually all capital-intensive industries have a massive investment in existing plant facilities, and they cannot afford to squander these resources through the wholesale replacement of working machinery. More importantly, the financial constraints on capital formation necessarily limit the rate at which new technologies are introduced. In this context, Joseph Engleberger, president of Unimation, Inc. (the nation's largest robot manufacturer), has dismissed predictions of galloping automation, noting that even the replacement of five percent of all blue-collar workers in Western industrialized nations would require investments totaling $3 billion in each of the next 40 years.[14] While microprocessor technology may be promising in its flexibility

[10]Diane Werneke, "Microelectronics and Office Jobs: The Impact of the Chip on Women's Employment," report prepared for the International Labour Office, 1982, pp. 115–24.

[11]Clive Jenkins and Barrie Sherman, *The Collapse of Work* (London: Eyre Methuen, 1979), p. 182.

[12]Mich McLean, "Sector Report: The Electronics Industry," background study prepared for the Organization for Economic Cooperation and Development, in *Technical Change and Economic Policy* (Paris: OECD, 1980).

[13]Richard W. Riche, "Impact of New Electronic Technology," *Monthly Labor Review*, March 1982, p. 39.

[14]Reed, "The Robots Are Coming."

and potential efficiency, industries must be able to afford the new acquisitions in order to use them.

A less tangible but perhaps equally important force limiting the expansion of computer technology lies in the attitudes of both workers and consumers. While a computer may be able to diagnose medical problems, its bedside manner may be less than comforting. Similarly, word processors and telephone answering systems may alter clerical roles, but most executives will not want to forgo the convenience offered by their personal secretaries. People can hear the best music in the comfort of their homes but flock to concert halls to hear lesser performances. Even on the assembly line, where robots may be perfectly suited for production processes, the aversion of managers and workers to such unfamiliar companions may hamper their smooth and rapid assimilation at the workplace. These psychological barriers cannot be factored into equations of economic efficiency, but they are likely to slow the pace of technological change nonetheless.

Will Workers Become Obsolete?

The picture which emerges when the functioning of capital markets and work organizations are considered is one of evolutionary rather than revolutionary change. With annual sales of robots well below 10,000 in a labor force of more than 100 million, it will be some time before computerized technologies make a major dent in aggregate employment levels. This perspective is emphasized by Robotics International, a professional group which polled 100 users and manufacturers of robots. Based on the responses, the group concluded that robots are likely to replace 440,000 rather than a million workers by 1990, and that all but five percent of the displaced workers would be retrained rather than dismissed.[15] The relative lack of union concern in the United States over aggregate job losses through automation also stems from this belief that the pace of innovation has been exaggerated. William Winpisinger, president of the

International Association of Machinists, has argued that the replacement of human skills with computerized machinery will occur slowly and that a shortage of skilled workers will remain our most pressing manpower problem.[16] No doubt, unions will continue to seek guarantees of job security in some industries, and collective bargaining may gradually extend to include management investment decisions.

In the more distant future, no one can be sure where new employment growth will occur. Expectations of a workless society still linger; as described in one forecast:[17]

Earning a living may no longer be a necessity but a privilege; services may have to be protected from automation, and given certain social status; leisure time activities may have to be invented in order to give new meaning to a mode of life that may have become economically useless for a majority of the populace.

The literature in recent decades has been replete with speculations on how people would cope with the loss of meaningful work roles, or how society would allocate and distribute wealth in the absence of strong ties between work and income.[18] Even for those who reject such forebodings, the belief in continued employment growth admittedly contains as much faith as foresight.

Still, there seems little likelihood that the worker will become obsolete in the foreseeable future. In one sense, past waves of automation have created dislocations, but it has been distributed throughout the labor force in the form of benefits and social progress—shorter workweeks, more vacation time, longer training and education, earlier retirement, child labor laws, and welfare and unemployment payments. We can expect this trend to continue, particularly as labor seeks assur-

---

[15]Lublin, "As Robot Age Arrives . . . "

[16]William W. Winpisinger, "Correcting the Shortage of Skilled Workers," *The AFL–CIO American Federationist*, June 1980, p. 21.

[17]Theodore J. Gordon and Olaf Helmer, "Report on a Long-Range Forecasting Study," in *Social Technology* (New York: Basic Books, 1966), pp. 81–82.

[18]James S. Albus, *People's Capitalism: The Economics of the Robot Revolution* (Kensington, Md.: New World Books, 1976); and Colin Hines and Graham Searle, *Automatic Unemployment* (London: Earth Resources Research, 1979).

ances of job security. Assuming a healthy rate of economic growth during a period of innovation and increasing automation, it is also likely that levels of aggregate demand will support the emergence of new goods and services. Rising expectations alone will cause Americans to translate productivity gains into higher standards of living instead of less work, a pattern which has held for centuries. The period of adjustment which lies ahead may not be painless, but it seems that work is here to stay.

Japan's Robots Produce Problems for Workers*

Ichiro Saga†

Although most Japanese view factory automation with awe and admiration, a hard look at the use of robots by a major car manufacturer suggests that such optimism is not warranted. Automation is subtly transforming the structure of employment in the auto industry and is adversely affecting the lives of workers, young and old.

Last spring the Nissan Motor Company gave blue-collar jobs to 2,650 new workers, but in 1983, it will hire less than half that number. A Nissan spokesman justified the reduction in recruitment by citing the continuing slow growth of the auto industry that has resulted from trade friction abroad and a sluggish market at home. He also pointed to the company's extensive investment in robots and other labor-saving equipment.

The rationale is revealing. Instead of a threat to employment, robots have been portrayed as mechanical wonders that actually increase job opportunities. But Nissan's new personnel policy suggests otherwise. Moreover, the strains produced by large-scale automation are beginning to affect the style and substance of the company's labor-management relations.

Until recently, Nissan union officials have been willing to take the company's word that automation is a must. Union President Ichiro Shioji repeatedly expressed his confidence that labor-management cooperation would be sufficient to surmount any difficulties arising from the introduction of robots.

But in September 1981, speaking before the 10th annual congress of the Federation of Automobile Workers, Mr. Shioji made an abrupt about-face. "The automobile industry employs a quarter of Japan's industrial robots, yet we have never opposed robotization on the grounds that it threatens jobs. But how long can we go on ignoring this problem?" he asked. "The time has come for us to change our basic policy concerning the introduction of robots on the shop floor."

Behind his militant get-tough stance is the realization that management is using robots to undermine the tradition of industrial harmony. The Nissan union is noted for its special "action" squad whose function is to keep an eye on dissident elements and prevent them from influencing rank-and-file members. The core of this group consists of older unionists, known as "non-career" workers, who are assigned to low-level administrative tasks and other duties indirectly related to production. Should office automation or robotization eliminate their jobs, Mr. Shioji might very well find his leadership in jeopardy.

Nissan's Murayama factory in Tokyo is a good example of what robotization holds for the future. It is equipped with 176 welder robots, and its mixed-flow production line can turn out three different types of cars at once.

The transfer of personnel has become a major problem for workers. In September 1974, just as full-scale automation got under-way at Murayama, 58 workers in the body shop were ordered to switch to another department. Of these, 46 went to the assembly and paint shops and six were reassigned to the forklift section. Six more employees, all of them foremen or deputy foremen, were shifted to another area.

At the time of the transfer, the section chief called each of the workers into his office and explained that the company had chosen the best men in his section for reassignment. Citing the unfavorable business climate, he appealed to their loyalty and asked for their cooperation.

When questioned by the author, however,

*Reprinted by permission of *The Wall Street Journal* ©Dow Jones & Co., Inc. 1983. All rights reserved.

†*Mr. Saga is a research assistant in labor relations at Tokyo University.* This article is a translated excerpt from the Japanese weekly magazine Ekonimusoto. The English version was prepared by the Asia Foundation's Translation Service Center.

none of the employees concerned felt they had been chosen because of their competence. One worker even told me, "We all know that management is eager to move us older workers out of the body shop. We don't see much future here anyway."

Automation has confronted workers with another serious problem: the dispatch of employees made redundant by robotization to other plants on temporary duty, ostensibly to "help out."

At the Murayama plant, as many as 70 percent of all workers have been temporarily reassigned at least once, either to another factory or to a different shop inside the same factory.

Recently, a new type of skilled laborer has appeared in machinery maintenance departments. He comes to the job equipped with a technical education acquired in high school as well as in the company, and a basic knowledge of computers and robot technology. Like operators in the oil industry, the new skilled workers are emerging as the shop-floor elite of the auto industry. The Murayama plant has about 300 such employees. They are all young laborers still in their 20s and early 30s who joined the company in the 1970s.

Taking young workers as a whole, however, the overwhelming majority have no prospects of ever belonging to such an elite. Their lot is to endure the frequent job reassignments management imposes on them. Some workers, complaining of psychological fatigue, have even quit.

Robot-led automation is steadily creating new divisions among younger laborers as those unable to adjust to the new mental strains drop out. One example is Takashi Yamazaki, a 35-year-old employee who entered the company upon graduating from high school. As assembly floor controller, it was his job to operate the computer that regulates production in the body shop. He took his work seriously, but being confined in a room with only the cold stare of a computer for company eventually depressed him.

A few years ago, he asked to be transferred to a Nissan sales outlet in Osaka, where he remained. According to friends, he is much happier in auto sales where at least there is human contact.

Automation is particularly bad news for older workers. Their traditional skills suddenly obsolete, many find themselves working under the supervision of younger employees. At the Murayama factory's machine processing shop, the foreman is 37, his assistant is 31, and most of the workers under him are in their early to middle 20s. The former deputy foreman, 47, has been demoted to the status of a rank-and-file employee.

Older workers tend to keep their feelings to themselves, finding no external release for pent-up frustrations. Although participating passively in quality control circles and other organized efforts designed to boost productivity, they react to the new work environment by withdrawing from their colleagues and losing enthusiasm for their jobs. The psychological impact of automation is far greater than outside observers imagine.

READING 41

Retraining of Workers for Automated Plants Gets Off to Slow Start*

Dale D. Buss†

Jim Smith could return to his familiar, comfortable electrician's job at General Motors Corporation's old St. Louis assembly plant now that truck production is picking up there.

But Mr. Smith, who was laid off last year when the auto maker suspended one shift at the plant, thinks he sees a better future elsewhere in the company. He is sticking with his training as a robot technician at GM's highly automated new plant here. The 52-year-old Mr. Smith and his 20 classmates, most of them middle-aged, are diligently studying the new technology in preparation for the plant's opening this summer.

Today's lesson: how to work on a programmable controller, the computer "brain" of an industrial robot. Scrawling in note pads, punching hand-held calculators, and consuming cup after cup of coffee, Mr. Smith and his classmates respond to the instructor like excited game-show contestants. Mr. Smith at one point even corrects the instructor's blackboard notation.

"What we're doing here with robots," Mr. Smith says after class, "is the sort of thing that American companies are going to have to do to compete. It's strictly our survival at stake."

It is natural for Mr. Smith to lead cheers for the automation that auto companies are installing. As a robot technician at one of GM's most-modern factories, he will be among the elite of U.S. autoworkers.

But for many workers in the automobile and other basic industries, computer-based automation isn't such a boon. While few of today's unemployed workers can blame their plight on technology, it's possible that technology will keep some from getting their jobs back.

Extent of Job Losses

Experts believe that within a few years, several hundred thousand metalworking positions alone will be automated out of existence. Thousands of white-collar employees also will be replaced by computers that design products, monitor inventory, or give instructions to the shop floor.

In theory at least, many of these displaced workers can be retrained for new jobs. That's already happening at trade schools such as the Detroit Engineering Institute, where graduating students, including many former autoworkers, find employment in such fields as air-conditioning repair. The Reagan administration also wants to help, asking $240 million for training of technologically displaced workers in fiscal 1984, up sharply from the $110 million allocated for this year.

Social critics, however, say most retraining efforts are either so limited or so ineffective that lasting damage already has been done. Harley Shaiken, who studies automation's social effects for the Massachusetts Institute of Technology, fears that industry "could already be creating a permanent technological underclass of unemployed, despairing people, particularly within certain areas of the country such as Detroit."

Despite its financial woes, the auto industry leads all others in bringing the computer age into the factory. Car companies already have installed about 3,200 robots—roughly half those in place in the country—and the Big Three auto makers expect to be using about 21,000 robots by 1990. Many automotive suppliers say that as soon as they can afford it, they will buy more robots too.

Higher-Quality Cars

The main attraction: A robot costs about $6 an hour to operate and typically does the job of two autoworkers, who each cost their

†*Dale D. Buss is a staff reporter of* The Wall Street Journal.

employer an average of about $20 an hour. Robots also turn out more consistent work, enabling them to make higher-quality cars.

Auto makers are embracing other high-tech equipment as well. At GM's Flint, Michigan, truck plant, inventory now is managed by computers, minimizing costly stockpiling. At Ford Motor Company's Dearborn, Michigan, engine plant, computers are all around the production line. One, for instance, matches pistons with the right-sized cylinders, replacing technicians who once performed the delicate measuring task. Another computer runs engines through a series of tests and prints the results.

Such technology, auto executives say, is needed for Detroit to become competitive with foreign car makers. And to the extent that this happens, they add, technology will save more jobs than it eliminates. Besides, "I don't expect the kind of (job) losses due to automation like those we've had due to our loss of volume," says Peter Pestillo, Ford's labor-relations vice president.

The United Auto Workers isn't against automation, either, particularly when it means using robots to perform hazardous jobs such as auto-body painting that can harm human workers. "In fact, the auto industry never moved as hard and fast in the direction of this sort of automation as it should have in the first place," says Kenneth Morris, a UAW executive board member.

The best case for the benefits of high automation, however, is made by new plants such as GM's Wentzville facility. By year end, the St. Louis-area factory could employ more than 5,000 now-jobless workers in producing a new line of front-wheel-drive luxury cars.

While assembly line jobs at Wentzville will be similiar to those in older GM plants, the new factory will make blue-collar superstars out of robot technicians such as Jim Smith. Some laid-off pipefitters, millwrights, and other tradesmen, in fact, uprooted their families and moved to Missouri from as far away as GM's Fremont, California, plant to snatch some of the select jobs.

The aim of their training is to teach the tradesmen enough of one another's skills that they can work in versatile "teams" to program,

maintain, and repair the 160 robots in the plant. GM figures such "cross-training" is the best way to prepare workers for dealing with the complexities of a robot; it also requires fewer technicians.

GM provides the tradesmen computerized refresher courses to hone their basic math and physics skills. Instructors don't grade the trainees, and GM allows them to go through all the instruction at their pace. At other plants, UAW tradesmen have struck over the issue of which worker does which job. At this one, bold blue-and-white signs placed throughout the training area urge the workers to "Trust the Process."

To a degree that is uncommon among traditionally militant auto tradesmen, many of the trainees seem to be doing just that. "There isn't anyplace else in the world that I could get the training I'm getting here," says Dennis Boyet, a 33-year-old toolmaker from St. Louis. "What I'm learning is something that's going to help me for the next several years."

Other rank-and-file autoworkers find technology makes some jobs more interesting. Herbert Hibbs fought boredom for a decade while inspecting parts coming off the line at Ford's Walton Heights, Ohio, stamping plant. Then six months ago, the company taught him how to use a hand-held, computerized inspection device and now, "I find my job so enjoyable and interesting that I get excited when I start talking about it," says Mr. Hibbs. "That's new for me."

Because of the lengthy recession, it's often hard for workers to tell whether automation has any negative effect on their jobs. When GM's Janesville, Wisconsin, assembly plant began producing J-cars last fall after a six-month retooling shutdown, there were 50 robots on an assembly line that hadn't had any before. But because the plant reopened with only one work turn instead of the two that had produced earlier models, it didn't occur even to local UAW officials that the new robots would have eliminated many jobs in a higher-volume operation.

Increasingly, though, there are workers like Robert Clark who see a connection between unemployment and automation. Mr. Clark was laid off two years ago from Ford's Lorain, Ohio, assembly plant because of slumping car sales. Now, says his UAW local, Mr. Clark and about 100 other low-seniority workers probably won't ever return because newly installed robots and other computerized equipment at the plant have made their jobs obsolete.

"It stinks, but you can't stop automation," says the 25-year-old Mr. Clark. He plans to stay in Lorain a few more months to see whether a recall is possible. "Then I'll go to some technical school if worse comes to worst."

Protection Argument

Other autoworkers believe that their union should do more to shield them from the effects of automation. In recent contract settlements, the UAW has won such job-security provisions as income guarantees for senior workers even while surrendering other benefits. Yet "we're being nickeled and dimed to death from (automation-related) job loss on the local level," says Michael Kozek, a local union official at GM's Bay City, Michigan, parts plant, where the company is doing more and more computer inspection of parts.

Worker distrust of automation also extends to new management methods that give employees a say in decisions involving manufacturing operations. Joseph Evans, a worker at GM's Tecumseh, Michigan, trim plant, suspects that "by saying 'we're going to involve you,' (auto companies) make it easier to bring in new automation." Some of Tecumseh's 600 workers are worried about job losses when GM installs about 70 computerized seat-sewing machines for the next model year.

The UAW's aim is to make job retraining, especially for positions outside the shrinking auto industry, part of national contracts. The union and GM currently run a small program in California to train laid-off GM workers for aerospace and computer-industry jobs. But the union's biggest retraining effort to date is a joint program with Ford, won in a 1982 contract, in which the company offers job counseling and tuition payments to laid-off workers interested in jobs outside the industry.

Presentation to Workers

About 1,000 jobless Ford workers gathered in a smoky union hall in the shadow of the company's River Rouge complex in Dearborn to hear about the program.

Included were the three Mendez brothers, laid-off workers without steady jobs these days and interested in training for new occupations. Victor, 34, wants Ford to help him get a two-year degree in automotive-emissions analysis, while Rudy, 29, wants to train for a license to be a moving contractor. Ken, 24, is interested in courses in electronics or robotics, "because that's where I see things going."

Robotics has an allure for a lot of laid-off autoworkers. The problem, according to researchers at the Upjohn Institute in Kalamazoo, Michigan, is that Michigan, for instance, could already be on the way to creating more robot technicians than the couple of thousand the state will probably need by 1990.

Philip Jajuga has already discovered that. The idle Garden City, Michigan, autoworker still can't find a job in the field 10 weeks after he completed a nine-month course in robotics. He has been turned down by more than 70 companies. "I'd like to know where the jobs are," says the 29-year old father of two children. "Sometimes I wonder if I wasted my time on this."

READING 42

Robotics and Their Effect on the Work Force*

Joseph Konowe†

As is usual with the introduction of new technology, much controversy has arisen as to whether the widespread introduction of robots into our industrial plants will, of itself, create a new industry and new jobs or whether robots will be a disaster to the millions of workers who will eventually be displaced by these "steel-collar" workers who do not belong to unions, do not need sick leave, vacation, coffee-breaks, cost-of-living increases, etc., and will work around-the-clock with nary a thought of overtime pay.

I should like to state, at this point, that while I realize nothing can stop the use of these robots in industry, I am emotionally opposed to the introduction of any new technology without the implementation of retraining programs and policies to relocate workers who will be displaced from their jobs and left with no hope for the future. I realize this is a formidable task because it will require that we do something drastic about the functional illiterates coming out of our existing school programs. It will take much schooling and on-the-job training to prepare displaced workers for the possibility of obtaining employment in high-tech fields and, further, training for other jobs in the service and information industries. Even in Japan, where the use of robots in various factories, particularly by auto manufacturers, was viewed with awe and fascination by the Japanese workers and their unions, there is now a subtle transformation of the structure of employment in the auto industry and it is adversely affecting the lives of workers, young and old.

I have taken the liberty of reproducing an article on this subject, which appeared in *The Wall Street Journal* of February 28 of this year and which addressed itself to the problems of robotics in Japanese plants. (See Reading 38.)

We must, here as in Japan, establish a curriculum in our high schools, if not sooner, to enable students, the future work force, to become proficient and comfortable, psychologically, in this new world of work. Our problem, as you all know, is that in the United States, there is an enormous shortage of mathematicians and scientists willing to teach in our school systems when they can earn three times as much and more money, by working for private industry. The most difficult part of retraining will be that most of those blue-collar workers will fall in the 35-to-55-year age bracket and most companies are loath to make an investment in workers whose tenure will be shorter than that of the young people coming out of school.

To address this complex problem will require the combined efforts of management, government, and labor and a very considerable outlay of money and much thought.

Just last month, there appeared before the Joint Economic Committee on Robotics of the Senate of the United States, a number of individuals who, it would appear, have given considerable time and study to the effects of robotics on the work force and, I might also add, the effects of robotics on American industry.

In an opening statement, the chairman of the committee, Senator Lloyd Bentsen, Democrat of Texas, noted that "The use of robots has soared across our nation and across the world by firms under pressure to raise productivity and reduce unit-labor costs."

In 1961 we began to hear speculation about robots, but sales really began to take off in 1979. There are some 22,000 sophisticated robots already in use worldwide, including 5,000 in the United States. Sales are predicted to rise at a phenomenal rate of 35 to 50 percent annually. By 1990, we could easily see from 100,000 to 150,000 robots being utilized in the

---

*Reprinted from an address given before the Industrial Relations Research Association, Philadelphia Chapter, April 12, 1983.

†*Joseph Konowe is Director, Industrial Trades Division, International Brotherhood of Teamsters.*

United States, with sales topping $2 billion annually. Ford and GM alone may well be using 30,000 robots between them by 1990, Bentsen said.

Before continuing with Senator Bentsen's observations, I should like to call your attention to one of the major fallacies of those people who speak of the creation of 800,000 new jobs in the labor force (U.S. Bureau of Labor Statistics). In the *New York Times* of March 21, 1983 under the headline, "IBM Joint Ventures, Etc.", it is noted that IBM and Matsushita will engage in a joint venture in Japan which will utilize Japanese-made computers. Similarly, IBM has also entered into joint ventures with Toshiba, and a little more than a year ago, IBM introduced a robot for sale here in the United States, made by Sankyo Seikei Manufacturing Company of Japan. Even better known is the joint General Motors-Toyota venture to produce cars in California using robots of U.S. technology but manufactured in Japan. Wherefrom will the supposed robot manufacturing jobs come if, in fact, Japanese-manufactured robots are the order of the day?

I think you will agree with me that unless government and labor can convince American industry to produce and buy robots made in this country, the problem of work force displacement and unemployment will become serious enough to provoke social unrest.

Lest you think I am a follower of the Luddite's who, in England in the 19th century, destroyed thousands of machines in the textile mills in an effort to halt the spread of the Industrial Revolution in their country, let me assure you that I am enormously impressed by the introduction of computers into our society and the benefits which have been derived therefrom. It seems to me that the vast difference between computer technology and that of robotics lies in the fact that the computers do not replace workers, but rather do jobs that humans cannot.

Functions that can be performed by the new generation of robots are growing monthly and a few examples of industries using them are: fruit picking, auto-body sanding and painting, car-welding, drilling bolt holes in F–16 Falcons, and the list is growing by leaps and bounds.

As to their performance, a robot used by Boeing to sand the wings of a cruise missile can accomplish the job in 46 minutes—a job which formerly took several workers eight hours to perform. General Dynamics has found that their F–16 robots are three to four times more productive than workers alone. GM has found that it can purchase a $50,000 robot and operate it at $1/3$ the hourly cost of a skilled worker. And many firms are finding that their robots are paying for themselves in three years or less and do the work of anywhere from 1.7 to 6 men and women. So, the rush to robots is easy to understand, especially by American firms who must compete head-on with Japan. While the first robots were developed here over 20 years ago, the Japanese government has heavily subsidized their use for several years. In fact, Japanese firms utilize over 14,000 robots now—60 percent of the total in use worldwide—and their enviable productivity records reflect it.

The need to boost productivity and compete with Japan and other nations means we cannot turn back the clock. Robots are here to stay. We need to utilize that technology to raise our productivity and to maintain markets and jobs. The issue is how best to deal with the human aspects of their use.

I should like to take a moment at this point to repeat part of a statement by John Andelin, assistant director of the Office of Technology Assessment, who testified before the Senate committee, because his description of robots clearly demonstrates the types and functions of these machines.

Computerized manufacturing—or, more simply, programable automation—is an umbrella term that applies to several types of automated equipment and systems that draw on computers, including robots, computer-aided design or CAD, computer-aided manufacturing or CAM, computer-aided process planning or CAPP, and automated materials-handling, storage, and retrieval systems. While robots seem to attract most of the attention of the media and other public commentators, it is important to realize that robots are only one component of a larger set of programable automated technology. It is also important to recognize that programable automation technologies are not new. For example, the beginnings of CAM may be found in the development of numerically controlled machine tools, while industrial robots were introduced in the early 1960s.

Following explanation concerning the differences between the economic and engineering estimate of the effects of these machines, Mr. Andelin said that the shortcomings of economic estimates are that economic models that project labor supply and industrial output separately may not capture the complex interactions of demographic and economic factors that influence the growth of the labor force and change in labor force participation by different groups within the population. Nor may they capture differences in the quality of the labor force, differences which may govern the ability of the labor force to adapt to changes in economic activity. Programmable automation may change not only the numbers and types of people working in manufacturing, but also the circumstances of work—what may be called the work environment.

This leads us back again to the question of educating, retraining, and relocating workers in order that they become useful and productive in the years which lie ahead.

Organized labor has been portrayed by various sources as facing a bleak future with the increasing onrush of industry to robotics. Faced with plant closings in old industrial areas, unions have devoted their time to arguing and negotiating contracts containing severance programs and, in a very few instances, retraining and relocating programs have been made part of the contract. This is true of the United Automobile Workers, the Steelworkers, and the Electrical Workers unions. John Naisbitt, in his best-selling book, *Megatrends*, notes that unions have been forced to fight automation in industries by sometimes accepting automation in exchange for job security. He cites the typographical field where the union ratified a 10-year contract that requires the company to employ 130 printers, but agrees to the layoff of 400 other printers in exchange. Naisbitt writes "That with robots in the second stage of technological innovation, the introduction of technology into the industrial workplace is on a collision course with much of the work force, organized or not."

MIT's Center for Policy Alternatives assis-

tant director, Robert Lund, finds that production and service jobs tended to become "deskilled" when technology is added. "Engineers' and supervisors' jobs, on the other hand," writes Lund, "tend to become more demanding." Harley Shaiken, also of MIT, concludes, "If labor does not find a way to control technology, then management will use technology to control labor."

I foresee that in the 21st century, millions of workers whose jobs have become obsolete as a result of their replacement by robots will have to be re-programed to enable our free enterprise system to survive. Not only will new jobs have to be created, but our whole social structure and working environment will have to be addressed, as well.

Much as the 97 percent of workers in agriculture found their way to jobs in manufacturing and service industries with the coming of the Industrial Revolution, so will the industrial workers have to find new jobs in service and information fields in order to remain useful citizens in our society.

Will the workweek have to be shortened to a national policy of 30 hours or less per week? Will vacation periods be prolonged? Will retirement policies of the present be reversed so that workers will be able to retire at a younger age rather than an older one as is now being projected? What will happen to our immigration policy? Will we remain the land of freedom with our doors open to people seeking to enter our shores from wherever and whenever the occasion arises? Who will pay for the education of our young people in the schools when their education becomes more complicated than now, in order to provide the highly skilled technicians demanded by automation and robotics? What will become of the aging communities in our midst which once so proudly boasted that they were the industrial heartland of our country? Will the government and industry cooperate in order for them to survive or shall they become the economic wasteland of our failure to perceive the enormous changes which swirl about us? These are the problems, my friends, for all of us here to wrestle with, because it will take our best minds to usher us into an era where high technology is the order of the day and where employment will have to be available for our work force, which will continue to grow for some years to come.

The necessity to provide jobs is not for workers alone, but for industry as well. Unemployed workers are poor customers and dropping sales demand a disaster for industry—manufacturing and retail—as well. Self-preservation makes partners of the producers and their customers.

So, let us not procrastinate. Let's get with it—it's later than we think.

Robotics Technology: The Implications for Collective Bargaining and Labor Law*

Terry L. Leap and
Allayne Barrilleaux Pizzolatto†

The human race is now poised on the brink of a new industrial revolution that will at least equal, if not far exceed, the first industrial revolution in its impact on mankind."[1] These words were spoken by James Albus, head of the robotics research lab at the National Bureau of Standards in Gaithersburg, Maryland. If that prediction holds true, then robotics will likely have a profound impact on the work force, personnel management, and unions. Changes in collective bargaining and labor law are also possible as robotics technology grows in the United States.

Robotics is a relatively new word in the American vocabulary and simply means the science of robots. But what exactly are robots? Although there is no universally agreed-upon definition, Webster describes a robot as "a machine in the form of a human being that performs the mechanical functions of a human being." Professionals in robotics define the robot as a mechanical device having a reasonably high level of intelligence, the ability to make elementary decisions, and the dexterity and flexibility to perform an intricate sequence of different motions without human intervention.[2] Robots are different from automatic machines in that they can be reprogrammed to carry out a number of functions and their adaptability competes closely with human talent. There is also the misconception that robots have human forms; in reality, they are being made in all shapes and sizes although they still perform human-like maneuvers.

Robots, depending on the nature of the task being performed, may offer the following advantages. One, productivity may be increased because of their ability to work at a faster and more continuous pace than their human counterparts. Two, quality of production may be improved due to the elimination of human error caused by fatigue, boredom, and inattention on the job. Three, safety hazards may be reduced or eliminated by placing robots in jobs that are dangerous and monotonous. And, four, robots are cost effective in many cases. An industrial robot costs approximately $50,000. When compared to an assembly line worker whose annual wage and benefit package may exceed $25,000 (not to mention recruitment, selection, training, absenteeism, and turnover costs) a robot pays for itself within two years.[3]

Assuming that organizational decision makers are aware of these advantages, it is likely that the use of robots will flourish in the coming decade. If this is the case, then it is equally likely that several issues involving the interface of collective bargaining, labor law, and robotics will be raised. This paper will discuss what we perceive to be the major developing labor law and collective bargaining issues surrounding the emergence of robotics.

Several areas appear to be especially ripe for change if robotics becomes a significant force in U.S. organizations. These areas are equal employment opportunity, union-management relations, health and safety, and compensation. Of course, the precise nature of these changes is speculative at this point.

*Reproduced from the November 1983 issue of the Labor Law Journal, published and copyrighted 1983 by Commerce Clearing House, Inc., 4025 W. Peterson Avenue, Chicago, Illinois 60646.

†Terry Leap is an associate professor of management at Clemson University, Clemson, South Carolina. Allayne Barrilleaux Pizzolatto is with the Department of Management at Louisiana State University, Baton Rouge, Louisiana.

[1] See Otto Friedrich, "The Robot Revolution, *Time*, December 8, 1980, p. 83, and J. W. Saverino, "Industrial Robots, Today and Tomorrow," *Robotics Age*, Summer 1980, cited in Parvez Salim, "The Robots Are Coming," *Professional Safety*, March 1983.

[2] Salim, "The Robots Are Coming," pp. 18–19.

[3] See "Robots" Are Taking over Many Jobs Nobody Wants—and Boosting Productivity," *Material Handling Engineering*, October 1979.

However, individuals dealing with the various administrative agencies that enforce federal and state laws, as well as union and management officials, must anticipate potential problems that may accompany the introduction of robotic technology in their organizations.

Despite the aforementioned advantages, the introduction and use of robots pose a threat (either real or imagined) to the status quo. Employees and union representatives are concerned about the effect of robotics on employment security. Personnel managers must evaluate the impact of robotics on recruitment, selection, training, and compensation programs. Persons assigned the task of negotiating and administering collective bargaining agreements will undoubtedly face the prospect of designing contract provisions that are somewhat different from those previously used in the labor relations arena.

EEO AND AFFIRMATIVE ACTION

Robots may encroach on jobs traditionally held by minorities and women. This may be a positive development if employees in protected groups are given the opportunity to advance to more responsible, rewarding, and higher-paying positions. For this to occur, organizations must have both the job openings for displaced minority and female employees as well as the training and development capabilities to facilitate their transfer to higher-level jobs.

If minority job advancement is not possible, then the impact of robotics may lead to increased problems under fair employment laws if a disparate impact is inflicted on a specific group protected under federal or state fair employment laws. For example, the elimination of a particular class of jobs in an organization which has been dominated by females could spur a Title VII suit unless these displaced employees are placed in equivalent or better jobs.

Furthermore, the introduction of robots in the production process could alter jobs, the work pace, and work schedule in such a manner so as to create a disproportionately less desirable working environment for certain protected groups. According to one observer:

"We often overlook the impact of robots on the jobs that remain. Today, if a worker assembling components has a daily quota of 100 units to fill, he can, for example, work flat out and assemble 60 in the first half of a shift leaving only 40 for a relatively unpressured second half. But when he is slotted between centrally programmed robots that dictate the pace,he becomes a mere cog in the machine. These things matter."[4]

As long as any negative consequences to the work environment posed by the introduction of robots do not single out and adversely affect a specific protected group, there should be no legitimate fair employment problems. When this is not the case, however, then the EEO doctrines dealing with disparate and unequal treatment come into play.[5]

Another potential area of concern pertains to the concept of "business necessity" as it is applied to fair employment practices. Traditionally, employers have been permitted to engage in limited discrimination against protected groups if such action can be justified because of excessive costs, differences in efficiency, or safety considerations. Robots will be introduced primarily because of their cost savings and increased efficiency vis-à-vis the human worker. An issue which must be addressed, therefore, is the extent to which costs must be decreased and efficiency improved if the introduction of robots has an adverse impact on minorities and females. This, of course, can lead to a serious discussion regarding how such cost savings, productivity changes, and efficiency improvements are measured.[6]

If members of a protected class are displaced by robotics technology, will fair employment laws and supporting regulations require some sort of retraining for suitable alternative employment? Will a certain amount of reverse discrimination in favor of racial minorities and females under the *Weber* dictum be allowed in order to protect these

---

[4]Friedrich, "Robot Revolution," p. 78.

[5]See, for example, the "Uniform Guidelines on Employee Selection Procedures," 29 CFR 1607 (1978).

[6]For an excellent discussion regarding the measurement of personnel-related costs and benefits, see Wayne F. Cascio, *Costing Human Resources: The Financial Impact of Behavior in Organizations* (Boston: Kent, 1982).

employees if their jobs are lost to robotics?[7] Many of the arguments for and against reverse discrimination set forth in *Weber* may apply here.[8]

Affirmative action programs required of organizations with federal government contracts or financial assistance may take on a new dimension if robotic technology proliferates in U.S. industries. Robots, if used extensively in an organization, may alter the racial, sex, or age composition of the personnel as well as the organizational structure of the firm or entity. If robots perform menial tasks (leaving the more complex and managerial duties to humans); then it is likely that a firm's affirmative action goals will change. The affirmative action program for a particular organization is primarily a function of the types of jobs to be filled, the labor market composition, the racial composition of the firm's employees, and the availability of training facilities both within the organization as well as in the relevant labor market. As previously mentioned, the use of robots may force or at least strongly encourage organizations to alter their training and development programs.

What is more difficult to predict is the magnitude of change regarding the concept of "relevant labor market" for human employees. If robots assume menial, routine, and lower-paying jobs, a firm's labor market for affirmative action purposes may expand geographically because the recruitment and selection process will focus on skilled and managerial personnel. In a somewhat more far-fetched vein, is it possible that robots will be considered the equivalent to nonminority employees under affirmative action programs?

UNION-MANAGEMENT RELATIONS

The introduction of robots in a unionized organization represents a technological change which management cannot normally make without first considering the needs of bargaining unit employees. Because robotics represents a significant alteration in production methods, it will elicit varying responses from unions, depending on the economic climate of the industry, financial condition of the firm, centralization of bargaining, and employment alternatives available to displaced employees, to name a few. Most unions have recognized the legitimacy of the employer's need to improve work methods and to develop more efficient operations, even when the result is a net reduction in permanent personnel. Nevertheless, nearly all unions seek to control the manner and rate of technological change if such change contributes to reduced manpower.[9]

Union policies toward technological change are not directly controlled by substantive labor law but are generally regarded as mandatory bargaining items which must be addressed by management at the union's insistence. Should managements attempt unilateral technological change without addressing union concerns at the bargaining table, they are likely to be the target of an unfair labor practice charge (bad faith bargaining) under Section 8(a)(5) of the National Labor Relations Act, as amended. Management's ability to install and use robots during the life of the collective bargaining agreement will depend primarily on the specific wording of the management rights clause.

Two contractual areas of direct concern, with regard to robotics, are seniority and layoff provisions. Both labor and management must design seniority and layoff provisions that will stand the test of equal employment opportunity laws as well as uphold the union's duty of fair representation to its constituents. The grievance mechanism will likely have to deal with cases in which employees with relatively high levels of seniority will be displaced by robots. Although other forms of technological change have created similar problems, the use of "human-like" robots may create two additional issues.

First, should robots be used if the incum-

---

[7]99 SCt 2721 (US SCt, 1979), 20 EP ¶30,026, reh'g denied (US SCt, 1979), EPD ¶30,266.

[8]See, for example, some of the issues raised in Terry Leap and Irving Kovarsky. "What Is the Impact of *Weber* on Collective Bargaining?" *Labor Law Journal* 31, no. 6 (June 1980), pp. 323–27.

[9]Harold W. Davey, Mario F. Bognanno, and David L. Estenson, *Contemporary Collective Bargaining*, 4th ed. (Englewood Cliffs, N.J.: Prentice-Hall, 1982), p. 294.

bent employee has approximately the same productive capability as the robot? Second, should it be possible for displaced employees to bump a robot off a job in a fashion similar to when senior employees bump their less senior counterparts during cutbacks? The second question also relates to the first in that the on-the-job capabilities of the human worker relative to the robot must be measured to determine whether bumping will be allowed.

Union organizing strategies and the structure of bargaining units may also change if robotics make significant in-roads into U.S. organizations. Robotics may make blue-collar jobs virtually obsolete, further eroding what has traditionally been the most heavily unionized category of employee. The precise change in bargaining unit composition is difficult to predict, but several considerations are worth mentioning.

One issue pertains to the increased technical expertise of bargaining unit employees as robots assume the tasks normally performed by unskilled and semiskilled workers. Professional and technical employees have generally been more difficult to organize than their less-skilled counterparts. Unions will have to become more creative in both their organizing tactics as well as the types of benefits included in collective bargaining agreements that cover professional-technical bargaining unit members. This may, for example, lead to a slight redefinition or expansion of the mandatory and permissive bargaining subjects in order to accommodate the concerns of highly trained and skilled employees.[10]

Furthermore, the coverage of supervisors under the NLRA may require alteration. For example, do persons who program robots to perform a certain task or job "formulate and effectuate management policies by expressing and making operative the decisions of the employer"?[11] If this is the case, the bulk of an organization's "human" personnel could be defined as supervisors and may, for all practical purposes, be excluded from any meaningful protection under federal labor relations law.[12] Another potential issue is whether persons responsible for programming robots to perform functions critical to an organization's security could be forced into bargaining units separate from other employees, much in the same fashion as plant guards have traditionally been partitioned into their own bargaining units.[13]

The types of grievances processed through the grievance mechanism may take on different forms in organizations that extensively use robots. In such organizations, employees are likely to be exposed to fewer tedious, monotonous, and dangerous jobs. Grievances involving discharges for excessive absenteeism, tardiness, and insubordination may decrease while disputes regarding professional prerogatives, job displacement, layoffs, seniority rights, and compensation-related issues may become more prevalent. labor arbitrators will have to become familiar with robotic technology, cost-benefit issues associated with the use of robots, and union-management problems that stem from robotics technology.

SAFETY AND COMPENSATION

One of the most often-cited reasons for using robots is that robots can perform monotonous, backbreaking and unsafe jobs, sparing their human counterparts from these tasks and facilitating compliance with OSHA. Robots have been used in the plastics, chemical, steel, and other industries primarily for safety-related reasons.[14] For example, robots are used to handle molten zinc, dry ice, heavy steel plates, artillery shells, fire brick, and other hot, toxic, or heavy materials.[15]

In addition to helping the employer adhere to the provisions of OSHA, improving safety measures through robotics also leads to decreased compliance costs because previously

[10]The well-known *Borg-Warner*, 356 US 342 (US SCt, 1958), 34 LC ¶71,492, categories of bargaining items have been widely held to include as a mandatory item those collective bargaining concerns that fall within the meaning of wages, hours, and working conditions. Most issues pertaining to robots would probably fall into this classification.

[11]*Bell Aerospace Co.*, 219 NLRB 384 (1975), 1974–75 CCH NLRB ¶ 16,031.

[12]See Section 2(11) of the Labor Management Relations Act.

[13]Ibid., Section 9(b)(3).

[14]Salim, "The Robots Are Coming," pp. 17–18.

[15]Ibid., pp. 18–21.

required shields, guards, ventilation devices, lighting, and periodic employee medical examinations are eliminated. As a firm's safety record improves worker's compensation insurance costs can also be expected to decrease.

Improved safety records and working conditions brought about by robots has additional spillover effects. One such effect might be the reduction of OSHA-related complaints by unions. Improved morale may also lead to fewer employee-initiated grievances and disciplinary problems involving legal entanglements. Workers who supervise or work alongside robots often appreciate the progressive, modernistic stance of their employer. Less-skilled employees are relieved of dangerous, boring, dirty, hot, and degrading jobs, all of which means a resurgence in self-dignity and employee morale. This in turn, should lead to a cooperative rather than a legally combative atmosphere between employees (or unions) and management.

Compensation

The introduction of robotics technology has a number of implications with regard to compensation programs. First, nonexempt employees who have legally been entitled to overtime pay under the Fair Labor Standards Act may find that the presence of robots curtails the need to work beyond the 40-hour work week. If this is the case, will an alteration of the FLSA be in order as a means of compensating those who have typically relied heavily on overtime pay? This may be accomplished, perhaps, through an arrangement where a certain category of employees who have regularly averaged a given amount of overtime over a specified period are granted a displacement allowance to compensate for their sudden loss of income. Even if such an arrangement is not incorporated into the FLSA, it could conceivably be included in collective bargaining agreements and would in all likelihood be deemed a mandatory bargaining item because of its direct effect on wages.

Robots obviously do not require retirement or group life and health insurance programs. A management decision to implement the use of robotics must take into account the cost savings associated with the elimination of these programs. Group insurance programs are generally required by state law to maintain a minimum number of participating employees in a life or health insurance program. It is conceivable that the extensive use of robotics in an organization could force the number of participants to fall below the legal minimum and jeopardize an established employee benefit program.[16]

Employees who are displaced because their positions have been eliminated by robotics technology may be forced into early retirement. Questions of adverse impact under the Age Discrimination in Employment Act may arise. In addition, problems may arise under the Employee Retirement Income Security Act, which regulates pension programs.

For example, should an employee whose job is filled by a robot be entitled to more liberalized vesting standards than would normally apply to an employee who is terminated?[17] If an employee is forced to retire early due to robotics would it be possible for an employer to make pension contributions on behalf of the displaced employee in excess of those allowed by ERISA? This may be necessary in a few cases in order to grant the employee a monthly annuity equivalent to the one that would have been received had the employee retired at the normal retirement age. Employers may want to liberalize vesting and funding provisions for displaced employees for reasons of social responsibility as well as to minimize the possibility of legal retaliation.

Robotics technology may lead to reduced workweeks and job-sharing arrangements as the need for the human component is re-

---

[16]Most state insurance codes require a minimum of 10 employees in an employer-sponsored group insurance program. As a practical matter, many organizations may be reluctant to sponsor group programs for only a few employees because of adverse selection and poor economies of scale, and high fixed costs.

[17]Vesting, under ERISA, pertains to an employee's right to receive all or part of an *employer's* contributions to a retirement program made on behalf of that employee in the event the individual is terminated or resigns. ERISA has three minimum vesting standards and the pension plan must meet one of those three standards.

duced in some organizations. More attention will be needed with regard to the composition of the pay and benefits package, especially with regard to vacation benefits, shift differentials, and supplemental unemployment benefits (SUBs). Vacation benefits and SUBs will likely be liberalized as robotics makes inroads into various industries while shift differentials may be eliminated for certain employee groups.

One question which must be addressed is the extent to which employers should share productivity gains brought about by robots with workers whose hours of employment and pay have been cut back. A logical means of doing this is through increased wages as well as paid vacation and SUB benefits. Another issue is to determine whether federal and state wage and hour laws will require modification to accommodate truncated workweeks and job-sharing arrangements.

Conclusion

Robotics technology has the potential for creating a new industrial revolution. The first industrial revolution was based on the substitution of mechanical energy for muscle power and the robotics-induced industrial revolution will be based on the substitution of electronic computers for the human brain in the control of machines and industrial processes.[18]

---

[18]J. W. Saverino, "Industrial Robots," p. 18.

The implications for such changes, if in fact they do occur, could be dramatic for the institution of collective bargaining and labor law. This article has attempted to delineate a number of issues that are likely to arise in the labor relations, EEO, health and safety, and compensation areas. The wider societal impact created by the extensive use of robotics that will also alter the role of work in our culture has been ignored here, but it is of major concern to industrial relations and management scholars.

A primary dilemma that must be faced as robotics becomes a significant force in certain industries is how and to what extent policymakers should alter the existing labor laws to reflect some of the issues discussed. Are policy changes to be preferred over mutually agreed-upon changes between labor and management? The latter strategy might be more desirable because robotics will be extensively used in some industries and very little in others. Furthermore, the impact of robotics will vary from one firm or industry to another, depending on the types of jobs for which they are used.

The bottom line, however, will be to introduce and use robotics in such a manner that will balance the impact on management and labor while, simultaneously, it avoids unnecessary legal problems. To accomplish this will require careful thought and preparation by top management, personnel specialists, and union officials with regard to some of the issues addressed here.

Author Index

This book has been set Compugraphic 8600 in 10 and 9 point Elante, leaded 2 points. Part numbers are 30 point Avant Garde Book; part titles are 20 point Avant Garde Book. Reading numbers and titles are 18 point Avant Garde Book. The size of the type page is 34½ by 52 picas.